ASSESSMENT STRATEGIES IN BEHAVIORAL MEDICINE

ASSESSMENT STRATEGIES IN BEHAVIORAL MEDICINE

Edited by

Francis J. Keefe, Ph.D.
Assistant Professor of Medical Psychology
Department of Psychiatry
Duke University Medical Center
Durham, North Carolina

James A. Blumenthal, Ph.D.
Assistant Professor of Medical Psychology
Department of Psychiatry
Duke University Medical Center
Durham, North Carolina

Grune & Stratton

A Subsidiary of Harcourt Brace Jovanovich, Publishers

New York   London
Paris   San Diego   San Francisco   São Paulo
Sydney   Tokyo   Toronto

Library of Congress Cataloging in Publication Data
Main entry under title:

Assessment strategies in behavioral medicine.

Bibliography
Includes index.
1. Psychodiagnostics.   2. Diagnosis.   I. Keefe,
Francis J.   II. Blumenthal, James A.   [DNLM: 1. Be-
havior.   2. Psychotherapy.   WM 420 A847]
RC469.A83   616.07′5′019   82-1112
ISBN 0-8089-1442-1   AACR2

Grune & Stratton, Inc.
111 Fifth Avenue
New York, New York 10003

Distributed in the United Kingdom by
Academic Press Inc. (London) Ltd.
24/28 Oval Road, London NW 1

Library of Congress Catalog Number 82-1112
International Standard Book Number 0-8089-1442-1

Printed in the United States of America

To our parents

Biographical Sketches

Francis J. Keefe is Assistant Professor of Medical Psychology in the Department of Psychiatry and Clinical Director of the Behavioral Physiology Laboratory at Duke University Medical Center. He received his doctorate at Ohio University and was a postdoctoral fellow at the Psychophysiology Laboratory at Harvard Medical School. Dr. Keefe has published many articles on the application of behavioral techniques to the treatment of physiological dysfunction and chronic disease.

James A. Blumenthal is Assistant Professor of Medical Psychology in the Department of Psychiatry and Senior Fellow at the Center for the Study of Aging and Human Development at Duke University Medical Center. He received his doctorate from the University of Washington and completed a predoctoral internship and postdoctoral fellowship at Duke University. Dr. Blumenthal's interests are in the areas of psychophysiology, cardiac rehabilitation, and psychological aspects of health and illness.

Contents

Part I
Behavioral Medicine: An Introduction

Part II
Assessment Strategies for Cardiovascular Disorders

Part III
Assessment Strategies for Disorders of the Central Nervous System

Part IV
Assessment Strategies for Behavioral Disorders

Part V
Assessment Strategies for Chronic Pain and Illness

Part VI
Assessment Strategies for Sexual Disorders

Part VII
Assessment Strategies for Disorders of Special Populations

Figures

Tables

Foreword

Life is short, and the art long; the occasion fleeting; and judgment difficult.*

{Hippocrates}

When we think of contemporary medicine, we tend to think of its flashy utilitarian aspects—triple bypass surgery and electronic protheses—often ignoring the subtle, relatively inconspicuous underpinnings that make contemporary medicine a scientific enterprise. This, however, was not always the case. Two thousand years ago medicine was an unanalyzed blend of superstition, custom, popular bias, and, especially within the Hippocratic school, systematic observation. But it was an unself-critical endeavor, without a directed and consistent empirical methodology.

The reliability and efficacy of modern scientific medicine have been a long time coming. Critical to this lengthy development was the reliance on experiment and directed observation. Harvey didn't arrive at the nature of the blood's circulation by sitting in the legendary philosophical arm chair—he did some testing. So did Pasteur. At the very cornerstone of effective testing is assessment, the subject of this book. The Hippocratic school of medicine flourished about 2400 years ago, yet it took almost another 2000 years until Harvey discovered the circulation of the blood about 300 years ago. And it was only 100 years ago that Pasteur developed the first vaccine for infectious disease. Thus, in recent times especially, medicine has been rocking from a still-continuing, still-accelerating explosion of knowledge. Behavioral medicine is part of that explosion, and assessment techniques within behavioral medicine are absolutely crucial to its further development as a rational and useful enterprise.

"Behavioral medicine," by that name at least, is now less than a decade old. Even the concepts that make it possible are, as historians reckon time, hardly any older. In 1973 I edited a very early book in the area.* On page 1 of that book I voiced the following concern:

> It can be all too easy to become fervently fascinated with a treatment method, caught up in a kind of *furor therapeuticus,* the practice and technology of which leaves little time and energy either for careful empirical evaluation of therapeutic efficacy, or for the analysis of underlying pathophysiology.

I am happy to say that the present volume, capably edited by Dr. James Blumenthal and by my old friend, Dr. Francis Keefe, totally avoids the pitfall of "furor therapeuticus"—enthusiasm and zeal for techniques that totally outstrips fundamental knowledge of relevant physiology and pathology, available data on outcome, and basic assessment techniques capable of measuring the effects of intended "treatments." In fact, this book contains a wealth of specific technical data. For most clinical syndromes there is a rather vast choice of *alternative methods of assessment,* together with guidance as to the specific advantages and disadvantages of each. There are specific chapters that deal with all the major areas of behavioral medicine: obesity, hypertension, smoking, coronary artery disease, Raynaud's disease, the measurement of higher brain functions, epilepsy, headache, sleep disorders, sexual disorders, and, most importantly, chronic pain. In the last part of the book there are also chapters that deal with assessment techniques within behavioral medicine for special populations—for patients with cancer, gender dysphoria syndromes, asthma, developmental disabilities, and self-injurious behaviors. The final chapter deals with assessment techniques applicable to the geriatric patient.

This wealth of factual material makes for less than breezy reading to be sure, but no one ever promised us that medicine, behavioral or otherwise, would be simple. Mere "clinical impression," for example, once led to widespread acceptance within medicine of the therapeutic value of bleeding and purging. With "judgment [so] difficult," there is ample reason for all of us in clinical work to have a vital interest in every valid assessment technique placed at our disposal. This excellent compilation by Drs. Keefe and Blumenthal takes a long step in that direction. This book is made to order for those interested in an up-to-date overview of the entire field of behavioral medicine, and this book will be a highly useful reference text for anyone working actively in one or more areas of behavioral medicine.

Lee Birk, M.D.
Associate Clinical Professor of Psychiatry
Harvard Medical School
Boston, Massachusetts

---

*Birk, L. (Ed). *Biofeedback: Behavioral medicine.* New York: Grune & Stratton, 1973.

Preface

Behavioral medicine is a field that has attracted a great deal of attention and interest. Much of the appeal of behavioral medicine lies in its attempt to integrate knowledge from the behavioral and biomedical sciences to reach solutions to practical problems of physical health and illness. Behavioral medicine is widely regarded as being broad in scope and thereby not limited to any one discipline or theoretical orientation; however, most of the published literature on behavioral medicine consists of reports of successful application of behavior therapy techniques to the treatment of a wide variety of medical disorders.

While a great deal has been written about treatment techniques such as biofeedback, relaxation training, and autogenic training, relatively little has been written regarding the role of assessment in behavioral medicine. The purpose of this book is to review methods of assessment currently employed in behavioral medicine. The application of both behavioral assessment and traditional psychological test instruments is considered.

The book is divided into six parts. In Part I we provide an introduction to the field of behavioral medicine. Readers who are unfamiliar with fundamental concepts, theoretical formulations, and assessment methods of behavioral medicine will find this section helpful. The remaining sections of the book examine assessment strategies used with particular medical disorders and populations. Each part contains chapters written by individuals who are specialists in their field. Each chapter provides an overview of those methods of assessment that are particularly relevant to the disorder under consideration. Assessment strategies developed to meet a broad spectrum of clinical needs are considered. These include: 1) identification of high risk individuals; 2) specification of presenting problems; 3) measurement of problems; 4) individualization of treatment strategies; and 5) evaluation of the potential for maintenance and generalization of behavior change.

Emphasis is placed on those assessment strategies that can be and are being incorporated into clinical practice.

Part II contains chapters on assessment techniques used for three cardiovascular disorders: hypertension, coronary heart disease, and Raynaud's disease. Part III examines strategies utilized for central nervous system disorders, including headaches, epilepsy, sleep disorders, and a variety of neurological disorders. Part IV describes assessment of two behavioral patterns that place individuals at risk for health problems: smoking and obesity. Part V examines assessment approaches that are useful for chronic pain and cancer patients. Part VI examines assessment methods used with sexual disorders, and Part VII focuses on assessment strategies used for special populations of patients. Methods of assessing problems encountered in children (developmental disabilities and asthma), the mentally retarded and institutionalized (self-injurious behavior), and geriatric patients are considered.

We would like to acknowledge many people who directly and indirectly contributed to this book. First, we would like to extend thanks to our many contributors for their excellent and timely contributions. Second, we would like to extend thanks to our colleagues, Drs. Richard Surwit and Redford Williams, whose support and encouragement were so important in the initial development of the book. We would also like to acknowledge the influence that our teachers and mentors, including Drs. Lee Birk, Steven B. Gordon, Hans O. Doerr, Joseph Becker, and Irving Alexander, had in shaping our thinking about behavioral medicine.

We would like to thank Dr. H. Keith H. Brodie, members of the Department of Psychiatry, and the staff of the Behavioral Physiology Laboratory for the support, assistance, and encouragement that they have given to us and to the role of behavioral medicine at Duke Medical Center. We would especially like to acknowledge Tricia Tenpenny for her valuable editorial assistance and the efforts of Cynthia Mongeon and Barbara Jackson in providing secretarial assistance. Finally, we would like to thank our families and closest friends for their understanding and encouragement during our work on this book.

Contributors

Denise Barnes, Ph.D., Clinical Assistant Professor, Department of Psychology, University of North Carolina, and Staff Psychologist, Geropsychiatric Institute, John Umstead Hospital, Chapel Hill, North Carolina

James A. Blumenthal, Ph.D., Assistant Professor of Medical Psychology, Department of Psychiatry, and Senior Fellow, Center for the Study of Aging and Human Development, Duke University Medical Center, Durham, North Carolina

Patrick A. Boudewyns, Ph.D., Associate Professor, Division of Medical Psychology, Department of Psychiatry, Duke University Medical Center, Durham, North Carolina

Charles J. Brown, Ph.D., Assistant Professor, Department of Psychology, University of Alabama, Birmingham, Alabama

Margaret A. Chesney, Ph.D., Director, Behavioral Medicine Program, Stanford Research Institute International, Menlo Park, California

Elaine Crovitz, Ph.D., Associate Professor of Medical Psychology, Department of Psychiatry, and Assistant Professor of Urology, Department of Surgery, Duke University Medical Center, Durham, North Carolina

Robert R. Freedman, Ph.D., Director, Laboratory of Behavioral Medicine, Lafayette Clinic, Wayne State University, Detroit, Michigan

Steve Herman, Ph.D., Medical Research Associate, Division of Medical Psychology, Department of Psychiatry, and Psychology Coordinator, O.A.R.S. Geriatric Evaluation and Treatment Clinic, Duke University Medical Center, Durham, North Carolina

Peter Ianni, M.A., Staff Psychologist, Laboratory of Behavioral Medicine, Lafayette Clinic, Wayne State University, Detroit, Michigan

Francis J. Keefe, Ph.D., Assistant Professor, Division of Medical Psychology, Department of Psychiatry, Duke University Medical Center, Durham, North Carolina

P. Scott Lawrence, Ph.D., Assistant Professor of Psychology, Department of Psychology, University of North Carolina, Greensboro, North Carolina

Sandra R. Leiblum, Ph.D., Clinical Associate Professor of Psychiatry and Director, Sexual Counseling Service, CMDNJ-Rutgers Medical School, Piscataway, New Jersey

Patrick E. Logue, Ph.D., Associate Professor of Medical Psychology, Department of Psychiatry, and Lecturer, Department of Psychology, Duke University Medical Center, Durham, North Carolina

Albert D. Loro, Jr., Ph.D., Assistant Professor of Medical Psychology, Department of Psychiatry and Behavior Change and Self-Control Program, Duke University Medical Center, Durham, North Carolina

Richard A. Lucas, Ph.D., Assistant Professor of Medical Psychology, Department of Psychiatry, Duke University Medical Center and Veterans Administration Hospital, Durham, North Carolina

Steven J. Lynn, Ph.D., Assistant Professor of Psychology, Department of Psychology, Ohio University, Athens, Ohio

Sarah M. McCarty, Ph.D., Assistant Professor, Department of Rehabilitation Medicine, Tufts University School of Medicine, Boston, Massachusetts

David I. Mostofsky, Ph.D., Professor of Psychology, Department of Psychology, Boston University, Boston, Massachusetts

Carole S. Orleans, Ph.D., Assistant Professor of Medical Psychology, Department of Psychiatry, Duke University Medical Center, Durham, North Carolina

Ray H. Rosenman, M.D., Senior Research Physician, Behavioral Medicine Program, Stanford Research Institute International, Menlo Park, California

Donald Scott, Ph.D., Clinical Psychologist, Department of Health Psychology, Miami Valley Hospital, Dayton, Ohio

Robert H. Shipley, Ph.D., Associate Professor of Medical Psychology, Department of Psychiatry, Duke University Medical Center, and Chief, Psychology Services, Durham Veterans Administration Medical Center, Durham, North Carolina

Alan D. Sirota, Ph.D., Assistant Professor, Department of Human Behavior, Brown University School of Medicine, Providence, Rhode Island

Gary E. Swan, Ph.D., Health Psychologist, Behavioral Medicine Program, Stanford Research Institute International, Menlo Park, California

Robert J. Thompson, Jr., Ph.D., Associate Professor and Head, Division of Medical Psychology, Department of Psychiatry, and Director, Duke Developmental Evaluation Center, Department of Pediatrics, Duke University Medical Center, Durham, North Carolina

Eric M. Ward, Ph.D., Assistant Professor of Neurology, Department of Neurology, Medical College of Wisconsin, Milwaukee, Wisconsin

Harold Ziesat, Ph.D., Assistant Professor of Psychiatry, Department of Psychiatry, University of Rochester Medical Center, Rochester, New York

PART I

Behavioral Medicine: An Introduction

Francis J. Keefe
James A. Blumenthal

1

Behavioral Medicine: Basic Principles and Theoretical Foundations

Behavioral medicine has received widespread recognition since 1976. This chapter, divided into three sections, provides an introduction to behavioral medicine. In the first, we discuss the definition of behavioral medicine. In section two, the origins of behavioral and psychosomatic medicine are contrasted. Finally, section three examines theoretical foundations and basic principles of assessment in behavioral medicine.

A DEFINITION OF BEHAVIORAL MEDICINE

The term *behavioral medicine* was first formally defined at the Yale Conference on Behavioral Medicine in 1977. At this meeting a group of behavioral and biomedical scientists known for their research contributions arrived at the following definition:

> Behavioral medicine is the field concerned with the development of behavioral science knowledge and techniques relevant to the understanding of physical health and illness and the application of this knowledge and these techniques to prevention, diagnosis, treatment and rehabilitation. . . .(Schwartz and Weiss, 1978a, p. 7)

This definition highlights the interdisciplinary nature of behavioral medicine. Behavioral medicine involves active collaboration between those trained in the behavioral sciences (e.g., psychologists, sociologists, epidemiologists), as well as those trained in medicine and allied health professions (e.g., neurologists, cardiologists, nurses, and physical therapists). The importance of basic research is also stressed in the definition. Basic research on behavioral factors has already contributed to our understanding of some diseases (e.g., Type A behavior and

3

coronary heart disease, discussed in Chapter 3). Much more basic research is needed. Practical applications of behavioral science concepts to assessment and treatment are also stressed in the definitions. Biofeedback, relaxation techniques, and a variety of operant conditioning techniques are among the behavioral techniques that have been shown to be effective in treating physiological dysfunction and disease (Shapiro and Surwit, 1976).

In addition to a formal definition, the boundaries of an emerging field are also determined by the activities of its members. A considerable amount of professional activity has taken place since the Yale Conference. As an outgrowth of the conference, the Academy of Behavioral Medicine Research was organized. This Academy, modeled along the lines of the National Academy of Science, is made up of distinguished scientists and serves to foster high-caliber research in behavioral medicine. Entry into the Academy is by invitation only. The Society of Behavioral Medicine, open to all behavioral and biomedical personnel who have an interest in this field, was founded shortly after the Academy. Since 1976 several journals, including the *Journal of Behavioral Medicine* and *Behavioral Medicine Abstracts,* have also appeared. An important additional development has been the establishment of a Behavioral Medicine Branch with study section status within the National Institutes of Health. This permits systematic peer review of federal funding requests for behavioral medicine research.

ORIGINS OF BEHAVIORAL AND PSYCHOSOMATIC MEDICINE

The emphasis on behavioral science applications to medical illness represents a marked shift from traditional psychological and psychiatric approaches. To appreciate the differences between these two approaches, the origins of behavioral and psychosomatic medicine must be considered.

The origins of psychosomatic medicine are directly related to the development of psychoanalysis. The term *psychosomatic* is derived from the Greek words *psyche* (meaning soul or mind) and *soma* (meaning body). It suggests "pertaining to mind and body" or "of mind and body." Originally, the psychosomatic model followed a "specificity" model, in which certain psychological dynamics contribute to specific physical disorders. Seven disorders were classified as psychosomatic: peptic ulcer disease, essential hypertension, bronchial asthma, thyrotoxicosis, rheumatoid arthritis, ulcerative colitis, and neurodermatitis (Alexander, French, & Pollack 1968). Alexander was aware of the organic predispositions of these diseases and proposed a psychological specificity theory that related certain personality traits to specific physiological manifestations. Alexander's specificity hypothesis was preceded by Flanders Dunbar who suggested that various personality constellations were etiologically associated with specific diseases and by Graham and coworkers who proposed that specific attitudes were related to specific medical disorders (Dunbar, 1943; Graham et al., 1962). For example, according to Graham and coworkers, acne reflects a feeling of being picked on or at, and wanting to be let alone; migraine headache reflects a feeling that something had to be achieved, and then release after the goal has been reached; and ulcerative colitis reflects a feeling of being injured, humiliated, or taken advantage of, and wanting to get rid of the responsible agent.

Empirical research has generally failed to support this specificity hypothesis, and other psychosomatic medicine models emerged. Those emphasizing biological adaptations to environmental stress gained widespread attention in the 1950s. For example, the general adaptation syndrome proposed tissue damage in response to chronic stress (Selye, 1956). While the theory did not propose for disease specificity, a study documented the stereotypic physiologic response patterns in humans (Lacey, Bateman, & Van Lehn, 1953). Similarly, Holmes and Rahe demonstrated that nonspecific life stresses, particularly in the form of life changes requiring social readjustment, often precede symptom formation and, therefore, play a causal (albeit nonspecific) role in the development of physical disease (Holmes and Rahe, 1967).

The early concepts of psychosomatic disorders recently have been expanded to include a more comprehensive definition (Weiner, 1977):

> Disease is a failure of adaptations, it is a biological phenomena. Because it is a biological phenomena, it deals with organism and interactions with their natural, social, and cultural environments. Disease is not only a matter of disturbance of the self-regulatory mechanisms within cells or of any one simple factor such as infection, nutritional deprivation, or the psychology of the diseased person (Weiner, 1977).

The emphasis on psychosocial factors is recognized in a 1977 definition of psychosomatic medicine (Lipowski, 1977). According to this definition, psychosomatic medicine involves (1) the study of the role of psychological, biological, and social factors in man's homeostasis; (2) a holistic approach to the practice of medicine; and (3) consultation-liaison psychiatry.

Other contemporary approaches to psychosomatic medicine place greater emphasis on biological psychiatry (Brady and Brodie, 1978). Within a relatively brief period of time, advances in medical technology have fostered tremendous growth in knowledge in neuroendocrinology, immunology, and psychopharmacology. There therefore remains a great deal of focus on understanding behavioral–biological interactions within the organism.

In contrast, behavioral medicine evolved from psychological, rather than medical or psychiatric, practice. Schwartz and Weiss note that while psychosomatic medicine emphasizes the etiology and pathogenesis of disease, behavioral medicine emphasizes the treatment and prevention of disease (Schwartz and Weiss, 1977; 1978a; 1978b). The latter emphasis is an important outgrowth of the relative failure of psychosomatic treatment to effectively modify physical symptoms or to reduce the prevalence of various disease states.

Additional historical developments have contributed to the emergence of behavioral medicine. First, since World War II, an increasing number of behavioral scientists have been working in close collaboration with biomedical scientists. The research and teaching done by psychologists, sociologists, epidemiologists, and other behavioral scientists has begun to significantly affect the training of physicians.

Second, empirical research in behavior therapy and behavior modification has clearly indicated the utility of behavioral concepts in treating many psychiatric disorders. Interest in extending the application of behavioral techniques to medical disorders has grown as their utility has become more apparent.

The third major development is technological. The development of inexpensive yet accurate biofeedback devices facilitates the study of physiological behavior responses in humans. Providing patients with accurate biological feedback has proven to be an effective treatment for many medical disorders (Keefe & Block, in press).

Finally, dissatisfaction is growing with respect to traditional medical and surgical approaches to many medical disorders. There are several examples: Long-term use of pharmacologic agents for chronic medical disorders is known to often lead to serious side effects (Leavitt, 1974). Surgical approaches for patients with acute problems (e.g., acute pain) have only limited success when used with more chronic patients (Caillet, 1968). As dissatisfaction with traditional treatment methods has increased, openness to alternative approaches has increased as well.

Sociopolitical reasons for the rise of behavioral medicine also should not be overlooked. Psychiatry has traditionally served as the connecting link between biomedical and behavioral science often at the exclusion of such disciplines as psychology, sociology, and epidemiology. Consequently, scientists have rallied around the field of behavioral medicine because it better represents their interests, needs, and beliefs. The criticisms of the psychosomatic medicine model are grounded in issues related to differences about the best way to conceptualize illness behavior, its antecedents and its modification. Professional concerns about authority and power, however, should remain independent so as not to confuse a sociopolitical issue with a scientific issue. The sociopolitical issue relates to what role nonmedical professionals play in the treatment of patients with medical disorders. The rationale for non-medically trained personnel should not be the inadequacies of their medically trained counterparts, but rather, should emphasize the unique contribution of each specialty.

THEORETICAL FOUNDATIONS AND BASIC PRINCIPLES OF ASSESSMENT

In this section, we first consider the major theories of behavior that have influenced the field of behavioral medicine. We then review basic principles derived from these theories that serve to guide the assessment process.

Theories of Behavior

Behavioral medicine is, by definition, a diverse field. Not surprisingly, a wide range of theoretical formulations has influenced this field. Although these theories may appear loosely related, they share one common characteristic: they are all theories of behavior. Each theory attempts to help explain, understand, and predict human behavior. A broad spectrum of human behavior has been addressed from a theoretical perspective. This spectrum includes patterns of physiological responding, overt motor behaviors, covert cognitive processes, and affective responses.

Theories of behavior form the conceptual bases of assessment in behavioral medicine. Theoretical models guide assessment efforts, pinpointing relevant aspects of behavior and suggesting fruitful assessment strategies.

This section considers a number of theoretical models of behavior. The models chosen for discussion do not represent an exhaustive list. Each, however, has had a major impact on behavioral medicine assessment and treatment efforts. These models form the theoretical foundations for many of the assessment strategies considered in subsequent chapters.

Classical Conditioning

Classical conditioning is a very basic form of learning. Through this form of learning, environmental events develop the ability to elicit physiological responses. Pavlov, a Russian physiologist, was the first to systematically study this learning phenomenon (Pavlov, 1927). In his study of gastric activity during digestion, he found that dogs often salivated in response to environmental events (e.g., the sight of an experimenter), and not simply to physical stimuli (e.g., ingestion of food). Later experiments demonstrated that this response was a learned one. Pavlov paired a previously neutral environmental stimulus (a bell) with an *unconditioned stimulus* that he knew reflexively elicited an *unconditioned response* (salivation). He found that after many such pairings, presentation of the neutral stimulus alone could produce a salivary response. Thus, through a process of learning a neutral stimulus—the bell—had become a *conditioned stimulus* capable of eliciting a physiological response.

Classical conditioning may have an important impact on certain medical disorders (Whitehead, Fedoravicius, Blackwell & Wooley, 1979). Nausea and vomiting are especially susceptible to this type of learning. This is evident in the response of many cancer patients to chemotherapy (discussed in Chapter 12). Chemicals administered during the chemotherapeutic process often produce reflexive nausea and vomiting. In this instance, the drugs used in chemotherapy constitute an unconditioned stimulus, and the physiological reaction, an unconditioned response. With repeated chemotherapy sessions, patients often develop nausea and vomiting responses in the presence of stimuli associated with treatment. Viewing a nurse or a doctor, or the simple anticipation of a visit to the hospital (conditioned stimuli) may produce vomiting.

Whitehead et al. have hypothesized that medical disorders susceptible to classical conditioning have symptoms that (1) are abrupt in onset, (2) occur in specific situations, (3) are associated with anxiety, and (4) are not affected by the response of the social environment (Whitehead et al., 1979). Classical conditioning is believed to have a major effect on symptoms of asthma, migraine headache, hypertension, and irritable bowel syndrome.

The classical conditioning model focuses assessment efforts on the relationship between patterns of phsyiological responding and antecedent environmental events. Treatment efforts are directed toward altering this relationship. Anxiety-reduction techniques that decrease autonomic arousal are especially helpful. Through a process of progressive relaxation training, autogenic training, hypnosis- or bio-feedback-assisted relaxation training, patients can acquire the ability to extinguish conditioned response patterns. This is accomplished by the patient's practice of an incompatible response (relaxation) in the presence of conditioned stimuli.

Operant Conditioning

Operant conditioning also emphasizes learned relationships between behavioral and environmental events. There are two fundamental differences between the operant and classical conditioning models. First, operant conditioning focuses on the role that environmental consequences play in modulating behavior. Second, behaviors most susceptible to operant conditioning are those that are overt and easily observed.

B. F. Skinner, an experimental psychologist, carried out much of the early experimental work on operant conditioning (Skinner, 1953). This work examined the role that response contingencies play in the acquisition and maintenance of simple motor behaviors in animals. When motor responses such as a key peck or bar press were followed by positive consequences, e.g., delivery of food, the likelihood of response decreased. Not only were the nature of consequences (positive versus aversive) found to be important, but the schedule under which they were delivered was critical. Responses that were positively reinforced intermittently were much more resistant to extinction than those reinforced on a continuous schedule.

Skinner maintained that the naturally occurring behaviors of humans could be analyzed from an operant conditioning perspective. The basic elements in this analysis were (1) a precise definition of the overt behavior of interest, (2) careful measurement of behaviors under natural circumstances, (3) tentative identification of relationships between behavior and environmental consequences, and (4) confirmation of the importance of environmental consequences by observing the results of systematic environmental manipulation on behavior. This approach, termed *applied behavior analysis,* greatly influenced the field of behavior therapy. Research has demonstrated that by positively reinforcing desired responses and withholding reinforcement from undesired responses, many maladaptive behavior patterns can be altered (Kanfer and Phillips, 1970; Bandura, 1977). In this work, particular emphasis was placed on the importance of social consequences. Behavior is often exquisitively sensitive to control by attention given by spouse, family, and friends.

Patients suffering from chronic medical disorders often develop maladaptive coping behaviors learned via operant conditioning mechanisms. Chronic pain patients, for example, may continue to exhibit pain behaviors (grimacing, complaining about pain, narcotic ingestion) long after the tissue pathology initially responsible for their pain has healed. In these patients, pain behavior results in powerful positive reinforcers in the form of solicitous attention from family members, avoidance of unwanted work and home responsibilities, and the addictive qualities of narcotics. Fordyce demonstrated that pain behaviors are reduced when the postive reinforcement for them is withheld and a variety of "well" behaviors are socially reinforced (Fordyce, 1976).

Medical disorders that produce highly overt behavioral symptoms apparent to both the patient and those in the immediate social environment (e.g., anorexia nervosa) are more likely to be influenced by operant conditioning factors. While the role of operant conditioning in the initial etiology of pathophysiological disorders is unclear, evidence clearly indicates that operant factors can function to maintain associated behavioral symptoms (Miller, 1972).

Miller stated that pathophysiologic response patterns can be learned via operant conditioning (Miller, 1972). He hypothesized that attention from a parent or spouse of a patient delivered immediately following a pathophysiologic symptom may serve to reinforce that symptom. This is an interesting hypothesis, but compelling evidence to support the importance of operant conditioning in the acquisition of pathophysiologic responses in medical patients has not yet been gathered. Operant conditioning techniques, however, can be quite effective in modifying established pathophysiologic responses. Operant conditioning procedures have been successfully applied to patients suffering from a variety of gastrointestinal, urogenital, neurologic and muscular disorders (Keefe and Block, in press).

Mixed Learning Models

The classical and operant conditioning models were initially developed in laboratory studies with animals. Attempts to apply these basic learning models to complex human behavioral interactions have met with several problems (Staats, 1981). In natural environments, the numbers of stimuli that may function to control behaviors are many and the range of relevant responses can be quite broad. Organismic variables, such as fatigue and drug effects, may mediate the control that environmental events exert over behavior. Finally, the prior history of the human organism is vastly more rich and complex that that of a laboratory animal. This long learning history may have an important impact on immediate behavior. To summarize, basic learning models are viewed by some as being too simple to explain human behaviors.

In order to deal with the complexity of human behavior, mixed learning models have been proposed. Mixed models of stimulus and response control have been suggested to explain complex symptom patterns (Kanfer and Phillips, 1970). Briefly, they indicate that elements of both classical and operant conditioning may be operating in a given case. For example, a fear of medical procedures may be acquired through a process of classical conditioning. Repeated pairings of physiologic arousal with stimuli in the hospital setting may lead to a conditioned fear of such settings. Conditioned fear leads the patient to avoid or escape any contact with medical procedures. Avoidance responses are then maintained via an operant conditioning process, i.e., by their positive consequences (reduction of fear and arousal). Such a mixed learning model directs assessment efforts to a wider class of variables. These include stimulus events, organismic variables, responses, contingency relationships, and consequences.

Stimulus events (S).   Relevant stimuli needing to be considered include not only physical or social stimuli, but the individual's own behavior, physiological responses, and thoughts.

Organismic variables (O).   The biological state, genetic background, and physical deficiences of the organism greatly contribute to learning and must be considered.

Responses (R).   A full range of verbal and motor responses are included in this class of variables. Responses may occur as part of a chain or sequence. One response (e.g., physiological arousal) may serve to mediate a host of others (e.g., headaches, avoidance behavior, intake of pain medication). In addition, complex learned responses such as a set of skills or cognitions, are often relevant.

Contingency relationships (K).   Schedules of reinforcement occurring in the natural environment are complex. Consequences usually occur on intermittent rather than continuous schedules.

Consequences (C).   Events that immediately follow responses are of obvious importance.

Discussing relationships between the various elements of the S-O-R-K-C model helps provide for a more comprehensive analysis of human behavior.

In summary, mixed learning models combine elements of classical and operant conditioning models with other learning concepts, such as response chains and mediating responses. In doing so, they extend basic learning theory to encompass more complex human interactions.

Recognition that multiple forms of learning may account for maladaptive behavior leads to multiple treatment recommendations. Techniques to reduce the potent effects of conditioned stimuli (e.g., relaxation) thus may be paired with social reinforcement techniques designed to increase the likelihood of adaptive behaviors. This multimodal treatment package approach is often used in behavioral medicine applications (Gottlieb, Strite, Koller, et al., 1977).

Modeling

Behaviors can also be acquired through observation of a model. Observing a competent model engaged in a task greatly facilitates subsequent performance on that task (Bandura, 1977). Modeling may have either negative or positive effects, for example, a child who views an anxious child's squeamish reaction to an injection is likely to develop anxiety when placed in a similar situation. In contrast, children who are shown a film of another child successfully coping with surgery are much more likely to successfully cope (Melamed and Siegel, 1975).

Modeling is considered as basic a form of learning as classical and operant conditioning. Bandura has stated ". . .virtually all learning phenomena resulting from direct experiences can occur on a vicarious basis through observation of other persons' behaviors and its consequences for them. . . ." (Bandura, 1969). Modeling is believed to be especially important in the acquisition of social behavior. Many of the sick-role behaviors displayed by patients who are ill are acquired via a modeling process. Observing a family member or friend's response to chronic illness or disease can affect that person's subsequent response to illness. The effects of modeling are strongest when the observer and model have many characteristics in common (such as age, sex, race, ethnic background) (Bandura, 1969). Individuals of different cultural and social backgrounds are known to respond to chronic illness and pain in very different ways (Sternbach, 1974). Vicarious learning occurring through observation of peer reference groups may well account for much of this diversity.

The concept of modeling influences assessment in behavioral medicine by directing attention to effects that behavior of individuals in the patient's social environment may have in teaching the patient response patterns. Providing patients with more appropriate models can greatly facilitate their ability to cope with such trauma as severe burns (Craig, 1978) or surgery (Melamed and Siegel, 1975).

Cognitive-behavioral Theories

There has been a great deal of interest in the 1970s in the role that cognitive factors play in learning. Prominent behavioral researchers have maintained (1) that cognitive processes are subject to learning and (2) that modifying covert cognitive processes can produce marked changes in overt behavior (Bandura, 1977; Mahoney, 1974; Meichenbaum, 1974).

Ellis and Beck have highlighted the role that errors in cognitive self-appraisals play in mediating maladaptive behavior (Ellis, 1971; Beck, 1976). Individuals with behavioral disorders, such as depression, often evaluate themselves in an illogical fashion. Through systematic errors in processing information these individuals distort the meaning of events around them. Common cognitive errors include *catastrophizing* (anticipating that any experience will have the worst outcome), *personlization* (taking responsibility for negative events), and *selective abstrac-tion* (selectively attending to negative features of an experience). Research has shown that training individuals to recognize these illogical thought patterns and to substitute more rational self-statements can produce major improvements in behavior.

Cognitive theories have expanded the focus of behavior theories beyond obvious overt responses to important covert responses. There are problems with this approach (Rachlin, 1977). As a theory, however, this approach attempts to take into account the unique role that language plays in human learning. Recent research has demonstrated the utility of the cognitive analysis in helping to explain the experience of chronic pain (Lefebvre, 1981).

In summary, cognitive–behavioral theories have only recently emerged as an important conceptual model of behavior. These theories, however, have strongly influenced assessment strategies in behavioral medicine. As the reader may note in subsequent chapters, assessment of cognitive factors is stressed.

Models of Self-regulatory Behavior

Humans are clearly capable of regulating their own behavior. While environmental events exert some control over behavior, the individual exerts control by choosing to pursue certain activities or by arranging the environment in such a way as to elicit desired behaviors. Self-regulation has long interested behavior theorists (Skinner, 1953; Ferster, 1965; Kanfer and Phillips, 1970). A number of theoretical models of self-regulatory behavior have been advanced to explain the mechanisms responsible for self-control. These models have three basic tenets: First, self-regulatory behaviors are learned through a variety of childhood and life experiences. Second, the ability of an individual to engage in self-regulation can become impaired or deteriorate as a result of psychological stress, physical injury, or trauma. When this happens, attempts at self-control weaken and powerful environmental factors can acquire control over behavior. Third, through a training process with behavioral techniques (such as relaxation or biofeedback training), self-regulatory skills can be strengthened and/or new methods of self-control learned. As self-control is enhanced, the individual is able to override competing environmental events responsible for maintaining maladaptive behavior patterns.

Self-control techniques work because they alter the level and strength of self-efficacy (Bandura, 1977). The role of cognitive processes in this model is central. Individuals who expect that their attempts to control their own behavior will be effective are more likely to initiate self-control efforts. If these self-control efforts are successful, expectations of self-efficacy are enhanced and the individual will persist. Many of the behavioral techniques utilized to enhance self-control, indeed, do give patients an immediate sense of control over their behavior, for example, a patient suffering from Raynaud's disease may discover, as a result of a brief autogenic or temperature biofeedback training session a capability to control peripheral blood flow (Keefe & Block, in press).

Mulholland (1977) has proposed that a cybernetic model can be used to explain self-regulation of behavioral and physiological responses. Concepts from engineering and electronics are used to analyze the dynamic effects that accurate feedback may have. According to this viewpoint, control over behavior can be enhanced by providing an individual with performance feedback. Individuals with behavior problems can be considered in an open-loop-system of behavioral control. In this system, the individual initiates a new course of behavior; this behavior then effects on the environment. The individual usually does not systematically attend to the effects of personal behavior and, thus, cannot correct it as effectively. In a closed-loop-system, however, ongoing feedback is provided to the individual. Positive feedback tells the individual that the correct course of action is being pursued; negative feedback indicates that a change is needed. Negative feedback tells the individual that the wrong course is being pursued. In biofeedback training, accurate feedback of changes in physiological responding can be provided via auditory (a beeping tone) or visual means (a needle on a meter or a moving dot on an oscilloscope). In other forms of behavioral treatment, performance feedback may take many forms, i.e., the comments of a therapist or a graph of changes occurring over treatment. The cybernetic model points out the potential positive effects of closing the feedback loop and providing corrective information.

Models of self-regulatory behavior direct attention to the importance of assessing the patient's capacity for, and current use of, self-control strategies. The success of self-management techniques (such as biofeedback in the treatment of disease) has suggested that these models of behavior are particularly important to behavioral medicine.

Basic Principles of Assessment

Several basic principles of assessment can be derived from the theories of human behavior reviewed here (Keefe, Kopel, & Gordon, 1978).

The first basic principle is that symptoms are defined in observable and measurable terms. Behavioral components of a medical symptom are often not immediately apparent to either the patient or the evaluator. Patients tend to describe their symptoms in vague and confusing terms. They see their symptoms simply as the by-product of underlying tissue pathology. The behavioral medicine perspective, in contrast, attempts to analyze the patient's presenting symptoms and style of coping as instances of behavior. Thus, diffuse complaints of cramping and tightness in the shoulders may be redefined in terms that are potentially observable and measurable. This tightness may be defined in terms of muscle tension of the upper trapezius muscle and may be measured via electromyography. Other relevant problems such as medication intake or activity level may also constitute targets for assessment efforts.

Redefining presenting symptoms in observable terms allows careful measurement and analysis. The behaviors observed vary with the medical disorder. For example, in assessing patients suffering from peripheral vascular disorders, the temperature of the extremities and frequency of vasospasm are especially important. In assessing patients suffering from sleep disorders, overt characteristics of the sleep pattern itself (length of time to sleep onset, number of napping episodes per day, etc.) may be critical.

A second basic principle of assessment is that interactions between behavior and environmental events are important. Many assessment strategies reviewed in this book are specifically designed to evaluate the role that physical and social stimuli play in controlling behavior. Analysis of present behavior–environmental interaction is stressed. Historical material is considered relevant insofar as it contributes to the understanding of current behavior.

A third basic principle is that assessment is directly linked to treatment efforts. One of the major strengths of behavioral medicine is the specificity of treatment programs utilized. All patients do not undergo a single treatment plan but rather, specific treatment procedures are matched to the needs of the individual patient.

A fourth basic principle is that behavioral measurements are repeated over time. In behavioral medicine, assessment is a continuing and integral part of the treatment process. Repeated measurements are needed to establish the reliability and validity of behavioral improvements. A minimum of three separate measurements are needed before, during, and after treatment (Kazdin, 1981).

The fifth, and final, basic assessment principle is that treatment techniques are introduced systematically. Whenever possible, assessment strategies are used to evaluate the efficacy of treatment. Single-case experimental designs, such as the reversal design or multiple-baseline design, permit one to rule out alternative explanations for effects obtained following the introduction of treatment (Hersen & Barlow, 1976). The intensive study of the single case is a basic objective of assessment efforts in behavioral medicine. As a scientific method, this approach may well advance our understanding of how behavioral factors influence physical health and illness.

SUMMARY

Behavioral medicine is a new field that is interdisciplinary in nature. This field recognizes the importance of contributions of behavioral and biomedical scientists to our understanding of how behavior affects health and illness. A major focus of behavioral medicine has been the clinical application of behavioral techniques to patients with medical disorders. Behavioral medicine can be differentiated from psychosomatic medicine in several ways: Psychosomatic medicine emphasizes etiology and pathogenesis of disease and has been strongly influenced by psychodynamic theory and biological psychiatry. Behavioral medicine emphasizes prevention and treatment of disease and has been most strongly influenced by conditioning and learning theories of human behavior. Theoretical models that have had a major impact on behavioral medicine include classical conditioning, operant conditioning, mixed learning models, modeling, cognitive–behavioral theories, and models of self-regulatory behavior. These models direct and guide assessment efforts. Several basic principles of assessment derived from these models can be delineated. These are (1) presenting symptoms are defined in observable and measurable terms; (2) current behavior–environmental interactions are important; (3) assessment information is linked to treatment efforts; (4) measurements of behavior are repeated over time; and (5) treatment techniques are introduced systematically to permit evaluation of outcome.

REFERENCES

Alexander, F., French, T., Pollack, K. *Psychosomatic specificity: Experimental study and results.* (vol. 1). Chicago: University of Chicago Press, 1968.

Bandura, A. *Principles of behavior modification.* New York: Holt, Rinehart & Winston, 1969.

Bandura, A. Self-efficacy: Toward a unifying theory of behavior change. *Psychological Review,* 1977, *84,* 191–215.

Beck, A. T. *Cognitive therapy and emotional disorders.* New York: International Universities Press, 1976.

Brady, J. P. & Brodie, H. K. H. *Controversy in psychiatry.* Philadelphia: W. B. Saunders, 1978.

Caillet, R. *Low back pain syndrome.* Philadelphia: Davis, 1968.

Craig, K. D. Social modeling influences on pain. In R. A. Sternbach (Ed.), *The Psychology of pain.* New York: Raven Press, 1978.

Dunbar, F. *Psychosomatic Diagnosis.* New York: Paul Bottomly, 1943.

Ellis, A. E. *Growth through reason: Verbatim cases in rational-emotive therapy.* North Hollywood, California: Wilshire, 1971.

Ferster, C. B. Classification of behavioral pathology. In L. Kramer and L. P. Ullman (Eds.), *Research in behavior modification: New developments and implications.* New York: Holt, Rinehart & Winston, 1965.

Fordyce, W. *Behavioral methods for chronic pain and illness.* St. Louis: C. V. Mosby, 1976.

Gottlieb, H., Strite, L., Koller, R., Madorsky, A., Hackersmith, V., Kleeman, M., & Wagner, J. Comprehensive rehabilitation of patients having chronic low back pain. *Archives of Physical Medicine & Rehabilitation,* 1977, *58,* 101–108.

Graham, D. T., Lundy, R. M., Benjamin L. S., et al: Specific attitudes in initial interviews with patients having different ''psychosomatic diseases''. *Psychosomatic Medicine,* 1962, *24,* 257–266.

Hersen, M. & Barlow, D. H. *Single case experimental designs: Strategies for Studying behavior change.* New York: Pergamon, 1976.

Holmes, T. H., & Rahe, R. H. The social readjustment rating scale. *Journal of Psychosomatic Research,* 1967, *11,* 213–218.

Kanfer, F. & Phillips, J. *Learning foundations of behavior therapy.* New York: Wiley, 1970.

Kazdin, A. Drawing valid inferences from case studies. *Journal of Consulting & Clinical Psychology,* 1981, *49,* 183–192.

Keefe, F. J., & Block, A. R. Biofeedback and behavioral medicine. In J. O. Cavenar & H. Keith H. Brodie (Eds.), *Critical problems in psychiatry, 1982–1983.* New York: Academic Press, in press.

Keefe, F. J., Kopel, S. & Gordon S. B. *A Practical Guide to Behavioral Assessment.* New York: Springer, 1978.

Lacey, H., Bateman, D. F., & Van Lehn, R. Autonomic response specificity: An experimental study. *Psychosomatic Medicine,* 1957, *15,* 8–21.

Leavitt, F. *Drugs and behavior.* Philadelphia: W. B. Saunders, 1974.

Lefebvre, M. F. Cognitive distortion and cognitive errors in depressed psychiatric and low back pain patients. *Journal of Consulting & Clinical Psychology,* 1981, *49,* 517–525.

Lipowski, Z. J., Lipsitt, D. R., & Walbrow, P. C. (Eds.), *Psychosomatic medicine: Current trends and clinical applications.* New York: Oxford University Press, 1977.

Mahoney, M. J. *Cognition and behavior modification.* Cambridge, Massachuseetts: Ballinger, 1974.

Meichenbaum, D. *Cognitive behavior modification.* Morristown, New Jersey: General Learning Press, 1974.

Melamed, B., & Siegel, L. J. Reduction of anxiety in children facing hospitalization and surgery by use of filmed modeling. *Journal of Consulting & Clinical Psychology,* 1975, *43,* 511–512.

Mulholland, T. B. Biofeedback as a scientific method. In G. E. Schwartz, & J. Beatty (Eds.), *Biofeedback: Theory & research.* New York: Academic Press, 1977.

Miller, N. E. Interactions between learned and physical factors in mental illness. *Seminars in Psychiatry,* 1972, *4,* 239–254.

Pavlov, I. *Conditioned reflexes.* London: Oxford University Press, 1927.

Rachlin, H. Reinforcing and punishing thoughts: A rejoinder to Ellis and Mahoney. *Behavior Therapy,* 1977, *8,* 678–681.

Schwartz, G. E., & Weiss, S. M. What is behavioral medicine? *Psychomsomatic Medicine,* 1977, *36,* 377–381.

Schwartz, G. E. & Weiss, S. M. Behavioral medicine revisited: An amended definition. *Journal Behavioral Medicine,* 1978a, *1,* 249–251.

Schwartz, G. E., & Weiss, S. M. Yale conference on behavioral medicine: A proposed definition of statement of goals. *Journal of Behavioral Medicine, 1978b, 1,* 3–14.

Selye, H. *The stress of life.* New York: McGraw-Hill, 1956.

Shapiro, D., & Surwit, R. S. Learned control of physiological function and disease. In H. Leitenberg (Ed.), *Handbook of behavior modification and behavior therapy.* New York: Prentice-Hall, 1976.

Skinner, B. F. *Science in human behavior.* New York: Macmillan, 1953.

Staats, A. W. Paradigmatic behaviorism, unified theory, unified theory construction methods, and the zeitgeist of separatism. *American Psychologist,* 1981, *36,* 239–256.

Sternbach, R. A. *Pain patients: Traits and treatment.* New York: Academic Press, 1974.

Weiner, H. *Psychobiology of human disease.* Amsterdam: Elsevier, 1977.

Whitehead, W. E., Fedoravicius, A. S., Blackwell, B., & Wooley, S. A behavioral conceptualization of psychosomatic illness: Psychosomatic symptoms as learned responses. In J. R. Macnamara (Ed.), *Behavioral approaches to medicine: Application and analysis.* New York: Plenum, 1979.

PART II

Assessment Strategies for Cardiovascular Disorders

Margaret A. Chesney
Gary E. Swan
Ray H. Rosenman

2

Assessment of Hypertension

National estimates indicate that 23.2 million adults between 18 and 74 years of age have hypertension, or high blood pressure. Of these, approximately 5 percent have elevated blood pressure as a result of a specific endocrine or renal disorder; the remaining 95 percent have essential hypertension, that is, elevated blood pressure not due to a specific cause. This chapter focuses on measurement issues relevant to the assessment and treatment of essential hypertension.

The blood pressure criteria that define essential hypertension are reviewed briefly in the first section of this chapter. In the second section, variables that influence blood pressure and its determination are discussed, including measurement procedures and situations, individual differences, and life style factors. These factors can confound treatment or experimental results for the clinician or researcher concerned with the assessment of an individual's basal or "true" blood pressure. On the other hand, for the clinician or researcher interested in the genesis of blood pressure elevation, these same factors may be central elements in treatment plans or research designs. The final section is an overview of the expanded role assessment can play in the exploration of the etiology of hypertension, in the evaluation of behavioral procedures for blood pressure reduction, and in patient adherence to antihypertensive regimens.

HYPERTENSION CRITERIA

Blood pressure is continuous. There is no clear division between normal and high blood pressure or hypertension. Similarly, hypertension is not a disease; it is a state of elevated blood pressure that is associated with end-organ complications

Table 2-1
Blood Pressure Cut-Points Associated with Increased Mortality

	Systolic BP	Diastolic BP
Men under 45	>130 mm Hg	> 90 mm Hg
Men over 45	>140 mm Hg	> 95 mm Hg
Women	>160 mm Hg	>95 mm Hg

and disease states. Historically, arbitrary cut points distinguishing high from normal blood pressure have been suggested; for example, the World Health Organization has defined hypertension as systolic blood pressures greater than 160 mm Hg, accompanied by diastolic blood pressures greater than 95 mm Hg.* These criteria were modified to correspond to blood pressures associated with reduced life expectancy (Kaplan, 1980). Blood pressure (BP) levels that are associated with a 50 percent or greater increase in mortality for men (classified by age) and women are given in Table 2-1. Still another criterion is offered by the Hypertension Detection and Follow-Up Program which reported significant treatment effects for diastolic blood pressure of 90 mm Hg and above (Hypertension Detection and Follow-Up Group, 1979, I and II).

These differing criteria indicate that a consensus is lacking on the definition of hypertension. In the absence of a standard definition, the clinician and the researcher are forced to select an operational definition and cut-points that are reliable, valid, and consistent with their immediate objectives for blood pressure measurement.

MEASUREMENT FACTORS

Initially, blood pressure determination or assessment may be considered straightforward, i.e., a patient's blood pressure assessment is synonymous with the two numbers indicated by the sphygmomanometer. However, blood pressure is not static and is influenced directly or indirectly by measurement procedures and situations, individual differences, and such life style variables as diet and smoking. As stated in the introductory section of this chapter, depending on the purpose of the blood pressure assessment, these influences may be contributors to error or elements of central importance to blood pressure measurement.

---

*For the reader not familiar with physiology, blood pressure is the pressure of the blood on the walls of the arteries. Systolic blood pressure is the maximum pressure occurring with contraction of the left ventricle of the heart, and diastolic blood pressure is minimum pressure occurring when the ventricle dilates between contractions. These points are most frequently determined by the Korotkoff method (presence or absence of sounds).

Measurement Procedures

Instrumentation

The procedure followed in measuring blood pressure can greatly influence the results. A key variable in this procedure is the instrument used. There are numerous devices for measuring blood pressure. The most common instruments rely on mercury–gravity or aneroid manometers. Both instruments consist of a compression cuff, a pressure source, and a manometer.

The compression cuff, connected to the pressure source and manometer, is placed around a patient's limb (typically, the upper arm). The amount of air pressure in the cuff is indicated on the manometer in terms of millimeters of mercury. The air pressure in the cuff is increased to the point where blood flow to the limb is occluded. The air pressure is then slowly released with the manometer indicating the dropping air pressure in the cuff. When the pressure is reduced to a point equal to the systolic pressure, sounds are heard through a stethoscope placed over the patient's brachial artery. When pressure in the cuff is reduced further, the point equal to the diastolic pressure is reached, and the sounds disappear.

The measurement of blood pressure in terms of millimeters of mercury is based on the mercury–gravity manometer, a straight, graduated glass tube with a reservoir containing mercury. The pressure in the cuff exerts equal pressure on the mercury in the reservoir, causing it to rise in the tube. Once calibrated, the mercury manometer provides an accurate measurement; recalibration is not necessary as long as the mercury is at the zero mark on the tube when no pressure is applied.

Because mercury manometers are bulky instruments, aneroid manometers were developed, which provide blood pressure readings on a calibrated dial. Variations of pressure in the compression cuff cause a bellows within the dial assembly to expand and compress, turning the needle of the dial. The more convenient aneroid manometer, however, requires frequent calibration and is probably less accurate.

Errors in measurement.   Accurate blood pressure measurement with manometers is more difficult than it may seem. Even with calibrated manometers, blood pressure measurement errors are common. The most frequent errors and the correct procedures to avoid them are presented in Table 2-2. To avoid measurement errors, it is recommended that individuals who take blood pressure measurements be thoroughly trained according to the guidelines of the Joint National Committee on Detection, Evaluation and Treatment of High Blood Pressure (Moser, 1977), and the American Heart Association (Kirkendall, Feinleib, Freis, and Mark, 1981).

Blood Pressure Machines

Simple machines capable of blood pressure measurement have been developed. The three types that are most frequently used will be discussed here. The first is a desk-top device that requires an operator. The second includes automatic

Table 2-2

Common Reports in Blood Pressure Measurement

Error	Correct Procedure
Cuff placed over clothing	Arm should be bared under cuff
Reinflating a partially inflated cuff when systolic blood pressure is inadvertently missed	Deflate cuff entirely; wait 30 seconds and reinflate
Improper positioning of arm	Arm should be resting on support with the subject's brachial artery at heart level
Inadequate number of readings in rapid succession	Take number of readings adequate for purpose, with at least 30 seconds between each reading
Improper cuff application	Cuff should be applied evenly and snugly with the bottom eduge of cuff 1 inch above antecubitafossa
Inaccurate reading of the mercury column	
Failing to calibrate equipment	Mercury column should be vertical and read at eye level
Improper size cuff	
	Establish and maintain a protocol to insure regular calibration of equipment
	Appropriate size cuffs should be used so that the bladder encircles the arm. Small (child) and large cuffs are available in addition to the standard size

instruments, and is stationary as well as ambulatory. The third consists of home blood pressure measuring units.

Infrasonic Blood Pressure Monitors

A number of automated blood pressure recorders are produced by Sphygmetrics, Inc. (Woodland Hills, California). The most common are the electronic infrasonic devices that use a pen on a rotating paper disk to record signals from an aneroid manometer in open communication with a cuff bladder. This device does not register Korotkoff sounds but senses arterial wall oscillations on a narrow subaudible frequency band. A technician is required to inflate and deflate the cuff.

This device has been used in a number of studies with somewhat mixed results (Voors, Foster, Frerichs, and Berenson, 1975; Cohen, Evans, Krantz, & Stokols, 1980). Fox and Phelps conducted an accuracy study of the Sphygemtrics Infrasonde device on 10 neonates and found high correlations between the device and direct arterial pressures (.90 diastolic; .94 systolic) (Fox and Phelps, 1981). In a similar study of adult women and adolescents, Van den Berg found that correlations between diastolic pressures in adolescents (-.69) were significantly lower than parallel correlations for adults (Van den Berg, 1980). The source of the reduced reliability was not found; however, the extent to which these results were due to anthropo-metric variables was studied and found to be negative.

A comparison study was conducted of the Sphygmetrics SR-2 and mercury manometers (Fortman, Marcuson, Bitter, and Haskell, 1980). Simultaneous blood pressures were recorded in 21 men and 50 women using the SR-2 unit. The machine measured slightly higher systolic and slightly lower diastolic pressures than the mercury manometers, but the differences were determined to be not significant clinically. Interpretation of the SR-2 disc was very reliable, with inter- and intrarater correlations between .99 for systolic and .94 for diastolic.

Despite this reported evidence of accuracy, there are several cautions when using Sphygmetrics' SR-2 instrument. First, the device must be repeatedly cali-brated; most researchers using this instrument calibrate it daily, prior to taking any measures. The second consideration is that the accuracy is widely influenced by ranges in room temperature. The third consideration involves interpretation of the disc recordings. Although most discs can be interpreted readily, approximately 5 to 7 percent do not fit set criteria and yield discrepant readings. Stanford Univer-sity is currently developing a standardized set of criteria for reproducible interpre-tations of these discs (Haskell, 1980).

The advantage of the Sphygmetrics instruments is that they provide "hard" blood pressure data that can be repeatedly scored by independent judges or raters. These instruments, however, necessitate the use of specially trained personnel and involve subjective judgments, a potential source of error. Another possible disad-vantage of this device is that it does not assess blood pressure in terms of Korotkoff sounds and, therefore, is not consistent with standard procedures for determining blood pressure.

Vita-Stat Automatic Blood Pressure Machines

Two models of automatic blood pressure instruments that utilize Korotkoff sounds in determining blood pressure are produced by Vita-Stat (St. Petersburg, Florida). One model is a coin-operated device that measures systolic and diastolic blood pressure using a looped cuff equipped with a microphone. After a start button is pressed, the cuff closes on the arm, inflates and slowly deflates, regis-tering systolic pressure at the appearance of Korotkoff sounds and diastolic pres-sure at the disappearance of sounds. The automatic operation, signal processing, and rejection of readings due to artifacts are controlled by a microprocessor.

Several reliability studies have been conducted with this device both in the laboratory and in the field. (Berkson, Whipple, Shireman, et al., 1979; Jordan and Chadwick, 1979; Polk, Rosner, Feudo and Vandenburgh, 1980). With one exception (Polk et al., 1980), these studies demonstrated that the Vita-Stat mea-sures fifth-phase diastolic blood pressure similarly to human technicians, but is more variable than technicians in measuring systolic blood pressure. Differences between the device and human technician readings are significant if the machines are not frequently calibrated. It is possible that a lack of calibration may have been a major source of error in the study that demonstrated markedly greater differences between the manual and machine readings than have been found in other studies (Polk et al., 1980).

There is also a desk-top Vita-Stat blood pressure machine that was designed for use in intensive care units. This machine utilizes the same blood pressure assessment circuitry, but differs from the larger unit in several ways. The portable Vita-Stat measures heart rate as well as blood pressure; it can be programmed to record these indices at time intervals and to sound an alarm when a monitored blood pressure rises above a set limit. One or two subjects may be simultaneously monitored using this device. Unlike the larger Vita-Stat, the cuff on the portable Vita-Stat is placed manually on the arm of the patient or subject but inflates and deflates automatically. This instrument has proved to be useful in laboratory research as it can take blood pressures in series. Furthermore, when a series of blood pressures is being taken, the previous blood pressures can be stored in memory and are utilized to decrease the time required for cuff deflation.

Ambulatory Monitors

There are numerous ambulatory blood pressure monitors available. These monitors consisted of blood pressure cuffs inflated and deflated by the wearer. The blood pressures are assessed by a microphone taped in place for detection of Korotkoff sounds. The sounds and time of measurement are automatically stored on a portable tape recorder for subsequent transcription.

Del Mar Avionics (Irvine, California) has developed an ambulatory monitor that is similar to those described above but has automatic cuff inflation and deflation. Blood pressure measurements are taken automatically, according to the program set by the clinician or researcher. This enables recording for up to 24 hours; the unit can also be used to record electrocardiograph signals. Blood pressure or other recorded cardiovascular data are stored on tape for subsequent transcription and scoring by a microprocessor.

Home Blood Pressure Units

A number of blood pressure instruments are available for home use. Consumer testing has found the mercury units to remain accurate for the longest time (Consumer Reports, 1979). However, the occasional leakage of mercury from these devices can be a hazard, especially if small children are in the home. The mechanical aneroid models, while lighter and more compact, require more frequent calibration than the mercury units. The electronic devices are the easiest to use when taking one's own blood pressure, but are delicate and tend to be less accurate than the mercury instruments.

In general, the home blood pressure units with built-in stethoscopes and the D-shaped metal ring on the cuff for tightening are easier to use alone. If patients are using home devices, it is advisable to have them calibrated with a standard mercury manometer every 6 months.

Measurement Situation

Until recently, the recommended setting for blood pressure assessment was a restful, quiet room. The subject or patient would rest for approximately 5 minutes in either a comfortable seated or recumbent position (Kaplan, 1980; Dustan, 1980). The blood pressure determined in this manner was considered to be the resting blood pressure. However, research cited below is suggesting that resting blood pressures may not be the best estimate of the blood pressure effect on end-organ disease.

Since an individual's blood pressure varies considerably, even within one sitting, multiple readings with at least 20 seconds intervening (to avoid venous congestion) provide a better assessment of a person's average or basal blood pressure than a single reading. Multiple readings also allow a more accurate classification of future blood pressure status. Others recommend taking, if possible, at least two blood pressures per day over multiple days to achieve a better estimate of true resting blood pressure (Kaplan, 1980; Dustan, 1980; Souchek, Stamler, Dyer, et al., 1979).

Blood pressure is not static but varies considerably over time, often remarkably so, even over 24 hours. Figure 2-1 illustrates this variability, showing two 24-hour systolic and diastolic pressure records. If blood pressures were taken immediately before and after sleep, the resulting blood pressure would be lower than if they were assessed throughout the entire day. This is true for the normotensive as well as the hypertensive person. Research has long documented the influence on blood pressure of such activities as exercise and emotional stress. However, recent findings suggest that much cognitive activity, and even speech, also influence blood pressure (Lynch, Thomas, Long, et al., 1980; Lynch, Long, Thomas, et al., in press). Specifically, blood pressure tends to show greater increases when speaking than those with lower resting baseline pressures.

Despite often-recited recommendations of control factors that influence blood pressure measurements, quiet readings may not always provide the most meaningful assessment of blood pressure. At times, the clinical or research purpose for blood pressure determination may indicate that other measurement situations are more significant than the resting situation. An early example of this was the assessment of blood pressure of patients during treadmill testing to determine the patient's blood pressure response to exertion and physical exercise. In assessing blood pressure, the clinician or researcher should use the situation that best corresponds to the objectives of measurement. For example, a physician may want a quiet, resting blood pressure for one person, but may want to contrast readings taken at rest with those taken while another patient is active, talking, at work, at home, or in the clinic to capture the effect these variables may have on blood pressure. Once the issue of the appropriate measurement is selected (for example, home and work blood pressure monitoring may require a portable device), the researcher or clinician should strive to provide valid and reliable assessments.

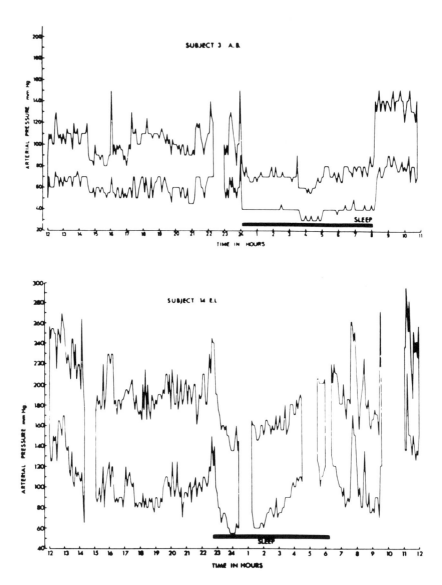

Fig. 2-1. The systolic and diastolic pressures recorded at 5-minute intervals in normotensive *(top)* and hypertensive *(bottom)* subject. The high pressures in the normotensive subject at 1600 and 2400 are due to a painful stimulus and coitus, respectively. (From Bevan AT and Honour AJ, Stott FN. *Clinical Science 36:*329, 1969. Reprinted with permission.)

Individual Differences

The assessment of blood pressure in behavioral medicine should consider the individual difference factors that are beyond control but nonetheless are key determinants of blood pressure. Leading this list of individual differences is genetic predisposition to hypertension. Based on twin- and family-aggregation studies, it has been suggested that as much as 60 percent of the population variance in blood pressure is attributable to genetic factors (Feinleib, 1978). The patient's family history should be obtained in order to estimate genetic predisposition to hypertension. In addition to genetic predisposition, the prevalence of hypertension is influenced by age, race, and sex.

Except in a few populations, blood pressure increases with age (Page, 1976). However, there are striking illustrations of populations in underdeveloped countries where blood pressures do not increase with age despite varying geographic areas, climates, and dietary customs. These individuals have been found to develop hypertension after moving from their homelands to more Western environments. In Western cultures, age-related trends are evident. In an examination of Bergen's study (1957) it was demonstrated that blood pressure rises slowly with age at the lower percentiles (Winklestein and Kantor, 1967). This rise is relatively faster at the upper percentiles, particularly after the decade that incudes men between 35 and 44 years of age.

There is clear evidence that genetic and environmental factors both play a role in determining the extent to which an individual's blood pressure will increase with age. Non-Caucasians, especially American blacks, show higher blood pressure elevation levels and disproportionately higher mortality rates than whites. In the Hypertension Detection and Follow-up Program (HDFP), for example, blood pressure and socioeconomic information was obtained for 158,906 adults in the United States communities (Hypertension Detection and Follow-Up Group, 1977). Overall, 18 percent of the whites and 37.4 percent of blacks had a diastolic blood pressure greater than or equal to 95 mm Hg, or reported that they were currently taking antihypertensive medication. This racial difference was in part, but not fully, associated with education. In the HDFP, education was found to be inversely associated with hypertension for race and sex, even when age was taken into account. This inverse relationship was more striking in the lower age groups and in blacks; it was less salient in overweight hypertensives. However, when education was taken into account statistically even at the higher education levels, the adjusted prevalence of hypertension in blacks was almost twice that in whites. Thus, the influence of education, although significant, does not explain the observed black-white difference in hypertension. Beyond their higher prevalence rates, blacks suffer a proportionately higher morbidity and mortality from hypertensive disease (U.S.P.H.S. Advance Data, 1976). Since the mid 1970s, this difference has been declining.

Blood pressure is a risk factor in both men and women. However, until age

45, systolic and diastolic blood pressure levels are lower for women than for men. The younger the woman, the greater the difference. After age 45, the systolic and diastolic blood pressure levels for women become even greater than those for men. However, elevated blood pressure in women may represent less risk than equivalent levels in men. Despite their lower rates, hypertensive women have three times the risk of developing cardiovascular disease as their normotensive counterparts (Kannel and Sorlie, 1975).

The individual differences in this section should be considered in the assessment of blood pressure. Each of these variables could mediate or set the limits for the effects of treatment. For example, a genetic predisposition for hypertension may influence the effectiveness of non-pharmacologic interventions such as stress-management or relaxation training. If such variables are assessed, their effects can be identified or controlled; if these variables are not taken into account, they could confound results or undermine effectiveness.

Life Style Factors

Increasing attention has focused on the influence of life style factors such as diet and stress upon an individual's blood pressure. As this influence is confirmed, the importance increases of assessing life style factors as part of blood pressure measurement. These factors may either be the target of behavioral medicine research and intervention or variables to be considered in order to prevent confounding research results and interfering with treatment effectiveness.

Among life style factors, weight has received confirmation as a significant correlate of blood pressure. Obesity, when initially seen in children, is strongly related to blood pressure levels (Heyden, Nelias, and Hames, 1980). Among children originally having mild blood pressure elevations and followed for 7 years, only overweight and weight gain differentiated between those who developed sustained hypertension and those whose blood pressure returned to normal levels (Heyden, Nelias, and Hames, 1980). Specifically, adult pressure tends to increase as weight is gained, and there is a higher prevalence of hypertension among obese persons. In the Nationwide Hypertension Evaluation Clinic screening of more than 1 million people, the group that identified itself as overweight had from 50 to 300 percent more hypertension (Stamler, Stamler, Ridelinger, et al., 1978). In the Chicago Coronary Prevention Evaluation Program, 216 men with mild hypertension or high normal blood pressure followed a nutritional, hygienic, non-pharmacologic treatment program which included recommendations for improved diet, exercise, and smoking reduction. Important for our purposes here, the treatment group showed a moderate change in weight that correlated significantly with blood pressure change. Of interest was that the achievement of "desirable" weight or near-desirable weight was not necessary to show meaningful blood pressure reductions (Stamler, Farinaro, and Mojonnier, 1980).

Reductions in blood pressure accompanying weight loss may be due to simultaneous reduction in salt intake. However, weight loss without salt restriction achieves significant blood pressure reduction in overweight hypertensive men and women (Reisen et al., 1978). Despite this finding, a substantial body of circumstantial evidence from cross-cultural, animal, and clinical research suggests that sodium intake and essential hypertension are related, and that decreases in sodium intake, blood volume, and potassium are involved with the control of blood pressure.

Habitual consumption of caffeine, nicotine, alcohol, and certain common non-prescription drugs (such as stimulants and antihistamines) is common in today's life styles. These substances have significant short-term effects on blood pressure. In measuring a patient's underlying blood pressure or response to treatment, it is important to assess recent consumption of these substances. A patient successfully reducing blood pressure, for example, could appear to be losing ground when he or she begins taking antihistamines to control common allergic reactions to pollens. Antihistamines tend to elevate blood pressure. Similarly, blood pressure measurements taken shortly after alcohol, caffeine, or nicotine consumption may be transiently elevated.

The link between transient and chronic stress and blood pressure is still at an early stage of investigation. Laboratory, applied, and epidemiologic research has consistently shown an association between various forms of stress and transient blood pressure responses (Kaplan, 1980; Henry and Stephens, 1977). Laboratory studies have encouraged speculation that chronic stress, accompanied by sustained blood pressure elevations, might lead over time to a resetting of the body's underlying or baseline blood pressure at a higher level (Dworkin, Filewich, Miller, et al., 1979). For example, individuals considered to be experiencing job stress (e.g., air traffic controllers), are at increased risk of hypertension when compared to other occupational groups (Jenkins and Hurst, 1978). A related study with children, found that children attending "noisy" schools, (e.g., schools in the air traffic corridor of Los Angeles International Airport), had higher blood pressures than children attending matched control (i.e., quiet) schools (Cohen et al., 1980).

Life style factors, like individual difference variables, are important components in the assessment of blood pressure and could facilitate the development of treatment or research plans. These plans might consider a patient's weight or life stress just as it might consider a patient's genetic predisposition; it might be directed toward reducing the patient's weight or life stress and, by doing so, reducing blood pressure.

CURRENT APPLICATIONS AND FUTURE DIRECTIONS

Within the field of behavioral medicine, behaviorally oriented assessment of blood pressure is needed to address major issues in hypertension. First, assessment of blood pressure and its accompanying psychosocial variables is needed to explicate the role that behavioral and psychosocial variables play in the etiology and maintenance of hypertension. Second, behavioral assessment is needed to evaluate the effectiveness of relaxation and biofeedback approaches to blood pressure control and prevention of end-organ complications. Third, behavioral assessment is needed to understand patient nonadherence to antihypertensive treatment regimens that include appointment-keeping, dietary changes, and medication.

Assessment of Mechanisms

The contribution that behavioral and psychosocial variables make to the hypertension problem is not without controversy. There appears to be little question about the effects of transient stress (internal and external) on the hemodynamics of blood pressure. (For reviews of this literature, see Kaplan, 1980; Shapiro, in press; Gutmann and Benson, 1971.) There is great controversy, however, about the extent to which stress can produce permanently elevated blood pressure or enhance its end-organ complications. To increase understanding of the stress–blood pressure relationship, clinicians and researchers have expanded blood pressure measurement to include such behavioral assessment procedures as diary-keeping and direct observation.

Behavioral Diaries

Daily logs or behavioral diaries can greatly assist the clinician in determining potential behavioral and environmental correlates of hypertension. Currently, behavioral diaries consist of having the patient self-monitor blood pressures taken at various times by the individual, technician, or machine. Corresponding to the blood pressures, the individual notes the activities in which he or she is involved. Additional recorded information may include thoughts or tension levels. Once collected, this information can be used to design an appropriate treatment plan tailored to those situations in which blood pressure is elevated. In the case of the hypertensive person, a portable blood pressure device can be used in conjunction with a diary to assess the relationship, if any, between perceived stress and increased blood pressure. If a relationship does emerge, the physician might suggest a combination of medication, coping-skills training, and life style modification. Even in the absence of a stress–hypertension relationship, the multiple blood pressure recordings could be of value by providing individuals with quasibiofeedback (i.e.; blood pressure changes in response to implementing treatment) or by determining the daily intrapersonal variability. Examples of typical log entries are presented in Figure 2-2.

Date	September 3	September 3
Time	6:45 A.M.	8:05 A.M.
Location	Home	Office
Situation	In bed, listening to radio, waking up	Walk into office and message on desk reads: "The boss wants to see you immediately."
Tension Level	15	75
Thoughts	I slept well. I feel good; wish I could go back to sleep	Uh oh, what have I done now? Sounds like I am in hot water
Blood Pressure	122/78	150/96

Fig. 2-2. Typical behavioral log entry.

Direct Observation

Direct observation of blood pressure responsivity in various situations can be of great value to the clinician or researcher. Obviously, the opportunity to observe an individual's behavioral and physiological responses to specific situations, such as controlled stressors, is of great value in delineation of the role of behavioral and psychosocial variables in the etiology of hypertension.

Assessment of Treatment Outcome

Today the primary treatment for hypertension is medication. A major issue in this treatment is the determination of the patient's particular dose-response. The advent of the newer blood pressure measurement procedures makes this information more accessible to the physician. Multiple measurements can be used to determine and adjust medication to maximize blood pressure reduction. The environmental responsivity of blood pressure has implications for evaluation of the effectiveness of antihypertensive medication. In addition to blood pressure taken in the medical clinic, clinicians and researchers are beginning to record blood pressure measurements taken at the worksite, in the home, and in other situations.

A parallel development has been the use of behavioral interventions such as relaxation and biofeedback (Seer, 1979; Agras and Jacob, 1979). As research established the stress–blood pressure relationship, investigators also have explored the effect of stress-reduction procedures on blood pressure. The effectiveness of these procedures may be expressed either in terms of reductions in basal blood pressure or in the decreased responsiveness to environmental stress. Therefore, it is important that the procedures outlined in this chapter, including ambulatory monitoring, behavioral diaries, and direct observation, be employed in the assessment of behavioral intervention outcome.

Assessment of Compliance

The effectiveness of all antihypertensive treatment requires appropriate patient compliance. Medication and behavioral interventions must be used daily to maintain their effectiveness. However, studies of adherence to standard antihypertensive medication regimens show that over 50 percent drop out of care within the first year (Wilber and Barrow, 1972; Caldwell et al., 1970), and only about two-thirds of those who remain under care take enough of their medication to achieve adequate blood pressure control (McKenney et al., 1973; Sackett et al., 1975).

Estimates of compliance to behavioral interventions have not been established. However, the behavioral change required to take medication is relatively simple; when the antihypertensive treatment regimen includes physician recommendations regarding dietary management and weight loss, the issues surrounding compliance become increasingly complex. Effective assessment of adherence behavior during the initiation and maintenance of treatment regimens is important to identify compliance barriers and to design strategies to improve compliance.

There are a number of methods for assessing compliance to antihypertensive treatment. The method used most often is clinical rating. However, ratings of patient compliance by their clinicians "is probably the least accurate and reliable of the assessment procedures, with the ratings being little better than chance estimates. . . ." (Dunbar, 1980). Other assessment methods include objective measures, such as pill counts, body weight, and, above all, blood pressures. However, these objective measures do not provide information about patterns of health behavior. Furthermore, pill counts are only reliable if the patient is unaware that they are being taken. Unobtrusive pill counts can be made in the home (Haynes, Taylor, Sackett, et al., 1980), and information about health behaviors can be obtained by observation of the patient's adherence to treatment recommendations by others (e.g., family members).

Self-reports, a more indirect method, while overestimating adherence, do correlate highly with the objective measures. Structured interviews and behavioral diaries can enhance self-report of compliance by eliciting information about a patient's compliant and noncompliant behavior patterns and daily habits. Reinforcers can be used in designing interventions to increase compliance and treatment effectiveness. Moreover, patients who admit their noncompliance upon direct questioning are more likely to respond positively to compliance interventions (Johnson et al., 1978).

SUMMARY

Assessment of hypertension has changed in recent years. Arguments over cut-points between normal and high blood pressure are being increasingly replaced by recommendations for considering blood pressure as a continuous variable, using age-weighting and multiple measurements under various conditions from supine resting to treadmill testing. Such procedural issues as calibration, proper positioning, and cuff inflation, while important, may be overshadowed by instrumentation, including ambulatory monitors, that is less sensitive to measurement errors.

The individual differences, life style, and environmental factors that influence blood pressure are being identified. When the measurement in question is an individual's basal blood pressure, these factors can confound assessment. When the measurement in question is identification of factors that may influence blood pressure variability, these factors take on an added importance. Assessment of hypertension can no longer be viewed in the same light as assessment of height; blood pressure is not static, but is dynamic and should be viewed in the context of the factors that influence its level. It may seem, then, that assessment of blood pressure and hypertension becomes overly complex. On the contrary, behavioral assessment of blood pressure will, by documenting the influence of individual differences, life style factors, and measurement settings, assist in identifying the etiology of essential hypertension. In the meantime, behavioral assessment, by clarifying the effectiveness of antihypertensive treatment through studies of non-adherence and through direct modification of blood pressure by stress-reduction procedures.

REFERENCES

Agras, S., & Jacob, R. Hypertension. In J. P. Brady, & O. Pomerleau (Eds.), *Behavioral medicine: Theory and practice;* Baltimore, Maryland: Williams & Wilkins, 1979.

Bergin-BØE, J., Humerfelt S., & Werdervang F. The blood pressure in a population. *Acta Med Scand* Suppl 321, 1957, *157*

Berkson, D. M., Whipple, I. T., Shireman, L., Brown, M. C., Raynor, W., Jr., & Shekelle, R. B. Evaluation of an automated blood pressure measuring device intended for general public use. *American Journal of Public Health*, 1979, *69*, 473–479.

Blood pressure kits. *Consumer Reports*, March 1979, 142–146.

Caldwell, J. R., Cobb, S., Dowling, M. D., & De Jongh, D. The dropout problem in antihypertensive therapy. *Journal of Chronic Disease*, 1970, *22*, 579–592.

Cohen, S., Evans, G. W., Krantz, D. S., & Stokols, D. Physiological motivational, and cognitive effects of aircraft noise on children. *American Psychologist*, 1980, *35*, 231–243.

Dunbar, J. M. Assessment of medication compliance: A review. In R. B. Haynes, M. E. Mattson, & T. O. Engebretson (Eds.), *Patient compliance to prescribed antihyper-*

tensive medication regimens: A report to the National Heart, Lung and Blood Institute, Bethesda, Maryland: National Institutes of Health, 1980 (NIH Publication No. 81-2102).

Dustan, A. Hypertension. In American Heart Associations: *Heartbook*. New York: Dutton, 1980.

Dworkin, B. R., Filewich, R. J., Miller, N. E., Craigmyle, N., & Pickering, T. G. Baroreceptor activation reduces reactivity to noxious stimulation: Implications for hypertension. *Science*, 1979, 1299–1301.

Feinleib, M. Genetics and family aggregation. In G. Onesti, & R. Klimt (Eds.), *Hypertension: Determinants, Complications and Interventions*. New York: Grune & Stratton Co., 1978.

Fortmann, S. P., Marcuson, R., Bitter, P. H., & Haskell, W. L. A comparison of the Sphygmetrics SR-2 automatic blood pressure recorder to the mercury sphygmomanometer in population studies. Unpublished manuscript, Stanford University, 1980.

Fox, L. L., & Phelps, D. L. Evaluation of a new indirect blood pressure system for neonates. Los Angeles: U.C.L.A. School of Medicine, Department of Pediatrics, 1981.

Gutmann, M. C., & Benson, H. Interaction of environmental factors and systemic arterial blood pressure: A review. *Medicine*, 1971, *50*, 543–553.

Haskell, W. Stanford University, personal communication, 1980.

Haynes, R. B.; Taylor, W., Sackett, D. L., Gibson, E. S., Bernholz, C. D., & Mukherjee, J. Can simple clinical measurements detect patient non-compliance? *Hypertension*, 1980, *2*, 757–764.

Henry, J. P., & Stephens, P. M. *Stress, health and the social environment: A sociobiologic approach to medicine*. New York: Springer-Verlag, 1977.

Heyden, S., Nelius, S. J., & Hames, C. G. Obesity, salt intake, and hypertension. *Journal of Cardiovascular Medicine*, 1980, 987–994.

Hypertension Detection and Follow-up Program Cooperative Group. Race, education and prevalence of hypertension. *American Journal of Epidemiology*, 1977, *106*, (5), 351–361.

Hypertension Detection and Follow-up Program Cooperative Group. Five-year findings of the hypertension detection and follow-up program: I. Reduction in mortality of persons with high blood pressure, including mild hypertension. *Journal of the American Medical Association*, 1979, *242*, 2562–2571.

Hypertension Detection and Follow-up Program Cooperative Group. Five-year findings of the hypertension detection and follow-up program: II. Mortality by race, sex and age. *Journal of the American Medical Association*, 1979, *242*, 2572–2577.

Johnson, A. L., Taylor, D. W., Sackett, D. L., Dunnett, C. W., & Shimizu, A. G. Self-recording blood pressure in the management of hypertension. *Canadian Medical Association Journal*, 1978, *119*, 1034–1039.

Jordan, S. C., & Chadwick, J. H. Evaluation of automatic blood pressure machines in the work setting. Paper presented at the National Conference on High Blood Pressure Control, Washington, D.C., 1979.

Kannel, W. B., & Sorlie, P. Hypertension in Framingham. In O. Paul (Ed.), *Epidemiology and control of hypertension*. Miami, Florida: Symposia Specialists, 1975.

Kaplan, N. *Clinical hypertension, (Ed. 2)*. Baltimore, Maryland: Williams & Wilkins, 1980.

Kirkendall, W. M., Feinleib, M., Freis, E. D., & Mark, A. L. *American Heart Association committee report: Recommendations for human blood pressure determination by sphygmomanometers.* Dallas, Texas: American Heart Association, 1981.

Lynch, J. J., Long, J. M., Thomas, S. A., Malinow, K. L., & Katcher, A. H. The effects of talking on the blood pressure of hypertensive and normotensive individuals. *Psychosomatic Medicine,* in press.

Lynch, J. J., Thomas, S. A., Long, J. M., Malinow, K. L., Chickadonz, G., & Katcher, A. H. Human speech and blood pressure. *The Journal of Nervous and Mental Disease,* 1980, *168,* 526–534.

McKenney, J. M., Slining, J. M., Nenderson, H. R., Devins, D., & Barr, M. The effect of clinical pharmacy services on patients with essential hypertension. *Circulation,* 1973, *48,* 1104–1111.

Moser, M., Guythur, J. P. & Finnerty, F. Report of the Joint National Committee on Detection, Evaluation, and Treatment of High Blood Pressure: A cooperative study. *Journal of the American Medical Association,* 1977, *237,* 255–261.

Page, L. B. Epidemilogic evidence on the etiology of human hypertension and its possible prevention. *American Heart Journal,* 1976, *91,* 527–534.

Polk, B. F., Rosner, B., Feudo, R., & Vandenburgh, M. An evaluation of the Vita-Stat automatic blood pressure measuring device. *Hypertension,* 1980, *2,* 221–227.

Reisin, E., Abel, R., Modan, M., Silverberg, D. S., Eliahou, H. E., & Modan, B. Effect of weight loss without salt restriction on the reduction of blood pressure in overweight hypertensive patients. *New England Journal of Medicine,* 1978, *298,* 1–3.

Rose, R. M., Jenkins, C. D., & Hurst, M. W. *Air traffic controller health change study.* Report to the Federal Aviation Administration under Contract No. DOT-FA73WA-3211, Boston University, Massachusetts, 1978.

Sackett, D. L., Haynes, R. B., Gibson, E. S., Hackett, B. C., Taylor, D. W., Roberts, R. S., & Johnson, A. L. Randomized clinical trials of strategies for improving medication compliance in primary hypertension. *Lancet,* 1975, *1,* 1205–1207.

Seer, P. Psychological control of essential hypertension: Review of the literature and methodological critique. *Psychological Bulletin,* 1979, *86* (5), 1015–1043.

Shapiro, A. P. Stress and hypertension. In H. Gavras and H. R. Brunner (Eds.), *Clinical Hypertension.* New York: Marcel Dekker, in press.

Souchek, J., Stamler, J., Dyer, A. R., Paul, O., & Lepper, M. H. The value of two or three versus a single reading of blood pressure at a first visit. *Journal of Chronic Diseases,* 1979, *32,* 197–210.

Stamler, J., Farinaro, E., Mojonnier, L. M., Hall, Y., Moss, D., & Stamler, R. Prevention and control of hypertension by nutritional-hygienic means: Long-term experience of the Chicago Coronary Prevention Evaluation Program. *Journal of the American Medical Association,* 1980, *234,* 1819–1823.

Stamler, R., Stamler, J., Riedlinger, W. F., Algera, G., & Roberts, R. H. Weight and blood pressure: Findings in hypertension screening of 1 million Americans. *Journal of the American Medical Association,* 1978, *240,* 1607–1610.

U.S.P.H.S. Advance Data, Number 1. Washington, D.C., 1976.

Van den Berg, B. J. Comparisons of blood pressure measurements by auscultation and Physiometrics Infrasonde recording techniques. *Hypertension,* supplement I, 1980, *2,* 8–17.

Voors, A. W., Foster, T. A., Frerichs, R. R., & Berenson, G. S. Some determinants of blood pressure in children age 5–14 years in a total biracial community—The Bogalusa heart study. Paper presented at the Epidemiology Session of the American Heart Association 27th Annual Meeting, Anaheim, California, 1975.

Wilber, J. A., Barrow, J. G. Hypertension—A community problem. *American Journal of Medicine*, 1972, *52*, 653–663.

Winklestein, W., Kantor, S. Some observations on the relationships between age, sex, and blood pressure. In J. Stamler, R. Stamler, & T. N. Pullman (Eds.), *The epidemiology of hypertension: Proceedings of an international symposium,* New York: Grune & Stratton Co., 1967, 70–81.

James A. Blumenthal

3

Assessment of Patients with Coronary Heart Disease

No one knows what causes heart attacks, and the known risk factors—high blood pressure, high cholesterol, smoking, stress, heredity—are valid only in a mass statistical way. Like a lot of patients, Lesher wanted an unambigious answer in an ambigious situation. And, like a lot of patients, he would have been the first to deride the medical profession for dogmaticism if I had given him a simple answer (Halberstam and Lesher, 1978).

Coronary heart disease (CHD) is the major disease of the 20th century. Despite advances in medical technology and increased awareness of preventive measures, more than 1 million Americans suffer a first myocardial infarction (heart attack, or MI) each year. Every minute of every day, someone in the United States is fatally stricken with an MI. A quarter of those who die are under the age of 65. Sudden death is the initial clinical manifestation in 20 to 25 percent of first events, and accounts for about 50 percent of all heart attack deaths. Close to two-thirds of all fatal MIs terminate outside the hospital, most of them within an hour of the onset of the acute physical symptoms.

In almost all cases, MI occurs in persons who have underlying atherosclerosis of the coronary arteries. Coronary atherosclerosis is a disease process in which the channel of the coronary artery becomes narrow and the blood supply to the heart is reduced. The major clinical manifestations of CHD include angina pectoris (AP), acute myocardial infarction (MI), arrhythmias-disturbances of the rhythm and electrical activity of the heart (e.g., brachycardia, tachycardia, premature atrial, and ventricular beats, etc.), and congestive heart failure (CHF). *Angina pectoris* results when a coronary artery is sufficiently narrowed to cause ischemia, or state of imbalance between the supply and demand for oxygen by the heart muscle. As a consequence, chest pain or discomfort are symptoms frequently experienced by the patient. Symptoms usually occur only intermittently, typically upon physical exertion or during emotional stress, whereby the need of the heart muscle for increased oxygen and blood exceeds the available supply. The pain associated with angina pectoris generally abates rather quickly with rest or medication, such as nitroglycerin. When the blood flow in one of the major coronary arteries supplying blood to the heart is blocked, the event is called coronary thrombosis, which may result in necrosis (tissue death) of portions of the heart muscle, resulting in *myocardial infarction*. The symptoms associated with acute myocardial infarction can be quite variable. They generally resemble those of angina pectoris, but are more intense, persist without interruption over a longer duration (i.e., more than an hour), and are generally unrelieved by rest or medication.

While a review of the diagnostic procedures for determining the presence of CHD is beyond the scope of the present chapter, several standard techniques are worth noting. The *electrocardiogram,* or EKG, is the recording of the electrical activity of the heart. The EKG is usually recorded from 12 sets of leads in which the recording of electrical potentials across pairs of electrodes provides information about the anatomy and function of the heart. Abnormal EKG patterns can provide evidence for the presence of myocardial infarction, myocardial ischemia, and cardiac arrhythmias. An area of the heart that has become scarred by MI can usually be identified by the resultant changes in EKG waveforms, specifically via the QRS complex. Similarly the early phase of an acute MI, or a reversible cardiac ischemia that occurs with AP, will often cause the ST segment to become displaced from baseline. EKG recording often (but not always) makes it possible to identify specific types of cardiac dysfunction.

Blood analyses are a second diagnostic method. When certain tissues are damaged, enzymes may be released into the blood stream. For example, necrotic cardiac tissue is frequently associated with elevated blood levels of serum glutamic oxalacetic transaminase (SGOT), a selected isoenzyme of creatinine phosphokinase (CPK). After an MI, enzyme levels may increase for a 24–48 hour interval, and then return to previous levels within 4–8 days.

Both of the above procedures are subject to a degree of error. For example, the EKG does not specifically identify the presence of coronary atherosclerosis. Consequently, the EKG can appear normal one moment, and abnormal subsequent to acute MI the next. Moreover, EKG abnormalities may not always be present with CHD.* For example, small lesions or lesions in ''silent'' areas of the myocardium may not reveal diagnostic changes. Similarly, because some delay between the onset of an MI and blood sampling may occur, enzyme analysis is not always conclusive in determining the presence of an MI. In addition, other disorders, such as cerebral infarction, liver disease, pancreatitis, acute cholecystitis, and neuromuscular disease, can produce elevations in plasma enzyme levels resembling

---

*EKG changes are almost always present in MI patients followed over time but may be absent on any given EKG record.

those found with an MI, though newer techniques for quantitating specific isoenzymes recently have made such diagnostic confusion less troublesome.

Cardiac catheterization is another well-known diagnostic procedure that is used to document the presence of CHD. It is typically performed to confirm the presence of lesions in coronary arteries and to assess the severity and extent of coronary atherosclerosis. The procedure involves entering a catheter through the patient's groin or arm, passing it through the peripheral vasculature into the heart, injecting a dye which is opaque to X ray beams, and then filming the coronary arterial blood flow. The procedure of cardiac angiography carries minimal risk and provides precise information regarding the state of the coronary vasculature. However, there are technical limitations: determination of the three-dimensional anatomy of coronary vessels employing a two-dimensional system requires multiple projections from various angles. Since selection of these angles is often random, and subjective estimates of the degree of occlusion or narrowing of a vessel are obtained, a small degree of error in this assessment is always present.

For a more detailed description of the assessment strategies employed in the determination of organic pathology of the heart, the interested reader is referred to two standard texts (Friedberg, 1966; Hurst, Logue, & Schlant, 1978).

The primary purpose of this chapter is to review the basic issues, problems, and procedures that are employed in the psychological assessment of patients with coronary heart disease. Psychological assessment, however, should not be misconstrued as the mere application of specific techniques, or the administration of certain tests. Rather, a psychological assessment is more broadly oriented to evaluating the person in a biopsychosocial context (Engel, 1977). While specific techniques and instruments will be reviewed, it is important to emphasize that such procedures are only aids in the collection of data. There exists a great diversity of conceptual orientations and procedures for psychological assessment (Bem and Allen, 1974; Maloney and Ward, 1976; Goldfried and Kent, 1972; Meehl, 1956). The main emphasis is on the need to integrate multidimensional approaches in the assessment of the whole person, including behavioral, cognitive, psychodynamic, and social considerations.

This chapter is divided into three major areas: (1) consideration of the assessment of individuals at risk for CHD; (2) review of the behavioral and psychological sequelae of cardiac illness; and (3) specific procedures and instruments for evaluating the CHD patient.

ASSESSMENT OF INDIVIDUALS AT RISK

Studies of initially healthy individuals since 1950 have demonstrated a significant association between specific characteristics of the individual and increased incidence and prevalence rates of CHD (Epstein, 1965; Keys, 1966; Simborg, 1970).

Gender. The inclusion of gender as a risk factor for ischemic heart disease is extremely important. Epidemiological evidence strongly supports the greater risk of CHD among men. For example, the approximate annual incidence rate among middle-aged men is about 2 percent, while the rate for women is less than .5 percent. Those women who do develop CHD almost always have hypercholesterolemia, hypertension, or smoke cigarettes, and may also have such characteristics as premature menopause or prolonged contraceptive use. History of pregnancy and fluctuations in menstrual cycle have also been suggested as relevant factors, but remain controversal (Oliver, 1974).

Age. Although coronary atherosclerosis is a disease process that begins early in life (Enos, Beyer, & Holmes 1965; Strong and McGill, 1962), it usually does not become clinically manifest until middle life. As a general rule, prevalence rates in the 40–50 age range are approximately two to three percent, but double that in the 50–60 age range. The likelihood for MI is extremely low in individuals under 40 years of age unless they have prominent risk factors, but the risk steadily increases throughout the period of middle and late adulthood, independent of other factors.

Hypercholesterolemia and hypertriglyceridemia. The relationship of serum cholesterol level to prevalence, incidence, and mortality rates of CHD has been demonstrated in numerous studies (Keys, 1970; Kannel et al., 1971). Moreover, the effect of dietary saturated fatty acids, polyunsaturated fatty acids, and cholesterol on levels of serum cholesterol in human beings has been well established (Erickson et al., 1964; Keys et al., 1965; Hegsted et al., 1965; Olson 1974). Several epidemiologic studies have failed to find a significant association between dietary practices and serum cholestoral (Keys et al., 1956; Nichols et al., 1976) thus prompting some investigators to minimize the role of diet (Mann, 1977). Therefore, it is generally agreed that diet is only one factor affecting serum cholesterol levels (Shekelle et al., 1981).

Data from the well-known prospective study in Framingham, Massachusetts (Dawber et al., 1957), found that elevated cholesterol levels represented the single most important risk factor for premature coronary heart disease in the United States. Recently, data have been combined from Framingham, Albany, Tucumseh, Los Angeles, Minneapolis, and Chicago (the American Pooling Project, 1978) to include 7,342 men from 39 to 59 years of age at baseline followed for a 10-year period (Pooling Project Research Group, 1978). Serum cholesterol levels below 225 mg percent were considered to be relatively benign, while levels in excess of 250 mg percent essentially double the relative risk in comparison to lower cholesterol levels.

Triglycerides appear to operate as an independent risk factor for CHD. Prospective studies have shown that triglyceride fasting levels are elevated in those individuals who subsequently develop MI (Olson, 1974). Levels in excess of 150 mg percent are considered potentially dangerous; levels in excess of 200 mg percent may require medical attention.

Hypertension. Blood pressure has been shown to be a significant predictor of the occurrence of CHD in a number of studies (Epstein 1965; Pooling Project Research Group, 1978; Dawber et al., 1957). Elevated blood pressure is generally considered to be in excess of 160 mm Hg systolic and/or 95 mm Hg diastolic. For example, a person whose systolic blood pressure is 160 mm Hg or higher has a five times greater risk of CHD compared to an individual with a systolic blood pressure of 120 mm Hg or under (Gordon and Kannel, 1972). As with serum cholesterol and triglycerides, CHD risk progressively increases with increased blood pressure; blood pressure in the 120/70 mm Hg range is generally regarded as normal.

The importance of systolic versus diastolic blood pressure has been a subject of debate. For example, data from the Framingham study (Kannel et al., 1971) suggest that diastolic blood pressure is most important in predicting CHD among adults less than 45 years of age, and systolic blood pressure is more important in those adults over 45. Recent evidence, however, has emphasized the greater importance of systolic blood pressure (Rabkin, Mathewson, & Tate, 1978). Regardless of which value is more important, the evidence is clear that blood pressure in excess of 160 mm Hg systolic and/or 95 mm Hg diastolic is a magnitude that warrants medical intervention.

Cigarette smoking. A number of studies (Simborg, 1970) show a strong statistical association between cigarette smoking and the risk of developing CHD. Retrospective and prospective epidemiological studies have demonstrated a dose-response effect of cigarette smoking and the risk of developing CHD (Epstein, 1965; Stamler, 1973). One-pack-a-day cigarette smokers are more than twice as likely to develop coronary heart disease as nonsmokers. Additional information concerning the practice of inhaling versus noninhaling has also shown a greater incidence for the inhaling group.

The mechanism by which cigarette smoking contributes to increased risk is not well established. Nicotine has been considered to be involved in the development of atherosclerotic plaque; however, recent evidence suggests that carbon monoxide, found in tobacco smoke, also has a damaging effect upon the arterial wall, leading to an increased permeability for various plasma components. It may also be responsible for increased atherosclerotic plaque development (Wald, 1976).

Diabetes mellitus. Studies (Stamler et al., 1966; Kannel et al., 1971) have shown that hyperglycemia and diabetes mellitus are risk factors for coronary disease. The Framingham study (Kannel et al., 1971) concluded that glucose tolerance is an important factor in arteriosclerotic disease in the three vascular beds (heart, head, and legs), but is most significantly correlated with the incidence of intermittent claudication. It is well established that coronary disease occurs with greater frequency among individuals who are diabetic than among those who are nondiabetic, especially in younger groups (Epstein, 1965; Kannel, and Gordon, 1974).

Family history.   Individuals with a family history of premature coronary disease are at a greater risk than those without a positive family history (Epstein, 1965). These genetic factors may operate through traditional risk factors, such as elevated cholesterol levels or blood pressure, through as yet undefined inherited metabolic traits, or indirectly, through psychological and behavioral processes, or other behavioral risk factors (e.g., obesity as a result of overeating, Type A pattern, etc.)

Sedentary life style.   A number of epidemiological studies have shown vigorous physical activity during work and leisure to be associated with reduced risk for CHD (Paffenbarger and Hale, 1975; Paffenbarger, Wing, & Hyde, 1978; Morris et al., 1973). Moreover, other studies have reported a variety of beneficial cardiovascular adaptations that occur with regular exercise (Clausen, 1977; Williams et al., in press). However, data are far from definitive. Recent reports demonstrate that exercise does not necessarily ensure protection from CHD (Thompson et al., 1979; Noakes et al., 1979). In summary, available evidence seems to suggest that continued exercise throughout adulthood may reduce the relative risk of premature CHD, although more carefully conducted epidemiological studies are needed.

Obesity.   The major epidemiological studies in the U.S. and Europe have not conclusively demonstrated obesity to be independently related to increased risk for CHD, despite the association of obesity with hyperlipidemia and hypertension. Part of the difficulty is isolating obesity from other risk factors such as physical inactivity, high blood pressure, or elevated cholesterol levels. The Framingham study (Kannel and Gordon, 1974) found the proportion of middle-aged men with one or more traditional risk factors increased as weight increased, and the overall incidence of CHD, CHF, and stroke to be higher among overweight than normal-weight men. Somatotype, or body build, has also been implicated as a risk factor, with endomorphic and mesomorphic types apparently being at greater risk.

Available evidence therefore appears to indicate that an overweight individual is at greater risk for the development of CHD than the normal weight individual. The grossly overweight person is particularly susceptible. Methods for determining if an individual is overweight include a general formula (e.g., height in cm − 100 = normal body weight in kg), expected weight tables, and such procedures as underwater weighing, skinfold thickness calibration, or determination of body mass or Ponderal index. The strengths and weaknesses of these procedures are discussed in Chapter 9.

Type A Behavior Pattern. The *Type A behavior pattern* refers to a constellation of overt behavioral characteristics and traits including excessive competitive drive, a persistent desire for recognition and personal advancement, enhanced aggressiveness and hostility, continuous involvement in multiple functions subject to deadlines, and a tendency to accelerate the pace of living. The converse, *Type B behavior pattern,* is defined as a relative absence of these characteristics. The Type A behavior pattern is not synonymous with "personality" or "stress reaction," but rather refers to the product of an individual difference characteristic and specific situational factors. The Type A behavior pattern has been shown to be related to increased risk of coronary disease in retrospective and prospective studies (Dembroski et al., 1978; Jenkins, 1976).

The Western collaborative group study project (WCGS) was initiated in 1960 and is regarded as the landmark study of the Type A pattern. Briefly, subjects underwent extensive medical evaluation and were followed over a 10-year period. The subjects consisted of more than 3,500 apparently healthy employed men from 39 to 59 years old at intake. Initially, of the 113 men who were found to have coronary disease, 80 men (71 percent) were judged to be Type A. Of the remaining sample, 257 men subsequently developed coronary disease during the mean period of 8½ years. One hundred and seventy-eight were classified as Type A, while only 79 were considered Type B. Thus, the Type A subjects exhibited 2.37 times the rate of new coronary disease compared to their Type B counterparts. The summary of the WCGS project is presented in Figure 3-1.

The National Heart, Lung, and Blood Institute (NHLBI) assembled a review panel of scientists to critically evaluate the Type A concept. They concluded that, "the review panel accepts the available body of scientific evidence as demonstrating that Type A behavior is associated with an increased risk of clinically apparent CHD in employed, middle-aged U.S. citizens. The increased risk is over and above that imposed by age, systolic blood pressure, serum cholesterol, and smoking and appears to be of the same order of magnitude as the relative risk associated with any of these factors" (NHLBI Forum, 1978).

Summary

Taken together, a composite cardiovascular risk profile can be constructed to assess the potential risk for the development of CHD. Table 3-1 presents a summary of the most significant factors.

PATTERNS OF ADAPTATION

Adaptation to heart disease follows a general temporal sequence beginning when symptoms are first noticed and extending throughout hospitalization and subsequent discharge. The *prehospital phase* refers to the interval between the

Table 3-1

Cardiovascular Risk Profile

Characteristic	Risk Profile	Risk
Age (years)	>65	+ +
	45–65	+
	<45	–
Sex	Male	+ +
	Female	–
Family history	MI<55	+ + +
	MI<65	+
	CVD<65	+
	absent	–
Cholesterol level (mg %)	≥270	+ + +
	240–269	+ +
	221–239	+
	≤220	–
Triglyceride level (mg %)	≥200	+ +
	151–199	+
	≤150	–
Blood pressure (mm Hg)	>160 (systolic) and/or >100 (diastolic)	+ + +
	140–159 (systolic) and/or 90–99 (diastolic)	+ + / +
	100–139 (systolic) and/or 69–89 (diastolic)	–
Smoking	> one pack per day	+ + +
	< one pack per day	+ +
	Stopped at least 5 years	+
	Nonsmoker	–
Behavior pattern	Type A (symptomatic)	+ + +
	Type A (asymptomatic)	+
	Type B (asymptomatic)	–
Exercise	None or some; irregular	+
	regular aerobic exercise	–
Obesity	Severe	+ +
	Moderate	+
	Mild	–

+ + + = severe; + + = moderate; + mild; – not significant.

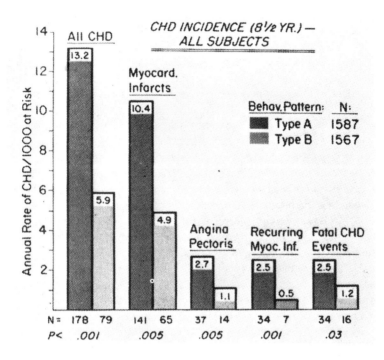

Fig. 3-1. Incidence of CHD in the Western Collaborative Group Study. The annual rate of incidence of CHD in 3154 subjects was studied prospectively in the WCGS project for 8½ years. The higher incidence of all forms of CHD in the Type A subjects is shown. Note, too, that recurring myocardial infarcts occurred 5 times as often and fatal CHD attacks approximately 2 times as often in Type A than in Type B subjects. N = number of cases. (From Friedman M., and Rosenman R.H.: Type A behavior pattern: Its association with coronary heart disease. *Annals of Clinical Research, 3,* 1971, 305. Reproduced with permission.)

initial signs of MI and admission to the hospital. The *acute phase* occurs when the patient is in the hospital, and typically lasts from 1 to 3 weeks. The *convalescent phase* represents the initial period of adjustment at home, and typically lasts from 2 to 8 weeks. Finally, the *rehabilitation phase* involves the long term adjustment and lasts up to 2 or more years post-MI.

Prehospital Phase

The most common reaction to symptoms of acute MI is ''no'' reaction. That is, most people simply fail to respond to their symptoms, perhaps in the hope that the symptoms will go away, or because the symptoms are not considered serious. The average time period between symptom onset and admission to a medical facility is usually about 3 hours, but may range from 1 hour to several days. In one study of coronary patients admitted to a coronary care unit (CCU), at least 50 percent took longer than 24 hours to seek help (Gentry and Haney, 1975).

Approximately 65 percent of the time between symptom onset and hospital arrival time involves what is termed *decision time,* a three-phase interval during which patients must (1) work through a cognitive sequence beginning with the initial perception of symptoms to the final realization that the nature and severity of their symptoms require medical treatment (Moss et al., 1969); (2) engage in self-treatment, using various medications; and (3) communicate with spouse, family, and friends to solicit advice on how to cope with the symptoms. This is also the interval when psychological factors may play their most important role in affecting patient behavior. Another 35 percent of the time between onset and hospital arrival involves the period of *medical preparation* (the time for the patient to contact the physician and for the physician to make necessary arrangements) (Moss and Goldstein, 1970). The remaining 10 percent is *transportation time* to the hospital.

Delay in seeking proper medical assistance is greatest when CHD patients attribute their symptoms to problems other than the heart. For example, Tjoe and Luria (1972) report that only 21 of 75 patients admitted to the CCU attributed their symptoms to a cardiac condition. Patients who recognize that something is wrong with their heart seek help sooner than persons who displace the cause of their symptoms to other organ systems (Hackett and Cassem, 1969), such as gall-bladder disease, ulcers, or indigestion. The tendency to mistake the origin of the cardiac symptoms unfortunately characterizes about 70 percent of patients experiencing either an initial or recurrent MI. Denial, or the tendency to ignore or minimize the true meaning of the condition, seems to be the primary factor leading to misattribution and, thus, unnecessary delay. Hackett and Cassem (1969) have shown that patients using ''minimal denial'' more often attribute their symptoms to the heart and generally make the decision to seek help themselves, as opposed to ''major deniers'' who more frequently list indigestion as the cause of their chest pain, and who also require advice and encouragement from family and friends before seeking medical attention.

Olin and Hackett (1964) describe a typical ''denier'' in their case report.

A 65-year-old medical technician had sustained a previous myocardial infarction ten years before his present admission. At that time he had experienced severe precordial pain which he attributed to indigestion. After being given morphine at home in preparation for the trip to the hospital, he started to dress for work because he felt so much better. He finally consented to hospitalization only because he 'liked the doctors so much.' In the current episode he again diagnosed his condition as stomach trouble and waited five hours before calling a doctor. He made the call only when the pain became unbearable.*

---

*From Olin, H. S., & Hackett, T. P. The denial of chest pain in 32 patients with acute myocardial infarction. *Journal of the American Medical Association,* 1964, *190,* 979–980. Copyright 1964, American Medical Association. Reprinted with permission.

Denial interacts with other factors, such as death concern, degree of preceived illness, and history of CHD, in affecting the patient's decision-making process (Alonzo, 1973). Patients classified as nondeniers (who readily admit to being anxious and apprehensive during the prehospital phase of illness), and who admit to high levels of death concern almost always make the decision to get medical care themselves. In contrast, those classified as deniers and as having a low level of death concern rely on the judgment of others. Similarly, patients who are nondeniers and who perceive themselves as seriously ill are generally self-referrals; patients using extreme denial and/or who view themselves as reasonably well despite their symptoms require advice from others. Finally, virtually every patient described as a nondenier who also has a history of CHD made the decision to seek medical attention; only 25 percent of those classified as deniers who do not have a positive history of CHD were self-referred (Williams and Gentry, 1978).

The patient's social context and the presence of prodromal symptoms (dizziness, fatigue, malaise, loss of appetite) can also interact with denial to foster delay and indecision (Alonzo, 1973). Gentry's (1975) excellent summary of preadmission behavior notes that patients experiencing symptoms at work, during a weekday, and in the presence of others are much more likely to respond more quickly, presumably because people around them are able to provide feedback concerning the nature and severity of symptoms, and can offer advice as to how to properly respond to such symptoms. Patients with a history of angina or other prodromal symptoms actually take longer to seek help than do those patients without symptoms, presumably because they are able to deny the fact that there is anything seriously wrong with them or because they consider the sensations benign variations of their usual symptoms.

One way to deal with denial during the prehospital phase is through the education of the patient and the family. Patients must learn to recognize the common signs of CHD. They should be taught that chest pain is by far the most common symptom of acute MI, and they should not be falsely reassured (denial) if they have not experienced difficulties in breathing, nausea, extreme weakness and fatigue, pain radiating down the arm, etc. Whether or not they can distinguish "new" symptoms from "old," they should be taught to take quick action and to not be indecisive about the need for assistance after the onset of symptoms. If the patient cannot accept the reality of the symptoms, then the family and/or physician should confront the patient and decide the most prudent course of action.

Physician education is also likely to provide more immediate help for the CHD patient (Gentry, 1975). While accurate diagnosis is essential, ambiguity in diagnosis unduly prolongs the preadmission period. As Hackett and Cassem (1969) report:

The physician employed the same maneuvers used by patients who delayed. He either blamed other organ systems or minimized the pain by calling it angina. In some cases, medication was given and the patient was instructed to wait. In other cases, an appointment was made for an office visit the next day. . . . One of the delaying doctors later admitted that he thought his patient was simply exaggerating his pain. In fact, this same physician doubted that his patient had true coronary disease until it was amply demonstrated angiographically.*

Physicians will often delay hospitalization because they are unfamiliar with their patients. The solution is for physicians to get to know their patients as quickly as possible, and to develop sensitivity to subtle signs and symptoms of altered cardiac function.

Acute Phase

The immediate and short-term reaction of patients to heart disease has been the subject of a large number of research investigations. An excellent comprehensive review of the literature (Doehrman, 1977) concluded that psychological problems are frequently present in a number of patients in the Coronary Care Unit (CCU), and that emotional factors play an important role in determining subsequent recovery.

The single-most important emotional feature of patients in the acute phase of illness is extreme fear and anxiety associated with life-threatening illness. At least 80 percent of patients in the CCU had some signs of being anxious, 58 percent were depressed, 22 percent were hostile, and 16 percent were agitated (Hackett et al., 1968). The content of anxious thought usually focuses on the realization of the possibility of sudden death, concerns about being abandoned, and the perception of various somatic symptoms, including shortness of breath, chest pain, fatigue, weakness, and disturbed heart rhythm. Awareness of physical symptoms provides evidence that a real medical problem is present, and that the condition may be serious. On the other hand, emotional disturbance in the CCU is rarely a cause for psychiatric consultation. Less than one third of CCU patients require psychiatric intervention; even fewer complain of emotional disturbance (Cassem and Hackett, 1973). While most patients may initially be quite anxious, anxiety tends to lessen after a few days in the CCU.

Strong feelings of depersonalization also characterize the patient in the CCU. Typically, the patient is in a new, unfamiliar environment in which he or she is treated as an object rather than as a person. For example, the patient may be referred to by staff as "the MI in 217" rather than "Mr. Jones, the man who just experienced an acute coronary event." The patient is usually aware of the ongoing surveillance of his or her medical condition; EKG, blood pressure, blood gases, and other functions are monitored to evaluate the patient's medical status. While these procedures can provide comfort and reassurance, they also increase feelings of depersonalization and loss of control. The patient is confined to the bed which further serves to reduce the feeling of power over his or her body. Although the

---

*From Hackett T. P., and Cassem, N. H. Factors contributing to delay in responding to the signs and symptoms of acute myocardial infarction. *American Journal of Cardiology,* 1969, *29,* 656. Reprinted with permission.

patient will usually submit to diagnostic procedures and cooperate with physicians, at the same time, the patient may feel a lack of control over his or her medical management. In addition, since the medical chart is open and readily available for all medical personnel to see, feelings of vulnerability, insecurity, and loss of privacy may become exacerbated.

Depression, which usually develops subsequent to anxiety, may have a more gradual onset, first appearing in the late stages of the CCU experience, and decreasing during the early stages of the convalescent period. Depression often becomes more pronounced several weeks after the patient returns home. Depression on the CCU can have important prognostic implications. Myocardial infarction patients characterized by a high level of depression upon admission to the CCU (as measured by scale 2 on the MMPI) are more prone to experience a recurrent MI within the first 12 weeks after discharge from the hospital (Cromwell, 1968).

Depression may be inferred from the presence of the following signs: sad facies, feelings of disinterest, disturbed sleep, feelings of pessimism and hopelessness, psychomotor retardation, loss of appetite, and crying spells. Also common is the guilt, frustration, and anger reflected in such statements as "why me?" and "what did I do to deserve this?" The content of depressive thought frequently takes the form of concern about self-esteem and self-concept. Many patients verbalize fears of loss of autonomy, income, social status, sexual functioning, and physical abilities. This is particularly true for the younger patient who was apparently in good health until the infarction. Moreover, patients experience frustration in being restricted by illness and forced into a dependency role, which they may feel conflicted about. Cassem and Hackett (1973) term the MI an "ego infarction," which aptly describes the psychological effects of sudden life-threatening illness. The depression exhibited by post-MI patients should not be considered pathological during the initial phase of the illness, however, and should be viewed as a normal grief reaction to a significant loss.

The reasons for psychological consultation are related to the timing of the referral (Cassem and Hackett, 1973). For example, most of the anxiety consultations occur on the first or second day of hospitalization. Consultations for signing out prematurely occur on day 2, and those for depression occur on days 3 to 5. Cassem and Hackett (1977) provide a concise description of events.

The typical patient, a few hours removed from his life-threatening experience with crushing chest pain, is anxious when he is admitted to the coronary care unit. At this point, this patient is preoccupied with death or its possibility as signaled by recurrence of pain or shortness of breath, a sense of imminent danger or doom, or simply the intimidation of the unknown. As the patient feels better, denial is mobilized. He may find it hard to believe that he really had a heart attack. If the damage is unconfirmed, he may protest his detention in the unit and insist on returning to important business obligations. By the third or fourth day, however, the implications of his cardiac injury begin to take the shape of a specific concern. As he becomes more cognizant of his true condition, despondency sets in. The more devastating the effects of the infarct, the more profound the depression is likely to be. If he also has premorbid abrasive personality traits, especially those centering on dependency or passivity, he may, after a "civil interval," start irritating or perplexing the staff by his behavior. Provocative behavior usually begins around the fourth day when the immediate threat to life seems to pass. It has been our experience that hostile, disruptive behavior in a coronary care unit patient on the first day is almost always due to anxiety and subsides as the sense of security increases. Patients who become difficult after the threat is over usually remain so, reverting to life patterns characterizing behavior styles prior to admission to the coronary care unit.*

The way patients cope with stress, and the mechanisms by which patients adapt to the CCU and to their illness have been widely studied. The most common defense mechanism is that of *denial*. As many as 20 percent of patients who were told that they suffered an MI refused to believe it (Croog, Shapiro, & Levine, 1971), and that at the time of discharge from the hospital, one third of all patients had no understanding of the physiology of CHD.

Denial is usually inferred from patients' responses to specific questions. For example, Gentry and coworkers (1973) asked patients only one question: "Did you feel afraid, frightened, or apprehensive at any time during your hospital stay so far?" The denier unequivocally stated "no," or "never," while the non-denier usually acknowledged fear and anxiety by such remarks as, "if someone says they're not scared, they're a liar." Hackett and coworkers (1968) evaluated denial by asking multiple questions and by inferring denial from behavior.

1. Does the patient minimize present symptoms?
2. Does the patient allude to there being nothing really wrong, that he or she is ready to go home?
3. Does the patient spontaneously mention fear of, or concern with, death, another MI, or invalidism?
4. Does the patient displace the source of symptoms to areas other than the heart?
5. Does the patient complain of symptoms unrelated to the cardiovascular system?
6. Does the patient chide physicians and staff for excessive and unnecessary restrictions in CCU?

Work by Gentry, Foster, & Haney (1972) provided quantitative measurement of psychological adjustment in patients in the CCU. They administered a battery of standardized tests measuring state and trait anxiety, situational depression, and perceived health status. Two groups of patients in the CCU with MI symptoms were rated. One group was classified as deniers, since they repudiated any fear or apprehension associated with their symptoms. A second group was labeled non-deniers, because they admitted to feelings of anxiety. The results of their study

---

*From Cassem, N. H., and Hackett, T. P. Psychological aspects of myocardial infarction. *Medical Clinics of North America*, 1977, *61*, 715. Reprinted with permission.

revealed that "nondeniers" had significantly higher levels of state anxiety across the first 5 days of hospitalization than did deniers. Nondeniers' scores actually decreased during hospitalization, and their perceived health status improved. There was no difference in trait anxiety or depression. Denial was thus demonstrated as a major determinant of anxiety experienced by patients in the CCU.

Denial has been shown to be related to subsequent morbidity (reinfarction) and mortality (survival). Gentry et al. (1972) observed that two of the eight CCU patients characterized as nondeniers died within the first 6 months after discharge from the hospital, while none of the eight patients classified as deniers died during the same interval. Hackett and coworkers (1968) also reported a small but significant percentage of deaths in those CCU patients whom they assessed as using minimal denial. While the number of subjects is extremely small, these preliminary data suggest that denial may be important in determining the immediate prognosis and survival of the acute MI patient. Garrity (1971) noted that the coronary patients who failed to adequately adjust to their illness while in the CCU had higher mortality rates during the 6-month period following discharge from the hospital than those patients who were better adjusted. Similarly, Cromwell, and coworkers (1977) found patients who were considered "excessive scanners" and "sensitizers" in the CCU to be more likely to suffer reinfarctions during the first 12 weeks at home.

A related style of coping is referred to as *isolation of affect*. In contrast to denial, the patient is aware of having suffered an infarct, but does not experience the negative affect (e.g., anxiety, depression, etc.) associated with the awareness. There has been little research on this defense mechanism, despite its relatively common occurrence.

Hypomania, a condition characterized by overactivity, restlessness, and accelerated behavioral tempo, represents another variation of denial. Hypomanic patients cope with stress by excessive physical or mental activity. They often report that they "stay on the go," and they may be aware that their activity serves to minimize their subjective distress. This style can be adaptive as long as it does not jeopardize the patient's physical well-being or interfere with medical care.

Finally, one of the more ominous ways of adapting to stress involves *regression*. The patient may feel hopeless and helpless, and may adopt an immature level of psychosocial functioning. This response to MI, if untreated, can be a precursor of "cardiac neurosis," a condition sometimes observed in patients during the convalescent and rehabilitative phases of recovery.

The small number of studies exploring demographic variables in relation to the CCU experience have all suggested that social factors are important. However, there is no uniform agreement as to what importance such factors have. For example, Croog and Levine (1969) and Dominion and Dobson (1969) found that persons of lower socioeconomic status experienced more difficulties in the hospital after an MI than persons of higher socioeconomic status. In contrast, Rosen and Bibring (1966) found that there was a positive relationship between socioeconomic status and anxiety, and suggested that those individuals of lower socioeconomic status actually use denial more effectively. Another study found that persons of higher socioeconomic status had better communication with doctors, but there was no difference in emotional response to MI among the patients within different socio-economic groups (Cassem and Hackett, 1977). Byrne (1980–1981) also noted the importance of socioeconomic variables in the recovery process and observed that patients employed in blue-collar occupations prior to MI had more state anxiety in response to MI than patients in white-collar occupations.

Age is another important demographic variable. Myocardial infarction patients in their 50s were found to be more depressed than either younger or older patients and to be more uncooperative during hospitalization (Rosen and Bibring, 1966).

Other relevant factors include race and education (Gentry and Haney, 1975), premorbid psychiatric history (Cay, Vetter, & Philip, et al., 1972), severity of ill-ness (Vetter et al., 1977), prior cardiac status, (Gentry and Haney, 1975), and characteristics of the CCU (Leigh et al., 1972).

Convalescant Phase

This phase begins with the patient's discharge from the hospital and contin-ues through the sixth to eighth week after discharge. During this period, the respon-sibility for the patient's care shifts from the hospital team to the patient and family. The family can be a strong source of support and is generally regarded as essen-tial for proper management of the patient. The physician becomes progressively less involved in direct patient care and often confines regular visits to 6–8 week follow-up evaluations.

Psychological problems are seldom resolved during the immediate period of hospitalization and intensive medical treatment. Wishnie, Hackett, & Cassem (1971) reported that at 6 months to 1 year post-MI, 88 percent of their patients were either anxious or depressed, 55 percent had sleep disorders, 38 percent had not returned to work for "psychological" reasons, and 83 percent complained of exces-sive weakness. Cassem and Hackett reported that in all of the patients' families, there was evidence of significant emotional conflict subsequent to the MI, in which 75 percent of the problems were a result of "differences over medical in-structions for convalescence," (Cassem and Hackett, 1973). Similarly, Tibblin, Lindstrom, & Ander (1972) reported that anxiety and irritability were noted 3 months post MI.

The convalescent phase of the patient's recovery is one in which there is heightened anxiety and apprehensiveness. Unlike the structured hospital setting, there is a great deal of ambiguity, and often a lack of specific guidelines when the patient returns home. During the 2-month period following MI, reports of anxie-ty, depression, weakness, fear of sexual arousal, disturbed sleep, and failure to return to work are among the most common complaints. The anxiety and depres-sion that so frequently are experienced by the MI patient may not be apparent unless the patient is asked specifically what bothers him (Wishnie et al., 1971).

Klein et al. (1967) concluded that features of "invalidism" usually began early in the convalescent experience of the patient with MI, and that early identification and treatment of emotional disturbance in the post-MI patient was essential for successful rehabilitation. "Cardiac neurosis" may become manifest during the 2-month period when the patient first returns home from the hospital. Paul Dudley White is generally credited with coining the term describing the "fear and anxiety about the heart" displayed by patients with (or even without) actual cardiac pathology (Glendy and White, 1937; Viko, 1925–1926). Hypochondriasis is the most common underlying behavioral feature, characterized by excessive worry about health and bodily functions, concerns of heart disease in relatives and friends, discomfort even with mild effort, and frequent fatigue and discomfort. Fear and anxiety is the cardinal feature of cardiac neurosis, and is often exacerbated by pain. Frequently, the pain may resemble angina pectoris in its location and description. On the other hand, vague or affect-laden descriptions should alert the physician to the possibility of psychological or unrelated physiological processes. Gastrointestinal disorders, neuromuscular conditions, or unrelated cardiovascular abnormalities (e.g., prolapsed mitral valve or cardiac arrhythmias) produce symptoms that frequently resemble coronary heart disease.

Excessive weakness is perhaps the most distressing symptom reported in patients in the convalescent phase. This symptom is most often due to muscle atrophy and to the systemic effects of prolonged immobilization. Bed rest can promote venous stasis and muscle atrophy that are mistakenly attributed to the damaged heart. Early progressive mobilization programs can serve to counter both the deleterious physical and psychological effects of prolonged bed rest; and in most cases, mobilization programs are recommended for recovering MI patients.

Rehabilitation Phase

The rehabilitation phase customarily refers to that period of time from approximately 2 months after the patient leaves the hospital to the 1-year anniversary of the onset of the illness. However, from a practical standpoint, the rehabilitation phase represents an ongoing, open-ended process of recovery and treatment. It is from this point on that the medical care often becomes open-ended, and guidelines designed to insure patients' continued progress becomes less specific. Usually, physicians' advice is to continue the treatment strategies that were instituted in the acute and convalescent stages: stop smoking, maintain diet and weight loss, adhere to medication regimens, receive proper rest, and exercise regularly. Many patients, for the first 6 to 12 months, may require specific behavioral, psychological, and medical intervention. After a year, however, the patient is expected to continue self-management, except for regular medical checkups.

The extent to which patients return to a normal, healthy life style is a function of physical, social, and psychological factors. As a general rule, the most ill patients have the most difficulty resuming normal activities. The greatest degree of physical impairment often requires the most adaptation and adjustment. In addition, such demographic variables as age, sex, occupational level, and socioeconomic status affect the illness's impact on an individual life style. Psychological factors also play a role, although it is not always easy to determine the extent to which psychological considerations affect subsequent recovery. However, as previously noted, many MI patients may be anxious or depressed, exhibit disturbed sleep, and, to a lesser degree, may not return to work. For a more detailed review of the literature, the interested reader is referred to several recent publications (Doehrman, 1977; Croog and Levine, 1977; Williams and Gentry, 1979).

Three general aspects of the rehabilitation phase have received the most attention: work, marital adjustment, and recreation.

Work

Most evidence suggests that the majority of CHD patients return to work within the first year post-illness. Approximately 50 percent return to work at the end of 3 months, 80 percent by 6 months, and 90 percent at the end of a year (Williams and Gentry, 1978). A number of psychological and demographic variables appear to predict whether or not an individual will return to work. These variables include age, severity of cardiac damage, socioeconomic status, and level of psychological impairment. The older the patient is, the more severe the cardiac illness, the lower the socioeconomic status and the more psychological distress, the less likely the patient is to return to work. Nagel et al. (1971) found 26 percent of their patients failed to return to work after 4 months. Anxiety and depression were present in 55 percent of patients still at home, and 52 percent of patients who had not returned to work were considered to have nonorganic disability. Similarly, Wynn (1967) studied over 400 patients with CHD and found significant emotional distress leading to vocational disability in 50 percent of his sample. He noted that 32 percent of the total sample were experiencing profound psychological problems, including anxiety and depression, which were interfering with their return to a normal daily routine. On the other hand, other studies suggest that psychological factors may be minimally responsible for a patient's return to work. For example, Groden (1967) reported that depression was only one factor that accounted for patient's failure to return to work after 1 year. In another study 13 percent of MI patients failed to return to work at the end of 1 year (Wenger et al., 1970). In fact, only 3½ percent of the total sample failed to return to work because of psychological reasons. About 45 percent of the patients followed up after discharge from the CCU failed to return to work within 3 to 9 months, but only 10 percent of these patients listed anxiety as a major problem (Wishnie et al., 1971). In general, the healthier the patient, the greater the social, economic, and personal resources available, and the less the perceived physical demands of the job, the greater the likelihood that the patient will return to work.

Marital Adjustment

Heart disease affects the spouse as well as the patient. Indeed, it has been suggested that while the patient may recover, the spouse may not (Crawshaw, 1974). Spouses of patients are fearful, anxious, and quite often depressed (Wishnie et al., 1971; Adsett and Bruhn, 1968; Croog et al., 1968; Skelton and Dominian, 1973). However, few programs involve the rehabilitation of the spouse (Adsett and Bruhn, 1968; Rahe et al., 1973; Granger, 1974; Hoebel, 1976).

Conflicts over compliance with medical prescriptions (e.g., diet, medication, and activity) are frequently reported. Wishnie et al. (1971) report that 6 to 9 months post-MI, emotional problems are present in three quarters of all families studied as a result of "difference over medical instructions." Oversolicitousness is another frequent complaint. Despite good intentions, if the spouse insists on taking over all household responsibilities, then accusations of overprotection are made. However, if the spouse shows restraint, accusations of lack of concern or sympathy may result. Usually the spouse feels reassured when the patient first returns home, but emotional distress, guilt, and irritability often occur in a sizable proportion of couples, and at 1 year, almost a third of all post-MI patients perceive their spouses as being more anxious (Croog and Levine, 1977).

Another significant problem for the post-MI patient and spouse is the return to prior level of sexual activity (Tuttle and Cook, 1964). Hellerstein and Friedman (1970), for example, have shown that the level of sexual activity reported by persons 1 year post-MI is about 60 percent of activity prior to illness, and less than half of the post-MI patients resume the same frequency of sexual intercourse as before the infarct. Patients attribute their decreased sexual activity to a variety of reasons: loss of interest (39 percent), spouse reluctance (25 percent), depression (21 percent), and anxiety associated with somatic concerns (18 percent). Stern and colleagues (1976) reported that 69 percent of a sample of MI patients returned to normal sexual activity during the first year post-MI. Depression was a significant factor in determining sexual adjustment. Only 58 percent of those patients who were depressed engaged in any sexual activity, while 93 percent of those patients judged to be non-depressed were able to resume some sexual activity.

The sexual functioning of the post-MI patient has, unfortunately, received relatively little attention. Several reasons for this neglect have been cited: (1) most cardiac patients are older and sex is often considered to be primarily for the young; (2) illness and sexuality are considered incompatible; and (3) many physicians and their patients are simply ignorant about basic sexual physiology.

Barlett was one of the first researchers to monitor physiologic function during sexual activity (Barlett, 1956). Three married couples between the ages of 22 and 30 years served as subjects. Heart rate rose during coitus, approached 170 beats per minute (bpm), and then rapidly dropped. Respiration rates showed a similar pattern. Subsequent work has provided a different picture of physiological response patterns among middle-aged adults. Holter monitoring equipment was used to assess the cardiovascular responses of 14 men with CHD during sexual intercourse with their wives in their natural environment. Heart rates during sexual activity were matched with previously recorded heart rates during exercise. The subjects' heart rates during coitus ranged from 90 to 144 bpm, with a mean of 101 bpm. Measurements taken 2 minutes before and after intercourse revealed mean heart rates of 89 bpm.

All too often, advice on sexual activity is either not given or presented in terms so global (i.e., take it easy, use common sense) as to be relatively useless. Two-thirds of patients who suffer MIs receive no advice from the medical team (Masters and Johnson, 1966). Significantly less information was given to heart patients about sexual activity than information on activities such as work, physical exertion, or diet (Cohen et al., 1976). Interestingly, data suggest that while physicians report that they do counsel their patients, most patients report that they receive no counseling (Croog and Levine, 1977; Wenger et al., 1970; Tuttle and Cook, 1964; Koller et al., 1972; Maser, 1979).

One excellent text discusses the problems of resuming normal sexual activity (Scheingold and Wagner, 1974). For the majority of patients with uncomplicated MI, full resumption of sexual functioning is appropriate and possible. The physical demands of sexual activity are roughly equivalent to climbing up several flights of stairs or a brisk walk. Certain coital positions may be less strenuous and, therefore, may be better for cardiac patients. For example, Douglas and Wilkes (1975) warn against tension induced by the male superior position, and Watts (1976) emphasizes the need for mutual selection of position by the couple, taking into consideration the couple's sexual preference.

Masturbation, extramarital sex, and sex among unmarried partners should also be discussed with the post-MI patient. The so-called "death in the saddle syndrome" refers to the higher rates of sudden death among MI patients during extramarital sex. These affairs often occur in unfamiliar surroundings, after a heavy meal, and under the influence of alcohol, each of which may induce excessive cardiovascular demands (Uneo, 1963).

Occasionally, impotence or ejaculatory incompetence may be side effects of medication. If medications are producing these effects, alternative pharmacological regimens should be explored. For the majority of heart patients, however, the following conclusions are appropriate:

> In view of the brevity of duration, the low frequency of the sexual act, the modest heart rate equivalent oxygen uptake, and the symbolic importance of conjugal sexual intercourse, most middle-aged men with atherosclerotic disease who are not in congestive heart failure can resume this important activity (Hellerstein and Friedman, 1970).

Recreation

One of the major goals of successful rehabilitation is improved quality of life. To this end, it is important to consider the interaction of psychological and physical limitations imposed by the illness. Physical capacity can be assessed and quantified using the unit of measurement known as metabolic equivalent (MET). One MET is defined as the energy expenditure/kg/minute of an individual sitting quietly in a chair. This amounts to about 1.4 calories/minute or 3.5 to 4 milliliters of oxygen/kg/minute. Table 3-2 provides a list of activities which have been assigned measurements in METs. Careful quantification of the individual's capacity for physical activity is important in helping patients to evaluate which activities they should participate in.

It is estimated that 40 percent of all patients suffering an MI report that they are less active and have reduced their level of athletic participation 6 months post-MI. In particular, strenuous activities such as cycling, tennis, team sports, and social dancing are affected. Routine household duties, gardening, and home repairs may be taken over by other household members.

Resumption of normal social and recreational pursuits is often related to the patient's improved mood, self-esteem, and self-confidence. Social support tends to come more from family and friends than from local mental health agencies or clergy. Religious practices generally remain constant, and are not altered after MI (Croog and Levine, 1972).

Summary

A sudden life-threatening illness occurs in a unique context for every individual. How the person copes with illness is a function of existing coping resources, prior experience in dealing with stress, social supports, and expectations for recovery. Mechanisms that were adaptive at one time or situation may not always be appropriate in new situations or at other times. For example, while some evidence suggests that denial enhances recovery in the acute phase, it may also contribute to non-compliance in the convalescent phase of recovery or in subsequent long-term medical management. It is not unusual for some patients to return to habits they gave up immediately after the onset of their illness. They may resume cigarette smoking and previous eating habits, become sedentary, discontinue regular use of medication, or accelerate their daily pace of living.

In general, emotional distress gradually subsides, and patients' long-term adjustment appears largely a function of their premorbid personality. All things being equal, the healthier the patient prior to illness, the greater the likelihood that recovery will be successful.

There are also developmental life crises that occur in adults that may become pronounced for an MI sufferer. The most obvious crisis involves the perception of physical decline which always accompanies normal aging. Perceived loss of function is especially acute for the MI patient, and may be exacerbated by additional losses (e.g., death in the family, children leaving home). Retirement also creates a crisis for many people; in those cases where the individual must accept forced or premature retirement, the loss is particularly distressing. Retirement also means the loss of status and money, as well as a new life style; both can produce anxiety.

An infarct forces the individual to confront his or her own mortality. Death, in terms of conscious awareness, can no longer be an abstraction, or something that happens "to others." Signs that one is aging—changes in vision, stamina, appearance—become even more apparent. One significant developmental process that occurs in adulthood involves a basic shift in time orientation (Neugarten, 1968): one stops counting "time since birth" and begins to think of life as "time yet to live." A myocardial infarction tends to make this shift more acute. With the awareness of death comes the recognition that one may not achieve all that one set out to achieve; one may not realize the income or status one has hoped for; one may not

Table 3-2

Approximate Metabolic Cost of Activities*

Metabolic Cost	Occupational	Recreational

1½–2 METs†
4–7 ml O_2/min/kg
2–2½ kcal/min
  (70 kg person)
	Desk work
	Auto driving‡
	Typing
	Electric calculating
	  machine operation
		Standing
		Walking (strolling 1.6 km or
		  1 mile/hr)
		Flying,‡ motorcycling‡
		Playing cards‡
		Sewing, knitting

2–3 METs
7–11 ml O_2/min/kg
2½–4 kcal/min
  (70 kg person)
	Auto repair
	Radio, TV repair
	Janitorial work
	Typing, manual
	Bartending
		Level walking (3.2 km or
		  2 miles/hr)
		Level bicycling (8.0 km or
		  5 miles/hr)
		Riding lawn mower
		Billiards, bowling
		Skeet,‡ shuffleboard
		Woodworking (light)
		Powerboat driving‡
		Golf (power cart)
		Canoeing (4 km or
		  2½miles/hr)
		Horseback riding (walk)
		Playing piano and many
		  musical instruments

3–4 METs
11–14 ml O_2/min/kg
4–5 kcal/min
  (70 kg person)
	Brick laying, plastering
	Wheelbarrow (45.4 kg or
	  10 lb load)
	Machine assembly
	Trailer-truck in traffic
	Welding (moderate load)
	Cleaning windows
		Walking (4.8 km or 3 miles/hr)
		Cycling (9.7 km or 6 miles/hr)
		Horseshoe pitching
		Volleyball (6-man
		  noncompetitive)
		Golf (pulling bag cart)
		Archery
		Sailing (handling small boat)
		Fly fishing (standing with
		  waders)
		Horseback (sitting to trot)
		Badminton (social doubles)
		Pushing light power mower
		Energetic musician

4–5 METs
14–18 ml O_2/min/kg
5–6 kcal/min
  (70 kg person)
	Painting, masonry
	Paperhanging
	Light carpentry
		Walking (5.6 km or
		  3½ miles/hr)
		Cycling (12.9 km or 8 miles/hr)
		Table tennis
		Golf (carrying clubs)
		Dancing (foxtrot)
		Badminton (singles)
		Tennis (doubles)
		Raking leaves
		Hoeing
		Many calisthenics

*Includes resting metabolic needs.

†1 MET is the energy expenditure at rest, equivalent to approximately 3.5 ml O_2/kg body weight/ minute.

‡A major excess metabolic increase may occur due to excitement, anxiety, or impatience in some of these activities, and a physician must assess his patient's psychological reactivity.

5–6 METs 18–21 ml O_2/min/kg 6–7 kcal/min (70 kg person)	Digging garden Shoveling light earth	Walking (6.4 km or 4 miles/hr) Cycling (16.1 km or 10 miles/hr) Canoeing (6.4 km or 4 miles/hr) Horseback (''posting'' to trot) Stream fishing (walking in light current in waders) Ice or roller skating (14.5 km or 9 miles/hr)
6–7 METs 21–25 ml O_2/min/kg 7–8 kcal/min (70 kg person)	Shoveling 10/min (4.5 kg or 10 lbs)	Walking (8.0 km or 5 miles/hr) Cycling (17.7 km or 11 miles/hr) Badminton (competitive) Tennis (singles) Splitting wood Snow shoveling Hand lawn-mowing Folk (square) dancing Light downhill skiing Ski touring (4.0 km or 2½ miles/hr) (loose snow) Water skiing
7–8 METs 25–28 ml O_2/min/kg 8–10 kcal/min (70 kg person)	Digging ditches Carrying 36.3 kg or 80 lbs Sawing hardwood	Jogging (8.0 km or 5 miles/hr) Cycling (19.3 km or 12 miles/hr) Horseback (gallop) Vigorous downhill skiing Basketball Mountain climbing Ice hockey Canoeing (8.0 km or 5 miles/hr) Touch football Paddleball
8–9 METs 28–32 ml O_2/min/kg 10–11 kcal/min (70 kg person)	Shoveling 10/min (6.4 kg or 14 lbs)	Running (8.9 km or 5½ miles/hr) Cycling (20.9 km or 13 miles/hr) Ski touring (6.4 km or 4 miles/hr) (loose snow) Squash racquets (social) Handball (social) Fencing Basketball (vigorous)
10 plus METs 32 plus ml O_2/min/kg 11 plus kcal/min (70 kg person)	Shoveling 10/min (7.3 kg or 16 lbs)	Running: 6 mph = 10 METs 7 mph = 11½ METs 8 mph = 13½ METs 9 mph = 15 METs 10 mph = 17 METs Ski touring (8 + km or 5 + miles/hr) (loose snow) Handball (competitive) Squash (competitive)

(Reprinted with permission from Fox SM, Naughton JP and Gorman PA: Physical activity and Cardiovascular health III. The exercise prescription; frequency and type of activity. *Modern Concepts Cardiovascular Disease* 41:6, June 1972.)

see all those places of one's dreams. Acceptance of life implies acceptance of death. Introspection and a search for spiritual and philosophical meaning often becomes intensified after the MI. For those MI victims who fail to come to terms with the meaning of life, the reality of death, and the limitation of time, the future may become one of frustration and despair. For those who accept life's limitations, reorder priorities, and modify life goals and expectations, successful rehabilitation can provide new energy and self-acceptance.

RELEVANT DOMAINS OF PSYCHOLOGICAL ASSESSMENT

Anxiety, Depression, and Psychopathology

A number of patients experience subjective emotional distress following an MI. Distress typically subsides by the end of the first week in the CCU, and then reappears during the convalescent phase after the patient has returned home (Cassem and Hackett, 1971). Denial is a common reaction to acute illness, and frequently serves to minimize self-reports of emotional disturbance. Moreover, marked response biases, such as defensiveness or social desirability, further serve to mask underlying distress. This is particularly true for situations where there is limited doctor–patient contact, such as a brief interview, or when the patient must complete an extensive battery of psychometric tests.

Self-rating Scales

The most common self-rating scales for depression are the Beck Depression Inventory (BDI) and the Zung Self-rating Depression Scale (SDS) (Beck et al., 1961; Zung, 1965). Both of these instruments were developed for estimating the severity of symptoms rather than diagnosing the patient's condition. Consequently, a patient may achieve a high score (indicative of depression), which may be secondary to another diagnosis (e.g., MI, or presenile dementia). Conversely, a patient may obtain a low score, and still be clinically depressed. A major shortcoming of these self-rating scales is that the items are readily transparent and do not provide adjustment for response set or different interpretations of the same item. A format which permits patients to elaborate on their responses and to reveal underlying response tendencies would be a useful complement to most depression self-rating scales.

Self-report measures of anxiety such as the Taylor Manifest Anxiety Scale (Taylor, 1955), Spielberger State-Trait Anxiety Questionnaire (Spielberger et al., 1970), and the Zung Self-rating Anxiety Scale (Zung, 1971) share strengths and weaknesses: they are objective, easily administered and scored, and are widely used. However, they are also subject to distortion, and should not be relied on exclusively for estimating symptom severity or for diagnostic purposes.

Clinicians using self-report measures should be aware of medical patients' tendency to characterize themselves in socially desirable ways. Frequently, the MI patient will present himself or herself as being free from worry, tension, or emotional stress. In order to partially control this response tendency, instruments which measure defensiveness (e.g., the K scale from the MMPI) and social desirability (e.g., the Edwards Social Desirability Scale (Edwards, 1953), or the Marlow Crowne Social Desirability Scale (Crowne and Marlowe, 1967), could be used to verify self-report scores. In many situations, establishing rapport and giving clear instructions may sufficiently motivate subjects to give honest responses. However, even a highly motivated patient may unconsciously distort his or her condition when unaware of this response set.

One of the most recent developments in the assessment of mood is the use of multiple affect scales such as the Profile of Mood States (POMS) (McNair et al., 1971) and the Multiple Affect Adjective Checklist (MAACL) (Zuckerman and Lubin, 1965). These instruments are standardized, objectively scored measures of multiple emotional states. The POMS for example, provides six factor scores, including tension, depression, fatigue, anger, vigor, and confusion. Again, the major shortcoming of these state measures is their failure to concurrently assess response set.

Multiple measures have been used in the more general assessment of psychopathology, and several instruments incorporate a measure or response set into their design. The best known multiple scale inventory is the Minnesota Multiphasic Personality Inventory (MMPI) (Hathaway and McKinley, 1943). The MMPI is a 566-item, true–false questionnaire that yields 4 validity scales, 10 clinical scales (including measures of hypochondriasis, depression, and psychopathology), and a variety of experimental scales. Comprehensive handbooks and numerous interpretive guides are available (Dahlstrom et al., 1972; Lacher, 1974; Carson, 1969). Another frequently used inventory is the Psychological Screening Inventory (PSI). The PSI is a 130-item, true–false questionnaire which yields scores on 5 subscales including alienation, social nonconformity, discomfort, depression, and defensiveness (Lanyon, 1973). A third multiple-scale instrument that has recently received a good deal of attention is the Hopkins Symptom Checklist (SCL-90) (Derogatis et al., 1974). The SCL-90 is comprised of 90 items which reflect 9 primary symptom dimensions: somatization; obsessive–compulsive; interpersonal sensitivity; depression; anxiety; phobic anxiety; paranoid ideation; hostility; and psychoticism. While the SCL-90 has been validated with both out- and in-patients, a major shortcoming is its failure to assess response bias. However, it may offer the clinician useful information along clinical dimensions that are relevant for post-MI patients.

Self-rating questionnaires need not focus solely on the ''self.'' It is becoming increasingly recognized that the context of behavior—the situation—is a primary determinant of behavioral and emotional reactions. The S-R Inventory of General Trait Anxiousness (Endler et al., 1962), Test Anxiety Questionnaire (Mandler and Sarason, 1952), and the Negative Evaluation Scale (Watson and Friend, 1969) are examples of anxiety inventories for specific situations (e.g., test-taking, social interactions). A variant of this form of self-rating is the Pleasant Event Schedule, a survey consisting of 320 events and activities which the patient is asked to rate on a 5-point scale of pleasantness (Lewinsohn and Libet, 1972). Depressed patients may report that they engage in relatively few pleasant activities compared to non-depressed individuals, and the scale may be useful in initial evaluation and repeated assessment of change.

Observer-rating Scales

Observer-rating scales represent a relatively new assessment technique. The Hamilton Psychiatric Rating Scale (Hamilton, 1967), the Phenomena of Depression Scale (Grinkler et al., 1961), and the NIMH Collaborative Depression Mood Scale (Raskin, 1965) are the most common observer rating scales for depression. Like self-report scales, these are not intended for diagnosis, but rather are designed to measure the clinical severity of depression. Unlike self-report, however, the observer-rating scales take into account data from all available sources concerning the patient's behavior during the preceding week. Consequently, the patient's subjective ratings probably represent a different dimension than the observer-ratings. Observer-rating scales that measure anxiety include the Hamilton Anxiety Scale (Hamilton, 1959) and the Zung Anxiety Status Inventory (Zung, 1971).

Semi-structured interviews, such as the Schedule for Affective Disorders and Schizophrenia (SADS), are employed for diagnosis as well as estimation of the severity of symptoms (Spitzer and Endicott, 1977). Its complexity is worthwhile when accurate diagnosis of depression is of utmost importance.

Observer-rating scales have not been used extensively in CHD patients. The use of relatives and immediate family members to assess the patient's recovery could, for example, prove a useful addition to standard test instruments. To date, observer rating scales appear to be underutilized in assessment of coronary patients; they appear to be a promising development in the future.

Interview

The clinical interview is the most basic and widely used method of assessment. Although it is usually supplemented by other diagnostic procedures, it is considered an essential component of any assessment procedure.

In general, the interview technique is directly related to psychotherapeutic theory and strategy. For example, Freud's technique of free association was designed to help the patient explore unconscious dynamics and reconstruct personality development. A behavioral interview (Linehan, 1977) relies on "self-report data" to formulate a functional behavioral analysis, generate hypotheses, and define target behaviors for subsequent modification.

In general, the interview represents a method for obtaining data about the patient in which verbal and nonverbal information is provided. As a technique, it is flexible and can be individualized to meet the unique needs and demands of a particular patient or specific situation. It is a procedure for assessing a patient's past, present, and future behavior, and it represents an essential component to virtually every assessment strategy.

Personality

Self-report Scales

Self-report measures are the most widely used instruments to assess personality functioning. The MMPI, as previously described, is the best known and is generally regarded as both reliable and valid. A number of studies have been conducted with coronary patients using the MMPI, and have been reviewed by Jenkins (Jenkins, 1971; Jenkins, 1976). In general, CHD patients tend to score higher on the "neurotic triad" scales 1(Hs), 2(D), and 3(Hy) than those individuals who remain healthy. Furthermore, the difference appears to be greater for those patients with angina pectoris than those who only develop MI. Hypochondriasis and hysteria scores were elevated in men before the development of angina, while those who developed MI were not different from those who did not develop any CHD on any MMPI scale (Ostfeld et al., 1964). The manifestation of CHD appears to impair coping mechanisms (e.g., lower scores on scales K, Repression, and Ego Strength) and also to elevate scales measuring Depression (2) and Anxiety (A). Jenkins (1971) concluded:

. . .that before their illness, patients with coronary disease differ from persons who remain healthy on several MMPI scales, particularly those in the "neurotic triad" (Hs, D, and Hy). These differences seem due largely to the high scores of persons in whom angina pectoris is about to develop rather than in those about to have myocardial infarction. The occurrence of manifest coronary disease increases the deviation of patients' MMPI scores further, and in addition, the breakdown of ego defenses becomes apparent. Patients with fatal disease tend to show greater neuroticism (particularly depression) in prospective MMPI's than those who incur and survive coronary disease.*

It should be emphasized, however, that there is a great deal of individual variability. Aside from the elevations of scales Hs, D, and Hy, there is no evidence that CHD patients exhibit greater psychopathology than nonmedically ill individuals. Moreover, the elevation of the neurotic triad scales is likely to occur in the context of any major medical illness and thus is not necessarily unique to the patient with CHD.

The Sixteen Personality Factor Questionnaire (16PF) also has been used extensively with CHD patients (Cattel et al., 1970). Factors O and C, which measure anxiety, apprehension, and hypochondriasis, have been found to be related to CHD patients by several investigators. In one study, patients who suffered fatal MIs were found to have exhibited higher scores on Factor O than those who survived (Caffrey, 1970). Bakker (1967) found patients with angina pectoris to have obtained the highest scores on neuroticism and anxiety. Ostfeld et al. (1964) administered the MMPI and 16PF prospectively to almost 2000 employed males in Chicago. Patients with angina pectoris scored particularly low on Factor C, which reflects such traits as

---

*From Jenkins, C. D. Psychologic and social precursors of coronary disease, I and II. *New England Journal of Medicine*, 1971, *284*, 251. Reprinted with permission of *New England Journal of Medicine*.

excessive worrying and hypochondriasis. Men with CHD also scored higher on L and Q_2 than the non-CHD controls, suggesting that CHD patients were more independent in social relations, more suspicious of others, and showed greater inner tension.

The MMPI and 16PF share several drawbacks: They are measures of psychopathology as well as personality and so may not be appropriate for psychological evaluations of medically ill, but otherwise "normal," individuals. Moreover, scores may have different meanings for medically-ill patients. For example, the "neurotic triad" frequently found in post-MI patients is not necessarily pathological and may not reflect the depression, excessive somatic preoccupation, and tension that are implied by the configuration. Rather, scores may represent real physical changes that occur secondary to the illness. Alternative personality inventories, such as the California Psychological Inventory (CPI) (Gough, 1957), Personality Research Form (PRF) (Jackson, 1967), Eysenck Personality Inventory (Eysenck and Eysenck, 1968), Guilford- Zimmerman Temperament Survey (Guilford and Zimmerman, 1949), Thurstone Temperament Survey (Thurstone, 1949), and Maudsley Personality Inventory (Eysenck, 1959) may be preferred. In addition, specific inventories such as the Myers-Briggs Scale, which measures Jungian constructs of thinking/perceiving and extroversion/introversion (Myers, 1962), the Regression-Sensitization Scale (Byrne, 1964), and various measures of locus of control may also be useful (Rotter, 1966; Collins, 1974; Kirscht, 1974; Levenson, 1976; Wallston et al., 1976).

There are a large number of self-report measures of "quality of life." George and Bearon (1980) reviewed the instruments frequently used in epidemiological research. For example, while the Cantril Ladder (Kilpatrick and Cantril, 1960) and the Affect Balance Scale (Bradburn, 1969) have been used in large-scale epidemiological studies, they also have clinical utility. The Life Satisfaction Index was developed for older persons, but may have application in CHD patients as well (Neugarten et al., 1961). Measures of self-esteem and self-concept such as the Self-Esteem Scale (Rosenberg, 1965), Self-Esteem Inventory (Coopersmith, 1967), and Tennessee Self-concept Scale (TSCS) (Fitts, 1965) may also prove useful. The TSCS was especially developed for clinical use. It consists of 100 items which assess five attitudinal domains, including physical, moral, personal, familial and social factors. Various subsets of items also yield other measures regarding self-actualization and personality integration.

Projective Techniques

Projective techniques are regarded by many clinical psychologists as the most basic and traditional of all instruments for assessing personality and classifying behavior into psychiatric schemata. The theoretical basis for projective testing is generally credited to Sigmund Freud. In his essay "Instincts and their Vicissitudes," Freud suggested that the ego unconsciously projected what was troublesome or painful on to someone or something else (Freud, 1915). Later, projection was expanded to include a more general mental process by which the individual attributes characteristics to a perceived subject which are, in fact, characteristics of the individual.

According to Rappaport and colleagues (1968), ". . . projective tests seek to avoid the necessity of scrutinizing vast amounts of life data, and of relying upon intuition. Successful or not, projective tests have the broadly proclaimed aim to *elicit*, to *render observable*, to *record* and to *communicate* the psychological structure of the subject. . ." There are four basic classes of projective techniques:

1. *Association.* The patient is asked to react to words, inkblots, etc. Examples might include the Rorschach, Holtzman, and Szondi tests (Rorschach, 1942; Holtzman et al., 1961; Szondi, 1965).
2. *Construction.* The patient must construct a story or picture. Examples include the Thematic Apperception Test and the Draw-A-Person Test (Murray, 1938; Machover, 1952).
3. *Completion.* The patient is asked to complete a stimulus. Examples of the techniques include the various Sentence Completion Tests (Holsopple and Migle, 1954; Rotter and Rafferty, 1950).
4. *Expression.* The patient is permitted free expression, such as painting, play, and so forth.

Projective tests have been widely used with coronary patients. For example, research has employed the Rorschach, TAT (Arlow, 1945; Thomas and Greenstreet, 1973; Détourney, 1970; Kemple, 1945; Cleveland and Johnson, 1962; Dreyfuss et al., 1966), and the Rosenzsweig Picture Frustration Test (Mordkoff and Golas, 1968). There are also projective tests for specialized populations, such as the elderly (Wolk and Wolk, 1971; Bellak, 1975). Although projective tests have been criticized for various practical and theoretical reasons, the current status of projective tests is such that the Rorschach, TAT, and Draw-A-Person tests remain important tools for many psychologists. However, since the TAT and Rorschach require considerable time to administer and interpret, they may not be appropriate for general screening purposes.

One projective technique that may be useful involves the sequential construction of a picture and a story. The patient is asked simply to (1) draw a picture of two people doing something, and then (2) make up a story with a beginning, middle, and end.

The following case studies represent examples of how such data can be useful, and also reflect some of the conceptual difficulties and practical limitations of projective testing.

In the first example, the patient was a 55-year-old businessman who was suffering from severe triple vessel coronary disease and appeared to have extensive atherosclerotic disease. Five years prior to his present evaluation he underwent aortofemoral bypass surgery. The procedure was apparently successful, but 3 years post-surgery he developed impotence. His story and picture are reproduced in Figure 3-2.

Fig. 3-2. Two men erecting a flag pole. One man is helping his neighbor install a new flag pole. Both men seem to help each other in difficult tasks around the house. Under current world conditions, the one man wants a flag pole. After it has been installed, the lanyard and flag are attached and properly raised for all to see.

His picture of two men erecting a flagpole can be easily recognized as his desire for sexual potency. Indeed, he subsequently requested a penile implantation to restore his sexual functioning. However, the broader psychological implications of his drawing, in terms of his need for recognition and self-esteem, and desire to regain his sense of power, are condensed in the picture.

In the second case, the patient was a 50-year-old professor who recently suffered an acute uncomplicated MI. He was referred for evaluation for problems associated with impaired memory and related cognitive functions. His drawing and story in Figure 3-3 are more subtle and open to alternate interpretations.

His work reveals an unconscious concern about being replaced by a younger man. At a conscious level, the patient acknowledged that his mental abilities were failing, and that he frequently had to pass work on to younger colleagues because of his cognitive difficulties. However, the father–son relationship contains basic elements of the Oedipal complex as perceived from the perspective of the adult: rivalry, competition, and the threat of castration are all present. While this study

Fig. 3-3. A Hair-raising Tale

Once upon a time, a man and his bald-headed son were walking down the street. They were laughing and talking about the fun they would have at the races. Suddenly, the father stopped short. He shouted "Tom, your hair is growing. At last you are going to have hair." Tom rubbed his head gently. "Oh, dad, poor dad. Now I have hair and you have only one strand. Maybe yours will grow too." They sat down on the curb and waited. Tom's hair continued to grow rapidly. It was now thick and bushy and growing very long— down to his shoulders. He wondered when it would stop. His father looked at that fine head of hair with envy.

As they sat there, Tom's hair continued to grow. It was now down to his chest and seemed to be growing faster. His father now became worried—what was happening to his son? He wondered if he should call a doctor but decided to wait a while. At last the hair stopped growing and then, abruptly fell out. Tom was bald again. Just then, the bus arrived and Tom and his dad climbed aboard. "You know dad, I'll bet on Saber Tooth in the third race," said Tom as they took a seat. "A good choice, son, I think you've got a winner."

can be interpreted in several different ways, the patient's unconscious fear and concern about being displaced provided an important insight into the patient's dynamics and helped clarify some of his anxieties during his rehabilitation.

Projective tests can therefore provide a useful addition to many of the more standard behavioral and psychometric approaches to the assessment of personality. The subtle meanings of projective productions, however, requires skilled and experienced judgments which can only be acquired by intensive training. Moreover, the emphasis of underlying personality constructs often cannot be translated into overt behavior.

Stressful Life Events

Stress is often regarded as a significant precursor of coronary disease. A series of 44 consecutive post-MI patients at Duke Medical Center were asked to indicate what factors they thought caused their illnesses. Table 3-3 shows that 59 percent of those surveyed thought that some form of stress was a significant contributor to their medical condition. Other research has also suggested a positive relationship between life stress and CHD (Jenkins, 1976; Jenkins, 1971; Theorell, 1974; Theorell and Rahe, 1974; Rahe and Romo, 1974; Rahe et al., 1974).

The association of stress and CHD appears to arise from the adaptation required to cope with the stressor. Stress exerts a strain on the individual and eventually results in organ damage. Attempts to quantify this process have involved the construction of numerous self-report scales to assess the degree of life change. The most widely used measures of life stress are the Social Readjustment Rating Scale (SRRS) and the Schedule of Recent Events (SRE) (Holmes and Rahe, 1967). The SRE is a self-administered, 43-item questionnaire in which the respondent is asked to indicate the number of life events (e.g., marriage, death of spouse, etc.) experienced over a given time interval. The SRRS includes the same set of items but assigns each event a specific weight or score based on the amount of social readjustment the various events required. The item "marriage" was arbitrarily selected as an anchor point, and mean values were obtained for each of the items on the SRE. These values, termed *life change units*, were then summed to obtain a total life-stress score.

In a number of retrospective studies, patients with MIs have been demonstrated to have experienced significant increases in life changes during the 6-month period prior to the onset of their symptoms (Theorell and Rahe, 1971). These changes were frequently related to occupational problems (Theorell and Rahe, 1974). The same study examined a small group of men from 45 to 66 years old who survived an MI and returned to their previous lifestyles. Changes in life events were observed to relate to elevated catecholamine levels in a number of the subjects.

The effects of life changes also seems to be strongly influenced by the psychosocial context in which these changes occur. Attempts to describe this context

Table 3-3
Patients' Perception of the Cause of Their Illness

Cause	N	%
Stress	26	59
Overweight	12	27
Smoking	9	20
Diet	8	18
Overwork	6	14
Heredity	6	14
Blood pressure	3	7
Sedentary life style	2	5
Age	2	5
Diabetes	1	2

have focused on such variables as developmental phase (Neugarten, 1973), control (Schultz and Brenner, 1977), and previous experience (Lazarus, 1979). There is not a single assessment device that takes into account the individual's perception of the stressfulness of a particular event, while providing a simultaneous description of the nature and extent of the behavioral, cognitive, and psychological coping strategies that the individual employed to adapt to the event.

Recently, however, a number of stressful life-event self-report scales have been developed that represent methodological and conceptual improvements over previous instruments. These include the Impact of Event Scale (Horowitz et al., 1979), the Life Experience Survey (LES) (Sarason and Johnson, 1976), and the Survey of Life Changes (Paykel et al., 1971).

The LES is a particularly promising instrument, in that specific life events and their perceived impact are independently considered, and individualized ratings are based on the respondent's experience of the events as being desirable or undesirable.

Similarly, the Impact of Event Scale is a 15-item scale designed to evaluate the conscious experiences of the individual in a particular stressful event. Reactions are classified as either *avoidance* (e.g., "I didn't let myself have thoughts related to it; I made an effort to avoid talking about it") or *cognitive intrusion* (e.g., "Images relating to it popped into my mind; I have difficulty falling asleep because of images or thoughts related to the event"). Preliminary measures of reliability and validity for the scale appear promising (Horowitz et al., 1979). There are a number of problems with all self-report measures, however. The respondent may consciously or unconsciously avoid admission of an event, may not be sufficiently motivated to recall all events, may forget events, or in some way or another distort the clinical picture (Jenkins et al., 1979).

Several observer-rating scales for assessing stress reactions are currently in use. These include the Stress Response Rating Scale which, like the Impact of Event Scale, consists of intrusion and denial subscales (Horowitz et al., 1979);

the Brief Psychiatric Rating Scale, which consists of 16 categories of observable signs and symptoms (Overall and Gorham, 1962); and the Coping Style Typology for conceptualizing stress coping strategies (Horowitz and Wilner, 1980).

The *SORC* model (Situational antecedents, Organismic variables, Response dimensions and Consequence) provides a general framework for assessing behavior that may have particular utility in assessing stress (Goldfried & Sprafkin). In stress evaluation in the cardiac patient, focus is placed on obtaining a detailed account of situations that precede the patient's feelings of anxiety or tension, evaluating such organismic variables as the physical condition and cognitive set of the patient, assessing response variables (including physiological responses, such as muscle tension, heart rate, and blood pressure), and determining the behavioral consequents, such as positive feelings of mastery, or decreased feelings of anxiety.

In order to evaluate the effect of a significant life event on the individual it is necessary to consider the psychosocial context in which the life change occurs: the perceived controllability of the event, the individual's past experience in dealing with such changes, the individual's adaptive resources, the degree of perceived distress, and the extent of the individual's preparation for the event. Moreover, no instrument currently available includes life events that may be unique to coronary patients; such an instrument could be of considerable value in assessing the impact of life events on coronary patients.

Type A Behavior Pattern

The *Type A behavior pattern* (TABP) refers to a particular constellation of psychological traits, overt behaviors, and response dispositions. Type A individuals are hard-driving, competitive, aggressive, impatient, time-urgent, and hypervigilant. Currently, TABP is considered to represent an integrated pattern elicited by particular situations. Those situations which involve competition and challenge or which threaten ''controllability'' appear to be most effective in stimulating Type A behavior in predisposed individuals.

Most of the published reports of various characteristics of the TABP employ fairly standard procedures for assessing characteristic verbal statements and voice and motor stylistics (e.g., loud, rapid, and staccato speech, tenseness of musculature). A structured interview has been developed which provides a suitable challenge to elicit the response style of the individual as well as the content of response. The interview has gone through a series of revisions, and the most recent version can be found in ''The Interview Method of Assessment of the Coronary Prone Behavior Pattern'' (Rosenman, 1978).

For classification purposes, a 4-point categorical system is usually employed: *A-1:* displaying fully developed TABP; *A-2:* displaying incompletely developed (i.e., less extreme) TABP; *B:* displaying an absence of TABP; *X:* displaying equivalent components of Type A and Type B characteristics.

Methodological studies have been conducted concerning the reliability and stability of the interview method for assessing TABP. In general, published reports suggest that interrater agreement is between 74 percent and 90 percent. Recent studies have also attempted to identify the essential elements of TABP. Expressive speech stylistics were found to be the best predictors of behavior pattern typing (Scherwitz et al., 1977). Volume and speed of speech were determined to be most responsible for TABP classification (Shucker and Jacobs, 1977).

The interview method permits flexibility and is generally recognized as the most valid TABP measure. However, it requires training for administration and classification, is a global and subjective procedure, and may be less sensitive for individuals who are not employed, middle class, white, and male.

Several other procedures have been used to assess TABP. Polygraph recordings of various physiological reactions of subjects listening to a specifically designed tape recording proved to have limited utility, as did a fairly extensive battery of performance tasks (Rosenman et al., 1964; Bortner and Rosenman, 1967; Friedman and Rosenman, 1960). Standard psychometric tests, such as the Thurstone Temperament Schedule, Eysenck Personality Inventory, Work Environment Scale, and Barrett Impulsiveness Scale, have been shown to be of little practical value in identifying Type A individuals. However, several questionnaires have been developed for the specific purpose of identifying individuals displaying TABP (Bortner, 1967; Wardwell and Bahnson, 1973; Vickers, 1973; Hinkle, 1972; Haynes et al., 1978).

The most well known, valid, and best-studied psychometric instrument for TABP assessment is the Jenkins Activity Survey for Health Prediction (JAS) (Jenkins et al., 1967). The JAS is a self-report inventory which was originally developed for use in the Western Collaborative Group Study (Rosenman, 1964). The JAS provides a continuous distribution of scores for Type A, as well as three separate factor analytically derived subscales: speed and impatience, hard-driving, and job involvement. The JAS can duplicate interview ratings in about 70 percent of cases (Jenkins et al., 1980; MacDougall et al., 1979). However, correlations between Type A JAS scores and interview have been low: correlations often fail to exceed 40 percent (Blumenthal et al., 1980).

The development and validation of the JAS has been reported in detail (Jenkins et al., 1980; Zyzanski and Jenkins, 1970; Brand et al., in press). While the JAS has the advantage of being easily scored and administered, it has been criticized for its cost (approximately $5.00 to score), vulnerability to distortion and response bias, unsuitability for use with retired persons, and poor predictive power for individuals. Several different forms of the JAS are now available for use with college students, women, and unemployed adults. While behavioral tests are also available for use with children (Butensky et al., 1976; Matthews, 1978), the problem of response equivalence of child and adult behaviors has not been adequately studied, and therefore cannot be recommended.

One of the major criticisms of TABP self-report measures is their failure to detect stylistic behaviors exhibited by Type A individuals. Moreover, there is some suggestion that Type A individuals have little insight into their own behavior. Recently, this issue was addressed through a systematic comparison of self-perceptions of Type A and Type B individuals on descriptive traits judged to be relevant to the coronary prone Type A behavior pattern (Herman et al., 1981). Item analyses performed on the data revealed that the personal traits most recognized by Type A (as opposed to Type B) individuals included those items which reflected socially acceptable forms of aggressiveness, an extroverted outlook on life, healthy autonomy, and ambition. A list of adjectives endorsed differentially by Type A and Type B individuals is found in Table 3-4. From this list, it may be possible for individuals to identify certain characteristics on their own that may place them at risk for the development of premature CHD. In addition, there are TABP features that Type A subjects fail to endorse. It may be appropriate for intervention efforts to help Type A individuals identify these characteristics to facilitate TABP modification. A brief screening device for the identification of Type A individuals is currently being developed at Duke University and should be validated on appropriate nonclinical and clinical (i.e., patients with CHD) samples.

NEUROPSYCHOLOGICAL ASSESSMENT

The question of impaired cognitive functioning is often raised as an important consideration for the coronary patient. Birren has noted ". . . while age appears to be accompanied by normal psychophysiological slowing, it is exacerbated by the presence of disease, particularly those diseases of a stress character . . ." (Birren, 1974). Not infrequently, patients with CHD complain of memory loss, problems with concentration and attention, and may occasionally display various aphasic signs and symptoms.

The relationship between physiological and neuropsychological functioning is complex (Eisdorfer and Wilkie, 1977). Szafran, for example, has suggested that decreased cardiac function, associated with decreased cerebral blood flow, may increase the amount of "neural noise," and subsequently interfere with efficient information processing (Szafran, 1968). Experimental studies have documented increased reaction time in patients with cardiovascular symptoms (Wilkie and Eisdorfer, 1972; Spieth, 1965; Botwinick and Storandt, 1974), although some evidence suggests mild blood pressure elevations provide a compensatory function (Obrist, 1964). Individuals with hypercholesterolemia improved their performance on the Halstead-Reitan battery when they reduced their cholesterol levels by at least 10 percent (Reitan and Shipley, 1963). For the post-surgical patient, cognitive changes appear even more common (Gilman, 1965; Silverstein and Kreiger,

Table 3-4

Percent Endorsing 65 ACL-Type A Scale Items by Interview Rating

Type A Scale Item	Interview Rating				Kendall's T Correlation
	B (n = 69)	X (n = 24)	A_2 (n = 193)	A_1 (n = 92)	
Calm (−)	77%	67%	56%	39%	− .23[a]
Quiet (−)	64	38	38	24	− .23[a]
Aggressive	32	46	57	62	18[a]
Assertive	35	58	58	66	.18[a]
Cautious (−)	71	79	56	47	− .17[a]
Mild (−)	48	54	34	24	− .17[a]
Outspoken	22	25	34	45	.15[a]
Strong	30	42	51	55	.15[a]
Individualistic	28	46	52	52	.14[a]
Loud	1	4	16	16	.14[a]
Quick	25	33	37	48	.14[a]
Self-confident	51	50	65	71	.14[a]
Silent (−)	38	29	21	17	− .14[a]
Slow (−)	12	13	4	2	− .14[a]
Easy-going (−)	68	58	49	46	− .13[a]
Energetic	49	58	67	70	.13[a]
Dominant	15	21	32	33	.12[a]
Masculine	46	63	67	66	.11[a]
Alert	78	83	82	91	.11[b]
Argumentative	23	38	35	41	.11[b]
Enterprising	39	46	51	57	.11[b]
Retiring (−)	10	4	3	2	− .11[b]
Shy (−)	23	25	19	11	− .11[b]
Enthusiastic	49	54	64	65	.10[b]
Forceful	26	38	40	44	.10[b]
Impatient	44	50	49	61	.10[b]
Patient (−)	52	54	49	37	− .10[b]
Relaxed (−)	46	58	29	34	− .10[b]
Withdrawn (−)	16	13	14	5	− .10[b]
Active	77	83	88	88	.09[b]
Determined	60	75	71	75	.09[b]
Excitable	17	17	25	29	.09[b]
Hurried	16	17	23	28	.09[b]
Irritable	7	4	17	16	.09[b]
Opinionated	26	21	33	38	.09[b]
Submissive (−)	7	13	5	2	− .09[b]
Tense	13	21	23	26	.09[b]
Demanding	35	38	43	47	.08
Leisurely(−)	28	33	23	19	− .08
Restless	17	21	26	28	.08

Self-centered	6	13	14	14	.07
Confident	67	71	77	76	.06
Gentle (−)	59	54	48	50	− .06
Stubborn	26	38	37	37	.06
Weak (−)	3	4	1	1	− .06
Dreamy (−)	12	25	15	9	− .05
Impulsive	15	33	24	25	.05
Meek (−)	4	8	3	2	− .05
Persevering	33	54	47	45	.05
Timid (−)	6	4	5	2	− .05
Unambitious (−)	1	4	2	4	− .05
Ambitious	52	54	63	59	.04
Bossy	7	17	14	13	.04
Industrious	68	75	77	75	.04
Persistent	54	63	60	61	.04
Apathetic (−)	6	0	3	3	− .03
Lazy (−)	7	8	7	10	.03
Reflective (−)	36	46	42	35	− .02
Unexcitable	9	4	7	9	.01
Contented (−)	32	38	34	33	.00
Hard-headed	30	33	30	32	.00
Hasty	4	17	11	7	.00
Hostile	4	0	3	3	.00
Feminine (−)	0	0	0	0	—
Headstrong	0	0	0	0	—

(−) = uncharacteristic of Type A
[a]$p < .001$; [b]$p < .01$

(From Herman, S. Blumenthal, J. A., Black, G., Chesney, M. Self-ratings of type A (coronary prone) adults: Do type As know they are As? *Psychosomatic Medicine*, 1981, *43*, 405–413. Copyright 1981 by The American Psychosomatic Society, Inc. Reproduced with permission.)

1960; Tufo et al., 1970). "Pump" time (time spent on the cardiopulmonary bypass apparatus), has been suggested as one mechanism by which patients sustain cerebral impairment (Kornfeld et al., 1965; Heller et al., 1970; Kolkka and Hilberman, 1980), although surgical survivors have been shown to sustain minimal dysfunction compared to those who die subsequent to surgery (Gilberstadt and Sako, 1967).

Aside from the effects that coronary disease and/or surgery may have on central nervous system integrity, advancing age plays a more dominant role in the determination of cognitive functioning. While it is generally agreed that some aspects of cognitive functioning decline during normal aging, normative data for older individuals are limited (Botwinick, 1977). This deficiency is unfortunate, since clinicians may find it difficult to determine if an observed level of cognitive functioning in a CHD patient is lowered beyond that which may be expected with normal aging. Normative data is just beginning to accumulate, but more research is clearly needed (Bak and Greene, 1980). This problem should not be underestimated, since one prerequisite for evaluation of brain dysfunction in adults is knowing what to expect in normal individuals. Research has suggested that the so-called "crystallized" functions, such as vocabulary, are relatively stable, while "fluid" abilities, such as motor problem-solving skills, decline with advancing age. Cognitive changes in coronary patients may (1) be normal for their respective age group; (2) represent an acceleration of generalized decline; (3) be specific to certain brain functions (e.g., memory, language skills, or psychomotor activity); or (4) reflect underlying psychiatric disturbance rather than true organic dysfunction.

The Wechsler Adult Intelligence Scale (WAIS) (Wechsler, 1958) is the best known and most widely used measure of intellectual functioning. It can assess overall intelligence, differential impairment, and lateralized dysfunction. In situations where more intensive neuropsychological evaluation is required, most clinicians rely upon a battery of tests, such as the Halstead Reitain or Luria-Nebraska Neuropsychological Batteries (Christensen, 1975; Golden et al., 1978; Reitan, 1966). Typically, this kind of detailed assessment is made only by psychologists with extensive experience with the various instruments. A pattern of scores and/or the presence of pathognomonic signs may suggest the nature of the brain disorder underlying the performance deficit (Russell et al., 1970; Walsh, 1978).

Several cautionary issues are worth noting. Behavioral tests for organicity rarely include normative data for elderly persons. The absence of this data is particularly evident for tests employing hypothesis testing (Goodglass and Kaplan, 1979). Consequently, many older people may be incorrectly labeled as "brain damaged" when they are, in fact, within the normal range of cognitive functioning. Moreover, the practical significance of the test results is of primary importance. Declines in cognitive abilities measured by neuropsychological tests are frequently irrelevant from a practical standpoint. That is, declines in test performance may not necessarily imply any perceived or real impairment in the subject's ability to perform routine tasks of daily living. Most clinicians recognize this situation, and consequently regard the approach to the task, and not just the test performance (i.e., scores on the test) as extremely important in understanding the individual's adaptive resources and potential for successful compensation or rehabilitation.

In many instances, a comprehensive neuropsychological evaluation is not appropriate. Rather, a brief screening measure that may give general estimates of the level of cognitive functioning may be all that is necessary, unless significant behavioral deficits are noted. Screening measures that have been widely used include the Mental Status Questionnaire (MSQ) (Kahn et al., 1960); the Short Portable Mental Status Questionnaire (SPMSQ) (Pfeiffer, 1975); the Mental Status Examination (Wells, 1945); and the Mini-Mental State (MMS) (Folstein et al., 1975). The latter scale may be particularly useful in middle-aged and elderly patients. The MMS includes 11 questions and requires only 5 or 10 minutes to administer. Multiple cognitive, perceptual, and motor functions are assessed, including the ability to reproduce geometric shapes; follow verbal and written commands; and provide information regarding orientation, memory and use of language.

Another useful screening measure of the efficiency of cognitive functioning is the Trail Making Test. The Trail Making Test (TMT) was originally considered to be a measure of general intellectual functioning but currently is used as a quick screening instrument for brain damage (Armitage, 1966; Reitan, 1958). The TMT consists of two parts. Each contains 25 circles on the back of a single piece of paper. Part A is comprised of circles numbered from 1 to 25, while Part B consists of 13 circles (numbered 1 to 13), and 12 circles (lettered A to L). In Part A, the circles are connected in numerical order; in Part B, the sequence alternates between number and letter (e.g., 1, A, 2, B, 3, C, etc.). The number of seconds to complete each task serves as the measure of performance. Most scoring systems do not count errors, since subjects are given immediate feedback and most subjects correct the sequence before resuming the task. Although the TMT is insufficient to diagnose brain damage (Reitan, 1974), it provides a brief screening for cortical dysfunction and may identify those individuals who require more intensive examination, particularly for lowered performance on Part B. Normative data are available (Davies, 1968). The specific indications for further evaluation are difficult to quantify. Such factors as aging and psychiatric disturbance (e.g., depression, anxiety, etc.) can serve to impair TMT performance in the absence of cortical dysfunction. However, some evidence suggests that the TMT may have less validity for older adults and consequently should be interpreted with caution (Schaie and Schaie, 1977). Since TMT performance is correlated with intelligence, the clinician must judge how the TMT scores compare to estimated levels of intellectual ability. Discrepancies between inferred level of intelligence (e.g., occupation, IQ, etc.) and TMT performance should be evaluated by more comprehensive assessment.

Many patients complain of impaired memory, and physicians frequently request an assessment of memory function. While numerous instruments are available, the most widely used include the Wechsler Memory Scale (Wechsler, 1945), (which combines verbal and nonverbal items), the Benton Visual Retention Test, (Benton, 1963), and the Graham-Kendall Memory for Designs Test (Graham and Kendall, 1960). A rapidly administered screening test that may have a good deal of merit is the Russell Revised Memory Scale (Russell, 1975). The Russell Scale is simple and easy to administer, requires a minimal amount of time to administer and score, and yields six separately scored aspects of memory function (short- and long-term verbal memory, short- and long-term figural memory, and verbal and figural retention ratios). While distant memory is not measured (Williams, 1968), this abbreviated version of the Wechsler Memory Scale is ideally suited for brief assessment of memory function. For a more detailed description of techniques and methods for a more comprehensive assessment of memory function, interested readers are referred to several texts (Goodglass and Kaplan, 1979; Barbizet, 1970; Lezak, 1976; Hecaen and Albert, 1978).

Occasionally, the clinician will want to assess the individual for aphasic signs and symptoms. A variety of aphasia tests are available, including the Boston Diagnostic Examination of Aphasia (Goodglass and Kaplan, 1972), the Minnesota Test for Differential Diagnosis of Aphasia (Schuell, 1965), and the Porch Index for Communicative Ability (Porch, 1967). The best-known instrument, with excellent validity and reliability, is the Halstead-Reitan Aphasia Screening Test (AST) (Heimberger and Reitan, 1961; Wheeler and Reitan, 1962). The AST provides an inexpensive, reliable, and rapidly administered and scored screening for receptive and expressive language, simple arithmetic skills, and psychomotor ability. A sensory perceptual examination is also available to evaluate the relative efficiency of the left and right sides of the body in recording auditory, visual, and tactile sensory input.

As with any screening device, there is always the possibility of identifying false-positives or missing false-negatives, i.e., misclassifying patients. There are many areas of brain–behavior relationships that are not reflected in the overt behavior of test performance; conversely, impaired performance is not necessarily indicative of organic impairment, but may reflect response style (e.g., carelessness or impulsivity), or psychiatric disturbance (e.g., depression, anxiety, or schizophrenia). Neuropsychological assessment must also take into account the context of the testing situation as well as the psychological status of the individual. Neglect of either factor could lead to an incorrect interpretation of test results.

HEALTH STATUS AND FUNCTIONAL CAPACITY

Coronary disease and its psychological consequences have an important effect on the individual's ability to function in the world. The technical term for this ability is the individual's *functional capacity*.

The major approaches to the assessment of functional capacity include the evaluation of subjective health, symptom reports, and measures of physical abilities (e.g., self-care skills and ability to perform various occupational and social roles). Determination of functional capacity is based in part on the patient's physical condition. Usually, the patient is referred by a physician who knows the patient's physical status and has documented the findings in medical records. Therefore, a careful review of medical records may provide useful information to the psychologist. Patients may occasionally report behavioral symptoms which require further medical consultation. For example, patients with chest pain may need more extensive cardiologic evaluation, including such procedures as radionuclide angiography, treadmill testing, or coronary angiography. Physical status, however, is only one component of the patient's overall functional capacity.

Perceived health is regarded as an important indicator of clinically measured health status, and is a significant determinant of post-illness adjustment (Garrity et al., 1978). The easiest and most accurate way to assess patients' perceived health is to ask them. A four-point rating scale (i.e., excellent, good, fair, poor) is a simple, direct method that has been found to be a generally valid index when compared to independent physicians' ratings (Maddox and Douglas, 1973). For example, in the Duke University longitudinal study, 64 percent of the doctor/patient ratings on the four-point scale were congruent, while only 36 percent were incongruent. Subsequent ratings revealed that the patients' initial health ratings were more predictive of future physician ratings than were physician ratings of future patient ratings. Thus, patients apparently knew more about their own health than physicians.

In addition, self-ratings of health can also be predictive of various indices of adjustment after illness. Health ratings were found to be predictive of morale after heart surgery and of subsequent relinquishment of the "sick role" (Brown and Rawlinson, 1975, 1976). Similarly, self-perception of health status was strongly associated with morale and return to work (Garrity, 1973). Data from a series of consecutive patients referred to a cardiac rehabilitation program at the Duke University Medical Center found a significant association between health ratings and compliance behavior. Of patients who initially rated their health as "excellent" or "good," 82 percent continued in the program for 1 year, while only 25 percent of the patients who rated their health as "fair" or "poor" remained in the program (Blumenthal, 1980). Health ratings combine perceptions of somatic impairment and functional impairment. These two aspects may be independent in many cases: consider the patient with significant three-vessel disease who is asymptomatic and able to function at a high level. Moreover, there is wide variation in individual response to illness, which can also affect self-perception of health. Self-ratings of health are therefore not simply a substitute for morale or self-concept, but represent a combined measure of the patient's subjective and objective health status.

Another common way to assess health is the more extensive self-report symptom questionnaire. The Cornell Medical Index (CMI) is the best-known and most widely used (Brodman et al., 1949). The CMI is composed of 195 *yes* or *no* questions and is divided into 12 physical symptom scales and 6 psychological symptom scales. CMI scores may be more valid for psychological than for physical health, but they are significantly correlated with physician-rated health status (Abramson, 1966; McCrae et al., 1976).

The integration of physician ratings with patient ratings probably represents the most realistic appraisal of that patient's health. Significant discrepancies between physician and patient ratings require further exploration.

There are a number of functional status indices currently available, including such measures as the Functional Status Index (Reynolds et al., 1974) and the OARS Functional Assessment Questionnaire (Pfeiffer, 1975). These measures are frequently used to assess elderly patients, however, and are not specifically designed for the post-MI patient. Instruments that may have more direct utility for the cardiac patient include the Activity of Daily Living Scale (Katz et al., 1963), the Sickness Impact Profile (Pollard et al., 1976; Bergner et al., 1976), and the Specific Activity Scale (Goldman et al., 1981).

Chest Pain (Angina Pectoris)

Pain is an elusive and yet universal experience. It is difficult to measure and, by its subjective nature, presents various methodological and conceptual difficulties. A variety of clinical diagnostic procedures are used to evaluate the patient with chest pain: coronary angiography, radionuclide angiography, and exercise treadmill testing are the most common.

For the psychologist, assessment is usually based on descriptions of symptoms, evaluation of situational and environmental factors, and determination of specific pathophysiology. In general, there are six dimensions relevant to the assessment of chest pain.

1. *Sensation.* Angina is typically described as having a deep, visceral quality. Adjectives, such as heavy, squeezing, aching, and pressure, are common descriptors.
2. *Location.* Angina pain is often located over or near the sternum but may also radiate or be limited to the left shoulder or arm.
3. *Duration.* Pain usually persists for at least 30 seconds but rarely for more than 30 minutes.
4. *Environmental factors.* Angina is often related to vigorous physical exertion or emotional stress.
5. *Severity.* There is a wide variation in the experience of the severity of symptoms for any single episode. In terms of general classification, the severity of the angina can be graded by such standard measures as the New York Heart Association's functional angina scale (CCNYHA, 1964), which has recently been shown to be predictive of morbidity (Dimsdale et al., 1980).
6. *Relief.* Those factors that relieve pain have important diagnostic significance. For example, with angina, pain is frequently relieved by vasodilators (such as nitroglycerine); or by lowering heart rate by rest or even by decreasing cardiac output (via the Val Salva maneuver).

Table 3-5
New York Heart Association Functional Classification

Class I	Patients with cardiac disease but without resulting limitation of physical activity. Ordinary physical activity does not cause undue fatigue, palpitation, dyspnea, or anginal pain.
Class II	Patients with cardiac disease resulting in slight limitation of physical activity. They are comfortable at rest. Ordinary physical activity results in fatigue, palpitation, dyspnea, or anginal pain.
Class III	Patients with cardiac disease resulting in marked limitation of physical activity. They are comfortable at rest. Less than ordinary physical activity causes fatigue, palpitation, dyspnea, or anginal pain.
Class IV	Patients with cardiac disease resulting in inability to carry on any physical activity without discomfort. Symptoms of cardiac insufficiency or of the anginal syndrome *may be* present even at rest. If any physical activity is undertaken, discomfort is increased.

Numerous systems for classifying the degree and extent of functional impairment are available (CCNYHA, 1964; Feinstein and Wells, 1977; Campeau, 1975; Peduzzi and Hultgren, 1979). The NYHA system is probably most widely used (see Table 3-5), although its reliability and validity are questionable (Selzer and Cohn, 1972).

Procedures used in the assessment of chronic pain syndromes have been used with coronary patients. For example, the McGill pain questionnaire may be used to systematically assess the verbal descriptors of pain (Melzack, 1975), while ratings of pain intensity and location can be assessed with a visual analogue scale (Woodforde and Mersky, 1972) and pain map (Keele, 1948). The use of behavioral diaries may hold particular promise. Keeping a daily log of episodes of chest pain in which severity, sensation, duration, and circumstances (e.g., precipitating events and consequents) may provide information regarding behavioral and situational determinants which can be used to tailor appropriate treatment interventions. There has been little effort to systematically gather data regarding the phenomenology of angina pectoris; much work in this area is needed.

COMPLIANCE

Nowhere is the problem of patient compliance more relevant than for patients with coronary heart disease. Current estimates of the magnitude of the compliance problem indicate that 20 to 80 percent of patients do not follow their prescribed medical regimens.

While noncompliance is not unique to coronary patients, the multimodal treatment of the CHD patient makes the compliance problem particularly relevant for such health-related areas as diet, exercise, medication, and smoking, all of which directly affect patients' health and prognosis. For example, an average of only 50 percent of all patients on long-term medication (e.g., antihypertensive drug regimens), special diets (e.g., low sodium or low cholesterol), or in structured exercise programs, adhere to the program.

Until recently, research has focused primarily on those social and demographic variables—age, sex, race, and socioeconomic status—which characterize noncompliant patients. In general, however, such factors have relatively small correlations with compliance behavior, have limited predictive value, and are not amenable to modification or change.

Since 1970, however, an increasing number of studies have attempted to define those characteristics of the patient and of the particular treatment regimen that might help to increase our understanding of the compliance problem. For example, comprehension of the treatment regimen, degree of satisfaction with care, and emotional stability are all positively correlated with adherence to treatment. In a recent Duke University study, assessment of patients prior to participation in a cardiac rehabilitation program was found to be useful in distinguishing program dropouts from those who maintained regular attendance (Blumenthal et al., 1981). Dropouts scored significantly higher on MMPI scales 1(Hypochondriasis), 2(Depression), 0(Social introversion), and A(Anxiety). They scored lower on scales Es(ego strength) and K(defensiveness). A discriminant function analysis showed impaired left ventricular function, low ego strength, and social introversion to be significant predictors of noncompliance behavior.

Adherence is also directly related to the treatment program itself. Compliance is likely to be lowest where the behavior has high economic cost, must be maintained over extended time periods, involves a complex medical regimen, and requires proscribed (rather than prescribed) behavior.

Assessment of patient compliance is usually based on (1) patient self-report, (2) observer ratings, or (3) clinical outcome. In the area of exercise compliance, for example, assessment may include having patients keep daily diaries of their exercise behavior. Patients are instructed to monitor their activity level (e.g., time and/or distance) and record those levels on either a chart or a graph. The pedometer can also be employed to assess activity levels (Saunders et al., 1978). A pedometer precisely records the distance a patient travels, and may be effective in providing an accurate index of exercise compliance. Most pedometers are about the size of a matchbook and can be unobtrusively clipped to the belt or pants, or pinned to a dress or blouse. More elaborate instruments, such as the Large Scale Integrated Motor Activity Monitor (La Porte et al., 1979), have been used for measuring activity in healthy adults. Such instruments may have more utility in assessing activity of coronary patients.

Observer ratings for exercise compliance include such measures as attendance records, time/distance recordings (both taken by medical staff), or activity logs (kept by the patient's spouse). The use of the clinical outcomes as an index of compliance is most common for compliance measures of smoking and diet. However, clinical outcome measures of exercise adherence, such as increased aerobic capacity, improved treadmill time, and lowered heart rate at submaximal exercise workload, are also related to the patient's physical condition. For example, a patient with a severely damaged left ventricle and inoperable coronary artery disease may not show the same kinds of training effects that typically accompany regular aerobic exercise over time in normal adults or in patients with less severe cardiac impairment. Similarly, hypertensive patients who do not reach their recommended blood pressure levels may be compliant in taking their medication, but may require larger doses or alternate drugs. It is important, therefore, to separate treatment outcomes from compliance behavior.

SUMMARY

The primary purpose of this chapter was to identify the behavioral and psychological dimensions relevant to the assessment of patients with coronary heart disease. The clinician must adopt a strategy for evaluating the patient, and for facilitating the implementation of an effective therapeutic program. Selection of specific instruments is largely a matter of personal preference based upon the clinician's experience, theoretical orientation, and specific reason for evaluation.

The field of assessment is in a state of transition. The 1950s were the years of the projective tests; the 1960s was the decade of the objective psychometric tests; and the 1970s was the decade of the behavioral tests. The 1980s may be a period of integration and synthesis. The assumption that people have certain stable, enduring characteristics that are responsible for overt behavior is compatible with the behavioral concepts of behavioral predispositions and response hierarchies that determine a given response in a particular context. Both traditional (i.e., psychodynamic) and learning (i.e., behavioral) approaches to assessment recognize the need to relate individual differences and situational variables to overt behavior. Continuing attention to situational variables is imperative. More precise strategies for assessing situations will certainly need to be developed.

The interview will remain the most important procedure for clinical evaluation. Behavioral interviews will likely receive more emphasis in efforts to define specific target behaviors and to identify behavioral antecedents and consequents. Additional attention will be given to the development of psychometric instruments to improve prediction and diagnostic precision. Self-report inventories will continue to be widely used. However, greater attention to the response tendencies which influence scores will be necessary. In addition, normative data must also be developed, particularly in recognition of the importance of age and the unique aspects of the study population. For example, the identical 1(Hs), 3(Hy), 2(D) MMPI profile may have a different interpretation if obtained from a coronary patient or a psychiatric patient. Similarly, peaks on scales 1(Hs) and 2(D) are relatively uncommon early in life, but become more common in later life; the reverse is true for scales 4(Pd) and 8(Sc). Therefore, it is necessary to recognize the importance of social and demographic factors when interpreting particular test scores.

Behavioral assessment has been generally underutilized in the assessment of coronary patients, and this situation should change rather dramatically as behaviorally oriented clinicians become more active in cardiac rehabilitation programs. Behavioral assessment will help to translate global behavioral tendencies into more concrete operational terms. The utility of assessing the coronary patient in such settings as the work environment has great potential which should be developed. The use of sophisticated instrumentation, such as halter monitors for recording EKG activity during a routine day, should provide an important addition to assessment strategies as clinicians attempt to integrate behavioral and psychophysiological factors in the assessment procedure.

There has been considerable progress in understanding the relationship between behavior and cardiovascular disease. Behavioral factors are considered most important in determining the clinical outcome of the illness. Cardiac rehabilitation is no longer an interest of a small handful of cardiologists, but has become a multidisciplinary field in which psychologists, physicians, exercise physiologists, vocational counselors, nurses, and nutritionists all play an active role. More precise assessment procedures should facilitate more effective intervention, which, in turn should not only prolong life, but also enhance the quality of life among victims of a disease that has significant physical, psychological, and social consequences.

REFERENCES

Abramson, J. H. The Cornell Medical Index (CMI) as an epidemiological tool. *American Journal of Public Health*, 1966, *56*, 287–298.

Adsett, C. A., & Bruhn, J. G. Short term group psychotherapy for post-myocardial infarction patients and their wives. *Canadian Medical Association Journal*, 1968, *99*, 577–584.

Alonzo, A. A. Illness behavior during acute episodes of coronary heart disease. Doctoral dissertation, University of California, Berkeley, 1973.

Arlow, J. A. Identification mechanisms in coronary occlusion. *Psychosomatic Medicine*, 1945, *7*, 195–209.

Armitage, S. C. An analysis of certain psychological tests used in evaluation of brain injury. *Psychological Monographs*, 1946, *60*, 1–48.

Bak, J. S., & Greene, R. L. Changes in neuropsychological functioning in an aging population. *Journal of Consulting and Clinical Psychology*, 1980, *48*, 395–399.

Bakker, C. B. Psychological factors in angina pectoris. *Psychosomatics*, 1967, *8*, 461–467.

Barbizet, J. *Human memory and its pathology*. San Francisco: Freeman, 1970.

Barlett, R. G. Physiologic response during coitus. *Journal of Applied Physiology*, 1956, *9*, 469–472.

Beck, A. T., Ward, C. H., Mendelson, M., Mock, J. E., & Erbaugh, J. An inventory for measuring depression. *Archives of General Psychiatry*, 1961, *4*, 561–571.

Bellak, L. *The TAT, CAT, and SAT in clinical use* (Edition 3). New York: Grune & Stratton, 1975.

Bem, D. J., & Allen, A. On predicting some of the people some of the time: The search for cross-situational consistencies in behavior. *Psychological Review*, 1974, *81*, 506–520.

Benton, A. L. *The Revised Visual Retention Test: Clinical and experimental applications* (Edition 3). New York: The Psychological Corporation, 1963.

Bergner, M., Bobbitt, R. A., Pollard, W. E., Martin, D. P., & Gilson, B. S. The sickness impact profile: Validation of a health status measure. *Medical Care*, 1976, *14*, 57–67.

Birren, J. E. Translations in gerontology from lab to life: Physiology and speed of response. *American Psychologist*, 1974, *29*, 808–815.

Blumenthal, J. A. Compliance and cardiac rehabilitation. Presented at the American College of Sports Medicine Annual Meeting, Las Vegas, Nevada, May 1980.

Blumenthal, J. A., McKee, D. C., Williams, R. B., & Haney, T. L. Assessment of conceptual tempo in the type A (coronary prone) behavior pattern. *Journal of Personality Assessment*, 1980, *45*, 44–51.

Blumenthal, J. A., Williams, R. S., Williams, R. B., & Wallace, A. G. The effects of exercise on the type A behavior pattern. *Psychosomatic Medicine*, 1980, *42*, 289–296.

Bortner, R. W. A short rating scale as a potential measure of pattern A behavior. *Journal of Chronic Diseases*, 1967, *22*, 87–91.

Bortner, R. W., & Rosenman, R. H. The measurement of pattern A behavior. *Journal of Chronic Diseases*, 1967, *20*, 525–533.

Botwinick, J. Intellectual abilities. In J. E. Birren, & K. W. Schaie (Eds.), *Handbook of the psychology of aging*. New York: Van Nostrand Reinhold, 1977.

Botwinick, J. L., & Storandt, M. Cardiovascular status, depressive affect and other factors in reaction time. *Journal of Gerontology*, 1974, *29*, 543–548.

Bradburn, N. H. *The structure of psychology and well-being*. Chicago: Aldine, 1969.

Brand, R. J., Rosenman, R. H., Jenkins, C. D., Scholtz, R. I., & Zyzanski, S. J. Comparison of coronary heart disease prediction in the Western Collaborative Group Study using the structured interview and the Jenkins Activity Survey assessments of the coronary prone type A behavior pattern. *Journal of Chronic Diseases*, in press.

Brodman, K., Erdmann, A. J., Lorge, I., & Wolff, N. G. The Cornell Medical Index: An adjunct to medical interview. *Journal of the American Medical Association*, 1949, *140*, 530–534.

Brown, J. S., & Rawlinson, M. The morale of patients following open heart surgery. *Journal of Health and Social Behavior*, 1976, *17*, 139–144.

Brown, J. S., & Rawlinson, M. Relinquishing the sick role following open heart surgery. *Journal of Health and Social Behavior*, 1975, *16*, 12–27.

Butensky, A., Farelli, V., Heebner, D., & Waldron, I. Elements of the coronary prone behavior in children and teenagers. *Journal of Psychosomatic Research*, 1976, *20*, 439–444.

Byrne, D. G. Effects of social context on psychological responses to survived myocardial infarction. *International Journal of Psychiatry in Medicine*, 1980–1981, *10*, 23–30.

Byrne, D. G. Repression-sensitization as a dimension of personality. *Progress in Experimental Personality Research*, 1964, *1*, 169–220.

Caffrey, B. A multivariate analysis of socio-psychological factors in men with myocardial infarction. *American Journal of Public Health*, 1970, *60*, 452–458.

Campeau, L. Grading of angina pectoris. *Circulation*, 1975, *54*, 522–523.

Carson, R. C. Interpretive manual to the MMPI. In J. N. Butcher (Ed.), *MMPI: Research developments and clinical applications*. New York: McGraw Hill, 1969.

Cassem, N. H., & Hackett, T. P. Psychiatric consultation in a coronary care unit. *Annals of Internal Medicine*, 1971, *75*, 9–14.

Cassem, N. H., & Hackett, T. P. Psychological rehabilitation of myocardial infarction patients in the acute phase. *Heart & Lung*, 1973, *2*, 382–388.

Cassem, N. H., & Hackett, T. P. Psychological aspects of myocardial infarction. *Medical Clinics of North America*, 1977, *61*, 711–721.

Cattel, R. B., Eber, H. W., & Tatsuoka, M. M. *Handbook for sixteen personality factor questionnaire*. Champaign, Illinois: Institute for Personality and Ability Testing, 1970.

Cay, E. L., Vetter, N. J., & Philip, A. E. Psychological status during recovery from an acute heart attack. *Journal of Psychosomatic Research*, 1972, *16*, 425–435.

Cay, E. L., Vetter, N. J., Philip, A. E., & Dugard, P. Psychological reactions to a coronary care unit. *Journal of Psychosomatic Research*, 1972, *16*, 437–447.

Christensen, A. L. *Luria's neuropsychological investigation manual*. New York: Spectrum Publications, 1975.

Clausen, J. P. Effect of physical training on cardiovascular adjustments to exercise in man. *Physiological Reviews*, 1977, *57*, 779–816.

Cleveland, S. E., & Johnson, D. L. Personality patterns in young males with coronary disease. *Psychosomatic Medicine*, 1962, *24*, 600–610.

Cohen, B. D., Wallston, B. S., & Wallston, K. A. Sex counselling in cardiac rehabilitation. *Archives of Physical Medicine and Rehabilitation*, 1976, *57*, 473–474.

Collins, B. F. Four components of the Rotter internal-external scale: Belief in a difficult world, a just world, a predictable world and a politically responsive world. *Journal of Personality and Social Psychology*, 1974, *29*, 381–391.

Coopersmith, S. *The antecedents of self-esteem*. San Francisco: California, W. H. Freeman, 1967.

Crawshaw, J. E. Community rehabilitation after acute myocardial infarction. *Heart & Lung*, 1974, *3*, 258–271.

Criteria Committee of the New York Heart Association, Inc. *Diseases of the heart and blood vessels: Nomenclature and criteria for diagnosis* (Edition 6). Boston: Little, Brown & Co., 1964.

Cromwell, R. *Stress, personality and nursing care in myocardial infarction*. National Institutes of Mental Health, Grants MH-09220 and MH-13614. Washington, D.C., 1969.

Cromwell, R. L., Butterfield, E. C., Brayfield, T. M., & Curry, J. J. *Acute myocardial infarction: Reaction and recovery.* St. Louis, Missouri: C. V. Mosby, Co., 1977.

Croog, S. H., & Levine, S. *The heart patient recovers.* New York: Science Press, 1977.

Croog, S. H., & Levine, S. Social status and subjective perceptions of 250 men after myocardial infarction. *Public Health Report,* 1969, *84,* 989–997.

Croog, S. H., & Levine, S. Religious identity and response to serious illness: A Report on heart patients. *Social Science and Medicine,* 1972, *6,* 17–32.

Croog, S. H., Levine, S., & Lurie, J. The heart patient and the recovery process. A review of the directions of research on social and psychological factors. *Social Science and Medicine,* 1968, *2,* 111–164.

Croog, S. H., Shapiro, D. S., & Levine, S. Denial among male heart patients. *Psychosomatic Medicine,* 1971, *33,* 385–397.

Crowne, D. P., & Marlowe, D. *The approval motive.* New York: John Wiley & Sons, 1967.

Dahlstrom, W. G., Welsh, G. S., & Dalhstrom, L. E. *An MMPI handbook: Clinical interpretation* (Vol. I). Minneapolis, Minnesota: University of Minnesota Press, 1972.

Davies, A. The influence of age on Trail Making Test performance. *Journal of Clinical Psychology,* 1968, *24,* 96–98.

Dawber, T. R., Moore, F. E., Mann, G. V. Measuring the risk of coronary heart disease in adult population groups. (The Gramingham Study). *American Journal of Public Health,* 1957, *47,* 4–24.

Defourney, M. Approche des phenomenes psychiques dans la maladie coronarienne. *Memoire de licence en psychologie,* Universite de Liege, 1970.

Dembroski, T. M., Weiss, S. M., Shields, J. L., Haynes, S. G., & Feinleib, M. *Coronary prone behavior.* New York: Springer-Verlag, 1978.

Derogatis, L., Lipman, R. S., Rickels, K., Uhlenhuth, E. H., & Covi, L. The Hopkins symptom checklist (HSCL): A measure of primary symptom dimensions. In P. Pichot (Ed.), *Psychological measurements in psychopharmacology: Modern problems in pharmacopsychiatry* (vol. 7). Basil: S. Karger, 1974.

Dimsdale, J. E., Hackett, T. P., Hutter, A. M., & Block, P. C. The risk of type A mediated coronary-artery disease in different populations. *Psychosomatic Medicine,* 1980, *42,* 55–62.

Doehrman, S. R. Psychological aspects of recovery from coronary heart disease: A Review. *Social Science and Medicine,* 1977, *11,* 199–218.

Dominion, J., & Dobson, M. Study of patients: psychological attitudes to a coronary care unit. *British Medical Journal,* 1969, *4,* 795–798.

Douglas, J. E., & Wilkes, D. J. Reconditioning cardiac patients. *American Family Physician,* 1975, *11,* 122–129.

Dreyfuss, F., Shannon, J., & Sharon, M. Some personality characteristics of middle aged men with coronary artery disease. *Psychotherapy and Psychosomatics,* 1966, *14,* 1–16.

Edwards, A. L. *Edwards Personal Preference Schedule.* New York: The Psychological Corporation, 1953.

Eisdorfer, C., & Wilkie, F. Stress, disease, aging and behavior. In J. E. Birren, & K. W. Schaie (Eds.), *Handbook of the psychology of aging.* New York: Van Nostrand Reinhold, 1977.

Endler, N. S., Hunt, J. McV., & Rosenstein, A. J. An S–R inventory of anxiousness. *Psychological Monographs*, 1962, *76*, 1–31.

Engel, G. L. The need for a new medical model: A challenge for biomedicine. *Science*, 1977, *196*, 129–136.

Enos, W. F., Beyer, J. C., & Holmes, R. H. Pathogenesis of coronary disease in American soldiers killed in Korea. *Journal of the American Medical Association*, 1955, *159*, 912–914.

Epstein, F. The epidemiology of coronary heart disease: A review. *Journal of Chronic Diseases*, 1965, *18*, 735–774.

Erickson, B. A., Coots, R. H., Mattson, F. H., Kligman, A. M. The effect of partial hydrogenation of dietary fats on the ratio of polyunsaturated to saturated fatty acids, and of dietary cholesterol upon plasma lipid in man. *Journal of Clinical Investigation*, 1964, *43*, 2017–2025.

Eysenck, H. J. *Manual of the Maudsley Personality Inventory*. London: University of London Press, 1959.

Eysenck, H. J., & Eysenck, S. B. G. *Eysenck Personality Inventory*. San Diego, California: Educational Testing Service, 1968.

Feinstein, A. R., & Wells, C. K. A new clinical taxonomy for rating change in functional activities of patients with angina pectoris. *American Heart Journal*, 1977, *93*, 172–182.

Fitts, W. *Tennessee Self-concept Scale manual*. Nashville, Tennessee: Counselor Recordings and Tests, 1965.

Folstein, M. F., Folstein, S. E., & McHugh, P. E. Mini-mental state. A practical method for grading the cognitive state of patients for the clinician. *Journal of Psychiatry Research*, 1975, *12*, 189–198.

Friedburg, C. K. *Diseases of the heart*. Philadelphia, Pennsylvania: W. B. Saunders, 1966.

Friedman, M., & Rosenman, R. H. Detection of overt behavior pattern A in patients with coronary disease by a new psychophysiological procedure. *Journal of the American Medical Association*, 1960, *173*, 1320–1335.

Freud, S. Instincts and their vicissitudes (1915). In J. Strachy (Ed.), *The Standard edition of the compete works of Sigmund Freud*. London: Hogarth Press, 1978.

Garrity, T. F. Social involvement and activeness as predictors of morale six months after first myocardial infarction. *Social Science and Medicine*, 1973, *7*, 199–207.

Garrity, T. F. Vocational adjustment after first myocardial infarction: Comparative assessment of several variables suggested in the literature. *Social Science and Medicine*, 1973, *7*, 705–707.

Garrity, T. F., Jones, G. W., & Marx, M. B. Factors influencing self-assessment of health. *Social Science and Medicine*, 1978, *12*, 77–81.

Garrity, T. F., & Klein, R. F. A behavioral prediction of survival among heart attack patients. In E. Palmer, & F. C. Jeffers (Eds.), *Predictions of life span*. Lexington, Massachusetts: Heath Publishing Co., 1971.

Gentry, W. D. Pre-admission behavior. In W. D. Gentry, & R. B. Williams (Eds.), *Psychological aspects of myocardial infarction and coronary care*. St. Louis, Missouri: C. V. Mosby Co., 1975.

Gentry, W. D., Foster, S., & Haney, T. Denial as a determinant of anxiety and perceived health status in the coronary care unit. *Psychosomatic Medicine*, 1972, *34*, 39–44.

Gentry, W. D., & Haney, T. Emotional and behavioral reaction to acute myocardial infarction. *Heart & Lung*, 1975, *4*, 738–745.

Gentry, W. D., Musante, G. J., & Haney, T. Anxiety and urinary sodium/potassium as stress indicators on admission to a coronary care unit. *Heart & Lung*, 1973, *2*, 875–877.

Gentry, W. D., & Williams, R. B. *Psychological aspects of myocardial infarction and coronary care* (Edition 2). St. Louis: Missouri: C. V. Mosby, 1979.

George, L. K., & Bearon, L. B. *Quality of life in older persons: Meaning and measurement*. New York: Human Sciences Press, 1980.

Gilberstadt, H., & Sako, Y. Intellectual and personality changes following open-heart surgery. *Archives of General Psychiatry*, 1967, *16*, 210–214.

Gilman, S. Cerebral disorders after open-heart operations. *New England Journal of Medicine*, 1965, *272*, 489–498.

Glendy, R. E., & White, P. D. The recognition and treatment of cardiac neurosis. *Medical Clinics of North America*, 1937, *21*, 449–465.

Golden, C. J., Hammeke, T. A., & Purisch, A. D. Diagnostic validity of a standardized neuropsychological test. *Journal of Consulting and Clinical Psychology*, 1978, *46*, 1256–1258.

Goldfried, M. R., & Kent, R. N. Traditional versus behavioral personality assessment: A comparison of methodological and theoretical assumptions. *Psychological Bulletin*, 1972, *77*, 409–420.

Goldfried, M. R., & Sprafkin, J. N. Behavioral personality assessment. In J. T. Spence, R. C. Carson, & J. W. Thibart (Eds.), *Behavioral approaches to therapy*, Morristown, New Jersey: General Learning Press, 974.

Goldman, L., Hashimoto, B., Cook, E. F., & Loscalzo, A. Comparative reproducibilities and validities of systems for the assessment of cardiovascular functional status: Advantages of a new specific activity scale. Unpublished manuscript, Harvard University, 1981.

Goodglass, H., & Kaplan, E. Assessment of cognitive deficit in the brain-injured patient. In M. S. Gazzaniga (Ed.), *The handbook of behavioral neurobiology*. New York: Plenum Press, 1979.

Goodglass, H., & Kaplan, E. *The assessment of aphasia and related disorders*. Philadelphia: Lea & Febiger, 1972.

Gordon, T., & Kannel, W. B. Predisposition to atherosclerosis in the head, heart and legs: The Framingham study. *Journal of the American Medical Association*, 1972, *221*, 661–666.

Gough, H. G. *Manual for the California Psychological Inventory*, Palo Alto, California: Consulting Psychologists Press, 1957.

Graham, F. K., & Kendall, B. S. Memory for designs test: Revised general manual. *Perceptual-Motor Skills*, 1960, *11*, 147–188.

Granger, J. W. Full recovery from myocardial infarction: Psychosocial factors. *Heart & Lung*, 1974, *3*, 600–610.

Grinkler, R. R., Miller, J., Sabahin, M., Nunn, R., & Nunnally, J. C. *The phenomena of depressions*. New York: Hoeber, 1961.

Groden, B. M. Return to work after myocardial infarction. *Scottish Medical Journal*, 1967, *12*, 297–301.

Guilford, J. P., & Zimmerman, W. S. *The Guilford-Zimmerman Temperament Survey: Manual of instructions and interpretations*. Beverly Hills, California: Sheridan House, 1949.

Hackett, T. P., & Cassem, N. H. Factors contributing to delay in responding to the signs and symptoms of acute myocardial infarction. *American Journal of Cardiology*, 1969, *29*, 651–658.

Hackett, T. P., Cassem, N. H., & Wishnie, H. A. The coronary care unit: An appraisal of its psychological hazards. *New England Journal of Medicine*, 1968, *279*, 1365–1370.

Halberstam, M., & Lesher, S. *A coronary event*. New York: Popular Library, 1978.

Hamilton, M. The assessment of anxiety status by rating. *British Journal of Medical Psychology*, 1959, *32*, 50–55.

Hamilton, M. Development of a rating scale for primary depressive illness. *British Journal of Social & Clinical Psychiatry*, 1967, *6*, 278–296.

Hathaway, S. R., & McKinley, J. C. *The Minnesota Multiphasic Personality Inventory manual*. Minneapolis: University of Minnesota Press, 1943.

Haynes, R. B., Taylor, D. W., & Sackett, D. L. *Compliance in health care*. Baltimore, Maryland: John Hopkins University Press, 1979.

Haynes, S. G., Feinleib, M., Scotch, N., & Kannel, W. B. The relationship of psychosocial factors to coronary heart disease in the Framingham study: II. Prevalence of coronary heart disease. *American Journal of Epidemiology*, 1978, *107*, 384–402.

Hecaen, H., & Albert, M. L. *Human neuropsychology*. New York: John Wiley & Sons, 1978.

Hegsted, D. M., McGandy, R. B., Myers, M. L., & Stare, F. J. Quantitative effects of dietary fat on serum cholesterol in man. *American Journal of Clinical Nutrition*, 1965, *12*, 281–295.

Heimberger, R. F., & Reitan, R. M. Easily administered written test for lateralizing brain lesions. *Journal of Neurosurgery*, 1961, *181*, 301–312.

Heller, S. S., Frank, K. A., Malm, J. R., Bowman, F. O., Harris, P. D., Charlton, M. H., & Kornfeld, D. S. Psychiatric complications of open heart surgery: A re-examination. *New England Journal of Medicine*, 1970, *283*, 1015–1020.

Hellerstein, H. K., & Friedman, E. H. Sexual activity and the post coronary patient. *Archives of Internal Medicine*, 1970, *125*, 987–999.

Herman, S., Blumenthal, J. A., Black, G., & Chesney, M. Self-ratings of type A (coronary prone) adults: Do Type As know they are As? *Psychosomatic Medicine*, 1981, *43*, 405–413.

Hinkle, L. E. An estimate of the effects of "stress" on the incidence and prevalence of coronary heart disease in a large industrial population in the United States. *Thrombosis: Risk factors and diagnostic approaches*. New York: Springer-Verlag, 1972, pp. 15–65.

Hoebel, F. L. Brief family interaction therapy in the management of cardiac-related high risk behavior. *Journal of Family Practice*, 1976, *3*, 613–618.

Holmes, T. H., & Rahe, R. H. The social readjustment rating scale. *Journal of Psychosomatic Research*, 1967, *11*, 219–225.

Holsopple, J., & Migle, F. *Sentence completion as a projective method for the study of personality*. Springfield, Illinois: Charles C. Thomas, 1954.

Holtzman, W. H., Thorpe, J. S., Schwartz, J. D., & Herron, E. W. *Inkblot perception and personality*. Austin, Texas: University of Texas Press, 1961.

Horowitz, M. H., & Wilner, N. Life events, stress, and coping. In L. W. Poon (Ed.), *Aging in the 1980s*. Washington, D. C.: American Psychological Association, 1980.

Horowitz, M., Wilner, N., & Alvarez, W. Impact of event scale: A measure of subjective stress. *Psychosomatic Medicine*, 1979, *41*, 209–218.

Hurst, J. W., Logue, R. B., Schlant, R. C., & Wenger, N. *The heart*. New York: McGraw Hill, 1978.

Jackson, D. N. *Personality Research Form manual*. Goshen, New York: Research Psychologists Press, 1967.

Jenkins, C. D. Psychologic and social precursors of coronary disease, I and II. *New England Journal of Medicine*, 1971, *284*, 244–255, 307–317.

Jenkins, C. D. Recent evidence supporting psychological and social risk factors for coronary disease. *New England Journal of Medicine*, 1976, *294*, 987–994, 1033–1038.

Jenkins, C. D., Hurst, M. W., & Rose, R. M. Life changes: Do people really remember? *Archives of General Psychiatry*, 1979, *36*, 379–384.

Jenkins, C. D., Rosenman, R. H., & Friedman, M. Development of an objective psychological test for the determination of the coronary prone behavior pattern in employed men. *Journal of Chronic Diseases*, 1967, *20*, 371–379.

Jenkins, C. D., Zyzanski, S. J., & Rosenman, R. H. Progress toward validation of a computer-scored test for the type A coronary prone behavior pattern. *Journal of Personality Assessment*, 1980, *45*, 44–51.

Kahn, R. L., Goldfarb, A. I., Polack M., & Peck, A. A brief objective measure for the determination of mental status of the aged. *American Journal of Psychiatry*, 1960, *117*, 326–328.

Kannel, W. B., & Gordon, T. Obesity and cardiovascular disease: The Framingham study. In W. L. Borland, P. D. Samuel, & J. Yudkin (Eds.), *Obesity Symposium*. New York: Charles Livingston, 1974.

Kannel, W. B., Gordon, T., Schwartz, M. J. Systolic versus diastolic blood pressure and the risk of coronary heart disease. The Framingham Study, *American Journal of Cardiology*, *1971, 27*, 335–346.

Katz, S., Ford, A. B., Moskowitz, R. W., Jackson, B. A., & Jaffe, M. V. Studies of illness in the aged. The index of ADL: A standardized measure of biological and psychosocial function. *Journal of the American Medical Association*, 1963, *185*, 914–919.

Keele, K. D. The pain chart. *Lancet*, 1948, *2*, 6–8.

Kemple, C. Rorschach method and psychosomatic diagnosis. Personality traits of patients with rheumatic disease, hypertensive cardiovascular disease, coronary occlusion and fractures. *Psychosomatic Medicine*, 1945, *7*, 85.

Keys, A. The individual risk of coronary heart disease. *Annals of the New York Academy of Sciences*, 1966, *134*, 1046–1056.

Keys, A. Coronary heart disease in seven countries. *Circulation*, 1970, *41*, 1–121.

Keys, A., Anderson, J. T., & Grande, F. Serum cholesterol response to changes in the diet. *Metabolism*, 1965, *54*, 747–787.

Keys, A., Anderson, J. T., Mickelsen, O., Adelson, S. F., & Fidanza, F. Diet and serum cholesterol in man: Lack of effect of dietary cholesterol. *Journal of Nutrition*, 1956, *56*, 39–56.

Kilpatrick, F. P., & Cantril, H. Self-achieving scaling: A measure of individuals unique reality worlds. *Journal of Individual Psychology*, 1960, *16*, 158–173.

Kirscht, J. P. Perceptions of control and health beliefs. *Canadian Journal of Behavioral Sciences*, 1974, *4*, 225–237.

Klein, R. F., Dean, A., Wilson, L. M., & Bogdonoff, M. D. The physician and post myocardial invalidism. *Journal of the American Medical Association*, 1967, *194*, 143–148.

Kolkka, R., & Hilberman, M. Neurologic dysfunction following cardiac operation with low flow, low pressure cardiopulmonary bypass. *Journal of Thoracic and Cardiovascular Surgery*, 1980, *79*, 432–437.

Koller, R., Kennedy, J. W., Butler, J. C., & Wagner, N. W. Counselling the coronary patient in sexual activity. *Postgraduate Medicine*, 1972, *51*, 133–136.

Kornfeld, D. S., Zimberg, S., & Malm, J. R. Psychiatric complications of open-heart surgery. *New England Journal of Medicine*, 1965, *273*, 287–292.

Lacher, D. *The MMPI: Clinical assessment and automated interpretation*. Los Angeles, California: Western Psychological Services, 1974.

LaPorte, R. E., Kuller, L. H., Kupfer, D. J., McPortland, R. J., Matthews, G., & Casperson, C. An objective measure of physical activity for epidemiologic research. *American Journal of Epidemiology*, 1979, *109*, 158–168.

Lanyon, R. I. *Psychological Screening Inventory manual*. Coshen, New York: Research Psychologist Press, 1973.

Lazarus, R. S. Ipsative-normative, process-oriented research on stress, coping and adaptation. Symposium presented at the Annual Meeting of the Western Psychological Association, San Diego, California. April 1979.

Leigh, H., Hofer, M. A., Cooper, J., & Reiser, M. F. A psychological comparison of patients in "open" and "closed" coronary care units. *Journal of Psychosomatic Research*, 1972, *16*, 449–456.

Levenson, H. Multi-dimensional locus of control in psychiatric patients. *Journal of Consulting and Clinical Psychology*, 1976, *44*, 580–585.

Lewinsohn, P. M., & Libet, J. Pleasant events, activity schedules and depression. *Journal of Abnormal Psychology*, 1972, *79*, 291–293.

Lezak, M. D. *Neuropsychological assessment*. New York: Oxford University Press, 1976.

Linehan, M. M. Issues in behavioral interviewing. In J. D. Cone, & R. P. Hawkins (Ed.), *Behavioral assessment*. New York: Brunner/Mazel, Inc., 1977.

MacDougall, J. M., Dembroski, T. M., & Musante, L. The structured interview and questionnaire methods of assessing coronary prone behavior in male and female college students. *Journal of Behavioral Medicine*, 1979, *2*, 78–83.

Machover, K. *Personality projection in the drawing of the human figure*. Springfield, Illinois: Charles C. Thomas, 1952.

Maddox, G. L., & Douglass, E. B. Self-assessment of health: A longitudinal study of elderly subjects. *Journal of Health and Social Behavior*, 1973, *14*, 87–93.

Maloney, M., & Ward, M. *Psychological assessment: A cknceptual approach*. New York: Oxford University Press, 1976.

Mandler, G., & Sarason, S. B. A study of anxiety and learning. *Journal of Abnormal and Social Psychology*, 1952, *47*, 166–173.

Mann, G. V. Diet-heart: end of an era. *New England Journal of Medicine*, 1977, 644–650.

Maser, F. T. Resumption of sexual activity following myocardial infarction. *Sexuality and Disability*, 1979, *2*, 98–114.

Masters, W. H., and Johnson, V. E. *Human sexual response*. Boston: Little, Brown & Co., 1966.

Matthews, K. A. Assessments and developmental antecedents of the coronary prone behavior pattern in children. In T. M. Dembroski, J. M. Weiss, J. L. Shields, S. G. Haynes, & M. Feinleib, (Eds.), *Coronary prone behavior*. New York: Springer-Verlag, 1978.

McCrae, R. R., Bartone, P. T., & Costa, P. T. Age, anxiety and self-reported health. *Journal of Aging and Human Development*, 1976, *7*, 49–58.

McNair, D. M., Lorr, M., & Droppleman, L. F. *Profile of Mood States: Manual*. San Diego, California: Educational and Industrial Testing Service, 1971.

Meehl, P. Wanted: A good cookbook. *American Psychologist*. 1956, *11*, 263–272.

Melzack, R. The McGill pain questionnaire: Major properties and scoring methods. *Pain*, 1975, *1*, 277–299.

Mordkoff, A. M., & Golas, R. M. Coronary artery disease and response to the Rosenzweig Picture-Frustration study. *Journal of Abnormal Psychology*, 1968, *73*, 381–386.

Morris, J. N., Chave, C. P., Adams, C., Sircy, C., Epstein, L., & Sheehan, D. J. Vigorous exercise in leisure time and the incidence of coronary heart disease. *Lancet*, 1973, *7799*, 333–339.

Moss, A. J., & Goldstein, S. The pre-hospital phase of acute myocardial infarction. *Circulation*, 1970, *41*, 737–742.

Moss, A. J., Wynar, B., & Goldstein, S. Delay in hospitalization during the acute coronary period. *American Journal of Cardiology*, 1969, *24*, 659–665.

Murray, H. A. *Explorations in personality*. New York: Oxford University Press, 1938.

Myers, I. B. *The Myers-Briggs Type Indicator: Manual*. Princeton, New Jersey: Educational Testing Service, 1962.

Nagel, R., Gangola, R., & Picton-Robinson, I. Factors influencing return to work after myocardial infarction. *Lancet*, 1971, *2*, 454–456.

National Heart, Lung, and Blood Institute Forum: Coronary prone behavior and coronary heart disease: A Critical review. Report of the coronary prone behavior review panel. Submitted to the National Heart, Lung, and Blood Institute, Washington, D.C.: 1978.

Neugarten, B. L. Adult personality: Towards a psychology of the life cycle. In B. L. Neugarten (Ed.), *Middle age and aging*. Chicago: University of Chicago Press, 1968.

Neugarten, B. L., Havinghurst, R. S., & Tobin, S. S. Measurement of life satisfaction. *Journal of Gerontology*, 1961, *16*, 134–143.

Neugarten, B. L. Personality changes in late life: A Developmental perspective. In C. Eisdorfer, & M. P. Lawton (Eds.), *Psychology of adult development and aging*. Washington, D. C., American Psychological Association, 1973.

Nichols, A. B., Ravenscroft, C., Lamphiear, D. E., Ostrander, L. D. Independence of serum lipid levels and dietary habits: The Tecumseh study. *Journal of the American Medical Association*, 1976, *236*, 1948–1953.

Noakes, T. D., Opie, L. H., Rose, A. G., & Kleynhans, P. H. Autopsy-proved coronary atherosclerosis in marathon runners. *New England Journal of Medicine*, 1979, *301*, 86–89.

Obrist, W. D. Cerebral ischemia and the senescent electroencephalogram. In E. Simonson, & T. H. McGavack (Eds.), *Cerebral ischemia*. Springfield, Illinois: Charles C. Thomas, 1964.

Olin, H. S., & Hackett, T. P. The denial of chest pain in 32 patients with acute myocardial infarction. *Journal of the American Medical Association*, 1964, 190, 977–981.

Oliver, M. F. Ischemic heart disease in young women: A re-appraisal of the sex factor. *Acta Cardiologica*, Supplement 20, 1974, 59–68.

Olson, A. G. Hyperlipidemia, lipoproteins, and coronary disease. *Acta Cardiologica*, Supplement 20, 1974, 37–45.

Ostfeld, A. M., Lebovits, B. S., Shekelle, R. P., & Paul, O. A prospective study of the relationship between personality and coronary heart disease. *Journal of Chronic Diseases*, 1964, 17, 265–276.

Overall, J. E., & Gorham, D. R. The brief psychiatric rating scale. *Psychological Reports*, 1962, 10, 799–812.

Paffenbarger, R. S., & Hale, W. E. Work activity and coronary heart mortality. *New England Journal of Medicine*, 1975, 11, 545–550.

Paffenbarger, R. S., Wing, A. L., & Hyde, R. T. Physical activity as an index of heart attack risk in college alumni. *American Journal of Epidemiology*, 1978, 108, 161–175.

Paykel, E. S., Prusoff, B. A., & Uhlenhuth, E. H. Scaling of life events. *Archives of General Psychiatry*, 1971, 25, 340–347.

Peduzzi, P., & Hultgren, H. N. Effect of medical versus surgical treatment on symptoms in stable angina pectoris. *Circulation*, 1979, 60, 888–900.

Pfeiffer, E. A short portable mental status questionnaire for the assessment of organic brain defect in elderly patients. *Journal of American Geriatric Society*, 1975, 23, 433–441.

Pollard, W. E., Bobbitt, R. A., Bergner, M., Martin, D. P., & Gilson, B. S. The sickness impact profile: Reliability of a health status measure. *Medical Care*, 1976, 14, 146–155.

The Pooling Project Research Group. Relationship of blood pressure, serum cholesterol, smoking habit, relative weight, and ECG abnormalities to incidence of major coronary events: Final report of the Pooling Project. *Journal of Chronic Diseases*, 1978, 31, 201–306.

Porch, B. E. *The Porch index of communicative ability*. Palo Alto: California: Consulting Psychologists, 1967.

Rabkin, S. W., Mathewson, F. A. L., & Tate, R. B. Predicting risk of ischemic heart disease and cerebrovascular disease from systolic and diastolic blood pressures. *Annals of Internal Medicine*, 1978, 88, 342–348.

Rahe, R. H., Bennett, L., Romo, M., Siltanen, P., & Arthur, R. J. Subjects' recent life changes and coronary heart disease in Finland. *American Journal of Psychiatry*, 1973, 130, 1222–1226.

Rahe, R. H., & Romo, M. Recent life changes and the onset of myocardial infarction and coronary death in Helsinki. In E. K. E. Gunderson, & R. H. Rahe (Eds.), *Life stress illness*. Springfield, Illinois: Charles C. Thomas, 1974.

Rahe, R. H., Romo, M., Bennett, L., & Siltanen, P. Recent life changes, myocardial infarction, and abrupt coronary death. Studies in Helsinki. *Archives of Internal Medicine*, 1974, 133, 221–228.

Rappaport, D., Gill, M. M., & Schafer, R. *Diagnostic psychological testing*. New York: International University Press, 1968.

Raskin, A. *NIMH Collaborative Depression Mood Scale*. Rockville, Maryland: National Institute of Mental Health, 1965.

Reitan, R. M. Methodological problems in clinical neuropsychology. In R. M. Reitan, & L. A. Davidson, (Eds.), *Clinical Neuropsychology: Current status and applications*. Washington, D. C.: V. H. Winston, 1974.

Reitan, R. M. A research program on the psychological effects of brain lesions in human beings. In N. R. Ellis (Ed.), *International review of research in mental retardation (vol. 1)*. New York: Academic Press, 1966.

Reitan, R. M. Validity of the Trail Making Test as an indicator of organic brain damage. *Perceptual & Motor Skills, 1958, 8,* 271–276.

Reitan, R. M., & Shipley, R. E. The relationship of serum cholesterol changes to psychological abilities. *Journal of Gerontology, 1963, 18,* 350–357.

Reynolds, W. J., Rushing, W. A., & Miles, P. Z. The validation of a functional status index. *Journal of Health & Social Behavior, 1974, 15,* 271–288.

Rorschach, H. *Psychodiagnostics*. New York: Grune and Stratton, 1942.

Rosen, J. L., & Bibring, G. L. Psychological reactions of hospitalized male patients to a heart attack: Age and social class differences. *Psychosomatic Medicine, 1966, 28,* 810–820.

Rosenberg, M. *Society and the adolescent self-image*. Princeton, New Jersey, Princeton University Press, 1965.

Rosenman, R. H. The interview method of assessment of the coronary prone behavior pattern. In T. M. Dembroski, S. M. Weiss, J. L. Shields, S. G. Haynes, & M. Feinlab, *Coronary prone behavior*. New York: Springer-Verlag, 1978.

Rosenman, R. H., Friedman, M., Strauss, R., Wurm, M., Kostichek, R., Hahn, W., & Werthessen, N. A predictive study of coronary heart disease: The Western Collaborative Group Study. *Journal of the American Medical Association, 1964, 189,* 103–110, 121–124.

Rotter, J. B. Generalized expectancies for internal versus external control of reinforcement. *Psychological Monographs, 1966, 80,* 1–28.

Rotter, J. B., & Rafferty, J. E. *Incomplete Sentences Blank: manual*. New York: Psychological Corporation, 1950.

Russell, E. W. The multiple scoring method for the assessment of complex memory functions. *Journal of Consulting and Clinical Psychology, 1975, 43,* 800–809.

Russell, E. W., Neuringer, C., & Goldstein, G. *Assessment of brain damage: A neurophysiological key approach*. New York: Wiley, 1970.

Sarason, I. G., & Johnson, J. H. The Life experience survey: Preliminary findings technical report number SCS-LS-001, U. S. Office of Naval Research, 1976.

Saunders, K. J., Goldstein, M. K., & Stein, G. H. Automated measurements of patient activity on a hospital rehabilitation ward. *Archives of Physical Medicine, 1978, 59,* 255–257.

Schaie, K. W., & Schaie, J. P. Clinical assessment and aging. In J. E. Birren, & K. W. Schaie (Eds.), *The handbook of the psychology of Aging* New York: Van Nostrand Reinhold, 1977.

Scheingold, L. D., & Wagner, N. N. *Sound sex and the aging heart*. New York: Human Science Press, 1974.

Scherwitz, L., Berton, K., & Leventhal, H. Type A assessment and interaction in the behavior pattern interview. *Psychosomatic Medicine*, 1977, *39*, 229–240.

Schucker, G., & Jacobs, D. R. Assessment of behavioral risk for coronary disease by voice characteristics. *Psychosomatic Medicine*, 1977, *39*, 219–228.

Schuell, H. *Minnesota Test for Differential Diagnosis of Aphasia*. Minneapolis, Minnesota: University of Minnesota Press, 1965.

Schultz, R., & Brenner, G. Relocation of the aged: A review and theoretical analysis. *Journal of Gerontology*, 1977, *32*, 323–333.

Selzer, A., & Cohn, K. Functional classification of cardiac disease: A critique. *American Journal of Cardiology*, 1972, *30*, 306–308.

Shekelle, R. B., Shryock, A. M., Paul, O., Lepper, M., Stamler, J., Liv, S., & Raynor, W. J. Diet, serum cholesterol, and death from coronary heart disease. The Western Electric Study. *New England Journal of Medicine*, 1981, *304*, 65–70.

Silverstein, A., & Krieger, H. P. Neurological complications of cardiac surgery. *Archives of Neurology*, 1960, *3*, 601–605.

Simborg, D. W. The status of risk factors and coronary heart disease. *Journal of Chronic Diseases*, 1970, *22*, 515–552.

Simon, A. B., Feinleib, M., & Thompson, H. K. Components of delay in the pre-hospital phase of acute myocardial infarction. *American Journal of Cardiology*, 1972, *30*, 476–482.

Skelton, M., & Dominion, J. Psychological stress in wives of patients with myocardial infarction. *British Medical Journal*, 1973, *2*, 101–103.

Spielberger, C. E., Gorsuch, R. L., & Luschene, R. E. *Manual for the State-Trait Anxiety Inventory*. Palo Alto, California: Consulting Psychologist Press, 1970.

Spieth, W. Slowness of task performance and cardiovascular diseases. In A. T. Welford, & J. E. Birren (Eds.), *Behavior, aging and the nervous system*. Springfield, Illinois: Charles C. Thomas, 1965.

Spitzer, R. L., & Endicott, J. *Schedule for affective disorders and schizophrenia—Lifetimes version (SADS-L)*. New York: New York Psychiatric Institute, 1977.

Stamler, J. Epidemiology of coronary heart disease. *Medical Clinics of North America*, 1973, *57*, 5–46.

Stamler, J., Berkson, D. M., Lindberg, H. A., Hall, Y., Miller, W., Mojonnier, L., Levinson, M., Cohen, O. B., & Young, A. D. Coronary risk factors: Their impact and their therapy in the prevention of coronary heart disease. *Medical Clinics of North America*, 1966, *50*, 229–255.

Stern, M. J., Pascale, L., & McLoone, J. B. Psychological adaptation following an acute myocardial infarction. *Journal of Chronic Diseases*, 1976, *29*, 513–526.

Strong, J. P., & McGill, H. C. The natural history of atherosclerosis. *American Journal of Pathology*, 1962, *40*, 37–49.

Szafran, J. Psychophysiological studies of aging in pilots. In G. A. Talland (Ed.), *Human aging and behavior*. New York: Academic Press, 1968.

Szondi, L. *Szondi Test manual*. New York: Grune and Stratton, 1965.

Taylor, J. A personality scale of manifest anxiety. *Journal of abnormal and Social Psychology*, 1955, *48*, 285–290.

Theorell, T. Life events before and after the onset of a premature myocardial infarction. In

B. S. Dohrenwend, & B. P. Dohrenwend (Eds.), *Stressful life events: Their nature and effects*. New York: Wiley Interscience, 1974.

Theorell, T., & Rahe, R. H. Psychological characteristics of subjects with myocardial infarction in Stockholm. In E. K. E. Gunderson, & R. H. Rahe, (Eds.), *Life stress and illness*. Springfield, Illinois: Charles C. Thomas, 1974.

Theorell, T., & Rahe, R. H. Psychosocial factors and myocardial infarction: An inpatient study in Sweden. *Journal of Psychosomatic Research*, 1971, *15*, 25–36.

Thomas, C. B., & Greenstreet, R. L. Psychobiological characteristics in youth as predictors of five disease states: Suicide, mental illness, hypertension, coronary heart disease and tumor. *John Hopkins Medical Journal*, 1973, *132*, 16–43.

Thompson, P. D., Stern, M. P., Williams, P., Duncan, K., Haskell, W. L. & Wood, P. D. Death during jogging or running. *Journal of the American Medical Association*, 1979, *242*, 1265–1267.

Thurstone, L. L. *Thurstone temperament schedule*. Chicago: Science Research Associates, 1949.

Tibblin, G., Lindstrom, B. & Ander, S. Emotions and heart disease. *Ciba Foundation Symposium*, 1972, *8*, 321–336.

Tjoe, S. L., & Luria, M. H. Delays in reaching the cardiac care unit: An analysis. *Chest*, 1972, *61*, 617–621.

Tufo, H. M., Ostfeld, A. M., & Shekelle, R. Central nervous system dysfunction following open-heart surgery. *Journal of the American Medical Association*, 1970, *212*, 1333–1340.

Tuttle, W. B., & Cook, W. L. Sexual behavior in post-myocardial infarction patients. *American Journal of Cardiology*, 1964, *13*, 140–153.

Uneo, M. The so-called coition death. *Japanese Journal of Legal Medicine*, 1963, *17*, 330–340.

Vetter, N. J., Cay, E. L., Philip, A. E., & Strange, R. C. Anxiety on admission to a coronary care unit. *Journal of Psychosomatic Medicine*, 1977, *21*, 73–80.

Vickers, R. A short measure of the type A personality. Unpublished manuscript. University of Michigan, Ann Arbor, Michigan, Institute of Social Research, 1973.

Viko, L. E. Cardiac neurosis associated with rheumatic valvular disease. *American Heart Journal*, 1925-26, *1*, 539–545.

Wald, N. J. Mortality from lung cancer and coronary heart disease in relation to changes in smoking habits. *Lancet*, 1976, 17, 136–138.

Wallston, B. S., Wallston, K. A., Kaplan, G. D., & Maides, S. A. Development and validation of the health locus of control scale. *Journal of Consulting and Clinical Psychology*, 1976, *44*, 580–585.

Walsh, K. *Neuropsychology: A clinical approach*, London: Churchill Livingston, 1978.

Wardwell, W. I., & Bahnson, C. B. Behavioral variables and myocardial infarction in the southeastern Connecticut Heart Study. *Journal of Chronic Diseases*, 1973, *26*, 447–461.

Watson, D., & Friend, R. Measurement of social-evaluation anxiety. *Journal of Consulting and Clinical Psychology*, 1969, *33*, 448–457.

Watts, R. J. Sexuality in the middle aged cardiac patient. *Nursing Clinics of North America*, 1976, *11*, 349–359.

Wechsler, D. A standardized memory scale for clinical use. *Journal of Psychology*, 1945, *19*, 87–95.

Wechsler, D. *The measurement and appraisal of adult intelligence*. Baltimore, Maryland: Williams & Wilkins, 1958.

Wells, F. L., & Ruesch, J. *Mental status examiner's notebook*. New York: The Psychological Corporation, 1945.

Wenger, N. K., Hellerstein, H. K., Blackburn, H. W., & Castranova, S. J. Uncomplicated myocardial infarction: Current physician practice in patient management. *Journal of the American Medical Association*, 1973, *224*, 511–514.

Wheeler, L., & Reitan, R. M. Presence and laterality of brain damage predicted from responses to a short aphasia screening test. *Perceptual & Motor Skills*, 1962, *15*, 783–799.

Wilkie, F., & Eisdorfer, C. Blood pressure and behavioral correlates in the aged. Paper presented at the Ninth International Congress of Gerontology, Kiev, U.S.S.R., 1972.

Williams, M. The measurement of memory in clinical practice. *Journal of Social and Clinical Psychology*, 1968, *7*, 19–34.

Williams, R. B., & Gentry, W. D. Psychological problems inherent in the cardiopathic state. In C. Long (Ed.), *Prevention and rehabilitation in ischemic heart disease*. Baltimore, Maryland: Williams & Wilkins, 1978.

Williams, R. S., Logue, H. E., Lewis, J. L., Barton, T., Stead, N. W., Wallace, A. G., & Pizzo, S. V. Physical conditioning augments vascular endothelial release of plasminogen activator in healthy adults. *New England Journal of Medicine*, in press.

Wishnie, H. A., Hackett, T. P., & Cassem, N. H. Psychological hazards of convalescence following myocardial infarction. *Journal of the American Medical Association*, 1971, *215*, 1291–1296.

Wolk, R. L., & Wolk, R. B. *The Gerontological Apperception Test*. New York: Behavioral Publications, 1971.

Woodforde, J. M., & Mersky, H. Some relationships between subjective measures of pain. *Journal of Psychosomatic Research*, 1972, *16*, 173–178.

Wynn, A. Unwarranted emotional distress in men with ischemic heart disease (IHD). *Medical Journal of Australia*, 1967, *2*, 847–851.

Zuckerman, M., & Lubin, B. *Manual for the Multiple Affect Adjective Checklist*. San Diego, California: Educational and Industrial Testing Service, 1965.

Zung, W. W. K. A rating instrument for anxiety disorders. *Psychosomatics*, 1971, *12*, 371–379.

Zung, W. W. K. A self-rating depression scale. *Archives of General Psychiatry* 1965, *12*, 63–70.

Zyzanski, S. J., & Jenkins, S. D. Basic dimensions within the coronary prone behavior pattern. *Journal of Chronic Diseases*, 1970, *22*, 781–795.

Robert R. Freedman
Steven J. Lynn
Peter Ianni

4

Behavioral Assessment of Raynaud's Disease

Raynaud's disease is a complex psychophysiological disorder of unknown etiology. Its symptoms may be extremely painful, interfere with activities of daily living, and cause social embarrassment due to obvious digital color changes. Conservative medical treatment has been mainly palliative, with patients instructed to wear warm clothing, avoid exposure to the cold, or move to a warmer climate. Pharmacologic and surgical treatments have been generally unsuccessful (Coffman and Davies, 1975). Patients treated with biofeedback (Freedman et al., 1981) and autogenic procedures (Surwit et al., 1978) show significant improvements in self-report and laboratory measures of vasospastic symptoms. Thus, behavioral medicine may have unique potential in the treatment of Raynaud's disease. Moreover, the fact that its symptoms are easily observed and accompanied by relatively clear physiological changes (digital artery vasospasms) make it an ideal area for the implementation of behavioral assessment techniques. These methods fall into two broad categories: the patient's own symptom report and the measurement of blood flow in the laboratory with or without vasoactive stimuli. After briefly discussing the symptoms and etiology of Raynaud's disease, specific assessment techniques within these two broad categories will be reviewed, along with their respective advantages and disadvantages. Attempts to relate these methodologies will be discussed, including research conducted in our laboratory. Since emotional stress may play a role in the precipitation of attacks, techniques for its assessment will be presented. Lastly, we will make specific suggestions for practitioners working with Raynaud's disease patients, and suggest possible avenues for future research.

Robert R. Freedman's research for this chapter was supported in part by Grant #HL23828 from the National Heart, Lung, and Blood Institute.

SYMPTOMS

Raynaud's disease is a disorder of the peripheral circulation characterized by episodic vasospasms and associated color changes in the fingers and, sometimes, the toes. The attacks are precipitated by cold exposure and/or emotional stress (Abramson, 1974). The attacks generally begin in the tips of one or more fingers and may eventually affect all the phalanges. The typical color progression is from pallor to cyanosis to rubor, although some patients may manifest only pallor or cyanosis; in others, rubor may be absent (Coffman and Davies, 1975). The initial pallor is due to digital artery vasospasm and resulting depletion of blood in the cutaneous vessels. The cyanotic phase is presumably caused by slow blood flow in dilated capillaries and vessels (McGrath and Penny, 1974). Patients typically complain of cold or numb fingers during these phases. The attacks, which can last from a few minutes to several hours, often terminate with reactive hyperemia, characterized by redness and painful, throbbing, or burning sensations.

The term *Raynaud's disease* refers to the primary form of the disorder, in which the attacks cannot be explained by connective tissue diseases (such as scleroderma, rheumatoid arthritis, or lupus erythematosus), traumatic vibration disease, occlusive arterial disease, thoracic outlet syndromes, or other disorders. It is five times more common in women than men (Spitell, 1972), with the age of onset from 11 to 30 years in 60 percent of one case series and from 11 to 40 years in 81 percent in another (Blain et al., 1951). In 75 percent of these cases, the disease ran a benign, chronic course for 5 to 55 years; the remaining 25 percent either suffered eventual tissue loss (ulceration, necrosis, and superficial gangrene) or submitted to sympathectomies due to symptom severity.

Presently, the diagnosis of Raynaud's disease is based on the following criteria (Allen and Brown, 1932): (1) episodes of bilateral color changes precipitated by cold or emotion, (2) absence of severe gangrene, (3) absence of any systemic disease that might account for the attacks, (4) duration of symptoms for at least 2 years. Using these criteria, a recent study in Denmark found a prevalence of 22 percent among women aged 21 to 50 (Olsen and Nielsen, 1978). The frequency and severity of the attacks generally increases during cold weather and, although the extremities are usually otherwise normal, sclerodactyly (tense and atrophic skin, deformed nails) occurs in approximately 10 percent of the patients (Gifford and Hines, 1978).

ETIOLOGY

The etiology of Raynaud's disease remains unknown, although several theories have been put forth to explain it. Raynaud hypothesized an overactivity of the sympathetic nervous system leading to an increased vasoconstrictor response to cold (Coffman and Davies, 1975), while Lewis postulated a "local fault'' in which precapillary resistance vessels were hypersensitive to local cooling (Lewis, 1929). Lewis produced ischemic attacks in the fingers of Raynaud's disease patients using local cooling, and also found local structural changes, such as intimal thickening and thrombosis. Although intraluminal thromboses have been found in pathologic and ateriographic studies of Raynaud's disease, it is unclear whether these changes are causal to the disorder or a result of it (Spurling et al., 1932; Allen, 1937). Lewis was criticized on the grounds that most of his patients had very advanced forms of the disease and that their vascular changes were therefore of a secondary nature (Coffman and Davies, 1975). Indeed, Lewis later reported three cases of mild Raynaud's disease where the precapillary vessels appeared normal (Lewis, 1938).

Evidence regarding Lewis' cold hypersensitivity hypothesis is mixed. Downey and Frewin (1973) measured the response of hand blood flow to a cold stimulus and recovery times after removal of the stimulus; they found no differences between patients with Raynaud's disease and normals. Miller and Walder (1972) measured finger blood flow and temperature before and after local cooling in normal subjects and patients with Raynaud's disease and also found no differences. However, Lottenbach (1971) found reduced heat elimination at 19°C in fingers of patients with Raynaud's disease when compared to normal controls. Chucker and coworkers, using thermography, found prolonged rewarming time after ice-water immersion of the hands in Raynaud's disease patients as compared to normals (Chucker et al., 1971). Another study found that local cooling of the hand enhanced reflexive sympathetic vasoconstriction following ice application to the neck in patients with Raynaud's disease or scleroderma but not in normal subjects (Jamieson et al., 1971).

In support of the theory of excessive sympathetic activity as the cause of Raynaud's disease, average hand blood flow in a group of patients with this disorder was found to be abnormally low when compared to normals (Peacock, 1959). After sympathetic release produced by body warming, hand blood flow in patients with mild forms of the disease rose to normal levels. Peacock argued that this normal vasodilitation was evidence against structural arterial disease. Willerson and coworkers found lower superficial digital blood flows in patients with Raynaud's disease as compared to normals and also suggested the hypothesis of increased sympathetic activity (Willerson et al., 1970). However, the failure of Downey and Frewin (1973) to find an increased reflex sympathetic vasoconstriction to a cold stimulus in afflicted patients argues against this theory.

Peacock (1959) also found an increased level of catecholamines in wrist venous blood in Raynaud's disease patients, which he took as evidence for continuous sympathetic vasoconstrictor hyperactivity. However, these results were not replicated in two other studies of patients with Raynaud's disease, or in patients with Raynaud's phenomenon due to scleroderma (Kontos and Wasserman, 1969; Mendlowitz and Naftchi, 1959; Sapira et al., 1972). Mendlowitz and Naftchi (1959) also studied digital blood pressure and flow in 20 Raynaud's disease patients before and after vasodilitation and identified two groups. In one group, the intrinsic vascular caliber after vasodilitation was normal, but vasomotor tone was high; in the second group, vascular caliber was decreased, but vasomotor tone was normal. It was hypothesized that the first group had heightened vasomotor tone but no organic obstructive disease, and that the second group had vascular obstruction, although it was not known whether this was a cause or an effect of the disease. As the researchers could not show increased epinephrine or norepinephrine levels in venous blood from the hands, or hypersensitivity to infused norepinephrine, the increased vasomotor tone of patients in the first group was attributed to heightened activity of sympathetic innervation.

Other research has examined physical properties of the blood in Raynaud's disease. Pringle and coworkers found blood hyperviscosity associated with hyperfibrinogenemia and increased erythrocyte aggregation, although these findings were not confirmed in later work (Pringle et al., 1965; Johnsen et al., 1977; McGrath et al., 1978). Two other studies failed to find increased plasma fibrinogen levels in patients with Raynaud's disease (Charles and Carmick, 1970; Jamieson et al., 1971).

In summary, a satisfactory explanation of the cause(s) of Raynaud's disease has not yet been found. Data for and against theories of increased sympathetic activity, catecholamine blood levels, blood viscosity, sensitivity to local cooling and vessel obstruction are relatively evenly divided (Halperin and Coffman, 1979). It is likely that only a multifactorial explanation of the disease will suffice, and that mechanisms other than physiological ones will be strongly implicated.

BEHAVIORAL ASSESSMENT METHODS

Self-report Methods

The patient's account of symptoms and their causes and effects constitutes a major source of data for assessment in Raynaud's disease. After referral from a diagnosing physician, the first step in the behavioral assessment process is the evaluation interview. We have included our interview protocol in the Appendix and will discuss the rationale for some of our procedures in the present section. We will then discuss the types of information obtained from symptom report cards, along with some of the problems encountered in defining attacks. Data from 838 cards will be presented to illustrate relationships among variables and to examine the effects of environmental factors on reported symptoms. Finally, we will review practical considerations in the duration of self-monitoring and will discuss an alternate assessment method involving the use of critical incidents.

Evaluation Interview

The evaluation interview is used to obtain a preliminary symptom picture for purposes of diagnosis and assessment of therapeutic change, to determine the environmental and psychological precipitants of attacks, and to assess the suitability of the patient for behavioral treatment. The interview procedure always includes a complete personal and family history of the patient in addition to the Raynaud's disease history. (The outline for part of the interview is shown in the Appendix.) In order to make a diagnosis of Raynaud's disease by the Allen and Brown criteria, it is necessary to establish the existence of symptoms for at least 2 years. This is not easy, as some patients experience one or two isolated attacks several years before their consistent occurrence. Other patients are not sure of exactly what constitutes an attack.

The progression of vasospastic color changes is not always consistent within a given patient (Coffman and Davies, 1975). Careful questioning during the interview will often help clarify the symptom picture. The patient should be encouraged to recall in as much detail as possible the first attack and the circumstances in which it occurred. One patient recalled that her fingers were white in her wedding picture and was thus able to establish the duration of her illness. Similar detail should be elicited for examples of typical, mild, and severe attacks. Many patients will experience situations in which symptoms virtually always occur, such as driving on a cold winter day. These *critical incidents* are useful for evaluating treatment outcome.

In order to develop the most effective treatment program for a particular patient, it is necessary to fully understand the causes and functions of symptoms. In addition to local and environmental cold, many vasospastic attacks are precipitated by stressful events.

One patient reported during the evaluation interview that when she felt overwhelmed by events over which she had little control, the probability of an attack was high. By learning to identify these events as soon as possible, she was able to better implement strategies learned during temperature biofeedback before the occurrence of a full-blown attack, thereby improving on symptom reductions obtained through biofeedback alone.

It is possible that social and psychological contingencies in the patient's life may serve to control or maintain symptoms. Another patient reported that as a result of her attacks, she avoided demands which her husband would otherwise place on her. Clearly, this problem had to be examined in more detail.

In addition to evaluating the antecedents and consequences of symptoms, it is important in the interview to assess the patient's perception of the prospective treatment. The patient may have doubts about participating in therapy, and may have fantasies of treatment and cure which could interfere with potential cooperation and involvement. For example, the patient may expect to be shocked by electrical equipment, entertain hopes for a magical cure and immediate symptom relief, or have a hopeless attitude which precludes the ability to envision a positive therapeutic outcome (Lynn and Freedman, 1979). In the evaluation interview, the patient is informed of the realities of behavioral treatment: the results which have been obtained thus far, the demands of the treatment schedule, and the necessity for accurate symptom reporting throughout a lengthy follow-up period.

Symptom Report Cards

The basic self-report instrument used to assess therapeutic change in the behavioral treatment of Raynaud's disease is the symptom report card. Patients are instructed to complete a card immediately following every attack. Symptom report cards are kept over a matter of months before, during, and after treatment. (The forms can be perforated and held in a binder.) Headings prompt the patient to record the specific circumstances of each attack, as well as the perceived cause and any methods which were used to inhibit or curtail the episode. Ratings of symptom severity and emotional stress are made from the scales provided, and the duration of the attack is recorded in minutes. Skin color changes that occur during the attack are also noted.

Most Raynaud's disease patients experience the classic, triphasic sequence of vasospastic symptoms (pallor, cyanosis, and rubor). This pattern is not always consistent across populations, however, and may change over time, particularly for patients who show symptom improvement. To assess therapeutic change it is therefore useful to define for each patient a minimal alteration of skin color which can then be logged as an attack. Behavioral treatment of Raynaud's disease emphasizes the detection of symptom onset at the earliest possible moment and the subsequent implementation of therapeutic strategies. Since blanching of the fingers usually occurs first, it is generally used as the minimal symptom criterion, regardless of the appearance of cyanosis or rubor. In some patients, symptom improvement is characterized by a lessening in duration of the blanching phase to the point where it is almost indiscriminate—yet some cyanosis remains. In these cases, it may be necessary to redefine the attacks in terms of the occurrence of cyanosis.

Although attack frequency is generally the most useful self-report measure for assessment of Raynaud's disease symptoms, there are exceptions. A few patients have reported virtually continuous vasospasms throughout their waking hours, rather than discrete phasic attacks. These patients have been instructed to complete symptom report cards at specific times each day, and to enter the severity and duration measures for symptoms occurring during the preceding interval.

Illustrative Self-report Data

Data from 838 symptom report cards obtained from 10 patients have been analyzed to determine the relationships among self-report variables and to examine the influence of environmental factors on Raynaud's symptoms. The mean weekly attack frequency of these patients was 27.0, with a standard deviation of 21.3. Reasonable agreement was found between an estimate of attack frequency obtained at the evaluation interview and the average frequency of attacks obtained from the cards ($r = .71, p < .05$). The median duration of vasospastic attacks was 15 minutes with a range from 1 to 240 minutes. A significant relationship ($r = .68, p < .05$) was found between symptom frequency and duration; patients with more frequent attacks also had longer ones. However, symptom severity as measured by a 1–10 scale was related neither to frequency nor duration. We have employed this scale primarily as a measure of pain experienced during attacks. This may be problematic since attacks can occur without physical sensations, and because some of the sensations which do occur may not be experienced as painful (e.g., tingling). Indeed, 49 percent of the attacks were rated as 1 or 2 on the 1–10 scale. Instead of a unidimensional severity scale, it may be more useful to develop a method of categorizing the sensations and the color changes which could then measure the effects of treatment.

Of the 838 reported attacks, 527 (62.9 percent) occurred indoors. Only 311 (37.1 percent) occurred outdoors. Indoor attacks were more severe ($\chi^2 = 32.79$, $p < .001$), and longer in duration ($\chi^2 = 35.6$, $p < .001$) than outdoor attacks. The most common circumstances in which attacks occurred were at work (26.8 percent), driving or riding in a car (19.6 percent), cooking or doing household chores (15.3 percent), and walking outdoors (11.3 percent). Attacks occurred with approximately equal frequencies throughout the waking hours of the day, with peaks during the intervals of 8:00 to 9:00 AM, 11:00 AM to noon, and 5:00 to 6:00 PM. Patients were usually driving to or from work or walking outdoors during these periods.

The distribution of perceived causes of attacks as recorded by the patients was: environmental cold (indoor or outdoor temperature), 47.4 percent; local cold (e.g., food, drinks, or water), 13.1 percent; emotional stress, 22.4 percent; and indeterminate, 17.1 percent. Significantly more ($\chi^2 = 87.87$, $p < .001$) attacks reported to be caused by local cold or emotional stress occurred indoors, as opposed to outdoors.

Sufficient data were obtained from eight patients to calculate attack frequencies for both colder (October through April) and warmer (May through September) months. Attacks were half as frequent in the warmer months; one patient reported no symptoms. A significant relationship was found between the warm and cold weather estimates of attack frequency ($r = .81$, $p < .01$).

Outdoor temperatures at the time and place of each of the 838 attacks were obtained from the U.S. Weather Service; their distributions are shown in Figure 4-1. Correlations between temperatures and attack frequencies for indoor and outdoor attacks were small and nonsignificant. Comparisons between the distributions in Figure 4-1 and the distributions of all hourly temperatures occurring during the time periods in which the symptom reports were obtained revealed no significant differences. That there is no relationship between indoor attack frequency and outdoor temperature is not surprising; the absence of a relationship between *outdoor* attack frequency and temperature may be due to variations in clothing, physical activity, local thermal environment (e.g., temperature inside a car), or psychological factors. It is quite possible that Raynaud's patients avoid the outdoors during cold weather. There is no simple relationship between absolute outdoor temperature and the occurrence of symptoms. Some patients have reported that temperature *changes* are more likely to cause attacks than the cold itself. Further research is needed to clarify these issues.

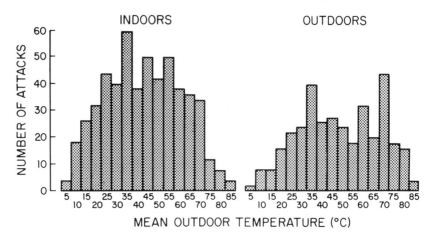

Fig. 4-1. Relationship between vasospastic attack frequency and outdoor temperature for attacks occurring indoors and outdoors.

Duration of Self-monitoring

It is clear that the vasospastic symptoms of Raynaud's disease are affected by a wide variety of physical and emotional factors. Since the environmental and psychological precipitants of attacks fluctuate over time, it is likely that the frequency, duration, and severity of attacks will fluctuate as well. Presumably, the length of symptom recording baseline periods will relate directly to the accuracy of the data obtained. However, this must be balanced against the realities of patient compliance.

During the pretreatment baseline period, some patients gradually paid increased attention to their symptoms as they engaged in the recording process, causing a progressive increase in reported frequency of attacks. We have found that this behavior generally reaches a plateau within a few weeks and we have thus adopted 1 month as the minimum baseline duration. Similarly, during the initial phases of behavioral treatment, some patients learn increased discrimination of symptoms, thereby reporting more attacks than they had previously reported. Data collected during the later stages of treatment may therefore be more accurate.

Although there is no clear relationship between outdoor temperature and symptom occurrence, weather is one factor in the constellation of symptom causes and must be taken into account in the recording process. It is necessary to establish the post-treatment recording period as one which is not warmer than the pretreatment period in order to provide a conservative measure of outcome. Ideally, follow-up data should be collected throughout an entire year of climatic changes after termination of treatment. Few patients are willing to complete symptom report cards for this extended period of time. However, most have been amenable to the use of a briefer reporting form over the interval. Since we have regarded attack frequency as the primary measure of therapeutic effectiveness, we have asked some patients to nightly record on a calendar the number of attacks they experienced that day. The calendar page is mailed to the laboratory at the end of the month. Compliance with this procedure over extended time periods has been generally good, although reminders by telephone or letter are often helpful.

Approximately 1 year from the beginning of the pretreatment baseline, patients should complete full-symptom report cards for 1 month. The weather during that month should be no warmer than that of the pretreatment month, to the extent that this is realistically possible. Comprehensive weather data for many locations in the United States is available from the U.S. Weather Service in Asheville, North Carolina, to aid in planning this process. At the end of the follow-up month it is useful to interview the patient to review the symptom report data and to elucidate successful and unsuccessful implementation of therapeutic procedures.

Critical Incidents

Since there are many causes of Raynaud's disease symptoms, it is unlikely that any one measure, be it attack frequency or finger blood flow under cold stress, will accurately reflect treatment outcome for all patients. However, there are certain naturally occurring circumstances in which patients consistently experience symptoms. One patient always had attacks while driving her old Volkswagen to work on cold mornings. It is likely that the combination of stressors in this situation accounted for the high probability of symptoms: environmental cold (the vehicle had inadequate heat), local cold (the steering wheel), and psychological stress (hurrying in rush hour traffic). After treatment with skin temperature biofeedback, this patient reported that she was able to consistently avert attacks in this situation. Her attack frequency recorded on the cards dropped from 28/week to less than 1/week; it has remained at this level for over 2 years. For this patient, the critical incident provided a naturalistic stressor that correlated well with overall reported occurrence of symptoms. Other such incidents we have observed include buying frozen foods, skiing, and having a cold drink in a social situation. Critical incidents that occur daily are the most useful in evaluating treatment outcome.

Comment

Self-report data have proven useful in the assessment of therapeutic change in Raynaud's disease patients. Several studies (Surwit et al., 1978; Keefe et al., 1979) have shown that reported attack frequency significantly declines in the course of behavioral treatment, and that reductions are maintained at 1 year follow-up (Freedman et al., 1981). In addition, we have found significant relationships between interview and self-report card estimates of attack frequency, and between warm and cold weather estimates of attack frequency. Although we regard attack frequency as the most reliable self-report outcome measure, the nature of the attack may change over time. It is therefore necessary to establish a minimal pattern of color changes and sensations which define an attack and to monitor these changes through the course of treatment.

Although Raynaud's symptoms are usually more frequent in the winter than in the summer, no relationship was found between absolute outdoor temperature and symptom frequency in our research. This relationship is confounded by factors such as clothing, physical activity, and time spent outdoors. The lack of correlation may also be due to the influence of other causal factors, such as local cold and psychological stress. To control for the effects of weather, it is recommended that symptom report cards be completed for 1-month periods before treatment, after treatment (no warmer than the pretreatment month), and 1 year from the pretreatment month. If situations can be identified in which the patient's symptoms virtually always occur, assessment of attack frequencies in these circumstances may prove to be the most valid outcome measure.

Assessment of Emotional Stress

It has been acknowledged that in some Raynaud's disease patients, symptoms are precipitated wholly or partially by emotional stress (Spitell, 1972; Blain et al., 1951). This is not surprising, since the attacks are clearly vasoconstrictive in nature, and since vasoconstriction has been produced in the laboratory in both normals (Cook, 1974; Ackner 1956) and Raynaud's patients (Mittelman and Wolff, 1939) using various psychological stressors. In support of this, many reported attacks appear to be triggered by emotional factors, illustrated by the following statement by Mrs. E., a Raynaud's sufferer:

> I went to talk to personnel at work about getting my old classification back. I have never been able to do shorthand well and they said I'd have to retake the test. I felt upset because I feel like I'm not getting anyplace. The attack occurred while I was in the personnel office.

It is our hypothesis that Raynaud's disease patients are affected in varying degrees by emotional stress. If this is true, patients whose symptoms are stress-related should benefit more from psychologically oriented therapies, such as cognitive stress management, than patients whose symptoms are not precipitated by stress. It would therefore be useful to develop methods to differentiate these patient types.

We will review the work of Mittelmann and Wolff in elucidating the stressful components of Raynaud's disease as well as our own attempts to develop repeatable laboratory techniques for the assessment of this aspect of the disorder. The use of psychological tests in the assessment of emotional stress in Raynaud's disease will also be addressed.

Interview Stress

Mittelmann and Wolff conducted a series of in-depth, emotionally stressful interviews with five Raynaud's "syndrome" patients while measuring finger temperature with a radiometer (Mittelmann and Wolff, 1959).

First, detailed personal histories were obtained in order to identify "significant experiences, stresses, and strains in the subject's daily existence." These topics were then discussed in interviews conducted at room temperatures of 20°C and 26°C and with the subject "adequately" or "inadequately" clothed. In one experiment, an adequately clothed subject's finger temperature fell 13.2°C while she was discussing difficulties with her family and experiencing a wide variety of emotions. She complained of tingling and pain in her fingers when her skin temperature reached 21.2°C. A control session during which there was no discussion showed little temperature drop, even though the room was cool.

This experiment illustrated that, at least in this patient, a combination of both reduced ambient temperature and emotional stress was necessary to produce a vasospastic attack. A subsequent interview with the same patient (but without adequate clothing) produced more severe symptoms. However, this attack occurred at a finger temperature of 22°C, demonstrating that there is no absolute skin temperature at which attacks occur.

We tried to replicate the Mittelmann and Wolff procedure in our laboratory on a 56-year-old woman with a 43-year history of idiopathic Raynaud's disease. The patient's right finger temperature stabilized at 23.7°C after a 16-minute adaptation period. Room temperature was maintained at 22.5°C. Pleasant topics (her summer vacation) were discussed during minutes 17 through 35, as a control for the effects of simply being interviewed. Throughout this time her finger temperature remained stable at 23.7°C. Over the next 22 minutes, her finger temperature fell to 23.4°C during a discussion of her failures at photography, at work, and the interference of her symptoms with her job. During the next 22 minutes, a series of seemingly highly stressful topics emerged: her hatred for her father, her parents' divorce, and severe embarrassment about her Raynaud's attacks at age 13. During this discussion she was extremely upset and cried at several points. However, during this period, her finger temperature rose to 23.6°C over 16 minutes. Thus, the discussion of stressful topics with this patient produced a single temperature reduction of only 0.3°C, which is less than the amount of natural variation she showed in the control session. It is unlikely that the patient's finger temperature "bottomed out," as she reached temperatures of 20°C in other laboratory sessions. Interestingly, her finger temperature increased during the last part of the interview, which appeared to be the most stressful.

Our failure to induce significant temperature decreases in this patient was notable since she had reported frequent attacks that appeared to be stress-related. Subsequent attempts to replicate the findings of Mittelmann and Wolff in other patients were also unsuccessful.

Singer (1974), in reviewing the effects of subject involvement in psychophysiological research, concluded that ". . . differences in the experimenter–subject relationship may alter the total meaning of the experimental situation so that different psychological and physiological mechanisms or responses are evoked by an otherwise identical test procedure.'' It is possible that uncontrolled factors such as these account for the discrepancies in results. It is also possible that some patients who report stress-related symptoms simply do not respond to certain stress-induction procedures. Since we wanted to develop standardized emotional stressors which could be repeated in a variety of experimental and clinical situations, another approach was tried.

Imagery Scripts

It was necessary to devise stressors which would be specifically relevant to persons with Raynaud's disease, but which could repeatedly be administered in identical form. Levenson produced differential respiratory responses in asthmatics and normals using a general stress film and one which was specifically stressful for persons with asthma (Levenson, 1979). Gelder and Mathews (1968) demonstrated forearm blood flow changes in phobic patients instructed to imagine stressful scenes compared to control periods. Self-reported anxiety correlated significantly with forearm blood flow. Lang (1979) has developed an instructed imagery technique in which subjects listen to tape-recorded scenes relevant to their clinical problem and then imagine them. Using this technique, he differentiated socially anxious from phobically anxious subjects on the basis of their heart rate responses to the imagined scenes. The above studies show that patient types can be distinguished on the basis of physiological responses to stressors having content relevant to the patient. Dugan and Sheridan (1976) showed that subjects produced average temperature decreases of 2°F by imagining their hands in cold water. Since instructed imagery techniques produced finger temperature changes, differentiated socially anxious from phobic patients, and could be easily adapted to utilize content relevant to Raynaud's symptoms, a procedure consisting of three imagery scenes was developed. To control for the effects of the imaging process, a script focusing on pleasant topics is used. Since Raynaud's patients are anxious about the cold, a script focusing on this theme was devised. Lastly, in reviewing the symptom report cards and interviews of pilot patients, it was found that themes of social anxiety, embarrassment, and being in a hurry occurred in many of them. A script focusing on these themes was therefore constructed. Each script is tape-recorded by the experimenter and is 3 minutes long. The session begins with a 16-minute adaptation period. The first script is played over headphones and the subject imagines it as vividly as possible for 2 minutes. A rest period then occurs. The second and third scripts are given in the same manner and separated by rest periods. The order of presentation of the three scripts is randomized.

Although this procedure must be regarded as experimental, the results obtained thus far are encouraging. Finger temperature responses to the cold and stress scripts have been generally negative with magnitudes up to $-2°C$, while responses to the neutral script have been minimal.

Psychological Tests

In addition to measuring physiological responses to emotional stressors in patients with Raynaud's disease, it would be useful to find psychological measures which are sensitive to stress in these patients. Our first approach to this problem was the administration of the MMPI to 12 Raynaud's patients. The mean T-scores for the 13 clinical scales, Welsh's A and R factors, and several experimental scales were obtained.

There were no mean scores above 69, the cutpoint for abnormal values. Results for individuals showed fewer scale elevations above 69 than would be expected by chance. A profile analysis, which examines relative scale elevations for each patient without regard to absolute scores, revealed no typical patterns. These findings were surprising, since many of the patients stated that their symptoms were often precipitated by emotional stress. We therefore expected to see elevations on scales related to anxiety: Hs, Hy, Pt, and Welsh's A. The MMPI, however, is a diagnostic instrument which taps the relatively enduring personality characteristics of individuals. It is possible that Raynaud's patients do not differ from normals in their stable personality qualities, but respond to transient stress conditions in characteristic ways. Surwit and coworkers found the Alienation scale of the Psychological Screening Inventory to be significantly related to finger temperature changes in a cold room (Surwit et al., 1979). However, no relationships were found with scales more closely related to stress and anxiety.

Spielberger's notion of state anxiety has proved useful in measuring the stress responses of our Raynaud's patients (Spielberger, 1972). State anxiety is conceptualized as a transitory emotional state or condition of the human organism that increases in intensity and fluctuates over time. Its level is high in circumstances that are perceived as threatening, regardless of the objective danger. The intensity of state anxiety should be low in nonstressful situations or in circumstances in which an existing danger is not perceived as threatening. The State Trait Anxiety Inventory (STAI) (Spielberger, 1972) has been shown to be sensitive to stress induced by threats of shock and failure, school examinations, surgery, pregnancy, dental procedures, and snake phobias. Kelly and coworkers obtained significant correlations between state anxiety and heart rate under stress caused by harassment during a serial subtraction task (Kelly et al., 1970).

During the month of October, each of 12 Raynaud's patients filled out two STAI A State scales at home. They were instructed to complete one copy according to how they felt just before an attack and another copy according to how they felt during an asymptomatic period. They also rated their perceived levels of stress at these times on a simple 0–100 scale of subjective stress units. Significantly higher state anxiety ($T = 2.23$, $p < .05$) and subjective stress ratings ($T = 2.57$, $p < .05$) were found during preattack periods in comparison to asymptomatic periods. The correlation between state anxiety and subjective stress ratings was r = .75 ($p < .001$). Thus, these measures might be useful in differentiating symptoms which are stress-related from those which are not, as well as in predicting the outcome of behavioral treatment.

Comment

Definitive data regarding the relationship between emotional stressors and peripheral blood flow in Raynaud's disease patients do not yet exist. Although Mittelmann and Wolff were able to produce large-magnitude finger temperature changes in a small number of patients, these results have not been replicated. Preliminary data from our laboratory show that recorded imagery scripts might be useful in producing stress-induced temperature responses in certain patients. This procedure is advantageous in that it is repeatable, yet its content can be manipulated to tap suspected stressful issues. However, it has not been validated in controlled studies.

Other data from our laboratory suggest that "state" rather than "trait" measures of anxiety are more useful in differentiating Raynaud's disease patients with stress-related symptoms. It would be useful to obtain state anxiety measures before and after behavioral treatment to relate changes in this variable to changes in peripheral blood flow and in reported symptoms. Since the 0–100 subjective stress scale correlated significantly with the STAI state scale, it can be repeatedly given to patients at many time points outside the laboratory. We have incorporated this scale into our symptom report cards to provide continuous assessment of the relationship between reported stress and symptom occurrence for each patient. Surwit and coworkers have shown that patients scoring lowest on the alienation scale of the Psychological Screening Inventory (Lanyon, 1973) had the greatest improvements in digital temperature after behavioral treatment (Surwit et al., 1979). This scale might therefore be a useful prognostic screening instrument, particularly if treatment resources are limited.

Assessment of Peripheral Blood Flow

Although patient reports play an important role in the assessment of Raynaud's disease symptoms, it would be useful to develop objective evaluation procedures which are not subject to the problems of compliance and bias inherent in self-report data. Since the vasospastic attacks of Raynaud's disease are accompanied by substantial changes in blood flow in the affected extremities, measurement of peripheral blood flow has been used in the differential diagnosis of this disorder and in the evaluation of treatment outcome.

In intact human extremities, blood flow can be measured only by indirect means. Behavioral studies have most often used the temperature of the skin as an index of peripheral blood flow. Measurement may be made on the surface of the skin (thermometry) or at a distance (thermography). Visual observation of portions of the peripheral circulation can be accomplished by capillary microscopy or angiography. Plethysmographic techniques measure changes in the volume of extremities and include pneumatic, girth, photoelectric, and ultrasonic methods. Although the behavioral-medicine professional will likely not have direct access to all of these procedures, it is likely that many of the procedures will be employed by collaborators from other areas (e.g., vascular surgery). We will therefore describe the most commonly used methods and examples of their use in the assessment of Raynaud's disease.

Thermal Methods

Thermometry. Skin surface temperature may be easily measured to an accuracy of .1°C using an electronic thermometer. The procedure involves attaching to the skin either a thermistor, whose electrical resistance changes with temperature, or a thermocouple, which generates a voltage proportional to its temperature. The appropriate electrical factor is then measured with an electronic meter.

The temperature of the left and right middle fingers was used to evaluate the effects of autogenic training and autogenic training plus temperature biofeedback in 32 Raynaud's disease patients (Surwit et al., 1978). Measurements were obtained at several points before and after treatment; patients were instructed to keep their hands warm and the room temperature was decreased from 26°C to 17°C over a 42-minute period. Both groups maintained significantly higher finger temperatures during post-treatment stress tests when compared to pretreatment tests and also when compared to waiting-list control groups.

The use of skin temperature or other thermal methods as indices of peripheral blood flow carries the risk of several sources of error. Skin temperature depends upon both the rate of heat supply to the skin and the rate of heat removal, i.e., upon the temperature and flow rate of the blood and the insulation and temperature difference between the skin and environment (Fletcher et al., 1949). Environmental factors, such as ambient temperature, air currents, and clothing, must be well-controlled. Even if this is done, physiological problems remain (Burton, 1948). The temperature of inflowing arterial blood may be affected by that of venous blood in adjacent vessels. Muscle blood-flow in the forearm tends to vary inversely with cutaneous flow and may affect finger circulation "downstream." The thermal capacity of tissues between the blood vessels and the skin surface varies with the size of the digit and the skin temperature. During conditions of constant temperature, thermal capacity remains relatively constant. If blood flow changes rapidly, however, changes in skin temperature may lag by several seconds or minutes. Lastly, skin temperature may fall, due to evaporation of perspiration, irrespective of changes in blood flow. The advantages of skin temperature measurement are mainly practical ones. High-quality instruments are relatively inexpensive, easy to apply, and do not require frequent calibration. The units of measurement (°C or °F) are easily used in statistical analysis, although their relationship to actual blood flow is not always clear.

Thermography. The human skin emits radiation primarily as a function of its temperature. Thermography is an electro-optical means of translating variations of surface temperature into visual images. Thermography was used to examine total digital rewarming time in 24 Raynaud's disease patients and 51 controls (Chucker et al., 1971). After immersion of both hands in ice water for 1 minute, only 2 patients achieved complete rewarming after 45 minutes, as opposed to 49 controls.

Like other thermal methods, thermography is an indirect measure of blood flow and, as such, is subject to the same sources of error. In addition, the required equipment is quite expensive. Its advantages lie in its fast response time (16 measurements/second), the capability of simultaneously measuring large surfaces, and the absence of physical contact with the object being measured.

Visual Methods

Capillary microscopy. Since vasospastic attacks occur at zero or near-zero levels of blood flow, the observation of the movement of red blood cells permits the determination of the complete standstill of capillary circulation (Maricq et al., 1976) as well as the measurement of cell velocities (Bollinger et al., 1977; Mahler et al., 1977). If the nailfold is moistened with immersion oil and observed under magnifications of approximately 50 × to 300 ×, the capillaries and red blood cells can be seen. Using this technique in a 16°C room, Maricq found that complete or intermittent standstill of capillary blood flow occurred in all 15 patients with Raynaud's phenomenon secondary to scleroderma, and in 5 of 6 patients with Raynaud's disease, but in none of the normal controls. By filming or video-taping the blood cells through the microscope and measuring the distance travelled over time, their velocity may be calculated. Under normal resting conditions the red blood cell velocities of Raynaud's disease patients were not different from those of controls (Bollinger et al., 1977), but with finger cooling by − 10°C air, the cell velocities were significantly slower. Complete flow stoppages also occurred significantly more frequently in the patients than in the controls during the cold stressor.

Since patients with Raynaud's disease may have very low levels of capillary blood flow, capillary microscopy may be a useful evaluation procedure (Maricq et al., 1976). Observation, however, is limited to a relatively small field of capillaries in the nailfold, and the thermal environment may be altered by the use of immersion oil. The calculation of cell velocities from films or videotapes is time-consuming, although automated techniques are being developed to facilitate the computations (Bollinger et al., 1977).

Angiography. This is a radiographic technique in which arteries are x-rayed using injected radioactive contrast agents. Results of this procedure were compared in 34 mixed Raynaud's phenomenon patients and 5 normal controls (Rosch et al., 1977). Raynaud's symptoms were classified as mild (occasional attacks with minimal functional impairment), moderate (daily attacks in cool weather with moderate functional impairment), or severe (frequent attacks with significant progression and ulcerations). Symptoms were related to vasospasms seen in the angiograms, graded on a five-point scale. Under resting baseline conditions, the patients had more severe vasospasms than the normals, but the degree of spasm did not significantly correlate with the severity of clinical symptoms. After hand immersion in cold water, the patients' degree of vasospasm was significantly greater than that of the controls. After treatment with intra-arterial reserpine the patients showed a significant decrease in cold-exposure vasospasm but not in baseline vasospasm. At 1 year follow-up the difference in cold spasm decrease between patients who rated their therapeutic results as excellent and those who rated them as poor was statistically significant.

Although angiography permits the visualization of arterial obstructions and vasospasm over a large area, it is an invasive procedure which involves risk to the patient. Objective quantification of the data is difficult.

Plethysmographic Methods

Pneumoplethysmography.   In this technique, a limb or digit is enclosed in a rigid container so that changes in volume in the enclosed part cause displacements of the substance (air or water) in the container. These pulsations are detected by a pressure transducer and output is displayed on a chart recorder or oscilloscope. If the limb is maintained at the level of the heart, the amplitude of the pulsations is closely related to total blood flow (Ackner, 1956). A similar method involves the measurement of changes in limb girth by encircling it with a strain gauge whose electrical resistance varies with changes in circumference. These procedures are most often employed in venous occlusion plethysmography, which determines blood flow from the increase in volume of the limb after venous outflow is occluded by a sphygmomanometer cuff.

Using this technique, Raynaud's patients showed significantly lower hand blood flows than normals when the temperature of the water in the plethysmograph was maintained at 32°C, 27°C, and 20°C (McGrath et al., 1978). The percentage decrease in flow with cooling was also greater in Raynaud's patients; similar changes were found in the contralateral, uncooled hands. Also using venous occlusion plethysmography, Jamieson and coworkers found similar results in Raynaud's disease and scleroderma patients using ice applied to the neck as the cold stimulus (Jamieson et al., 1971).

Venous occlusion plethysmography is relatively well-accepted because it permits the calculation of blood flow in absolute units. However, venous occlusion alters blood flow, and it is difficult to know if all veins are actually occluded (Cooper et al., 1949). Continuous measurement is not possible since blood flow must be permitted to return to resting values between occlusions.

Photoelectric plethysmography.   Pulse waves may also be detected using an infrared light source to transmit through, or reflect light from, a segment of tissue and converting the light to electricity with a photodetector. Since infrared light is scattered by blood, the output of the photodetector is related to the volume of blood within the tissue (Stern et al., 1980). However, since a suitable method of calibration for this technique has not yet been developed, it provides only a relative measure of blood flow.

Pulse amplitude recovery time was measured with this method in 12 Raynaud's patients and 11 controls after immersion of both hands in ice water for 1 minute (Chucker et al., 1973). Recovery times (time required for amplitude to reach pre-stress baseline) were longer for patients than controls (significance not tested), and agreed in each case with measurements obtained with thermography. The digital pulse wave disappeared completely in Raynaud's disease patients (number not specified) but not in controls when room temperature was lowered to 18°C (Mishima et al., 1978). An electronic integrator was used to analyze the pulse volumes of three Raynaud's disease patients during temperature biofeedback training (Freedman et al., 1979b). The average correlation between integrated pulse volume and adjacent finger temperature was .67.

As noted, photoplethysmography provides only a relative measure of blood flow. In addition, it is subject to error, due to changes in physical characteristics of the blood (e.g., hematocrit and orientation of red blood cells) which do not affect other plethysmographic methods. The advantages of photoplethysmography lie in the ease of transducer application and in the fact that it detects primarily cutaneous, rather than total, blood flow.

Doppler ultrasound.   In this procedure, high-frequency sound waves transmitted towards and reflected by the red blood cells moving within a vessel are detected by an electronic receiver. The red cells shift the transmitted frequency by an amount proportional to their velocity (the Doppler effect). This frequency shift can provide an audible signal as well as a visual record of pulse waves on a chart recorder (Strandness, 1975).

In the diagnosis of Raynaud's disease, Doppler ultrasound has been used mainly to detect the presence or absence of vessel occlusions, and thereby differentiate between Raynaud's disease and Raynaud's phenomenon. Of 27 patients presenting with symptoms of these disorders, 10 were found to have occlusion of the digital artery by the ultrasound method, all later confirmed by arteriograms (Yao et al., 1972).

The output waveform of the Doppler flow meter is only proportional to relative blood velocity. Determination of true velocity requires knowledge of the angle between the ultrasonic beam and the flowing blood, which is impossible to delineate in practicality. Doppler ultrasound is particularly useful in the detection of deep venous thromboses, which are inaccessible to most noninvasive procedures (Strandness, 1975).

Other Methods

Isotope clearance. The rate of disappearance of a radioisotope from the skin is proportional to the rate of blood flow within it. Finger blood-flow rates obtained by this method have been found to correlate significantly ($r = .95$) with those determined by venous occlusion plethysmography when 133^{xe} was used as the isotope (Chumoskey, 1972).

Coffman and Cohen (1971) postulated that isotope clearance rate represented capillary flow, that values obtained by venous occlusion plethysmography measured total finger flow, and that the difference between these values represented arteriovenous shunt flow. Using $Na^{13}I$ as the isotope, they found that patients with Raynaud's phenomenon or primary Raynaud's disease had significantly smaller total and capillary fingertip blood-flows than normals, and that arteriovenous shunt flow was only smaller in a 20°C room.

This technique may be useful for determining digital blood flow as it does not require occlusion. The results discussed above were contradicted by those of a later study, in which no differences were found between Raynaud's disease patients and normals (Nielsen, 1978). In addition, it is unclear whether the disappearance rate represents capillary or total skin blood flow.

Digital blood pressure. Finger systolic pressure (FSP), defined as the highest cuff pressure where pulses can be detected during cuff deflation (Brown, 1972), may be recorded using a small occluding cuff on the proximal phalanx attached to a pressure gauge and a distal strain gauge plethysmograph to detect pulses. Since the pallor of a Raynaud's attack may be due to digital artery closure, FSP should fall to zero during this period. FSP was measured in 18 Raynaud's disease patients and 22 normals while cooling the finger with a small water-filled cuff on the midphalynx (Nielsen, 1978). Sixty-one percent of the patients showed digital artery closure between 20°C and 10°C, as opposed to none of the controls. By adding body cooling with a water-filled blanket, closure was provoked in all but one of the remaining patients, as opposed to none of the controls.

Given the excellent differentiation of Raynaud's patients from normals, it is possible that the FSP technique will be useful in evaluating treatment outcome in Raynaud's disease. This study illustrates that a combination of local and environmental cold is probably necessary to reliably produce vasospastic symptoms. However, Nielsen (1978) does not report the appearance of actual attacks in his study. The FSP technique cannot be used to obtain continuous measurements as cuff occlusion is necessary. It would be desirable to use this technique to simultaneously measure several digits.

Comment

Skin temperature has been the most commonly employed measure of blood flow in behavioral studies of Raynaud's disease given the ease of transducer application, relative lack of expense, and availability of interval data for statistical analysis. It is recommended that a measure of perspiration, such as skin conductance, be simultaneously recorded to control for potential error due to this factor. If blood flow is rapidly changing, a concomitant plethysmographic measure may be obtained to control for time lag errors.

Thermography is advantageous over thermometry in its rapid response time and capability to simultaneously monitor many skin surfaces. The high cost of the thermographic equipment would probably prevent its use by most behavioral clinicians and researchers. However, data obtained by this method could help map the distribution of blood-flow changes occurring due to behavioral treatments.

Although capillary microscopy is not routinely employed in many laboratories, its relatively low cost and capability of detecting very low rates of blood flow recommend its use in the assessment of Raynaud's disease, particularly in the observation of actual vasospastic attacks. Angiography, while available in many radiology departments, is an invasive procedure involving risk to the patient.

Venous-occlusion plethysmography has been regarded as the best method for determining blood flow in the extremities since the swelling in volume of the occluded limb may be directly converted to standard flow units (Ackner, 1956). The disturbance caused by the occlusion, however, and the lack of continuous measurement, detract from its accuracy and usefulness. Pneumatic and girth methods may be used without occlusion to determine true volumetric changes for individual pulses if suitable calibration standards are employed. The pneumatic and girth methods both summate the changes in blood volume in both skin and muscle, even though these may change in opposite directions (Brown, 1972). However, since finger blood-flow is of primary interest in Raynaud's disease, and muscular circulation in the fingers is relatively low, this does not present a serious problem.

The analysis of pulse wave shapes obtained with strain gauge, photoelectric, or ultrasonic sensors has received little attention in the assessment of Raynaud's disease and an evaluation of them must await further research.

If the isotope clearance method is validated in further research, it may replace venous occlusion plethysmography, since it provides continuous data and does not require occlusion. Similarly, the results obtained on finger systolic pressure appear promising but remain to be validated.

Thermal Stressors

Since the vasospastic attacks of Raynaud's disease are precipitated, at least in part, by local or environmental cold, a variety of thermal stressors have been used as diagnostic and assessment instruments. We have reviewed above a number of studies in which Raynaud's patients were differentiated from normals on the basis of peripheral circulatory responses to cold stress. We now will discuss studies in which cold stressors have been used to evaluate the outcome of behavioral treatment. Since many of these treatments, (e.g., biofeedback and autogenic training), emphasize self-control of finger temperature, we will also examine the relationship between this phenomenon and vasospastic symptom improvement.

Cold Chamber

Surwit, Keefe, and coworkers have conducted several studies in which the outcome of behavioral treatments for Raynaud's disease was evaluated using a chamber within which temperature decreased from 26°C to 17°C over a 42-minute period. Subjects, wearing only terry cloth robes, were seated in the chamber before and after treatment and were instructed to keep their hands as warm as possible. In the first study, subjects who had received autogenic training and biofeedback maintained significantly higher finger temperatures after treatment than before treatment and when compared to waiting list controls (Surwit et al., 1978). Nineteen of the original 32 subjects were retested 1 year later and finger temperatures had returned to pretreatment levels (Keefe et al., 1979). This was attributed to subjects' lack of compliance with treatment procedures. However, subjects continued to report significantly fewer vasospastic attacks. This raises the crucial issue of the relationship between self-report and laboratory data. There are two logical explanations of the discrepancy found in this study: It is possible that subjects truly were having fewer attacks and that the cold chamber procedure is not a good index of symptomatology. It is also possible that subjects were actually having more attacks but were not accurate symptom reporters.

Local Cold Stress

The use of cold stress as an assessment procedure in our laboratory has differed in two respects from the technique just described. Since many Raynaud's attacks seemed to be triggered by cold objects (such as iced drinks), we chose to employ local, rather than environmental, cold. In addition, we wanted to increase the likelihood that the results of skin-temperature biofeedback training would generalize beyond the laboratory setting (Lynn and Freedman, 1979). To accomplish this, a gradually increasing cold stressor was introduced during biofeedback training. In this procedure, the subject rests a finger on a thermoelectric device which maintains a constant temperature regardless of the thermal load (Fig. 4-2). Skin temperature feedback is provided by a thermistor attached to the fingertip, 1 cm from the edge of the cooling surface. The temperature of this surface is decreased from 30°C to 20°C at a rate of 1°C/minute, and held at 20°C for 10 minutes. Subjects are instructed to increase finger temperature as much as possible during this period using the feedback. This is a difficult task, since the temperature of the cooling surface remains constant regardless of the amount of blood flow.

Figure 4-3 displays data from a patient who increased the temperature of her right middle finger from 23.6°C to 25.0°C while resting it on the thermoelectric cooler. A greater temperature increase was shown in the same finger of the contralateral hand.

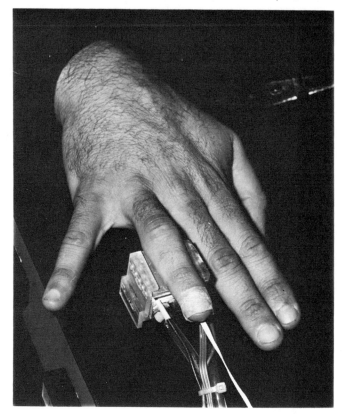

Fig. 4-2. Thermoelectric cooling device used during biofeedback training. (Design and construction by Samuel Wasson, P.E., and James Szopo, Lafayette Clinic.)

Six Raynaud's disease and two scleroderma patients have received six sessions of this cold desensitization procedure following six sessions of temperature biofeedback alone (Freedman et al., 1979a). The mean weekly frequency of vasospastic attacks decreased from 30.3 during the month prior to treatment to 12.7 at 1-year follow-up ($t = 3.11$, $p < .02$). Mean temperatures of the finger under cold stress significantly related ($r = -.64$, $p < .05$) to symptom frequency at the 1-year follow-up; patients with higher finger temperatures had fewer attacks. Differences in finger temperatures between baseline and cold stress periods were also significantly related to follow-up attack frequency ($r = -.68$, $p < .05$). However, finger temperatures from the hand not under cold stress did not correlate significantly with symptom frequency.

Temperature Control and Treatment Outcome

In the study described above, we also examined the relationship between finger temperatures obtained during feedback training without cold stress and attack frequency reported at the 1-year follow-up. Here, differences in finger temperatures

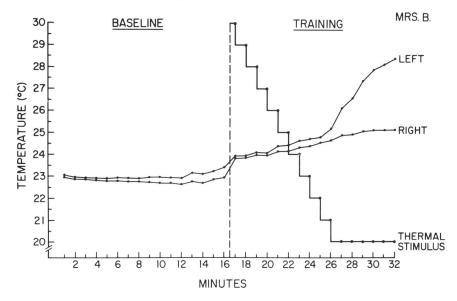

Fig. 4-3. One session of a patient receiving feedback of temperature of right fourth finger, resting on thermal stimulus.

between baseline and feedback periods were significantly correlated with symptom frequencies ($r = -.85, p < .01$); absolute finger temperatures were not. Similar findings were obtained in another study of temperature feedback and Raynaud's disease and phenomenon (Freedman et al., 1981).

We have also examined the relationship between reported attack frequency and the ability of Raynaud's patients to control finger temperature without feedback or cold stress. Patients were instructed to increase finger temperature as much as possible during two 24-minute periods: one prior to biofeedback/cold desensitization training, and one after the completion of training (Freedman et al., 1979a). Patients were rarely able to increase finger temperature above baseline during either 24-minute period. However, absolute temperatures were significantly ($F = 17.78, p < .0001$) warmer in the post treatment session ($\bar{x} = 27.2°C$) than in the pretreatment session ($\bar{x} = 24.5°C$).

Temperature differences between the two sessions were significantly related to attack frequencies reported at the 1-year follow-up ($r = -.68, p < .05$), as were absolute temperatures during the final session ($r = -.88, p < .01$).

Comment

It is obviously desirable to develop objective laboratory procedures that could reliably reflect the outcome of treatments for Raynaud's disease. That such procedures do not exist is due to our lack of understanding of the pathophysiology of Raynaud's disease symptoms and to the difficulty of noninvasive measurement of blood flow, particularly at low levels. It is unclear whether local cold, environmental cold, or a combination of the two, cause Raynaud's attacks. The work of Nielson showed that both types of thermal stress were needed to provoke digital artery closure in most Raynaud's patients (Nielsen, 1978). In addition, it is likely that, at least in some patients, psychological stress plays a role in the provocation of attacks.

Given this complex situation, it is not that surprising that results of a cold-chamber stress test failed to correlate with patient symptom reports 1 year after treatment (Keefe et al., 1979). Data from our laboratory showed that 1-year follow-up symptom reports were significantly related to finger temperatures during conditions with and without local cold stress. However, our procedures were not as rigorously evaluated as those of Surwit and colleagues: we did not retest subjects in the laboratory at the follow-up point. Furthermore, it is not known which parameters of blood flow should be used in laboratory assessment procedures. We found that finger temperature changes during feedback were related to follow-up symptom frequencies as well as absolute temperatures during a post-treatment, nonfeedback test session.

We have noted earlier that under some conditions, skin temperature may not be an accurate measure of peripheral blood flow. Indeed, data from Mittelmann and Wolff (1939) and from our laboratory show that there is no absolute temperature below which finger temperature must fall for an attack to occur.

It is thus possible that finger temperature may not sufficiently correspond to blood flow to serve as an accurate means of assessment. It is also possible that finger temperature is an adequate measure, but that combinations of stressors (environmental cold, local cold, and psychological) are necessary as stimuli.

Ambulatory Monitoring

We have discussed some of the problems encountered in the use of laboratory stress procedures and patients' self-report data in the assessment of Raynaud's disease patients. In order to evaluate the patient under the environmental and emotional stresses of daily life, it would be useful to develop measures of peripheral blood flow and psychological stress which could be used outside the laboratory. We have employed radiotelemetry, Medilog cassette tape recording, and the 0–100 subjective stress scale for this purpose.

Telemetry

Two channels of a six-channel Signatron FM telemetry transmitter and receiver have been used to monitor fingertip and environmental temperatures in Raynaud's patients outside our laboratory. The system has an effective range of approximately 100 meters and requires the patient to wear a small backpack containing the transmitter and antenna.

In one telemetry session, we obtained some interesting results. The patient first established a stable temperature baseline in the laboratory and was then sent outdoors wearing a tee shirt; the air temperature was 19°C. He sat on a park bench on the hospital grounds with instructions to keep his hands as warm as possible using the techniques he learned in biofeedback training. He was able to raise his finger temperature about 1°C above baseline during his first 5 minutes outdoors. He then lost control and finger temperature dropped about 2°C, but increased, as he regained control, to about 2°C above baseline. At this point, he was harassed by a hospital security guard. His finger temperature then dropped substantially due to this intrusion. Although we were able to examine temperature control and the effects of stress outside the laboratory, telemetry is limited by the fact that the patient must remain within a short distance of the telemetry receiver.

Medilog™ Cassette Recording

A miniature tape recorder has been developed to detect transient electrocardiogram (ECG) abnormalities in the natural environment over prolonged periods of time (Holter, 1961). Patients are sent home with the Holter monitor for 10–24 hours, with instructions to engage in typical activities, especially those that produce symptoms, and to keep an accurate diary of all events and symptoms. The correlation of ECG with event diary data has been a valuable diagnostic tool, particularly when the data collection period has been extended to 48 hours (Kennedy et al., 1978). Patient acceptance of these procedures has been good, with the majority of them keeping accurate diaries (Bleifer et al., 1976).

Holter monitoring technology has recently been developed to include procedures for obtaining continuous skin and ambient temperature recordings. The system which we employ (Medilog™, manufactured by Oxford Medical Instruments, Oxford, England) can record four channels of data for 24 hours on a standard tape cassette. The recorder is 11.2 × 8.6 × 3.6 cm; it weighs 400 gm. It is equipped with two channels that record finger and ambient temperatures to an absolute accuracy of 0.1°C, an ECG channel and an event-marker time-code channel. Playback is done at 16, 25, 32, or 60× real time on a separate unit. The recorder is worn on a belt or shoulder strap with the finger temperature thermistor taped to the volar surface of the middle finger. The ambient temperature thermistor is worn on a wrist strap. Wires are concealed under the patient's clothing and are colored to minimize visibility. ECG is monitored using disposable electrodes in a Lead III configuration. Patients are sent home for 2 consecutive days with this device. They can remove the transducers to shower and sleep and are given extra adhesive tape and ECG electrodes for reattachment. They are also given event diary cards which they are instructed to fill out hourly as well as when any symptoms occur. Stress ratings on the 0–100 scale are made by the patient every hour and for the period just preceding a Raynaud's attack. In addition, the patient is instructed to press the event marker button at the onset of every attack to to log the time from the digital clock on the recorder in the event diary.

The results of a portion of one recording are graphed in Figure 4-4. The patient reported four attacks during this period, occurring at finger temperatures ranging from 23.5°C to 26.0°C, and stress ratings from 30 to 75. As in previous work (Mittelmann and Wolff, 1939), it can be seen that there is no absolute level of finger temperature at which attacks must occur. Similarly, the levels of reported stress experienced prior to each attack are variable. It is possible, however, that in a given patient there is an optimal combination of finger temperature, ambient temperature, and level of psychological stress which reliably produces attacks. We are currently testing this hypothesis by obtaining data on a large number of patients. We are also employing this method to evaluate the outcome of behavioral treatment for Raynaud's disease. If temperature biofeedback, for example, is successful in ameliorating the patient's symptoms, one might expect higher finger temperatures after treatment than before treatment, given equivalent levels of thermal and emotional stress.

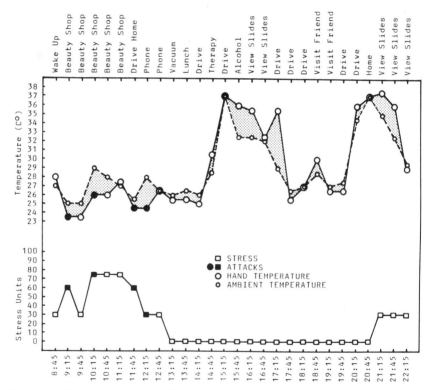

Fig. 4-4. Relationship between finger temperature, ambient temperature, and reported stress during ambulatory monitoring. Difference between finger and ambient temperature is denoted by shading. Four attacks occurred between 9:15 AM and 12:15 PM.

SUMMARY

Raynaud's disease is a peripheral circulatory disorder characterized by episodic vasospasms in the fingers and toes. Increases in sympathetic activity, catecholamine blood levels, blood viscosity, and sensitivity to local cooling have all been implicated as its cause but none have been proven. Although the disease is not uncommon its symptoms rarely occur in the laboratory, either spontaneously or under cold stress. This, and the fact that blood flow is difficult to measure noninvasively, has led to limited knowledge of the pathophysiology of Raynaud's disease. It is, therefore, not surprising that an objective laboratory method of Raynaud's disease symptom assessment has not been developed.

Although behavioral medicine workers have typically used skin temperature as the sole measure of blood flow in the assessment of Raynaud's disease, it is recommended that additional physiological measures be employed to control for possible errors due to sweating and thermal lag. Since close collaboration with other medical professions is likely, alternative methods of blood flow measurement should be explored; they may yield new knowledge. Differences in peripheral blood flow between Raynaud's disease patients and normals have generally been more prominent during cold stress than under resting baseline conditions. However, the use of cold stressors as outcome measures in the behavioral treatment of Raynaud's disease has not been proven definitive.

Since Raynaud's attacks are probably caused by combinations of local cold, environmental cold, and emotional and psychological stress, it is possible that no single stressor will adequately measure symptomatology. Little attention has been paid thus far to the use of psychological stressors in the assessment of Raynaud's disease. Stressors which are both salient and repeatable may be useful in distinguishing patient types and in determining outcome. State measures of anxiety may also be valuable for the same purposes.

The problem of multiple symptom causes may be dealt with in some patients by the use of critical incidents. These are naturally occurring events (such as driving on a cold day), which virtually always cause attacks due to the combination of precipitating factors. Decreased symptomatology in these circumstances maintained over an extended time period would represent good evidence of therapeutic improvement.

The critical incidents approach obviously requires the use of self-report data. The major instrument for the collection of this form of data has been the symptom report card or diary. We have found attack frequency, as determined from these cards, to be the most useful self-report measure of Raynaud's symptoms. Satisfactory correspondence was found between separate interview and diary estimates of attack frequency. In addition, a high correlation was found between warm- and cold-weather estimates of attack frequency. Although no relationship was found between absolute outdoor temperature and attack frequency, twice as many attacks occurred during the colder months. In determining treatment outcome, it is therefore necessary to ensure that post-treatment measurement periods are no warmer than pretreatment periods.

The relative accuracy and reliability of laboratory and self-report methods for the assessment of Raynaud's disease symptoms require further investigation. It is possible that new procedures, such as ambulatory monitoring, will aid in this purpose. Hopefully, the respective contributions of both behavioral and traditional medicine will prove mutually beneficial in furthering our understanding of Raynaud's disease.

REFERENCES

Abramson, D. *Vascular disorders of the extremities*. New York: Harper & Row, 1974.

Ackner, B. Emotions and the peripheral vasomotor system. *Journal of Psychosomatic Research*, 1956, *1*:3–20.

Allen, E. The peripheral arteries in Raynaud's disease: An arteriographic study of living subjects. *Proceedings of the Mayo Clinic*, 1937, *12*:187–192.

Allen, E., & Brown, G. Raynaud's disease: a critical review of minimal requisites for diagnosis. *American Journal of Medical Science*, 1932, *183*:195–197.

Blain, A., Coller, F., & Carver, G. Raynaud's disease: A study of criteria for prognosis. *Surgery*, 1951, *29*:387–397.

Bleifer, S., Harris, T., Oliver, G., Wenger, N. & Yarnall, S. Ambulatory ECG monitoring. *Patient Care*, 1976, *1*:1–27.

Bollinger, A., Mahler, F., & Meier, B.: Velocity patterns in nailfold capillaries of normal subjects and patients with Raynaud's disease and acrocyanosis. *Bibliotheca Anatomica*, 1977, *16*:142–145.

Brown, C. Instruments in psychophysiology. In N. Greenfield, & R. Sternbach (Eds.), *Handbook of psychophysiology*. New York: Holt, Rinehart, and Winston, 1972.

Burton, A. Temperature of skin: Measurement and use as index of peripheral blood flow. In V. Potter (Ed.): *Methods in medical research*. Chicago: Yearbook Publishers, 1948.

Charles, R., & Carmick, E. Skin temperature changes after griseofulvin. *Archives of Dermatology*, 1970, *101*:331–336.

Chucker, F., Fowler, R., & Hurley, C. Photoplethysmometry and thermography in Raynaud's disorders. *Angiology*, 1973, *24*:612–618.

Chucker, F., Fowler, R., Motomiya, T., Singh, B., & Hurley, W. Induced temperature transients in Raynaud's disease measured by thermography. *Angiology*, 1971, *22*:580–593.

Chumoskey, J. Skin blood flow by 133Xe disappearance validated by venous occlusion plethysmography. *Journal of Applied Physiology*, 1972, *32*:432–435.

Coffman, J., & Cohen, A. Total and capillary fingertip blood flow in Raynaud's phenomenon. *New England Journal of Medicine*, 1971, *285*:259–263.

Coffman, J., & Davies, W. Vasospastic diseases: A review. *Progress in Cardiovascular Diseases*, 1975, *18*:123–146.

Cook, M. Psychophysiology of peripheral vascular changes. In P. Obrist, A. Black, J. Brener, and L. DiCara (Eds.), *Cardiovascular psychophysiology.* Chicago: Aldine, 1974.

Cooper, K., Gross, K., Greenfield, A., Hamilton, D., & Scarborough, H. A comparison of methods for gauging the blood flow through the hand. *Clinical Science,* 1949, *8:* 217–234.

Downey, J., & Frewin, D. The effect of cold on blood flow in the hands of patients with Raynaud's phenomenon. *Clinical Science,* 1973, *44:*279–287.

Dugan, M., & Sheridan, C. Effects of instructed imagery on temperature of hands. *Perceptual & Motor Skills,* 1976, *42:*12.

Fetcher, E., Hall, J., & Shaub, H. The skin temperature of an extremity as a measure of its blood flow. *Science,* 1949, *110:*422–432.

Freedman, R., Ianni, P., Hale, P., & Lynn, S. Treatment of Raynaud's phenomenon with biofeedback and cold desensitization. *Psychophysiology,* 1979a, *16:*182.

Freedman, R., Lynn, S., Ianni, P., & Hale, P. Biofeedback treatment of Raynaud's disease and phenomenon. *Biofeedback and Self Regulation,* 1981, *6:*355–365.

Freedman, R., Sattler, H., & Ianni, P. Analysis of photoplethysmographic data. *Psychophysiology,* 1979b, *16:*182.

Gelder, M., & Mathews, A. Forearm blood flow and phobic anxiety. *British Journal of Psychiatry,* 1968, *114:*1371–1376.

Gifford, R., & Hines, E. Raynaud's disease among women and girls. *Circulation,* 1957, *16:*1012–1025.

Halperin, J., & Coffman, J. Pathophysiology of Raynaud's disease. *Archives of Internal Medicine,* 1979, *139:*89–92.

Jamieson, G., Ludbrook, J., & Wilson, A. Cold hypersensitivity in Raynaud's phenomenon. *Circulation,* 1971, *44:*254–264.

Johnsen, T., Nielsen, S., & Skovborg, F. Blood viscosity and local response to cold in primary Raynaud's phenomenon. *Lancet,* 1977, *2:*1001–1002.

Keefe, F., Surwit, R., & Pilon, R. A 1-year follow-up of Raynaud's patients treated with behavioral therapy techniques. *Journal of Behavioral Medicine,* 1979, *2:*385–391.

Kennedy, J., Chandra, V., Sayther, K., & Caralis, D. Effectiveness of increasing hours of continuous ambulatory electrocardiography in detecting maximal ventricular ectopy. *American Journal of Cardiology,* 1978, *42:*925–930.

Kelly, D., Brown, C., & Shaffer, J. W. A comparison of physiological and psychological measurements on anxious patients and normal controls. *Psychophsyiology,* 1970, *6:* 429–441.

Kontos, H. A., & Wasserman, A. J. Effect of reserpine in Raynaud's phenomenon. *Circulation,* 1969, *39:*259–266.

Lang, P. Emotional imagery and visceral control. In R. Gatchel, & K. Price (Eds.): *Clinical applications of biofeedback: Appraisal and status.* New York: Pergamon, 1979.

Lanyon, R. *Psychological Screening Inventory: Manual.* New York: Research Psychologists Press, 1973.

Levenson, R. Effects of thematically relevant and general stressors on specificity of responding in asthmatic and non-asthmatic subjects, *Psychosomatic Medicine,* 1979, *41:*28–39.

Lewis, T. Experiments relating to the peripheral mechanism involved in spasmodic arrest of circulation in fingers, a variety of Raynaud's disease. *Heart,* 1929, *15:*7–101.

Lewis, T. The pathological changes in the arteries supplying the fingers in warm handed people and cases of so-called Raynaud's disease. *Clinical Science*, 1938, *3:*287–300.

Lottenbach, K. Vasomotor tone and vascular responses to local cold in primary Raynaud's disease. *Angiology*, 1971, *22:*4–8.

Lynn, S., & Freedman, R. Transfer and evaluation of biofeedback treatment. In A. Goldstein, & F. Kanfer (Eds.), *Maximizing treatment gains—transfer enhancement in psychotherapy.* New York: Academic Press, 1979.

Mahler, F., Meier, B., Frey, R., Bollinger, A. & Anliker, M. Reaction of red blood cell velocity in nailfold capillaries to local cold in patients with vasospastic disease. *Bibliotheca Anatomica*, 1977, *16:*155–158.

Maricq, H., Downey, J., & LeRoy, E. Standstill of nailfold capillary blood flow during cooling in scleroderma and Raynaud's syndrome. *Blood Vessels*, 1976, *13:*338–349.

McGrath, M., Peek, R., & Penny, R. Raynaud's disease: Reduced hand blood flows with normal blood viscosity. *Australian and New Zealand Journal of Medicine*, 1978, *8:* 126–131.

McGrath, M., & Penny, R. The mechanisms of Raynaud's phenomenon, part 1. *Medical Journal of Australia*, 1974, *2:*328–333.

Mendlowitz, M., & Naftchi, N. The digital circulation in Raynaud's disease. *American Journal of Cardiology*, 1959, *4:*480–484.

Miller, I., & Walder, D. Raynaud's disease and cooling of the fingers. *British Journal of Surgery*, 1972, *59:*313.

Mishima, Y. Pathophysiology of Raynaud's phenomenon. *Journal of Cardiovascular Surgery*, 1978, *19:*521–526.

Mittelmann, B., & Wolff, H. Affective states and skin temperature: Experimental study of subjects with "cold hands" and Raynaud's syndrome. *Psychosomatic Medicine*, 1939, *1:*271–292.

Nielsen, S. Raynaud phenomenon and finger systolic pressure during cooling. *Scandanavian Journal of Clinical Laboratory Investigation*, 1978, *38:*765–770.

Olsen, N., & Nielsen, S. Prevalence of primary Raynaud's phenomenon in young females. *Scandinavian Journal of Clinical & Laboratory Investigation*, 1978, *38:*761–765.

Peacock, J. A comparative study of the digital cutaneous temperatures and hand blood flows in the normal hand, primary Raynaud's disease, and primary acrocyanosis. *Clinical Science*, 1959, *8:*25–33.

Peacock, J. Peripheral venous blood concentration of epinephrine and norepinephrine in primary Raynaud's disease. *Circulation Research*, 1959, *7:*831–837.

Pringle, R., Walder, D., & Weaver, J. Blood viscosity and Raynaud's disease. *Lancet*, 1965, *3:*1085–1088.

Rosch, J., Porter, J., & Grolino, B. Cryodynamic hand angiography in the diagnosis and management of Raynaud's syndrome. *Radiology*, 1977, *55:*807–814.

Sapira, J., Rodnan, G., Scheib, E., Klaniecki, T., & Rizk, M. Studies of endogenous catecholamines in patients with Raynaud's phenomenon secondary to progressive systemic sclerosis. *American Journal of Medicine*, 1972, *52:*330–337.

Singer, M. Engagement–involvement: A central phenomenon in psychophysiological research. *Psychosomatic Medicine*, 1974; *36:*1–17.

Spielberger, C. Anxiety as an emotional state. In C. Spielberger (Ed.), *Anxiety: Current trends in theory and research* (Vol. 1). New York: Academic Press, 1972.

Spitell, J. A., Jr. Raynaud's phenomenon and allied vasospastic conditions. In J. F. Fairbairn, J. L. Juergens, & J. A. Spitell, Jr. (Eds): *Peripheral vascular diseases*. Philadelphia: W. B. Saunders Co., 1972.

Spurling, R., Jelsma, F., & Rogers, J. Observations in Raynaud's disease with histopathologic studies. *Surgical Gynecology & Obstetrics*, 1932, *54*:584–593.

Stern, R., Ray, W., & Davis, C. *Psychophysiological recording*. New York: Oxford University Press, 1980.

Surwit, R., Bradner, M., Fenton, C., & Pilon, R. Individual differences in response to the behavioral treatment of Raynaud's disease. *Journal Consulting and Clinical Psychology*, 1979, *47*:363–367.

Surwit, R., Pilon, R., & Fenton, C. Behavioral treatment of Raynaud's disease. *Journal of Behavioral Medicine*, 1978, *1*:323–335.

Willerson, J., Thompson, R., & Hookman, P. Reserpine in Raynaud's disease and phenomenon. *Annals of Internal Medicine*, 1970, *72*:17–27.

Yao, S., Gourmas, C., Papathanasion, K., & Irvine, W. A method for assessing ischemia of the hand and fingers. *Surgery, Gynecology, and Obstetrics*, 1972, *135*:373–378.

Appendix: Interview Protocol

1. When did your symptoms first begin?
2. Please describe your symptoms.

   A. Where do they occur? Hands? Both Hands? Feet? Both feet? Face?
   B. What sequence of color changes occurs? White? Blue? Red?
   C. Are these changes always the same?
   D. What do your hands, feet, or face feel like during each color change? Cold? Numb? Burning? Tingling? Painful?

3. How long does a typical attack last? A mild attack? Your worst attack?
4. How frequent are your attacks?

   A. In what month do you tend to get the most attacks? *How many?*
   B. In what month do you tend to get the least attacks? *How many?*
   C. When your problem was the worst, how frequently did you have attacks?
   D. When your problem was the least troublesome, how frequently did you get attacks?
   E. What is the longest period that you have experienced without an attack?
   F. What is the longest period in cold weather that you have experienced without an attack?

5. Do you wear any special clothing to prevent attacks?
6. Do you regulate the room temperature in any way to decrease attacks? What room temperature do you feel most comfortable?
7. Assuming you are not wearing protective clothing, what outside temperature would begin to create problems for you?
8. When you are wearing protective clothing, at what temperature do you begin to have problems?
9. In what circumstances are you most likely to get attacks?
10. When you get an attack, what do you do? Do you do anything to try to curtail it?
11. What kinds of events, thoughts, or feelings tend to precipitate an attack? (Try to be specific.)
12. When you get an attack, how do you feel, what do you think? (Try to be specific.)
13. Does Raynaud's disease prevent you from doing anything?
14. If you didn't have Raynaud's, how would your life change?
15. Are you taking medication or being treated in some way? How?
16. How helpful has your treatment been?
17. How helpful do you think this treatment will be?

PART III

Assessment Strategies for Disorders of the Central Nervous System

Patrick Logue
Sarah M. McCarty

5

Assessment of Neurological Disorders

NEUROLOGICAL DISORDERS

The field of clinical neuropsychology has emerged from an interdisciplinary union between psychology and neurology. Davison defines clinical neuropsychology as a set of *"comprehensive* approaches to *applied* problems concerning the *psychological* effects of brain damage in *humans"* (italics his) (Davison, 1974). Davison emphasizes comprehensive in his definition because complex brain functions require a wide variety of psychological measures to tap the diversity of deficits which may occur with any particular central neurological disorder. Furthermore, given the extensive research in neuropsychology, it is no longer sufficient to simply determine whether a patient has "brain damage." Questions which can be addressed by the clinical neuropsychologist also include the localization of the disorder within the brain, its etiology, and the rehabilitative and prognostic implications of the patient's deficits. A simple screening test is inadequate to meet these demands. At the very least, a neuropsychological battery should include measures of basic motor and sensory functions, memory, language functions, visuospatial abilities, and a variety of higher cognitive functions.

There are two basic approaches to neuropsychological assessment. One is the battery approach, in which a standard battery of tests is given to all patients. The Halstead-Reitan Battery (Reitan and Davison, 1974) and the Luria-Nebraska Neuropsychological Battery are examples of this approach (Golden et al., 1978). The Halstead-Reitan Battery consists of neuropsychological tests to measure adaptive functioning, intelligence, expressive/receptive language, simple and complex motor performance, sensory/perceptual functions, attention, and concentration. The Halstead-Reitan Battery (in different versions for differing age ranges) can

The authors wish to thank Dr. David Power for his comments on this manuscript.

take 6 to 8 hours to administer; it requires considerable experience to interpret. The Luria-Nebraska Battery is an attempt to quantify Luria's qualitative approach. It consists of a series of very brief single examinations that cover a wide range of functions and, typically, takes less time to administer than the Halstead-Reitan Battery.

A second approach to neurological assessment is eclectic; various tests are used depending on the patient's presenting symptoms and the clinician's hypothesis about the patient's deficits. Lezak provides a good summary of this approach (Lezak, 1976).

Regardless of the approach used, patterns of neuropsychological test performance vary as a function of such variables as the location of the brain lesion, its etiology, its size, its momentum, the age of the patient at the lesion's onset, the current age of the patient, the time since the onset of the lesion, and the premorbid abilities of the patient.

Given these complexities, four levels of inference have been suggested to interpret neuropsychological test scores (Reitan, 1974). The first type of inference involves the level of performance. The patient's test scores are compared to the means or cutoff scores of a standardization sample and are judged to be normal or impaired. The second inference involves pathognomonic signs of neurological dysfunction, such as aphasia or constructional apraxia. Such signs are not always present in brain-damaged patients with lesions in a given location, particularly in patients with chronic, static, or slowly progressive lesions, but they rarely occur in the absence of brain damage. The third kind of inference involves the patterns of obtained scores. Certain patterns occur more frequently with specific types and/or locations of brain damage; these patterns will be discussed more fully below. The fourth type of inference involves comparing the functional efficiency of the two sides of the body. Consistent motor or sensory deficits on one side can be related to dysfunction on the contralateral side of the brain. The Halstead-Reitan Battery was specifically designed to permit these multiple levels of inference. However, it is also possible to use the Halstead-Reitan criteria regardless of the measures used, as long as those measures vary enough to provide the necessary information.

This chapter is divided into two major sections. The first addresses some of the variables affecting neuropsychological test performance in adults. The second part describes some common neurological disorders and their concomitant behavioral deficits.

VARIABLES AFFECTING TEST PERFORMANCE

Lateralization of Lesion

Language

The most intensely studied lateralized functions are language functions, which include the expression and comprehension of spoken and written language. The best information to date suggests that language resides primarily in the left hemisphere (LH) in 96 percent of right-handed people *(dextrals)* and in 70 percent of left-handed people *(sinistrals)*. Fifteen percent of sinistrals are right-hemisphere (RH) dominant for language, and 15 percent have bilateral representation of language function (Milner, 1974). The percentages for language in the LH are lower among those who suffer brain lesions at an early age, especially for sinistrals. However, assuming some period of normal language development, aphasic disorders are much more likely to result from LH than RH lesions. There are many excellent reviews of the complexities of language disorders which cannot be covered here (see Heilman and Valenstein, 1979; Hecaen and Albert, 1978; Eisenson, 1973).

The aphasia screening test of the Halstead-Reitan Battery provides a brief assessment of aphasic symptoms. The Luria-Nebraska Battery contains sections for both expressive and receptive (i.e., impressive) speech, reading, and writing. In addition, there is a wide variety of more extensive aphasia examinations, such as the Porch Index of Communicative Ability, the Boston Diagnostic Aphasia Examination, and the Minnesota Test for the Differential Diagnosis of Aphasia (Porch, 1967; Goodglass and Kaplan, 1972; Schwell, 1957). Basic functions which must be assessed in a comprehensive aphasia exam include the fluency and accuracy of spoken language, the ability to report what is heard, the ability to communicate in writing, and the comprehension of oral and written language. Primary sensory and motor deficits must be ruled out as the major source of impairment. Although the presence of aphasia may be determined by a neuropsychologist, more detailed evaluation and remediation are often carried out by speech pathologists.

Spatial Skills

Although the right hemisphere has been found to have some very rudimentary receptive language functions (Parsons, 1970; Smith and Burklund, 1966; Sperry, 1966), it appears to be primarily involved in the processing of nonverbal spatial information. The actual mechanisms and classification of RH functions are the subject of debate (Hecaen and Albert, 1978; Arrigoni and De Renzi, 1964; Benton, 1979; Piercy, 1964). It has not been resolved whether hemispheric difference is related to the type of material being processed (e.g., verbal or nonverbal) or the way in which each hemisphere processes the information (e.g., analyzing and naming vs. organizing into wholes) (Hecaen and Albert, 1978). However, clinically, right posterior lesions frequently lead to deficits in the performance of nonverbal tasks. Such deficits include spatial disorientation, problems in color perception, and difficulties in recognizing faces (Benton, 1979), as well as inability to perceive tonal patterns (Piercy, 1964; Goodglass, 1977), constructional apraxia, and so on.

Constructional apraxia, defined as the inability ''to organize elements in correct spatial relationships so that they form an entity'' (Benton, 1979), is one of the most commonly discussed spatial deficits. This includes the inability to draw something and the inability to construct from a model, such as a block design. Such deficits occur more frequently with right-posterior than with left-posterior lesions (Parsons, 1970; Arrigoni and De Renzi, 1964; Benton, 1979; Piercy, 1964; Hecaen, 1962). Approximately 62 percent of 151 patients with posterior RH lesions had constructional apraxia, whereas 40 percent of 206 patients with posterior LH lesions showed this deficit. This difference is not as striking as for other lateralized functions.

Many measures of constructional apraxia have been developed. Some of the more common are copying designs such as a Greek cross or the Bender Gestalt Test figures, constructing block designs as on the Wechsler Adult Intelligence Scale (WAIS), three-dimensional block building, and building match-stick figures. Right- and left-hemisphere-damaged patients may do poorly on block design with about equal frequency, whereas three-dimensional block building and copying figures are much more frequently impaired in those with RH lesions (Benton, 1979). In addition, a given patient with RH damage will not necessarily fail all constructional tests. There is some controversy concerning the nature of LH vs RH constructional apraxia. Some argue that errors resulting from LH lesions are due to disruption in the programming of movements, whereas errors associated with RH damage are of a visual-spatial, perceptual nature (Lezak, 1976; Hecaen and Albert, 1978). Consequently, patients with LH lesions tend to preserve the gestalt of figures while distorting details; those with RH damage fail to preserve the gestalt. It remains unclear whether these differences are a matter of severity of perceptual dysfunction or are indeed qualitative differences (Benton, 1979).

The Verbal and Performance subtests of the WAIS and Wechsler-Bellevue Intelligence Test have been found to reflect, to some extent, the lateralized verbal vs spatial functions of the brain. With some consistency findings show that patients with LH lesions have significantly lower verbal scores than performance scores, and patients with RH damage have lower performance scores than verbal scores (Balthazar and Morrison, 1961; Doehring and Reitan, 1961; Fitzhugh et al., 1962; Klove, 1959; Klove, 1974; Reed and Reitan, 1963; Reitan, 1955; Reitan, 1970; Satz, 1966; Vega and Parsons, 1969). Not all patients with lateralized lesions will show a verbal–performance discrepancy. When it occurs, it must be interpreted within the context of a larger battery of more specialized neuropsychological tests. Verbal–performance discrepancies are reported to be more pronounced in patients with cerebrovascular and neoplastic lesions than in those with head trauma (Reitan, 1973). Several studies have reported Verbal–Performance discrepancies to be greater in patients with acute (new or progressive) lesions than in those with chronic static lesions (Fitzhugh et al., 1962; Fitzhugh and Fitzhugh, 1964; Fitzhugh et al., 1961; Klove and Fitzhugh, 1962).

Memory

Memory functions also tend to be lateralized. Unilateral lesions of the hippocampus, which lies within the temporal lobe, produce differential memory deficits. Bilateral hippocampal lesions produce profound and all-encompassing deficits in memory for new information. Mamillary bodies, parts of the thalamus, and the fornix are also important in the consolidation of new information. Although the traditional right–left distinction has been between auditory and visual memory, (Parsons, 1970; Piercy, 1964; McFie, 1975; Smith and Sugar, 1975) it is probably more appropriate to distinguish between verbal and nonverbal memory (Hecaen and Albert, 1978). Many verbal stimuli are auditory, but left hippocampal damage may also lead to deficits in memory for written (visual) material. Many nonverbal tasks are visuospatial ones, but right hippocampal lesions may also impair tonal memory or memory for auditory patterns (Piercy, 1964; Hecaen, 1962). The Russell revision of the Wechsler Memory Scale is based on this verbal–nonverbal distinction (Russell, 1975; Logue and Wyrick, 1979; McCarty et al., 1980; Power et al., 1979; Ziesat et al., 1980). The original Wechsler Memory Scale is primarily a test of verbal memory; the only nonverbal task is visual reproduction (Wechsler, 1945). Consequently, the Wechsler Memory Quotient may decrease in LH damage (Prigatano, 1978). The memory scale on the Luria-Nebraska Battery assesses both verbal and nonverbal memory functions. The memory and location scores for the Tactual Performance Test of the Halstead-Reitan Battery reflect nonverbal memory skills; the Wechsler Memory Scale is often used as a measure of verbal recall in conjunction with the Halstead-Reitan Battery. Lezak presents a wide variety of other memory function tests, including those which assess retrieval of old information, immediate recall of material specific to various sensory modalities, and the ability to retain new information after repeated trials (Lezak, 1976).

Sensory and Motor Functions

Basic sensory and motor functions are also lateralized; the functions of each side of the body are contralaterally represented in the brain. An exception to this general principle is that the LH seems to exert some control over motor and sensory functions on both sides of the body (Sperry, 1966; Piercy, 1964; McFie, 1975; Teuber, 1962). The primary motor areas are located in the posterior frontal lobes; the primary sensory areas, in the anterior parietal lobes. Motor and sensory integrative areas extend anteriorly and posteriorly, respectively, from the primary areas. The Halstead-Reitan Battery and the Luria-Nebraska Battery both assess motor and sensory functions of varying levels of complexity on both sides of the body. For example, finger oscillation on the Halstead-Reitan Battery compares simple motor speed on the right and left. Finger agnosia examines the ability to identify which finger is touched when the eyes are closed, a simple sensory function. The Tactual Performance Test assesses more complex sensorimotor integration and problem-solving abilities when the patient is using the preferred hand, the non-preferred hand, and both hands.

Unilateral neglect (also called unilateral imperception or inattention) is a secondary sensory deficit which may involve tactile, visual, and/or auditory sensory modalities. Although patients with this symptom are able to see, hear, and feel, they often fail to attend to stimuli from the side of their bodies contralateral to the brain lesion which is typically on the right. In copying drawings, they may leave out one side of the figure. They may fail to read one side of a word or sentence. In extreme cases, they express the opinion that half of their bodies do not seem to belong to them. Even in the absence of such marked symptoms, they may show extinction (or suppression) to double simultaneous stimulation. That is, these patients will detect unilateral tactile, visual, or auditory stimulation, but when both sides are simultaneously stimulated, the patients will not perceive the stimulation to the contralateral side. Patients who originally show severe unilateral neglect eventually show only suppression on double simultaneous stimulation as recovery progresses (Heilman, 1979). The imperception portion of the sensory–perceptual examination in the Halstead-Reitan Battery is a structured procedure for detecting such suppressions (Reitan and Davison, 1974).

Unilateral neglect most commonly results from lesions in the inferior parietal lobe. Lesions of the dorsolateral frontal lobe or cingulate gyrus may also produce these symptoms (Heilman, 1979). Right parietal lesions produce unilateral neglect significantly more frequently than left parietal lesions (Parsons, 1970; Piercy, 1964; Heilman, 1979). One is therefore more likely to see neglect of stimuli on the left side of the body. Although auditory, tactile, and visual neglect may all be present, they need not all occur together.

Apraxia

Another function which lateralizes is apraxia, specifically ideomotor and ideational apraxia. Generally, apraxia is the inability to carry out skilled or purposeful movements. Apraxia is not due to primary motor deficits, failure to comprehend verbal instructions, or general intellectual deterioration (Hecaen and Albert, 1978; Geschwind, 1969; Heilman, 1979). The distinction between ideomotor and ideational forms is subject to debate (Hecaen and Albert, 1978). Most commonly, ideomotor apraxia is the inability to pantomime the use of an object (e.g., stirring coffee with a spoon) or to perform a movement in the absence of an object (e.g., raise a hand); ideational apraxia is the inability to correctly manipulate objects (Piercy, 1964). The distinction made by Hecaen and Albert is between single simple gestures (e.g., wave goodbye) and complex gestures that involve a sequence of movements (e.g., lighting a candle with a match). It is not known whether ideational apraxia is simply a more severe apraxia than ideomotor apraxia or a separate syndrome. However, the clinical presentation of these types of apraxia and their localizing significance are less ambiguous.

The apraxic patient may show any of the following symptoms: clumsiness in the execution of motor behaviors, oversimplification of the response; the use of a body part as an object (e.g., the use of a finger for a key rather than pantomiming holding, inserting, and turning a key); total failure to execute the desired movement; or incorrect use of objects. There may be differences in the patient's ability to perform in response to a verbal command as opposed to the ability to imitate. Impairment of performance is usually equal for both hands, but may occur for the left hand only. Patients may not spontaneously complain of apraxia. They may think their left hand's clumsiness to be normal and may have right hemiparesis. Consequently, it is important to test for apraxia even in the absence of complaints (Hecaen and Albert, 1978; Heilman, 1979).

Ideational and ideomotor apraxia result from posterior LH lesions. Other varieties may occur with lesions of the corpus callosum or frontal lobes. Since patients with ideomotor and ideational apraxia are also often aphasic, care must be taken to ensure that their failure to appropriately respond to commands is not solely due to an inability to understand the spoken command. Heilman, in his excellent description of the assessment of apraxia, recommends asking the patient (a) to repeat the examiner's request, (b) to point to the object appropriate for a specific action, and (c) to pick out the correct action from several executed by the examiner.

The Aphasia Screening Test of the Halstead-Reitan Battery contains an item for assessing apraxia (''show me how you would use a key''); the Luria-Nebraska Battery has several; Heilman[47] presents a flexible unstandardized set of procedures.

Apraxia and the lateralizing signs (previously discussed) are seen in patients with focal lesions, such as infarction (especially of the middle cerebral artery), tumor, arteriovenous malformation and trauma, and also in later stages of Alzheimer's disease (Heilman, 1979).

Emotion

Patients with lateralized lesions may differ in both their expression of emotion and in their ability to perceive the emotional expressions of others (Valenstein and Heilman, 1979). Aphasia patients with LH lesions tend to have difficulty understanding the words of others but may be able to interpret the affect conveyed by the pitch, tempo, and tonal contours of speech, and by facial expressions. Conversely, patients with RH lesions may understand words but not the affective, nonlinguistic qualities of speech. The expressive abilities of patients with LH and RH lesions may parallel their receptive abilities, with LH patients expressing emotion through appropriate intonation despite linguistic difficulties, and RH patients using words which may convey affect but which are not accompanied by appropriate inflections or facial expressions. These differences between LH and RH patients may account for previous descriptions of aphasics as displaying catastrophic reactions to their disabilities while RH patients seem inappropriately indifferent (Goldstein, 1948).

Diaschisis may occur in both acute and chronic conditions (Smith, 1975). Diaschisis is the disruption of function of intact portions of the brain by lesions located elsewhere in the brain. Diaschisis may lead to false lateralizing signs in the later stages of expanding lesions, such as tumor, or in the early stages of lesions of rapid onset, such as head trauma or stroke. It is more likely to occur with large lesions. The exact mechanism of diaschisis is not understood, however, it is likely that diaschisis results from disruptions of cerebrospinal fluid dynamics, altered metabolism, increased pressure from a mass lesion, and/or edema.

Anterior versus Posterior Locus of Lesion

Less is understood about the significance of anterior vs posterior locus of lesion than about lateralization. Although posterior lesions tend to produce relatively obvious deficits, anterior lesions tend to have subtle effects which are difficult to quantify (Damasio, 1979; Meier, 1974). Consequently, opinion on the frontal lobes has ranged from the conviction that the lobes are the seat of higher cognitive functions, to the observation that frontal lobe lesions may produce no discernable deficits at all (Damasio, 1979).

Patients with frontal lobe lesions may perform within the normal range on standard intelligence tests, especially if the lesion is in the anterior frontal lobes (Damasio, 1979; Smith, 1964). However, Milner reports decreases in verbal fluency in patients with left frontal lobectomy (Milner, 1964); Hecaen and Albert report such deficits accompanying left or right frontal lesions, but much greater with those on the left (Hecaen and Albert, 1978). Posterior left frontal damage may produce right hemiplegia and Broca's aphasia with nonfluent output and relatively intact comprehension (Benson, 1979). Patients with right frontal lesions may show deficits in visuoconstructive tasks and spatial (Damasio, 1979), as do patients with right posterior lesions.

Generally, self-regulation of behavior may be impaired. Frontal lobe patients do especially poorly on the Wisconsin Card Sorting Test, in which they must sort cards to correspond to a criterion (color, shape, etc.) which periodically changes. Patients must utilize feedback on the correctness of their responses to determine the criterion. Those with frontal lesions tend to continue sorting to the first criterion even when it is no longer correct (perseveration). They may be able to verbalize the correct criterion, but seem unable to use this information to change their behavior. The ability to shift strategies or mental sets is also tapped by Part B of the Trail Making Test, which is now part of the Halstead-Reitan Battery. Clinical descriptions of patients with frontal lobe lesions indicate that they may be oblivious to social norms, somewhat impulsive, and inappropriate in their behavior. Real or anticipated consequences to their behavior may have no influence. They may have difficulty in planning and executing daily activities and in initiating behavior. They tend to be forgetful, in that they "forgot to remember." These patients may be relatively docile, with occasional, short-lived outbursts in the face of frustration. They also tend to be quite distractible. It has been hypothesized that their deficits relate to impaired orienting responses and attentional deficits, and to the disconnection of the frontal lobes for the limbic system which mediates emotional responses (Damasio, 1979).

Frontal lobe syndromes are quite variable, depending on the age at which damage was sustained, the time elapsed since the lesion, the patient's premorbid abilities, the locus of the lesion within the frontal lobes, the size of the lesion, and so on (Damasio, 1979).

Acute versus Chronic Lesions

A number of early studies (Fitzhugh et al., 1962; Fitzhugh et al., 1961; Klove and Fitzhugh, 1962) indicate that lateralizing signs on the Wechsler-Bellevue Intelligence Scale are less pronounced among chronic brain-damaged patients or those who have recovered from acute lesions than among patients with acute, rapid-onset, or progressive lesions. Chronic brain-damaged patients tend to show more uniform and less-pronounced deficits than acute patients. The performances of the latter are more uneven, with greater severity of specific deficits. Similarly, the level of impairment on Halstead-Reitan and Luria-Nebraska Battery tests is greater for acute patients than for patients with chronic, static, or slowly progressive lesions, and those recovering from acute lesions (Fitzhugh et al., 1962; Fitzhugh et al., 1961; Russell et al., 1970; Reitan, 1966).

Demographic Characteristics

In making determinations about the status of cognitive functioning, it is necessary to know what levels of performance might be considered normal. Normal test performance varies as a function of such demographic characteristics as age, educational level, and gender.

Age

The relationship of age to neuropsychological and intelligence test performance has been the most widely studied. Increasing age is related to decreasing performance on some tests of cognitive function; the reasons are less clear.

On the WAIS, sharp declines in scaled scores are not seen in cross-sectional studies until relatively late in life, e.g., after age 70. Even then, the declines are not great, especially for verbal subtests (Birren and Morrison, 1961; Botwinick, 1977; Doppelt and Wallace, 1955; Goldstein and Shelly, 1975; Siegler and Botwinick, 1979). Mean verbal subtest scores for those over 70 are reported to be less than one standard deviation below the mean achieved by Wechsler's 20-to-34-year-old standardization group (Wechsler, 1955). Subjects aged 75 and older fall more than one standard deviation below the mean for the 20-to-34-year-old group on all performance subtests, especially on the digit symbol test. Botwinick noted that the "classic aging pattern" for the WAIS is characterized by higher verbal than performance subtest scores (Botwinick, 1977). Consequently, such a verbal–performance discrepancy in an older person would not be interpreted in the same way as for a younger person. (These comments apply to standard scores; IQs are age-corrected.)

Short-term memory functions, such as those tapped by the Logical Memory, Visual Reproduction, and Associate Learning subtests of the Wechsler Memory Scale probably decline earlier and more sharply than the intellectual functions measured by the WAIS, e.g. in the subject's 50s (Hulicka, 1966; Kear-Colwell and Heller, 1978; McCarty et al., 1980). Although cross-sectional declines are steeper than those seen on the WAIS, longitudinal declines are not great. McCarty et al. found significant longitudinal declines only on visual reproduction and the hard associate portion of associate learning.

Little systematic age-related change is seen in performance on the Halstead-Reitan Battery between the ages of 15 and 45 (Reitan, 1967). However, many authors have demonstrated a relationship between older age and performance on Halstead-Reitan Battery measures in cross-sectional samples (Goldstein and Shelly, 1975; Reitan, 1967; Bak and Greene, 1980; Botwinick and Storandt, 1974; Davies, 1968; Fitzhugh et al., 1964; Klisz, 1978; Prigatano and Parsons, 1976; Reed and Reitan, 1963; Reed and Reitan, 1963; Reitan, 1955; Reitan, 1973; Vega and Parsons, 1967; Wood et al., 1979). There is reasonable agreement that performance decreases with age on the Category Test, total time of the Tactual Performance Test, and Parts A and B of the Trail Making Test. Results are somewhat less consistent for the Seashore Rhythm Test, the Speech Perception Test, the memory and location scores of the Tactual Performance Test, and Finger Tapping. The correlations between age and Halstead-Reitan test scores tend to be higher among normals than among brain-damaged patients; brain damage is the most important variable for the latter (Reitan, 1956). Significant differences among older and younger subjects were reported in all areas of the Luria-Nebraska Battery except reading, writing and arithmetic (Marvel et al., 1979).

Although there is some agreement concerning the effects of age on specific tests, the common characteristics of the tests showing age-related changes, and delineating the affected cognitive functions, are less clear. One hypothesis is that RH functions are more vulnerable and decrease more than LH functions. In addition to the classic aging pattern on the WAIS, more tests measuring RH functions on the Halstead-Reitan Battery show declines than those measuring LH functions or generalized functions (Klisz, 1978).

A more common distinction is made between fluid and crystallized intelligence (Cattell, 1963). Fluid intelligence involves new learning or problem-solving, whereas crystallized intelligence involves old learning and stored information. The WAIS information and vocabulary subtests are the most often cited tests of crystallized intelligence. Reitan invokes a similar categorization which he has variously called active problem-solving vs recall of stored information and brain-sensitive vs education variables (Fitzhugh et al., 1964; Reed and Reitan, 1963; Reitan, 1955). The above studies have reported that older subjects perform significantly worse than younger subjects on active problem-solving or brain-sensitive tests and equally well or better than younger subjects on stored information or education-related tests. Diffusely brain-damaged patients may show similar patterns, but they may also show decreases on tests reflecting crystallized intelligence (Kahn and Miller, 1978; Overall and Gorham, 1972).

The extent to which age-related motor slowing contributes to age-related differences on the various tests is not known. However, studies of the WAIS indicate that these differences are not due entirely to slowing (Botwinick, 1977; Doppelt and Wallace, 1955).

It must be noted that there is large variability among elderly people in cognitive abilities, and that not all normals show the patterns of decline described here. There is a tendency among people with higher levels of ability during their younger years to maintain well and perform relatively well when they are older (Botwinick, 1977; Siegler and Botwinick, 1979). In addition, such variables as health, educational level, and distance from death may influence performance in the old (LaRue and Jarvik, 1978; Siegler, 1975).

Educational Level

It is important to understand the relationship between educational level and test performance for two reasons: educational experiences themselves may have an influence on test performance, and educational level provides a rough estimate of premorbid intelligence. Since brain lesions may be accompanied by reduced IQ scores, clinicians frequently use the relatively stable and quantifiable level of education as an index of premorbid IQ. A general correlation of .70 between level of education and IQ in adults (Matarazzo, 1972). Education is one of the two most powerful predictors of IQ in the 1955 WAIS standardization sample (Wilson et al., 1979). Other authors also report significant relationships between various WAIS scores and education (Birren and Morrison, 1961; Botwinick and Storandt, 1974; LaRue and Jarvik, 1978; Finlayson et al., 1977; Granick and Friedman, 1967; Overall and Levin, 1978). Those who have compared the influence of age and education on intelligence test performance have found education to be more important than age (Birren and Morrison, 1961; Granick and Friedman, 1967).

Since Wechsler memory scale scores have been reported to correlate highly with IQ scores in both normal and brain damaged subjects (Hall and Toal, 1957; Fields, 1971). It is not surprising that education has been found to be more important than age in performance on the Wechsler memory scale logical memory, visual reproduction, and associate learning subtests (McCarty et al., 1980).

The relationship between education and Halstead-Reitan Battery measures appears less strong than between education and WAIS scores (Finlayson et al., 1977). Studies on the Halstead-Reitan Battery have used non-brain-damaged groups of different composition; the results are therefore somewhat contradictory. Among psychiatric patients, there are no significant correlations between education and test scores (Prigatano and Parsons, 1976). However, significant correlations are found for medical patients (Vega and Parsons, 1967), and significant differences among education groups are found for the Finlayson et al. mixed psychiatric, medical, and normal group (Finlayson et al., 1977). A comparison of the results of the latter two studies suggests that education influences scores on the Category Test, the Seashore Rhythm Test and the Speech Perception Test. Tactual Performance Test memory and location scores are unrelated to education in both studies. There is disagreement regarding tactual performance test total time and finger tapping. The trail-making test was not included in the Vega and Parsons study; however, Finlayson et al. and Botwinick and Storandt report significant differences on this test among education groups (Finlayson et al., 1977; Botwinick and Storandt, 1974). The relationship between education and Halstead-Reitan Battery scores is less strong among brain-damaged than non-brain-damaged subjects (Prigatano and Parsons, 1976; Vega and Parsons, 1967; Finlayson et al., 1977). Marvel et al. report significant main effects for education for all sections of the Luria-Nebraska Battery (Marvel et al., 1979).

Gender

There is some indication that normal adult females perform better on verbal tasks (vocabulary, logical memory) than males: normal adult males perform better on gross motor tasks (finger tapping, dynomometer), visuospatial tasks (picture completion, block design, and visual reproduction), and quantitative tasks (arithmetic) than females (Dodrill, 1979; Kupke et al., 1979; McGlone, 1978; McGlone, 1973). However, the number of studies on these differences is relatively small and subjects vary across studies in terms of age and neurologic status. When gender differences are found for various tests, they support the contention that males perform better on visuospatial and motor tasks while females perform better on verbal tasks. However, the effect of gender is not strong enough to provide consistent differences across studies on a given measure.

Other Variables

The size of a lesion obviously influences the severity of cognitive deficit, but it does so in interaction with the locus of the lesion. It is likely that a large lesion in any location will disrupt more functions than a smaller lesion in the same region, but lesions in some areas of the brain will produce less pronounced effects generally. For example, large frontal lesions produce less impairment of cognitive functioning than posterior lesions of the same size (Barbizet, 1970; Chapman and Wolff, 1959). The age at which the lesion occurs also interacts with size and locus. Very early lesions, even if they involve an entire hemisphere, may not produce the profound effects seen with smaller lesions later in life (Piercy, 1964).

Although personality variables may play many roles in both the effects of brain damage and recovery, one point is especially important in assessment: patients with hysterical neurosis or hysterical personality disorders may overemphasize their symptoms. It is therefore tempting to dismiss all their symptoms as psychogenic. Such a patient warrants increased rather than decreased efforts in assessment, since he or she is not immune to central neurologic disorders.

A history of alcohol abuse may produce effects which complicate assessment of other disorders. Deficits occur in chronic alcoholics include impairment of abstract reasoning and conceptual abilities (Goldstein, in press) in the absence of impairment on standard intelligence tests. Furthermore, these patients show adequate performance on simple perceptual-motor tasks, such as copying geometric forms, but show deficits in perceptual-motor tasks involving complex visuospatial relations or problem-solving, such as block design or embedded figures. Chronic alcoholics do especially poorly on the Category Test.

The next section describes some of the etiologies of brain damage and their influence on test performance.

NEUROLOGIC DISORDERS

Cerebrovascular Accident

Cerebrovascular accident (CVA), or stroke, consists of an interruption of the blood supply to the brain and typically involves one of the larger arteries. It occurs with the highest frequency in the 50-to-70 age range. Stroke is most commonly produced in one of three ways:

1. Thrombosis—a local narrowing of the vessel, with eventual complete blockage (thrombus), which cuts off the blood supply to the rest of the artery and to the surrounding brain tissue.
2. Embolism—an occlusion by material such as a blood clot, fat body, or bacterial clump which travels from a remote site, finally lodging as the vessel narrows.
3. Hemorrhage—a rupture of the vessel wall releasing blood into surrounding tissue. Not only is the blood supply cut off, but the escaping blood acts as a foreign space-occupying body.

The first type, thrombosis, accounts for over half of all CVAs. The other two types represent less than 20 percent each. Hemorrhagic stroke, while relatively low in occurrence, is most likely fatal (Chusid and McDonald, 1967).

When stroke occurs, it is typically complete in seconds to hours. It is therefore a relatively high-velocity or rapid-onset lesion which produces strong lateralizing signs. The patient is likely to display such pathognomonic signs as aphasia, right hemiplegia, ideational or ideomotor apraxia (if the stroke occurs in the left hemisphere), and left hemiplegia, constructional apraxia, or neglect if it occurs in the right hemisphere (Heilman, 1974; Levine and Mohr, 1979). There may be a strong discrepancy between verbal and performance IQ scores, with verbal scores significantly lower in the LH patient, and performance scores lower in the RH patient. The patient may show severe sensory or motor deficits on the side contralateral to the lesion. The specific behavioral effects depend on the type of CVA, the brain area affected, and to some extent the personal characteristics of the individual (dominant hand, age, gender, educational level, and so on).

Recovery may range from minimal to almost complete (Banister, 1978; Walton, 1977). Because of the severity of deficits which accompany stroke and the potential for recovery, it is important that rehabilitation begin as early as feasible and be multidisciplinary in nature. The neuropsychologist often serves as a liaison among the various therapeutic disciplines and the family. Supportive therapy with the family is usually a part of the rehabilitation process.

Neoplasm

Neoplasms, or tumors, can be divided into three general types: encapsulated, infiltrating, and metastatic. Encapsulated tumors have definite boundaries and are often cyst-like. Accordingly, they are usually operable. Infiltrating tumors, by contrast, do not present definite boundaries between healthy tissue and the tumor itself. Accordingly, they are often treated with combinations of surgery, drugs, and radiation. Metastatic tumors typically arise in some remote area of the body such as the lungs or breasts, and spread throughout the body, including the brain. As such, they are multifocal in site and effects (Baker, 1958).

Depending on type and locus, a tumor can produce its effects through increased intracranial pressure, direct tissue destruction, and direct pressure effects on other brain structures. With the exception of metastatic tumors, the classic pattern of a neoplastic disorder is that of a lateralized, progressive, relatively localized lesion. Since tumors are relatively low-velocity lesions, the acute signs of constructional apraxia, aphasia, and striking variability in IQ test performance characteristic of vascular lesions may not occur until relatively late in the course of the disorder (Smith, 1966; Smith, 1966). In addition, because of the space-occupying nature of a neoplastic disorder and the possibility of disrupting,brain area connections, effects that are not consistent with the immediate locus of brain damage may sometimes occur (diaschisis). Nonetheless, lateralizing signs usually do appear. These may include right-left differences on motor measures (finger tapping, dynomometer), the sensory exam, and the Tactual Performance Test of the Halstead-Reitan Battery, or differences in right- and left-hemisphere indicators on the Luria-Nebraska Battery. Generalized deficits may also appear on such measures as the Trail Making Test and the Category Test.

Survival rates in certain carcinomas have increased progressively since the early 1970s. Neuropsychologists will increasingly be faced with the sequelae of successful treatment. Treatment with radiation and/or drugs may result in a general loss of higher level adaptive functions and problem-solving skills superimposed on the lateralized effects of the tumor itself (Hochberg and Slotnick, 1980). Further, a later degenerative process can begin weeks to years after treatment. It is presently not known how frequently this occurs (Hochberg and Slotnick, 1980).

Closed Head Trauma

Closed head trauma involves a blow to the head in which the skull and brain are not penetrated, although skull fracture may occur. It represents a significant and relatively frequent source of brain damage in the general population, most particularly in children and young adults. After a blow to the skull, the brain is subjected to rapid acceleration and deceleration. It may slam against the opposite side of the skull, sometimes producing more serious damage than the original blow; this is the *contra coup* effect. Because of the shape of the brain and the interior of the skull, the temporal, frontal, and prefrontal areas are particularly vulnerable to injury. Following impact, the brain may hemorrhage; if that patient dies, an autopsy may show multiple small bleeds. Tearing of arteries and veins may produce potentially life-endangering hemorrhages. Edema within several minutes of the injury is common and can be life-threatening.

The closed head injury may be initially described as involving simple fracture; concussion, in which the impact of the brain against the skull has produced transient loss of consciousness and neuronal dysfunction; or contusion, in which the brain has been bruised.

If the patient is unconscious for an extended length of time, he or she has entered into a coma. Various rating scales have been developed to measure depth of coma, such as the Glasgow Coma Scale (Jennett, 1976; Jennett and Teasdale, 1981). This scale assesses eye-opening (spontaneously, to speech, to pain, or none), verbal response (oriented, confused, inappropriate, incomprehensible, or none), and motor response (obey commands, localize pain, flexion to pain, extension to pain, or none). Assessments are made several times daily, and the level of each response is quantified and plotted so that overall level and duration of coma can be easily visualized. The categories produce good agreement among observers.

Once the patient is fully conscious, amnesia poses a potential problem. The patient may lack the ability to store new experiences and may not recall this period of time later. This is called anterograde amnesia. The patient may also be unable to recall a period of time immediately before the blow to the head (retrograde amnesia). Retrograde amnesia resolves to varying degrees over a longer period of time, with ''islands'' of previous events recalled and expanded in no particular order. Depending on the severity and site of the injury, almost any other behavioral anomaly can also occur, including aphasia, constructional apraxia, personality changes, concentration problems, and significant decreases in formal intelligence.

After the acute phase, the patient enters the recovery phase. The most rapid recovery occurs during the first 6 months. During this time, increases in all cognitive functions are generally seen. Patients often continue to recover over a more extended time period, for example, 1 to 3 years. Verbal skills, as reflected by verbal IQ, tend to return earlier than nonverbal ones.

Chronic Sequelae

Consistent with the high probability of selective damage to the frontal and temporal areas, the most usual sequelae to closed head injury are memory deficits (Lezak, 1976; Klove and Cleeland, 1972; Fuld and Fisher, 1977), losses in higher adaptive functions (Lezak, 1976), and personality changes (Lezak, 1976; Damasio, 1979). Residual deficits are often subtle (Klove and Cleeland, 1972; Groher, 1977;

Gronwal and Wrightson, 1974). Only a relatively thorough neuropsychological assessment can detect residual deficits (Dikmen and Reitan, 1978). However, it is just those deficits which can prevent successful return to work or school: premature attempts to resume such activities can seriously delay or impede recovery. Consequently, neuropsychological assessment is essential to enlightened planning.

Memory.   Immediate or sensory memory, such as that tested by digit span, is often intact even in an individual with a significant memory disturbance. Long-term memory also appears to be relatively resistant to disturbance. It is the intermediate or short-term memory for new information which is most likely to show deficits following closed head trauma (Watson and Heilman, 1975). Consequently, Wechsler Memory Scale scores are generally affected (Brooks, 1976). In addition, the more complex the material, the less likely it is to be retained by brain-damaged individuals. Finally, if frontal areas are damaged, the patient may also display a peculiar memory disturbance called "forgetting to remember" (Watson and Heilman, 1975). The patient fails to initiate retrieval of information when appropriate, but can retrieve if cued to do so. The patient can remember but may not try.

Adaptive functions.   Cognitive functions (variously called biological intelligence, higher adaptive functions, abstract reasoning, or problem-solving skills) have been related to frontal-lobe functioning. Patients who have frontal lesions may display adequate IQ scores but be totally unable to deal with new and complex situations rapidly and appropriately. They lack the ability to "think on their feet." This may be especially apparent in impaired performance on the Category Test or Part B of the Trail Making Test of the Halstead-Reitan Battery.

Personality disturbances.   A variety of personality changes have been associated with closed head injury. With or without hard evidence of frontal lobe damage, one of the most common effects is the loss of self-regulatory mechanisms. The patient may appear apathetic, showing very little tendency to initiate behavior. At the same time, he or she may be less able to inhibit impulses and may exhibit extreme emotional lability when frustrated or under stress (Damasio, 1979). The patient may function adequately only in very structured situations.

Post-concussion Syndrome

Even after minor injuries, patients may present symptoms such as dizziness, headaches, difficulty in concentration, changes in personality, and memory problems. This condition may not be linked to hard evidence of physical damage and may disappear after a few months. Occasionally, particularly when secondary gains may be present or predisposing personality patterns exist, the symptoms may persist for years. Neuropsychological and personality assessment are helpful in treatment planning for these patients. Affect which is inappropriately cheerful given the nature of the symptoms is especially indicative of a "functional" etiology (Lezak, 1976).

Dementia

Dementia involves a general decline in cognitive functioning beyond that which can be expected on the basis of normal aging. Acute, reversible dementia can result from toxic states, metabolic disorders, electrolyte imbalance, subdural hematoma, and a variety of non-neurological physical disorders (Lipowski, 1975; Eisdorfer and Cohen, 1978). Normal-pressure hydrocephalus produces a reversible dementia that has subtle symptoms of slower onset. Pseudodementia, in which depression, anxiety, or other psychiatric disorders produce signs similar to those of early chronic dementia, is also reversible (Kiloh, 1961; Folstein and McHugh, 1978; Post, 1975). In contrast, Alzheimer's and Huntington's diseases are progressive and irreversible degenerative disorders. Multi-infarct dementia, although not reversible, may involve periods of stabilization and recovery of function between the occurrences of small strokes: the probability of further strokes may be decreased by controlling hypertension. Over 50 percent of dementias are of the primary degenerative or Alzheimer's type (Eisdorfer and Cohen, 1978; Tomlinson et al., 1970); to 17 percent are of the multiinfarct type (Wells, 1977); the remainder are of other etiologies, including reversible processes (Wells, 1977).

Alzheimer's Disease

Alzheimer's disease was described by Alzheimer in 1907. It was considered to be a presenile dementia, occurring before 60 years of age, and distinct from senile dementia, occurring after age 60, and thought to be inevitable. The presenile syndrome was thought to be quite rare; the majority of early dementias were assumed to be of vascular etiology. However, subsequent research indicated that Alzheimer's disease accounts for more than 50 percent of the diagnosed dementias and that no anatomical or behavioral differentiation can be made between presenile and senile dementia (Eisdorfer and Cohen, 1978).

Alzheimer's disease involves characteristic changes in the cellular structure of the brain which occur to a lesser degree in normal aging: senile plaques, neurofibrillary tangles, and granulovacuolar degeneration (Tomlinson et al., 1970; Blessed et al., 1968; Tomlinson et al., 1968; Wells, 1978). Typically, the brain shrinks in size, resulting in an increase in the size of the ventricles (Wells, 1978). There also are changes in the concentrations of various neurotransmitters in the brain (Davies, 1977; Perry and Perry, 1977). Behaviorally, the changes are equally striking. A classic description of the behavior associated with Alzheimer's disease follows (Mayer-Gross et al., 1960):

The disease usually begins with an *impairment of memory* for recent events and a *failure of efficiency* in the usual activities of the patient's life. Belongings are mislaid, appointments forgotten. A tidy, meticulous man begins to walk in a daze, an efficient housewife lets the soup evaporate (Mayer-Gross et al., 1960, p. 489).

Neuropsychologically, the pattern which emerges depends on the progress and severity of the disease. In the early stages, there is a consistent and significant loss of memory functions disproportionate to other cognitive deficits such as verbal abilities and problem-solving skills. The patient's IQ scores decrease over time, but the initial loss is subtle. Later, a loss in higher adaptive functioning and a decrease in inhibitory functions related to frontal lobe degeneration often occurs. Aphasia, constructional apraxia, and personality changes appear. There are deficits at this point on the majority of neuropsychological tests, including the WAIS. Finally, the patient becomes severely incapacitated in all areas of functioning and is not testable.

There is always the danger of a false–positive diagnosis of dementia in elderly patients. Pseudodementia can be easily mistaken for early Alzheimer's disease.

Pseudodementia

Pseudodementia is a psychiatric disturbance which mimics early signs of Alzheimer's disease, such as decreases in problem-solving skills and memory deficits. Studies of the frequency of pseudodementia among patients diagnosed with Alzheimer's or chronic brain syndrome report that 20 to 42 percent of the patients sampled show no deterioration over time. In fact, they have psychiatric disorders, often depression (Dorfman, 1967; Marsden and Harrison, 1972; Nott and Fleminger, 1975).

Differentiation between depression and dementia is difficult because of the similarity of their symptoms, and because depression frequently occurs in the early stages of Alzheimer's disease (Ciompi, 1968; Gustafson and Hagberg, 1975; Katzman and Karasu, 1975). Some studies estimate that 50 percent of their demented patients are depressed (Katzman and Karasu, 1975; Liston, 1977). A valid differentiation between Alzheimer's disease and pseudodementia is essential, since pseudodementia generally is treatable.

Depressed patients show milder cognitive impairments than demented patients. In addition, pseudodemented patients show no pathognomonic signs such as aphasia, apraxia, agraphia, and so on. Unfortunately, this can also be said of many early Alzheimer patients (Nott and Fleminger, 1975). Further, psychiatric patients may improve in performance on repeated testing, whereas demented patients generally do not (Walton, 1958). A careful history can be illuminating, especially if there is a history of psychiatric disorder. Treatment for depression will result in improved cognitive functioning for both demented and pseudodemented patients

(Sternberg and Jarnik, 1976). However, demented patients will continue to display some impairment, thereby clarifying the diagnosis.

Multi-Infarct Dementia

Multi-infarct dementia occurs in 7 to 17 percent of dementia cases (Wells, 1977). It consists of small, occlusive strokes that occur in small vessels. Since the infarctions may produce areas of destruction anywhere in the brain, the neuropsychological pattern is, by definition, a variable one. Patients may retain good general abilities, adaptive functions, and memory, while clearly suffering from discrete deficits, such as suppressions in one of more of the sensory modalities under double, simultaneous stimulation. Decreases on the WAIS and Wechsler Memory Scale are much less severe in multi-infarct dementia than in Alzheimer's disease (Perez et al., 1975; Perez et al., 1975). Further, while Alzheimer's course is a consistent decline, multi-infarct dementia shows discrete episodes with stabilization or some recovery of function between episodes.

Since the behavioral and medical course of the disease is stepwise, the rehabilitation potential for multi-infarct dementia is more promising from both the medical and psychological viewpoint. Appropriate medical care may reduce the probability of further damage and decline. Cognitive retraining strategies, such as memory-enhancement techniques, may assist the patient in remaining a productive member of society.

Studies have illustrated the use of memory enhancement techniques (Crovitz, 1979; Jones, 1974; Patton, 1972). While the problems of generalization and reduced learning in the brain-damaged patient are yet to be resolved, these techniques do appear promising. Among the various procedures that have been used are:

1. visual mnemonics, in which the patient creates a visual image, usually bizarre, of the thing(s) to be remembered
2. pegging, in which verbal "pegs" (one = bun; two = shoe, etc.) are created on which to visually "hang" lists of things to be remembered
3. active rehearsal and retrieval strategies
4. reviewing material at increasingly larger time intervals

Normal Pressure Hydrocephalus

Normal pressure hydrocephalus involves a temporary increase in cerebrospinal fluid (CSF) pressure, followed by a return to normal CSF pressure as alternate routes of absorption are activated. Although the ventricles remain distended, the usual effects of an increased intracranial pressure, such as papilledema or blinding headaches, may not occur. Cognitive abilities may be well-preserved, although the typical symptom triad is confusion, ataxia, and incontinence (Wells, 1978). The initial build-up in pressure can be produced by three causes: obstruction in CSF flow, decreased CSF absorption, and increased CSF production.

In early normal pressure hydrocephalus, the patient is in no obvious acute medical distress. He or she may present with medical and behavioral symptoms that resemble Alzheimer's disease, such as an increased ventricular size and decreased memory function. However, patients with normal pressure hydrocephalus rarely display the profound and consistent memory disturbance characteristic of Alzheimer's. If the patient is not seriously confused, there may be only a few deficits on neuropsychological tests. The successful implantation of a shunt to drain fluid can prevent further damage or progression of the disorder.

Huntington's Disease

Huntington's disease is a slowly progressive, inherited, and degenerative disorder. It is transmitted through an autosomal dominant gene; each of the offspring of a Huntington's patient has a 50 percent chance of developing the disorder. The symptoms usually begin after the twenties and thirties. Consequently, patients typically have children before they know whether they are transmitting the disease. The most marked neuronal changes occur in the caudate nucleus and putamen (basal ganglia), where neuronal degeneration leads to ventricular dilation. Later in the course of the disease, there are variable amounts of degeneration in the cortex and thalamus (Caine et al., 1978). Because of its initial and primary locus in the basal ganglia, it has recently been grouped with Parkinson's disease, progressive supranuclear palsy, and thalamic disorders, as a subcortical dementia, although cortical involvement invariably occurs at some point in the course of the disease (McHugh and Folstein, 1975; Joynt and Shoulson, 1979).

There typically are four components to Huntington's disease: choreiform movements, psychiatric symptoms, apathy, and cognitive deficits. Any of the first three may present first in the affected patient (Caine et al., 1978; McHugh and Folstein, 1975; Joynt and Shoulson, 1979). The latter three symptoms will be discussed most fully here, since the movement disorder has no direct implications for cognitive functioning.

Psychiatric Symptoms

A significant portion of Huntington's disease patients display major psychiatric symptoms sometime during the course of their illness, ranging from anxiety and irritability to psychotic episodes, including schizophrenia-like symptoms, mania, or psychotic depression (Caine et al., 1978; McHugh and Folstein, 1975; Joynt and Shoulson, 1979). It is not known whether the psychiatric symptoms are reactions to the stress of Huntington's and are consistent with premorbid personality patterns, or whether they are the direct result of neuropathologic changes associated with the disease (Caine et al., 1978).

Suicide is a definite possibility among depressed Huntington's patients. Those Huntington patients who are depressed respond well to medication and electroconvulsive therapy, and that manic depressives respond well to phenothiazines, but not lithium (McHugh and Folstein, 1975). Patients may be extremely sensitive to rapid changes in medication, exhibiting such symptoms as incontinence, hypomania, somnolence, and disorientation (Caine et al., 1978). Given the risk of suicide in this population, treatment for depression is especially warranted, but it must be approached with caution in terms of dosages and careful monitoring of patient reactions.

The MMPI profiles of Huntington's patients are frequently elevated (Boll et al., 1974; Norton, 1975). Severity of psychopathology on the MMPI tends to correlate highly with severity of cognitive dysfunction (Boll et al., 1974). Psychopathology is not unique to Huntington's patients; however, as it appears with about equal frequency among heterogeneous groups of brain damaged patients (Boll et al., 1974; Norton, 1975).

Apathy

Apathy has repeatedly been observed in Huntington's patients. Its severity increases as cognitive impairment increases. It may alternate with periods of restlessness, irritability, and even violent outbursts. This apathetic appearance is attributed to problems in planning, structuring, and initiating ideas and activity (Caine et al., 1978). Patients complained of being overwhelmed by too much information and failed to spontaneously initiate activity. Patients were able, however, to sustain interest and participation in structured activities. Although they showed pride in projects they completed, they rarely worked on them independently. Strong emotional involvement also tended to counteract the apparent apathy. For example, opportunities to leave the hospital sometimes brought forth unsuspected disabilities. These findings suggest that apathy is at least partially due to difficulties in sorting information and in sufficiently organizing that information to begin an activity.

Cognitive Deficits

Cognitive deficits in Huntington's disease patients are progressive and generalized (McHugh and Folstein, 1975; Aminoff et al., 1975). Early in the course of the disease, there may be slightly greater deficits in right parietal lobe constructional abilities and detailed memories than in other functions (Caine et al., 1978; Butters et al., 1978). As impairment progresses, the discrepancy between verbal and performance IQ scores grows, with relative sparing of verbal skills (McHugh and Folstein, 1975; Norton, 1975; Butters et al., 1978). Performance on Halstead-Reitan Battery measures becomes uniformly impaired and is considerably in excess of deficits revealed by the WAIS (Boll et al., 1974; Norton, 1975). Finally, overall declines in all IQ and neuropsychologic test scores grow in severity, until the patient becomes untestable.

Given the increasingly pervasive cognitive losses and the apathy found in these patients, considerable supervision is required at some point in the disease process. The vast majority of families eventually must make decisions about institutional care for these patients.

Parkinson's Disease

Parkinson's disease has several diverse etiologies, including encephalitis, arteriosclerosis, ingestion of major tranquilizers, various toxic reactions, some metabolic disorders, and some degenerative disorders. In idiopathic parkinsonism the etiology is unknown. Neuropathologically, parkinsonism consists of depigmentation and neuronal loss in the substantia nigra and a decrease in dopamine levels in the basal ganglia. Consequently, it is frequently treated with levodopa, a precursor to dopamine, which crosses the blood-brain barrier. Previous less-successful treatments included a variety of anticholinergic drugs, thalamotomy, and pallidectomy (Pincus and Tucker, 1978).

There are three major motor features in parkinsonism. *Tremor* occurs primarily when the patient is at rest and decreases during voluntary movement. *Rigidity* results from increased muscle tone in antagonistic muscle groups. It produces a stooped posture, with slight flexion of the knees, hips, neck, and elbows. Patients complain of weakness; in reality, they need extra effort to overcome the increased muscle tone. *Bradykinesia* is difficulty in initiating and sometimes terminating movement. For example, parkinsonians have trouble beginning to walk, and then may run into a wall before they are able to stop. Levodopa typically reduces rigidity and bradykinesia and somewhat alleviates tremor (Pincus and Tucker, 1978).

Affective changes noted in some parkinsonians include apparent apathy and depression (Pincus and Tucker, 1978; Reitan and Boll, 1971; Talland, 1962; Loranger et al., 1972). However, it is difficult to assess the presence of depression since these patients are also hypokinetic and have "masked" faces. It is not known whether the depression is a reaction to the disease, a direct result of neuropathological processes, or due to decreases in serotonin levels as a result of treatment with levodopa (Pincus and Tucker, 1978).

There is some disagreement concerning the cognitive changes found in Parkinson's disease. They are certainly less frequent than those found in Huntington's disease. Impairment for some patients has been reported for a wide variety of measures (Reitan and Boll, 1971; Loranger et al., 1972; Riklan and Levita, 1969; Riklan et al., 1976), while other studies have found only minimal deficits (Talland, 1962). Those parkinsonians with more severe motor symptoms tend to show greater cognitive deficits (Loranger et al., 1972; Riklan and Levita, 1969).

There are several possible reasons for the disagreement among studies of cognitive functioning. Different etiologies may lead to different cognitive changes; Riklan and Levita note that post-encephalitic patients most often show cognitive deficits. In addition, some methods of treating movement disorders may contribute to cognitive impairment, although this is less likely with levodopa. Finally, depression and apathy can affect performance on tests of cognitive functioning. However, it is important to be alert to the possibility of cognitive deterioration in parkinsonians, and to accordingly plan patient care.

Multiple Sclerosis

Multiple sclerosis (MS) is a degenerative disease of the central nervous system in which the myelin sheath that coats the neuron process degenerates. The patient has a series of acute attacks followed by partial to complete recovery. Although there are some indications that precipitating internal events, such as high fever or emotional disturbance, may trigger an attack, the patient and physician typically are unable to predict the disease's course and rate of progression. There is no known MS treatment at this time (Walton, 1977). The etiology is also unknown, but it is thought not to be genetic. Those born in colder climates have a higher incidence of MS, even when they later move to warmer areas.

Medical diagnosis of MS in its early stages is extremely difficult. Symptoms often are obscure, mild, and transitory. Further, they tend to be the type of symptom that is often associated with hysterical or psychosomatic complaints, such as blurred vision, paresthesia, and transitory incoordination. For this reason, the early MS patient is often labeled as hysteric (Pincus and Tucker, 1978). However, even patients with hysterical and hypochondriachal tendencies are not immune to MS; therefore, the MMPI may not be particularly useful in the early stages in such patients. Further, MS patients are frequently found to have elevations on the neurotic triad of the MMPI (Canter, 1951; Dodge and Dolstoe, 1971; Gilberstadt and Farkas, 1961; Shontz, 1955), although it is not known whether this reflects premorbid personality, a reaction to MS, or an actual component of MS.

After the initial stage, the neuropsychological and behavioral effects of MS are reasonably consistent. The most common finding is motor disturbance. The patient may show bilateral impairment, particularly in complex motor tasks such as the tactual performance test of the Halstead-Reitan Battery. Typically, higher-level adaptive functions are significantly but less profoundly affected than motor functions (Matthews et al., 1970; Reitan et al., 1971; Goldstein and Shelly, 1974; Ross and Reitan, 1955). There may also be visual anomalies (Reitan et al., 1971).

Functional versus Organic Disorders

The ability of neuropsychological tests to differentiate functional and organic disorders was challenged by a 1968 study. The results suggested that the most widely validated neuropsychological test battery, the Halstead-Reitan, is ineffective in differentiating between chronic schizophrenic and chronic organic patients (Watson et al., 1968). However, Heaton et al., in their excellent review, conclude that "all psychiatric diagnostic groups except chronic/process schizophrenics perform better than organics on neuropsychological tests." They suggest that the use of neuropsychological tests is clearly justified in most settings which do not include a high proportion of process or chronic schizophrenics (Heaton et al., 1978). Other studies further indicate that schizophrenia can be differentiated from acute neurological conditions (Heaton et al., 1979), and that neurological patients can be differentiated from some other psychiatric groups (Matthews et al., 1966). Both personality and neuropsychological assessment techniques are recommended when there is a question of a functional disorder (Watson et al., 1978).

Drug Effects

Anti-seizure medication has relatively benign effects on neuropsychological test performance in adults (Dodrill, 1975; Dodrill, 1975; Dodrill and Troupin, 1977). Dilantin, for example, at normal and high-dosage levels, appears to produce a decrease in motor functioning without the corresponding decrease in higher cortical functions (Dodrill, 1975). Negative effects of other drugs may be even less severe (Dodrill and Troupin, 1977). In contrast, phenobarbitol and its derivatives have been related to decreased levels of verbal learning potential, particularly in children (Matthews and Harley, 1975).

Psychotropic medication either has no effect or a positive effect on neuropsychological test performance (Howard et al., 1975; Heaton et al., 1978). However, with long-term administration, there is "significant positive relationship between the doses of major tranquilizers used and the degree of neuropsychological impairment in chronic schizophrenics . . ." (Heaton et al., 1978). The incidence of tardive dyskinesia after chronic phenothiazine use is well-documented and supports aforementioned conclusion.

SUMMARY

We have described some variables which influence performance on neuropsychological tests, and some patterns of impairment associated with various neurological disorders. There is a wide variety of tests available today which are specifically designed to answer questions about a person's cognitive functioning and neurological status (Reitan and Davison, 1974; Golden et al., 1978; Lezak, 1976). This is a vast improvement over the standard test battery of WAIS, Rorschach, and Bender-Gestalt, and vague questions about "organicity." It is possible to provide a relatively comprehensive description of an individual's strengths and deficits, to describe the etiology and locus of some neurologic lesions, and, in many instances, to make broad prognostic statements. However, we still lack a meaningful description of brain function and dysfunction. For example, constructional abilities are no doubt dependent on a variety of diverse functions; constructional apraxia may occur through any of these functional systems. It is probably not the "inability to make something" which is the most meaningful deficit in a given patient, but a deficit in visual analysis or in visuomotor integration that disrupts construction and several other measurable skills. Our current vocabulary and tests do not reflect brain–behavior relationships very well. More meaningful ways of describing functions and dysfunctions, and of evaluating them, will only come with increased understanding of these relationships. Therefore, it will evolve slowly. Understanding the relationship between the brain and developing behavior in children is an especially large challenge.

We can now measure recovery of function through repeated neuropsychological evaluations; it remains for us to accurately predict and control recovery. Concerted efforts are beginning in the development of cognitive retraining programs aimed at cognitive deficits and personality changes.

Due to the complexity of the brain–behavior relationship, fairly extensive training is required for a specialization in clinical neuropsychology. The general clinician may not want to assume responsibility for detailed neuropsychological assessment. However, through workshops and a rapidly expanding literature, it is now possible to gain sufficient background to know when a referral for more complete neurological or neuropsychological assessment is warranted.

REFERENCES

Aminoff, M. J., Marshall, J., Smith, E. M., et al. Pattern of intellectual impairment in Huntington's chorea. *Psychol Med*, 1975, *5*, 169–172.

Arrigoni, G., & DeRenzi, E. Constructional apraxia and hemispheric locus of lesion. *Cortex*, 1964, *1*, 170–197.

Bak, J. S., & Greene, R. L. Changes in neuropsychological functioning in aging population. *J Consult Clin Psychol*, 1980, *48*, 395–399.

Baker, A. B. *An outline of clinical neurology*. Dubuque, Iowa: Kendal Hunt, 1958.

Balthazar, E. E., & Morrison, D. H. The use of Wechsler intelligence scales as diagnostic indicators of predominant left-right and indeterminate unilater brain damage. *J Clin Psychol*, 1961, *17*, 161–165.

Banister, R. *Brain's clinical neurology* (Ed. 5). New York: Oxford Medical Publications, 1978.

Barbizet, J. *Human memory and its pathology*. San Francisco: W. H. Freeman, 1970.

Benson, D. F. *Aphasia*. In K. M. Heilman, & E. Valenstein (Eds.), *Clinical Neuropsychology*. New York: Oxford University Press, 1979.

Benton, A. L. Visuoperceptive, visuospatial, and visuoconstructive disorders. In K. M. Heilman, & E. Valenstein, (Eds.), *Clinical neuropsychology*. New York: Oxford University Press, 1979.

Birren, J. E., & Morrison, D. F. Analysis of the WAIS subtests in relation to age and education. *J Gerontol*, 1961, *16*, 363–369.

Blessed, G., Tomlinson, B. E., & Roth, M. The association between quantitative measures of dementia and of senile changes in the cerebral grey matter of elderly subjects. *Br J Psychiatry*, 1968, *114*, 797–811.

Boll, T. J., Heaton, R., & Reitan, R. M. Neuropsychological and emotional correlates of Huntington's chorea. *J Nerv Ment Dis*, 1974, *158*, 61–69.

Botwinick, J. Intellectual abilities. In J. E. Birren, & K. W. Schaie (Eds.), *Handbook of the psychology of aging*. New York: Van Nostrand Reinhold, 1977.

Botwinick, J., & Storandt, M. *Memory, related functions and age*. Springfield, Illinois: Charles C. Thomas, 1974.

Brooks, D. N. Wechsler memory scale performance and its relationship to brain damage after severe closed head injury. *J Neurol Neurosurg Psychiatry,* 1976, *39,* 593–601.

Butters, N., Sax, D., Montgomery, K., et al. Comparison of the neuropsychological deficits associated with early and advanced Huntington's disease. *Arch Neurol,* 1978, *35,* 585–589.

Caine, E. D., Hunt, R. D., Weingartner, H., et al. Huntington's dementia. *Arch Gen Psychiat,* 1978, *35,* 377–384.

Canter, A. MMPI profiles in multiple sclerosis. *J Consult Psychol,* 1951, *15,* 253–256.

Catell, R. B. Theory of fluid and crystallized intelligence: A critical experiment. *J Educ Psychol,* 1963, *54,* 1–22.

Chapman, L. F., & Wolff, H. G. The cerebral hemispheres and the highest integrative function of man. *AMA Arch Neurol,* 1959, *1,* 357–424.

Chusid, J. G., & McDonald, J. J. Correlative neuroanatomy and functional neurology. Los Altos, California: Lange Medical Publications, 1967.

Ciompi, L. On the relations between depression, brain damage and the aging process. In C. Muller, & L. Ciompi (Eds.), *Senile dementia.* Bern, Switzerland: Hans Huber, 1968.

Crovitz, H. F. Memory retraining and brain damaged patients: The airplane list. *Cortex,* 1979, *15,* 131–134.

Damasio, A. The frontal lobes. In K. M. Heilman, & E. Valenstein (Eds.), *Clinical neuropsychology.* New York: Oxford University Press, 1979.

Davies, A. D. M. The influence of age on trail making test performance. *J Clin Psychol,* 1968, *24,* 96–98.

Davies, P. Cholinergic mechanisms in Alzheimer's disease (abstract). *Br J Psychiat,* 1977, *131,* 318–319.

Davison, L. A. Introduction. In R. M. Reitan, & L. A. Davison, (Eds.), *Clinical neuropsychology: Current status and applications.* Washington, D.C.: V. H. Winston & Sons, 1974.

Dikmen, S., & Reitan, R. M. Neuropsychological performance in post-traumatic epilepsy. *Epilepsia,* 1978, *19,* 177–183.

Dodge, G. R., & Dolstoe, R. H. The MMPI in differentiating early multiple sclerosis and conversion hysteria. *Psychol Rep,* 1971, *29,* 155–159.

Dodrill, C. B. Diphenylhydantoin serum levels, toxicity, and neuropsychological performance in patients with epilepsy. *Epilepsia,* 1975, *16,* 593–600.

Dodrill, C. B. Effects of sulthiame upon intellectual, neuropsychological, and social functioning abilities among adult epileptics: Comparison with diphenylhydantoin. *Epilepsia,* 1975, *16,* 617–625.

Dodrill, C. B. Sex differences on the Halstead-Reitan battery and on other neuropsychological measures. *J Clin Psychol,* 1979, *35,* 236–241.

Dodrill, C. B., & Troupin, E. S. Psychotropic effects of carbamazepine in epilepsy: A double blind comparison with phenytoin. *Neurology,* 1977, *27,* 1023–1038.

Doehring, D. G., & Reitan, R. M. Behavioral consequences of brain damage associated with homonymous visual field defects. *J Compar Physiol Psychol,* 1961, *54,* 489–492.

Doppelt, J. E., & Wallace, W. L. Standardization of the Wechsler adult intelligence scale of older persons. *J Abnorm Soc Psychol,* 1955, *51,* 312–320.

Dorfman, W. Is there a "reversible" chronic brain syndrome? *Psychosomatics,* 1967, *8,* 293–295.

Eisdorfer, C., & Cohen, D. The cognitively impaired elderly: Differential diagnosis. In M. Storandt, I. C. Siegler, & M. F. Elias (Eds.), *The clinical psychology of aging*. New York: Plenum Press, 1978.

Eisenson, J. *Adult aphasia*. Englewood Cliffs, New Jersey: Prentice-Hall, 1973.

Fields, F. R. J. Relative effects of brain damage on the Wechsler memory and intelligence quotients. *Dis Nerv Syst*, 1971, *32*, 673–765.

Finlayson, M. A. J., Johnson, K. A., & Reitan, R. M. Relationship of level of education to neuropsychological measures in brain-damaged and nonbrain-damaged adults. *J Consult Clin Psychol*, 1977, *45*, 536–542.

Fitzhugh, K. B., & Fitzhugh, L. C., & Reitan, R. M. Influence of age upon measures of problem solving and experiential background in subjects with long-standing cerebral dysfunction. *J Gerontol*, 1964, *19*, 132–134.

Fitzhugh, K. B., Fitzhugh, L. C., & Reitan, R. M. Wechsler-Bellevue comparisons in groups with "chronic" and "current" lateralized and diffuse brain lesions. *J Consult Psychol*, 1962, *26*, 306–310.

Fitzhugh, K. B., & Fitzhugh, L. C. WAIS results for Ss with longstanding, chronic, lateralized and diffuse cerebral dysfunction. *Percept Mot Skills*, 1964, *19*, 735–739.

Fitzhugh, K. B., Fitzhugh, L. C., & Reitan, R. M. Psychological deficits in relation to acuteness of brain dysfunction. *J Consult Psychol*, 1961, *25*, 61–66.

Folstein, M. F., & McHugh, P. R. Dementia syndrome of depression. In R. Katzman, R. D. Terry, & K. L. Bick (Eds.), *Alzheimer's disease: Senile dementia and related disorders*. New York: Raven Press, 1978.

Fuld, P. A., & Fisher, P. Recovery of intellectual ability after closed head injury. *Devel Med Child Neurology*, 1977, *19*, 495–502.

Geschwind, N. The apraxias and agnosias. In G. A. Talland, & N. C. Waugh (Eds.), *The pathology of memory*. New York: Academic Press, 1969.

Gilberstadt, H., Farkas, E. Another look at MMPI profile types in multiple sclerosis. *J Consult Psychol*, 1961, *25*, 440–444.

Golden, C. J., Hammeke, T. A., Purisch, A. D. Diagnostic validity of a standardized neuropsychological battery derived from Luria's neuropsychological tests. *J Consult Clin Psychol*, 1978, *46*, 1258–1265.

Goldstein, G. Contributions of clinical neuropsychology to psychiatry. In P. E. Logue, & J. M. Schear (Eds.), *Clinical neuropsychology: A multi-disciplinary approach*. Springfield, Illinois: Charles C. Thomas, in press.

Goldstein, G., & Shelly, C. H. Similarities and differences between psychological deficit in aging and brain damage. *J Gerontol*, 1975, *30*, 448–455.

Goldstein, K. *Language and language disturbances*. New York: Grune & Stratton, 1948.

Goldstein, G., & Shelly, C. H. Neuropsychological diagnosis of multiple sclerosis in a neuropsychiatric setting. *J Nerv Ment Dis*, 1974, *158*, 282–290.

Goodglass, H. Aphasiology from clinic to laboratory. Presidential address, International Neuropsychological Society, 1977.

Goodglass, G., & Kaplan, E. *The Assessment of Aphasia and related disorders*. Philadelphia: Lea & Febiger, 1972.

Granick, S., & Friedman, A. S. The effect of education on the decline of psychometric test performance with age. *J Gerontol*, 1967, *22*, 191–195.

Groher, M. Language and memory disorders following closed head trauma. *J Speech Hear Res*, 1977, *20*, 212–223.

Gronwal, D., & Wrightson, P. Delayed recovery of intellectual functioning after minor head injury. *Lancet,* 1974, *2,* 605–609.

Gustafson, L., & Hagberg, B. Dementia with onset in the presenile period. Part II. Emotional behaviour, personality changes and cognitive reduction in presenile dementia: Related to regional cerebral blood flow. *Acta Psychiat Scand,* 1975, supplement *257,* 9–71.

Hall, J. C., & Toal, R. Reliability (internal consistency) of the Wechsler memory scale and correlation with the Wechsler-Bellevue intelligence scale. *J Consult Psychol,* 1957, *21,* 131–135.

Hecaen, H. Clinical symptomatology in right and left hemispheric lesions. In V. B. Mountcastle (Ed.), *Interhemispheric relations and cerebral dominance.* Baltimore, Maryland: The Johns Hopkins Press, 1962.

Hecaen, H., & Albert, M. L. *Human neuropsychology.* New York: Wiley-Interscience, 1978.

Heaton, R. K., Baade, L. E., & Johnson, K. L. Neuropsychological test results associated with psychiatric disorders in adults. *Psychol Bull,* 1978, *85,* 141–162.

Heaton, R. K., Vogt, A. T., Hoehn, M. M., et al. Neuropsychological impairment with schizophrenia vs acute and chronic cerebral lesions. *J Clin Psychol,* 1979, *35,* 46–53.

Heilman, K. M. Neglect and related disorders. In K. M. Heilman, & E. Valenstein (Eds.), *Clinical neuropsychology.* New York: Oxford University Press, 1979.

Heilman, K. M. Apraxia. In K. M. Heilman, & E. Valenstein (Eds.), *Clinical neuropsychology.* New York: Oxford University Press, 1979.

Heilman, K. M. Neuropsychologic changes in the stroke patient. *Geriatrics,* 1974, *29,* 153–160.

Heilman, K. M., & Valenstein, E. *Clinical neuropsychology.* New York: Oxford University Press, 1979.

Hochberg, F. H., & Slotnick, B. Neuropsychologic impairment in astrocytoma survivors. *Neurology,* 1980, *30,* 172–177.

Howard, M. L., Hogan, T. P., & Wright, M. W. The effects of drugs on psychiatric patients' performance on the Halstead-Reitan neuropsychological test battery. *J Nerv Ment Dis,* 1975, *161,* 166–171.

Hulicka, I. M. Age differences in Wechsler memory scale scores. *J Genet Psychol,* 1966, *109,* 135–145.

Jennett, B. Prognosis after head injury. In P. J. Vinken, & G. W. Bruyn (Eds.), *Handbook of clinical neurology,* Vol. 24. New York: American Elsevier, 1976.

Jennett, B., & Teasdale, G. *Management of head injuries.* Philadelphia: F. A. Davis, 1981.

Jones, M. K. Imagery as a mnemonic aid after left temporal lobectomy: Contrast between material-specific and generalized memory disorders. *Neuropsychologia,* 1974, *12,* 21–30.

Joynt, R. F., & Shoulson, I. Dementia. In K. M. Heilman, & E. Valenstein (Eds.), *Clinical neuropsychology.* New York: Oxford University Press, 1979.

Kahn, R. L., & Miller, N. E. Assessment of altered brain function in the aged. In M. Storandt, I. C. Siegler, & M. F. Elias (Eds.), *The clinical psychology of aging.* New York: Plenum Press, 1978.

Katzman, R., & Karasu, T. B. Differential diagnosis of dementia. In W. S. Fields (Ed.), *Neurological and sensory disorders in the elderly.* Miami, Florida: Symposia Specialists, 1975.

Kear-Colwell, J. J., & Heller, M. A normative study of the Wechsler memory scale. *J Clin Psychol*, 1978, *34*, 437–442.

Kiloh, L. G. Pseudo-dementia. *Acta Psychiat Scand*, 1961, *37*, 336–351.

Klisz, D. Neuropsychological evaluation in older persons. In M. Storandt, I. C. Siegler, & M. F. Elias (Eds.), *The clinical psychology of aging*. New York: Plenum Press, 1978.

Klove, H. Relationship of differential electroencephalographic patterns to distribution of Wechsler-Bellevue scores. *Neurology*, 1959, *9*, 871–876.

Klove, H. Validation studies in adult clinical neuropsychology. In R. M. Reitan, & L. A. Davison (Eds.), *Clinical neuropsychology: Current status and applications*. Washington, D.C.: V. H. Winston & Sons, 1974.

Klove, H. & Cleeland, C. S. The relationship of neuropsychological impairment to other indices of severity of head injury. *Scand J Rehab Med*, 1972, *4*, 55–60.

Klove, H., & Fitzhugh, K. B. The relationship of differential EEG patterns to the distribution of Wechsler-Bellevue scores in a chronic epileptic population. *J Clin Psychol*, 1962, *18*, 334–337.

Kupke, T., Lewis, R., & Rennick, P. Sex differences in the neuropsychological functioning of epileptics. *J Consult Clin Psychol*, 1979, *47*, 1128–1130.

LaRue, A., & Jarvik, L. F. Aging and intellectual functioning: Great expectations? In L. F. Jarvik (Ed.), *Aging into the 21st century: Middle agers today*. New York: Gardner Press, 1978.

Levine, D. N., & Mohr, J. P. Language after bilateral cerebral infarctions: Role of the minor hemisphere in speech. *Neurology*, 1979, *29*, 927–938.

Lezak, M. D. *Neuropsychological assessment*. New York: Oxford University Press, 1976.

Lipowski, Z. J. Organic brain syndromes: Overview and classification. In D. F. Benson, & D. Blumer (Eds.), *Psychiatric aspects of neurological disease*. New York: Grune and Stratton, 1975.

Liston, E. H. Occult presenile dementia. *J Nerv Ment Dis*, 1977, *164*, 263–267.

Logue, P. E., & Wyrick, L. Initial validation of Russell's revised Wechsler memory scale: A comparison of normal aging vs dementia. *J Consult Clin Psychol*, 1979, *47*, 176–178.

Loranger, A. W., Goodell, H., McDowell, F. H., et al. Intellectual impairment in Parkinson's syndrome. *Brain*, 1972, *95*, 405–412.

Marsden, C. D., & Harrison, M. J. G. Outcome of investigation of patients with presenile dementia. *Br Med J*, 1972, *2*, 249–252.

Marvel, G. A., Golden, C. J., & Hammeke, T., et al: Relationship of age and education to performance on a standardized version of Luria's neuropsychological tests in different patient populations. *Int J Neurosci*, 1979, *9*, 63–70.

Matarazzo, J. D. Wechsler's measurement and appraisal of adult intelligence. Baltimore, Maryland: Williams and Wilkins Co., 1972.

Matthews, C. G., Cleeland, C. S., & Hopper, C. L. Neuropsychological patterns in multiple sclerosis. *Dis Nerv Syst*, 1970, *31*, 151–170.

Matthews, C. G., Shaw, D. J., & Klove, H. Psychological test performances in neurologic and "pseudo-neurologic" subjects. *Cortex*, 1966, *2*, 244–253.

Matthews, C. G., & Harley, J. P. Cognitive and motor-sensory performance in toxic and nontoxic epileptic subjects. *Neurology*, 1975, *25*, 184–188.

Mayer-Gross, W., Slater, E., & Roth, M. *Clinical psychiatry* (Ed. 2). Baltimore, Maryland: Williams & Wilkins Co., 1960.

McCarty, S. M., Logue, P. E., & Power, D. G., et al: Alternate-form reliability and age-related scores for Russell's revised Wechsler memory scale. *J Consult Clin Psychol,* 1980, *48,* 296–298.

McFie, J. *Assessment of organic intellectual impairment.* London: Academic Press, 1975.

McGlone, J. Sex differences in functional brain asymmetry. *Cortex,* 1978, *14,* 122–128.

McGlone, J., & Kertesz, A. Sex differences in ceregral processing of visuospatial tasks. *Cortex,* 1973, *9,* 313–320.

McHugh, P. R., & Folstein, M. F. Psychiatric syndromes of Huntington's chorea: A clinical and phenomenologic study. In D. F. Benson, & D. Blumer (Eds.), *Psychiatric aspects of neurological disease.* New York: Grune and Stratton, 1975.

Meier, M. J. Some challenges for clinical neuropsychology. In R. M. Reitan, & L. A. Davison (Eds.), *Clinical neuropsychology: Current status and applications.* Washington, D.C.: V. H. Winston & Sons, 1974.

Milner, B. Hemispheric specialization: Scope and limits. In H. O. Schmitt, & F. G. Worden (Eds.), *The neurosciences: Third study program.* Cambridge, Massachusetts: MIT Press, 1974.

Milner, B. Some effects of frontal lobectomy in man. In J. M. Warren, & K. Akert (Eds.), *The frontal granular cortex and behavior.* New York: McGraw-Hill, 1964.

Norton, J. C. Patterns of neuropsychological test performance in Huntington's disease. *J Nerv Ment Dis,* 1975, *161,* 276–279.

Nott, P. N., & Fleminger, J. J. Presenile dementia: The difficulties of early diagnosis. *Acta Psychiat Scand,* 1975, *51,* 210–217.

Overall, J. E., & Gorham, D. R. Organicity versus old age in objective and projective test performance. *J Consult Clin Psychol,* 1972, *39,* 98–105.

Overall, J. E., & Levin, H. S. Correcting for cultural factors in evaluating intellectual deficit on the WAIS. *J Clin Psychol,* 1978, *34,* 910–915.

Parsons, O. A. Clinical neuropsychology, in C. D. Spielberger (Ed.), *Current topics in clinical and community psychology, Vol. 2.*

Patton, E. M. The ancient art of memory. Arch Neurol, 1972, *26,* 25–32.

Perez, L. I., Gay, J. R. A., Taylor, R. L., et al. Patterns of memory performance in the neurologically impaired aged. *J Canad Sci Neurologiques,* 1975, *1,* 347–355.

Perry, E. K., & Perry, R. H. Cholinergic and GABA systems in dementia and normal old age (abstract). *Br J Psychiat,* 1977, *131,* 319.

Piercy, M. The effects of cerebral lesions on intellectual function. *Bri J Psychiatry,* 1964, *110,* 310–352.

Pincus, J. H., & Tucker, G. J. *Behavioral neurology.* New York: Oxford University Press: 1978.

Porch, B. E. *The Porch index of communicative ability.* Palo Alto, California: Consulting Psychologists Press, 1967.

Post, F. Dementia, depression and pseudodementia, In D. F. Benson, & D. Blumer (Eds.), *Psychiatric aspects of neurological disease.* New York: Grune and Stratton, 1975.

Prigatano, G. P. Wechsler memory scale: A selective review of the literature. *J Clin Psychol,* 1978, *34,* 816–832.

Prigatano, G. P., & Parsons, O. A. Relationship of age and education to Halstead test performance in different patient populations. *J Consult Clin Psychol,* 1976, *44,* 527–533.

Reed, H. B. C., & Reitan, R. M. Changes in psychological test performance associated with the normal aging process. *J Gerontol,* 1963, *18,* 271–274.

Reed, H. B. C., & Reitan, R. M. A comparison of the effects of the normal aging process with the effects of organic brain-damage on adaptive abilities. *J Gerontol,* 1963, *18,* 177–179.

Reed, H. B. C., & Reitan, R. M. Intelligence test performances of brain damaged subjects with lateralized motor deficits. *J Consult Psychol,* 1963, *27,* 102–106.

Reitan, R. M. Behavioral manifestation of impaired brain functions in aging. Paper presented at the meeting of the American Psychological Association, 1973.

Reitan, R. M. Certain differential effects of left and right cerebral lesions in human adults. *J Compar Physiol Psychol,* 1955, *48,* 474–477.

Reitan, R. M. The distribution according to age of a psychologic measure dependent upon organic brain dysfunction. *J Gerontol,* 1955, *10,* 338–340.

Reitan, R. M. Methodological problems in clinical neuropsychology. In R. M. Reitan, & I. A. Davison (Eds.), *Clinical Neuropsychology: Current Status and Application.* Washington, D.C.: V. H. Winston & Sons, 1974.

Reitan, R. M. Objective behavioral assessment in diagnosis and prediction. In A. L. Benton (Ed.), *Behavioral change in cerebrovascular disease.* New York: Harper & Row, 1970.

Reitan, R. M. Psychologic changes associated with aging and with cerebral damage. *Mayo Clinic Proc,* 1967, *42,* 653–673.

Reitan, R. M. Psychological testing after craniocerebral injury. In J. R. Youmans (Ed.), *Neurological surgery,* Vol. 1. Philadelphia: W. B. Saunders, 1973.

Reitan, R. M. The relationship of the Halstead-Reitan impairment index and the Wechsler-Bellevue total weighted score to chronological age (abstract). *J Gerontol,* 1956, *11,* 447.

Reitan, R. M. A research program on the psychological effects of brain lesions in human beings. In N. R. Ellis (Ed.), *International review of research in mental retardation.* New York: Academic Press, 1966.

Reitan, R. M., & Boll, T. J. Intellectual and cognitive functions in Parkinson's disease. *J Consult Clin Psychol,* 1971, *37,* 364–369.

Reitan, R. M., Davison, L. A. (Eds.), *Clinical neuropsychology: Current status and applications.* Washington, D.C.: V. H. Winston & Sons, 1974.

Reitan, R. M., Reed, J. C., & Dykken, M. L. Cognitive, psychomotor and motor correlates of multiple sclerosis. *J Nerv Ment Dis,* 1971, *153,* 218–224.

Riklan, M., & Levita, E. *Subcortical correlates of human behavior.* Baltimore, Maryland: Williams & Wilkins Co., 1969.

Riklan, M., Whelihan, W., & Cullinan, T. Levodopa and psychometric test performance in parkinsonism—five years later. *Neurology,* 1976, *26,* 173–179.

Ross, A. T., & Reitan, R. M. Intellectual and affective functions in multiple sclerosis. *AMA Arch Neurol Psychiat,* 1955, *73,* 663–677.

Russell, E. W. A multiple scoring method for the assessment of complex memory functions. *J Consult Clin Psychol,* 1975, *43,* 800–809.

Russell, E. W. Revision of the Wechsler Memory Scale: An attempt to clarify ambiguities in scoring. *J Clin Neuropsychol,* 1979, *1,* 343–345.

Russell, E. W., Neuringer, C., & Goldstein G. *Assessment of brain damage: A neuropsychological key approach.* New York: Wiley-Interscience, 1970.

Satz, P. Specific and nonspecific effects of brain lesions in man. *J Abnorm Psychol,* 1966, *71,* 65–70.

Schuell, H. Minnesota test for the differential diagnosis of aphasia. Minneapolis, Minnesota: University of Minnesota Press, 1957.

Shontz, E. C. MMPI responses of patients with multiple sclerosis. *J Consult Psychol*, 1955, *19*, 74.

Siegler, I. C. The terminal drop hypothesei: Fact or artifact? *Exper Aging Res*, 1975, *1*, 169–185.

Siegler, I. C., McCarty, S. M., & Logue, P. E. Cross-sectional and longitudinal patterns of three Wechsler memory scale subtests. *Manuscript submitted for publication*, 1980.

Siegler, I. C., & Botwinick, J. A long-term longitudinal study of intellectual ability of older adults: The matter of selective subject attribution. *J Gerontol*, 1979, *34*, 242–245.

Smith, A. Intellectual functions in patients with lateralized frontal tumors. *J Neurol Neurosurg Psychiatry*, 1966, *29*, 52–59.

Smith, A. Neuropsychological testing in neurological disorders. In W. J. Friedlander (Ed.), *Advances in neurology*. New York: Raven Press, 1975.

Smith, A. Verbal and nonverbal test performance of patients with "acute" lateralized brain lesions (tumor). *J Nervous Mental Disorders*, 1966, *141*, 517–523.

Smith, A. Changing effects of frontal lesions in man. *J Neurol Neurosurg Psychiatry*, 1964, *27*, 511–515.

Smith, A., & Burklund, C. W. Dominant hemispherectomy: Preliminary report on neuropsychological sequelae. *Science*, 1966, *153*, 1280–1282.

Smith, A., & Sugar, O. Development of above normal language and intelligence 21 years after left hemispherectomy. *Neurology*, 1975, *25*, 813–818.

Sperry, R. W. Brain bisection and mechanisms of consciousness. In J. C. Eccles (Ed.), *Brain and conscious experience*. New York: Springer-Verlag, 1966.

Sternberg, D. E., & Jarvik, M. E. Memory functions in depression. *Arch Gen Psychiat*, 1976, *33*, 219–224.

Talland, G. A. Cognitive function in Parkinson's disease. *J Nerv Ment Dis*, 1962, *135*, 196–205.

Teuber, H-L. Effects of brain wounds implicating right or left hemisphere in man: Hemisphere differences and hemisphere interaction in vision, audition and somesthesis. In E. B. Mountcastel (Ed.), *Interhemispheric relations and cerebral dominance*. Baltimore, Maryland: The Johns Hopkins Press, 1962.

Tomlinson, B. E., Blessed, G., & Roth, M. Observations on the brains of demented old people. *J Neurol Sciences*, 1970, *11*, 205–242.

Tomlinson, B.E., Blessed, G., & Roth, M. Observations on the brains of nondemented old people. *J Neurol Sciences*, 1968, *7*, 331–356.

Valenstein, E., & Heilman, K. M. Emotional disorders resulting from lesions of the central nervous system. In K. M. Heilman, & E. Valenstein (Eds.), *Clinical neuropsychology*. New York: Oxford University Press, 1979.

Vega, A., & Parsons, O. A. Relationship between sensory-motor deficits and WAIS verbal and performance scores in unilateral brain damage. *Cortex*, 1969, *5*, 229–241.

Vega, A., & Parsons, O. A. Cross-validation of the Halstead-Reitan tests for brain damage. *J Consult Psychol*, 1967, *31*, 619–625.

Wechsler memory scale in psychiatric patients over 65. *J Ment Sci*, 1958, *104*, 1111–1118.

Walton, J. N. *Brain's diseases of the nervous system* (Ed. 8). New York: Oxford Medical Publications, 1977.

Watson, C. G., Davis, W. E., & Gasser, R. B. Separation of organics from depressives with ability and personality based tests. *J Clin Psychol,* 1978, *34,* 393–397.

Watson, R. T., & Heilman, K. M. The differential diagnosis of dementia. *Geriatrics* 1975, *29,* 145–154.

Watson, C. G., Thomas, R. W., Anderson, D., et al. Differentiation of organics from schizophrenics at two chronicity levels by use of the Reitan-Halstead organic test battery. *J Consult Clin Psychol,* 1968, *32,* 679–684.

Wechsler, D. *Manual for the Wechsler adult intelligence scale.* New York: Psychological Corporation, 1955.

Wechsler, D. A standardized memory scale for clinical use. *J Psychol,* 1945, *19,* 87–95.

Wells, C. E. Chronic brain disease: An overview. *Am J Psychiat,* 1978, *135,* 1–13.

Wells, C. E. Diagnostic evaluation and treatment in dementia. In C. E. Wells (Ed.), *Dementia,* Ed. 2. Philadelphia: F. A. Davis. 1977.

Wilson, R. S., Rosenbauer, G., & Brown, G. The problem of premorbid intelligence in neuropsychological assessment. *J Clin Neuropsychol,* 1979, *1,* 49–53.

Wood, W. G., Elias, M. F., Pentz, C. A., et al: Age differences in neuropsychological performance among healthy well-educated subjects. Paper read at the meeting of the Gerontological Society, 1979.

Ziesat, H. A., Logue, P. E., & McCarty, S. M. Psychological measurement of memory deficits in dialysis patients. *Percept Mot Skills,* 1980, *50,* 311–318.

Patrick A. Boudewyns

6

Assessment of Headache

Headache is man's most common pain complaint. Of a sample of 1,809 volunteers, 50.2 percent of the females and 48.9 percent of the males reported having, at some time in their lives, disabling and severe headache (Ziegler, 1976). Both the plethora of over-the-counter headache remedies and media advertisements for headache remedies support this assertion. Since most headaches are not the result of an underlying disease process, treatment usually involves prescription of pain medication. Thus, patients who suffer from chronic, severe, and disabling headache run risks that are inherent with any chronic drug usage. Recent studies of behavioral evaluation and treatment of headache appear to offer effective non-drug alternatives to the traditional medical approach (Diamond et al., 1978; Wickramasekera, 1973; Budzynski et al., 1973; Cox et al., 1975; Holroyd and Andrasik, 1978; Mitchell and White, 1977). This chapter will first describe the common medical diagnostic nomenclatures for headache, and then contrast them with a behavioral approach to the assessment and management of headache.

MEDICAL DIAGNOSIS OF HEADACHE

The terminology used to describe the various types of headaches has never been consistent. In 1962 an attempt to put order into the area was made by an Ad Hoc Committee on *Classification of Headache* of the National Institute of Neurological Diseases and Blindness (Friedman et al., 1962). The Committee's report resulted in the rather complex nomenclature shown in Table 6-1.

Diamond and Medina tried to simplify things by classifying headaches into three categories: (1) *traction and inflammatory headaches,* caused by identifiable diseases or disorders, such as allergies, infections, and cervical osteoarthritis; (2) *vascular-type headaches,* or migraine, cluster, facial, opthalmoplegic, hemiplegic, toxic, and hypertensive headaches; and (3) *psychogenic headaches,* including depression, conversion, delusion, and anxiety headaches (Diamond and Medina, 1976). In the latter classification, *depression* and *anxiety* headache are used instead of *muscle contraction headache.* Obviously, Diamond's classification implies more of a psychosomatic or psychogenic component to some common headache types than is suggested by the Ad Hoc Committee's report.

Regardless of the classification, more than 90 percent of all headaches seen by the clinician are benign, that is, "involve psychogenic or psychophysiologic factors rather than permanent structural changes or serious illness" (Diamond, 1976). These headaches are considered "functional," while those that result from an underlying disease process are termed "organic" (Miller, 1979). Because the quantity of organic disorders or diseases that may present as headache is considerable and often difficult to diagnose, a thorough medical and neurological examination is required. This is of particular importance if there has been no history of headache, or if there has been some change in the nature of the pain of a diagnosed functional headache.

To allow appreciation for the complexity of the problem, the following are only

Table 6-1

The 1962 Ad Hoc Committee's Classification of Headache

Vascular headache of migraine type
    "Classic" migraine
    "Common" migraine
    "Cluster" headache
    "Hemiplegic" and "opthalmoplegic" migraine
    "Lower half" headache
Muscle contraction headache
Combined headache: Vascular and muscle contraction
Headache of nasal vasomotor reaction
Headache of delusional conversion or hypochondrical states
Non-migranous vascular headaches
Traction headache
Headache due to overt cranial inflammation
Headache due to disease of ocular, aural, nasal and sinusal, dental, or other cranial or neck structures
Cranial neuritides
Cranial neuralgias

(Adapted from Friedman, A. P., Finley, K. H., Graham, J. R., et al. Classification of headache. Journal of the American Medical Association, 1962, *179,* 717–718.)

some of the etiologies that may present as headache: chronic nasal allergy (sinus-itis), primary and secondary polycythemia, subdural hematoma, pituitary tumor, nasopharyngeal neoplasm, posteria fossa lesion, basilar invagination, chronic mastoiditis, bony anomalies (anywhere in the head), carotid or middle-cerebral arterial occlusion, vestibrobasilar occlusion, venous sinus thrombosis, cerebral hemorrhage, subarachnoid hemorrhage, cerebral aneurysm, glaucoma, dental path-ology, neuralgia (occipital and facial), meningitis, encephalitis, systemic infec-tions, and hypertension. If no underlying cause can be found using the Ad Hoc Committee's nomenclature, several diagnostic options are available. These in-clude: (1) several types of "vascular headache of the migraine type," (2) mus-cle contraction headache, (3) delusional conversion or hypochondriacal headache, and (4) combined headache. Common alternative terms for these syndromes will be noted in the following discussion.

Migraine Headache

As shown in Table 6-1, the Ad Hoc Committee defined two types of migraine, *classic* and *common*. Estimates of prevalence vary, but approximately 8 to 12 per-cent of patients seen in general practice present with migraine. Most researchers agree that about twice as many women as men suffer from this type of headache. Patients usually describe the pain of migraine as "throbbing" or "stabbing." It is often accompanied by nausea and vomiting, and usually is "unilateral," with pain usually recurring on the same side of the head from one attack to the next.

Classic migraine usually involves preheadache symptoms known as the prodromal phase. This phase can include unusual sensory experiences (visual "flashes," or scotoma), with increased sympathetic activity. Prodromes may last from a few minutes to several hours. Physiologically, the cause of the symp-toms is thought to be vasoconstriction of the intracranial vessels, which, in turn, reduces oxygen and increases carbon dioxide and lactic acid levels in the brain (ischemia). The headache phase itself involves vasodilation which may cause what Graham terms a "rebound effect," where "sympathetically powerful systemic vessels contract and create a rebound rise in the blood pressure which causes the vessels to fill excessively and pulsate wildly" (Graham, 1976).

In common migraine, the prodromal phase is not well-defined, and usually consists of vague autonomic experiences. The headache phase is much the same as in classic migraine, except that it is less often unilateral. Common migraine is often associated with events or environmental stimuli, such as certain days of the week or time in the menstrual cycle. Common migraines are usually less severe, although attacks may last longer. Both types of migraine tend to start after pu-berty and lessen in frequency and intensity after middle age; menopause may bring relief for some women.

There is little evidence for a well-defined personality type for migraine suf-ferers, but in general they are described as obsessive, perfectionistic, goal-oriented, and rigid.

Heredity plays a role in migraine. From 50 to 60 percent of migraine patients report that at least one parent also suffered from the disorder (Lance and Anthony, 1966). Yet, when studies of twins are reviewed, evidence for a genetic factor is less impressive. Certainly, genetics are not the sole determinant in migraine (Refsum, 1968).

The Ad Hoc Committee defined three other types of "vascular headache of the migraine type": hemiplegic and/or opthalmoplegic migraine, lower-half headache, and cluster headache (Friedman et al., 1962). The first two are rare. Both are "headaches featured by sensory and motor phenomenon which persists during and after headache," implying perhaps a very complex physiological pattern of the intracranial vasodilation and constriction occurring at the same time. Lower-half headache is just as implied by the term; headache occurring in the lower face and caused by a vascular mechanism. Cluster headache is much more common, and presents some special difficulties for behavioral assessment.

Cluster Headache

The prodromal phase for cluster headache (also known as *Horton's cephalgia and histamine cephalgia),* is either undefined or nonexistent, but the headache is often accompanied by autonomic responses such as flushing, sweating, rhinorrhea, and lacramation. The most distinct feature of cluster headaches are that they occur in groups separated by long remissions. The remissions make it difficult to research the effects of treatment, since a long follow-up is necessary. Unlike migraine, cluster headache occurs much more commonly in men than in women. Interestingly, Graham has pointed out that those women who do suffer from cluster headache usually have masculine features. Psychologically, cluster headache sufferers are described as needing to appear strong, masculine, and assertive, as a defense against an underlying tendency to be passive and dependent (Graham, 1976).

Muscle Contraction Headache

The most common form of functional headache is the muscle contraction, or tension, headache. The cause of this type of head pain is presumed to be continued involuntary contraction of the scalp and neck muscles, although muscle contraction can be a factor in any headache type. As already noted, tension headache is so often accompanied by emotional upset that some clinicians prefer the terms "anxiety" or "depression" headache to describe the same syndrome (Diamond and Medina, 1976). Certainly, headache is one of several symptoms often seen in severely depressed and anxious patients.

Muscle contraction headache is most often described as "band-like" or involving pressure or constriction of the scalp. It is usually located in the occipital region, and may extend into the neck and posterior shoulder girdle musculature or up into the temples. It usually occurs in conjunction with stressful interpersonal situations, although some patients complain of waking up with a tension headache.

"Wake-up headaches" are the most severe, and when they occur patients can expect little relief for the rest of the day. Expectancy factors may play a role here. The expectation that the pain will persist may actually increase tension and thereby increase pain; producing a vicious cycle of pain and anxiety feeding each other.

In its severe state, muscle contraction headache is described in terms similar to those used by vascular headache sufferers and is accompanied by nausea. Psychologically, tension headache sufferers may be described as depressed and anxious. Often, they may appear overly dependent on their spouse, friends, and relatives.

Hysterical (Conversion), Hypochondrical, and Delusional Headache

Hysterical headache is usually described as severe and constant. Incredibly, it may last for years, night and day, with no change in intensity. It is often associated with other unusual symptoms, such as tingling sensations or numbness, and may be described as extending out from the head into the arms and back. Complaints are often vague. After interviewing hysterical headache patients, one may come away feeling that while these patients talk much about the severity of the pain, they still appear to have an attitude of indifference about it. This *la-belle-indifference,* as it is sometimes labeled, is more commonly seen in classic examples of hysterical conversion (e.g., glove anesthesia). If distinctions are made, *la-belle-indifference* would probably not be found in hypochondrical patients.

The concept of "secondary gain" is often used to explain hysterical pain. The assumption is that the patient's pain serves to control others, especially relatives and close friends, and helps patients meet their dependency needs. Patients with hysterical pain are seen as having repressed anger which is converted (thus the term "conversion" headache) to somatic symptoms rather than being directly expressed. Regardless of theory, most hysterical types do have problems with direct expression of emotion and effective treatment must address itself to this.

Two other factors distinguish hysterical headaches. As with migraine, there is a high familial incidence of headache, and hysterical headaches occur more commonly in women than in men. If the dynamic interpretation of repressed rage and anger is true, we might expect to see a reduction in the number of female patients diagnosed as having hysterical headache, as direct expression of negative feelings by women becomes more accepted in the culture.

Delusional headache is marked by its bizarre nature. Often the location of delusional pain is unusual (e.g., a small spot in the center of the head). Patients may also describe the pain in a bizarre manner (e.g., "It feels like my head is full of snakes"), and they may be inconsistent in their description from one day to the next. Delusional pain also tends to "move around" in its bodily location. These patients are usually described as having "borderline" personalities, may have a thought disorder, and often carry diagnosis of schizophrenia.

Unfortunately, all of these psychological categories are too often (mis)used to describe troublesome patients who do not respond well to treatment, and who continue to seek medical help without success (''crocks''). When considering a diagnosis of hysterical or delusional headache, it may be helpful to realize that *all* pain, regardless of cause, will have both psychological (psychogenic) and physiological (somatogenic) influences. Understanding how these influences interact to account for the patient's sensitivity to pain is a difficult but important diagnostic consideration. For instance, although hysterical headache has a larger psychogenic component than classical migraine, this does not mean that pain is not experienced by both types of patients; or that the hysterical patient is malingering. Some professionals dismiss hysterical pain as not real. This is inaccurate and demonstrates a lack of knowledge of both psychoanalytic theory and the nature of pain as it is empirically understood. Regardless of the cause, pain is a valid experience and can be evaluated only indirectly by self-report and patient behavior.

Psychological evaluation, especially the Minnesota Multiphasic Personality Inventory (MMPI), can be helpful in diagnosing suspected hysterical or delusional headache. If hysterical or delusional headache is determined, the patient should be referred for the appropriate psychological or psychiatric treatment.

Mixed Headache

The 1962 task force described mixed headache as a ''combination of vascular headache of the migraine type and muscle contraction headache prominently coexisting in an attack.'' This form of headache may be more common than originally thought. For many patients, a less-severe muscle contraction headache appears to initiate a more severe vascular-type pain. At least one recent study found involuntary scalp muscle contraction to be even more severe for some vascular headaches than for muscle contraction headache (Philips, 1977).

BEHAVIORAL ASSESSMENT OF FUNCTIONAL HEADACHE

The basic assumption underlying the behavioral approach to headache is that the headache is considered to be strongly affected both by environmental stimuli and the patient's own response to stress and pain. Control these factors and you can control the pain. Evaluation involves obtaining baseline recordings of headache frequency, and of events and experiences occurring just prior to, during, and following headache. These occurrences can be classified under the headings; stimulus factors (S), organismic factors (O), and response factors (R). The reader who is familiar with learning theory will note the familiar $S \rightleftharpoons O \rightleftharpoons R$ model. This model is shown with the dotted arrow pointing from R to S implying that response factors ultimately do affect the environment.

The Pain Log: Monitoring the S → O → R System

All patients are asked to keep a pain log similar to the one shown in Table 6-2 prior to treatment in order to establish a baseline of headache frequency and intensity, as well as to determine what stimulus and response factors affect the pain. The time needed to establish an adequate baseline depends on the frequency of the headache. Usually a few weeks is enough, although in some cases, (e.g., cluster headaches) it can be difficult to record an adequate baseline in that short a time. For most migraine or tension headaches, 3 to 6 weeks is sufficient. Patients are required to maintain the log throughout treatment and follow-up in order to determine changes in pain and behavior.

Besides serving as a way of evaluating treatment outcome, the pain log also serves as information to the patient that can be therapeutic in and of itself. Many patients, even those who have been suffering from headaches for years, are not aware of the environmental stimuli that trigger their pain. When they keep an accurate log, they are often surprised to see that most of their headaches occur at certain places (e.g., at work), or more frequently during certain days of the week. Patients often resist the notion that some stressful aspect of their lives is causing the pain; they feel that to admit this implies weakness and a lack of self-control. During an initial interview, patients usually will admit that there are stress factors which *seem* to initiate headache, but point out (defensively) that they also experience headaches during periods of relatively little stress. Since most people think in "all-or-none" terms when it comes to headache (e.g., either all headaches or no headaches are caused by stress), they then wholly dismiss the stress hypothesis. The headache log allows the patient to accurately determine what portion of their headaches are related to specific environmental stimuli. It is often found to be a much greater percentage than was first thought. Learning theorists and behavior therapists might also point out that simply having patients keep track of their headaches may reduce their frequency. It is known, for example, that having overweight patients write down everything they eat will result in weight reduction. With headache, however, this does not seem to be the case (Mitchell and White, 1977). Simply keeping track of frequency and intensity does not significantly alter the pain, but is nevertheless vital to the behavioral treatment process. Patients who generally have an "all-or-none" attitude about pain are often unaware of the reduction in frequency or intensity of the pain unless accurate records are kept. Seeing small reductions in frequency and/or intensity is reinforcing, motivating the patient to continue with the treatment program and giving the patient a sense of mastery and self-control essential to any effective behavioral treatment.

Stimulus Factors

As can be seen in Table 6-2, the first part of the pain log relates to those environmental stimuli that initiate, or at least relate to, headache. The patient is asked to record the date, time, place of onset, emotional state, and/or what they

Table 6-2
Sample Pain Log

		Stimulus Factors			Organismic Factors				Response Factors	
Date	Time	Place	Feeling state thoughts behavior	Length of time	Location	Intensity (1–5)	Description and comment about related experience	Behavior in response to pain	Effect on activities
5/9	5:30 AM	After work	Tired	3 hours	back	2	Hard day at work; usually gives me headache	Aspirin Nap	Didn't talk to my wife
5/11	8:30 PM	Going home from meeting	Tired; angry about meeting	all night	back	5	Long school board meeting; argued with board members	Aspirin Went to bed	Didn't sleep well

were thinking or doing just prior to onset. For this part of the log it may be helpful to give patients examples of the types of descriptive terms to use. Non-verbal patients, when asked to describe their feelings just prior to headache, will often write down "bad," "sick," or some other general term.

Organismic Factors

This part of the log is used to record physiological experiences prior to and during headache. These include *length of time* the patient experienced the pain; *location*, (i.e., where the pain is experienced); *intensity* (1-to-5-scale); *description of the pain* (i.e., throbbing, continuous); and *correlated experiences* (autonomic reactivity, such as hot flashes, cold hands and feet, and visual or auditory experiences). Although frequency may also be considered an organismic factor, these data can be determined from the stimulus part of the log.

Keeping an accurate record of experience during headache is important for several reasons. First, a patient's description (prior to treatment) of headache may be inconsistent with what he or she writes in the log. Initial descriptions tend to focus on the more severe headaches experienced by the patient. As already noted, some patients commonly have a less severe tension headache set off a more severe vascular headache. Thus, if patients can learn to recognize early signs of headache onset and control the less-severe head pain, they will reduce the number of more severe headaches.

Correlated physiological experiences are also significant. Patients are often unaware of the physiological experiences occurring prior to or during a headache that may signal probable onset. In one study in our lab, 9 out of 10 migraine headache sufferers were unable to say whether or not their hand temperature changed during and/or prior to a headache. When asked to observe their hand temperature with a portable thermister, during onset and before taking medication, all 10 patients reported temperature decreases just prior to the onset of pain. This fact has treatment implications; hand-warming may be an effective therapy for vascular headache.

Response Factors

The third section of the log inquires about *how the patient behaved as a result of pain*. Whether or not he or she went to bed to relax, took medication, etc. This part of the log should also include, when possible, the impact the pain had on significant others (e.g., were plans disrupted). In some cases, it is helpful to have significant others also keep a pain log on the patient.

TREATMENT CONSIDERATIONS

Unlike the more traditional medical treatment, behavioral evaluation is not distinct from treatment, and cannot be fully understood apart from it. The purpose of this section is to emphasize that in behavioral therapy, the evaluation process is in itself part of the treatment, and vice-versa. A more detailed discussion of this treatment program can be found elsewhere (Boudewyns and Massey, 1982).

Behavioral treatment for functional headache is best applied at all levels of the $S \rightleftarrows O \rightarrow R$ model. Most treatment outcome studies for headaches have concentrated on the organismic level by demonstrating how various relaxation techniques can affect head pain (Wickramsekera, 1973; Budzynski et al., 1973; Cox et al., 1975; Sargent et al., 1973). However, it has also been demonstrated that simply attending to the stimulus and response levels alone is effective in reducing functional headache (Holroyd and Andrasik, 1978; Mitchell and White, 1977).

Treatment procedures aimed at identifying and influencing the stimuli which are found to set off pain are generally called *stimulus control procedures*. These techniques have been shown to be most effective when used in the treatment of insomnia but should be considered when dealing with any chronic pain (Bootzin, 1973; Borkovec, 1979). With stimulus control techniques it is assumed that environmental stimuli have often become conditioned to elicit autonomic activity which, in turn, can bring on headache. For instance, if a job situation is at times anxiety-provoking, conditioning may eventually bring on a "generalization effect," such that the individual will experience anxiety to even relatively benign aspects of the work situation. This can be so severe that patients will "learn" to be tense as soon as they enter their place of work, long before any real threat is posed. Stimulus control procedures would aim at reducing these conditioned stimuli when possible by eliminating or changing them. If for example, an executive finds it difficult to relax in his or her office, he or she might be encouraged to change office procedures and redecorate office for a more "relaxing decor." Softer lights, music, and tighter controls on telephone calls and interruptions could be some of the stimulus control procedures suggested.

The next step in behavioral treatment is directed at the organismic factors. There are two aspects to this part of the treatment. First, the patient is trained to relax. Second, the patient is asked to change the way he or she thinks about the situation. Ellis has effectively argued that it is not the environmental stimuli which *cause* anxiety but the way in which we *think* about the stimuli (Ellis, 1962). Obviously, the executive's office is not really physically dangerous. If he or she would stop long enough to think about that, he or she would realize that at some level of consciousness the beliefs are irrational and that many of the day-to-day situations which appear to produce anxiety, if looked at more rationally, will seem less threatening. This form of therapy is called *rational emotive therapy or rational behavior therapy,* or sometimes *cognitive ecology.*

There are several relaxation techniques available, (e.g., progressive muscle relaxation (Jacobson, 1938; Bernstein and Borkovec, 1973); autogenic training (Sargent et al., 1973; Schultz and Luthe, 1969); and meditative exercises (Benson, 1975). In addition to these techniques, or used alone, electromyographic (EMG) biofeedback (for muscle contraction headache) and thermal biofeedback (for vascular headache) have also been shown to be helpful.

The third aspect of treatment, *contingency management,* involves managing the effects of the patient's responses to the pain. Common areas that are identified here are amount and manner in which the pain medication is taken, response of spouse to the pain, and how the pain affects the daily lives of those around the patient. The assumption here is that significant others can inadvertently reinforce pain behaviors and actually sensitize the patient to the pain or maintain the negative effects of the pain beyond what would normally be expected.

Many spouses admit that although they may feel empathy for their mate, the chronic interruptions in family plans and social activities caused by their pain often makes them angry. Spouses are encouraged to remain empathetic but not to continue to organize their lives around the patient's pain behavior. If the patient appears to be deriving secondary gain or is being reinforced for pain behavior, then the significant others are asked to change *their* behavior to reduce the effect of this contingency.

Case Study

Joan, 36 years old, had suffered from headaches since puberty. She had been divorced for 6 years, and had two children: a 6-year-old girl and a 9-year-old boy. She worked days as a secretary and was attending night school to learn accounting. For the last 3 years, her headaches had become more frequent and severe. When she started to have ischemic attacks prior to and during some of her headaches she consulted her physician who referred her to a neurologist. The neurologist diagnosed migraine, and prescribed the usual medication. Joan consulted our clinic, stating that while the medications were effective in reducing the pain, they often made her so "tired and groggy" they interfered with her busy life.

The pain log revealed that Joan's life was indeed busy. Further, it became very clear that migraine was not the only headache type. In fact, she appeared to experience tension headaches almost daily. These in turn would, on occasion, set off a migraine. It could not be determined from the baseline record which factors predicted tension headache followed by migraine. Nevertheless, there was a definite pattern to the muscle contraction pains. They usually (75 percent of the time) occurred after work, during a time when Joan reported feeling hurried and, sometimes, "aggravated." Further inquiry revealed that this was the time she picked up her children from the day-care center, and it was always a difficult time. Joan had to travel a 25-minute expressway route from work to the center on a tight time table. She had to work until 5:00 PM and was required to pick up the children before 5:30. Unusually heavy traffic, or leaving work late, made her schedule impossible.

Treatment involved the usual relaxation training, including EMG biofeedback. Probably more significant than this, however, was the suggestion that she talk to her boss about changing her working hours from 8:30 AM to 5:00 PM to 8:00 AM to 4:30 PM. It was also suggested that she take that extra time to practice her relaxation; perhaps, even to stop off at her apartment for a few minutes before picking up the children.

Joan did get her hours changed, and had seven biofeedback sessions. Headache frequency and severity were reduced significantly and pain medication usage was almost completely eliminated.

Of course, not all cases are this straightforward, but it does illustrate how simply tracking headaches made treatment obvious.

MEASURING OUTCOME OR EFFECTIVENESS

Although not all treatment outcome studies have been favorable, those with negative results have usually concentrated on a single aspect of the $S \rightleftharpoons \bar{O} \rightarrow R$ model. In general, the outcome literature lacks long-term clinical program evaluation. Few studies have looked at the effects of comprehensive treatment programs using sufficient follow-up. Several reviews of this literature might be of interest (Diamond et al., 1978; Silver and Blanchard, 1978; Budzynski, 1978; Cox, 1979).

THE EXPERIENCE OF SELF-CONTROL

Perhaps the most important outcome of behavioral treatment is that the patient achieves a sense of mastery or self-control over pain, essential if treatment is to be effective in the long run. Behavioral treatment may require a long-term change in behavior, or even in lifestyle. If patients realize that they can control their own pain and gain the reassurance that this brings, then they will be motivated to continue practicing relaxation and maintaining behavior change.

After therapy, patients tend to fall back into previous behavior patterns once their pain is relieved. When their headache returns they may lose confidence in the technique, not sensing that they have fallen back into old behavior patterns. For this reason, long-term follow-up contacts with patients and significant others are necessary to help maintain motivation and gains.

SUMMARY

Most, perhaps greater than 90 percent (Lance, 1975), of all headache complaints are not the result of organic disease or any known underlying physiological structural defects. These headaches are considered functional or benign, but must be treated. Recommended medical treatment, depending on the type of headache, involves prescribing pain medication, which, while often quite effective, when used on a chronic basis can lead to dependency and addiction and present the problems encountered in any chronic use of drugs.

Behavioral assessment and treatment approaches to headache have been proven effective in the management of most types of functional headache. This chapter outlined a behavioral approach to the assessment of headache and compared it with the traditional medical diagnostic nomenclature. Behavioral assessment allows for the evaluation of environmental factors that appear to "set off" pain, and response factors that affect the patient's environment.

Underlying the behavioral approach is the assumption that functional headaches are considered to be significantly affected by environmental stimuli and the patient's own responses to stress and pain. Control or change these factors and you can control the pain. In the behavioral approach to headache, assessment inevitably becomes part of the treatment process.

REFERENCES

Benson, H. *The relaxation response.* New York: William Morrow, 1975.

Bernstein, D. A., & Borkovec, T. D. *Progressive relaxation training: A manual for the helping professions.* Champaign, Illinois: Research Press, 1973.

Bootzin, R. Stimulus control of insomnia. Paper presented at a symposium, the Treatment of Sleep Disorders, American Psychological Association, Montreal, 1973.

Borkovec, T. D. Pseudo (experiential) insomnia and idiopathic (objective) insomnia: Theoretical and therapeutic issues. *Advances in Behavior Research and Therapy,* 1979, 2, 27–55.

Boudewyns, P. A., & Massey, E. W. Behavioral management of headache. In P. Boudewyns & F. Keefe (Eds.): *Behavioral medicine in general medical practice.* Menlo Park: Addison-Wesley, 1982.

Budzynski, T. Biofeedback in the treatment of muscle-contraction (tension) headache. *Biofeedback and Self-Regulation,* 1978, 3; 409–434.

Budzynski, T. H., Stoyva, M. M., Adler, C. S., & Mullaney, D. J. EMG biofeedback and tension headache: A controlled outcome study. *Psychosomatic Medicine,* 1973, 35; 484–496.

Cox, D. J. Nonpharmacological integrated treatment approach to headaches. *Behavioral Medicine Update,* 1979, 1; 14–20.

Cox, D. J., Freundlich, A., & Meyer, R. G. Differential effectiveness of electromyograph feedback, verbal relaxation instructions and medication placebo with tension headache. *Journal of Consulting and Clinical Psychology,* 1975, 43; 892–898.

Diamond, S. Psychogenic headache: Treatment including biofeedback techniques. In O. Appenzeller, (Ed.); *Pathogenesis and treatment of headache.* New York: Spectrum, 1976.

Diamond, S., Diamond-Falk, J. & Deveno, T. Biofeedback in the treatment of vascular headache. *Biofeedback and self-regulation,* 1978, 3; 385–408.

Diamond, S., & Medina, J. The headache history—key to diagnosis. In O. Appenzeller (Ed.); *Pathogenesis and treatment of headache.* New York: Spectrum, 1976.

Ellis, A. *Reason and emotion in psychotherapy.* New York: Lyle Stuart, 1962.

Friedman, A. P., Finley, K. H., Graham, J. R., Kunkle, H. G., Ostfeld, A. M., & Wolff, H. G. Classification of headache. *Journal of the American Medical Association,* 1962, 179; 717–718.

Graham, J. R. Headache related to a variety of medical disorders. In O. Appenzeller (Ed.); *Pathogenesis and treatment of headache.* New York: Spectrum, 1976.

Holroyd, K. A., & Andrasik, F. Coping and the self-control of chronic tension headache. *Journal of Consulting and Clinical Psychology,* 1978, 46; 1036–1045.

Jacobson, E. *Progressive Relaxation.* Chicago: University of Chicago Press, 1938.

Lance, J. W. *Headache.* New York: Charles Scribners & Sons, 1975.

Lance, J., & Anthony, M. Some clinical aspects of migraine: A prospective survey of 500 patients. *Archives of Neurology,* 1966, 15; 356–361.

Miller, J. Q. A clinical neurologist's approach to headache. *Behavioral Medicine Update,* 1979, 1; 13–14.

Mitchell, K. R., & White, R. G. Behavioral self-management: An application to the problem of migraine headaches. *Behavior Therapy,* 1977, 8; 213–221.

Philips, C. A psychological analysis of tension headache. In S. Rachman (Ed.), *Advances in medical psychology.* Oxford, England: Pergamon Press, 1977.

Refsum, S. Genetic aspects of migraine. In P. J. Vinken, & G. W. Bruyn (Eds.); *Handbook of clinical neurology*. New York: John Wiley and Sons, 1968.

Sargent, J. D., Green, E. E., & Walters, E. D. Psychosomatic self-regulation of migraine headache. In L. Burk (Ed.); *Biofeedback: Behavioral medicine*. New York: Grune and Stratton & Co., 1973.

Schultz, J. H., & Luthe, W. *Autogenic training* (Vol. 1). New York: Grune and Stratton & Co., 1969.

Silver, B. V., & Blanchard, E. B. Biofeedback and relaxation training in the treatment of psychophysiological disorders: Or, are the machines really necessary. *Journal of Behavioral Medicine*, 1978, *1;* 217–239.

Wickramasekera, I. Temperature feedback for the control of migraine. *Behavior Therapy and Experimental Psychiatry*, 1973, *4;* 343–345.

Ziegler, D. K. Epidemiology and genetics of migraine. In O. Appenzeller (Ed.); *Pathogenesis and treatment of headache*. New York: Spectrum, 1976.

David I. Mostofsky

7

Assessment of Epilepsy

The quantity of publications on both behavioral medicine and assessment gives testimony to the renewed interest in the problems which each presents. Behavioral medicine has forced a reconsideration of preconceived notions and parochially developed theories on health and disease. The emergence of this area—in its scholarly, scientific and political aspects—may indeed constitute a major revolution in this century, in medicine and in the delivery of health services. As for assessment, it is reasserting its rightful place, after a long period of dormancy and silence. To be sure, issues of assessment have never left the concerns of the psychodiagnostic, personnel, or industrial communities of psychology. But for most of medicine and social science, only the Fisherian models of analysis and design seem to be relevant for most specialists. These models are based upon group data in which population parameters are estimated, usually in an attempt to demonstrate outcomes that can be said to be significantly different from chance (Fisher, 1925). The joint consideration of the two topics, behavioral medicine and assessment, is particularly appropriate and timely, especially since there are special demands that enterprises in the name of behavioral medicine place on assessment needs. Among the more prominent issues are analytic strategies for single case designs, multiple baseline and multivariate analyses for n = 1 studies, and medical conditions that preclude direct procedures for demonstrating stimulus control.

The epilepsies (the preferred label for the clinical syndrome) have themselves become the object of renewed interest. Although one of the oldest of conditions described in medical history (Temkin, 1971), it is only since the 1970s that the behavioral sciences have attempted to apply their theories and skills to this complex manifestation. While many results of a neurology–psychology collaboration have been gratifying and promising, the tip of the iceberg has hardly been revealed. The assessment issues surrounding the specific behavioral medicine stance to the epilepsies are numerous and poorly understood. Despite ambiguities and uncertainties, the literature is vast. It is doubtless impossible to suggest that this chapter will provide an exhaustive review, or that it will attempt to approach that ideal. The interested reader will find an extensive library of monographs and articles on epilepsy, including a KWIC 18,000-item indexed bibliography covering 1950 to 1975 (Penry, 1976), as well as many shorter bibliographies (including a list of books available on request from the Epilepsy Foundation of America). This chapter will review the salient features of epileptic disorders and indicate the role of assessment for the clinician or researcher. The emphasis follows the observation attributed to former HEW Secretary John Gardner, that "the important yield of education is not how to do it, but how to think about it."

EPILEPSY

Neurological Considerations

Symptomatic of a disorder of the central nervous system, epilepsy is not in itself a disease. It is recognized by the recurrent sudden seizures due to abnormal electrical discharges of brain cells. The consequences of these "electrical storms" are varied, complex, and at times unpredictable, since the immediate anatomical area of the electroparoxysms (or their projections) will ultimately define the manifestations. Because of the varieties of symptoms, they are more correctly termed "the epilepsies," although we will use the popular and less-awkward reference: epilepsy. The symptom complex is characterized by several features:

1. It consists of recurrent paroxysmal aberrations of brain activity and function. The single incidence or transient episode does not in itself warrant this diagnostic label of epilepsy. The changes may be noted in electroencephalograph (EEG) data and in behavioral performance (motoric, cognitive, sensory, or total loss of consciousness), either singly or in combination. No single criterion is sufficient to define the condition.
2. The seizures are brief and self-limited (with rare exceptions, in which case a medical emergency then exists). The first aid of choice for dealing with an epileptic episode is "benign neglect" (Khoshbin, 1976). Forceful or aggressive resuscitation or intervention in the course of the seizure is contraindicated, and the benevolent bystander should simply be calm without trying to restrain or revive the patient, or at most, remove objects which could injure the epileptic, loosen tight clothing, and allow the patient to rest once the seizure passes. To call for an ambulance on such occasions (except if the patient reenters successive seizures without regaining consciousness) only contributes to the patient's embarrassment and health expenses.
3. The seizures may be of diverse etiologies. Ultimately, predisposition to elec-

trical paroxysms will be attributed to improper chemistry at the neurotransmitter level or to the dynamics of the sodium–potassium balance (the *sodium pump*). Such imbalances may be the result of infinitesimal lesions (which begin prenatally), or to gross vascular and anatomical anomalies, cortical scarred tissue, toxicities, or tumors. The histories of such conditions may be unknown or obscured.

4. The seizures are secondary to the repeated abnormal electrical discharges from neural aggregates in the brain. Clearly, numerous conditions may lead to seizures, but not all seizures are *epileptic* seizures (e.g., those seizures secondary to a heart attack).

5. The source of the paroxysmal disorder resides within the brain itself. Every person is subject to seizures if exposed to convulsant chemicals or to electroshock, but only those with epilepsy will experience seizures in the absence of precipitating conditions. This is not to suggest that external events or covert states cannot be catalytic in triggering seizures; the opposite appears to be more consistent with clinical and research experience.

Finally, the problem of epilepsy is of greatest concern for pediatric populations, with the onset and perhaps the psychologically most-damaging phase occurring in childhood. A small number may "outgrow" their epilepsy; some will have their first diagnosis during puberty or adolescence; and others will not have their first "fit," "convulsion," or "attack" until adulthood (in which case trauma or tumor are highly suspect). Epilepsy per se need not impose intellectual handicaps (i.e., retardation), although many retarded persons suffering from diffuse brain damage will also have a seizure problem.

Epidemiologically, it is estimated that 1 to 2 percent of the population are affected by epilepsy. There are more Americans with an epileptic disorder than with cancer, tuberculosis, cerebral palsy, muscular dystrophy, and multiple sclerosis combined (Epilepsy Foundation of America, 1975). The estimated cost to government (for welfare, Social Security disability payments, Medicaid, Medicare, special education, and vocational rehabilitation) and to the individual (for hospitalization, drugs, special education, and therapy) reached the staggering figure of $4.37 *billion* (Epilepsy Foundation of America, 1974).

The medical management of epileptic disorders relies most heavily on pharmacologic agents (anticonvulsants). Approximately 80 percent of epileptic patients are controlled by medication (Masland, 1976). When a lesion is surgically accessible such treatment may be recommended, but these procedures account for a miniscule fraction of the cases. The most recent development, the use of implanted cerebellar stimulation, has been met with wide skepticism if not rejection, and does not currently constitute accepted medical practice (Cf., Lubar & Deering, p. 67). Each treatment tactic presents its own undesirable costs: Drugs have their risks of toxicity and side effects. Surgery has its potential for possible residual "weaknesses" (if not total abolition) of selected motor and cognitive functions.

To these must be added the cost, inconvenience, and stigma of taking medication, as well as social and psychological restrictions imposed by the disorder and its treatment. The parochial medical approach to the pathophysiology of epilepsy and its management leaves much unanswered, as has been noted elsewhere (Mostofsky, 1980).

The traditional view in both medicine and the social–behavioral sciences is clouded with ambiguities and inaccuracies. For example, most medical text presentations on epilepsy take great pains to elucidate the abnormalities of neuronal activities and its representation in EEG evaluations. There then usually follows a discussion on the range of available anticonvulsants which may be prescribed for the various conditions, together with recommended dosages and warning about possible side effects. Some medical texts will carefully note the dangers of misinterpreting diagnostic data, the fact that EEG abnormalities will not always be accompanied by clinical symptoms, and the importance of balancing the cost of seizure control with healthy development and a decent quality of life. Neurologists and epileptologists acquire expertise in the many skills necessary for EEG administration and their interpretation. When found to be a disorder, the patient's problem will eventually be identified by one or more entries of the International Classification System (e.g., partial seizures, generalized seizures with complex symptomatologies, etc.) (Gastaut, 1970). By itself, the neurological verdict with its different diagnostic inputs will inadequately reflect the problem that epilepsy presents. After all is said and done, the patient's problem is not with a spike-and-wave discharge or other abnormal EEG element. It is, more often, with the serious disruption and impairment of personal and interpersonal behaviors. The International Classification System for all its utility in pointing to neuroanatomical loci and neurological processes is not able to speak to the other dimensions of the epilepsy problem. It cannot (nor does it presume to) comment on the seriousness of functional loss, nor whether three *petit mal* attacks/week are "worse" or "better" than two *grand mal* attacks/month, nor whether a patient is likely to achieve "control" by medication. Indeed, the very concept and criteria for "control" in epilepsy are subject to quite different referents. For the physician who first sees a patient with many daily seizures, there is justifiable comfort when medication restricts the incidence to several/week. Neither the patient nor the patient's family may share such satisfaction, especially when the condition continues to interfere with personal growth and "normal" living. Such persons continue to search for a "wonder drug" or mystical treatment that can totally eliminate every single seizure.

Texts in the social sciences, for their part, have been disproportionately preoccupied with citing studies that describe the relationship of epilepsy to mental health disorders. In doing so, they give credence to an established link between the two, while touting the oft-reported statistic that "80 percent of those with epilepsy have achieved control through medication" (Epilepsy Foundation of America, 1975). Given the ambiguity of the criterion used to define control, one must view such statements with great skepticism.

Behavioral Considerations

Epilepsy is perhaps unique among central nervous system disorders, with respect to the role of social and psychological variables. Personality, environment, and reinforcement may substantially contribute to the aggravation and precipitation of seizures, to the mental health and personal functioning of the patient, and even to the treatment and rehabilitation program designed to offer relief. We have elsewhere considered many of the issues (Balaschak and Mostofsky, 1980), and a comprehensive review of behavioral treatment strategies has been discussed (Mostofsky and Balaschak, 1977; Mostofsky, 1980).

The traditional psychosocial interest in epilepsy has largely been patterned after conventional mental health topics (i.e., specification of functional limitations and comparison to normal groups). The population of persons with epilepsy has been the subject of numerous epidemiologic surveys; psychometric test batteries, and studies of family and social relations. Quite often results of personality, IQ, and neuropsychological evaluations have been shown to be statistically significant compared to their nonepileptic counterparts (Hermann, 1972). From such studies (many deficient in rigorous control and analysis), some have advocated confirmation of the age-old concept of an "epileptic personality" (Aretaeus, 1856). While that concept deserves rejection as both wrong and dangerous, there is probably good reason to suspect that persons with a long epileptic history and frequent or intense seizures *do* present risk for serious psychological problems, though hardly anything that ought to be characterized as purely an epileptic syndrome (Tizard, 1962; Mostofsky, 1979). Fortunately, behavioral problems often respond to therapeutic programs, and their etiologies become understandable in the light of the enduring harsh and adverse environment which their seizure condition creates. Under such constant assault, one could hardly expect anything less than a "maladaptive" outcome.

The relationship between clinical psychology and the person with epilepsy is perhaps most understandable. Elements of the seizure itself, including the aura and prodromal phases, are accompanied by distortions of the patient's normal behavior, mood, and affect, and are suggestive of the conditions one is accustomed to view among the seriously mentally ill. The analogy is not lost on either the patient or those in the patient's environment.

Dynamic psychoanalytic theory has considered the "psychosomatic" nature of epilepsy (Fenichel, 1945). In this view, the symptom complex is seen as organically prearranged, although the appearance of the syndrome sometimes seems dependent on (and, in some cases, triggered by) cognitive factors. Within a rigid psychoanalytic framework the epileptic seizure is compared to a "spell of affect," differing from the nonepileptic variety only by the presence of certain organically predisposed personalities. The characteristic EEG changes are said to represent this disposition. One description of the features of such personalities (i.e., those predisposed to react to certain stimuli or to pressures of certain dammed-up states with the production of an archaic syndrome which is the explosive convulsive discharge) has been formulated as follows:

Clinical experience indicates that epileptic personalities are (a) generally very narcissistically oriented, showing the described features of an archaic ego and always ready to substitute identifications for object relationships, and (b) show very intense destructive and sadistic drives which have been repressed for a long time and which find an explosive discharge in the seizure. The repression of the destructive drives is due to an intense fear of retaliation, which often is very conspicuous in the clinical picture. (Fenichel, 1945, p. 226).

Other clinical proposals have focused on the possible link between psychopathology and epilepsy, examined later in this chapter. The fascination with such studies is most prominent in those cases of epilepsy where the EEG focus is prominent in the temporal lobe of the brain and where, as a consequence, complex automatisms (e.g., lip-smacking, aimless movements, detached staring) mimic the behaviors commonly associated with psychiatric conditions. While these stereotyped associations persist, they are not substantiated to any meaningful degree by empirical research.

Behavioral treatment protocols (Mostofsky & Balaschak, 1977) have been developed to deal with reinstatement of seizure control, especially for patients who appear refractory to medication or are in other ways failing to effectively cope with their problems. While traditional psychotherapeutic models have been shown to be of great value in such instances, the popular treatments of choice are overwhelmingly in biofeedback and the behavior therapies (Lubar & Deering, 1981). The subjects will generally have participated in a minimum of 16 sessions before progress can be expected to become observable, although most subjects will have been in training for many months, with daily or multiple experimental days/week and with each session lasting an hour or more and carried out in well-equipped laboratories. ''Trainer units'' (stripped-down versions of the research models) are commonly provided for continued home use, with provisions for recording and for off-line analysis of the biofeedback data.

While various theoretical and procedural rules have been advanced, the results are often unquestionably dramatic (Lubar & Deering, 1981). It should be obvious nonetheless that these techniques require equipment resources not common to most facilities, and that candidates for this for this treatment option must be available and prepared to devote many long hours during training and for follow-up; a condition which is often difficult to satisfy for a procedure which is decidedly costly and still viewed with skepticism in many quarters. Understandably, the search for a more efficient ''breakthrough'' is being aggressively pursued, although currently there is no comparable nonmechanical equivalent for the EEG–biofeedback instrumentation system.

Behavior therapy approaches to epilepsy control differ little in principle from their applications in other areas. Essentially, the judicious use of reward and punishment is implemented to extinguish definable trigger stimuli or conditions which precipitate or aggravate seizures. (Even when such stimuli are unspecifiable, the techniques are used on the assumption that the seizure behavior complex follows the laws of learning.) The same methods are used to instate or strengthen periods of nonseizure activity. Among the techniques that have demonstrated success (Cf. Mostofsky & Balaschak, 1977) are the established protocols for positive reinforcement, punishment, contracting, time out, and relaxation training. It is not evident at this time which technique in this category is best-suited for which patients or conditions. The reported results, however, range from almost total control to total failure. The techniques have been successful with patients who have seizures due to inoperable tumors as well as for those who are multiply handicapped by retardation and other neurological disorders (Mostofsky & Balaschak, 1977). Part of the difficulty in the confidence of ascribing success or failure rests with the remissions for which epileptic seizures are notorious, as well as the complex natural environment where most of the procedures are executed. In general, the gains are greatest where the therapist (or other personnel) have maximal opportunity for implementing the intervention strategy and where continued, consistent, and careful execution of the therapeutic program can be assured.

Biofeedback procedures involve training the subject to generate higher frequency rhythms (usually in the range 12–16 Hz), while suppressing 4–7 Hz activity and/or spikes or paroxysmal discharges. Hardware containing the necessary logic for the NAND conditions (i.e., feedback contingent on the sensed presence of a given frequency for a specified duration *and no* concurrent slow wave or spike activity) and for frequency analysis used in determining the feedback consequences vary in design and construction and are not available as off-the-shelf units. The results of such feedback training have been rewarding, especially since the patients that participate are usually selected from among the more difficult cases.

The first reported case (Sterman and Friar, 1972) involved a 23-year-old woman who had a long history of epileptic seizures which were uncontrollable by medication. The patient underwent EEG-biofeedback training in which she was taught to increase sensory motor rhythm brain wave activity (12–16 Hz). With training, her seizure frequency dropped from one-to-four/month to near-zero levels. More adequately controlled single-case studies have lent support to the efficacy of EEG-biofeedback in the treatment of epilepsy. Lubar and his colleagues (Lubar, in press) used a double-blind design in which neither patients nor the laboratory technicians who conducted the training knew what type of feedback was being used. An A-B-A design was also used. During the A-phase, patients were given feedback for a brain-wave pattern other than the sensory-motor rhythm. During the B-phase, patients were given sensory-motor rhythm feedback. The results showed that epileptic attacks dropped dramatically when sensory-motor rhythm feedback was provided, and stayed at high levels when this feedback training was not in effect.

Even on occasions where the primary behavioral objectives are other than modification of the seizure episodes, remediation of ancillary personality and mental health problems is often accompanied by a clinically improved neurological status. Whether by use of orthodox reinforcement contingencies or by cognitive behavior modification techniques (e.g., self-control procedures), the clinical gains are often dramatic, even when corresponding medical interventions appear unsuccessful.

Not infrequently patients adopt superstitious and ritualistic practices in an effort to exert anticonvulsant self control. Mostofsky and Balaschak (1977) have cited several examples. In one case, the patient had a sensation of warmth just prior to a seizure and was able to interrupt the progression of the seizure by getting angry. In another case, the patient reported that she could prevent a seizure by remaining motionless and concentrating. One 17-year-old retarded patient would pray whenever she thought a seizure was about to occur.

The potential for secondary gain by occasioning seizures is not to be minimized. Although an increase in seizures may lead to further ostracism and interpersonal difficulties, the seizures may well provide sufficient immediate gratification in the already restricted life of the patient so as to acquire an undesirable level of habit strength. The many contingencies which may modulate the reinforcement of seizures will be found both in the subjective life space of the patient, as well as within patient contact with significant others (family, friends, school, employment). It is not clear how an understanding of personality variables (or, for that matter, reinforcement variables) can account for the course of the epileptic crisis, but it seems certain that these variables account for more than a trivial portion of the variance.

Whether one is persuaded by dynamic and cognitive theories or by behavioral reinforcement theories, the implications of non-organic factors in the comprehensive treatment of seizure disorders are important. If nothing else, the implications speak to the influence exerted by family, friends, counselors, nurses, therapists, teachers, and employers on the threshold for seizures and on quality of normative functioning which can be provided for those with epilepsy. In a real sense, *each is a potential therapist, and each is a resource for providing data in the assessment process.* At the very least, the message of behavioral medicine highlights the complex interdependencies between the neurological and psychological mechanisms that contribute to the maintenance of seizure problems. The following observation by Rodin (1968) superbly reflects this point:

> The great majority of neurophysiological and neurochemical investigations still deal with the "epileptic focus" or the properties of the "epileptogenic neuron." These are important studies, but they are likely to be insufficient in providing the final answer to the problem . . . [one should also ask] what are the factors that are responsible for the spread of abnormal electrical activity in this particular patient? Even more important would be the question: How does the patient's condition differ on the five days of the week when he is seizure-free from that of the sixth day then he has an attack (Rodin, 1968, p. 343).

These realizations, however, do not by themselves fully convey the range of considerations which must be appreciated for any meaningful assessment activity. It is clear that the mandate of assessment extends beyond the simple medical diagnostic evaluations and/or conventional psychodiagnostic test batteries.

ASSESSMENT AND EPILEPSY

Too often the organization of discussions on assessment as it relates to the respective needs of clinical and research enterprises fails to communicate the distinctly separate contexts in which the dictionary definition ("to appraise; to place a value") is applied. In the case of epilepsy, these issues may refer to the context wherein the application of assessment procedures is to the condition of the disorder itself and to the effect(s) of those suffering its consequences (the *assessment of objects*). There are yet other and different issues concerned with another context, that of assessing the method used for description, prediction, and baseline determination (the *assessment of technology*). Finally, there are issues relevant to the context concerned with the particular procedure(s) used for quantification and data representation (the *assessment of analytic models*). Each context presents its own problems for assessment; each differs with respect to the state of the art, the methodologic pitfalls, and the range of alternatives available to the clinician and researcher. In epilepsy, appropriate measures will be concerned with details of the neurological condition, as well as with the person and the family. The results of test batteries about a person with epilepsy may help us to make an educated guess about how well the person will do in later life (school, socialization, vocation, etc.); what chances there are for natural remission or for overcoming handicap; how likely the patient is to be a "controlled epileptic," and to comply with drugs, therapy, self-improvement. Thus, these test batteries have a dual purpose: (1) a predictive role, wherein reliable prognosis for subsequent functioning can be estimated, and wherein rational criteria for selection among the many treatment alternatives can be developed; and finally (2) to enable the development of baseline profiles so that chance fluctuations can be subsequently partitioned from explainable changes.

To appreciate the nature of assessment programming for epilepsy, it may be convenient to classify the problems as responses to three questions: What is to be assessed? How should assessment be conducted? What are the results of the assessment effort? Such a classification allows for an examination of the separate contexts in which the term assessment may be applied.

The Assessment of Objects

Prominent in this category is the matter of the epilepsy syndrome itself; its neurological and other medical characteristics. A host of additional "objects of assessment" deserve attention, among them: the family constellation, with its dynamic and reinforcement properties; the school and/or place of employment, with its attendant contingencies; the community, with its social values and support resources; and the constitution, personality, and general functioning of the person with the problem. To satisfy the goals for this assessment context, the obvious access to medical records and the competent interpretation of psychometric evaluations are prerequisite. The decision to carry out assessment for any object element will depend on many factors, most importantly the accessibility to such information. Even when such data appears to be available, the careful therapist or researcher should be sensitive to countless sources of error and confoundation. There may be inadequate or incomplete information; there may be serious questions on the reliability of self-reports and the reports of others. One must be equally sensitive to the distortions in evaluations that may be attributable to side effects of a medication regimen, or obscured by the presence of multiply handicapping disabilities. Even when a firm medical diagnosis appears on record, there is considerable wisdom in guarding against misdiagnosis and different kinds of errors. Not infrequently, an EEG may be "overread" or an inexpert clinician may be overwhelmed by the presenting case, and a misdiagnosis nonetheless becomes part of the official record. Above all, one should be mindful of the fact that seizure disorders are notoriously subject to fluctuations, oscillations, biorhythmic correlates, and placebo effects. To tease out the separate ingredients of assessment, a mechanical selection of standardized test batteries will surely fall short of a meaningful effort. The therapist's clinical insights will often lead to constructing test instruments of his or her own design, or to the judicious integration of selected sections of more popular psychodiagnostic batteries. There are not any firm guidelines for a comprehensive epilepsy assessment battery, although several valiant attempts have been reported (Batzel et al., 1980; Dodrill, 1978; Sarver and Howell, 1980). Even so, separate formulations exist, primarily tailored to academic, vocational, or mental health objectives.

The relationship of psychodiagnostic indices in epilepsy as they reflect mental health psychopathologies or neuropsychological deficits remains controversial. Whether from factor-analyzed interviews (Bagley, 1971), or from MMPI and WAIS results (Stevens et al., 1972) the dilemma of the-chicken-and-the-egg remains ambiguous. In practice, the therapist's course of action may be but trivially affected even if such information could be easily made available. To burden the patient and others with excessive test protocols cannot be justified, as may seem reflected by the popular activities of many health service deliverers.

The application of experimental analysis of behavior to epilepsy can be profitable, both in refining our understanding of the syndrome as well as in the implementation of effective programs of intervention and adjunct treatment (Cataldo et al., 1980). In this instance, one would be more concerned with the identification and manipulation of environmental factors than with the covert and intrapsychic status. To ascertain the various parameters, questionnaires, structured interview guides, behavior-coding forms, and similar devices constructed locally and, when possible, tailored to fit the special requirements of the problem are employed. We have described one such outline in an earlier report (Mostofsky and Balaschak, 1977).

1. Patient description—age, sex, level of retardation (if any), and other significant characteristics
2. Symptoms and diagnosis—behavioral description of the seizure and its classification
3. Etiology of the seizure disorder—form, time of onset, duration of disorder
4. EEG information
5. Medication before and/or during treatment
6. Setting in which the treatment takes place—institution, home, laboratory, outpatient facility
7. Baseline data—number of seizures, time period of baseline, who reported the data
8. Trigger—stimuli or events known to set off a seizure
9. Aura—presence or absence, and its described form
10. Treatment procedure
11. Therapist—age, gender, experience, orientation
12. Treatment schedule
13. Medication after treatment
14. Results and follow-up level of success; specific information as to long- and short-term follow-up

The above should only be viewed as an *outline*, and represents our estimate of the minimal information necessary for every patient prior to embarking on behavioral interventions.

It should be observed that while assessment in the context of ''object'' is decidedly descriptive, it will undoubtedly prove to have significant utility for predictive purposes as well. Knowledge of the patient and of the environment may by itself suggest the relative ease of instituting a particular behavioral treatment program, with its dependence on team cooperation, allied therapists, patient compliance, and long-term tolerance to inconvenience, medication side effects, etc. Aside from classical medical and psychological considerations, treatment (or research strategy) is limited by the technical resources available. Some protocols require special expertise or sophisticated hardware, and despite any evidence for promise, one is unlikely to succeed with any protocol without a reserve of the necessary competencies. If geography or economics require drastic alterations of established paradigms, the likelihood of effective outcome is seriously jeopardized.

Assessment of Technology

Assessment protocols include those that involve regional cerebral blood flow measurement, averaged evoked potentials, EEG telemetry, ''sensory motor rhythm'' biofeedback training, or habituation and desensitization procedures for the sensory precipitated epilepsies.

Given the decision to assess one or more domains of the epilepsy problem, there remain numerous alternatives leading to its accomplishment. In part, the selection of any particular strategy will be governed by the same principles that control a therapist's or experimenter's choice in any situation, i.e., temperament, history of training, comfort, and expertise with an assessment style. Not to be forgotten are considerations of cost, time, and availability of personnel. In this context, the assessment is of the technology itself: How reliable is it? How valid? How generalizable?

The possible technologies for epilepsy include *"paper and pencil" methodologies* (the administration of standardized, ad hoc inventories and test batteries covering personality, intelligence, and neuropsychological aspects of functioning); while MMPI, WAIS (or WISC), and Reitan are among the more favored instruments they do not exhaust the range of possibilities available to the psychologist. A second technique is *interview and nonverbal measurements* (the analysis of language content and videotape recordings during interview or treatment sessions as well as in the natural environment). These data permit a richer appreciation of both the intensity and quality of the patient's behavior during epileptic episodes as well as during interictal periods. Third, *operant derived methodologies* are used, in addition to conventional behavior therapy operations involving reward and punishment. These items include the use of multiple baselines, titration procedures, and analyses which might reveal evidence of behavioral contrast or induction. For purely diagnostic objectives one might also consider *human operant conditioning paradigms,* particularly avoidance, differential reinforcement of low-rate behavior, and reversal shift learning). Technology assessment issues may be considered independent of the specific condition of epilepsy, although the complex and confusing array of signals which the seizure forms and the patient behavior jointly emits add meaning to the usual concerns of reliability and validity identified with this context. In large measure, the standard caveats stated for test construction enterprises also obtain here. In addition, the technology includes evaluations of treatment effectiveness. We are not discussing the particular statistical model or the pitfalls of significance determination. Rather, we are focusing on the need to provide a comprehensive assessment—a multidimensional view—of treatment outcome. The focus is on the possible changes (good and bad) that intervention produces. One may well encounter situations where EEG normalization is not found, nor is an appreciable decrease in seizure frequency noted. At the same time, one should search other areas of the problem: Has the intensity of the seizure changed? Are the same number of seizures now differently distributed during the day or week? (Perhaps seizure episodes now occur only in the home, for instance, and not during school?) In our clinical activities, we try to provide for a minimum 2-month baseline and 18-month follow-up. Treatment effects may vary slowly not only during the active portion of therapy, but even during phases of follow-up. One hopes for technological and cost-effective breakthroughs in epilepsy. While experimental prototypes have been developed, we cannot realistically expect in the near future to benefit from certain necessary luxuries which would improve assessment capabilities, e.g., extensive third-party cost recovery; or portable, miniaturized telemetric systems.

Assessment of Analytic Models

This third set of assessment issues include the commonly repeated hortatives and admonitions that accompany discussions of statistics and experimental design. However, research and clinical activities in epilepsy have generally failed to capitalize on the sophisticated models currently available. The overwhelming style of analysis continues to follow a predominantly conventional, univariate approach, with occasional forays into factor analysis. Many otherwise-suitable selections from both uni- and multivariate techniques go untouched. Rarely have scaling procedures, function fitting, or simulation attempts been undertaken. Even at this basic level of development in behavioral epileptology, sufficient data can be procured to permit a test of the viability of new techniques (Hersen & Barlow, 1976; Kaplan & Litrownik, 1977). And although much epilepsy research is plagued by the inability to create a true agronomic Fisher (Fisher, 1925) Group Design, the old saw statistical analysis is inappropriate—deserves a firm and loud rejection. Methodologies for dealing with quantitative precision in single-case designs have begun to enter the mainstream of operant research and the behavior therapies. Tactics built upon autocorrelation and spectral analysis (among many others) should be better represented in all clinical and research areas concerned with epilepsy.

SUMMARY

Epilepsy is a disorder in which the seizure is the most disruptive element for normal functioning. It is a complex medical and behavioral-science problem. Behavioral medicine has inspired renewed consideration of both the biological and psychological aspects, so that the epileptic syndrome may be better understood, and so that more effective treatment and rehabilitation can be achieved. Seizures can occur at any age; they affect a significant population in the United States, many of whom are children. Seizures are neurologically recognized to be recurrent paroxysmal abnormal brain discharges, although the specific mechanisms responsible for their generation, propagation, or maintenance is not completely understood. Neurological assessment involves evaluation of EEG, brain structure, neuropsychological test performance, and blood chemistry. Diagnosis follows the international classification system (the terms *grand mal, petit mal,* and *temporal lobe epilepsy* have been officially replaced, though without popular acceptance), which is most valuable for its correlation with EEG parameters and for its differential recommendations for medication programs. The medical treatments of choice largely are pharmacologic, and only in some cases surgical or a Ketogenic diet.

For many persons with epilepsy, these techniques fail to provide satisfactory seizure control. For many as well, there is visible evidence of disruption in the social, academic, or family life.

There is also a convincing body of data that emotional or situational stimuli trigger, provoke, or precipitate seizures, if the predisposition for their elicitation already exists. The implication is that a sensible approach to a better understanding of the disorder and to the design of more effective treatment protocols would be the incorporation of psychosocial considerations with primary medical management. The design of treatment strategies presumes adequate assessment. It has been suggested in this chapter that assessment can be applied to three separate domains and that the particular context in which assessment is used carries with it a number of issues and decisions. Assessment, therefore, may refer to (1) the object—the extent and ingredients of evaluation for what or who is being assessed; (2) the technology—the evaluation of the instruments used in assessment; and (3) the analysis—the examination of the logical and mathematical rigor in the evaluation of outcomes. Within these three classes are included the range of variables and test instruments that are common to assessment in other areas of behavioral medicine. Perhaps the single difference important for assessment in epilepsy is to recognize the seizure as "another kind of behavior" subject to the same laws governing other behaviors and, as such, subject to the same inexplicable lawlessness and idiosyncracies is all too familiar in other psychological, medical, and behavioral medicine challenges.

The promise refined assessment activity holds for epilepsy is a better understanding of the seizure mechanism and, as a corollary, the design of more effective treatment programs. Achieving success will mean a clinically significant reduction in seizures, a significant improvement in the quality of life, a less-costly health liability (both economic and psychological), with an accompanying reduction in medication, social stigma, and personal restriction.

REFERENCES

Aretaeus, J. *The extant works of J. Aretaeus, the Cappodocian.* London: The Sydenham Society, 1956.

Bagley, C. Social, psychological, and neurological factors and behavior disorders in epileptic children: A taxonomic study. *Acta Paedopsychiatrica,* 1971, *38,* 78–79.

Balaschak, B. A., & Mostofsky, D. I. Seizure disorders, In E. J. Marsh and L. G. Terdal (Eds.), *Behavioral assessment of childhood disorders.* New York: Guilford Press, 1980.

Batzel, L. W., Dodrill, C. B., & Fraser, R. T. Further validation of the WPSI vocational scale: Comparisons with other correlates of employment in epilepsy. *Epilepsia,* 1980, *21,* 235–242.

Cataldo, M. F., Russo, D. C., Bird, B., L., & Varni, J. W. Assessment and management of chronic disorders. In J. Ferguson and C. B. Taylor (Eds.), *Comprehensive handbook of behavioral medicine*. Holliswood, New York: Spectrum, 1980.

Dodrill, C. B. A neuropsychological battery for epilepsy. *Epilepsia* 1978, *19*, 611–623.

Epilepsy Foundation of America. *Basic statistics on the epilepsies*. Philadelphia: F. A. Davis, 1975.

Fenichel, O. *The psychoanalytic theory of neurosis*. New York: W. W. Norton, 1945.

Fisher, R. A. *Statistical methods for research workers*. Edinburgh, Scotland: Oliver & Boyd, 1925.

Gastaut, H. Clinical and electroencephalogal classification of epileptic seizures. *Epilepsia*, 1970, *11*, 102–113.

Haynes, S. N., & Wilson, C. C. *Behavioral assessment*. San Francisco: Jossey-Bass, 1979.

Hermann, B. P. Psychological effects and epilepsy: A review. *American Psychological Association Journal Supplement*, MS, 1430, 1977, 1(i) 16.

Hersen, M., & Barlow, D. H. *Single case experimental designs*. New York: Pergamon Press, 1976.

Kaplan, R. M., & Litrownik, A. J. Some statistical methods for the assessment of multiple outcome criteria in behavioral research. *Behavior Therapy*, 1977, *8*, 383–392.

Khoshbin, S. Epileptic seizures: An introduction. Unpublished manuscript. Childrens Hospital Medical Center, Boston, 1976.

Lubar, J. F. EEG operant conditioning in intractable epileptics: Controlled multidimensional studies. In L. White, & B. Tursky (Eds.), *Clinical biofeedback: Efficacy and mechanisms* (in press).

Lubar, J. F., & Deering, W. M. *Behavioral approaches to neurology*. New York: Academic Press, 1981.

Mash, E. J., & Terdal. L. G. (Eds.). *Behavioral assessment of childhood disorders*. New York: Guilford Press, 1980.

Masland, R. L. Epidemiology and basic statistics on the epilepsies: Where are we? Paper presented at the Fifth National Conference on the Epilepsies. Washington, D.C., 1976.

Mostofsky, D. J., & Balaschak, B. Psychobiological control of seizures. *Psychological Bulletin*, 1977, *84*, 723–750.

Mostofsky, D. I. Epilepsy. In L. G. Pearlman (Ed.), A report of the Third Mary E. Switzer Memorial Seminar National Rehabilitation Association, Washington, D.C., 1979.

Mostofsky, D. I. Paroxysmal disorders of the central nervous system. In S. M. Turner (Ed.), *Handbook of Clinical Behavior Modification*. New York: J. Wiley, 1980.

Penry, J. K. (Ed.). Epilepsy bibliography: 1950–1975. DHEW Publication No. (NIH) 76-1186 PHS-NIH, Bethesda, Maryland, 1976.

Rodin, E. A. *The prognosis of patients with epilepsy*. Springfield, Illinois: Charles C. Thomas, 1968.

Russo, D., Bird, B. L., & Masek, B. J. Assessment issues in behavioral medicine. *Behavioral Assessment*, 1980, *1*, 1–18.

Sarver, G. S., & Howland, A. Epilepsy. In R. H. Woody (Ed.), *Encyclopedia of clinical assessment*. San Francisco: Jossey-Bass, 1980.

Sterman, M. D., & Friar, L. Suppression of seizures in an epileptic following sensorimotor EEG training. *Electroencephalography and Clinical Neurophysiology*, 1972, *33*, 89–95.

Stevens, J. R., Milstein, V., & Goldstein, S. Psychometric test performance in relation to the psychopathology of epilepsy. *Archives of General Psychiatry,* 1972, *26,* 532–538.

Temkin, O. *The falling sickness: A history of epilepsy from the greeks to the beginnings of modern neurology.* (Ed. 2) Baltimore, Maryland: Johns Hopkins, 1971.

Tizard, B. The personality of epileptics: A discussion of the evidence. *Psychological Bulletin,* 1962, *59,* 196–210.

Woody, R. H. (Ed.). *Encyclopedia of Clinical Assessment.* San Francisco: Jossey-Bass, 1980.

P. Scott Lawrence

8

Behavioral Assessment of Sleep Disorders

Sleep disorders are one of the most common complaints made to physicians, psychologists, and other mental health professionals. A recent survey of over 1,000 representative households in the Los Angeles metropolitan area found an overall prevalence of current or previous sleep disorders in adults of 52.1 percent (Bixler et al., 1979). This included a prevalence of 42.5 percent for insomnia, 11.25 percent for nightmares, 7.1 percent for excessive sleep, 5.3 percent for sleeptalking, and 2.5 percent for sleepwalking. These problems were often chronic, with average durations ranging from 7 to 14 years. They were also often associated with other physcial and mental health problems. Although sleep medication remains the most common treatment for sleep disorders, the effectiveness of alternative behavioral treatment procedures is increasingly being recognized. A number of reviews have evaluated behavioral treatments for insomnia (Bootzin and Nicassio, 1978; Coates and Thoresen, 1977; Knapp et al., 1976; Montgomery et al., 1975; Ribordy and Denney, 1977). Although insomnia is the most frequently investigated sleep disorder, other sleep disorders, such as nightmares, sleep apnea, and excessive daytime sleepiness are receiving increasing attention (Cellucci and Lawrence, 1978 a, b; Mitler et al., 1975; Roffwarg, 1979).

Less known, however, are recent developments in the assessment of sleep disorders. These include the development of a new diagnostic classification of sleep and arousal disorders, more sophisticated and better-validated self-report, behavioral and physiological measures of sleep, and improved methods for evaluating the relationship between sleep variables. This chapter will review the definition and classification of sleep disorders; describe self-report, behavioral, and physiological measures of sleep; and discuss the assessment of causal variables related to sleep problems.

DEFINITION AND CLASSIFICATION OF
SLEEP DISORDERS

Any adequate assessment of sleep disorders requires a precise definition of each disorder. Unfortunately, until 1979, the various forms of sleep disorders were subsumed under the terms "insomnia" or "inadequate sleep." It is now recognized that sleep disorders represent a large array of distinct but related sleep disturbances that take place during the day or at night. These disturbances may either be caused by or be independent of other medical and psychological problems. The large number of terms to describe distinct sleep problems have been interchangeably and inconsistently used. For example, the terms "nightmares" and "sleep terrors" have not been adequately differentiated. This confusing use of diagnostic terminology pointed to a need to develop a classification system for sleep disorders.

One of the most significant advancements in the assessment of sleep disorders occurred with the publication of the Diagnostic Classification of Sleep and Arousal Disorders by the Association of Sleep Disorders Centers (ASDC) and the Association for the Psychophysiological Study of Sleep (APSS) in 1979 (Roffwarg, 1979). This classification system is the culmination of 4 years work by the Sleep Disorders Classification Committee of the ASDC. The system was developed out of a need for an inclusive organization of sleep and arousal disorders encountered by researchers and clinicians. The resulting diagnostic entities incorporate both clinical descriptions and interrelationships between client complaints and physiological data furnished by polysomnographic recordings. A broad cross-section of professionals, including basic sleep researchers and experienced sleep diagnosticians, were involved in the development of this diagnostic system. The outline of Diagnostic Classification of sleep and arousal disorders is presented in Appendix A.

A classification system defines four major categories of sleep and arousal disorders. *Disorders of initiating and maintaining sleep (DIMS)* are traditionally viewed as insomnias and are a heterogeneous group of conditions that are considered to be responsible for inducing disturbed or diminished sleep. The Diagnostic Classification of Sleep and Arousal Disorders subdivides the DIMS (insomnias) into subcategories depending on presumed causes (psychophysiological, psychiatric disorders, use of drugs and alcohol), correlated symptoms (respiratory impairment, nocturnal myoclonus and "restless legs"), age of onset (childhood-onset), or the absence of abnormality (short sleeper, no objective findings).

The *DIMS: psychophysiological* subcategory is used when the sleep disturbance is provoked or maintained by emotional arousal. Sleep loss may be brief and determined by situational factors, or may be persistent and maintained by chronic tension or the conditioning of arousal to bedtime stimuli. The *DIMS associated with psychiatric disorders* subcategory is used when the insomnia is believed to be secondary to a primary psychiatric disorder, such as a personality or an affective disorder. The *DIMS associated with use of drugs and alcohol* subcategory is used when the insomnia is related to the use of or withdrawal from CNS depressants, stimulants, or other drugs.

The *DIMS associated with sleep-induced respiratory impairment* is applied in cases where insomnia results from frequent cessations of breathing, lasting from 20 to 130 seconds during sleep. Persons with this form of sleep apnea typically have short sleep latencies but wake up several times during the course of the night, sometimes gasping for air, snoring, or choking. The *DIMS associated with nocturnal myoclonus and "restless legs"* subctegory is used when insomnia is associated with periodic episodes of repetitive and highly sterotyped leg-muscle jerks. The individual reports an uncomfortable, creeping sensation inside the calves when sitting or lying down. This disorder is seen predominantly in middle-aged and older individuals of both sexes. Patients have a higher incidence of leg cramps, disruption of bedclothes, and falling out of bed than the general population. Nighttime observations from a bed partner are extremely important in diagnosing this disorder since the sleeper is often unaware of the leg movements.

The *DIMS associated with other medical, toxic, and environmental conditions* subcategory is generally used when a loss of sleep results from a symptom of a medical condition. For example, diseases which cause pain, shortness of breath, coughing, or abnormal movements may cause sleep disturbances. *The DIMS associated with other DIMS conditions* is used when an individual's sleep is interrupted repeatedly during rapid eye-movement (REM) sleep or where other abnormal physiological features are correlated with insomnia.

Childhood-onset DIMS is characterized by a lifelong history of poor sleeping which originates during infancy or childhood. The individual is a consistently poor sleeper independent of emotional variations.

The *no DIMS abnormality* category is used for two types of sleepers: *the short sleeper* and the *pseudo-insomniac*. The *short sleeper* sleeps considerably less than the average person of the same age, sleeps continuously, and does not complain of sleep difficulties. Short sleep is at one end of the normal sleep continuum. The *pseudo-insomniac* complains of insomnia, but this complaint is at variance with laboratory evidence of normal sleep length and patterns. The pseudo-insomniac diagnosis requires persistent subjective complaints of insomnia coupled with polysomnographic recordings repeatedly within normal limits. The person must not be showing hypochondriasis, malingering, or other psychological disturbances.

The second category of sleep disorders, *Disorders of excessive somnolence (DOES)*, are a varied group of functional and organic conditions. The chief symptoms include inappropriate and undesirable sleepiness during waking hours, decreased cognitive and motor performance, excessive sleep, unavoidable napping, increased total sleep, and difficulty in achievement of full arousal on awakening.

The *DOES psychophysiological* subcategory is used when the individual shows temporary or persistent tendency to weariness, excessive sleeping, bedrest, and daytime napping when confronted with stress. Most sleeping problems in this category are transient responses to life changes (lasting less than 3 weeks), such as illness or death, marital separation, divorce, or job loss or changes. The *DOES associated with psychiatric disorders* is used when excessive daytime sleepiness, a proclivity for napping, or prolonged sleep at night is viewed as secondary to a psychiatric disorder. Excessive daytime sleepiness is frequently reported in the initial stages of many mild depressive disorders as well as in the depressed phase of the bipolar affective disorder. Excessive sleep is also occasionally associated with other psychiatric conditions, such as dissociative somatoform, fugue, amnesia, and the schizophrenic disorders. The *DOES associated with use of drugs and alcohol* is used when daytime sleepiness is associated with the use of central nervous system (CNS) depressants, or tolerance to or withdrawal from CNS stimulants. Daytime sleepiness typically occurs when doses of stimulants (taken to counteract daytime DOES symptoms) wear off. Moderate-to-high dosages of various drugs used for therapeutic purposes-antiseizure and antihypertensive medications, major and minor tranquilizers, tricyclic antidepressants, antihistamines, muscle relaxants, and alcohol—can cause excessive daytime sleepiness.

The *DOES associated with sleep-induced respiratory impairment* occurs in two forms: *sleep apnea DOES syndrome* and *alveolar hypoventilation DOES syndrome*. Sleep apnea DOES syndrome, the most common form of sleep-related respiratory impairment, is more frequently called obstructive upper-airway apnea. It is caused by an obstruction of tissue structures which prevent breathing during sleep. This potentially lethal condition is associated with inordinately loud snoring and excessive daytime sleepiness. Some patients deny drowsiness or any impairment of alertness. The attacks tend to be prolonged, lasting over an hour, and some individuals report blackouts, disorientation, and periods of automatic behavior associated with amnesia. Once asleep, the person is very difficult to arouse. A common symptom in children is the reappearance of enuresis after complete toilet training. Older children often show increased difficulties in school, consisting of learning problems, hyperactivity, and daytime sleeping or grogginess. Many individuals report diffuse headaches lasting several hours upon awakening. The *DOES associated with nocturnal myoclonus and "restless legs"* subcategory is identical to the DIMS subcategory, except that the individual complains of excessive daytime sleepiness and is unaware of arousing during the night or leg jerks. *The DOES associated with narcolepsy* consists of frequent, uncontrollable attacks of daytime sleepiness and frequent sleep-onset REM periods reported as vivid sensory images at sleep onset. Another symptom, cateplexy, consists of a daytime attack of muscle weakness resulting in partial or total body collapse. The cataleptic is often aware of his or her surroundings during these attacks. Sleep paralysis (the person is unable to move), may occur at entry into or emergence from sleep. Narcoleptics frequently remain undiagnosed and become depressed because of their sleeping problems and resulting interpersonal difficulties.

Idiopathic CNS hypersomnolence DOES syndrome consists of constant daytime sleepiness despite lengthy, nonrefreshing naps. Total nighttime sleep is lengthy and these persons have difficulty awakening. The *DOES associated with other medical, toxic, and environmental conditions* is identical to the related DIMS subcategory but excessive daytime sleepiness is the predominant symptom. Endocrine and metabolic disorders, nutritional deficiency states, uremia, liver failure, toxic encephalopathies, neurosyphilis, numerous infections, degenerative states, and CNS trauma are some of the conditions which can cause excessive daytime sleepiness. *The DOES associated with other DOES conditions* subcategory refers to various other conditions that cause daytime sleepiness. This includes Kleine-Levin syndrome, which consists of recurrent periods of exceedingly prolonged sleep with intervening periods of normal sleep. Also included are sleepiness associated with menstruation, voluntarily chronic sleep deprivation, and sleep drunkeness, which is a prolonged state of confusion upon awakening.

The *no DOES abnormality* subcategory is used to refer to two types of sleep conditions. The *long sleeper* sleeps considerably more than most persons of the same age group, but the sleep is otherwise normal. These persons may require from 12 to 14 hours of sleep each night. The No DOES abnormality subcategory is also used for persons who complain of daytime sleepiness, but whose reports are not confirmed by the external observations of others, such as family members.

The third category of sleep disorders, *Disorders of sleep–wake schedule,* is a collection of conditions that share an initial misalignment between sleeping, waking, and the day–night cycles in which we live. The individual usually complains that he or she cannot sleep and be awake when he or she wants to. There is no abnormality of sleep per se, but only a lack of correspondence between sleeping and the individual's (or society's) expectations of when sleep should occur. Transient sleep schedule problems can occur due to a rapid time zone change (jet lag), or due to a change in a work schedule or shift. Persistent sleep schedule problems can occur from rotating shift work, recurrent time zone changes, or inconsistent sleep schedules. For unknown reasons, some individuals have sleep-onset and awakening times that are stable, but either consistently earlier or later than desired for social and occupational purposes.

The fourth category of sleep disorders, *Dysfunctions associated with sleep, sleep stages, or partial arousals,* is traditionally called *parasomnia.* This group of conditions consists of undesirable physical phenomena that either appearing exclusively in sleep or are exacerbated by sleep. These conditions are not directly causal in sleep disturbances but result from CNS activation, usually transmitted into skeletal muscle or autonomic nervous system channels. They are frequently associated with specific sleep stages or partial arousal, and are abnormal behaviors and medical symptoms which appear in sleep. A diverse set of sleep disorders fall into this category including sleepwalking, sleep terror, nightmares, sleep-related epileptic seizures, sleep-related cluster headaches, and sleep-related asthma.

This diagnostic system, although representing a significant advancement in the classification if sleep disorders, has many limitations, many of which are admitted by its originators. First, no evidence attests to the reliability of the specific diagnostic categories. Although these categories were derived by consensus, there is no guarantee that in actual clinical application, two independent investigators will apply the same diagnostic label to a given set of clinical symptoms. Second, the diagnostic validity of the classification scheme is not known. The developers of this system point out that the diagnostic boundaries must continue to be evaluated as research explores the mechanisms of action of the various disorders. The diagnostic system is only a provisional working construct requiring much revision. A third criticism is that most of the data used to develop the categories come from verbal client reports of symptoms or psychophysiological measures. Very little use was made of systematic self-observation by patients or behavioral observations of persons living with the patients. Despite these problems, the classifications may improve research and treatment of sleep disorders by providing standard diagnostic labels.

SELF-REPORTS

In at least some respects, the client knows more about his or her sleep problem than anyone else. Therefore, the analysis of one's own sleep should be taken very seriously despite the potential for bias. Client self-reports can be obtained through the use of interviews, general sleep questionnaires, or rating scales.

Interviews

Interviews can be used to obtain a diverse set of general information, including complaints, medical history, current medical and psychological difficulties, family history of sleep problems, and sleep history. The interview serves several other purposes as well: It can be use to educate the client as to the components of sleep assessment and why various assessment procedures such as psycholphysiological measurements, self-observations, and observations by others are required. The interview can also help to identify misconceptions regarding sleep that, if not corrected, can interfere with treatment. Most clients are completely unaware of the extreme range of sleep disorders and the diverse set of factors that influence sleep; and unless these are explained, the extended assessment procedures required in analyzing sleep disorders may seem monotonous and unnecessary.

In some cases, the client's self-report may be the behavior in need of change, as in the case of the client who is sleeping only 7 hours nightly, and believes that everyone should get at least 8 hours. Self-reports have been shown to be as reliable as most other types of measurements (Walsh, 1967). In Walsh's review of the literature, he found that 13 of 27 studies demonstrated high validity for interview data, and 3 of 7 studies demonstrated high validity for questionnaire data.

Sleep Questionnaires

General sleep questionnaires are used to obtain information on the specifics of a client's sleep problem, including the behaviors which characterize it, the client's typical sleep habits, thoughts, arousal, or other antecedents which provoke poor sleep.

A sleep-habits questionnaire in use with adults has recently been modified for use with children (Anders et al., 1978). It consists of 68 multiple-choice and yes-or-no items addressing such topics as bed and waking times on weekends and weekdays, awakening at night, incidence and frequency of naps, time to fall asleep, daytime sleepiness and sleep attacks, episodic sleep disturbances, waking energy levels, attentiveness, and school performance. This questionnaire was used to assess the sleep disorders and daytime sleepiness of children from 10 to 13 years of age. Daytime sleepiness did not frequently occur with these children when compared to college students. Unfortunately, no reliability or validity data are reported on this or other sleep questionnaires. As the authors suggest, if the scale is valid and reliable, it may be useful for screening children who are failing in school and who also have sleep problems.

Rating Scales

A variety of rating scales have been developed to measure various sleep difficulties. They are primarily useful in evaluating the subjective feelings of clients when more objective measures are not possible. Typical scales measure degree of restedness in the morning, general satisfaction with the night's sleep, difficulty in getting to sleep, or dream pleasantness. Four-to-nine point scales generally are used.

Recently, Karle and co-workers developed a set of rating scales for the functional analysis of dreams that have great potential for the assessment of nightmares (Karle et al., 1980). There are two sets of scales: one set measures dream process variables, and the second set measures dream content variables. The first process scale, feeling intensity refers to the overall feeling level of the dream. The second process scale, dreamer activity, refers to the actions of the dreamer in response to the dream events. The third process scale, dream clarity, measures the coherence of the dream as well as the amount of distortion present. The fourth process scale, dreamer expression, measures how intensely the dreamer shows his or her feelings about the dream events. Although the process scales are probably most useful in the assessment of nightmares, there are four content scales that focus on context. The setting scale describes what part of the dreamer's life relates to the setting in the dream. The second, origin of feeling scale, defines what part of the dreamer's life relates to the feeling in the dream (present, past, mixed, or no feeling). The two additional content scales are a character scale and an overall rating scale.

Karle et al. (1980) report a series of experiments which include evaluations of the reliabilities of the process and content scales. In one study, interjudged reliablity coefficients for the process scales ranged from .88 to .97. The percentages of interrater agreement for the content scales ranged from 96.2 percent to 99.4 percent. These scales can provide more detailed analyses of changes resulting from the treatment of nightmare sufferers than simple frequency counts of the number of nightmares. Systematic desensitization of daytime fears was found to reduce nightmare frequency (Cellucci and Lawrence, 1978a). A similarity between the themes of the subject's nightmares and themes of the daytime fears was also found. It is possible that Karle et al.'s scales of dream quality might better reflect the effects of treatments of daytime fears on nightime sleep than gross measures of nightmare frequency or intensity.

Kazarian, Howe, and Csapo (1979) have developed a 24-item Sleep Behavior Self-Rating Scale in order to assess various sleep-incompatible behaviors associated with a person's bedroom or bed. This was administered to 121 normal subjects and 81 clinical subjects in order to determine the reliability and validity of the scale. The scale proved to have both high test–retest reliability ($r = .88$), and internal consistency (Kruskal-Wallis-20 coefficients for the two samples of .72 and .76). The scale was found to discriminate between insomniac and non-insomniac subjects based on sleep latency but not based on total hours of sleep. The scale was also found to be relatively independent of anxiety and depression as measured by the manifest anxiety scale and the Zung depression scale. The scale thus appears to have some validity as an indicant of sleep latency independent of anxiety or depression.

BEHAVIORAL OBSERVATION

Although the client's goal self-reports or ratings of sleep are extremely important in obtaining information about sleep patterns, these reports can be subject to both intentional and unintentional bias. Clinicians and researchers should not quickly dismiss these measures, since they are not all susceptible to the same degree of inaccuracy (Bootzin and Nicassio, 1978). Inaccurate reporting can be reduced by making the subject's task more specific and less ambiguous. Ciminero and coworkers agree with this view and note that self-monitoring provides reliable data most often when subjects are provided with specific instructions and are highly trained in the actual self-monitoring task (Ciminero et al., 1977).

Daily Sleep Logs

The daily use of sleep logs (completed immediately upon waking in the morning) is now standard procedure in the assessment of insomnia, and provides a concrete, unambiguous task. Because these logs are filled out every morning, they provide the clinician with a continuous, ongoing picture of the client's sleep behavior. Clients typically self-monitor behaviors such as the time they went to bed, time they fell asleep, number of times they awakened during the night, number of minutes to resume sleep, number of nightmares, time awakened in the morning, and the time up in the morning. Also included are scales for rating the more subjective aspects of sleep. An example of a daily sleep log is privided in Appendix B.

Sleep logs can be "returned" simply by having the client phone in the data on a daily basis, which time the client can be socially reinforced for collecting the data. Alternatively, a brief sleep log can be printed on self-addressed postcards to be mailed daily.

Cellucci and Lawrence (1978b) have used sleep logs to determine the relationship between several sleep variables. They have 29 subjects record the following information daily on a sleep log for 8 weeks: ratings of average and maximum anxiety for that day, time to bed, approximate time to sleep, number of awakenings unrelated to a disturbing dream, subsequent time to fall back to sleep, difficulty falling asleep, wake up time, degree of restedness, sleepwalking, sleeptalking, nightmares, nightmare intensity, and pleasantness of other dreams. These variables were then correlated. A large variation in the individual patterns was found, suggesting that an individual's observed pattern of relationships between sleep variables and/or anxiety might be used in formulating a treatment plan. For example, anxiety reduction interventions (such as systematic desensitization) might be most effective with persons for whom a correlation exists between anxiety rating and one or more sleep difficulties. Alternative treatments, such as stimulus control or paradoxical intention, might be used for subjects who show no relationship between anxiety measures and sleep problems.

Self-monitoring of sleep behavior is not only useful for assessment purposes, it can be therapeutic as well. Unfortunately, this reactivity effect of the self-monitoring of sleep can interfere with the objective evaluation of the effectiveness of treatment techniques. One week of self-monitoring was effective in reducing sleep latency in severe insomniacs (Jason, 1975). A similar reactivity effect was found for mild insomniacs, but not for severe insomniacs (Shealy, 1979). However, even following self-observation, the severe insomniacs in Jason's study and the moderate insomniacs in Shealy's study still had significant sleep onset problems.

In most research studies, a spouse/roommate reliability check procedure is used to verify the accuracy of the client's reports from daily sleep logs. Such reliability checks cannot be used with client's sleep behavior. For example, they may be told to check when the client is asleep by using the following criteria: (1) eyes closed, (2) no voluntary movement for 10 minutes, and (3) failure to respond when his or her name is whispered by the spouse/roommate. The spouse/roommate is provided with a separate questionnaire on which to record sleep data. Witnessed contracts have been used prior to treatment in which the client and the spouse/roommate agree to provide as accurate data as possible and not to be in collusion. It is possible generally to obtain from 30 to 60 percent of spouses/roommates to collect reliability data. Collecting such data is frequently not easy. Roommates are often asleep before the subjects fall asleep and are usually not awake when subjects awaken during the night or in the morning. It is best usually to have a spouse/roommate collect data only a few nights throughout the recording period; otherwise their own sleep may become disturbed.

When spouse/roommate reliability checks are made, they are generally quite high. Tokarz and Lawrence (1974) obtained reliabilities ranging from .91 to .99.

Turner and Ascher (1979) obtained a reliability for sleep latency of .84, and also found that data obtained from daily sleep logs were not influenced by social acquiescence or the tendency to give socially approved responses.

Other Observational Methods

A number of investigators have used sedative-hypnotic agents as a dependent measure (Lick and Haffler, 1977; Turner and Ascher, 1979). Using sleep medication as a dependent variable assumes that such medication is a negative outcome of disturbed sleep. Reductions in the use of sleep medication may reflect an increase in confidence in the effectiveness of other methods to improve sleep.

Parents can accurately observe the sleep behavior of their children. Graziano and Mooney (1980) conducted a study with families of 6 to 12 year old children who had long histories of nighttime fears. The children were taught self-control techniques aimed at reducing these fears. Assessments were provided by the parents through direct home observations and parent meetings with the investigators. During the parent meetings, parents completed a fear strength questionnaire which described their children's nighttime fears on dimensions of frequency, intensity, duration/event, disruption of the child's, parental, and siblings' behavior during each fear episode, the general seriousness of the problem as perceived by the parents, the degree of school interference, and the disruption of the child's social adjustment. A 120-item fear survey was also administered during the parent meetings.

Each night the parent directly observed and recorded the nighttime fear behaviors of their children. These measures included the number of minutes the child required to get to bed after being asked, the number of minutes the child took to fall asleep, the avoidance and delay behaviors displayed (crying, getting out of bed, arguing, asking for a glass of water, or something else), a rating of the child's willingness to go to bed, and a recording of whether the child was afraid on that particular night. Four week test–retest reliabilities of the fear strength questionnaire ranged from .44 to .99 and for the home observations ranged from .00 to .01.

Nicassio and Bottzin (1974) used a pupillography measure taken during the day. This dependent variable was chosen based on the observation that pupil diameter in a dark room varies with the subject's drowsiness. The procedure requires a subject to sit in a dark room for 15 minutes while the pupil diameter is repeatedly photographed. A subject who is alert and has slept well the night before will maintain his or her pupils at maximum dilation throughout the entire 15 minutes. The more tired, less well-slept, subject's pupils will begin to constrict earlier.

Knapp and coworkers have suggested that various sensing devices be used to detect changes in body movements, respiration, or other responses associated with sleep onset. These devices include microswitches which trigger elapsed time clocks and common stopwatches (Knapp et al., 1976). Subjects could indicate they are awake by calling the therapist's answering service at regular intervals, or by logging radio and/or television advertisements. These latter procedures, however, are highly disruptive of sleep. Recent advancements in telecommunication technology may soon make possible the measurement of sleep behavior in the subject's home. The current impracticalities of obtaining physiological measures of sleep in the client's home necessitate obtaining such data in a sleep laboratory.

SLEEP LABORATORY ASSESSMENT

Precise, continuous measurements of sleep behavior throughout the night can only be obtained in a sleep laboratory. A staff of highly trained personnel observes and records sleep data from a client. Although the data obtained in a sleep laboratory are highly reliable, sleep laboratories have several disadvantages that have restricted their use by clinicians and behavioral researchers (Kelley and Lichstein, 1980). They require very expensive equipment. Sleep laboratories can usually accommodate only a few subjects each night. Changes in sleep behavior observed in the laboratory may not necessarily reflect similar changes in the natural sleeping environment. Finally, all-night physiological assessment is extremely costly and technically impractical.

The three basic measures employed in the sleep laboratory are the electroencephalogram (EEG), the electromyogram (EMG), and the electro-oculogram (EOG). Each of these variables measures some correlate of sleep. The EEG measures moment-to-moment changes in the electrical activity from the brain via surface electrodes, and is used to score sleep stages and waking. The chin/cheek EMG measures electrical activity from the submental or masseter muscles, which are tonically inhibited during REM sleep. The EOG records voltage changes resulting from shifts in position of the eyeball. Rapid eye movements during sleep indicate REM sleep.

One of the most significant advances in sleep research has been made through polysomnographic recordings. Sleep occurs in cycles of NREM (non-rapid eye movement) sleep and REM sleep. A sleep period of 6.5 to 8.5 hours typically consists of four to six sleep cycles; each sleep cycle consists of four stages of NREM sleep followed by a period of REM sleep. NREM sleep stage occurs directly upon falling asleep and consists of a low-voltage EEG with slowing to theta frequencies, alpha-activity less than 50 percent, and no sleep spindles, K-complexes, or REMs. (Sleep spindles and K-complexes are particular EEG wave forms). Stage 1 normally assumes only 4–5 percent of total sleep. REM sleep stage 2 usually accounts for 45–55 percent of total sleep time and consists of sleep spindles and K-complexes against a relatively low-voltage, mixed-frequency EEG background. NREM sleep stage 3 consists of 20–50 percent high-voltage, slow EEG waves. It often occurs only during the first third of the sleep period and usually comprises 4–6 percent of total sleep time. NREM sleep stage 4 consists of more than 50 percent high-voltage, slow EEG waves and constitutes 12–15 percent of total sleep time. Because of their physiological similarities, NREM stages 3 and 4 are often combined and are referred to as "deep" NREM sleep. During REM sleep, brain activity and metabolism increases, and dreaming occurs. A low-voltage, fast-frequency, non-alpha EEG record occurs. REM sleep usually constitutes from 20–25 percent of total sleep time.

Other physiological measures are employed depending on the specific sleep disorder. For example, measures of throat muscle activity (glossal pharyngial EMG), rib muscle activity (intercostal EMG), chest movement (thoracic respiration), and air flow at the mouth are useful in studying or diagnosing various forms of sleep apnea. Measures of activity in the thigh muscles (quadricepts EMG) or shin muscles (anterior tibial EMG) are useful in the diagnosis or study of nocturnal myoclonus or "restless legs" syndrome. The continuous and simultaneous recording of several physiological variables during sleep is a *polysomnogram*.

Subjects should spend several nights in the sleep laboratory to insure that representative nights of sleeping occur. At least one habituation night (with the electrodes attached but no recordings being taken), should be included. Unless the effects of sleep medication are of interest, subjects should be off medication for at least 15 days. Visual scoring of polysomnographic recordings can be done by dividing the protocols into 30-second segments using the scoring manual of Rechtschaffan and Kales (1968). An alternative, time-consuming method of scoring the data involves recording directly onto magnetic tape and then analyzing the tapes with an electronic scoring system (Gaillard and Tissot, 1973). The printed results contain a minute-by-minute sleep stage analysis, comments on the presence of artifacts or body movements, and numerical values for other measures such as eye movements, muscle tone, cardiac rate, respiration, or peripheral EMG.

Conclusions can be drawn by observing the correlations between the various physiological recordings. For example, a sleep apnea patient might show a reduction in rib and throat muscle activity, respiration, and air flow at the mouth with the onset of sleep. As the patient gasps and wakes up, these responses may resume until the patient falls asleep again. Some sleep phenomena are associated only particular stages of sleep as reflected on EEG records. Therefore, the polysomnographic recordings can be used for differential diagnostic purposes. Nightmares occur only during REM sleep, but night terror attacks occur during NREM sleep. As another example, narcoleptics fall directly into REM sleep, whereas individuals with idiopathic CNS hypersomnolence fall into normal NREM sleep. Both types of individuals complain of severe daytime sleepiness.

RELATIONSHIPS BETWEEN SLEEP MEASURES

There has been considerable interest in the relationship between self-report, behavioral, and physiological measures of sleep. In the past, physiological measures have been viewed as the only "true" measures of sleep difficulty (Bootzin and Nicassio, 1978). Such interpretations are unfortunate, since verbal reports have been found to be reliable, and because verbal reports may assess somewhat different information about sleep than physiological measures. As noted earlier, the verbal report of sleep difficulties may, in some cases, be the main behavior in need of modification. Measures obtained from sleep logs have correlated more highly with physiological measures of sleep than global self-report estimates taken during the initial interview (Carskadon et al., 1976). Freedman and Papsdorf (1976) obtained evidence that subjects improved at estimating sleep latency with repeated practice, resulting in greater agreement with EEG measures. It is not known whether providing feedback to clients on their self reports in the sleep laboratory will increase the accuracy of their reports once they return to their natural environment.

As part of a systematic attempt to compare self-report, behavioral and physiological measures of sleep difficulty, Kelley and Lichstein (1980) invented a sleep assessment device that presents auditory cues to which the subject is to respond throughout the night. This device consists of two timers, a tone generator, and a cassette tape recorder which are housed in an attaché case. The device is placed about 1 meter from the subject's head and plugged into regular house (AC) current. Every 10 minutes, the device presents a 1-second tone and the tape recorder turns on and records for 10 seconds. The subject is instructed to respond, "I'm awake," to each tone heard during the night. A series of 10 seconds of recordings (totaling about 8 minutes playing time) captures an entire night's sleep data.

In a sleep laboratory, Kelley and Lichstein (1980) compared the results from this sleep assessment device to data obtained through a sleep log completed each morning and EEG recordings. Sleep latency measures obtained from the sleep device correlated .90 or better with EEG measures of latency. The device, however, tended to overestimate latencies for subjects who vacillated between wakefulness and light sleep. The sleep device correlated .97 with subjective estimates of latency obtained from the sleep logs, indicating extremely high validity for this self-report measure. The self-report estimates, however, may be atypically accurate, since the device may function as a cue to the subject as to when he or she falls asleep. The self-report measure of latency correlated .75 with EEG stage 1 sleep and .93 with EEG stage 2 sleep. The lower correlation of the subjective estimate of latency with stage 1 sleep may mean that subjects perceive stage 1 sleep as being awake, rather than asleep, as is assumed in the EEG scoring criteria.

The sleep assessment device also provided valid estimates of total sleep time, correlating .91 with EEG estimates of total sleep time, and .92 with self-report ratings of total sleep time. The device underestimated total sleep time by a constant 30 minutes, due to its insensitivity to short runs of light sleep. This is consistent with the notion that normal subjects may perceive themselves as awake during stage 1 EEG measured sleep. As Kelly and Lichstein (1980) point out, their device does not allow the measurement of the various stages of sleep. Furthermore, it has not been validated with clinically-referred insomniacs. It nevertheless provides further evidence to support the reliability of sleep log measures of latency and total sleep. It also suggests that inexpensive sleep assessment devices may be a reliable and useful measure of sleep in naturalistic settings.

ASSESSMENT OF CAUSAL FACTORS

A diverse set of factors have been found to relate to sleep difficulties, and an attempt should be made to isolate possible sleep-disrupting variables in each client's life through various assessment strategies.

A thorough evaluation of physical factors involved in sleep difficulties is indispensable. Medical conditions which cause pain, breathing difficulties, or other discomfort are particularly likely to disrupt sleep. Such conditions include asthma, angina, ulcers, arthritis, migraine, and cluster headaches. Some drugs used to treat these medical problems may affect sleep adversely. Some pharmacological agents for asthma contain adrenaline which causes arousal and interferes with sleep (Bootzin and Nicassio, 1978). Other drugs that interfere with sleep include antimetabolites, cancer chemotherapeutic agents, thyroid preparations, anticonvulsant agents, monoamine oxidase (MAO) inhibitors, adrenocorticotropic hormone (ACTH), oral contraceptives, alpha-methyl-DPOA, and propranolol. These drugs interfere with sleep onset and may also cause frequent sleep interruptions (Roffwarg, 1979). There are also drugs whose withdrawal often leads to sleep problems. These include diazepam, the major tranquilizers, sedating tricyclic antidepressants, illicit drugs (such as marijuana, cocaine, phencyclidene, and the opiates), and, occasionally, agents that contain aspirin (Roffwarg, 1979). Some of the above drugs suppress REM sleep; intense dreaming can occur during withdrawal. Similarly, drugs to treat insomnia can exacerbate other medical disorders. Some sleep medications depress the brain's respiratory centers, compounding the breathing difficulties of asthmatics.

Another cause of sleep difficulty is the regular intake of CNS stimulants. Most prevalent among these is caffeine (taken in the form of coffee, tea, and soft drinks). Caffeine, in amounts equivalent to four cups of coffee taken just before bedtime, increased awakenings from sleep (Karacan et al., 1973). Cigarette smoking has also been found to be associated with sleep difficulty (Soldatos et al., 1980). When the sleep difficulties of 50 smokers and 50 non-smokers who did not differ in personality patterns or drug consumption were compared, the smokers spent 15 minutes (average) longer to fall asleep than the non-smokers, and spent almost 20 minutes longer awake during the night than non-smokers, presumably due to the stimulant effects of nicotine. When eight chronic smokers abstained from smoking, their sleep patterns significantly improved.

Although occasional use of alcohol may facilitate sleep in some individuals, excessive alcohol intake severely interferes with normal sleep patterns. Such clients typically complain of frequent awakenings during the night, difficulty falling asleep again in the morning, and insufficient total sleep. EEG sleep records show fragmented REM sleep periods and reduced REM sleep. Deep NREM sleep (stages 3 and 4) diminished during withdrawal from alcohol.

Drugs aimed at relieving insomnia can themselves function to disrupt sleep. This is called ''drug-dependency insomnia'' in the literature (Bootzin and Nicassio, 1978). The client typically finds the sleep medication ineffective after about two weeks of continuous use. Drug tolerance develops; larger and larger doses are required to have an effect. When the pills are abruptly withdrawn, the client frequently has severely disturbed sleep with frightening nightmares. These disturbing experiences reinforce the client's sense of need for the medication. Thus, he or she continues to take the drugs despite obtaining only light, frequently disrupted sleep.

A host of environmental circumstances can be related to the quality of sleep. Bedroom ventilation, humidity, temperature, and light conditions need careful assessment. Interfering noise can result from other persons in the house not yet asleep, outside noises, or a snoring or restless bedmate. The comfort of one's bed, especially the pillow and mattress, may be important determinants of sleep. For some sleep problems, a simple environmental modification of one of the above can be as effective as a complicated and time-consuming treatment program.

The routines established surrounding sleep should also be assessed. Persons who have frequent work shift schedule changes or who frequently change time zones often have difficulty sleeping. Some people engage in arousing activities prior to bedtime which may interfere with sleep. The extent to which a person engages in vigorous exercise, reads upsetting books, or gets involved in anxiety-producing conversation prior to bedtime should be assessed.

A variety of cognitive factors are implicated in sleep disorders. A survey of chronic insomniacs found that most blamed their insomnia on cognitive arousal rather than on somatic factors (Lichstein and Rosenthal, 1980). Some of the misconceptions that can interfere with sleep include views that we all need 8 hours of sleep; we have to think, worry, analyze, and plan while lying in bed; we can't function well after a poor night's sleep; we should keep the same sleep schedule as others in our family; all sleep difficulties are stress-related; and the belief that temporary bouts with insomnia indicate a chronic problem. The treatment of sleep difficulties may be more effective if its focus (i.e., motor, automatic, or cognitive) matches the affected response modality (Lichstein and Rosenthal, 1980). The assessment of specific cognitive variables related to sleep difficulties suggests that cognitively oriented treatments, such as attribution therapy, paradoxical intention, or thought-stopping, might be particularly useful with some sleep disorders.

A number of psychological variables, in particular anxiety and depression, have traditionally been viewed as causes of sleep difficulties. Although it is true that frequently anxious and depressed persons have problems sleeping, it is often difficult to determine whether these emotional states cause the sleep difficulties or whether continuing sleep difficulties cause the anxiety or depression. Sleep and other psychological factors may be related to or independent of each other. As

Bootzin and Nicassio (1978) suggest, in cases in which psychological problems accompany sleep disturbance, it is best to provide separate interventions to each, rather than assuming that improvement in one will automatically produce parallel improvement in the other.

Most of the research on the relationship of sleep difficulties to emotional states has focused on comparing the sleep disturbances of various diagnostic groups. In one of the most systematic of these studies, all-night EEG sleep studies were used to differentiate normal subjects, primary depressed patients, and primary insomniac patients (Gillin et al., 1979). Compared to normal subjects, the depressed patients showed less total sleep, longer sleep latencies, more early morning time awake, more intermittent time awake, less delta sleep, less sleep efficiency, and shorter latencies. Insomniacs when compared to depressed patients, showed more early morning time awake, shorter REM latencies, and greater REM densities. Compared to normal subjects, insomniac patients showed less total sleep time, longer sleep latencies, less delta sleep, and less sleep efficiency. Using a discriminant function analysis, eight sleep variables were used to accurately distinguish depressed patients from insomniacs.

Roffwarg (1979) reports a number of relationships between psychiatric diagnosis and sleep difficulties. Neurotic patients most frequently report difficulty falling asleep and frequent awakenings at night. Excessive pre-bedtime rituals can also interfere with sleep. Depressed patients often complain of early morning awakening. Roffwarg also suggests a short REM latency associated with reduced stages 3 and 4 NREM sleep can serve as a biological marker of depression. Bipolar depressives frequently have excessive sleep but still awaken unrefreshed. Manic patients frequently show a very long sleep latency, but once asleep awaken refreshed after only 2 to 4 hours of sleep. Severely anxious or depressed patients may be taking psychotropic medications, which further can complicate their sleep difficulties.

Cellucci and Lawrence (1978b) developed a procedure for determining the relationship between sleep disturbances and emotional states for individual clients. They had students who reported two or more nightmares per week record anxiety ratings and sleep observations for 8 weeks. All the subjects recorded the following information daily: two ratings (on a 10-point scale) that indicated their general (average) and maximum anxiety for that day, time to bed, approximate time to sleep, number of awakenings unrelated to a disturbing dream, subsequent time to fall back to sleep, difficulty falling to sleep (on a 5-point scale), wake-up time, degree of restedness (on a 4-point scale), sleepwalking, sleeptalking, nightmares and their intensity (on a 10-point scale), and, finally, recall for other dreams and their pleasantness (on a 10-point scale). The anxiety questions were completed prior to retiring, while the remainder of the recording form was completed immediately upon awakening. The various anxiety, nightmare, and sleep variables were then correlated within individual subjects. Generally positive relationships between anxiety and nightmares and between nightmares and other measures of sleep disturbance were found. However, large individual differences were found in the patterns of significant correlations. For some subjects, nightmares were highly correlated with anxiety ratings; for others, nightmares were more highly correlated with other sleep variables. This study suggests that the relationships between emotional variables and sleep variables may differ considerably from one client to another. The exact nature of this relationship for a given client may be important for determining the most appropriate form of intervention for that client.

Sleep disorders have also been found to be related to poor sleep habits and scheduling (Tokarz and Lawrence, 1974; Bootzin, 1976). Insomniacs often go to bed at night and get up in the morning at very irregular times. Hauri (1975) hypothesizes that such irregular habits, which may include napping during the day, create circadian rhythm disturbances and upset various bodily cycles. Other poor sleep habits may include using the bed for purposes other than sleep, such as reading, watching television, eating, conversing, or worrying about the next day's events. As a result, the bed becomes a cue for a variety of activities other than sleep.

The above factors represent a sample of the large array of variables related to sleep difficulties. Although very little is known about the relationship between these assessment variables and the effectiveness of specific interventions, ignoring them and choosing an inappropriate treatment strategy could lead to a worsening of sleep difficulties. For example, suggesting that a person with drug-dependency insomnia discontinue taking the medication during treatment aimed at changing sleep habits and cognitions could lead to severe nightmares, thus increasing his or her dependency on the sleep medication. A functional assessment of a person's sleep disorder prior to the initiation of treatment is of critical importance.

SUMMARY

Much progress has been made since 1970 in the development of assessment strategies for the evaluation of sleep disorders. With advances in our knowledge of the variety of biological and behavioral variables which influence sleep have come increased recognition that a variety of assessment strategies are necessary for a thorough evaluation of sleep disorders. Some of these assessment methods utilize the client's own assessment of his or her own sleep problems; other methods rely on the observation of persons who live with the client; still others require a sophisticated sleep laboratory capable of polysomnographic recordings. No method should be viewed as primary, as each is capable of providing useful although somewhat different information about the individual's sleep behavior.

Despite advancements in our knowledge of assessment strategies, much is yet to be learned. Better methods for assessing sleep disorders in the natural environment need to be developed. Disorders such as sleep apnea and nocturnal myoclonus can only be diagnosed in the sleep laboratory. As a result, many persons with these disorders probably go undetected and may suffer much of their lives. Improved methods for training observers of poor sleepers, whether parents or spouses/ roommates, need to be developed. Ways of increasing the reliability of the various self-reports need further development. Most of the dependent variables chosen are based purely on the client's complaints. Little is known about which measures of sleep are the most significant for the physical and emotional health of the client. In addition, very little is known about which sleep variables are most useful for determining the most effective treatment approaches for particular individuals. Furthermore, better methods are needed for assessing the relationship between various sleep measures and the daily activities, habits, diet, and emotional states of the individual.

REFERENCES

Anders, T. F., Carskadon, M. A., Dement, W. C., & Harvey, K. Sleep habits of children and the identification of pathologically sleepy children. *Child Psychiatry and Human Development*, 1978, *9*, 56–63.

Bixler, E. O., Kales, A., Soldatos, C. R., Kales, J. D., & Healey, S. Prevalence of sleep disorders in the Los Angeles metropolitan area. *American Journal of Psychiatry*, 1979, *186*, 1257–1262.

Bootzin, R. R. Self-help techniques for controlling insomnia. In C. M. Franks (Ed.), *Behavior therapy: Techniques, principles and patient aids*. New York: Biomonitoring Applications, Inc., 1976.

Bootzin, R. R., & Nicassio, P. M. Behavioral treatments for insomnia. In M. Hersen, R. Eislery, & P. Miller (Eds.), *Progress in behavior modification*, Vol. 6. New York: Academic Press, 1978.

Carskadon, M. A., Dement, W. C., Mitler, M. M., Guilleminault, C., Zarcone, V. P., & Spiegel, R. Self-reports versus sleep laboratory findings in 122 drug-free subjects with complaints of chronic insomnia. *American Journal of Psychiatry*, 1976, *133*, 1382–1388.

Cellucci, A. J., & Lawrence, P. S. The efficacy of systematic desensitization in reducing nightmares. *Journal of Behavior Therapy and Experimental Psychiatry*, 1978a, *9*, 109–114.

Cellucci, A. J., & Lawrence, P. S. Individual differences in self-reported sleep variable correlations among nightmare sufferers. *Journal of Clinical Psychology*, 1978b, *34*, 721–725.

Ciminero, A. R., Nelson, R. O., & Lipinski, D. P. Self-monitoring procedures. In A. R. Ciminero, K. Calhoun, & H. E. Adams (Eds.), *Handbook of Behavioral Assessment*, New York: John Wiley & Sons, 1977.

Coates, T. J., & Thoresen, C. E. Behavioral self management in the treatment of insomniac: Clinical and research issues, Appendix A. *How to sleep better: A drug free program for overcoming insomnia*. Englewood Cliffs, New Jersey: Spectrum, 1977.

Freedman, R., & Papsdorf, J. Biofeedback and progressive relaxation treatment of insomnia: A controlled, all-night investigation. *Biofeedback and Self-Regulation*, 1976, *1*, 253–271.

Gaillard, J. M., & Tissot, R. Principles of automatic analysis of sleep records with a hybrid system. *Comparative Biomedical Research*, 1973, *6*, 1–13.

Gillin, J. C., Duncan, W., Pettigrew, K. D., Frankel, B. L., & Snyder, F. Successful separation of depressed, and insomniac subjects by EEG sleep data. *Archives of General Psychiatry*, 1979, *36*, 85–90.

Hauri, P. Psychology of sleep disorders: Their diagnosis and treatment. Paper presented at the Symposium on Sleep and Dreams of the 83rd Annual Convention of the American Psychological Association, Chicago, 1975.

Jason, L. A. Rapid improvement in insomnia following self-monitoring. *Journal of Behavior Therapy and Experimental Psychiatry*, 1975, *6*, 349–350.

Karacan, I., Booth, G. H., & Thornby, J. I. The effect of caffeine and decaffeinated coffee on nocturnal sleep in young adult males. Paper presented at the Annual Meeting of the Association for the Psychophsiological Study of Sleep, San Diego, California, 1973.

Karle, W., Carriere, R., Hart, J., & Woldenberg, L. The functional analysis of dreams: A new theory of dreaming. *Journal of Clinical Psychology*, 1980, *36*, 5–78.

Kazarian, S. S., Howe, M. G., & Csapo, K. G. Development of the sleep behavior self-rating scale. *Behavior Therapy*, 1979, *10*, 412–417.

Kelley, J. E., & Lichstein, K. L. A sleep assessment device. *Behavioral Assessment*, 1980, *2*, 135–146.

Knapp, T., Downs, D. L., & Alperson, J. R. Behavior therapy for insomnia: A review. *Behavior Therapy*, 1976, *7*, 614–625.

Lichstein, K. L., & Rosenthal, T. L. Insomniacs' perceptions of cognitive versus somatic determinants of sleep disturbance. *Journal of Abnormal Psychology*, 1980, *89*, 105–107.

Lick, J., & Heffler, D. Relaxation training and attention placebo in the treatment of severe insomnia. *Journal of Consulting and Clinical Psychology*, 1977, *45*, 153–161.

Mitler, MM., Guilleminault, C., Orem, J., Zarcone, V. P., & Dement, W. C. Sleeplessness, sleep attacks, and things that go wrong in the night. *Psychology Today*, 1975, *9*(7), 45–50.

Montgomery, I., Perkin, G., & Wise, D. A review of behavioral treatments for insomnia. *Journal of Behavior Therapy and Experimental Psychiatry*, 1975, *6*, 93–100.

Nicassio, P., & Bootzin, R. A comparison of progressive relaxation and autogenic training as treatments for insomnia. *Journal of Abnormal Psychology*, 1974, *83*, 253–260.

Rechtschaffen, A., & Kales, A. (Eds.). A manual of standardized terminology, techniques and scoring system for sleep stages of human subjects. PHS Publ. No. 204, Government Printing Office, Washington, D.C., 1968.

Ribordy, S. C., & Denney, D. R. The behavioral treatment of insomnia: An alternative to drug therapy. *Behaviour Research and Therapy*, 1977, *15*, 39–50.

Roffwarg, H. P. Diagnostic classification of sleep and arousal disorders, *Sleep*, 1979, *2*, 1–137. (First edition prepared by the Sleep Disorders Classification Committee of the Association of Sleep Disorders Centers.)

Shealy, R. C. The effectiveness of various treatment techniques on different degrees and durations of sleep-onset insomnia. *Behavior Research and Therapy*, 1979, *17*, 541–546.

Soldatos, C. R., Kales, J. D., Scharf, M. B., Bixler, E. O., & Kales, A. Cigarette smoking associated with sleep difficulty. *Science,* 1980, *207,* 551–553.

Tokarz, T. P., & Lawrence, P. S. An analysis of temporal and stimulus factors in the treatment of insomnia. Paper presented at the Eighth Annual Meeting of the Association for Advancement of Behavior Therapy, Chicago, 1974.

Turner, R. M., & Ascher, L. M. Controlled comparison of progressive relaxation, stimulus control, and paradoxical intention therapies for insomnia. *Journal of Consulting and Clinical Psychology,* 1979, *47,* 500–508.

Walsh, W. B. Validity of self-report. *Journal of Counseling Psychology,* 1967, *14,* 18–23.

Appendix A: Outline of Diagnostic Classification of Sleep and Arousal Disorders

DMS: Disorders of Initiating and Maintaining Sleep (Insomnias)

- Psychophysiological
    Transient and situational
    Persistent
- Associated with psychiatric disorders
    Symptom and personality disorders
    Affective disorders
    Other functional psychoses
- Associated with drugs and/or alcohol
    Tolerance to or withdrawal from CNS depressants
    Sustained use of CNS stimulants
    Sustained use of or withdrawal from other drugs
    Chronic alcholism
- Associated with sleep-induced respiratory impairment
    Sleep apnea DIMS syndrome
    Alveolar hypoventilation DIMS syndrome
- Associated with sleep-related (nocturnal) myoclonus and "restless legs" syndrome
    Sleep-related (nocturnal) myoclonus DIMS syndrome
    "Restless legs" DIMS syndrome
- Associated with other medical, toxic, and environmental conditions
- Childhood-onset DIMS
- Associatd with other DIMS conditions
    Repeated REM sleep interruptions
    Atypical poloysomnographic features
    Not otherwise specified*
- No DIMS abnormality
    Short sleeper
    Subjective DIMS complaint without objective findings
    Not otherwise specified*

This appendix has been adapted from Roffwarg, H. P. Diagnostic classification of sleep and arousal disorders. *Sleep*, 1979, 2, 1–137.

*This entry is intended to leave place in the classification for both undiagnosed ("don't know") conditions and additional (as yet undocumented) conditions that will be described in the future.

DOES: Disorders of Excessive Somnolence

- Psychophysiological
    Transient and situational
    persistent
- Associated with psychiatric disorders
    Affective disorders
    Other functional disorders
- Associated with use of drugs and/or alcohol
    Tolerance to or withdrawal from CNS stimulants
    Sustained use of CNS depressants
- Associated with sleep-induced respiratory impairment
    Sleep apnea DOES syndrome
    Alveolar hypoventilation DOES syndrome
- Associated with sleep-related (nocturnal) myoclonus and "restless legs" syndrome
    Sleep-related (nocturnal) myoclonus DOES syndrome
    "restless legs" DOES syndrome
- Narcolepsy
- Idiopathic CNS hypersomnolence
- Associated with other medical, toxic, and environmental conditions
- Associated with other DOES conditions
    Intermittent (periodic) DOES syndromes
        Kleine-Levin syndrome
        Menstrual-associated syndrome
    Insufficient sleep
    Sleep drunkenness
    Not otherwise specified*
- No DOES abnormality
    Long sleeper
    Subjective DOES complaint without objective findings
    Not otherwise specified*

Disorders of the sleep–wake schedule

- Transient
    Rapid time-zone change ("jet lag") syndrome
    "Work shift" change in conventional sleep–wake schedule

---

*This entry is intended to leave place in the classification for both undiagnosed ("don't know") conditions and additional (as yet undocumented) conditions that will be described in the future.

- Persistent
    Frequently changing sleep–wake schedule
    Delayed sleep phase syndrome
    Advanced sleep phase syndrome
    Non-24-hour sleep–wake pattern
    Irregular sleep–wake pattern
    Not otherwise specified*

Dysfunctions associated with sleep, sleep stages, or partial arousals (parasomnias)

- Sleepwalking (somnambulism)

- Sleep terror (pavor nocturnus, incubus)

- Sleep-related enuresis

- Other dysfunctions
    Dream anxiety attacks (nightmares)
    Sleep-related bruxism
    Sleep-related headbanging (jactatio capitis nocturnus)
    Familial sleep paralysis
    Impaired sleep-related penile tumescence
    Sleep-related painful erections
    Sleep-related cluster headaches and chronic paroxysmal hemicrania
    Sleep-related abnormal swallowing syndrome
    Sleep-related asthma
    Sleep-related cardiovascular symptoms
    Sleep-related gastroesophageal reflux
    Sleep-related hemolysis (paroxysmal nocturnal hemoglobinuria)
    Asymptomatic polysomnographic finding
    Not otherwise specified*

---

*This entry is intended to leave place in the classification for both undiagnosed (''don't know'') conditions and additional (as yet undocumented) conditions that will be described in the future.

Appendix B: Daily Sleep Log

NAME _____
DATE_____

Try to keep these forms in the same place (i.e., on a table next to your bed) so that they will be within easy access for you to fill out each morning upon awakening. Please fill out this questionnaire each morning as soon as you wake up or, at latest, within 30 minutes of waking. Make sure you fill this form out each morning *before you leave your room*. The date given above is for the day on which it is filled out *(not the date when you went to bed)*. Please refrain from consuming alcohol or other drugs, and especially from taking sleeping pills within at least 3 hours prior to going to bed.

ALL INFORMATION ON THIS QUESTIONNAIRE WILL BE STRICTLY CONFIDENTIAL.

1. What time did you first get in bed to go to sleep last night? _____

2. How many times did you get out of bed (once you had initially gotten in to go to sleep) before you finally fell asleep? _____

3. If you got out of bed after you initially got in to bed to go to sleep, then please list how long you were out of bed in each instance (in minutes).
    1st time _____ 2nd time _____ 3rd time _____
    4th time _____ 5th time _____ 6th time _____
    7th time _____ 8th time _____ 9th time _____
    10th time _____
    (Please check back to #2. See that you included all the times out of bed).

4. What was the time of the last instance in which you got into bed and did not get out again until you were asleep? _____

5. What time did you fall asleep last night? _____

6. How much difficulty did you have in falling asleep initially last night?
    1. No difficulty _____   4. Quite a bit difficulty _____
    2. Very little difficulty _____   5. Much difficulty _____
    3. Moderate difficulty _____

7. How many times, if any, did you awaken last night? _____

8. If you did awaken last night, what time was it when you woke up? _____

What time did you fall asleep? _____

If more than once: time awakened _____   time asleep _____

                              time awakened _____   time asleep _____

9.   What time did you get up this morning? _____

10.   How rested did you feel this morning?
   1.   Very rested _____   3.   Not very rested _____
   2.   Moderately rested _____   4.   Not rested at all _____

PLEASE CHECK TO SEE THAT YOU'VE FILLED OUT ALL
RELEVANT QUESTIONS.

PART IV

Assessment Strategies for Behavioral Disorders

Albert Loro
Carole S. Orleans

9

Behavioral Assessment of Obesity

This chapter presents guidelines for the behavioral assessment of obesity. The goal in obesity assessment is to identify the obese condition and to determine the relative importance of behavioral, psychological, biological, and social factors in the etiology and maintenance of obesity. To achieve this goal, a comprehensive assessment protocol is necessary. An example of such a protocol is described, which outlines and explains some of the standard assessment methods and measures for assessing obesity and its contributing factors. In addition, several useful strategies for conceptualizing obesity are presented and discussed, with a review of several critical clinical and behavioral assessment issues.

OBESITY

Scope of the Problem

Obesity is the most common metabolic disorder in affluent societies, and the primary malnutrition problem in the United States (Bray, 1978a). It is usually estimated that between 40 and 50 million Americans are obese (Bray, 1979). A national health and nutrition survey was conducted in 1979; *obesity* was defined as 20 percent or more over ideal body weight, based on the revised Fogarty Conference tables of 1973 (Bray, 1979). According to this survey, of American adults from 25 to 74 years of age, 27.8 percent of females and 15 percent of males are obese. Taken together, these figures indicate that approximately 21 percent of the adult American population is obese. At the same time, medical research findings link obesity and the overconsumption of calories to several degenerative diseases (Bray, 1978b). The high correlation of obesity with diabetes mellitus, hypertension, cardiovascular disease, and other chronic debilitating diseases is striking, and the complications an obese patient faces during or following surgery or child-birth are multiple and severe. Additionally, sociopsychologic studies indicate that obesity stimulates social prejudice (Allon, 1975), occupational discrimination (Mayer, 1968), and discrimination in college admissions (Canning and Mayer, 1966). Obesity also results in psychological and developmental problems (Katahn, 1980). In short, obesity can be a significant social, psychological, and physical liability in a society that equates thinness with health, beauty, and social accep-tance. Finally, the health-related economic costs to the obese individual and soci-ety have not been systematically estimated. Approximately $80 million/year is spent on appetite-suppressant drugs (Stuart and Davis, 1972); the annual income of the U.S. diet industry was estimated at $10 billion in the early 1970s (Allon, 1973). We do not know the amount of added health care costs obese patients pro-duce, although we can speculate that this figure is significant.

Nature of the Problem

Obesity is a heterogeneous disorder of multiple origins. Biological, nutrition-al, behavioral, psychological, and social factors play varying roles in the cause and maintenance of the obese condition across different individuals. However, most professionals agree that overeating, underactivity, or both are responsible for up to 95 percent of obesities in America today. There is little professional consensus, however, and growing controversy about the constraints that certain biological, biochemical, and psychological factors place on a person who becomes obese and attempts to lose weight (Rodin, 1981; Wooley et al., 1979). For some obese patients, it may be more appropriate, safer, and healthier to maintain their obese bodyweight than to attempt to reduce and be unsuccessful (Jordan, 1973). For other obese individuals, there appear to be biochemical factors, particularly ab-normalities in the sodium–potassium pump processes, that mitigate against total cellular thermogenesis and weight reduction (De Luise et al., 1980).

Definition of the Problem

Obesity refers to an excessive accumulation of adipose tissue and should be distinguished from *overweight*, which refers to deviation from standards based on desirable weight charts (e.g., Metropolitan Life Insurance Company, 1959) de-rived for actuarial purposes. Desirable weight tables are generally compiled to predict longevity and, in some cases, morbidity for insurance purposes. There are, however, several interpretation problems with these tables. For example, one can be overweight without being obese, and one could possibly be obese without being overweight, although this condition is rare. Specifically, individuals with large, well-developed muscle mass (e.g., weight-lifters or football players) may be overweight according to standard tables but not obese (Katahn, 1980). Their overweight condition is a result of muscle tissue which tends to be more dense, weigh more, and occupy less space/unit of volume than adipose tissue. In contrast, a sedentary or disabled person could be underweight according to the standard tables, yet overfat.

OBESITY STATUS

An adequate obesity assessment must indicate whether the individual is, in fact, obese. As noted previously, there is an essential difference between overweight and overfat. Since obesity is most accurately defined as an excessive accumulation of body fat, and since the latter is only crudely reflected by body weight, a more valid measure is essential. Various sophisticated assessment techniques have long been available to obesity researchers (Garrow, 1978), but relatively few have been employed by clinicians (Mahoney et al., 1979). Moreover, there is no indisputable criterion for when body fat is "excessive" or for when percent over ideal body weight indicates obesity, although 20 percent over ideal body weight is generally considered obese (Mahoney et al., 1979). Since the average behavioral clinician does not have the necessary instruments or technology for direct measurement of body fat, indirect assessment methods are more feasible and popular (Rogers et al., 1980). Most of these methods have relied upon body weight as a predictor of body fat, but there has been much debate as to the optimal weight-derived index of obesity (Feinstein, 1959; Garrow, 1978; Keys et al., 1972; Mayer, 1968). There is an additional controversy about how much overweight constitutes too much (Andres, 1980; Hanna et al., 1981). In clinical research, the most popular indices of obesity have been the following: (1) bodyweight, (2) percent overweight based on height and sex norms, (3) anthropometry, and (4) transformations of height–weight ratios as in the Ponderal index (W/H^3) and the body mass index (W/H^2). The reliability and validity of these indices range from poor to relatively good depending on such parameters as age, sex, muscularity, and the degree of obesity (Mahoney et al., 1979). Some indices (e.g., the Ponderal index) appear to be heavily influenced by height and therefore biased (Powers, 1980); others are relatively stable across different heights, at least in overweight populations (Bray, 1978a; Powers, 1980).

The clinician or applied researcher, however, has been interested in more than the degree of obesity. Change in obesity status before, during and after treatment has been a major concern, and some of the dependent variables employed have included:

1. Absolute change in body weight (kg/lb lost) $(W_1 - W_2)$
2. Weight reduction index (where ideal weight is derived from actuarial tables) (lb lost/lb overweight $\times$ initial weight/ideal weight $\times$ 100)
3. Percent of excess body weight lost $(W_1 - W_2)/(W_1 - IW)$ (IW = ideal weight derived from actuarial tables)

4. Percent of body weight lost $(W_1 - W_2)/W_1$ (W_1 = initial body weight)
5. Changes in one of the previously noted height–weight ratios (e.g., body mass or Ponderal Index)

Mayer (1968) and others (Bellack and Rozensky, 1975; Garrow, 1978) have cogently criticized these weight dependent indices of obesity. If the applied researcher is interested in body fat and its presumed physiological correlates, then it is important to understand that these variables are poorly reflected by body weight. In fact, Mayer (1968) warns that these indices only correlate approximately 0.60 with body fat. A person can be "overweight" according to height–weight tables and still be normal or below average in fat content (e.g., muscular football players). Moreover, several studies have reported losses of body fat which were actually greater than observed losses in body weight (Boileau et al., 1971; Dempsey, 1964; Moody et al., 1969). These results were apparently due to increases in lean body mass (muscle) which masked fat reductions when body weight was used as the criterion of improvement (Rogers et al., 1980). In these cases, it is necessary to evaluate additional parameters such as arm, waist, and chest circumference to detect increases in muscle tone while bodyweight remains the same or slightly increases (Loro et al., 1979; Steel, 1977).

The most valid measures of body fat are densitometric techniques that employ total body density to estimate fat content. Although innovation continues in body fat estimation technology (Powers, 1980), the more conventional densitometric methods employ Archimedes' principle of volume displacement in water. Subjects are weighed and then immersed so that their underwater weight (corrected for lung and intestinal gases) can be measured. After several auxiliary measurements, these values are employed in an equation which estimates body density. From body density, one can estimate body fat (Behnke and Wilmore, 1974; Powers, 1980). The average nonobese American male is from 11 to 14 percent fat (standard deviation [SD] = 6 percent) (Allen et al., 1956; Durnin and Rahaman, 1967; Durnin and Womersley, 1974; Garrow, 1978). Densitometric methods can estimate body fat with reliabilities of .90 and higher. Unfortunately, densitometric methods require elaborate and expensive instrumentation and significant amounts of time. They are, consequently, of little practical use to the clinician. There are alternative methods which are more practical, less expensive, and less time-consuming.

Several researchers (Mayer, 1968; Powers, 1980; Wilson, 1978) have recommended skinfold thickness measures as an alternative to unsatisfactory weight-dependent indices and unfeasible densitometric methods. Skinfold measures capitalize on the fact that approximately half of the body's fat deposits are directly underneath the skin. The skinfold caliper is a relatively inexpensive instrument which allows accurate measurement of subcutaneous fat. By taking measures of skinfolds at various body sites, researchers derived equations which reliably predicted body fat. One of the most popular of these equations was developed by Allen et al., (1956) based on 10 skinfold sites. Research by Durnin and his colleagues (Durnin and Rahaman, 1967; Durnin and Womersley, 1974) suggests even simpler equations based on four skinfold sites (biceps, triceps, subscapular, and suprailiac). Although the Allen and Durnin equations have been among the most widely used, several equations are available (Powers, 1980). Skinfold thickness has been extensively researched by body composition specialists and the results are generally favorable (Rogers et al., 1980). It is less reliable in the extremely obese or underweight, and the method is susceptible to a myriad of technical errors (Johnson and Stalonas, 1977; Powers, 1980). There is a general consensus, however, that skinfold thickness provides a much better index of obesity than weight-dependent measures. Rogers and his colleagues (1980) reported after scanning the numerous studies in this area, that "skinfold measures of body fat correlate with the more accurate densitometric estimates at about .75 reliability." These assessment strategies are discussed in detail in a later section.

HEALTH RISK

The strong correlation between obesity and health risk is important from an epidemiological standpoint. It is also important for the researcher or therapist to assess these risks in each individual case. In fact, the inadequacy of many popular indices of obesity argues for a broader assessment that takes individual risk factors into account. For example, Rogers et al., (1980) following a comprehensive and intensive study of the clinical assessment of obesity recommended, "that we should begin to regard health risk indices as equally [if not more] important dependent variables [than] either weight or body fat estimates." These measures provide necessary relevant information and allow for a more comprehensive assessment of initial obesity status as well as more sophisticated insights into therapeutic improvements than do body weight or skinfolds alone. Since medical health risks are often considered the domain of medical specialists, the collaboration of qualified medical personnel in the assessment of these medical factors is essential. For an adequate measurement of health risk, Rogers et al., (1980) suggested the following multidimensional assessment battery: (1) blood pressure; (2) serum lipids and lipoproteins (cholesterol, triglycerides, and high- and low-density lipoproteins); (3) Stress electrocardiogram; (4) Assessment of aerobic capacity (maximum oxygen volume); and (5) Psychological status and adjustment. In addition to reflecting initial risk levels, changes in these variables may help assess the impact of treatment, both from a short- and long-term perspective.

METHODS OF ASSESSMENT

A variety of methods have been used to determine the presence of obesity. Some of these methods are more sophisticated and valid than others (Stuart and Davis, 1972). The two most commonly used professional methods of determining obesity are reference to height–weight tables (or another index derived from these tables) and the measurement of subcutaneous skinfolds. Because of their frequent use, these methods will be presented here and discussed in detail.

Assessment of Obesity With Height–Weight Tables

Tables of average or ideal body weights have been available in the United States since 1912 (Stuart and Davis, 1972). They are periodically updated (i.e., in 1929, 1943, 1959, and 1965) (Seltzer and Mayer, 1965; Stuart and Davis, 1972). Initially, these tables were based upon the weight and height of women and men at various ages, but the population samples of insurance policy-holders were not representative of the general population. A second limitation of the average weight tables was the fact that they reflected a rise in weight with age of upper- and middle-class socioeconomic groups. This unintentionally implied maturity-onset obesity was, if not desirable, at least acceptable and, possibly, the norm.

In later tables, (1943 and 1959), several improvements were attempted. Though still based upon data derived from insurance policy-holders, the age distribution was replaced with a designation of desirable or ideal body weights for men and women of differing heights and frame sizes. These designations were formulated from the actuarial experience of insurance underwriters. While these tables were considered an improvement over the earlier versions, the standards still did not provide adequate guidelines for distinguishing between small, medium, and large frames, nor did they standardize the conditions of weigh-ins. Subsequently, the estimated weights without clothing for men and women were believed to be approximately 8 and 5 pounds less, respectively, than the stated tabular weights (Stuart and Davis, 1972). An example of the standard height–weight tables used to determine percent overweight are illustrated in Tables 9-1 and 9-2.

Interpreting data from representative and standardized height–weight tables requires considerable caution, especially since overweight is not synonymous with obese. In otherwords, the correlation between weight in excess of standard tables and more direct measures of obesity is close but not always consistent (Stuart and Davis, 1972). This is especially true in children, adolescents, the aged, and special populations (e.g., the developmentally disabled). In regard to the matter of equating the conditions of overweight and obesity, the Public Health Service has cautioned clinicians and researchers:

> It cannot be overstressed that assigning a label of obese to any one person or group of persons should come only after a comprehensive assessment of all pertinent factors. The sex of the subject, age, body type, and state of health, along with specific measurements such as skinfold thickness must be considered in determining if a person is obese. Comparing any individual or group in terms of their heights and weights with a given set of averages or standards does *not* give adequate information on which to assess obesity since such comparisons imply weight not fatness (USPHS, 1966).

Table 9-1

Desirable Weights for Women (Age 25 and over)*

(Height without shoes)		Weight in pounds according to frame (in outdoor clothing)		
Feet	Inches	Small Frame	Medium Frame	Large Frame
4	8	92–98	96–107	104–119
4	9	94–101	98–110	106–122
4	10	96–104	101–113	109–125
4	11	99–107	104–116	112–128
5	0	102–110	107–119	115–131
5	1	105–113	110–122	118–134
5	2	108–116	113–126	121–138
5	3	111–119	116–130	125–142
5	4	114–123	120–135	129–146
5	5	118–127	124–139	133–150
5	6	122–131	128–143	137–154
5	7	126–135	132–147	141–158
5	8	130–140	136–151	145–163
5	9	134–144	140–155	149–168
5	10	138–148	144–159	153–173

*For women between 18 and 25, subtract 1 pound for each year under 25. (Reproduced with permission from the Metropolitan Life Insurance Company, New York, New York. Derived from data of the 1959 Build and Blood Pressure Study, Society of Actuaries.)

Table 9-2

Desirable Weights for Men (Age 25 and over)

(Height without shoes)		Weight in pounds according to frame (in outdoor clothing)		
Feet	Inches	Small Frame	Medium Frame	Large Frame
5	1	112–120	118–129	126–141
5	2	115–123	121–133	129–144
5	3	118–126	124–136	132–148
5	4	121–129	127–139	135–152
5	5	124–133	130–143	138–156
5	6	128–137	134–147	142–161
5	7	132–141	138–152	147–166
5	8	136–145	142–156	151–170
5	9	140–150	146–160	155–174
5	10	144–154	150–165	159–179
5	11	148–158	154–170	164–184
6	0	152–162	158–175	168–189
6	1	156–167	162–180	173–194
6	2	160–171	167–185	178–199
6	3	164–175	172–190	182–204

(Reproduced with permission from the Metropolitan Life Insurance Company, New York, New York. Derived from data of the 1959 Build and Blood Pressure Study, Society of Actuaries.)

Several researchers repeat this same caution (Seltzer and Mayer, 1976; Bellack and Rozensky, 1975; Katahn, 1980), and criticize the singular use of information from standard tables to determine obesity and evaluate progress in weight reduction treatment (Wilson, 1978). On the other hand, standardized tables afford the practicing clinician a fast, inexpensive, convenient, and useful way to determine percent overweight. Further, this assessment is understandable to the client and may have clinical or research implications (Hanna et al., 1981). The assessment of obesity with standard height–weight tables will probably continue for these reasons and, if cautiously interpreted, they can add an important dimension to the comprehensive assessment of obesity.

Assessment of Obesity with Skinfold Thickness Measures

Of all the various indirect measures of body fat, the measurement of skinfold thickness appears to offer the greatest overall promise in terms of validity, reliability, and practicality. While there are some procedural and practical problems with the accurate and consistent assessment of skinfold thickness (Garrow, 1978; Johnson and Stalonas, 1977), this measure seems to be a less biased and more sensitive means of assessing obesity (Seltzer and Mayer, 1967) than the standard height–weight tables. Since approximately half of total body fat is deposited in subcutaneous tissues, it is readily available for observation and assessment. Body fat is typically deposited in a layer of adipose tissue which, in many parts of the body, is only loosely attached to the underlying body tissue. Often clinical inspection alone is sufficient to determine whether a person is obese (Powers, 1980). In questionable cases the clinician can pinch the skin between the thumb and forefinger, attempt to pull it away from the underlying tissue, and determine the presence of excess adipose tissue. Basically, the skinfold thickness calipers were developed to make the process of manually pinching skinfold more systematic and standardized (Powers, 1980). Also, skinfold measures allow a comparison between indirect and direct laboratory methods of determining body fat, such as underwater weighing and ultrasonic techniques.

Skinfold Measurements that Indicate Obesity

There are marked age and gender differences in the distribution and amount of subcutaneous fat. For infants, children, and adolescents, relatively few broad epidemiological studies have been undertaken using skinfold measurements as the means of evaluating fat content. However, data from several studies (Seltzer and Mayer, 1965; Foman, 1974; 10 State Nutrition Survey, 1972) have been used to establish approximate upper limits of normal in children and adults. For example, the upper limits for the 1-year-old male is 15mm, 14mm at 2 years, 15mm at 10 years and 16mm at 18 years. The upper limit for a male 28 years and older is 22mm, while the upper limit for a female 30 years and older is 30mm.

The rationale for these norms was developed by Seltzer and Mayer (1965).

Using the triceps skinfold measurement, they suggested that skinfold measures greater than one standard deviation above the mean would constitute obesity. Therefore, approximately 84 percent of the population would fall below this point which was designated as the lower limit of obesity for white Americans; 16 percent of the population was defined as obese.

The values for infants and children up to 5 years of age are less certain than for older children because they are derived from cross-sectional data and most of this research is poorly controlled (Powers, 1980). Also, the ''normal'' fat content of infants and very young children is not known. Further, since longitudinal data for children are sketchy, it is not known with certainty if a higher body fat content in very early life portends later obesity (Powers, 1980). These norms are then, an approximate guide for determining obesity at different ages. Unlike the height–weight tables, they have the advantage of being independent of height or body frame.

Skinfold Thickness Variations

There are sex differences in subcutaneous fat distribution which affect skinfold thickness. In adult men, approximately 11 percent to 14 percent of body weight is subcutaneous fat tissue. In adult women, approximately 18 to 24 percent of body weight is subcutaneous fat tissue (Garrow, 1978; Mahoney et al., 1979; USPHS, 1966). These differences are reflected in skinfold measurements that are consistently larger in nonobese women than in nonobese men.

Skinfold Measurement Calipers

Although skinfold measurement is in itself a simple procedure, it must be performed under standard conditions to be valid. The two major instruments available for measuring skinfolds are the Harpenden caliper and the Lange caliper. The Lange caliper is the only one commercially produced in the United States. Its 1981 cost is approximately $155.00. (The Lange caliper is available from Cambridge–Scientific Industries, Cambridge, Maryland 21613.) The Harpenden caliper is a slightly different kind of caliper with a vise-type pincer mechanism. It is produced in England by British Indicators, Ltd. (St. Albans, Hertfordshire, England), and is slightly more expensive than the Lange caliper. Plastic calipers (for example, the Ponderax), although less costly, have inadequate springs and incorrect tension. An easy-to-use Arthrogauge is in the testing phase; it is a flat sheet of plastic with notches for accommodating different size skinfolds. The Lange or Harpenden caliper is the most useful caliper, since standards for obesity have been established with these instruments (Powers, 1980).

Triceps Skinfold versus Other Sites

Selection of the skinfold site remains controversial. The skinfold overlying the main point of the triceps of the non-dominant arm has been used most frequently in the large epidemiological studies, and most available studies establishing the upper limits of "normal" at different ages are based on this measurement. The triceps skinfold has the great advantage of easy accessability (i.e., it does not require that the patient disrobe). Other sites have been used in comparison studies, including points over the biceps muscle, above the iliac crest, immediately under the costal margin, and close to the umbilicus.

The major problem with the triceps skinfold is that accurate determination of the midpoint of a left or nondominant triceps is difficult, and an error in placement of the caliper can markedly skew readings. Some investigators have recommended that the subscapular skinfold be used because fat is distributed more uniformly. For this reason, placement of the caliper is not as critical and subscapular skinfold measurements are most easily reproduced, even by relatively inexperienced investigators (Powers, 1980). However, in terms of validity, the triceps skinfold measurement correlates more closely with density values obtained from underwater weighings than does the subscapular skinfold measurement (Seltzer and Mayer, 1965; 1967). From a clinical assessment standpoint, the triceps skinfold measurement is best if only one measurement is to be made. If measurement of two sites is feasible, the triceps and subscapular skinfolds are the best choices.

Procedures for Skinfold Measurement

The skinfold caliper to be used should be calibrated to exert a pressure of about 10 g/mm^2 and the pressure should be constant over a range of openings from 2 to 40 mm. The Lange caliper has a jaw surface which consists of a mobile flat metal piece; care is required to prevent misalignment. The contact surface between the jaw of the caliper and the skin should be from 20 to 40 mm. Readings are made to the nearest 0.5 mm.

Measurement of the triceps skinfold is as follows: A small mark is made on the left upper arm, halfway between the top of the olecranon and the tip of the acromial process with the arm flexed at a 90 degree angle. (In young children, this midpoint often appears higher than expected and is not necessarily at the point of the widest arm circumference.) A line is drawn vertically above the olecranon to cross the midpoint. The subject's arm then hangs straight and relaxed for the measurement. The examiner uses his or her left thumb and index finger to grasp and lift the triceps skinfold parallel with the long axis of the arm half an inch proximal to the cross mark. The calipers are applied to the fold below the fingers so that the pressure at the point measured is exerted by the caliper tips, not the fingers. If the deep fatfold appears anchored to the intermuscular septum, or if the main bulk of the triceps muscle is not directly felt with the thumb and forefinger just deep to the fatfold, the position should be rechecked, as it is probably too medial or lateral. (In infants, the muscle-subcutaneous fat interface must be clearly identified, because the calipers are often placed too deep.) The dial should be read 2 to 3 seconds after the caliper tips are placed on the fatfold. Two readings at the selected site are made, and the average is recorded (Seltzer and Mayer, 1965; Powers, 1980).

Whenever feasible, the subscapular skinfold can also be measured. For proper use of standardized tables, the left side should be used. The fatfold below the scapula tip is located and the same procedure as described above is followed. Precise localization of the site for this measurement is less critical than for the triceps fatfold measurement.

Sources of Skinfold Measurement Errors and Problems

Measurement of skinfold, and particularly of the triceps fatfold, is subject to a number of technical errors (Zerfas et al., 1977). These errors include: use of the wrong arm, incorrect measurement of the midarm point, and incorrect caliper placement. The common errors are itemized in Table 9-3. Burkinshaw, Jones, and Krupowicz (1973) found wide variability in recorded triceps fatfold measurements among three observers who each measured skinfold thickness in 21 subjects three times. Loro, Fisher, and Levenkron (1979) however, obtained high percentages of agreements among trained observers when measuring triceps skinfolds in 51 mildly and moderately overweight females.

More importantly, Johnson and Stalonas (1977) conducted a study to investigate the use of skinfold thickness measures as a dependent variable in an obesity treatment program and to determine whether the triceps measures alone (the most convenient site for skinfold measures) sufficed to provide valid data. Reliability estimates across different assessors were variable, although within assessor reliability estimates were very high. Correlations between skinfold measures and weight were unsatisfactory. According to the authors, the published standards for determining obesity on the basis of the triceps measure (Seltzer and Mayer, 1965) identified only 8 percent of the subjects as obese despite their characterization as ''visually overweight and averaging weight 40 percent over insurance table norms.'' Johnson and Stalonas (1977) concluded that there are several difficulties in obtaining reliable caliper reading and these are inherent in the assessment operation. For example, variations could occur in site selection, pinching the skin, applying calipers, and recording. The more simple operation of measuring subjects on a

Table 9-3
Errors in Triceps Skinfold Measurement

- Wrong arm (should be left arm)
- Midpoint of arm or posterior plane incorrectly measured or marked
- Arm not relaxed by side during measurement
- Examiner uncomfortable
- Finger-thumb pinch or caliper placement too deep (muscle) or too superficial (skin)
- Caliper jaws not at marked site
- Reading done too early or too late (should be 2 to 3 seconds after caliper is applied)
- At time of reading, pinch not maintained or caliper handle not fully released

(Adapted from Zerfas et al., 1977)

balance-bar scale can be contrasted with this procedure. Furthermore, the reported relationships between skinfold thickness measures and weight are based primarily on nonobese subjects. With more subcutaneous skin tissue to measure and more ways to measure it, one can expect higher variability in skinfold thickness measures of obese subjects. They emphasize that skinfold measures should be used only as an adjunct measure in weight reduction programs and list a number of precautions that should be followed if reliable information is to be obtained (see Table 9-4).

Other Assessment Methods

Some investigators have measured various diameters to estimate body fatness. Measurement of the mid-upper arm circumference has been widely used in developing countries, primarily to evaluate undernutrition in children. However, mid-upper arm circumference can easily be used to evaluate obesity. The midpoint of the non-dominant upper arm is obtained in the same way as for the triceps skinfold measurement. The measuring tape is applied to the skin around the entire arm with a snug tension but not so tightly applied as to cause an indentation. This method has the advantage of requiring very inexpensive equipment (less than $1.00, as compared to $155.00 for the Lange caliper).

Steinkamp et al. (1965) found close correlations between measurements of several body diameters and densitometry. They used 20 measurements in their investigation, including height and weight, 14 different diameters and circumferences, and 4 skinfold measurements. Correlation of these anthropometric measures with density estimates of body fat was high, r = .98. However, measurement of these circumferences is not in wide clinical use (Powers, 1980).

Ultrasonic and radiographic techniques have been used to estimate fat content. Soft x-rays can be useful in assessing the thickness of subcutaneous fat. Since fat is less dense than muscle and other lean body mass components, fat is less opaque on x-rays. Estimates of bodyfat from skinfold measurements were found to correlate highly with estimates of fat from x-rays (Garn, 1957). However, radia-

Table 9-4
Precautions in Skinfold Assessment

- Measurements should be obtained over four sites (biceps, triceps, subscapular, and suprailiac).
- The same observers should perform measurements throughout the assessment period.
- Site identification by skin markings, though often impractical, tends to increase inter- and intra-observer consistency.
- Skinfold measurements are an index of subcutaneous fat which may represent 50% of total adipose tissue and should be considered as an important criterion against which to evaluate the total health benefits of a weight reduction program.

(Adapted from Johnson & Stalonas, 1977)

tion dose limits the usefulness of this technique. Hawes et al. (1972) have compared fat content estimates using ultrasound, radiography, skinfold, and thigh circumference measurements over the greater trochanter and iliac crest. There are close correlations between radiography and skinfold and circumference measures. The authors conclude that ultrasound may provide one of the safest, most valid estimates of subcutaneous fat (Powers, 1980). From a clinical assessment standpoint, however, the use of ultrasound procedures is probably impractical and from a cost standpoint, prohibitive.

A BEHAVIORAL APPROACH TO ASSESSMENT FOR OBESITY TREATMENT

A behavioral approach dictates several important classes of variables to be assessed in analyzing the pattern of behaviors contributing to obesity. In deciding which variables should be changed to facilitate weight loss or control, the behavioral clinician considers each of the following: (1) the overt maladaptive behaviors contributing to an energy imbalance; (2) antecedent stimulus variables, which elicit or set the stage for the maladaptive behaviors; (3) organismic variables, including biological and psychological variables; and (4) consequences of maladaptive behaviors, including the reactions of significant others. Each of these variables needs careful assessment in planning a comprehensive treatment program (Goldfried and Davison, 1976).

The Energy Balance

The obese individual is (or was), by definition, in a state of positive energy imbalance, i.e., calories consumed exceed(ed) calories spent. This generalization is misleading in its simplicity, however, since an energy imbalance may develop in one or more of the following ways: (1) the individual may consume an excessive amount of calories, (2) The individual may expend too few calories, and/or (3) The individual may suffer from an energy conversion anomaly which adversely affects lipid metabolism and deposition of adipose tissue. Wooley and her colleagues (1979) have presented convincing evidence to support the notion that some obese individuals have developed propensities towards positive energy balances after reducing and regaining excess weight. In addition, research noting the reduced activity of the red-cell sodium-potassium pump suggests that biochemical factors may have a role in the pathophysiology of some types of obesity (DeLuise et al., 1980).

After considering the above biochemical and physiological factors, an adequate assessment battery should help the clinician determine the client's current and past energy balance, and the perceived level of difficulty (based on history) for establishing a negative energy balance, i.e., creating a caloric deficit by consuming fewer calories than one expends. There are no simple or unequivocal tests for determining energy conversion anomalies (Garrow, 1978). However, assessment of daily energy intake and output can be accomplished via caloric consumption records and physical activity charts. In both instances, the margin for error is large. Caloric intake records have been consistently inaccurate in the few studies that have closely examined their validity. Assuming a client keeps accurate caloric intake records, misrepresentations may stem from the reactivity of self-monitoring (Romancyzk, 1974), uncertainties about food and drink quantities, variations in the caloric value of differing brands of the same food, and individual differences in the net caloric absorption from particular foods. Direct observation of eating behavior may be difficult to arrange; only self-monitoring places the client in a position to independently monitor and regulate intake after treatment. Specific training and periodic ''reliability'' checks with feedback to the client may yield the best of both worlds.

On the energy-output side of the equation, accurate portable calorimeters are now available for naturalistic assessment of basal and activity-elevated metabolic rate. Unfortunately, these devices are expensive and somewhat complicated, making them impractical for most clinicians. Records of physical activity have been used by some researchers, but their reliability and validity have not been assessed. A cruder index of physical activity can be obtained from pedometers attached to the waist and adjusted for stride length. Although their validity remains unassessed, preliminary evidence suggests that pedometer measures may be reliable indices of change in the quantity of gross motor activity (Straw et al., 1981). Again, pedometers and activity records serve a useful function in providing activity feedback to the client.

Response Characteristics: A Closer Look

As Mischel (1968) has pointed out: ''in behavioral analysis the emphasis is on what a person does in situations rather than on inferences about what attributes he has more globally.'' In other words, the behavioral assessment of response variables should focus on situation-specific samples of maladaptive eating behaviors and exercise activity. Specifically, the behavioral clinician should gather extensive data about the topography of eating and activity, including the duration, frequency, pervasiveness, and intensity of caloric intake and output.

At the individual level, assessment of eating behaviors and activity patterns requires careful monitoring and recording of response topography. Katell et al., (1979) provide an excellent example of this behavioral approach. They directly observed and recorded an obese client's eating behaviors in both an analog laboratory setting and a natural setting. Behaviors recorded included bites, sips, utensil drops, and utensil down time. In addition, the client completed a daily caloric intake diary which required information about the antecedents to eating i.e., location, time, subjective rating of hunger, emotional state, and presence of others, as well as information about the act of eating or drinking, e.g., the duration, amount, and type of calories consumed. Since these behaviors may need to be changed during a weight reduction program, they are important targets for initial behavioral assessment. At the same time, the behavioral clinician needs to be aware of conflicting evidence about actual differences in the eating behaviors of obese and non-obese individuals. In several well-designed studies, no significant differences were identified in the caloric consumption or eating style of obese, overweight and normal weight subjects (Hill and McCutcheon, 1975; Mahoney, 1975; Milich et al., 1976; Wooley and Wooley, 1975). This controversy implies that caloric intake data must be assessed as well as other relevant information about exercise patterns, activities, and lifestyle in order to identify a client's behavioral patterns and design a suitable, appropriate intervention program. In some cases, it may be better to facilitate changes in a client's exercise habits and leisure time activities than to radically change eating habits (Loro, 1981; Loro et al., 1979).

At a global level, the overall pattern of eating leading to excessive caloric intake can usually be identified via self-monitoring and a caloric intake record (see Fig. 9-1). Obese clients typically exhibit some irregular eating habits, i.e., meal skipping, snacking, etc., and may also show considerable variability in the nutritional adequacy and appropriateness of their meals (Loro et al., 1979; McReynolds et al., 1976). Specifying areas of relatively normal eating and drinking behaviors and identifying the physical, cognitive, emotional, and social correlates of acceptable behavior can point the way to effective weight control. Mapping out maladaptive patterns is crucial to treatment design. Exploring the timing, duration, and content of meals (both the caloric and nutritive value) helps to establish these patterns. Identifying activities and events which accompany both adaptive and maladaptive eating suggests possible treatment interventions (Loro et al., 1979).

One pattern typical of obese clients involves vacillating between excessively strict dieting or fasting and overeating or binging. Dieting patterns are often major contributors to overeating (Loro & Orleans, 1981). Obese clients often complain of no breakfast and a very light lunch, and nonetheless maintain or gain weight for that day. This is frustating experience particularly if the client expects weight loss. In a similar vein, many dieters protest recommendations for three balanced meals daily, stating that they diet better by avoiding meals. On closer inspection, however, meal avoidance or prolonged fasting seems to result in overeating. Loro and Orleans (1981) carefully outline how excessively strict dieting or fasting sets the stage for overeating by producing extreme hunger, feelings of self-deprivation, and depression or fatigue related to low blood-sugar level and prolonged self-denial. When these aversive physical and emotional consequences reach a peak, the individual may overeat or binge (i.e., consume an enormous amount of calories in a very short time). In these circumstances, overeating or bingeing is powerfully and negatively reinforced by relieving, albeit temporarily, these aversive conditions. Often, the overeater under these circumstances experiences anguish,

Name_____   Today's Weight _____

Date	Time	Place	Alone or with whom	Associated activity	Feeling state(s)	*Food:* Amounts, types and how prepared *Liquids:* Amounts and types (compute calories)	Other relevant information

Fig. 9-1. Self-monitoring record of caloric intake.

shame, and self-hate after the initial relief. Unfortunately, these negative consequences are too delayed in time to inhibit overeating or bingeing. These negative experiences set the stage, in some cases, for purging via self-induced vomiting, or laxative or diuretic abuse. Detailed guidelines for behaviorally assessing binge eating and bingeing/purging practices and their controlling stimuli are provided elsewhere (Loro and Orleans, 1981; Orleans and Barnett, 1980). The point to be made is that any pretreatment assessment must include a careful study of the eating-and-dieting pattern that contributes to obesity. Similar care must be taken to measure activity levels. Periods of excessive exercise can be linked to periods of excessive self-denial, and may ultimately lead to a binge. In establishing regular, appropriate eating and exercise habits, baseline as well as treatment practices must be carefully monitored.

Stimulus Antecedents

In considering the role of antecedent stimulus events, a distinction can be drawn between those events that elicit emotional and autonomic responses, and those events that function primarily as cues for maladaptive instrumental responses. For instance, in dealing with maladaptive emotional response, like anxiety or depression, the behavioral clinician operates under the assumption that some cognitive, physiologic, or external stimulation is eliciting these states (Goldfried and Davison, 1976). Since maladaptive emotional responses often are linked to behaviors resulting in obesity, their antecedents require special attention and have been most often studied as antecedents for overeating (Loro and Orleans, 1981).

Boredom, anxiety, frustration, and positive anticipation are important antecedents for overeating or bingeing (Loro and Orleans, 1981). Many times, emotional responses can be linked to concurrent external events or activities. In these cases, the individual can learn to control or avoid external triggers for emotional states that trigger overeating. In other cases, cognitions or self-talk will play a major role in generating feeling states leading to overeating. For example, how an individual labels an internal stress and appraises his or her coping abilities can be the critical variable in determining emotional response. In most circumstances involving a pattern of consistent emotional antecedents for overeating, the therapist and the client must attempt to identify, measure, and control contributors to these emotional states. We have found that a rating scale similar to the SUDS (subjective units of discomfort scale) scales initially developed to measure anxiety (Wolpe, 1969), can be adopted for almost any feeling state (boredom, tension, frustration, despair, pessimism), and incorporated into daily caloric records (Fig. 9-1). The client rates the response intensity on a 1-to-10 scale at the time of every eating episode, both before and after eating occurs. Numerical ratings can be related to ongoing external events, and changes in ratings after eating can point out possible reinforcements for maladaptive eating behaviors.

Previously, it was believed that eating was regulated by biological cues associated with hunger and satiety. Yet, studies in the 1970s have shown the significance of external food- and meal-related stimuli, and suggested that some obese persons may be over-responsive to external cues, and relatively under-responsive to the internal cues normally associated with hunger and satiety (Schachter and Rodin, 1974). These findings initially spurred behavioral clinicians to carefully examine the relationship of eating to external cues involving the availability, smell, sight, and taste of foods, as well as meal times and settings. In fact, behavioral treatments that revolutionized weight control technology taught clients to use stimulus control strategies to regulate these external stimuli (Stuart, 1967, 1971). Recent research questions the original stimulus control treatment assumptions (Loro et al., 1979; Rodin, 1981), but for some obese clients, environmental and stimulus control of food-related cues is necessary for weight-reduction (McReynolds et al., 1976).

Internal or biological antecedents for overeating should be assessed in some cases. When external cues do not suggest a consistent pattern, or when their regulation does not sufficiently control overeating, antecedent internal states may be playing a crucial role. Rodin (1981) found that people who are visually overresponsive to the sight of food may also show the overproduction of insulin while viewing food preparation and preparing to eat. This physical overresponsiveness can lead to or reinforce overeating, which in turn produces reinforcing biological changes.

In a related vein, medical problems potentially related to faulty eating patterns must be carefully assessed as one set of antecedents. The energy imbalance of the obese individual rarely stems from hormonal irregularities and energy conversion anomalies, but these factors should not be overlooked. For example, hypoglycemia and various neurological defects or diseases can contribute to binge or compulsive eating (Loro and Orleans, 1981; Wermuth et al., 1977). These excessive eating episodes result in significant energy imbalances. A complete medical evaluation and continuous medical monitoring for serious conditions that may contribute to overeating or under activity or result from treatment are strongly recommended. Nutritional deficits related to fad dieting and electrolyte imbalances related to self-induced vomiting or purgative abuse are two other serious conditions that may result as the individual attempts to lose weight using his or her own dieting techniques (Russell, 1979).

In assessing discriminative stimuli that set the stage for maladaptive instrumental behaviors, the therapist must obtain detailed information on the precise nature of the situation in which the individual overeats or under-exercises. This information should include the time, place, social circumstances, and ongoing activities accompanying the maladaptive behavior. These data are typically collected on self-monitoring forms (see Fig. 9-1). Some activities are more likely to be associated with maladaptive eating practices than others (e.g., watching sports events on television, shopping, or eating in a restaurant). Likewise, social circumstances may either facilitate or inhibit eating depending on the consequences they foreshadow. For example, many obese clients will not overeat or eat at all in front of family and friends, yet they consume enormous numbers of calories when they are alone. Social reinforcement patterns can explain the development of a wide range of discriminative cues for the onset and termination of eating.

Finally, how the individual interprets an event can be an important determinant of stimulus antecedents for maladaptive eating and exercise behaviors. The issue of defining the effective stimulus has prompted many behavioral clinicians to examine the significant role played by physiological and cognitive states in setting the stage for maladaptive behaviors. These processes are usually referred to as organismic variables (Goldfried and Davison, 1976).

Organismic Variables

Many times, the behavioral clinician may need to focus not on environmental or stimulus variables but on cognitions, feelings, and other mediating factors in order to understand and modify behavior. Even though one individual's attitudes, beliefs, and expectations may often be modified by changes in overt behavior, there are times when such organismic variables should themselves be the targets for direct modification.

One type of mediator consists of the client's expectations about success in weight reduction. The way in which an obese client labels or categorizes an event can affect his or her emotional reactions in those situations (Ellis, 1962; Mahoney and Mahoney, 1976). For example, many chronic obese clients hold high expectations for fast and easy weight loss. These unrealistic expectations are usually followed by short-lived, moderate success and consequent feelings of disappointment about not reaching the initial, unreasonable goal. Typically, this disappointment leads to despair, and eventual relapse (Marlatt and Gordon, 1979) especially if the client has not acquired the necessary and appropriate relapse prevention skills (Rosenthal and Marx, 1979).

In addition to interpreting situations in ways that can create problems, a person may also create difficulties in labeling behavior. To the extent that an obese client perceives his or her maladaptive behavior as indicative of a lack of "willpower," inadequate metabolism, or other factors over which he or she has limited control, the problem will be compounded. Another important mediating cognitive variable in obesity assessment consists of the standards for self-reinforcement and ultimate success. Obese clients generally expect too much weight loss in too short a time with too little effort (Loro et al., 1979). Unfortunately, this fallacy is propagated in the media and played up in gimmicky come-ons for weight loss schemes. Even though an obese client may be functioning at an appropriate level of proficiency in weight reduction according to acceptable clinical standards (e.g., losing 1 to 2 lb/week in an outpatient behavioral program), his or her primary problem may result from the incorrect belief that this performance is not good enough or not fast enough. Detecting cognitive problems and negative self-statements has been described by Mahoney and Mahoney (1976) as "cognitive ecology." They suggest positive self-statements to counter unrealistic expectations and incorrect beliefs. Generally, obese clients need to develop realistic expectations, based on accurate information about their individual patterns and performance.

As noted in the previous section about antecedents, behavioral clinicians must pay particularly close attention to any physiological or biological factors that could contribute to maladaptive behavior or complicate the weight reduction process. Included would be one or more of the following: (1) complications from any number of obesity related disorders, such as diabetes, hypertension, gout, or arthritis; (2) the direct and indirect effects of medications taken; (3) the client's general energy level and capacity for physical exercise; and (4) any other important physiological and constitutional factors which might influence behavior. It is not uncommon, for example, for obese clients to experience problems with water retention. In women, these difficulties frequently coincide with menstrual periods and can produce significant weight gains in spite of close dietary adherence. As in other behavioral medicine problems, a thorough assessment for obesity treatment generally requires a complete physical exam with laboratory tests (see Bray et al., 1976, for a comprehensive evaluation flow chart). After assessing organismic variables, the behavioral clinician then focuses on the behaviors to be changed.

Finally, in order to make meaningful, useful, and sensible treatment recommendations, clinicians must understand all of the following factors and their unique contribution to, or influence on, caloric intake and energy expenditure (Rogers et al., 1980).

1. Knowledge about nutrition and dietetics
2. Knowledge about exercise and physical activity
3. Attitudes about one's obesity
4. Attitudes about one's body
5. Expectations about treatment
6. Current eating patterns
7. Current activity patterns
8. Knowledge about structuring and organizing time
9. Attitudes about exercise
10. Family and social factors related to caloric intake and expenditure
11. Level of social skills, especially assertiveness and anger control
12. Family history of obesity

Consequent Variables

In determining whether a behavior "pays off," or is reinforced, both the timing and nature of the consequences must be carefully assessed. For example, the neurotic or addictive paradox (Mowrer, 1950) refers to behavior having immediate positive consequences and long-term negative ones, as in the cases of overeating, alcohol abuse, or smoking. In the case of overeating, often a precursor of obesity, there are few behaviors that are more pleasurable, readily accessible, tasty and socially acceptable than eating. A frequently existing negative consequence for obese clients is the reaction of others to their obesity. These punishing reactions can result in obese clients isolating themselves from the public (Millman, 1980). Unfortunately, from a behavior change perspective the negative consequences from overeating are too delayed in time from the actual eating behavior to effectively control caloric intake.

A behavioral assessment includes determining the full range of immediate and delayed consequences of overeating and underexercising. Positive and negative consequences should be studied. Likewise, consequences for desired eating and exercise practices should be assessed, since the dual goal of behavioral treatment programs is to *decrease* reinforcement for maladaptive behaviors and to *increase* reinforcements for adaptive substitutes. The daily caloric intake record (Fig. 9-1) can be modified to collect this information. An interview can often furnish critical guidelines for detecting reinforcement patterns, or the reinforcement survey schedule (see Cautela and Kastenbaum, 1967) can be administered, assisting the client in identifying possible new reinforcers for adaptive behaviors.

Social consequences are particularly important, even if the individual claims that all significant others disapprove of overeating and even if significant others could be helpful in arranging for appropriate eating, for example, by avoiding junk food and choosing restaurants in which "natural" or low-calorie foods are served. In some cases, well-intentioned positive consequences may in fact be negative. Many obese clients report that apparent efforts by family and friends to be helpful are actually aversive. These might include a parent taking away food from an obese adolescent, or a friend commenting on the caloric value of an individual's plateful of food. At the same time, social responses planned to be unpleasant may actually reinforce maladaptive behaviors. Loro and Orleans (1981) report how disapproval may actually reinforce rebellious overeating among obese binge eaters, and suggest counter-control tactics to avoid inadvertently reinforcing maladaptive behaviors. Likewise, Stuart and Davis (1972) report that spouses' critical attention to faulty eating may reinforce, rather than extinguish, overeating. During behavioral assessment, it is important to identify individuals who are positive and consistent in their support of the client, as well as individuals who are intrusive, punitive, and provocative. Behavioral treatment programs for obesity often successfully include significant others in reprogramming social consequences for overeating (Saccone and Israel, 1978).

In addition to the timing and type of reinforcement, the clinician should observe the frequency of reinforcement. In the case of obese clients who face a long, difficult, and frustrating journey to weight control, there usually is a need for frequent rewards. Early rewards to enhance adherence to the program, consistent and significant intermediate rewards to maintain sustained efforts, and long-range rewards for reaching goal weight and maintaining that weight are in order.

CRITICAL FACTORS AND ASSESSMENT ISSUES IN
OBESITY: A CLINICAL APPROACH

Obesity results from consuming more calories than one expends. But as we have shown, a variety of factors influence food consumption and day-to-day activities. Thus, obesity is not a single disease entity, but rather a complex, multifaceted disorder that encompasses *psychological, behavioral, environmental, and biological factors* (Bray, 1978a). In obesity treatment assessment, each of the four factors must be explored. This section focuses on critical psychological, behavioral, and environmental aspects of obesity (Loro, 1979). For a thorough description of important biological and medical problems that present with obesity, the reader is referred to work by Bray, Jordan, and Sims (1976) and Jordan, Levitz, and Kimbrell (1977).

There are several critical psychological factors to consider when assessing a patient for obesity treatment. First and probably most important is the patient's history of psychologic and psychiatric disturbance. It is essential to determine whether the patient has experienced any untoward effects, such as anxiety, depression, or disturbance of body image, during prior attempts at weight reduction. These types of psychological problems are generally more common in patients who have been obese since childhood or adolescence, and are less common in patients who became obese in adulthood (defined as life after age 19) (Grinker et al., 1973). Psychiatric problems associated with obesity treatment can typically be handled with psychotherapy or psychiatric consultation.

With the history of psychiatric disturbance, it is necessary to evaluate the patient's current psychological functioning. Sensible weight reduction is a demanding and lengthy task, and the professional must assess the patient's capacity to cope with the rigors of dieting. Frequently, the physician or a designiated associate may need to provide some type of psychological or emotional support during the weight reduction program. It is especially important to determine whether the patient is experiencing significant life changes, such as a change in marital status, job, or environment. During such times of lifestyle change and readjustment, it is *not* recommended that an obese patient initiate a long-term weight reduction program (Jeffrey and Katz, 1977). It is additionally necessary to determine the number of years a patient has been obese, and whether the patient has a previous history of anorexia nervosa, bulimia (binge eating) or bulimarexia (the bingeing-purging pattern) (Loro and Orleans, 1981). When a professional encounters these eating disorders, psychiatric and/or psychological consultation is necessary, and referral may be advisable. After compiling the above data, the professional can accurately estimate a patient's readiness for, and probably responsiveness to, a comprehensive obesity treatment program. Success is most likely in patients who are early in stages of obesity, who developed obesity during adulthood rather than childhood, who have *no* previous history of attempted weight loss with failure to lose weight or with prompt regaining of lost weight, and who have an understanding physician and family.

Certain types of behavioral data are also necessary when evaluating a patient for obesity treatment. Behavioral questions should include number of previous attempts at weight loss, the presence of a yo-yo pattern (repetitive cycles of aborted diets associated with marked weight losses and weight gains), and current physical activity level. The general probability of successful weight loss is inversely proportional to the number of previous attempts at weight reduction. Additionally, if a patient demonstrates a yo-yo pattern of weight loss and gain and has a sedentary lifestyle, that patient's chance of being successful in obesity treatment is relatively low.

A detailed account of the patient's daily eating behavior and activity patterns, as well as information about early feeding experiences and family attitudes/pressures toward food and weight loss could shed light on these behavioral factors. In this regard, it is important to determine the role of food in the family, (i.e., if food was used as reward or punishment, and if the patient is being pressured to reduce). Some obese patients act out against authority or parental figures who are subtly or overtly coercing them to reduce their weight. This acting out tends to consist of secretive overeating and may require psychotherapeutic intervention.

As we have noted, the assessment of the patient's nutritional knowledge and expectations about the amounts and types of food that are allowed during a dietary program is vital. Patients frequently lack adequate nutritional knowledge and tend to make inappropriate and unrealistic choices about foods while dieting. In all cases, the clinician needs to evaluate the patient's thoughts, feelings, and behaviors in relation to food in order to properly assess the roles that food, eating, and activity play in the patient's life. From these data, the clinician can identify problematic cognitive, emotional, and behavioral patterns that require change.

Finally, a variety of environmental issues must be considered when assessing a patient for obesity treatment. The most important environmental considerations include family and social factors. The emotional and psychological support available to the patient should be analyzed, as well as the number and types of non-food-related activities and interests. Successful weight reduction and weight control require a supportive social and family system, major lifestyle restructuring to lift the central focus of life from food and drink, and realistic considerations about structuring time and activities. It is also important to assess the frequency with which a person comes in contact with food, and if these contacts result in consumption. In some cases, careful consideration may need to be given the patient's occupation, especially if it is directly involved in food preparation and/or results in regular inactivity.

In summary, the proper assessment of an obese patient requesting treatment requires a thorough consideration of psychological, behavioral, environmental, and biological factors. All four contribute to obesity and may complicate or interfere with treatment.

The Role of Personality Assessment and Psychological Tests

Reviews of the obesity treatment literature consistently show that organismic variables such as demographic characteristics, personality measures, and psychopathology have *not* been reliably related to treatment outcome (Bellack, 1975; Jeffrey et al., 1978; Stunkard and Mahoney, 1976; Weiss, 1977). Valid predictor variables are most likely identified by focusing on what a person *does* (i.e., behavior) in specific situations rather than on what a person believes, prefers, or thinks (Wilson, 1980). There is supportive evidence, however, for the clinical and individualized use of empirically based psychometric instruments (such as the MMPI or Bell Adjustment Inventory) to identify psychological or adjustment problems prior to treatment (Leon, 1976; 1979; Weiss, 1977). Without therapeutic attention, these problems tend to complicate and impede standard behavioral weight reduction treatment (Loro et al., 1979).

ASSESSING TREATMENT OUTCOME

Assessing Change

The same measures used during pretreatment baseline assessment should be used post-treatment, to document pre- to post-treatment changes in eating, exercise behaviors, weight, and body fat. If caloric records or activity logs were used to identify and quantify eating/exercise practices, they should be used in the same form after treatment. Any precautions introduced to enhance the accuracy of self-report for these measures should be included at post-treatment assessments (i.e., observed weigh-ins vs self-reported weight). Likewise, weight or skinfold thickness measures should be exactly duplicated. The addition of measures such as percentage of desired loss, or degree to which treatment goals have been achieved may also be included. But, without duplicating pretreatment measures, the validity of post-treatment results can be compromised (Wilson, 1978).

Issues related to selecting appropriate treatment controls are beyond the scope of this chapter. However, control groups are needed to establish the link between treatment and outcome. In some cases, a correlational approach can be used to clarify the means whereby change occurs. If, for instance, stimulus control procedures are central to an intervention, clients' compliance with prescribed stimulus control strategies should be monitored. Likewise, if self-reward practices are central to treatment, they should be carefully monitored. Critical external supports for change in eating and exercise can be estimated by asking clients to rate the degree or adequacy of support they received. Also, significant others can make these ratings. Practical methods for determining factors that influence treatment outcome and the mechanisms of desired behavior change, are provided in the next section, which addresses the assessment of how treatment outcomes are maintained.

These guidelines apply equally to end-of-treatment measures. More has been written about assessing pre- to post-treatment changes than assessing maintenance of change. In particular, the reader is referred to Gormally et al. (1977) and Wilson (1978). The following section concentrates on measurement of factors related to long-term maintenance of behavioral change in weight control programs.

Assessing Maintenance of Treatment Outcomes

Maintenance is the *sine qua non* of successful obesity treatment. Only if treatment-produced changes in weight, eating, and exercise practices are maintained is treatment successful. Maintenance remains the toughest problem in obesity treatment, as in the treatment of other addictive behaviors requiring significant lifestyle change, e.g., smoking, alcoholism, and drug addiction (Marlatt and Gordon, 1979). Even the most successful behavioral treatments are more effective in producing initial weight loss than long-term maintenance (Jeffrey et al., 1978; Stunkard, 1977). In order to establish and understand the maintenance of treatment outcomes, careful follow-up monitoring is needed (Wilson, 1978). Two types of measures are discussed in this chapter: longitudinal extensions of pre- and post-treatment measures, and measures designed specifically to illuminate the maintenance/relapse process.

Longitudinal Follow-up

In most cases, it is important to extend pre- and post-treatment measures into the follow-up period. The main purpose of longitudinal assessment is to evaluate long-term outcome. High-risk relapse periods can be identified and focused relapse prevention training could be offered during these periods (Rosenthal and Marx, 1979).

We recommend at least four follow-ups, at intervals of 6 weeks, 12 weeks, 6 months, and 12 months. Although 18-month-and-longer follow-ups are desirable, long-term follow-ups present many practical problems. Wilson (1978) recently made several specific practical suggestions for increasing the probability of obtaining long-term follow-up data in weight loss studies:

1. Making maintenance procedures and long-term follow-up an integral part of the study's design, and presenting this information to clients prior to treatment. In this way, clients who commit themselves to treatment are also commiting themselves to follow-up.
2. Instituting frequent personal contact between the therapists and clients, so as to minimize attrition. These contacts could be made by phone or mail, and may serve as a maintenance strategy on their own.
3. Instituting a contingency contracting system with refundable deposits. Clients will lose their deposits if they do not provide follow-up data.

Another practical question concerns the measures to be used. Ideally, measures should be administered in the same form used in pre- and immediate post-treatment assessments. This usually involves an actual weigh-in and careful daily diet and exercise records. If weigh-ins cannot be arranged, consider obtaining the client's permission to contact his or her physician to verify self-reported follow-up weights. Sometimes knowing (or just believing) that a researcher will objectively verify self-report increases the accuracy of self-report. For instance, graduates of a "quit smoking clinic" reported more truthfully on their post-treatment smoking status when informed that a test of carbon monoxide levels would be administered to get a physical index of their smoking behavior (Ohlin et al., 1976).

A third practical question concerns which variables, other than weight, should be explored at follow-up to describe long-term weight control. We recommend including a measure of the mechanism whereby maintenance is expected or hypothesized to occur. If, for instance, a clinician hypothesizes that only those clients who maintain their new eating and exercise regimens will maintain or continue to lose, then some measure of eating and exercise habits could be incorporated at follow-up (Chapman and Jeffrey, 1979). Likewise, if stable changes in irrational thinking about eating are believed to be at the base of an effective treatment, maintenance of these "intervening variables" should be assessed. Even administering such measures at a single follow-up point can be extremely beneficial.

Stuart and Guire (1978), in an exemplary follow-up study, contacted 721 Weight Watchers graduates 12 to 15 months after they had achieved their goal weights. These researchers developed a 33-item questionnaire that included questions about weight and weight maintenance, in addition to questions about continued use of behavioral self-management techniques, continued involvement in Weight Watchers, lifestyle changes supporting weight maintenance, altered self-concept, and tensions related to weight management as measured by the restrained eating scale (developed by Herman and Polivy, 1975). Variables were dictated by their theory of weight maintenance. In this study, continuity in self-management and treatment predicted successful maintenance. Continued attendance of Weight Watchers' meetings, particularly by returning to one's initial group, continuous use of behavioral self-control techniques, and the adoption of lifestyle changes supporting maintenance (e.g., increased exercise) discriminated successes from backsliders. Of course, these results need to be replicated because follow-up data, including weight, were based primarily on self-report. For example, it could be argued that only those with the best maintenance provided follow-up data, and therefore reported the greatest success in changing eating and exercise habits. But in spite of the questionable validity of these results, this study represents a step toward identifying how maintenance is achieved.

There is perhaps one more requirement of longitudinal follow-up. Care should be taken to determine possible negative or positive "side effects" of weight loss. Advocates of a symptom substitution explanation for the success of behavioral treatment of obesity or other addictive behaviors might argue that superficial changes in eating behavior could cause increased stress or anxiety, or lead the dieter to substitute other forms of anxiety control that might be just as *undesirable* (e.g., increased tobacco, alcohol, or drug abuse). Behavior therapists who seek to program replacements (e.g., relaxation or regular exercise) for overeating as a form of stress management might argue that changes in weight would be accompanied by *positive* shifts in self-efficacy, self-esteem, and lifestyle or stress management habits. Few studies of obesity or other health lifestyle change programs have included measures of possible positive or negative side effects. Again, the Stuart and Guire study (1978) stands out. They asked follow-up questions concerning exercise level and mastery over mood and found that those maintaining weight loss reported positive changes in mood management and exercise.

Exploring Maintenance Factors and Relapse

In addition to establishing the long-term maintenance of treatment outcomes, one may wish to clarify the mechanisms of maintenance and relapse, which entails a slightly different measurement approach. Empirical and theoretical guidelines exist for selecting variables to study. Research to find predictors of maintenance of obesity treatment results offer useful empirical guidelines. In most cases, personality and demographic variables have not predicted treatment success (Jeffrey et al., 1978; Weiss, 1977). Certain weight-related variables seem to influence maintenance: higher initial weight and childhood-onset obesity tend to correlate negatively with weight-loss maintenance (Stuart and Guire, 1978; Weiss, 1977). But the most promising results have come from studies of behavioral correlates of maintenance. Two variables stand out: continued use of self-management practices, and self-reinforcement style.

Permanent weight-control involves lifelong changes in eating and exercise habits. The most successful treatments involve teaching self-management skills (such as self-monitoring and stimulus control) to achieve and maintain these changes. Clinicians and researchers have increasingly evaluated self-management practices as a dimension of outcome and maintenance. Most studies have been based on the eating and exercise diaries described earlier (Cohen et al., 1980), and/or on questionnaires or interviews asking about self-management techniques (Chapman and Jeffrey, 1979; Cohen et al., 1980; Perri and Richards, 1977; Stuart and Guire, 1978). Behavioral observations (meal length, bite size and frequency, etc.) have also been employed (Kattell et al., 1979).

There has been little consistency across studies in method or focus of assessment, and self-control practices are not always assessed during maintenance (Johnson et al., 1980). This may partially account for the inconsistency in specific findings across studies. For example, adherence to stimulus control procedures did not discriminate success and failure in two studies (Chapman and Jeffrey, 1979; Perri and Richards, 1977), but did in a third study (Stuart and Guire, 1978). Substantiating self-report through direct observation might better demonstrate the influence of self-control practices in weight loss and maintenance. This has been the case with studies of self-reinforcement as a specific self-management technique.

We would expect maintenance of changed eating practices to relate to patterns of self-reward for behavior change. Successful weight control requires sustained use of self-management techniques in the natural environment. Setting reasonable goals, self-monitoring, self-appraisal, and self-reward are crucial. In some studies, self-reinforcement style was identified as a variable influencing initial and long-term weight loss. Rozensky and Bellack (1974) compared 12 subjects who had successfully lost 15 pounds on their own with 12 subjects who tried to lose weight and failed. They elicited actual samples of self-reinforcement behavior using a structural verbal recognition memory task (Bellack and Tillman, 1974). Successful weight-losers consistently administered more positive self-reinforcement than nonlosers. Perri and Richards (1977) compared college students who had succeeded in losing weight to a group that failed to change their overweight/overeating problems. A structured interview protocol was used to determine the self-management techniques subjects used, finding that successful dieters used self-reward significantly more often. Successful weight-losers also reported more positive feedback from significant others. Chapman and Jeffrey (1979) contacted subjects completing a behavioral weight loss program and a 7-month follow-up. Questionnaire reports of sustained attention to principles and practices of self-reward and self-standard setting correlated significantly with maintenance of weight loss verified by actual weigh-ins. Self-reward has also been found to predict outcomes of lifestyle programs in other areas like smoking, dating, and studying (Newman, 1971; Perri and Richards, 1977; Condiotte and Lichtenstein, 1981). Assessing self-reinforcement practices during maintenance can add a great deal to understanding how maintenance is achieved.

Another way to approach maintenance is to examine how relapse occurs and is resisted. Marlatt and Gordon (1979) are the pioneers of this approach. They have studied relapse among smokers, alcoholics, and drug addicts completing abstinence-oriented treatment, and developed a cognitive–behavioral model of the relapse process. The chief obstacles to maintenance are high-risk relapse situations for which the individual lacks coping skills. Relapse episodes commonly involve feeling angry, frustrated, or tense, dealing with interpersonal conflict, or coping with social pressures. Whether a person backslides or remains abstinent depends on coping skills and a sense of self-efficacy, i.e., the belief that one can enact the coping behaviors needed to resist relapse. Bandura's (1977) self-efficacy theory, central to the Marlatt and Gordon relapse model, asserts that expectations of personal efficacy influence the initiation, persistence, and strength of coping responses. Finally, this model explains the easy course from a single slip to a full-blown relapse by positing an abstinence violation effect; this leads to intense guilt and personal attributions for failure, and serves to undermine self-efficacy. The model suggests ways to assess, control and intervene in the relapse process.

Rosenthal and Marx (1979) have applied the Marlatt and Gordon model to a group of dieters treated with behavioral approaches. First, they studied relapse after treatment to identify high-risk relapse situations. They found that situations involving inability to deal with depression, anger, or boredom, or to cope with positive social events like parties or celebrations, were frequently involved in relapse episodes. They then designed and evaluated a relapse prevention program to teach dieters in advance to analyze high-risk situations, to use global problem-solving strategies in order to avoid relapse, and to prevent feelings of deprivation by increasing the daily ratio of ''fun''–''obligatory'' activities. Dieters who received this training during their treatment did not differ at end of treatment from those who did not. But those that received relapse prevention training maintained their losses better. Weight loss from initial weight to a 60-day follow-up was significantly greater for dieters trained in relapse prevention. Dieters armed with relapse prevention techniques made more external attributions and felt less guilty following a slip, and felt less influenced by ''lack of willpower'' or ''internal weakness.''

In sum, Rosenthal and Marx (1979) have shown that the model developed by Marlatt and Gordon is clinically useful when applied to obesity. Results point to the value of new maintenance assessments, including measures of self-efficacy. Several practical measures of self-efficacy during maintenance could also be borrowed from studies of smoking cessation programs. DiClemente (1979), for instance, asked newly abstinent smokers who had quit either on their own or in a formal program to use 7-point, Likert-type ratings to indicate how sure they were they would avoid smoking in each of 12 high-risk situations (e.g., ''when alone and feeling nervous,'' ''with friends at a party''). These ratings were summed to get a single self-efficacy score, which reflected global self-efficacy. Successful maintainers judged at a 5-month follow-up had higher post-treatment self-efficacy scores than recidivists. Condiotte and Lichtenstein (1981) developed a similar instrument using ratings for 48 common smoking situations. They found that self-efficacy scores increased from pre- to post-treatment assessments. In addition, higher post-treatment scores were associated with less recidivism and longer prerelapse intervals in a 3-month follow-up. Similar measures might be applied to predicting maintenance and recidivism among dieters.

SUMMARY

This chapter presents guidelines, procedures, and strategies for the behavioral assessment of obesity. The dual goals of obesity assessment are to identify the obese condition and to determine the relative importance of behavioral, psychological, environmental, social, and biological factors in the etiology and maintenance of obesity. To achieve these goals, a comprehensive assessment protocol is described and explained. This protocol includes the standard obesity assessment methods and describes relatively new behavioral assessment procedures. These behavioral methods are particularly important when designing weight reduction treatment programs. In addition, several useful assessment strategies are presented and discussed; these discussions focus on clinical issues in weight reduction treatment. Finally, the authors suggest ways to improve treatment outcome, increase the quality of long-term follow-up studies, and facilitate the maintenance of weight lost during treatment.

REFERENCES

Allen, T. H., Peng, M. T., Chen, K. P., Huang, T. F., Chang, C., & Fang, H. S. Prediction of total adiposity from skinfolds and the curvilinear relationship between external and internal adiposity. *Metabolism*, 1956, *5*, 346–352.

Allon, N. The stigma of overweight in everyday life. In G. A. Bray (Ed.), *Obesity in perspective*, Vol. 2, part 2. Washington, D.C.: Government Printing Office, 1973.

Allon, N. Fat is a dirty word: Fat as a sociological and social problem. In A. Howard (Ed.), *Recent advances in obesity research:I*. London: Newman, 1975.

Andres, R. Influence of obesity on longevity in the aged. In, *Aging, cancer and cell membranes*, Vol. 7, Advances in cancer biology series. New York: Stratton Intercontinental Medical Book Corporation, 1980.

Bandura, A. Self-efficacy: Toward a unifying theory of behavioral change. *Psychological Review*, 1977, *84*, 191–215.

Behnke, A. R., & Wilmore, J. H. *Evaluation and regulation of body build and composition*, Englewood Cliffs, New Jersey: Prentice-Hall, 1974.

Bellack, A. S. Behavior therapy for weight reduction. *Addictive Behaviors*, 1975, *1*, 73–82.

Bellack, A. S., & Rozensky, R. H. The selection of dependent variables for weight reduction research. *Journal of Behavior Therapy and Experimental Psychiatry*, 1975, *6*, 83–84.

Bellack, A. S., & Tillman, W. The effects of task and experimenter feedback on the self-reinforcement behavior of internals and externals. *Journal of Consulting and Clinical Psychology*, 1974, *43*.

Boileau, R. A., Buskirk, E. R., Hortsman, D. H., Mendez, J., & Nicholas, W. C. Body composition changes in obese and lean men during physical conditioning. *Medical Science in Sports*, 1971, *3*, 183–189.

Bray, G. A. (Ed.). *Recent advances in obesity research:II*. London: Newman, 1978a.

Bray, G. A. Definition, measurement, and classifications of the syndromes of obesity. *International Journal of Obesity*, 1978b, *2*, 99–112.

Bray, G. A. (Ed.). Obesity in America. Washington, D.C.: DHEW-NIH No. 79-359, 1979.

Bray, G. A., Jordan, H. A., & Sims, E. A. H. Evaluation of the obese patient: I. An algorithm. *Journal of the American Medical Association*, 1976, *235*, 1487–1491.

Brightwell, D. R., & Sloan, C. L. Long-term results of behavior therapy for obesity. *Behavior Therapy*, 1977, *8*, 898–905.

Burkinshaw, L., Jones, P. R., & Krupowicz, D. W. Observer error in skinfold thickness measurements. *Human Biology*, 1973, *45*, 273–279.

Canning, H., & Mayer, J. Obesity: Its possible effect on college acceptance. *The New England Journal of Medicine*, 1966, *275*, 1172–1174.

Cautela, J. R., & Kastenbaum, R. A reinforcement survey schedule for use in therapy, training, and research. *Psychological Reports*, 1967, *20*, 1115–1130.

Chapman, S. L., & Jeffrey, D. B. Processes in the maintenance of weight loss with behavior therapy. *Behavior Therapy*, 1979, *10*, 566–570.

Cohen, E. A., Gelfand, D. M., Dodd, D. K., Jensen, J, & Turner, C. Self-control practices associated with weight loss maintenance in children and adolescents. *Behavior Therapy*, 1980, *11*, 26–37.

Condiotte, M. M., & Lichtenstein, E. Self-efficacy and relapse in smoking cessation programs. *Journal of Consulting and Clinical Psychology*, in press.

DeLuise, M., Blackburn, G. L., & Flier, J. S. Reduced activity of the red-cell sodium-potassium pump in human obesity. *The New England Journal of Medicine*, 1980, *303*, 1017–1022.

Dempsey, J. Anthropometrical observations on obese and non-obese young men undergoing a program of vigorous physical activity. *Research Quarterly*, 1964, *35*, 275–287.

DiClemente, C. C. *Self-efficacy and smoking cessation maintenance*. Unpublished manuscript, 1979, Texas Research Institute of Mental Sciences, Houston, Texas.

Durnin, J. V. G. A., & Rahaman, M. M. The assessment of the amount of fat in the human body from measurements of skinfold thickness. *British Journal of Nutrition*, 1967, *21*, 681–689.

Durnin, J. V. G. A., & Womersley, J. Bodyfat assessed from total body density and its estimation from skinfold thickness: Measurements on 481 men and women aged from 16 to 72 years. *British Journal of Nutrition*, 1974, *32*, 77–97.

Ellis, A. *Reason and emotion in psychotherapy*, New York: Lyle Stuart, 1962.

Feinstein, A. R. The measurement of success in weight reduction: An analysis of methods and a new index. *Journal of Chronic Diseases*, 1959, *10*, 439–456.

Foman, J. J. *Infant nutrition* (Ed. 2). Philadelphia: W. B. Saunders & Co., 1974.

Garn, S. M. Roentgenogrammetric determinations of body composition. *Human Biology*, 1957, *29*, 337–353.

Garrow, J. S. *Energy balance and obesity in man* (Ed. 2). Amsterdam: Elsevier/North Holland Biomedical Press, 1978.

Goldfried, M. R., & Davison, G. C. *Clinical behavior therapy*. New York: Holt, Rinehart, & Winston, 1976.

Gormally, J., Moscati-Buese, E., Clyman, R., & Forbes, R. R. Research design issues for behavioral treatment of obesity. *Journal Supplement Abstract Service Catalog of Selected Documents in Psychology*, 1977, *7*, 34.

Grinker, J., Hirsch, J., & Levin, B. The affective responses of obese patients to weight reduction: A differentiation based on age at onset of obesity. *Psychosomatic Medicine*, 1973, *35*, 57–63.

Hanna, C. F., Loro, A. D., Jr., & Power, D. D. Differences in the degree of overweight: A note on its importance. *Addictive Behaviors*, 1981, *6*, 61–62.

Hawes, S. F., Albert, A., Healy, M. J. R., & Garrow, J. S. A comparison of soft tissue radiography, reflected ultrasound, skinfold calipers and thigh circumference for estimating the thickness of fat overlying the iliac crest and greater trochanter. *Proceedings of the Nutrition Society*, 1972, *31*, 91A–92A.

Herman, C. P., & Polivy, J. Anxiety, restraint, and eating behavior. *Journal of Abnormal Psychology*, 1975, *84*, 666–672.

Hill, S. W., & McCutcheon, N. B. Eating responses of obese and non-obese humans during dinner meals. *Psychosomatic Medicine*, 1975, *37*, 395–401.

Jeffrey, D. B., & Katz, R. C. Take it off and keep it off: *A behavioral program for weight loss and healthy living*. Englewood Cliffs, New Jersey: Prentice-Hall, 1977.

Jeffery, R. W., Wing, R. R., & Stunkard, A. J. Behavioral treatment of obesity: The state of the art in 1976. *Behavior Therapy*, 1978, *9*, 189–199.

Johnson, W. G., & Stalonas, P. Measuring skinfold thickness: A cautionary note. *Addictive Behaviors*, 1977, *2*, 105–107.

Johnson, W. G., Wildman, H. E., & O'Brien, T. The assessment of program adherence: The Achilles heel of behavioral weight reduction. *Behavioral Assessment*, 1980, *2*, 297–301.

Jordan, H. A. In defense of body weight. *Journal of the American Dietetic Association*, 1973, *62*, 17–21.

Jordan, H. A., Levitz, L. S., & Kimbrell, G. M. Psychobiological factors in obesity. In E. D. Wittkower and H. Warnes (Eds.), *Psychosomatic medicine: Its clinical applications*. Hagerstown, Maryland: Harper & Row, 1977.

Katahn, M. Obesity. In R. H. Woody (Ed.), *Encyclopedia of clinical assessment*. San Francisco: Jossey-Bass, 1980.

Katell, A., Callahan, E. J., Fremouw, W. J., & Zitter, R. E. The effects of behavioral treatment and fasting on eating behaviors and weight loss: A case study. *Behavior Therapy*, 1979, *10*, 579–587.

Keys, A., Fidanza, F., Karvonen, M. J., Kimura, M., & Taylor, H. L. Indices of relative weight and obesity. *Journal of Chronic Diseases*, 1972, *25*, 329–343.

Leon, G. R. Current directions in the treatment of obesity. *Psychological Bulletin*, 1976, *83*, 557–578.

Leon, G. R. Cognitive–behavior therapy for eating disturbances. In P. C. Kendall and S. D. Hollon (Eds.), *Cognitive–behavioral interventions: Theory, research, and procedures*. New York: Academic Press, 1979.

Loro, A. D., Jr. Critical psychological, behavioral, and environmental issues in assessment for obesity treatment. In J. B. Parker (Ed.), *Psychotherapeutics*. Birmingham, Alabama: Southern Medical Association, 1979.

Loro, A. D., Jr. Treatment of eating disorders. In P. A. Boudewyns, & F. J. Keefe (Eds.), *Behavioral medicine for the primary care physician*. Reading, Massachusetts: Addison-Wesley, in press.

Loro, A. D., Jr., Fisher, E. B., Jr., & Levenkron, J. C. Comparison of established and innovative weight reduction treatment procedures. *Journal of Applied Behavior Analysis*, 1979, *12*, 141–155.

Loro, A. D., Jr., Levenkron, J. C., & Fisher, E. B., Jr. Critical clinical issues in the behavioral treatment of obesity. *Addictive Behaviors*, 1979, *4*, 383–391.

Loro, A. D., Jr., & Orleans, C. S. Binge eating in obesity: Preliminary findings and guidelines for behavioral analysis and treatment. *Addictive Behaviors*, 1981, *6*, 155–166.

Mahoney, M. J. Fat fiction. *Behavior Therapy*, 1975, *6*, 416–418.

Mahoney, M. J., & Mahoney, K. *Permanent weight control: A total solution to the dieter's dilemma*. New York: Norton, 1976.

Mahoney, M. J., Mahoney, K., Rogers, T., & Straw, M. K. Assessment of human obesity: Measurement of body composition. *Journal of Behavioral Assessment*, 1979, *1*, 327–349.

Marlatt, G. A., & Gordon, J. R. Determinants of relapse: Implications for the maintenance of behavior change. In P. Davidson (Ed.), *Behavioral Medicine: Changing health lifestyles.* New York: Brunner/Mazel, 1979l

Mayer, J. *Overweight: Causes, costs, and control.* Englewood Cliffs, New Jersey: Prentice-Hall, 1968.

McReynolds, W. T., Lutz, R. N., Paulsen, B. K., & Kohrs, M. B. Weight loss resulting from two behavior modification procedures with nutritionists as therapists. *Behavior Therapy,* 1976, *7,* 283–291.

Metropolitan Life Insurance Company. New weight standards for males and females. Statistical Bulletin, 1959, *40,* 2–3.

Milich, R. S., Anderson, J., & Mills, M. Effects of visual presentation of caloric values on food buying by normal and obese persons. *Perceptual and Motor Skills,* 1976, *42,* 155–162.

Millman, M. *Such a pretty face.* New York: W. W. Norton & Co., 1980.

Mischel, W. *Personality and assessment.* New York: Wiley, 1968.

Moody, D. L., Kollias, J., & Buskirk, E. R. The effect of a moderate exercise program on body weight and skinfold thickness in overweight college women. *Medical Science in Sports,* 1969, *1,* 75–80.

Mowrer, O. H. *Learning theory and personality dynamics.* New York: Ronald, 1950.

Newman, A. The effect on reinforcement of intention statements and/or execution of self-control in smokers and ex-smokers. *Addictive Behaviors,* 1977, *2,* 15–20.

Ohlin, P., Lundh, B., & Westling, H. Carbon monoxide blood levels and reported cessation of smoking. *Psychopharmacology,* 1976, *49,* 263–265.

Orleans, C. S. & Barnett, L. R. Bulimarexia: Guidelines for behavioral assessment and treatment. Paper presented at the 14th Annual Convention of the Association for Advancement of Behavior Therapy, New York, November, 1980.

Perri, M. G., & Richards, C. S. An investigation of naturally occurring episodes of self-controlled behaviors. *Journal of Counseling Psychology,* 1977, *24,* 178–183.

Powers, P. S. *Obesity: The regulation of weight.* Baltimore, Maryland: Williams & Wilkins Co., 1980.

Rodin, J. Current status of the internal-external hypothesis for obesity: What went wrong? *American Psychologist,* 1981, *26,* 361–372.

Rogers, T., Mahoney, M. J., Mahoney, K., Straw, M. K., & Kenigsberg, M. I. Clinical assessment of obesity: An empirical evaluation of diverse techniques. *Journal of Behavioral Assessment,* 1980, *2,* 161–181.

Romanczyk, R. G. Self-monitoring in the treatment of obesity: Parameters of reactivity. *Behavior Therapy,* 1974, *5,* 531–540.

Rosenthal, B. S., & Marx, R. D. A comparison of standard behavioral and relapse prevention weight reduction programs. Paper presented at the 13th Annual Association for the Advancement of Behavior Therapy convention, San Francisco, California, December, 1979.

Rozensky, R. H., & Bellack, A. S. Individual differences in self-reinforcement style and performance in self- and therapist-controlled weight reduction programs. *Behavior Research and Therapy,* 1974, *14,* 357–364.

Russell, G. F. M. Bulimia nervosa: An ominous variant of anorexia nervosa. *Psychological Medicine,* 1979, *9,* 429–448.

Saccone, A. J., & Israel, A. C. Effects of experimenter versus significant other-controlled reinforcement and choice of target behavior on weight loss. *Behavior Therapy*, 1978, *9*, 271–278.

Schachter, S., & Rodin, J. (Eds.). *Obese humans and rats*. Potomac, Maryland: Lawrence Erlbaum Associates, 1974.

Seltzer, C. C., & Mayer, J. A simple criterion of obesity. *Postgraduate Medicine*, 1965, *38*, A101–A107.

Seltzer, C. G., & Mayer, J. Greater reliability of the triceps skinfold over the subscapular skinfold as an index of obesity. *The American Journal of Clinical Nutrition*, 1967, *20*, 950–953.

Steel, J. M. Measurement of triceps skinfold thickness during the treatment of obesity. *Obesity and Bariatric Medicine*, 1977, *6*, 20–22.

Steinkamp, R. C., Cohen, N. L., Siri, S. W. E., Sargent, T. W., Walsh, H. E. Measures of body fat and related factors in normal adults: I. Introduction and methodology. *Journal of Chronic Diseases*, 1965, *18*, 1279–1289.

Straw, M. K., Mahoney, K., Rogers, T., & Mahoney, M. J. Assessment of human obesity: Measurement of energy intake and expenditure. Unpublished manuscript. Bowman-Gray School of Medicine, Wake Forest University, Winston-Salem, North Carolina, 1981.

Stuart, R. B. Behavioral control of overeating. *Behavior Research and Therapy*, 1967, *7*, 198–204.

Stuart, R. B. A three dimensional program for the treatment of obesity. *Behavior Research and Theory*, 1971, *9*, 177–186.

Stuart, R. B., & Davis, B. *Slim chance in a fat workd: Behavioral control of obesity* (professional edition). Champaign, Illinois: Research Press, 1972.

Stuart, R. B., & Guire, K. Some correlates of the maintenance of weight lost through behavior modification. *International Journal of Obesity*, 1978, *2*, 225–235.

Stunkard, A. J. Behavioral treatments of obesity: Failure to maintain weight loss. In R. B. Stuart (Ed.), *Behavioral self-management: Strategies, techniques and outcome*. New York: Brunner/Mazel, 1977.

Stunkard, A. J., & Mahoney, M. J. Behavioral treatment of the eating disorders. In H. Leitenberg (Ed.), *Handbook of behavior modification and behavior therapy*. Englewood Cliffs, New Jersey: Prentice-Hall, 1976.

Ten State Nutrition Survey, 1968-1970. Washington, D.C.: U.S. Department of Health, Education and Welfare, 1972.

U.S. Public Health Service. Obesity and health. Publication No. 1485. Washington, D.C.: U.S. Government Printing Office, 1966.

Weiss, A. R. Characteristics of successful weight reducers: A brief review of predictor variables. *Addictive Behaviors*, 1977, *2*, 193–201.

Wermuth, B. M., Davis, K. L., Hollister, L. E., & Stunkard, A. J. Phenytoin treatment of the binge-eating syndrome. *American Journal of Psychiatry*, 1977, *134*, 1249–1253.

Wilson, G. T. Methodological considerations in treatment outcome research on obesity. *Journal of Consulting and Clinical Psychology*, 1978, *46*, 687–702.

Wilson, G. T. Behavior modification and the treatment of obesity. In A. J. Stunkard (Ed.), *Obesity*. Philadelphia: W. B. Saunders Co., 1980.

Wolpe, J. *The practice of behavior therapy*. New York: Pergammon, 1969.

Wooley, O. W., & Wooley, S. C. The experimental psychology of obesity. In T. Silverstone,

& J. Finchman (Eds.), *Obesity: Pathogenesis and management.* Lancaster, Pennsylvania: Medical and Technical Publishing Co., 1975.

Wooley, S. C., Wooley, O. W., & Dyrenforth, S. R. Theoretical, practical and social issues in behavioral treatments of obesity. *Journal of Applied Behavioral Analysis,* 1979, *12,* 3–25.

Zerfas, A. J., Shorr, I. J., & Neumann, C. G. Office assessment of nutritional status. *Pediatric Clinics of North America,* 1977, *24,* 253–272.

Carole S. Orleans
Robert H. Shipley

10

Assessment in Smoking Cessation Research: Some Practical Guidelines

Since 1975, behavioral science researchers and clinicians have made great progress refining smoking control treatment programs and solving the associated measurement problems (McFall, 1978; Pechacek, 1979). This chapter presents a practical overview of the major assessment issues in smoking control research, and presents recommendations based on rapidly growing research findings. It is organized into several sections so it can be used as a reference for clinicians and researchers to evaluate smoking control treatments.

The first section presents guidelines for assessing smoking behavior for the purpose of evaluating smoking control treatments. It describes and critically evaluates various measures of smoking rate, focusing on indispensible self-report measures. Commonly used self-report measures are discussed with respect to their accuracy, reactivity, and "palatability," or acceptability to subjects. Several corroborating measures are introduced: physiological measures of biochemical exposure, informant reports, and unobtrusive assessments.

The greatest progress in the measurement of smoking behavior has come through work to validate physiological indices of smoking status, smoking rate, and biochemical exposure (e.g., daily tar, nicotine, and carbon monoxide intake). This research is reviewed, focusing on practical indices of carbon monoxide absorption, thiocyanate production, and nicotine absorption. The sensitivity, specificity, cost, and convenience of these measures for smoking control research are discussed. The value of these measures as indices of smoking health risks is appraised. The section concludes with guidelines for matching specific physiologic measures to specific assessment needs.

The third section concerns measuring the process and outcome of smoking control treatments. Our focus is on multicomponent behavioral smoking cessation treatments combining nonsmoking skill training and aversive smoking, and on newer, controlled smoking and nicotine-fading procedures. Therefore, we recommend assessing compliance with treatment procedures and measuring important "nonspecific" treatment parameters, screening subjects for aversive smoking and safeguarding their health by assessing the physiological impact of aversive smoking procedures, and measuring smoking substance and smoking topography in controlled smoking regimens.

The final section addresses the measurement of pre- to post-treatment change. We present some "rules of thumb" for post-treatment evaluations, and discuss abstinence measures and the problem of treatment and assessment dropouts. We also advise assessing treatment "side-effects," and exploring the maintenance and relapse process in long-term follow-ups. The chapter concludes with an appendix containing sample pre- and post-treatment questionnaires; the questionnaires reflect recommendations made throughout the chapter and serve as a model or practical reference.

MEASURING SMOKING RATE

The most basic concern in assessing smoking behavior is to quantify the amount a person smokes. For smoking cessation treatment research, this usually involves determining smoking status, that is, abstinence or nonabstinence, and the number of cigarettes smoked daily. Measures of smoking rate are discussed first in this chapter, reserving a discussion of abstinence for a later section on the measurement of change. Since any comprehensive assessment of smoking behavior should include the assessment of brand smoked, total biochemical exposure (i.e., daily tar, nicotine, and carbon monoxide intakes) and the compound physiologic effects and health risks of that exposure, these measures are addressed later in the chapter.

The most typical measure of smoking is number of cigarettes smoked daily. There is, however, nothing sacred about this measure (McFall, 1978). One could, for instance, measure a larger unit (packs consumed), or smaller units (puffs taken), or measure instead levels of biochemical exposure (e.g., mg of nicotine absorbed). We begin with number of cigarettes per day because it is most commonly employed by smokers and researchers alike. Since it is practical and widely used, it facilitates comparisons across smokers and studies. It correlates well with more complex assessments of smoking behavior; we therefore recommend it as the basic index of smoking behavior.

Most smoking control studies rely exclusively on self-report information about smoking rate. In a sample of 30 studies published between 1975 and 1978, Frederiksen, Martin, and Webster (1979) found that 93 percent of the studies employed some form of self-report smoking rate. Of that group, 36 percent used self-report alone, and 60 percent combined self-report and observational measures. Only 14 percent used indirect assessment (corroborator report or physiolog-ical measures) to verify self-report. Like McFall (1978), we strongly advise some verification of self-report data. Our preference is for physiologic verification, since physiologic measures also furnish data about biochemical exposure and health risks. But we expect that self-report will remain the basic dependent measure in smoking treatment research as perhaps the most accurate measure of smoking rate.

There are several excellent reviews of major methodological issues in self-monitoring (Fremouw and Brown, 1980; Kazdin, 1974; Nelson, 1977). Of special concern in using any self-reported date are *reactivity, accuracy,* and *"palata-bility."* Selecting a self-report measure involves a compromise between accuracy, reliability, and palatability.

Reactivity is present whenever behavior changes as a result of the self-monitoring procedure. In smoking cessation research, tallying cigarettes smoked often results in a decrease in that number. But when used as an assessment device versus treatment method, the reactivity would be unwanted. The accuracy of self-monitoring refers to the agreement between self-recorded data and data col-lected using other measures. Thus, self-recorded smoking is accurate inasmuch as it agrees with data recorded by family and friends, and/or with relevant physi-ologic indices of biochemical exposure. When relying on self-monitoring to evalu-ate treatment results, it is essential to maximize accuracy while minimizing reactivity.

A third parameter of practical importance is the palatability, or acceptabil-ity, of the self-monitoring regimen to its user. Self-recording methods which are perceived as onerous (i.e., high response cost) are likely to result in noncom-pliance, subversion, or withdrawal from the treatment (e.g., Condiotte & Lich-tenstein, 1981). For example, smoking diaries are popular ways to facilitate functional analyses of smoking (Danaher and Lichtenstein, 1978). However, per-sons asked to continuously record detailed descriptions of the circumstances of their smoking behavior may fail to do so, comply only sporadically, estimate prior to a session, or drop out of the treatment or the study. Although an exten-sive self-monitoring system appears scientifically exact, it may engender unknown noncompliance that seriously undermines accuracy. To help raise the palatability of any self-monitoring method, all data collected by participants should be acknowl-edged and used by the therapist or experimenter, and should have some clear value or meaning (i.e., be reinforcing) for subjects. Several variations in self-monitoring method are discussed below with regard to their reactivity, accuracy, and palatability.

Frequency of Self-monitoring

Frederiksen, Epstein, and Kosevsky (1975) systemically compared contin-uous recording of when each cigarette was smoked each day, once-daily record-ing of the total number of cigarettes, or once-weekly telephone reports of daily

cigarette consumption. Their findings suggest that continuous monitoring of cigarettes smoked, while potentially very accurate, is highly reactive and not palatable. Accuracy proved greatest in the continuous monitoring condition. However,
accuracy was high with all three monitoring conditions (greater than 85 percent
agreement with informants' reports). Continuous recording proved more reactive,
producing reduced smoking after 3 weeks of self-monitoring, and was also judged
least palatable. In fact, 25 percent of participants in the continuous monitoring
condition failed to complete the study, noting excessive self-monitoring demands
as their reason for quitting. It thus appears that continuous monitoring is probably *not* the best assessment method, unless it is included as a treatment adjunct to
reduce smoking among highly motivated subjects. The subjects themselves selected the daily rating procedures as the best assessment compromise, but little
recommends daily (over weekly) self-monitoring. Either of these intermittent recording methods was palatable, accurate, and relatively nonreactive.

Timing of Self-recording

Kanfer (1970) suggested that recording an undesirable behavior, like smoking a cigarette, prior to the behavior may disrupt it, and thus be more reactive
than recording the behavior after it occurs. Empirical evidence on this hypothesis
is mixed (Karoly and Doyle, 1975; Rozensky, 1974). The smoking of a cigarette
actually cannot be monitored prior to its occurrence. Therefore, the question is
one of monitoring the intention or urge to smoke vs recording the occurrence of
smoking.

Target of Self-monitoring

Abrams and Wilson (1979) found self-monitoring of nicotine consumption
(by monitoring number of cigarettes × nicotine/cigarette) to be more reactive than
simply monitoring the number of cigarettes. For regular smokers accustomed to
counting cigarettes or packs/day, nicotine intake may be more salient or more
threatening than cigarette intake. Nicotine monitoring might thus be problematic
where assessment of stable smoking rates is desirable, but valuable where reduced
smoking is desired (Foxx and Brown, 1979).

Knowledge of Accuracy Checks

Knowledge of accuracy checks increases accuracy of self-report. Thus, self-
recording of smoking will be more accurate if subjects believe that the experimenter will verify their accuracy (Evans et al., 1977).

Retrospective Global Self-report

Retrospective global self-report is commonly used. The subject or client is
asked, "how many cigarettes do you usually smoke per day?" Obviously low in
reactivity, this measure is presumed to be high in palatability, since it is unlikely

to elicit resistance. The only remaining question, then, concerns its accuracy. Vogt (1977) noted a presumed digit bias, with half of 98 smokers reporting smoking 20, 30, or 40 cigarettes per day. Twenty-two percent of the subjects gave different estimates of daily cigarette consumption on questionnaires administered an hour apart. Nevertheless, reported daily cigarettes correlated moderately ($r = .55$) with a combination of biochemical measures of smoke exposure (expired air carbon monoxide and plasma thiocyanate).

Shipley (1981) obtained a correlation of .75 between self-estimates of number of cigarettes smoked over the past week and expired air carbon monoxide (COa) levels. Subjects' knowledge that COa measures would be taken may have increased self-report accuracy. Specifying time frame in the question (e.g., cigarettes smoked over the past week) may produce greater accuracy than more open-ended queries (e.g., "How many cigarettes do you usually smoke?"). While such global, retrospective estimates are probably less accurate than self-monitoring, they have the advantage of being lower in reactivity and are highly palatable. When combined with verifying physiologic measures, global self-reports are an acceptable basic rate measurement.

Informant Reports

Outside observation of the subject's natural smoking behavior theoretically represents a measurement ideal. It is, however, difficult to find objective observers, and experimenter observation in controlled laboratory sessions is likely to be quite reactive. Although high correlations ($\approx .90$) between self-reports and informant's reports of smoking behavior have been reported (Ober, 1968; Shipley, 1981), informants generally are friends or relatives of the subjects; it cannot be known to what extent high agreement reflects collusion rather than measurement accuracy. For this reason, we recommend physiological assessments over informant reports for corroborating smoking behavior.

Unobtrusive Measures

Perhaps 90 percent of social science research is based on self-report data (Webb et al., 1966). Webb and coworkers advocate non-reactive, unobtrusive measures based on natural records of the behaviors being measured. Nonobtrusive naturalistic measures seem particularly promising for measuring the effectiveness of system-wide smoking control interventions (at worksites, hospitals, or schools). For instance, McFall (1978) suggests counting cigarette butts in ashtrays as an unobtrusive measure of cigarette consumption. Counting them, and measuring their length, Auger et al., (1972) assessed the impact of an antismoking poster campaign on smoking in specific settings. Likewise, in worksites selling cigarettes at low cost (e.g., Veterans Administration Medical Centers), the impact of interventions aimed at reducing smoking could be measured by cigarette sales at the worksite.

VERIFYING SELF-REPORT: PHYSIOLOGICAL MEASURES

Verifying self-report has been the single greatest problem facing researchers evaluating smoking cessation treatment. False reports of abstinence following treatment have been noted in experimental, clinical, and worksite programs (Brockway et al., 1975; Ohlin et al., 1976; Rosen and Lichtenstein, 1977). Collaborator verification represents, at best, an imperfect solution. Fortunately, systematic research has identified several physiologic correlates of smoking behavior and indices of biochemical exposure. These tools are useful both to verify self-report data and to detect changes in smoking-related health risks.

Three biochemical correlates of smoking behavior have received particular attention: carbon monoxide levels in expired air; thiocyanate levels in serum, urine, and saliva; and nicotine/cotinine levels in serum, urine, and saliva. These measures are described below in a practical review that emphasizes their advantages and disadvantages in discriminating smokers and nonsmokers, and in indicating treatment-induced changes in smoking rate, smoking patterns, and related health risks.

We strongly advise combining self-report with one or more physiologic measures to evaluate any smoking control program. Ironically, physiologic measures are likely to increase the truthfulness or validity of self-report. More adolescents reported their smoking when they believed saliva samples would be analyzed for an objective index of smoking (Evans et al., 1977). Likewise, one-third of allegedly abstinent graduates of a quit-smoking clinic confessed to smoking when challenged with discrepant physiologic evidence (Ohlin et al., 1976). This desired reactive effect can be profitably exploited by clinicians and researchers. Bogus physiologic measures were used to convince subjects that the experimenter could "read" their true feelings and beliefs (Jones and Sigall, 1971). Under these circumstances, subjects were more likely to report socially undesirable feelings and beliefs. A similar strategy could be used to convince subjects that the researcher has independent evidence of smoking behavior. This alone, even without true verification, would be expected to improve the validity of self-report. A bogus physical index may be useful when actual physiological data cannot be analyzed for all subjects.

Alveolar Carbon Monoxide

Definition and Health Risks

Carbon monoxide (CO), a by-product of tobacco combustion, is one of the most hazardous compounds in tobacco smoke. Cigarettes vary in CO content, and a listing of CO contents of major brands should be consulted to estimate daily CO exposure (Jenkins et al., 1979). CO quickly displaces oxygen in the blood to form carboxyhemoglobin (COHb), thereby reducing vital oxygen supply to body tissue. This has been directly linked to smoking-related illnesses, including cardiovascular disease, chronic obstructive pulmonary diseases, and fetal damage in pregnant mothers (Frederiksen and Martin, 1979; Wald et al., 1975). The estimated half-life of CO in the body is only 3 to 5 hours, and even less under conditions of heightened physical activity (Frederiksen and Martin, 1979; Horan et al., 1978; Lando, 1975).

Measurement Procedures

COHb concentrations can be directly measured in blood samples or reliably estimated using non-invasive breath sampling. CO saturation in expired alveolar air (COa), expressed in parts/million (ppm), is linearly related to COHb concentration (Jones et al., 1958; Stewart et al., 1976). Using portable analyzers that require no backup laboratory facilities, COa can be reliably measured in less than 2 minutes (Lando, 1975; Horan et al., 1978; Hughes et al., 1978). Subjects hold their breath for 20 seconds, then expel the first portion of their expired breath, exhaling the last portion into a small polyvinyl bag. Energetics Science, Inc. (Hawthorne, New York 10542) manufactures a portable Ecolyzer with needed supplies for about $2,000.

Specificity

Vulnerability to influence by nonsmoking-related CO sources limits the specificity of COa measures for smoking (Frederiksen and Martin, 1979). First, ambient CO levels affect COa and COHb measures. Ambient CO is elevated by passive smoking and numerous environmental pollutants, including auto exhaust and other products of incomplete combustion (Stewart et al., 1976). Exposure to secondhand smoke in any poorly ventilated or confined area can relatively quickly raise nonsmokers' COa levels to those of smokers. Second, a range of personal factors influences CO uptake and elimination. An individual's activity level influences how quickly CO is eliminated; greater activity levels produce more rapid elimination. Likewise, poorly understood constitutional factors, drug treatment effects (e.g., phenobarbitol and disphenylhydantion increase CO levels), and alcohol use can influence CO absorption and elimination or lead to measurement error (Frederiksen & Martin, 1979). Adding an inexpensive filter to the portable COa analyzers removes interference caused by alcohol use, but other sources of ambient CO exposure and possible measurement error must be monitored.

Discriminating Smokers and Nonsmokers

Notwithstanding their sensitivity to nonsmoking influences, COHb and COa levels successfully discriminate smokers from nonsmokers. Smokers typically have COHb levels two to three times higher than those of nonsmokers, with mean nonsmoker COHb levels under 2 percent and mean COHb levels above 4 percent among regular smokers (Russell, 1973; Turner, 1976). COa levels of 20 to 40 ppm are typical for regular smokers, while 3 to 5 ppm levels are expected for nonsmokers (Cohen et al., 1971; Frederiksen and Martin, 1979; Goldsmith and Aronow, 1975; Horan et al., 1978). Lando (1975) found a range from 36 to 80 ppm for regular smokers, and 5 to 11 ppm for smokers claiming abstinence after treatment.

Vogt and coworkers recommend 8 ppm as the threshold for dichotomizing smokers and nonsmokers (Vogt et al., 1977). They also caution against reliance on COa levels as a measure for habitual smoking among "atypical smokers," including those smoking less than one-half pack per day and those who do not inhale. Because of its short half-life, COa is not a good measure for detecting low-level or episodic smoking. Overnight abstinence could easily bring a smoker's COa levels down to those of a nonsmoker's (Henningfield et al., 1980).

Several precautions can be taken to minimize the disadvantages of the brief CO half-life. Hughes et al. (1978) recommend a time lapse of at least 30 minutes following smoking before estimating daily COa, and stress the importance of standardization and careful reporting of time since last smoking. Horan et al. (1978) suggest choosing a standard time of day for COa measures, preferably towards the end of the day. Henningfield and coworkers were able to correctly identify six of eight people who had smoked only three cigarettes that day by analyzing samples of COa collected late in the day (Henningfield et al., 1980). Horan et al. also advise impromptu assessment and avoid informing smokers of the actual half-life of carbon monoxide.

Measuring Smoking Rate and Rate Changes

Several studies have shown a dose–response relation between COa and smoking rate. Correlations between COa and smokers' self-reported daily smoking rates typically range from .40 to .60 (Horan et al., 1978; Lando, 1975; Vogt et al., 1977). The within-subject dose–response correlation has also been fairly high (Henningfield et al., 1980), but COa-level variability is the norm, reflecting the dependence of CO on time since last smoking, type of tobacco smoked, and variations in how it is smoked.

The 3 to 5 hour CO half-life makes the time since the last smoking episode a critical determinate of CO measures (Horan et al., 1978; Hughes et al., 1978). Vogt et al. (1977) found a correlation of .45 between COa level and time since last cigarette and postulated that the high positive correlation between CO and self-reported daily smoking levels ($r = .48$ in their study) was chiefly due to the strong natural relationship between the frequency of smoking and the time since last cigarette. However, holding minutes constant since last cigaretts, Shipley (1980) still found a partial correlation of .44 between COa and subject report of smoking following a treatment program.

Many other parameters of smoking topography and tobacco product influence CO levels (Frederiksen and Martin, 1979). For example, levels generally increase with the number of cigarettes smoked within a fixed time period, and the closer together in time they are smoked. Likewise, CO delivery is generally higher with filtered cigarettes and with greater depth of inhalation.

Because of their sensitivity to smoking rate, substance smoked, and smoking pattern or topography, CO measures are key in evaluating both the medical safety of aversive smoking treatment procedures and the health risks of controlled-smoking regimens adopted by individuals unable to quit smoking (e.g., Frederiksen et al., 1977; Hall et al., 1979). (The uses of COa measures for these purposes are discussed later in this chapter.)

The chief advantages of COa measures include their reliance on non-invasive procedures, the relatively low cost of reliable assessment instruments, the simplicity of data collection and analysis, and the value of COa as a direct measure of health risk. COa measures can discriminate smokers from nonsmokers and reflect important changes in the parameters of smoking behavior. Finally, smokers can get immediate feedback of smoking harms with COa measures, and see rapid improvements after even moderate changes in smoking behavior. In fact, COa feedback has been effectively used to motivate healthy smokers to change their smoking habits (Orleans and Shipley, 1982).

Thiocyanate Measures

Definition and Health Risks

Thiocyanate (SCN) levels in blood serum, urine, and saliva are useful indices of smoking behavior. The hydrogen cyanide in tobacco smoke is transformed, primarily by the liver, to thiocyanate, a salt less toxic than cyanide (Pettigrew and Fell, 1972). Thiocyanate in the body has a half-life of 10 to 14 days before it is excreted through urine, sweat, and saliva (Butts et al., 1974; Densen et al., 1967). This long half-life makes thiocyanate levels much less dependent on time since last cigarette than CO measures (Vogt et al., 1977). In addition, evidence has shown SCN to be a reliable and valid index of smoking status and rate.

SCN levels currently can provide only limited information about the health risks of smoking. Harmful effects of elevated SCN levels are not fully known (USPHS, 1976; Vogt et al., 1977), outside of those involving uncommon visual disturbances (e.g., tobacco amblyopia) and vitamin B_{12} deficiencies (*British Medical Journal,* 1976; Pettigrew and Fell, 1973).

Measurement Procedures

Thiocyanate levels may be measured in the blood, urine, or saliva. Saliva sampling is the least invasive, least expensive to analyze and, luckily, most sensitive in assessing smoking rate (Prue et al., 1980).

Basically, saliva samples are collected using cotton rolls held in the mouth for 2 to 3 minutes. Samples are immediately sealed in airtight containers and frozen to prevent evaporation and deterioration of SCN compounds.

Thiocyanate analyses are performed using colormetric procedures, either with standard laboratory equipment or with more expensive automated analyzers (Butts et al., 1974; Pechacek et al., 1980; Pettigrew and Fell, 1973; Prue et al., 1980). For a laboratory which already has a spectrophotometer, costs for additional equipment could be as low as $100 (Prue et al., 1980). Including costs for collection materials, costs for colormetric analysis range from $2.90/sample (Laboratory of Physiological Hygiene, University of Minnesota, Minneapolis, Minnesota 55455) to $5.00 per sample (University of Mississippi School of Medicine, Jackson, Mississippi 39216).

We recommend two resources for details concerning collection of SCN measures. Prue et al. (1980) offer a useful evaluation of problems related to improper collection and storage practices and discuss checks on the reliability of laboratory procedures and the effects of variations in smoking patterns. Another valuable resource is the saliva sample collection manual and demonstration film by Pechacek et al. (1980).

Specificity

SCN measures have a greater specificity for smoking than CO measures, as they are subject to fewer nonsmoking influences, and smoking represents the primary influence on SCN levels. But certain environmental cyanides must also be taken into account, including regular consumption of large amounts of certain vegetables (e.g., yams, cabbage, broccoli, turnips, garlic, horseradish), certain alcoholic beverages high in preformed thiocyanate (e.g., beer and stout ale), (Dastur et al., 1972; Prue et al., 1980), and industrial exposures to cyanide compounds (Dacre and Tabershaw, 1970). In addition, passive smoking can elevate saliva thiocyanate levels (Pekkannen et al., 1976).

Discriminating Smokers and Nonsmokers

One-shot SCN measures have successfully discriminated smokers from nonsmokers. Butts and coworkers found that nonsmokers averaged 44 micromoles/liter of thiocyanate in contrast to an average 177 micromoles/liter for cigarette smokers, and 90 micromoles/liter for cigar smokers (Butts et al., 1974). Very similar data were reported with mean SCN levels of 46 micromoles for nonsmokers and 86 micromoles for smokers (Pettigrew and Fell, 1973).

Butts et al. recommend 85 micromoles/liter as a cutoff, since that level resulted in only 1.8 percent false-positives and 6.7 percent false-negatives. Research at the University of Minnesota indicated that an 85 micromoles cutoff successfully discriminates smokers from nonsmokers, even in instances of low-level and sporadic smoking (Luepker et al., 1980; Pechacek et al., 1979). Their data have shown SCN to be a valuable discriminator among smokers who smoke infrequently or have an atypical pattern. Among eighth-grade students in one large study, the 62.5 percent who reported smoking more than one pack/week have SCN levels greater than or equal to 85 micromoles/liter, compared to only 2.9 percent of the reported nonsmokers. Luepker et al. (1980) indicate that the 85 micromoles/liter cutoff enables sensitive discrimination between extremely infrequent adolescents smoking (a few cigarettes per month) and those smoking fewer than 20 cigarettes per week. Vogt et al. (1977) recommend a more conservative 200 micromoles/liter cutoff: Benfari et al. (1977) advise a 95 micromoles/liter cutoff to minimize false-positives and false-negatives in populations where expected smoking rates approach 60 percent.

Measuring Smoking Rate and Rate Changes

Several studies have shown a useful dose-response relationship between SCN and smoking rate. Butte et al. (1974) found a positive correlation (r = .46) between SCN levels and self-reported daily smoking rate. Luepker et al. (1980) found positive correlations between SCN levels and the number of cigarettes reportedly smoked in both the last day (r = .41) and the last week (r = .37), even among low-level and episodic smokers. In addition, a positive correlation (r = .37) was found between various self-report categories (never smoke, smoke a few cigarettes a month, daily smoke fewer than 20, or more than 20 cigarettes, etc.), and SCN levels in this adolescent population. When only considering smokers, SCN levels and daily reported smoking rate correlations increased to near .50 (Luepker et al., 1980; Vogt et al., 1977).

Several studies have shown that SCN levels are reliable indices of treatment-produced abstinence 10 to 14 days after quitting (Pechacek et al., 1980; Prue et al., 1980). Little evidence relates SCN levels to different tobacco types, or different patterns or parameters of cigarette smoking. These are promising areas for future investigation.

In summary, SCN measures can discriminate smokers from nonsmokers, and reflect treatment-induced changes in smoking status and smoking rate. The chief advantages of non-invasive saliva SCN measures (relative to CO measures), are the long SCN half-life, and the ability to detect low-frequency and episodic smoking. SCN measures are less susceptible to nonsmoking influences than CO measures. Chief drawbacks of saliva SCN are requirements for storing and freezing samples, the expense of laboratory analysis, and an unknown sensitivity to important changes in the pattern or topography of smoking.

Combining Carbon Monoxide and Thiocyanate Measures

CO and SCN measures have different advantages, disadvantages, and sources of variance for measuring smoking behavior, biochemical exposure, and smoking health risks. The choice between these measures depends on the investigator's particular assessment needs. When documenting abstinence, SCN measures are preferable. When a measure of smoking-related health risks is desired, CO measures are better, and should be used in impromptu assessments as outlined earlier. It will often be beneficial to employ both measures. Vogt et al. (1977) recommend both measures to minimize error in identifying smokers. They found a correlation of .57 between alveolar CO and serum SCN measures. These measures correlated more highly with each other than either did with reported daily smoking. Combining an 8 ppm CO cutoff and a 100 micromoles/liter SCN cutoff, they distinguished between smokers and nonsmokers at a 99 percent accuracy level.

Nicotine and Cotinine Measures

Nicotine is a major ingredient of tobacco smoke, and nicotine intake is clearly related to a number of smoking health risks, most particularly those involving cardiovascular disease (e.g., Hammond et al., 1976). Estimates of nicotine present in saliva, urine, or blood have also been used to validate smokers' self-reports (Evans et al., 1977; Horning et al., 1973; Isaac and Rand, 1972; Paxton and Bernacca, 1979; Pomerleau et al., 1978). Unfortunately, nicotine has a half-life of only 30 minutes in the body. This short half-life, and nicotine's relatively great susceptibility to passive smoking (Horning et al., 1973; Isaac and Rand, 1972) and to variations in smoking habits affecting nicotine delivery (substance smoked, frequency and depth of inhalation, etc.), limit its value as an index of smoking rate.

To overcome some of the drawbacks related to the short half-life of nicotine, some researchers have examined blood levels of cotinine, a nicotine metabolite that has a half-life of approximately 30 hours (Zeidenberg et al., Vunakis, 1977). Cotinine measures are beginning to be examined for their success discriminating smokers from nonsmokers. Zeidenberg et al. (1977), for instance, found that 53 percent of the variance in cotinine levels was associated with variance in daily nicotine consumption.

COORDINATING ASSESSMENT TO TREATMENT METHODS AND GOALS

Assessment strategies in smoking cessation research depend on treatment methods and goals and measurement objectives. There is no single "best" approach. In this section, we discuss a range of assessment approaches potentially suitable for evaluating the major treatments developed to help people quit and control their smoking and we pay special attention to measures of treatment process and methods for safeguarding the health of participants.

Multicomponent Treatment Packages

A major smoking-cessation treatment program combines cognitive and behavioral self-management procedures. Nonaversive procedures can be exclusively employed (Brockway et al., 1977; Katz et al., 1977; Pomerleau et al., 1978), or combined with aversive smoking (Danaher, 1977; Hackett and Horan, 1979; Lando, 1977, 1978; Powell and McCann, 1979), or other aversive conditioning techniques (Conway, 1977). Nonaversive procedures generally involve some combination of the following: stimulus control procedures; training in nonsmoking skills and coping techniques (e.g., incompatible responses, relaxation procedures); positive reinforcement and contingency contracting, and cognitive restructuring. Broad-spectrum programs combining nonaversive techniques and aversive smoking generally have been the most successful (e.g., Bernstein and McAlister, 1976; Orleans, 1980; Pechacek, 1979).

Regardless of the particular combination of treatment procedures, treatment process measurements are needed to operationalize the treatment and to permit research determining the relative impact of different procedures.

As a first step, the clinician/researcher should clearly describe treatment procedures so others can replicate them. Some investigators publish or provide a therapist's manual (Lando, 1976), or the self-management materials and manuals used by clients (Conway, 1975; Danaher and Lichtenstein, 1978; Pomerleau and Pomerleau, 1977; Powell and McCann, 1979). It may be valuable to measure client compliance with self-management guidelines, since some studies have shown treatment effectiveness to depend on the degree to which self-management guidelines are followed (Danaher et al., 1978; Pomerleau et al., 1978). For instance, Pomerleau and coworkers asked clients to simply estimate the number of daily smoking logs they completed, and found that this index of cooperation and compliance with instructions predicted abstinence 8 weeks after treatment. One study of unaided quitters found that frequent and consistent use of specific self-management skills (e.g., self-reinforcement) and a variety of skills predicted long-term maintenance of nonsmoking (Perri et al., 1977).

Any important treatment believed to have a therapeutic effect should be assessed. If, for instance, a support group or therapist is believed to be helpful, as is generally the case (Bernstein and McAlister, 1976), then measures of cohesiveness (Yalom, 1970) or therapist support should be included. Or, in programs teaching quitters to mobilize support in their natural environments, ratings by quitters and/or significant others of actual support provided can be valuable. Danaher et al. (1978) obtained support ratings from spouses of pregnant quitters. Perri et al. (1977) found quitters' outside support ratings predicted long-term outcomes.

In most cases, it is valuable to ask participating subjects to rate the different components of multicomponent packages. Katz et al. (1977) asked clients to rank order the helpfulness of several treatment components, and found that those judged most helpful were social support provided by the group, self-monitoring, graphing results, stimulus-control procedures, and support from family and friends. Components rated least helpful were antismoking films and brochures. These ratings can identify components for objective study or comparison in subsequent investigations. See the sample "End-of-Treatment Questionnaire" (Appendix).

Finally, whenever an investigation compares the effectiveness of different treatment procedures, particularly when a minimal treatment or placebo control is used, expectancies regarding treatment efficacy should be assessed. Using a 5-point rating scale, different smoking cessation strategies (e.g., rapid smoking, relaxation, covert sensitization) elicited different expectancies for positive outcome (Hynd et al., 1978).

Monitoring the Impact of Aversive Smoking

Developing effective aversive smoking techniques represents a major advance in smoking cessation technology (Orleans et al., 1981). Rapid smoking, the most widely applied of the original smoking aversion procedures, was pioneered by Lichtenstein and his colleagues (Lichtenstein et al., 1973). It involves inhaling once every 6 seconds until smoking becomes extremely unpleasant or intolerable, and takes place during controlled laboratory sessions with participants abstinent outside of sessions. The theoretical rationale for rapid smoking was to employ an aversive stimulus intrinsic to the act of smoking. Moreover, rapid smoking proved more effective than other aversive conditioning procedures (e.g., electroshock aversion) by significantly boosting quit rates (Bernstein and McAlister, 1976; Orleans, 1980). Following early clinical studies, several researchers studied variations influencing treatment success, examined the physiological effects and possible harms of rapid smoking, and sought to develop medically safe alternatives to the rapid inhalation procedure. These alternatives include normal-paced or focused smoking (Danaher, 1977; Hackett and Horan, 1979; Lando, 1976), smoke-holding (Kopel et al., 1979), rapid puffing without inhalation (Powell and McCann, 1979), and taste aversion (Tori, 1978). This section summarizes measures used to monitor the impact of aversive smoking techniques, and emphasizes assessments needed to safeguard the health of participants.

Measures of the Aversive Procedure

Researchers must operationally define the aversive smoking procedures they use and their context. Danaher's (1977) interim summary of research on rapid smoking identified a number of parameters that may affect outcome, including amount of time spent smoking; number and scheduling of treatment sessions; criteria for terminating aversive smoking (either a certain number of sessions or until smoking urges have ceased); and size and supportiveness of treatment groups. Quantifying these variations appears as important for newer, safer aversive smoking techniques, such as normal-paced smoking or smoke-holding. Likewise, the brand(s) of cigarettes smoked and average nicotine and CO levels should be noted, since these factors influence the aversiveness and intensity of physiological reactions. In addition, the physical setting in which smoking occurs should be carefully described (room size, ventilation, etc.), since these factors determine ambient CO levels that in turn affect the safety and effectiveness of smoking procedures (Orleans et al., 1981).

Other process variables influence the success of rapid smoking treatment.

Poorer outcomes may be associated with smoking between sessions, shallower levels of inhalation, and lower levels of subjective aversiveness (Danaher, 1977; Merbaum et al., 1979). Any important variable related theoretically or empirically to treatment outcome should routinely be measured and reported, if not studied. For instance, many researchers obtain routine numerical ratings of smoking unpleasantness (Danaher, 1977; Kopel et al., 1979), or use standard symptom checklists (Merbaum et al., 1979; Miller et al., 1977).

Physiological Effects of Aversive Smoking

Studies of the physiological effects of rapid smoking strongly demonstrate the need to carefully pretest any potentially harmful smoke aversion procedure in order to determine its medical risks. These studies have shown that rapid smoking constitutes a cardiovascular stress with potentially hazardous consequences for persons with cardiopulmonary dysfunction (Hall et al., 1979). Basically, the nicotine and CO in cigarettes combine to increase myocardial oxygen demand while decreasing oxygen supply, potentially causing ischemia or fatal arrhythmia. Focusing on these potentially hazardous hemodynamics, most physioloigcal studies have evaluated aversive smoking's effects on vital signs, a variety of blood gas concentrations, and blood nicotine levels (Danaher et al., 1976; Miller et al., 1977; Hall et al., 1979; Hynd et al., 1976).

In the most carefully controlled and comprehensive of these studies, Hall and coworkers evaluated the relative medical risks of rapid- and normal-paced smoking. They concluded that rapid smoking, as they used it, does not present a significant medical risk for young healthy smokers who have undergone medical screening to insure good health and "physiologic normality." They also cautioned that the safety of this stressful aversive smoking technique for smokers with compromised cardiopulmonary function could not be judged from their results with healthy smokers. Lichtenstein and Glascow (1977), reviewing the literature on the riskiness and physiological effects of rapid smoking, reached similar conclusions. They recommend several precautions to safeguard normal healthy subjects when using a rapid smoking technique, which include informed consent, careful medical screening, physician approval, and limited duration of exposure.

Research on the medical risks of rapid smoking was conducted *after* widescale implementation of the technique, an error that should not be repeated. Any potentially risky smoke aversion technique should be pretested for medical risks and physiological effects. Care must be taken to define and/or recognize potential risk.

Some aversive smoking procedures are less risky than others. Procedures less toxic than rapid smoking can be more widely applied and may be safely used with high-risk subjects (e.g., the obese, pregnant, elderly, and known cardiovascular or respiratory disease sufferers). Most studies evaluating relative risks have been done with healthy smokers. Danaher et al. (1976) and Hall et al. (1979) found normal-paced smoking less risky than rapid smoking. Pechacek and coworkers found the warm, smoky, air procedure (involving normal-paced smoking with warm cigarette smoke directed into the smoker's face), to cause greater cardiopulmonary stress than normal-paced smoking (Pechacek et al., 1979). Orleans et al. (1981) found two non-inhalation, smoke-holding procedures, including that developed by Kopel et al. (1979), to cause less change in vital signs and CO elevations than normal paced smoking or Tori's taste-satiation procedure (1978), both of which involve inhaling smoke.

Prejudging riskiness can, however, be difficult and misleading. All smoking, even if no more harmful than ''normal'' cigarette smoking, is harmful. There are some smokers for whom even normal-paced smoking, a procedure less harmful than rapid smoking (Danaher et al., 1976; Hall et al., 1979) could be too risky (i.e., pregnant smokers and myocardial infarction victims). Also, a procedure which superficially appears to be less stressful than normal-paced or rapid smoking for healthy smokers may not be. The overall impact of the many parameters affecting riskiness of a procedure (e.g., ambient CO concentration, tobacco product used, depth of inhalation, amount and duration of smoke exposure) can be difficult or impossible to estimate and must instead be determined through careful pretesting. For instance, contrary to prediction, Orleans et al. (1981) found that the taste-satiation technique (Tori, 1978) of alternating smoke-holding and inhalation did not differ from a matched, normal-paced smoking procedure involving twice as much inhalation, in its effects on heart rate, blood pressure, and CO absorption. Likewise, Pechacek et al. (1979) evaluated the effects of the warm, smoky, air procedure and found that 3 of 13 carefully screened and apparently healthy young men displayed myocardial arrythmias during the procedure.

Our intent is to alert researchers to the need for pretesting, and not to furnish comprehensive guidelines for designing this basic research. If you are using an aversive smoking procedure with known physiological effects, you should have clear assurance from past research of its safety for your intended population and use. In evaluating results of previous pretesting, make sure pretesting was conducted under conditions that simulate your treatment conditions (Lichtenstein and Glascow, 1977). In this regard, since most subjects receiving aversive smoking treatments will be abstinent before sessions, and since many physiological reactions to smoking depend on time since last cigarette, a period of abstinence (usually 8 to 12 hours) should precede experimental smoke aversion trials. For instance, smoking one cigarette raises heart rate only 5 beats/minute (bpm) after a period of regular smoking, but 20 bpm after overnight abstinence (Elliott and Thysell, 1968). All procedural and topographical parameters affecting tobacco smoke exposure in experimental pretesting should be stated and replicated. Changing the type of cigarette smoked, duration and timing of inhalation and breaks, or altering the physical setting (e.g., room size, ventilation, ambient CO levels) of aversive smoking can significantly alter physiological results. Such departures from pretesting procedure make adequate assessment of risks to your subjects difficult. Likewise, departing from subject selection and screening procedures used in pretesting may make it impossible to judge the risks of a given procedure for your intended population. A medical review of pretesting results should be obtained to evaluate the potential safety of smoking procedures for your intended treatment population, and to assist in subject selection and screening procedures.

Conservatism should be the rule when implementing any potentially risky technique. Subjects should be carefully screened and advised of possible harm as part of informed consent procedures. In screening, medical history data are usually collected, using a brief symptom checklist and interview and sometimes accompanied by data from a physical exam (Danaher et al., 1976; Miller et al., 1977). Predefined high-risk subjects (the obese, pregnant, or elderly) and those with a history of cardiovascular or respiratory symptoms (e.g., high blood pressure, diabetes, chronic obstructive pulmonary disease, stroke, or coronary heart disease) frequently are excluded. In a conservative screening, Hall et a. (1979) excluded all subjects from a rapid smoking procedure whose baseline physiological measures fell outside of accepted normal limits. Physician approval, based on full understanding of potential harms of experimental procedures, is generally required in addition to informed consent from subjects whenever a procedure may be particularly risky (e.g., rapid smoking), or when subjects are particularly at risk by virtue of a physical illness or preexisting condition. We have included a short symptom checklist in our Pre-Treatment Questionnaire along with several questions to alert the researcher to possible health problems (Appendix). A more detailed screening questionnaire including questions about occupational health risks that might possibly confound the perils of smoking has been developed by Hall et al. (1979) and can be obtained directly from those authors.

As an additional precaution to minimize danger with high-risk procedures or participants, physiologic monitoring can be employed during sessions. Maximum heart rate, blood pressure, and carbon monoxide levels might be established as criteria for continuing or discontinuing procedures (Orleans et al., 1981). Measures should be sensitive to the most important physiologic consequences of these smoking procedures, and easy to administer in treatment sessions.

WHEN ABSTINENCE IS NOT THE GOAL

Special assessments are needed for treatments which have as their goal not total abstinence but reduced health risks via reduced exposure to the hazardous constituents of cigarette smoke. Many smokers have no desire to give up cigarettes entirely (Gallup, 1974), or find it impossible to quit. For them, controlled smoking to reduce health risks is one option. Frederiksen and his colleagues (Frederiksen et al., 1977; Frederiksen and Simon, 1978) have pioneered controlled smoking treatments which parallel the recent success of controlled drinking programs for alcoholics (Sobell and Sobell, 1978). The goal of controlled smoking programs is to teach smokers to limit their cigarette consumption, and to choose their brands and smoking style to limit their exposure to tar, nicotine, carbon monoxide, and the other hazardous constituents of cigarette smoke. Other smokers, particularly heavy smokers, may wish to decrease their dependence on nicotine as a step toward total abstinence. Nicotine-fading programs involve planned brand-switching to gradually reduce nicotine intake in a stepwise fashion. Nicotine fading was found to be highly effective when combined with a daily self-monitoring of nicotine and tar intake, and setting a target quit date (Foxx and Brown, 1979). Promising results were also obtained with nicotine fading as a step toward abstinence (Jaffe et al., 1978; Prue et al., 1981).

Controlled Smoking

The goal of controlled smoking treatment is to reduce smoking health risks by reducing intake of harmful tobacco smoke constituents. Controlled smoking regimens may be the ultimate goal for smokers unable (or unwilling) to quit. Assessment must determine both that overt smoking patterns have changed, *and* that resultant health risks have decreased. It is possible to adopt presumably safer smoking habits that are in fact no less risky. For instance, many American smokers have switched to cigarettes lower in tar and nicotine to reduce health risks (Gori, 1976). Unfortunately, many who switch brands and/or decrease their consumption actually avoid health benefits by compensating in other ways, for instance, by unwittingly smoking a greater number to achieve the same daily nicotine dose. Likewise, smokers who limit the number of cigarettes they smoke may inhale more deeply, puff more frequently, or smoke a greater portion of each cigarette. The estimation of smoking health risks depends on careful assessment of type and number of cigarettes smoked, the individual's smoking topography, and the individual's exposure to harmful smoke constituents.

Monitoring the brand and number of cigarettes smoked is straightforward. Actually, since combining measures of brand and rate improves estimation of health risks, this may become a standard practice, even when abstinence is the treatment goal. In a survey of recent smoking research reports, however, Frederiksen et al. (1979) found that the reporting of cigarette brand was rare. Cigarette brands can be easily determined by self-report or observations. Going beyond self-reports, Foxx and Brown (1979) collected cigarette butts and empty cigarette packages to verify that subjects were smoking assigned brands in a nicotine-fading program. However, except in cases of very frequent brand switching, self-reports of rate and substance would be palatable, sufficiently accurate, and non-reactive.

Measuring smoking topography is more complicated; standard topographic assessment procedures have not been developed. Basically, topography measures should reflect parameters of smoking behavior which influence absorption of, or exposure to, hazardous tobacco smoke constituents. Frederiksen et al. (1979) have defined at least eight imporant parameters: (1) puff frequency; (2) puff duration; (3) interpuff interval; (4) amount of tobacco used (the difference between tobacco weight before and after smoking a cigarette); (5) cigarette duration; (6) puff volume; (7) puff intensity (puff volume divided by puff duration); and (8) puff distribution (the location on the cigarette where each puff is taken relative to the proximal or distal end of the cigarette). Basically, the more smoke that is inhaled and the greater the depth of inhalation, the greater the biochemical exposure.

Retrospective self-reports have been used to reflect such parameters as depth of inhalation, number of puffs, and amount of tobacco used (Russell et al., 1973; Vogt, 1977). When finer grained measures of consumption have been used (such as number of puffs taken, or estimated level of mouth nicotine exposure), results have closely paralleled those of simple rate measures (O'Banion et al., 1980; Leventhal and Avis, 1976; Robinson and Young, 1980). Evidence challenging the accuracy of self-report topographical data has led Frederiksen and colleagues to measure smoking topography directly sometimes with videotape recordings (Frederiksen and Simon, 1978; Frederiksen et al., 1977). Two obvious drawbacks of topographical measurement are its requirements for trained observers and (reactive) laboratory environments. To overcome these drawbacks, newly developed instrumentation permits mechanical recording of topography (eliminating the need for observers) and portable instruments permit assessment in the smoker's natural environment (Creighton et al., 1979; Henningfield et al., 1980). Fine-grained topographical assessment is indicated when evaluating those programs that teach smokers to modify their smoking topography. But, it is of unquestionable value for programs whose goals include reducing the number of cigarettes smoked, or smoking "safer" brands to limit intake of harmful smoke constituents. Better measures for these programs are estimates of intake of harmful substances combined with physiological indices of actual biochemical exposure.

Harmful cigarette smoke constituents include nicotine, tar (the particulate matter in cigarette smoke), and the poisonous triple gases, carbon monoxide, hydrogen cyanide, and nictric oxide (Gori, 1976; Prue et al., 1981). Several publications list the average amounts of some or all of these substances in commercial brand cigarettes (Jenkins et al., 1979; Ross, 1976a,b). These can be consulted to develop estimates of actual biochemical exposure, based on rate measures and brand reports. Measures of nicotine intake can be employed with related measures to gauge severity of nicotine dependency (Fagerstrom, 1978; see Appendix). For most purposes, however, physiological indices of biochemical exposure (COa, SCN, serum, nicotine) are better. It is not necessary to index absorption of all major harmful substances, since the same topographical factors (e.g., depth and duration of inhalation) control the absorption of many different gaseous and particulate smoke constituents (e.g., nicotine, hydrogen cyanide, CO). One index will usually suffice. Using such indices, Frederiksen and Simon (1978) obtained data on the relative harmfulness of various smoking topographies. Evidence suggests that smokers can be taught to accurately track their own CO levels with frequent CO feedback (3 to 5 times daily), and to maintain their discrimination of CO levels in the abstinence of such feedback (Martin and Frederiksen, 1980).

Nicotine Fading

The chief goal of nicotine fading as a step toward abstinence is reducing nicotine intake while holding constant the number of cigarettes smoked. Since nicotine and tar are very highly correlated, nicotine-fading procedures achieve reductions in both tar and nicotine. Consulting listings of common tobacco smoke constituents, individuals select brands for stepwise nicotine reduction. As noted, some investigators have requested actual cigarette-end counts to determine the type and amount of the cigarettes smoked (Foxx and Brown, 1979). Prue et al. (1979) took the additional step of documenting reduced health risks by measuring alveolar CO and saliva SCN levels.

ASSESSMENT AFTER TREATMENT: THE NEW MEASUREMENT FRONTIER

This section presents some "rules of thumb" concerning the measurement of treatment outcome both immediately after treatment and into the long-term follow-up phase. Guidelines for measuring smoking rate and status (smoking or abstinent), and for dealing with dropouts are presented. Subsequent sections address the comprehensive assessment of long-term treatment outcomes. The emphasis in each section is on smoking cessation, rather than controlled smoking, programs.

Pre- to Post-treatment Changes in Smoking Rate and Status

In order to evaluate pre- to post-treatment change, the same measure must be applied at two or more points. McFall (1978) has pointed out, for example, that it would be questionable to establish baseline smoking by self-monitoring of cigarette consumption, and then to measure post-treatment change from this baseline by obtaining global retrospective self-reports. Likewise, Shipley et al. (in press) recommend using the same criterion interval at each measurement point to define smoking behavior.

Measurement interval is the time period over which smoking is monitored or estimated. Shipley et al. (in press) surveyed principal authors of recent smoking treatment reports, and found great variability in measurement intervals both across and within studies. They recommend a 1-week interval at each measurement point to define both smoking rate and abstinence. Thus, at 6-month follow-up, a person who had not smoked over a 1-week interval would be classified as abstinent. Some may consider a 1-week interval too "liberal." The authors further suggest that research reports include, by treatment condition, the proportion of the subjects who smoked at some time during the follow-up period but who were abstinent throughout a subsequent measurement interval (i.e., "slippers"). Subtracting these subjects from the recommended follow-up abstinence figures (determined over a 1-week interval) would yield a "pure" or conservative abstinence rate. This reporting convention would also resolve a pronounced disagreement, revealed by the survey, over how to classify slippers: 52 percent of the respondents reported classifying slippers as smokers, and 44 percent classified them as abstinent.

If physiological assessments are to be included in follow-up assessments, they should also be obtained before treatment. Only in this way can the researcher document reduced biochemical exposure and health risk. If objective verification of self-report cannot be obtained at each follow-up, perhaps it can be obtained at a reasonable expense for a random sample of participants, or at only one important follow-up (i.e., 6 months, or 1 year). If the therapist/researcher cannot reach clients for direct observation and physiologic measurements, substitute means of verifying self-report should be introduced for longitudinal follow-ups (e.g., informant reports).

Traditionally, both smoking rate and abstinence status are reported as outcome measures. *Rate* is often expressed as a percentage of daily baseline smoking. *Abstinence status* is usually categorical—smoking or abstinent. These two complementary measures have different measurement requirements and require different statistical analyses. Abstinence is likely to be measured with higher accuracy, less reactivity, and greater palatability than smoking rate, and can be more accurately confirmed than rate by physiological measures, such as SCN. It is less sensitive to changes in methods of assessments. That is, if baseline assessment is by self-monitoring of each cigarette smoked, and follow-up assessment is by global retrospective self-report, the categorization of smoking or abstinence might still be accurately made. It would be unwise, however, to rely on abstinence classifications as the sole dependent measure. Abstinence status is a nomial scale datum, most appropriately analyzed with non-parametric procedures, and, as such, has less power than rate data to reveal subtle differences in outcome. Both rate and abstinence data should be reported for each measurement point with physiological verification of self-reports.

One issue in assessing change in smoking is the question of how to count "switchers," people who continue to use tobacco by switching to products other than cigarettes. A survey of smoking-cessation researchers showed much disagreement, with 48 percent classifying switchers as smokers and 32 percent classifying them as abstinent (Shipley et al., in press). Shipley and colleagues recommend reporting all tobacco use. However, they believe the use of pipes, cigars, chewing tobacco or snuff should not be confounded in research reports with the use of cigarettes. Thus, abstinence should mean cigarette abstinence, with the use of tobacco substitutes reported separately by experimental condition.

Another problem concerns how to handle dropouts, or those who fail to complete post-treatment assessments. We advise treating dropouts as failures—that is, counting them as smokers vs abstainers. We also recommend reporting outcome data on three groups of participants: those attending all sessions, those attending at least one third of sessions, and other dropouts. We discuss ways to deal with attrition in follow-up assessments in the next section.

Assessing Maintenance and Relapse after Treatment

Treatment aimed at smoking cessation, or at long-term shifts to safer smoking, is only successful if treatment-produced changes are maintained. Maintenance of treatment results is the most important goal and the most difficult achievement of smoking-control treatments. Hunt and Bespalec (1974) reviewed over 100 studies of smoking cessation treatments and plotted a relapse curve from the available follow-up data. This curve, strikingly similar for smokers, alcoholics, and drug addicts completing abstinence-oriented treatment (Hunt et al., 1971), showed that only 25–30 percent of abstainers at the end of treatment were still off cigarettes 1 year later. Relapse rates of even treatments producing highest initial abstinence approach 50 percent at 1-year follow-up, and treatment itself does not seem to help new exsmokers avoid relapse: a similar relapse curve is observed for treated smokers and smokers who quit on their own (Horn, 1978; Moss, 1979; Orleans, 1980). Understanding and reducing relapse is crucial in smoking control; careful follow-up is required to achieve this understanding.

Two types of measures are discussed in this section. Follow-up measures usually consist of longitudinal extensions of pre- and post-treatment measures to determine *if* and *when* relapse occurs. Unfortunately, while these measures are crucial, they do not provide information about *how* maintenance is achieved or *how* relapse comes about. Only with a second group of measures designed to illuminate the maintenance/relapse process can we move toward designing treatments to protect new exsmokers against relapse. Progress developing these measures is highlighted in this section.

Longitudinal Follow-up Measures

The major purpose of longitudinal assessment is to describe long-term treatment outcome. The relapse curve plotted by Hunt and his colleagues (Hunt et al., 1971; Hunt and Bespalec, 1974) shows most relapses occurring in the first 3 months post-treatment. Frequent follow-up contacts should include measures taken during this 3-month high-risk relapse period. To show stability of treatment results, we recommend three follow-up evaluations, at 6 weeks, 6 months, and 1 year; 18 month and longer follow-ups are desirable. Although it is assumed that little relapse occurs after a year of abstinence, few researchers have verified this assumption with longer-term follow-up (Lichtenstein and Rodrigues, 1977).

Many practical problems can make long-term follow-up difficult or inconvenient. To make it easier to contact quit-smoking participants, we recommend informing participants in advance of the procedures and importance of follow-up assessment; obtaining the names of at least two persons who will be able to furnish the participant's address and telephone number in the event of a move; and collecting a refundable deposit, with refunds for participating in each follow-up assessment.

Another major practical question concerns which follow-up measures to administer. The same measurement and measurement interval should ideally be employed at each measurement point. Physiological assessment or corroborating reports at only some measurement points, or with only a portion of the participants, violates this principle. But *some* data are better than *no* data. In all cases the methods and any variability in assessment should be reported. People who cannot be reached for follow-up should be counted as smokers.

Measuring Treatment Side Effects

Perhaps because cigarette smoking is such a circumscribed behavior, research seldom includes multidimensional treatment outcome measures to assess effects of treatment or smoking cessation on important life functions and related lifestyle health risks. This omission is not unique to smoking cessation outcome studies, characterizing research on alcohol (e.g., Nathan & Lansky, 1978) and weight loss (Loro & Orleans, 1982) programs as well. But multidimensional assessment is important in studying any program to change addictive behavior. Advocates of a symptom substitution explanation for the successful behavioral treatment of smoking (or other addictions) might argue that changes in smoking increase stress or anxiety levels or cause exsmokers to substitute other forms of anxiety control that might be just as undesirable (e.g., overeating, increased alcohol, marijuana, or other drug use). In fact, addictive behaviors do appear to be related in the few controlled studies which have addressed their interrelationship (e.g., Kozlowski, 1978; Miller, 1979). On the other hand, behavior therapists who seek to program replacements for smoking (e.g., as by teaching alternative stress management skills) would expect changes in smoking to be accompanied by positive shifts in affect, health lifestyle, or stress management habits.

To date, few studies of smoking control programs have incorporated measures of positive or negative treatment "side-effects," and these have relied almost exclusively on retrospective assessments: that is, subjects are asked after treatment whether they gained or lost weight and whether they feel more or less irritable, nervous, depressed, etc. than before quitting (e.g., Hecht, 1978; Pederson & Lefcoe, 1976). Only prospective studies using baseline (pretreatment) and posttreatment measures avoid the bias inherent in retrospective reports: successful exsmokers may minimize adverse side-effects and or exaggerate improvements in their lifestyles, and relapsers may exhibit the opposite tendency. For instance, Graham and Gibson (1971) found significantly more recidivists than successful quitters recalling increased nervousness and irritability after quitting. In two other retrospective studies, 20-40 percent of exsmokers reported no negative withdrawal effects (Hecht, 1978; Pederson & Lefcoe, 1976).

Following empirical or theoretical guidelines, you may focus on general treatment or quitting side-effects, or on program-specific variables like the use of substitute stress-management techniques, or the frequency of nonsmoking self-rewards. The timing of side-effect measures will reflect expectations concerning the particular effect monitored. If one is primarily interested in documenting withdrawal effects, one could choose intensive measurement during the first few weeks after quitting. If one wanted to examine weight gain, or the adoption of a regular exercise regimen, one would need less intense longer-term assessments. Repeated assessment is desirable for many side-effects, but asking clients too frequently for follow-up reports will backfire, engendering high levels of noncompliance (e.g., Condiotte & Lichtenstein, 1981).

Quitting smoking probably has different short-term and long-term effects on anxiety levels and mood. We know little about these effects. Even relatively short-term withdrawal effects (increased anxiety, irritability, restlessness, craving, decreased concentration) have been poorly studied. Shiffman and Jarvick (1976), who charted physical and emotional withdrawal effects over the first two weeks after quitting, employed a 26-item questionnaire factor-analyzed to yield 5 factors: craving, physiological discomfort, physical symptoms, arousal level, appetite. Interestingly, their well-known findings showing greatest psychological discomfort during the first week after quitting are based on only three questions: "Do you feel more calm than usual? Do you feel content? Are you less nervous than usual?" Validated anxiety, depression, and mood indicators have only rarely been used to monitor withdrawal effects or the longer-term positive or emotional consequences of smoking cessation (Condiotte & Lichtenstein, 1978; Pomerleau et al., 1978).

Paralleling mood changes, the stress-management habits adopted by new exsmokers should be explored. Substitutes for smoking can be positive as with increased exercise and the use of relaxation skills, or negative as with increased alcohol or drug use. Asking clients about their caffine intake, their use of mood control drugs, marijuana, and alcohol should be routine. A commonly feared side-effect of quitting, particularly among women, is weight gain (USDHEW, 1976). Studies of unaided quitters show new exsmokers frequently turning to food as a substitute (e.g., Hecht, 1978; Peterson & Lefcoe, 1976). However, weight gain is by no means universal, with average gains generally under 10 pounds and occurring chiefly in the first few weeks following treatment (e.g., Pomerleau et al., 1979; Powell & McCann, 1979). Tobacco substitutes should also be monitored, particularly given the recent upsurge in the use of chewing tobacco among former smokers (e.g., Ellis, 1978). Finally, positive side-effects on health and well-being should be assessed. Smoking-related and stress-related symptoms (pain, headache, or sleep difficulties) often show immediate improvement. For instance, smokers have been found to have longer sleep latencies than nonsmokers, but, this difference decreases dramatically immediately after abrupt quitting (Soldatos et al., 1980). Physiological verification of self-reported smoking rates can give incidental evidence of improved physical functioning. Perceived well-being is seldom assessed, however, many exsmokers report feeling more in control of their lives and show an increased belief in their ability to control their health (Hecht, 1978; Shipley, in press). To identify some of these changes sample questionnaires request pre- and post-treatment ratings in addition to collecting information about alcohol, drug and caffeine intake (see Appendix).

To these basic measures, additional program-specific measures can be easily added. For instance, pre- and post-treatment muscle tension should be assessed for subjects receiving treatment including muscle relaxation training. For treatment emphasizing physical exercise to facilitate nonsmoking, one might want to include estimates of exercise levels or physiologic verification of exercise status. Similarly, assessment of worksite smoking interventions should consider assessing side effects related to job satisfaction and performance (Orleans and Shipley, 1982).

Exploring the Maintenance/Relapse Process

In addition to establishing the long-term maintenance of treatment results, it is important to clarify the mechanisms of initial treatment success, maintenance, and relapse. This entails a very different measurement approach. There are empirical and theoretical guidelines for selecting variables to study (Orleans, 1981).

Predicting End-of-treatment Success and Maintenance

One goal of assessment is to identify individual difference variables affecting treatment outcome and maintenance, so as to ultimately tailor treatment to individual smokers. In pursuing this goal, most studies have taken an empirical "shotgun" approach by investigating many (sometimes hundreds) predictor variables. Reviews of these efforts between 1950 and 1970 (Kozlowski, 1979; Matarazzo and Saslow, 1960; Smith, 1970), and our own extensive review of this literature since 1970, have failed to find consistent, reliable patient-by-treatment interactions, and have found few variables related to treatment success. Predictors of end-of-treatment and long-term outcomes have differed (Pomerleau et al., 1978). Even where correlates are found, the absolute levels of difference between successful and unsuccessful quitters have generally been too small to yield practical predictors of success. The "shotgun" strategy is non-productive and inefficient, since the choice of possible predictor variables has generally not reflected coherent theoretical notions concerning mechanisms of initial change or maintenance.

More promising results have come from studies based on theories of the quitting and maintenance process. In an earlier section, we discussed the importance of measuring treatment agents hypothesized to cause change in smoking behavior (e.g., procedural components, non-specific factors). Our focus here is on active

agents in the maintenance process. Retrospective studies of people who have successfully quit smoking and maintained their success, vs those who failed in an
attempt to quit, suggest that success is more likely in the presence of continued
use of self-reinforcement, continued social support and reinforcement for nonsmoking, and continued use of a variety of self-management nonsmoking skills (Newman, 1977; Perri and Richards, 1977; Perri et al., 1977; Rozensky and Bellack,
1974). Each study meets the minimum requirement for studying the maintenance
process—that of including some measure of a mechanism whereby maintenance
is expected or hypothesized to occur. The findings, however, are weakened by the
retrospective nature of the maintenance-process studies.

Repeated longitudinal assessments of self-management practices associated
with change and maintenance are needed. (Perri and Richards and colleagues; Perri
and Richards, 1977; Perri, Richards and Schultheis (1977) used a comprehensive
structured interview protocol to examine behavioral self-control methods associated with short- and long-term success in self-initiated smoking control projects.
This protocol contains much of interest for the researcher evaluating smoking control programs. As another model, the sample questionnaires in the Appendix include several questions dealing with self-management practices theoretically related to maintenance.

Predicting and Exploring Relapse

Another way to approach the question of maintenance is to examine how
relapse occurs and is resisted. Marlatt and Gordon (1979) have been the pioneers
of this approach. Using post-relapse questionnaires to study the relapse process
in smokers, alcoholics, and drug addicts completing abstinence-oriented treatments, they developed a preliminary cognitive-behavioral model of the relapse
process. According to that model, chief obstacles to maintenance are high-risk
relapse situations for which the individual lacks coping skills (Marlatt and Gordon, 1979). Relapse episodes for new exsmokers commonly were found to involve
dealing with feelings of anger, frustration, or tension; interpersonal conflicts; and
social pressures to smoke. Powell and McCann (1979), using a "Return to Smoking Questionnaire," identified similar relapse circumstances. According to Marlatt
and Gordon, whether a person relapses or remains abstinent when confronting a
high-risk situation depends on the degree to which he or she possesses needed
coping skills, and a related sense of self-efficacy—the belief that one can enact
the coping behaviors necessary to resist relapse. Bandura's (1977) self-efficacy
theory, central to the Marlatt and Gordon model, asserts that expectations of personal efficacy influence the initiation, persistence, and strength of coping responses. Finally, this model explains the easy course from a single slip to a full-blown
relapse, by positing an "abstinence violation effect," involving intense guilt and
personal attribution for failure that undermines self-efficacy at the very time that
expectations of benefits from smoking increase.

A strong relationship has been found between maintenance and self-efficacy. Studies have advanced several practical measures of self-efficacy for exploring the maintenance process. DiClemente (1981), for instance, asked new exsmokers to use 7-point Likert-ratings to indicate how sure they were that they could avoid smoking in each of 12 high-risk situations (e.g., when alone and feeling nervous, or with friends at a party). Ratings were summed to get a single self-efficacy score reflecting global self-efficacy appraisal. Successful maintainers judged at a 5-month follow-up had higher post-treatment self-efficacy scores than relapsers. Condiotte and Lichtenstein (1981) developed a similar instrument, using ratings for 49 common smoking situations. In this and another study (McIntyre et al., 1980), higher post-treatment efficacy scores were associated with less relapse. Also documented was a high correspondence between clusters of smoking situations in which relapsing subjects experienced low self-efficacy, and the situations in which the first cigarette "slip" actually occurred. Moreover, related mood and self-efficacy data collected during the follow-up period indicated cognitive processes similar to those hypothesized by Marlatt and Gordon's (1979) "abstinence violation effect."

These studies establish the importance of self-efficacy appraisal and clearly indicate directions for relapse prevention programs. Rosenthal and Marx (1979), for instance, have shown that Marlatt and Gordon's model has clinical utility when applied to obesity. They used this model to develop a relapse prevention training protocol that significantly enhanced maintenance of weight loss following a standard behavioral weight loss treatment. Applications to smoking cessation are forthcoming. It will be interesting to examine how self-efficacy ratings relate to actual use of coping skills during the maintenance period, integrating what we learn about relapse with what we learn about maintenance. Moreover, the research spurred by Marlatt and Gordon's innovative conceptual approach provides a valuable model for theoretically-based investigations of the mechanisms of relapse and maintenance in smoking cessation treatments and in programs treating other addictive behaviors and lifestyle health risks.

REFERENCES

Abrams, D. B., & Wilson, G. T. Self-monitoring and reactivity in the modification of cigarette smoking. *Journal of Consulting and Clinical Psychology*, 1979, 47, 243–251.

Aronow, W. S., Goldsmith, J. R., Kern, J. C., & Johnson, L. L. Effect of smoking cigarettes on cardiovascular hemodynamics. *Archives of Environmental Health*, 1974, 28, 330–332.

Auger, T. J., Wright, E., & Simpson, R. H. Posters as smoking deterrents. *Journal of Applied Psychology*, 1972, 56, 169–171.

Bandura, A. Self-efficacy: Toward a unifying theory of behavioral change. *Psychological Review*, 1977, 84, 191–215.

Benfari, R. C., McIntyre, K., Benfari, M. J., Baldwin, A., & Ockene, J. The use of thiocyanate determination for indication of cigarette smoking status. *Evaluation Quarterly*, 1977, *1*, 629–638.

Bernstein, D. A., & McAlister, A. The modification of smoking behavior: Programs and problems. *Addictive Behaviors*, 1976, *1*, 89–102.

Best, J. A., Bass, F., & Owen, L. E. Mode of service delivery in a smoking cessation program for public health. *Canadian Journal of Public Health*, 1978, *68*, 469–473.

British Medical Journal. Cigarette smoking in pregnancy, *British Medical Journal*, 1976, *2*, 492–493.

Brockway, B., Steinman, G., Edelson, J., & Gruenewald, K. Nonaversion procedures and their effect on cigarette smoking. *Addictive Behaviors*, 1977, *2*, 121–128.

Butts, W. C., Kuehneman, M., & Widdowson, G. W. Automated method for determining serum thiocyanate to distinguish smokers from nonsmokers. *Clinical Chemistry*, 1974, *20*, 1344–1348.

Cohen, S. I., Perkins, N. M., Ury, H. K., & Goldsmith, J. R. Carbon monoxide uptake in cigarette smoking. *Archives of Environmental Health*, 1971, *22*, 55–60.

Condiotte, M. M., & Lichtenstein, E. Self-efficacy and relapse in smoking cessation programs. *Journal of Consulting and Clinical Psychology*, 1981, *49*, 648–659.

Conway, J. B. Behavioral self-control of smoking through aversive conditioning and self-management. *Journal of Consulting and Clinical Psychology*, 1977, *45*, 348–357.

Conway, J. B. A handbook of self-control procedures for cigarette smokers. Journal Supplement Abstract Service *Catalog of Selected Documents in Psychology*, 1975, *5*, 285.

Creighton, D. E., Noble, M. J., & Whewell, R. T. A portable smoking pattern recorder. *Biotelemetry Patient Monitoring*, 1979, *6*, 186–191.

Dacre, J. C., & Tabershaw, I. R. Thiocyanate in saliva and sputum. *Archives of Environmental Health*, 1970, *21*, 47–49.

Danaher, B. G. Research on rapid smoking: Interim summary and recommendations. *Addictive Behaviors*, 1977, *2*, 151–166.

Danaher, B. G., & Lichtenstein, E. *Become an ex-smoker*. Englewood Cliffs, New Jersey: Prentice-Hall, Inc., 1978.

Danaher, B. G., Lichtenstein, E., & Sullivan, J. M. Comparative effects of rapid and normal smoking in heart rate and carboxyhemoglobin. *Journal of Consulting and Clinical Psychology*, 1976, *44*, 556–563.

Danaher, B. G., Shisslak, C. M., Thompson, C. B., & Ford, J. D. A smoking cessation program for pregnant women: An exploratory study. *American Journal of Public Health*, 1978, *68*, 896–898.

Dastur, D. K., Quadros, E. V., Wadia, N. H., Desai, M. M., & Bharucha, E. P. Effect of vegetarianism and smoking on vitamin B_{12} thiocyanate and folate levels in the blood of normal subjects. *British Medical Journal*, 1972, *3*, 260–263.

Densen, P. M., Davidow, B., Bass, H. E., & Jones, E. W. A chemical test for smoking exposure. *Archives of Environmental Mental Health*, 1967, *14*, 865–874.

DiClemente, C. C. Self-efficacy and smoking cessation maintenance. *Cognitive Therapy and Research*, 1981, *5*, 175–187.

Elliott, R., & Thysell, R. A note on smoking and heart rate. *Psychophysiology*, 1968, *5*, 280–283.

Ellis, B. H. How to reach and convince asbestos workers to give up smoking. In J. Schwartz

(Ed.), *Progress in Smoking Cessation: International Conference on Smoking Cessation*. New York: American Cancer Society, 1978.

Evans, R. I., Hansen, W. B., & Mittlemark, M. B. Increasing the validity of self-reports of smoking behavior in children. *Journal of Applied Psychology*, 1977, *62*, 521–523.

Fagerstrom, K. Measuring degree of physical dependence to tobacco smoking with reference to individualization of treatment. *Addictive Behaviors*, 1978, , 235–241.

Foxx, R. M., & Brown, R. A. Nicotine-fading and self-monitoring for cigarette abstinence or controlled smoking. *Journal of Applied Behavior Analysis*, 1979, *12*, 111–125.

Frederiksen, L. W., Epstein, L. H., & Kosevsky, B. P. Reliability and controlling effects of three procedures for self-monitoring smoking. *The Psychological Record*, 1975, *25*, 255–264.

Frederiksen, L. W., & Martin, J. E. Carbon monoxide and smoking behavior. *Addictive Behaviors*, 1979, *4*, 21–30.

Frederiksen, L. W., Martin, J. E., & Webster, J. S. Assessment of smoking behavior. *Journal of Applied Behavior Analysis*, 1979, *12*, 653–664.

Frederiksen, L. W., Miller, P. M., & Peterson, G. L. Topographical components of smoking behavior. *Addictive Behaviors*, 1977, *2*, 55–61.

Frederiksen, L. W., & Simon, S. J. Modification of smoking topography: A preliminary analysis. *Behavior Therapy*, 1978, *9*, 946–949.

Fremouw, W. J., & Brown, J. P. The reactivity of addictive behavior to self-monitoring: A functional analysis. *Addictive Behaviors*, 1980, *5*, 209–217.

Gallup Opinion Index. Public puffs on after ten years of warnings. *Gallup Opinion Index*, 1974, 108:20–21.

Goldsmith, J. R., & Aronow, W. S. Carbon monoxide and coronary heart disease: A review. *Environmental Research*, 1975, *10*, 236–248.

Gori, B. G. Low-risk cigarettes: A prescription. *Science*, 1976, *194*, 1243–1246.

Graham, S. & Gibson, R. W. Cessation of patterned behavior: Withdrawal from smoking. *Social Science and Medicine*, 1971, *5*, 319–337.

Hackett, G., & Horan, J. J. Partial component analysis of a comprehensive smoking program. *Addictive Behaviors*, 1979, *4*, 259–262.

Hall, R. G., Sachs, D. P. L., & Hall, S. M. Medical risks and therapeutic effectiveness of rapid smoking. *Behavior Therapy*, 1979, *10*, 249–259.

Hammond, E. C., Garfinkel, L., Seidman, H., & Lew, E. A. "Tar" and nicotine content of cigarette smoke in relation to death rites. *Environmental Research*, 1976, *12*, 263–274.

Hecht, E. A retrospective study of successful quitters. Paper presented at the meeting of the American Psychological Association, Toronto, 1978. (E. A. Hecht, 2414 Brocklawn Drive, Temple, Texas 76501.)

Henningfield, J. E., Stitzer, M. L., & Griffiths, R. R. Expired air carbon monoxide accumulation and elimination as a function of number of cigarettes smoked. *Addictive Behaviors*, 1980, *5*, 265–267.

Henningfield, J. E., Yingling, J., Griffiths, R. R., & Pickens, R. An inexpensive portable device for measuring puffing behavior by cigarette smokers. *Pharmacology, Biochemistry and Behavior*, 1980, *12*, 811–813.

Horan, J. J., Hackett, G., & Linberg, S. E. Factors to consider when using expired air carbon monoxide in smoking assessment. *Addictive Behaviors*, 1978, *3*, 25–28.

Horn, D. Who is quitting—and why. In J. L. Schwartz (Ed.), *Progress in Smoking Cessation: Proceedings, International Conference on Smoking Cessation.* New York: American Cancer Society, 1978.

Horning, E. C., Horning, M. G., Carroll, D. I., Stillwell, R. N., & Dzidic, I. Nicotine in smokers, nonsmokers and room air. *Life Sciences,* 1973, *13,* 1331–1346.

Hughes, J. R., Frederiksen, L. W., & Frazier, M. A carbon monoxide analyzer for measurement of smoking behavior. *Behavior Therapy,* 1978, *9,* 293–296.

Hunt, W. A., Barnett, L. W., & Branch, L. G. Relapse rates in addition programs. *Journal of Clinical Psychology,* 1971, *27,* 455–456.

Hunt, W. A., & Bespalec, D. A. An evaluation of current methods of modifying smoking behavior. *Journal of Clinical Psychology,* 1974, *30,* 431–438.

Hynd, G. W., O'Neal, M., & Severson, H. H. Cardiovascular stress during the rapid smoking procedure. *Psychological Reports,* 1976, *39,* 371–375.

Hynd, G. W., Stratton, T. T., & Severson, H. H. Smoking treatment strategies, expectancy outcomes, and credibility in attention-placebo control conditions. *Journal of Clinical Psychology,* 1978, *34,* 182–186.

Isaac, P. F., & Rand, M. J. Cigarette smoking and plasma levels of nicotine. *Nature,* 1972, *236,* 310.

Jaffe, J. H., Kanzler, M., Cohen, M., & Kaplan, T. Inducing low tar/nicotine cigarette smoking in women. *British Journal of Addiction,* 1978, *73,* 271–281.

Jenkins, R. A., Quincy, R. B., & Geurin, M. R. Selected constituents in the smokes of U.S. commercial cigarettes: "Tar", nicotine, carbon monoxide and carbon dioxide. National Technical Information Service, U.S. Department of Commerce, Springfield, Virginia, 1979.

Jones, E. E., & Sigall, H. The bogus pipeline: A new paradigm for measuring affect and attitude. *Psychological Bulletin,* 1971, *76,* 349–364.

Jones, R. H., Ellicott, M. F., Cadigan, J. B., & Gaensler, E. The relationship between alveolar and blood carbon monoxide concentrations during breath holding. *Journal of Laboratory and Clinical Medicine,* 1958, *51,* 553–564.

Kanfer, F. Self-monitoring: Methodological limitations and clinical application. *Journal of Consulting and Clinical Psychology,* 1970, *35,* 148–152.

Karoly, P., & Doyle, W. W. Effects of outcome expectancy and timing of self-monitoring on cigarette smoking. *Journal of Clinical Psychology,* 1975, *31,* 351–355.

Katz, R. C., Heiman, M., & Gordon, S. Effects of two self-management approaches on cigarette smoking. *Addictive Behaviors,* 1977, *2,* 113-nd119.

Kazdin, A. E. Self-monitoring and behavioral change. In M. J. Mahoney, & C. E. Thoreson (Eds.), *Self control: Power to the person.* Monterey, California: Brooks/Cole, 1974.

Kopel, S. A., Suckerman, K. R., & Baksht, A. Smoke holding: An evaluation of physiological effects and treatment efficacy of a new nonhazardous aversive smoking procedure. Paper presented at the meeting of the Association for Advancement of Behavior Therapy, San Francisco, 1979.

Kozlowski, L. T. Psychosocial influences on cigarette smoking. In N. Krasnegor (Ed.), *The Behavioral Aspects of Smoking, NIDA Research Monograph 26.* Washington, D.C.:USGPO (Pub. #017-024-00947-4), August, 1979.

Lando, H. A. Manual for a broad-spectrum behavioral approach to cigarette smoking. *Journal Supplement Abstract Service Catalog of Selected Documents in Psychology,* 1976, *6,* 113.

Lando, H. A. An objective check upon self-reported smoking levels: A preliminary report. *Behavior Therapy*, 1975, *6*, 547–549.

Lando, H. A. Stimulus control, rapid smoking and contractual management in the maintenance of nonsmoking. *Behavior Therapy*, 1978, *9*, 962–963.

Lando, H. A. Successful treatment of smokers with a broad-spectrum behavioral approach. *Journal of Consulting and Clinical Psychology*, 1977, *45*, 361–366.

Leventhal, H., & Avis, N. Pleasure, addiction and habit: Factors in verbal report or factors in smoking behavior? *Journal of Abnormal Psychology*, 1976, *85*, 478–488.

Lichtenstein, E., & Glasgow, R. E. Rapid smoking: Side effects and safeguards, *Journal of Consulting and Clinical Psychology*, 1977, *45*, 815–821.

Lichtenstein, E., Harris, E., Birchler, G. R., Wahl, J. M., & Schmahl, D. P. Comparison of rapid smoking, warm smoky air, and attention placebo in the modification of smoking behavior. *Journal of Consulting and Clinical Psychology*, 1973, *40*, 92–98.

Lichtenstein, E., & Rodrigues, M. R. P. Long-term effects of rapid smoking treatment for dependent cigarette smokers. *Addictive Behaviors*, 1977, *2*, 109–112.

Loro, A. D. & Orleans, C. S. The behavioral assessment of obesity. In F. J. Keefe & J. Blumenthal (Eds.), *Assessment Strategies in Behavioral Medicine*, New York: Grune & Stratton, 1982, pp. 225–260.

Luepker, R. V., Pechacek, T. F., Murray, D. M., Johnson, C. A., Hurd, P., & Jacobs, D. Saliva thiocyanate: A chemical indicator of cigarette smoking in adolescents. Unpublished manuscript, 1980. (Available from R. V. Luepker, Laboratory of Physiological Hygiene, School of Public Health, Minneapolis, Minnesota 55455).

Marlatt, G. A., & Gordon, J. R. Determinants of relapse: Implications for the maintenance of behavior change. In P. Davidson (Ed.), *Behavioral medicine: Changing health lifestyles*. New York: Brunner-Mazel, 1979.

Martin, J. E., & Frederiksen, L. W. Self-tracking of carbon monoxide levels of smokers. *Behavior Therapy*, 1980, *11*, 577–587.

Matarazzo, J. D., & Saslow, G. Psychological and related characteristics of smokers and nonsmokers. *Psychological Bulletin*, 1960, *57*, 593–613.

McFall, R. M. Smoking cessation research. *Journal of Consulting and Clinical Psychology*, 1978, *46*, 703–712.

McIntyre, K., Mermelstein, R., & Lichtenstein, E. Predicting abstinence from smoking using measures of self-efficacy and physical dependence. Paper presented at the meeting of the Association for Advancement of Behavior Therapy, New York, 1980.

Merbaum, M., Avimer, R., & Goldberg, J. The relationship between aversion group training and vomiting in the reduction of smoking behavior. *Addictive Behaviors*, 1979, *4*, 279–285.

Miller, L. D., Schilling, A. F., Logan, D. L., & Johnson, R. L. Potential hazards of rapid smoking as a technique for the modification of smoking behavior. *New England Journal of Medicine*, 1977, *297*, 590–592.

Miller, P. M. Interactions among addictive behaviors. *British Journal of Addiction*, 1979, *74*, 211–212.

Moss, A. J. Changes in cigarette smoking and current smoking practices among adults: United States, 1978. National Center for Health Statistics, *Advance Data*, 1979, *52*, 1–15.

Nathan, P. E. & Lansky, D. Common methodological problems in research on the addictions. *Journal of Consulting and Clinical Psychology*, 1978, *46*, 713–726.

Nelson, S. K. Behavioral control of smoking with combined procedures. *Psychological Reports*, 1977, *40*, 191–196.

Newman, A. The effect of reinforcement of intention statements and/or execution of self-control in smokers and exsmokers. *Addictive Behaviors*, 1977, *2*, 15–20.

O'Banion, D., Armstrong, B. K., & Ellis, J. Conquered urge as a means of self-control. *Addictive Behaviors*, 1980, *5*, 101–106.

Ober, D. C. Modification of smoking behavior. *Journal of Consulting and Clinical Psychology*, 1968, *32*, 543–549.

Ohlin, P., Lundh, B., & Westling, H. Carbon monoxide blood levels and reported cessation of smoking. *Psychopharmacology*, 1976, *49*, 263–265.

Orleans, C. S. Quitting smoking: Promising approaches and critical issues. In *Smoking and Behavior*, Institute of Medicine Report No. 1, Washington, D.C.: National Academy of Sciences, IOM Publication No. 80-001, 1980.

Orleans, C. S. *Assessment after treatment: A new frontier in smoking cessation research.* Paper presented at the meeting of The Association for Advancement of Behavior Therapy, Toronto, 1981.

Orleans, C. S., & Shipley, R. H. Worksite smoking cessation initiatives: Review and recommendations. *Addictive Behaviors*, 1982, *7*, 1–16.

Orleans, C. S., Shipley, R. H., Williams, C., & Haac, L. A. Behavioral approaches to smoking cessation, 1969–1979. I. A decade of research progress. *Journal of Behavior Therapy and Experimental Psychiatry*, 1981, *12*, 125–129.

Orleans, C. S., White, M. L., & Nagey, D. A. Comparative physiological effects and aversiveness of four nonhazardous aversive smoking procedures: Alternatives for the pregnant smoker. Paper presented at the meeting of the Association for Advancement of Behavior Therapy, Toronto, 1981.

Paxton, R., & Bernacca, G. Urinary nicotine concentration as a function of time since last cigarette: Implications for detecting faking in smoking clinics. *Behavior Therapy*, 1979, *10*, 523–528.

Pechacek, T. F. Modification of smoking behavior. In N. A. Krasnegor (Ed.), *The behavioral aspects of smoking*. NIDA research Monography, Washington, D.C.:USGPO, DHEW Publication No. (ADM) 79-882, 1979.

Pechacek, T. F., Danaher, B. G., Hall, R. G., Sachs, D. P. & Hall, S. M. *Evaluation of cardiopulmonary effects in response to the warm smoky air procedure.* Paper presented at the meeting of the Society of Behavioral Medicine, San Francisco, December 1979.

Pechacek, T. F., Luepker, R. V., & Pickens, R. C. Advances in the measurement of smoking behavior. Paper presented at the meeting of the Society of Behavioral Medicine, New York, 1980.

Pechacek, T. F., Murray, D., & Luepker, R. *Saliva sample collection manual.* Unpublished manuscript, 1980. (Available from T. F. Pechacek, Laboratory of Physiological Hygiene, School of Public Health, Minneapolis, Minnesota 55455).

Pederson, L. L., & Lefcoe, N. M. A psychological and behavioral comparison of exsmokers and smokers. *Journal of Chronic Diseases*, 1976, *39*, 431–434.

Pekkanen, T. J., Elo, O., & Hanninen, M. L. Changes in nonsmokers' saliva thiocyanate levels after being in a tobacco smoke-filled room. *World Smoking and Health*, 1976, *1*, 37–59.

Perri, M. G., Richards, C. S., & Schultheis, K. R. Behavioral self-control and smoking reduction: A study of self-initiated attempts to reduce smoking. *Behavior Therapy,* 1977, *8,* 360–365.

Perri, M. G., Richards, C. S. An investigation of naturally occurring episodes of self-controlled behaviors. *Journal of Counseling Psychology,* 1977, *24,* 178–183.

Pettigrew, A. R., & Fell, G. S. Microdiffusion method for estimation of cyanide in whole blood and its application to the study of conversion of cyanide to thiocyanate. *Clinical Chemistry,* 1973, *19,* 466–471.

Pomerleau, O. F., & Pomerleau, C. S. *Break the smoking habit: A behavioral program for giving up cigarettes.* Champaign, Illinois: Research Press, 1977.

Pomerleau, P. F., Adkins, D., & Pertschuk, M. Predictors of outcome and recidivism in smoking cessation treatment. *Addictive Behaviors,* 1978, *3,* 65–70.

Powell, D. R., & McCann, B. S. The effect of multiple treatment and multiple maintenance procedures on smoking cessation. Unpublished manuscript, 1979. (Available from D. R. Powell, American Health Foundation, 320 E. 43rd Street, New York, New York 10017.)

Prue, D. M., Martin, J. E., & Hume, A. S. A critical evaluation of thiocyanate as a biochemical index of smoking exposure. *Behavior Therapy,* 1980, *11,* 368–380.

Prue, D. M., Krapfl, J. E., & Martin, J. E. Brandfading: The effects of gradual changes to low tar and nicotine cigarettes on smoking rate, carbonmonoxide and thiocyanate levels. *Behavior Therapy,* 1981, *12,* 400–416.

Robinson, J. S., & Young, J. C. Temporal patterns in smoking rate and mouth-level nicotine exposure. *Addictive Behaviors,* 1980, *5,* 91–95.

Rosen, G. M., & Lichtenstein, E. An employee incentive program to reduce cigarette smoking. *Journal of Consulting and Clinical Psychology,* 1977, *45,* 957.

Rosenthal, B. S., & Marx, R. D. A comparison of standard behavior and relapse prevention weight reduction programs. Paper presented at the annual meeting of the Association for Advancement Behavior Therapy, San Francisco, 1979.

Ross, W. S. Poison gases in your cigarettes—Part I: Carbon monoxide. *Reader's Digest,* 1976a, *109,* 114–118.

Ross, W. S. Poison gases in your cigarettes—Part II: Hydrogen cyanide and nitrogen oxides. *Reader's Digest,* 1976b, *109,* 92–98.

Rozensky, R. H., & Bellack, A. S. Behavior change and individual differences in self-control. *Behavior Research and Therapy,* 1974, *12,* 267–268.

Rozensky, R. H. The effect of timing of self-monitoring behavior on reducing cigarette consumption. *Journal of Behavior Therapy and Experimental Psychiatry,* 1974, *5,* 301–303.

Russell, M. A. H. Blood carboxyhemoglobin changes during tobacco smoking. *Postgraduate Medical Journal,* 1973, *49,* 684–687.

Russell, M. A. H., Wilson, C., Patel, U. A., Cole, P. V., & Feyerabend, C. Comparison of effects on tobacco consumption and carbon monoxide absorption of changing to high and low nicotine cigarettes. *British Medical Journal,* 1973, *4,* 512–516.

Ryan, F. J. Cold-turkey in Greenfield, Iowa: A follow-up study. In W. L. Dunn (Ed.), *Smoking Behavior: Motives and Incentives.* Washington, D.C.: V. H. Winston, 1973.

Schmahl, D. P., Lichtenstein, E., & Harris, D. E. Successful treatment of habitual smokers with warm, smoky air and rapid smoking. *Journal of Consulting and Clinical Psychology,* 1972, *38,* 105–111.

Shewchuk, L. A. Smoking cessation programs of the American Health Foundation. *Preventive Medicine*, 1976, *5*, 454–474.

Shiffman, S. M., & Jarvik, M. E. Smoking withdrawal symptoms in two weeks of abstinence. *Psychopharmacology*, 1976, *50*, 35–39.

Shipley, R. H. Maintenance of smoking cessation: Effects of follow-up letters, smoking motivation, muscle tension and health laws of control. *Journal of Consulting and Clinical Psychology*, 1981, *49*, 982–985.

Shipley, R. H., Rosen, T. J., Williams, C. Measurement of smoking: Surveys and some recommendations. *Addictive Behaviors*, in press.

Smith, G. M. Personality and smoking: A review of the empirical literature. In W. A. Hunt (Ed.), *Learning Mechanisms in Smoking*. Chicago, Aldine Publishing Company, 1970.

Sobell, M. A., & Sobell, L. C. *Behavioral treatment of alcohol problems: Individualized therapy and controlled drinking*. New York: Plenum Press, 1978.

Soldatos, C., Kales, J. D., Scharf, M. D., Bixler, E. O., & Kales, A. Cigarette smoking associated with sleep difficulty. *Science*, 1980, *207*, 551–552.

Stewart, R. D., Stewart, R. S., Stamm, W., & Seelen, R. P. Rapid estimation of carboxhemoglobin level in fire fighters. *Journal of the American Medical Association*, 1976, *235*, 390–392.

Tori, C. D. A smoking satiation procedure with reduced medical risk. *Journal of Clinical Psychology*, 1978, *34*, 574–577.

Turner, J. A. M. Confirmation of abstinence from smoking. *British Medical Journal*, 1976, *2*, 755.

USDHEW. *Adult use of tobacco—1975*. Bethesda, Maryland: National Institutes of Health, National Cancer Institute, 1976.

USPHS. *The health consequences of smoking: 1975*. USGPO, Washington, D.C.: DHEW Publication No. (CDC) 76–8704, 1976.

Vogt, T. M. Smoking behavioral factors as predictors of risks. In M. E. Jarvik, J. W. Culler, E. R. Gritz, T. M. Vogt, & L. S. West (Eds.), *Research on smoking behavior*. NIDA Research Monograph 17. USDHEW Public Health Service, National Institute of Drug Abuse, DHEW Publication No. (ADM) 78-581, 1977, 98–110.

Vogt, T., Selvin, S., Widdowson, G., & Hulley, S. Expired air carbon monoxide and serum thiocyanate as objective measures of cigarette exposure. *American Journal of Public Health*, 1977, *67*, 545–549.

Wald, N., Howard, S., Smith, P. G., & Bailey, A. Use of carboxyhemoglobin levels to predict the development of diseases associated with cigarette smoking. *Thorax*, 1975, *30*, 133–140.

Webb, E. J., Campbell, D. T., Schwartz, R. D., & Sechrest, L. *Unobtrusive measures: Nonreactive research in the social sciences*. Chicago: Rand McNally, 1966.

Yalom, I. D. *The theory and practice of group psychotherapy*. New York: Basic Books, Inc., 1970.

Zeidenberg, P., Jaffe, J. H., Kanzler, M., Levitt, M. D., Langone, J. J., & Vunakis, H. V. Nicotine: Cotinine levels in blood during cessation of smoking. *Comprehensive Psychiatry*, 1977, *18*, 93–101.

Appendix: Sample Pretreatment, End-of-treatment, and Follow-up Questionnaires

No single set of measures (or questionnaires) will be suitable for all smoking control programs. We have argued for measures tailored to the specific programs and procedures under study. Therefore, we offer the following questionnaires only as examples. They arise from our work evaluating multicomponent behavioral smoking cessation programs combining training in nonsmoking skills with aversive smoke holding.

The pretreatment questionnaire gathers information on a number of demographic, smoking history, and individual difference variables which may affect outcome, including measures of current tobacco habit (including Fagerström's (1978 tolerance questionnaire), past quitting history, social supports, quitting motivation, and expectations for success in smoking control since many of these variables have been found to predict quitting success. Some administrative issues are also covered (e.g., source of referral, addresses of informants). This questionnaire includes a brief sympton checklist for screening subjects for aversive smoking and questions for obtaining physician approval when a medical risk is present. Two additional symptom checklists are included, chiefly to establish baseline data for later determinations of changes in mood (e.g., depression, irritability, anxiety) or in possible smoking-related activities (e.g., exercise, overeating, coffee drinking, alcohol use). We have emphasized the need for comprehensive assessment before and after treatment, and at each follow-up point. Our pretreatment and follow-up instruments include questions concerning substance smoked and self-reported smoking rate and are used in conjunction with physiological measures to verify self-report.

Both the end-of-treatment and follow-up questionnaires assess the circumstances and extent of any post-treatment smoking, the use and strength of a variety of nonsmoking skills, and expectations for success. They also repeat pre-treatment questions concerning smoking-related symptoms and habits, to document positive and negative treatment side effects. The end-of-treatment questionnaire rates the helpfulness of a variety of treatment components. As we have designed it, the follow-up questionnaire is suitable for repeated use at follow-up (e.g., 6 months, 1 year, 18 months, etc.). At each administration, we explain that this confidential information is used to improve the treatment program, and we congratulate those who are still abstinent, advising those who have relapsed that quitting often involves a gradual process and that many successful exsmokers have tried to quit and failed before final success. Relapsers are encouraged to consider another attempt at changing their smoking habits, and are informed that we are willing to provide additional treatment or direct them to other quitting resources in the community.

As we have discussed, additional measures will undoubtedly be required, depending on the specific purpose of an investigation. Selecting measures should always be guided by specific hypotheses, relevant theory, and research. For example, if an investigator were interested in the predictive potential of self-efficacy beliefs, an instrument should be designed or selected to specifically and comprehensively assess smoking-cessation self-efficacy (e.g., DiClementi, 1981).

PRETREATMENT QUESTIONNAIRE

CONFIDENTIAL SMOKING QUESTIONNAIRE

Date _____

Name _____ Sex _____ Age _____ Marital status _____

Home address _____ Work address _____

Home phone _____ Work phone _____

Occupation _____

Are you currently employed? _____ Full-time _____ Part-time

_____ Retired _____ Not working

Education (check highest level completed):

_____ Did not complete high school _____ High school graduate _____ Some college

_____ College graduate _____ Some post-graduate training _____ Post-graduate degree

Please give the following information on someone not living in your home who will
always know your address:

Name _____

Address _____ Phone _____

Please give the following information on a friend or relative who would be able to
tell us about your smoking behavior:

Name _____ Phone _____

Address _____

Part A: Tobacco Habit

1. How old were you when your began smoking regularly
   (at least one pack/week): _____

*2. Exactly what brand do you smoke (include if it's
    menthol, longs, filtered, etc)? _____

*3. In an average day, how many cigarettes do you usually
    smoke? _____

4. How many cigarettes would you estimate you smoked
   per day over the past week? _____

*5. On the average, how much of a cigarette do you smoke? ___ About 1/3 ___ About 2/3
                                                            ___ All of it

*6. Do you inhale? ___ Always ___ Sometimes

*7. Do you smoke more during the morning than the rest of
    the day? ___ Yes ___ No

*8. How soon after you wake up do you smoke your first
    cigarette? _____

*9. Which cigarette would you most hate to give up?

*10. Do you find it difficult to refrain from smoking in places where it is forbidden e.g., while shopping, at the library or cinema, etc?

_____ Yes _____ No

*11. Do you smoke if you are so ill that you are in bed most of the day?

_____ Yes _____ No

*12. In the past two years, have you changed the number of cigarettes you smoke, switched brands, changed your inhaling habits, or otherwise changed your smoking habits? If so, please give details _____

_____ Yes _____ No

Part B: Quitting History

1. How many times have you deliberately attempted to quit smoking, and succeeded for at least 24 hours?

2. How long ago was your most recent serious attempt to quit smoking?

3. What is the longest period of time you were able to stay off cigarettes after quitting on your own (not counting any times you were forced to quit, for example, because you were sick)?

4. In your past quitting attempts, were you most likely to go back to smoking:

a) When you were ___ irritated ___ sad ___ happy ___ anxious

b) In the ___ morning ___ midday ___ evening ___ night

c) While drinking ___ alcohol ___ coffee ___ nothing ___ other

d) When ___ alone ___ with others

e) At ___ work ___ home ___ other

5. What help have you sought in the past to help you quit cigarettes (clinics, doctors, filters, books, etc): _____

Part C: Social support

1. Which of the following people are currently smokers (circle):

Mother   Father   Spouse/Mate
Roommate(s)   Office mate(s)
Closest friend
Closest work associate(s)
Child living at home
Child living away from home

*from Fagerstrom, K. Measuring degree of physical dependence to tobacco smoking with reference to individualization of treatment. Addictive Behaviors, 1978, 3, 235-241.

2. How many people in your household are

___ smokers ___ exsmokers ___ nonsmokers

3. About what percentage of your close friends are

___ smokers ___ exsmokers ___ nonsmokers

4. How many children 13 years old or younger are living in your home? ___

5. Are there any people who have been trying to get you to quit smoking?

___ Yes ___ No

If Yes, who (e.g., friend, relative, etc)?

6. How much support and understanding do you expect from family and friends for your quit smoking effort?

0--------------------------100

None   Very very much   ___
                                               Rating

Part D: Estimation Choose a number from 0 to 100 to answer each question.

1. To what extent do you desire to quit smoking?

0--------------------------100

Not at all   Very very much   ___
                                               Rating

2. As a result of your efforts in this clinic, what do you estimate is your probability of quitting during the clinic?

0----------------------------100   _____
No change   Can't fail   Rating

3. What is the probability that you will be a nonsmoker 6 months after this clinic?

0----------------------------100   _____
Poor   Excellent   Rating

4. If you are successful in quitting cigarettes, do you foresee any significant negative side effects lasting more than a month or so? (e.g., weight problems, nerves, difficulty concentrating)

_____ Yes _____ No

If Yes, what problems do you anticipate? _____

_____

5. If you could learn to smoke in a way less damaging to your health, would you prefer this to complete quitting?   _____ Yes   _____ Maybe   _____ No

Part E: Health

1. Do you believe smoking adversely affects your health?

0----------------------------100   _____
Not at all   Very very much   Rating

2. About how many close friends or relatives do you know whose health has been adversely affected by smoking? _____

3. Have you ever been advised by a physician to quit smoking?

_____ No

_____ Yes, because of a specific illness _____ Specify _____

_____ Yes, for general health reasons

4. Have you ever had:

a) A heart attack   Yes _____ No
b) Any indication of heart trouble   Yes _____ No
c) A stroke   Yes _____ No
d) High blood pressure   Yes _____ No
e) Shortness of breath climbing stairs   Yes _____ No
f) Emphysema   Yes _____ No
g) Tuberculosis   Yes _____ No
h) Bronchitis   Yes _____ No
i) Decreased blood flow to your limbs   Yes _____ No
j) Diabetes   Yes _____ No
k) Asthma   Yes _____ No
l) Anemia   Yes _____ No
m) Pregnancy (at present time)   Yes _____ No

5. If you checked "Yes" for any of the conditions or illnesses, may we contact your physician for routine screening information:

      _____ Yes   _____ No

6. Would you like us to contact your doctor to describe your progress after the clinic?

      _____ Yes   _____ No

7. Please give name and address of your personal physician:

_____

_____

8. Over the past month, have you suffered from:	Never	Rarely (less than once a week)	Often (once or twice a week)	Frequently (two or more times a week)
a) Headaches	____	____	____	____
b) Sleep difficulties	____	____	____	____
c) Stomach upset	____	____	____	____
d) Tight muscles	____	____	____	____
e) Dizziness	____	____	____	____
f) Pain	____	____	____	____
g) Heart racing or palpitations	____	____	____	____
h) Nervous sweating	____	____	____	____

9. Have you seen a mental health professional in the past 2 years?

Yes _____ No _____

If Yes, please briefly describe: _____

10. Using a 100-point scale, please rate the degree in which each item applied to you during the past week:

0----------50----------100

Not at   Somewhat   Very
all   characteristic characteristic

Characteristic:

_____ a) Smoking-related physical symptoms like wheezing, coughing, shortness of breath

_____ b) Stamina, good energy level

_____ c) Good productivity, got things done

_____ d) Right appetite for me

_____ e) Restlessness, tension, impatience, etc.

_____ f) Irritability

_____ g) Sociability

_____ h) Overeating

_____ i) Getting enough physical activity, exercise

_____ j) Sharp sense of smell and taste

_____ k) Sadness, depression

_____ l) Feeling in control of your life

_____ m) Efficiency in getting things done

_____ n) Good concentration

_____ o) Feeling addicted to tobacco

p) Feeling physically healthy
q) Good general self-esteem
r) Lethargy

Part F: Other habits

1. Do you use other forms of tobacco (snuff, chewing tobacco, pipes, cigars)?

    _____ Yes   _____ No

2. How many cups or glasses of caffeinated beverage (coffee, tea, cola) have you averaged each day over the past week? _____

3. How many alcoholic drinks (beer, glasses of wine, mixed or single-shot hard drinks) have you had over the past week? _____

4. Please describe any mood-altering medications which you have taken over the past week, giving the drug name(s), strength and how often you take the medication (mood altering medications include tranquilizers, antidepressants and stimulants).

    _____

    _____

5. We are interested in possible changes in marijuana smoking as a result of quitting cigarette smoking. Would you be willing to disclose, in coded form, information about marijuana usage (This information would remain confidential)?

    _____ Yes   _____ No

6. Present weight _____   Height _____

Confidential End-of-treatment Questionnaire

Date _____

Name _____

1. How helpful were each of the following aspects of the clinic program? Use the following rating scale:

0---100

Not at all   Very very helpful;
helpful; could   indispensible
have done without

_____ a) Carbon monoxide feedback
_____ b) Discussing nonsmoking skills
_____ c) Discussing how to avoid relapse
_____ d) Group interaction and support
_____ e) Handouts
_____ f) Learning deep breathing
_____ g) Normal paced smoking in one session
_____ h) Smoke-holding in sessions
_____ i) Therapist interaction and support
_____ j) Other _____ (please specify)

2. Have you smoked at all (outside of sessions) since starting the Quit Smoking Clinic?

_____ Yes   _____ No

If you have smoked, please complete a) through f) below.

a) Exactly how many cigarettes would you estimate you smoked per day over the past week? _____

b) What is the approximate total number of cigarettes you have smoked since the start of the clinic? _____

c) What is the brand of cigarettes you smoked? _____

d) About how many days after starting the clinic did you have your first cigarette? _____

e) Briefly describe your smoking since starting the clinic. _____

_____

f) If you are still smoking, to what extent do you desire to quit? Choose a number from 0 to 100.

0------------------------------100

_____
Rating

3. If you are presently not smoking, please complete 3a) through d) below. Otherwise, go on to question 4. For each item use one rating from 0 to 100.

a) How often in the past week have you experienced urges to smoke?

0------------------------------100
None of the   All of the
time   time

_____
Rating

b) Over the past week, how strong, on the average, have your smoking urges been?

0---------------100

Hardly noticeable   Extremely strong   Rating _____

c) How easy or difficult is it for you to resist smoking urges?

0---------------100

Very very easy   Very very difficult   Rating _____

d) How confident are you that you can succeed in resisting these urges and controlling your smoking?

0---------------100

Not at all   Extremely   Rating _____
confident   confident

4. What is the probability that you will be a nonsmoker 6 months from now?

0%---------------100%   _____ %

5. Using a 100-point scale, please rate how much each item applied to you during the past week:

0---------50---------100

Not at all   Somewhat   Very
characteristic   characteristic   characteristic

_____ a) Smoking-related physical symptoms like wheezing, coughing, shortness of breath

_____ b) Stamina, general energy level

_____ c) Good productivity, got things done
_____ d) Right appetite for me
_____ e) Restlessness, tension, impatience
_____ f) Irritability
_____ g) Sociability
_____ h) Overeating
_____ i) Getting enough physical activity, exercise
_____ j) Sharp sense of smell and taste
_____ k) Sadness, depression
_____ l) Feeling in control of your life
_____ m) Efficiency in getting things done
_____ n) Good concentration
_____ o) Feeling addicted to tobacco
_____ p) Feeling physically healthy
_____ q) Good general self-esteem
_____ r) Lethargy

6. About how many times per day in the past week have you used each of the following techniques to help you control your smoking?

Number of times per day in the past week:

_____ a) Cigarette replacements/substitutes (e.g., chewing gum, doodling, mints, bending paper clips)
_____ b) Rewarding yourself for not smoking
_____ c) Avoiding places or activities associated with smoking
_____ d) Deep breathing or using another relaxation technique
_____ e) Walking, jogging or other aerobic activity

309

f) Overeating at meals or snacks
_____ g) Getting encouragement and support from others
_____ h) Talking yourself out of a cigarette (e.g., rehearsing reasons for quitting, "pep talks")
_____ i) Calling for follow-up telephone messages
_____ j) Using drugs, medications, or alcohol
_____ k) Using self-help materials (a book, tape, etc)
_____ l) Other

7. Since the start of the treatment program, have you used other forms of tobacco, (pipes, cigars)? _____ Yes _____ No

If Yes, please indicate substances and the number of times used over the past week _____

8. How many cups or glasses of caffeinated beverage (coffee, tea, cola) have you averaged each day over the past week? _____

9. How many alcoholic drinks (beer, glasses of wine, single-shot hard or mixed drinks) have you had over the past week? _____

10. Please describe any mood-altering medications which you have taken over the past week, giving the drug name(s), strengths, and how often you take the medication (mood altering medications include tranquilizers, antidepressants, and stimulants).

_____

_____

11. We are interested in possible changes in marijuana smoking as a result of quitting cigarette smoking. Would you be willing to disclose, in coded form, information about marijuana usage?(This information would remain confidential.)

_____ Yes _____ No

12. Present weight _____

Confidential Follow-up Questionnaire

Name _____   Date _____

Address _____

Home phone _____   Business phone _____

1. Have you smoked at all since complete the Quit Smoking Clinic?

    ____ Yes   ____ No

   If you have smoked, please complete a) through h) below. If not, go on to question 2.

   a) Exactly how many cigarettes would you estimate you smoked per day over the past week? _____

   b) What is the approximate total number of cigarettes you have smoked since the end of the clinic? _____

   c) What is the brand of cigarettes you smoked? _____

   d) About how many days after completion of the clinic did you have your first cigarette? _____

   e) Briefly describe your smoking since completing the clinic.
   _____

f) If you are still smoking, to what extent do you desire to quit? Choose a number from 0 to 100.

0---100
Not at all   Very very much

_____
Rating

g) Would you be interested in attending another program designed to help you control your smoking?

_____ Yes   _____ No

If yes, would you prefer learning to smoke in a way less damaging to your health over total quitting?

_____ Yes   _____ Maybe   _____ No

h) Describe the circumstances of your first cigarette after the clinic:

When you were _____ irritated _____ sad _____ happy _____ anxious

In the _____ morning _____ midday _____ evening _____ night

While drinking _____ alcohol _____ coffee _____ nothing

When _____ alone _____ with others

At _____ work _____ home _____ other

2. If you are presently not smoking, please complete 2a) through d). Otherwise, go on to question 3. For each item use one rating from 0 to 100.

a) How often in the past week have you experienced urges to smoke?

0---100
Not of the time   All of the time

_____
Rating

b) Over the past week, how strong, on the average, have your smoking urges been?

```
0------------------------100                    _____
Hardly noticeable        Extremely noticeable      Rating
```

c) How easy or difficult is it for you now to resist smoking urges?

```
0------------------------100                    _____
Very very easy           Very very difficult       Rating
```

d) How confident are you that you can succeed in resisting these urges and controlling your smoking?

```
0------------------------100                    _____
Not at all               Extremely                 Rating
confident                confident
```

3. What is the probability that you will be a nonsmoker 6 months from now?

```
0%------------------------100%                  _____ %
```

4. Using a 100-point rating scale, please rate how much each item applied to you during the past week:

```
0------------------50------------------100
Not at all          Somewhat           Very
characteristic      characteristic     characteristic
```

_____ a) Smoking-related physical symptoms like wheezing, coughing, shortness of breath

_____ b) Stamina, good energy level

_____ c) Good productivity, got things done

_____ d) Right appetite for me

_____ e) Restlessness, tension, impatience

_____ f) Irritability
_____ g) Sociability
_____ h) Overating
_____ i) Getting enough physical activity, exercise
_____ j) Sharp sense of smell and taste
_____ k) Sadness, depression
_____ l) Feeling in control of your life
_____ m) Efficiency in getting things done
_____ n) Good concentration
_____ o) Feeling addicted to tobacco
_____ p) Feeling physically healthy
_____ q) Good general self-esteem
_____ r) Lethargy

5. How many times, per day in the past week have you used each of the following techinques to help you control your smoking?

Number of times per day in the past week:

_____ a) Cigarette replacements/substitutes (e.g., chewing gum, doodling, mints, bending paper clips)
_____ b) Rewarding yourself for not smoking
_____ c) Avoiding places or activities associated with smoking
_____ d) Deep breathing or using another relaxation technique
_____ e) Walking, jogging or other aerobic activity
_____ f) Overeating at meals or snacks
_____ g) Getting encouragement and support from others
_____ h) Talking to yourself out of a cigarette (e.g., rehearsing reasons for quitting, "pep talks")

i) Calling for follow-up telephone messages

j) Using drugs, medication or alcohol

k) Using self-help materials (a book, tape, etc)

l) Other

6. Since the end of the treatment program, have you used other forms for tobacco (pipes, cigars)?   Yes _____ No _____

   If yes, please indicate substances and the number of times used over the past week.

7. How many cups/glasses or caffeinated beverage (coffee, tea, cola) have you averaged each day over the past week?

8. How many alcoholic drinks (beer, glasses of wine, single-shot hard or mixed drinks) have you averaged over the past week? _____

9. Please describe any mood-altering medications which you have taken over the past week, giving the drug name(s), strengths, and how often you take the medication (mood altering medications include tranquilizers, antidepressant and stimulants).

   _____

10. Present weight _____

11. We are interested in possible changes in marijuana smoking as a result of quitting cigarette smoking. Would you be willing in the future to disclose, in coded form, information about marijuana usage?(This information would remain confidential.)

    _____ Yes   _____ No

316

12. Over the past month, have you suffered from:

	Never	Rarely (less than once a week)	Often (once or twice a week)	Frequently (two or more times a week)
a) Headaches				
b) Sleep difficulties				
c) Stomach upset				
d) Tight muscles				
e) Dizziness				
f) Pain				
g) Heart racing or palpitations				
h) Nervous sweating				

13. Have any of your relatives or close friends started or stopped smoking since you attempted to quit?   Yes _____   No _____
If yes, please describe _____

How do you think your attempt to quit influenced these changes ? _____

_____

PART V

Assssment Strategies for Chronic Pain and Illness

Francis J. Keefe, Charles Brown
Donald S. Scott, Harold Ziesat

11

Behavioral Assessment of Chronic Pain

Chronic pain is a major national medical problem. The costs of chronic pain, in terms of hospitalization, insurance claims, and disability payments are staggering. This is evident if we examine data on just one type of chronic pain—back pain. Patients suffering from chronic back pain rank eleventh of 194 diagnostic groups in terms of number of days spent in hospitals in the United States (Chaffin, 1974). In 1977, in Washington state alone, there were 10,535 claims for workmen's compensation due to back pain, amounting to $63.5 million (Loeser, 1980). The total cost of chronic low back pain to our society may be as much as $100,000/ patient (Bonica, 1974).

Physicians often have great difficulty managing the chronic pain patient. Traditional medical and surgical approaches to treating chronic pain often are ineffective or contraindicated because patients lack evidence of obvious tissue pathology responsible for their pain. Physicians, having little to offer such patients, may view them as an untreatable group of "crocks, losers, and malingerers."

While pain is obviously a highly subjective experience, "an unpleasant sensory and emotional experience associated with actual or potential tissue damage," (IASP Subcommittee on Taxonomy, 1979), it has a profound impact on behavior. There is increasing awareness among physicians of the importance of behavioral factors in chronic pain (Bonica, 1977). A number of maladaptive behaviors are associated with chronic pain, including excessive reliance on addictive medications, excessive utilization of health services, avoidance of both work and exercise (Fordyce, 1978), and a hostile, manipulative approach to interpersonal relationships (Timmermans and Sternbach, 1974).

*We would like to thank the following participants in our psychology of pain seminar for their critical comments on this chapter: Norm Anderson, Marcia Angle, Linda Barnett, Janis Kupersmidt, David Miller, Nancy Milliken, Janice Nici, John Roeback, Anne Rosentiel, Barry Schapira, Al Scovern, Eric Shaw, and Betty Wolfe.

Since 1970, behavioral treatment techniques have emerged as a viable alternative in the management of chronic pain patients. Behaviorally oriented treatment programs, using either operant conditioning techniques (Fordyce et al., 1973; Seres and Newman, 1976; Sternbach, 1974; Swanson et al., 1976), or cognitive behavior therapy procedures (Gottlieb et al., 1977; Rybstein-Blinchik, 1979) have attempted to modify maladaptive behavior patterns in chronic pain patients. These programs clearly are successful in reducing addictive pain medication intake and in increasing the general activity level of chronic pain patients. While behavioral treatment procedures for chronic low back pain have been described in detail, little attention has been given to behavioral assessment. Several reviews dealing with the measurement of experimental and clinical pain have appeared (Merskey, 1973; Huskisson, 1974; Wolff, 1978), but none of these address behavioral assessment.

This chapter will provide a critical review of behavioral assessment strategies used with chronic pain patients. We begin with a consideration of the etiology of chronic pain syndromes, and briefly discuss principles underlying behavioral treatment approaches. We then describe various behavioral assessment techniques, consider their application to chronic pain, and critically evaluate their utility. The review ends with a discussion of some of the clinical, methodological, and ethical issues involved in behavioral assessment with this patient population.

ETIOLOGY OF CHRONIC PAIN

The term *chronic pain* is usually used to describe a pain that is benign in origin and that is present on a constant, daily basis for longer than 6 months (Sternbach, 1974). The word "benign" does not refer to a lack of severity, but rather to pain which is not the result of a malignant disease process, such as cancer. Although chronic pain is not the result of a life-threatening malignancy, it may very well be a result of trauma, physical injury, or another type of organic disorder.

Attempts have been made to categorize chronic pain patients into two distinct groups: *organic* pain patients and *psychogenic* pain patients. Those who advocate a behavioral approach to chronic pain strongly disagree with this dichotomization (Sternbach, 1974; Fordyce, 1976). The term "psychogenic pain" is not very useful when dealing behaviorally with chronic pain patients. First, patients experience pain in much the same way, regardless of whether the primary contributing factors are associated with psychological stress, physical disease, or trauma (Sternbach, 1974). Second, most chronic pain cases involve multiple etiologic factors (Bonica, 1974). Physiologic and behavioral factors may interact to produce a vicious cycle: The patient who injures his or her back may become depressed and inactive. Inactivity tends to weaken muscles supporting the spine; thereby placing more stress on injured tissues which increases pain and strengthens the tendency to reduce activity (Fordyce, 1976). Third, the crude state of physical diagnostic procedures in this area makes it difficult (if not impossible) to definitively exclude tissue pathology as a basis for the patient's complaint (Bonica, 1977). Attempts to surgically remedy pain have iatrogenic effects that further complicate the clinical picture. Scar tissue, resulting from repeated surgeries, cannot be detected through diagnostic tests but may be an important neurophysiologic factor in the persistence of chronic pain (Caillet, 1968).

Our understanding of the etiology of chronic pain syndromes is far from complete. Chronic pain is typically the result of a complex interplay of neurophysiological, behavioral, and psychological factors (Bonica, 1977).

Neurophysiologic Factors

One or a combination of neurophysiologic factors may lead to chronic pain. Chronic pain of a vascular nature, such as migraine headache, is thought to be due to vasospasms which stimulate nerve fibers. Neuralgias, usually occurring in the mouth and face, are due either to nerve degeneration (e.g., trigeminal neuralgia) or disease processes (e.g., post-herpetic neuralgia) (Bond, 1977). Causalgias, usually involving the upper extremities, are due to peripheral nerve degeneration secondary to trauma. Musculoskeletal pain, believed to be involved in many chronic back pain problems, is thought to be due to chronic muscular hyperactivity (Bonica, 1977). Such hyperactivity has been shown to be associated with histological changes of the connective tissue (Awad, 1973).

Neurophysiological factors important in the onset of acute pain may become less important as pain becomes chronic. For example, MacNab (1977) has stated that acute low back pain may have a neurogenic basis (cauda equina tumor), a vascular basis (aortic aneurysm), a viscerogenic basis (pancreatic disease), a discogenic basis (degenerative disc disease), or a spondylogenic basis (scoliosis, spondylolisthesis). A survey of patients suffering from chronic low back pain (Fernback et al., 1976), however, indicates that patients suffering from discogenic, spondylogenic, or no identifiable neurophysiologic factors make up the vast majority of chronic back pain patients.

The management of most acute pain problems is based on diagnosis of the underlying tissue pathology and appropriate treatment. Conservative treatment procedures are used whenever possible (Caillet, 1968). Treatment typically consists of bed rest, bed exercises, analgesic and/or sedative-hypnotic medications, traction, corseting, and eventually, gradual reconditioning through flexibility exercises (Caillet, 1968). For those patients who do not experience relief with conservative treatment, or who show advancing neurological deficits, surgical procedures are sometimes considered (Caillet, 1968).

There is frank recognition of the limitations of conventional surgical treatment procedures for chronic pain (Aitken, 1959; Hirsch, 1965; Leavitt et al., 1972). One problem confronting surgeons with chronic pain patients is that these patients do not show obvious evidence of underlying tissue pathology that can be surgically corrected (Loeser, 1980). For example, in one survey, the number of low back pain patients who had evidence of hard neurologic signs (e.g., muscle atrophy and weakness, bladder or bowel control problems, positive myelogram), suggesting obvious tissue pathology in the spinal nerves was less than 28 percent (Loeser, 1980). Because of such problems, at most major medical centers, chronic pain patients are carefully screened to maximize the possibility of surgical success (Caillet, 1968).

Why do chronic pain patients with no "hard" evidence of tissue pathology continue to experience pain? One possible reason is that neurophysiological factors that are not surgically correctable, e.g., muscle spasm or vasospasm, may be operating (Bonica, 1977). Another reason is that chronic pain may lead to marked behavioral and emotional deficits that serve to maintain pain and associated behaviors (Fordyce, 1976; Keefe & Brown, 1982).

Behavioral Factors

When pain persists over long time periods, its potential to influence behavior is great (Fordyce, 1976). Fordyce (1976) has emphasized the importance of learning in understanding the behavior of the chronic pain patient. He states that through a conditioning process, patients learn behavior patterns that help them reduce pain; but these same behavior patterns may actually serve to maintain pain, however.

The development of pain behavior patterns can be conceptualized as occurring over three stages, *acute, prechronic,* and *chronic.* Table 11-1 depicts some of the characteristic responses that occur at each stage.

In response to acute pain, most individuals engage in patterns of overt motor behavior, cognitive-affective, and physiological responses as summarized in Table 11-1. These responses serve an important adaptive function. For example, a temporary decrease of activity has been recognized for centuries as an effective agent in healing tissue pathology responsible for pain (Hilton, 1863). Anxiety associated with acute pain motivates the patient to take appropriate steps to cope with pain. For most patients, the acute pain experience is a brief period during which they display the behavioral pattern described, experience a marked decrease in pain, and resume normal function. A fraction of patients, however, continue to experience pain, and begin to exhibit more firmly entrenched behavior patterns. At this point, the patient enters the prechronic stage.

During the prechronic stage, pain patients may take an active stance in dealing with pain (Keefe & Brown, 1982). They report that they "push" themselves because they "refuse to give in" to pain; they often display a high level of physical activity and minimal pain-medication intake. These periods of active coping alternate with passive periods, with a very low level of activity and high pain-medication intake. Thus, during the prechronic stage pain patients are attempting to assume a more normal lifestyle (Keefe & Brown, 1982). If they are able to do so gradually and without exacerbating their pain, they are much more likely to

Table 11-1

A Proposed Developmental Perspective on Chronic Pain Behavior*

Stages	Response System		
	Overt behavior	Cognitive/affective	Physiological
Acute (0–2 months)	Temporary decrease in activity	Belief that pain is controllable through medical treatment	Reactive muscle spasm
	Temporary reliance on pain medications	Active coping style	Autonomic arousal
	Seeking help from health professionals	Anxiety	
Prechronic (2–6 months)	Alternating patterns of increasing/decreasing activity withdrawal from/reliance on pain medications	Recognition that pain may not be entirely controllable medically	During periods of intense pain reactive muscle spasm autonomic arousal
	Reduced contact with doctors	Active coping style alternates with passive	
	Working/attempting to work	Denial of depression	
		Focus on physical symptomatology	
		Pain quite variable in intensity	
		Pain reactive to stressors	
Chronic (6–24 months, plus)	Long-term pattern of decrease in activity	Belief that pain is uncontrollable	Chronic muscle spasm secondary to posturing and guarding
	Addiction to narcotic agents	Passive coping style	Decreased autonomic arousal
	Doctor "shopping" with numerous treatment failures	Depression	Deficits in muscle strength and endurance secondary to disuse
		Strong preoccupation with pain and bodily complaints	
	Not working/on disability	Pain varies little in intensity	Development of other psychophysiologic disorders (e.g., muscle contraction headaches)

Decreasing evidence of organic pathology (vertical label at left, spanning Acute through Chronic stages)

*From Keefe, F. J., Block A. R., & Williams, R. Behavioral treatment of the prechronic vs chronic pain patient. Unpublished paper presented at the American Pain Society, New York, 1980.

continue to effectively cope with pain and perhaps become pain free. If they repeatedly push themselves too hard, experience flare-ups or severe pain, and become bedridden and dependent on medication, the powerful positive consequences of these behaviors (e.g., pain medication, financial compensation, avoidance of work responsibilities), may exert control over the patient's behavior, and the patient enters the chronic stage (Keefe & Brown, 1982). The longer a patient has pain, the more likely it is that positive consequences for pain behavior are available (Fordyce, 1976).

The behavioral patterns displayed during the chronic pain stage have been described by many authors (Bonica, 1977; Fordyce, 1976; Sternbach, 1974) and are summarized in Table 11-1. At the chronic stage—12 months or more—patients display stereotyped and firmly entrenched response patterns. Family and friends have, by this time, begun to treat the patient in a different way. Solicitous attention is often given to chronic pain patients whenever they display pain (Fordyce, 1976). In many cases, family members may encourage the patient to be inactive and take pain medication. The response of the social environment to the chronic pain patient needs to be considered in both assessment and treatment efforts (Sternbach, 1974).

BEHAVIORAL TREATMENT OF CHRONIC PAIN

The hallmark of behaviorally oriented pain management is an emphasis on observable behavior. Experiences of pain and emotional sequelae are seen as less important than those things the patient does that can be more directly measured, as it frequently is easier to change the behavioral patterns of chronic low back pain patients than to modify their perception of pain. However, it is commonly observed that changes in behavior precede and facilitate reports of pain reduction (Sternbach, 1978).

Efforts to modify the behavior of chronic pain patients are based on two approaches: operant conditioning and self-control procedures. The operant conditioning approach is examplified by the work of Fordyce (1976). According to this viewpoint, pain behaviors initially elicited by tissue pathology may, over time, function as operants. That is, they come under the control of environmental consequences. Such pain behaviors as medication abuse, reductions in physical activity, and verbal or non-verbal expressions of pain are often followed by positive reinforcement. Reinforcement comes both from pain reduction (e.g., with narcotics) and the patient's social environment (e.g., solicitous attention from close friends and often [unwittingly] by health professionals). Through a process of conditioning, pain behaviors may continue even after the original pathological stimulus for pain no longer appears important. Treatment involves shifting positive reinforcement contingencies from "pain" to "well" behaviors, such as walking, smiling, discussing topics other than pain, and participating in social and recreational activities. Pain patients are typically hospitalized in special wards in which staff members use social reinforcement to reward gradual approximations of "well" behavior.

Among the self-control procedure used by behavior therapists in the treatment of chronic pain are relaxation training, biofeedback, self-hypnosis, assertion training, and cognitive restructuring techniques. These different techniques teach the patient to recognize associations between antecedents and pain behaviors. Unlike operant conditioning techniques, these approaches also emphasize instructing the patient in specific methods for altering or breaking this association. In so doing, primary responsibility for behavior change is placed on the patient rather than the social environment.

Traditional approaches to treating chronic low back pain have been evaluated on the basis of pain relief. Both the validity and utility of assessment techniques are, therefore, largely based on their correlation with pain reports (Wolff, 1978). The behavioral approaches discussed above view many behaviors exhibited by the pain patient as important in their own right. For example, patterns of analgesic/narcotic intake or functional activity level are equally as important as reports of pain (Fordyce, 1976). The goal of behavioral rehabilitation encompasses a range of relevant target behaviors.

METHODS OF ASSESSMENT

Behavioral assessment serves essentially two purposes: identifying and measuring target behaviors; and identifying those variables that control the occurrence of target variables (Nelson and Hayes, 1979). Behavioral assessment techniques used with chronic pain patients focus almost exclusively on the first goal. Techniques are typically used to evaluate treatment programs carried out on specially designed pain wards or with groups of outpatients. The specific target behaviors measured are usually selected on an a priori theoretical basis as being of central importance (Fordyce, 1976). Effects of behavioral intervention are measured across one or more of three response systems: subjective, behavioral, and physiological (Keefe & Brown, 1982). In this section, we consider those techniques of behavioral assessment used to measure responses in each of these systems. We describe the techniques, summarize the literature regarding their application, and evaluate them.

Subjective Response System

Behavior therapists initially spurned self-report measures (Azrin et al., 1961). The reliability and validity of self-report were presumed to be quite poor. Routine use of more objective observational measures were thought to preclude the need for subjective measures (Azrin et al., 1961). However, as behavior therapists began working with pain patients, the need to monitor subjective report became apparent for several reasons (Keefe & Brown, 1982). First, pain is a stimulus that elicits behaviors particularly during the acute and prechronic stages. Behavior patterns differ during periods of intense pain and during periods of little pain. Second, the pain report can have powerful effects. Patients who show improvements in behavior but who continue to complain of pain may elicit responses from family members and physicians that can reverse whatever gains have been made.

Efforts to behaviorally assess the subjective responses of pain patients to chronic pain have involved two approaches. The first approach involves a direct report of pain. The second involves examination of personality variables.

Self-report of Pain

Chronic pain patients almost invariably regard pain sensation as the most important target behavior. This may sharply contrast with the clinician's goal. Although pain may not be the primary focus of behavioral interventions, the self-report of pain is obviously a relevant measure of improvement. Assessment methods measure one or more of the following: pain intensity, location, and quality.

Pain intensity ratings have long been used in pain assessment (Wolff, 1978). The two most commonly used intensity rating methods are magnitude estimation and visual analogue scales (VAS). Magnitude estimation procedures involve asking the patient to either numerically (e.g., from 1 to 100), or verbally (e.g., none, slight, moderate, severe, excruciating) rate pain. Magnitude estimation scales have been the primary strategy used for self-report of pain since 1930, and are widely employed (Greenhoot and Sternbach, 1974; Swanson et al., 1976). Researchers in Great Britain and elsewhere have advocated the use of the visual analogue scale as a superior method to magnitude estimation procedures in sensitivity. The VAS is a line, usually 100 mm in length, whose endpoints are anchored by descriptive terms, such as ''no pain'' and ''pain as bad as it can be.'' The VAS is administered by giving the patient a sheet of paper with the scale drawn upon it and asking that a mark be placed along the line indicating the current level of pain. Visual analogue scales are slightly more difficult for patients to understand than magnitude estimation procedures. When both visual analogue and magnitude estimation procedures are compared in clinical settings, correlations of over $r = .80$ are obtained (Ohnhaus and Adler, 1975; Woodforde and Merskey, 1972). The VAS is more sensitive to variations in pain (Joyce et al., 1975). The sensitivity of the VAS to pain variations makes it a very good tool for behavior therapists using self-control procedures with pain patients.

Measures of pain intensity can be made using psychophysical techniques as well. One approach employs a tourniquet or pressure algometer to induce pain; the patient is then asked to match the intensity of the pain stimulus to the clinical pain level. The tourniquet pain method was most extensively used in the early 1970s, by Beecher, Sternbach, and their colleagues (Smith and Beecher, 1969; Smith et al., 1966; Smith et al., 1968; Sternbach, 1974; Sternbach et al., 1974). Sternbach routinely took three tourniquet measures of pain: clinical pain level (the time in seconds for the patient to experience pain equivalent to the clinical pain), pain tolerance (the time in seconds taken until the patient reaches the limit of tolerance for the ischemic pain), and the tourniquet pain ratio (calculated by dividing the time to reach clinical pain level by the time to reach maximum pain tolerance and multiplying the result by 100 percent. Sternbach and coworkers (1974) demonstrated the reliability of this procedure, but numerous reports question its validity. Sternbach (1974) presented evidence that the tourniquet ratio scores decreased following analgesic neurosurgery. More recently (Sternbach et al., 1977), the tourniquet pain ratio was found insensitive to the administration of various analgesic dosage levels. Ziesat (1978) found that the tourniquet ratio scores correlated with the patient estimates of pain on a 0- to-100 scale, the perceived impact of pain on daily activity, and with measures of hypochondriasis and reactive depression. Given that emotional factors such as hypochondriasis, depression, and pain intensity are often confounded, it is difficult to determine how much of the tourniquet pain ratio scores actually relate per se to the intensity of pain. A recent report (Moore et al., 1979) raises additional questions about assumptions underlying the use of the tourniquet pain ratio. Sternbach has assumed a mathematical, linear relationship between pain intensity and time to reach clinical pain level or pain tolerance. Moore et al. (1979) found that report of pain intensity increases as a sigmoid function, rather than as a linear function, of time. Finally, the ethical problem of inflicting additional pain on chronic pain patients in the absence of a compelling medical justification argues against routine application of such methods (Sternbach, 1978).

Research indicates that verbal pain descriptors provide a psychophysically valid alternative that overcomes many of the limitations inherent in the tourniquet pain ratio method. Both Tursky (1976) and Gracely (Gracely et al., 1978) describe the rationale and experimental techniques used to develop series of verbal pain descriptors. Briefly, both investigators have used cross-modality matching techniques to evaluate sets of pain descriptors that could be used to describe two dimensions of the pain experience, sensory intensity of the pain (i.e., how much the pain hurts), and the affective reaction to pain (i.e., how unpleasant the pain feels). Numerous studies were conducted by both investigators to develop a 10 to 15 word list that clearly discriminates between these dimensions of pain. Each list of pain descriptors was then evaluated in a second series of cross-modality matching tests, in which subjects were required to match the force of their hand grip, length of a line, and white noise to the particular descriptor presented. Using such cross-modality matching procedures, ratio scales of sensory and affective descriptors have been developed. These are the only measures of pain intensity that have been investigated that allow determinations about the relationship between different levels of perceived pain. With such scales, we can determine whether a particular verbal report of pain is two, three, or four times more intense than a second report of pain. Gracely has conducted several studies indicating that such pain descriptors are relatively bias-free, reliable, and objective. Recent studies suggest that these verbal descriptors provide useful methods for discriminating between the different dimensions of intensity and affective reaction to pain. In one experiment, (Gracely et al., 1978), the effects of intravenous administration of 5 mg of diazepam were evaluated by having subjects rate the intensity and affective aspect of electric shocks delivered immediately before and after drug administration. Results indicated significant decreases in the affective dimension of pain with no change in perception of the intensity of pain. The verbal descriptors are presently being tested by Tursky and Gracely in clinical situations with chronic pain patients to determine their clinical utility. The development of such scales is a significant advance in pain assessment and cannot help but aid the behavioral assessment of various chronic pain conditions.

Measures of pain location can be made using a pain map. First described by Keele (1948), a pain map is a simplified, human outline. The patient shades in those body areas in which pain is experienced. Mooney and coworkers (1976) routinely use pain maps in their evaluation of chronic low back pain. They report that the maps help identify those patients who complain of anatomically implausible pain and those who may be exaggerating pain. Although scores derived from pain maps correlate highly with the hypochondriasis and hysteria scales of the MMPI (Ransford et al., 1976), it is not clear whether this result reflects appropriate somatic concern or personality style.

Measures of chronic pain quality have been taken using an adjective checklist, the McGill pain questionnaire (Melzack, 1975). The checklist consists of 102 adjectives divided into 20 categories that describe three major dimensions of pain—sensory, affective, and evaluative. An example of a sensory dimension is the temporal category, which includes the following descriptors: flickering, quivering, pulsing, throbbing, beating, and pounding. Patients check one item in each relevant category that refers to their pain experience. The McGill pain questionnaire yields a measure of pain quality, by examining classes in which a word is chosen; and a measure of pain intensity, by examining the relative position of the word checked within each category.

Leavitt, and colleagues (1979) used a modified version of the McGill pain questionnaire in a study comparing low back pain patients with definite neurological findings vs. those patients without such findings. Definite differences between the two groups occurred: Patients who had demonstrable organic disease tended to be consistent and very specific in their use of descriptors. Patients without disease pathology tended to be vague and more diffuse in describing their pain.

The McGill pain questionnaire has only begun to be widely applied in clinical settings (Jones and Wolf, in press). It has been criticized because it is long; the words may be difficult for some patients to understand; and the separation between affective, sensory, and evaluation dimensions seems to be statistically invalid (Leavitt et al., 1978; Reading and Newton, 1978; Crockett et al., 1977). A variation on the McGill pain questionnaire, using a card sort technique, appears to have the potential to eliminate some of these problms (Reading and Newton, 1978). In conclusion, adjective checklists are one means of systematically assessing pain quality, but they have not been shown to be superior to anecdotal reports.

Comments. Although we have questioned the reliability and validity of self-reports of pain, they are clinically and theoretically important. Physicians rely on their patients' pain reports to diagnose and treat chronic pain. Patients have a history of experiences with physicians beginning in childhood that teaches them how important their reports of pain are in eliciting professional help. For patients who experience acute, intermittent, or variable pain (e.g., vascular headaches), measures of pain intensity provide an assessment of an important stimulus variable that elicits certain pain behaviors. Examining relationships between such perceived pain stimuli and pain behaviors may be helpful in assessment with such patients. In chronic patients, pain behavior is typically not as closely related to pain intensity ratings. Measures of pain intensity are still relevant, however. Chronic pain patients who show improvements in behavior (e.g., reduced medication and increased activity) but who continue to complain of severe pain are likely to elicit responses from family members (e.g., encouragement to decrease activity) and physicians (e.g., additional medical or surgical interventions) that may reverse whatever gains have been made. Subjective measures of pain are valid and, in our opinion, are necessary components in the behavioral assessment of chronic pain. Of the various techniques reviewed, pain intensity ratings are the most widely applied in behavioral programs for chronic pain. Research does not support the validity of pain location and pain quality measures at present.

Pain intensity ratings have several advantages: They are much more systematic and valid than global, anecdotal reports. They are easily understood and are inexpensive. Finally, they lend themselves to repeated measurement.

Pain intensity measures have several inherent limitations. Cultural, ethnic, and social influences are reputed to bias these ratings. Zborowski (1969) found that white, Anglo-Saxon, Protestant patients report pain in an unemotional fashion, whereas Italians and Jewish patients tend to complain more and to be emotional about pain. Pain intensity ratings are higher in female patients than males (Folkard et al., 1976). In addition, patients who stay at home have higher pain ratings than those who work.

In addition to inherent limitations, several problems exist in the way that pain intensity ratings are used in behavioral treatment programs. First, patients have been asked to make too many ratings. For example, patients are sometimes asked to record pain intensity every hour, on the hour, for weeks (Elton et al., 1979). Behavioral clinicians have noted the difficulty they experience in getting patients to complete such records (Peck and Kraft, 1977). Fewer ratings would enhance both the reliability and validity of such measures. Second, pain intensity ratings tend to vary over the day, so that ratings taken during the morning do not reflect those taken in the afternoon (Folkard et al., 1976). Accordingly, treatment sessions should be held at the same time each day. A third difficulty is that pain intensity ratings vary with activity level. Measures taken on an interval-sampling basis (every 1 to 4 hours) may not reflect the importance of functional level; ratings taken before and after a standard set of activities might be more valid in measuring pain. A fourth problem is the lack of normative data on both level and variability of pain intensity ratings in chronic pain patients. The natural history of acute pain patients has been studied (Finneson, 1973; Pearce and Moll, 1967), but comparable data are not available on chronic pain patients. The pattern of pain in chronic pain patients undoubtedly varies with pathology. This notion is supported by Spangfort's (1972) analysis of over 2,000 low back pain patients who underwent surgery. The single, most important factor responsible for the incidence of persistent pain was found to be the degree of initial disc herniation. The use of longer baselines can aid in establishing individual norms for chronic pain patients.

Pain intensity ratings may not show much change as a result of behavioral treatment. Behavioral treatment programs evaluated by the use of global self-reports of pain (Cairns et al., 1976; Newman et al., 1978), or no subjective pain reports (Gottlieb et al., 1977) have appeared to be quite successful. However, similar programs using more precise pain intensity measures have only shown sustained decreases in pain ranging from 10 to 19 percent (Ignelzi et al., 1977; Swanson et al., 1979; Keefe et al., 1981; Jones and Wolf, in press).

Finally, there is need for additional research on measures of pain quality and location. While pain intensity ratings may show modest changes over treatment, substantial changes in location or quality may occur. We have seen chronic pain patients who were treated with relaxation procedures show a much less diffuse pain pattern over time. The use of multimodal subjective measures of chronic pain needs full investigation.

Personality Variables

Behavior therapists have begun to appreciate the fact that many objective psychological tests possess greater reliability and validity than most self-report measures commonly used in behavior therapy (Kanfer, 1975).

Objective psychological tests allow for comparisons of patients on one or more personality variables with normative reference groups. Scoring procedures are standardized, minimizing interpretation bias.

Minnesota Multiphasic Personality Inventory. The Minnesota Multiphasic Personality Inventory (MMPI) is probably the most commonly used psychological test instrument for the assessment of personality characteristics of chronic low back pain. This test is a 540-item, true-false inventory that provides a description of the patient on 3 validity scales and 10 clinical scales. The MMPI has been widely used in the assessment of low back pain; for purposes of discussion we shall focus on this application. The MMPI has been used in studies of back pain patients to describe the typical back pain patient's personality type, to predict response to medical or surgical treatment, and to evaluate outcome.

Descriptive studies indicate that lower back pain patients are likely to have elevated hysteria depression (Hy), (D), and hypochondriasis (Hs) scales (e.g., Sternbach et al., 1973; McCreary et al., 1977; Gentry et al., 1974). This profile, with the elevated "neurotic triad," indicates a high degree of depression, denial of emotional conflicts, and expression of needs through somatic symptoms.

The studies which have used the MMPI to predict response to surgical or other medical treatment are summarized in Table 11-2. Only those studies which are prospective are included. Examination of this table yields several conclusions. First, elevations on the Hy and Hs scales have been shown to predict poor outcome in the majority of studies. Second, elevations on the D scale and the somatization subscale of the MMPI-168 have been found to be predictive, though in fewer studies. Third, the MMPI predictions are generally equivalent to, or less valid than, ratings of prognosis made by physicians prior to treatment.

The MMPI has been used as an outcome measure to examine personality changes both after surgery and conservative treatment. While pathology statistically significantly decreases following treatment, the magnitude of the improvements is slight (Sternbach and Timmermans, 1975). Since the MMPI is largely based on global traits and attitudes and less on manifest behavior, the likelihood for marked change to appear is slight.

The low back pain scale (Lb) of the MMPI was devised to help differentiate between patients with known organic pathology and patients with an absence of known pathology (Hanvik, 1951). The items were selected on the basis of their ability to differentiate between the two patient groups. In clinical practice, patients are identified by whether or not they surpass the empirically derived cutoff score. The subsequent empirical tests of this scale have produced mixed results. Although Tsushima and Towne (1979) found that their own empirically derived cutoff score could correctly classify 75 percent of their cases, this does not represent statistical significance. In addition, Freeman et al. (1976), found in their test that the Lb scale had little clinical utility.

Other objective psychological tests.   Two other multidimensional personality questionnaires used with chronic pain patients are the SCL-90 (Derogatis et al., 1975) and the Middlesex Hospital Questionnaire (Crown and Crisp, 1966). Both measure personality variables, but are symptom- rather than trait-oriented. The somatization scale of the Middlesex Hospital Questionnaire has been found to be highly predictive of outcome to conservative treatment. Items dealing with decreased sexual interests, decreased appetite, and sleep difficulties are highly predictive of outcome (Wolkind and Forrest, 1972). Like the MMPI Hs scale, the somatization scale assesses general physical health complaints not directly related to back pain. The SCL-90 has been used to measure the efficacy of biofeedback treatment for chronic back pain patients. Various behavioral and emotional symp-

Table 11-2
A Summary of Studies Using the MMPI to Predict Outcome of Treatment for Low Back Pain Patients

Authors	Population	Predictors	Criteria	Treatment	Results
Wiltse, & Rocchio (1975)	63 females 67 males; low back pain with sciatica and no prior surgery	MMPI individual scale and combinations	Surgeon ratings of outcome on 5-point scale, 1 year post-treatment.	Chemonucleolysis	Combined Hy and Hs scale scores correlate negative with outcome (.60)
Waring, Weisz, & Bailey (1976)	14 females 20 males; scales average number prior to surgery equals .75	MMPI individual scales	Surgeon rating of organic and functional outcome months post treatment.	Surgery (type unspecified)	No significant correlations
Blumetti, & Modesti (1976)	8 females 34 males: 40 of 42 patients had prior surgery	MMPI individual scales	Patient ratings of pain on 2-point scale (pain alleviated or abolished vs no change made).	Rhizotomy Cordotomy Dorsal column stimulator implantation or stearo-toxic thalamotomy	High scores on Hy and Hs predict poor outcome
Gentry, Newman, Goldner, & Von Baeger (1977)	35 patients; 33 of 35 had previous surgery	MMPI individual scales	Patient ratings on three variables: employment status; pain; and functional activity level. Follow-up time varied, averaging 18 months.	Surgery (type unspecified)	Functional activity negatively correlated with Mf scale; pain rating negatively correlated with Mf and positively correlated with R
Toomey, Ghia, More, & Gregg (1977)	38 patients	MMPI	Patients classified as responders vs non-responders on basis of daily pain ratings.	Acupuncture	Only the R scale predicted poor outcome

334

Study	Sample	MMPI measure	Criterion measure	Treatment	Findings
Caslyn, Spengler, & Freeman (1977)	22 males	MMPI-168 (5 subscales)	Responders had a 50% reduction in pain for 2 weeks.	Unspecified	High somatization scores and high depression scores predict poor outcome
Pheasant, Gilbert, Goldford, & Herron (1979)	49 females. 54 males; 34 of 103 patients had prior surgery	MMPI	Ratings by orthopedic surgeon and psychologist 6 and 12 months post-treatment.	Surgery (type unspecified)	Hs and Hy predict poor response
Turner, McCreary, Robinson, & Dawson (in press)	82 females. 53 males; non-surgical	MMPI	Patient ratings of pain on a 10-point scale; Patient ratings of functional improvement on a 5-point scale.	Conservative	Hs correlates positively with pain intensity and negatively with return to functional activity; Hy, D and Pt correlate positively with pain intensity
McCreary, Turner, & Dawson (in press)	46 females, 30 males; non-surgical	MMPI invidual scales	Same as above and patients classified in 2 categories (successful vs unsuccessful)	Conservative	Hs correlates positively with pain and negatively with return to activity D correlates positively with pain; "Poor risk codes" are those in which two highest scores are Hs, D, Hy, or Sc.

toms decreased with treatment. An interesting finding was that improvements noted in the tendency to somatize and obsessive–compulsiveness on the SCL-90 were more significant and achieved by more subjects than pain decreases (Hendler et al, 1977).

Other objective assessment instruments evaluate patients on such variables as their levels of depression and anxiety, marital satisfaction, and attitudes toward health. The Health Index (Sternbach et al., 1973) taps the following dimensions: self-concept as an invalid, manifest depression, perceived impact of pain on daily activities, and the tendency to engage in "pain games" with medical personnel (Sternbach, 1974b). Sternbach has used the Health Index as both a baseline measure, at the beginning of treatment, and an outcome measure, at the end of his 4-week inpatient treatment program. This questionnaire is brief, easily administered, and sensitive to behavioral change. A major weakness, however, shared with the SCL-90 is the lack of validity scales built into the instrument; it is quite possible for a patient to misrepresent him- or herself.

Comments.   The MMPI is the only objective psychological testing instrument that has been extensively used with chronic pain patients. In chronic low back pain patients, it appears to predict response to medical or surgical treatment, although it has not been used to predict response to behavioral treatment to date.

There are several problems with predictive studies. They are not well-controlled, so that it is unclear whether results are due to spontaneous remission or regression toward the mean. Further, these studies involve a variety of populations, treatments, and follow-up techniques. Since assessment techniques have mainly relied on patient's self-report data or physician impressions at follow-up, it is not surprising that Hy and Hs scale elevations predict poor response. People who score high on these scales are prone to complain about somatic symptoms, deny emotional problems, and unlikely to change their verbal behavior, even if their functional activity level and pain level have changed. In the MMPI is to be validated as a prognostic tool, changes in function, i.e., relevant daily activities (e.g., activity level, work status, drug intake), should be more adequately assessed.

The MMPI has several problems as an outcome measure. It is long, trait-oriented; and may irritate patients who interpret the test as suggesting their pain is "in their head." The brevity and symptom-orientation of the Middlesex Hospital Questionnaire and SCL-90 suggest that they are more appropriate for repeated measurements. However, the latter two instruments lack validity scales, whereas the MMPI has well-established validity scales.

Surprisingly, no studies have used ongoing self-assessment of pain-relevant mood changes (ratings of depression, marital distress, etc.) in chronic pain patients. Self-report of affect is routinely used in behavioral treatment of depression and a variety of other disorders, and could be used to monitor cognitive and affective reactions to the experience of chronic pain. Research by Copp (1974) suggests that pain patients vary in the cognitive coping statements they use with pain. Assessment of cognitive coping skills may aid behavioral clinicians in identifying controlling variables that can be used in treatment.

Behavioral Responses

Measurement of observable behaviors is the sine qua non of behavioral assessment. Basically, two methods have been used in the assessment of chronic pain: *self-observation* and *direct observation.*

Self-observation

Self-observation is the most common method used in the behavioral assessment of chronic pain (Fordyce, 1976; Keefe & Brown, 1982). It involves a three-step procedure. The patient is first given a definition of the target behavior and usually is provided with a standard data-recording format. Second, the patient is instructed to observe the target behavior. Observations may continue for weeks or months, as the patient progresses in treatment. Third, the patient summarizes the data to help evaluate performance changes. One of the most important features of behavioral self-observation is that it is carried out by the patient in natural settings. Self-observation promotes behavior change by increasing a patient's awareness of important target behaviors. It is one of the least expensive assessment strategies available, and thus widely used. In behavioral treatment programs for chronic pain, patients have been asked to observe and keep records of one or more of the following: physical activity, exercise, and medication.

Fordyce and his colleagues developed a procedure for monitoring activity level, or "uptime," that is widely used in behavioral management programs for chronic pain patients (Fordyce et al., 1973; Fordyce, 1976). Patients make hourly entries on a standard data sheet indicating the duration of time spent in each of three categories: reclining, sitting or standing, and walking. The time spent in each category, as well as the patient's daily "uptime" (the total time spent sitting or standing *plus* walking) is recorded and graphed on an ongoing basis. Similar measures of activity level have been used in both inpatient (Greenhoot and Sternbach, 1974; Cairns et al., 1976; Swanson et al., 1979) and outpatient behavioral treatment programs (Brena and Unikel, 1976).

A second behavior patients are frequently asked to monitor is their participation in exercise programs, usually set up by physical therapists. Patients record the number of repetitions of various flexion exercises, such as sit-ups, straight-leg raises, or pelvic tilts (Cairns et al., 1976). They may be asked to record their mileage while walking or bicycling (Greenhoot and Sternbach, 1974). Increased tolerance to exercise is considered one of the most important signs of improvement.

Self-observation of medication intake is used in behavioral outpatient programs for chronic pain (Brena and Unikel, 1976). Patients keep daily records of the amount and type of medications they use.

Direct Behavioral Observation

Direct observation of behavior in naturalistic settings is generally considered the most fundamental, objective, and valid method of behavioral assessment. Direct observation procedures have been used in several studies in chronic pain patients.

Ward observation.   One major advantage of treating the chronic pain patient in an inpatient setting is the plentiful opportunity available to observe the patient. The observers typically are nurses, staff members, or specially trained research assistants. They are provided with a definition of the target behavior and instructions as to how to record the behavior. The most common targets have been medication intake and pain behavior.

Measures of medication intake are routinely taken by ward staff (Seres and Newman, 1976; Greenhoot and Sternbach, 1974; Fordyce et al., 1973; Swanson et al., 1979). In order to compare the potency of different medications, several scaling procedures have been developed. These procedures rate the analgesic effects of medication as compared to a baseline of 1 mg of morphine injected intramuscularly (Fordyce et al., 1973; Halpern, 1977). The validity of these scaling techniques is unknown. Some investigators employ pill counts, and examine changes in the quantity of pills consumed over a given period of days. Drugs are typically grouped by type (e.g., amitryptline, morphine) and category (e.g., antidepressant, narcotics).

Rating scales are most widely employed clinically to measure pain behavior. Swanson and coworkers (1979) described a rating scale technique used by nurses on a pain ward. Nurses rated three types of pain behavior once each shift: bodily expression of pain; facial or vocal pain behavior; and dependent, manipulative behavior. (The guidelines for each category were provided to the nurses but have not been published.)

A good example of the use of rating scales is found in the work of Gottlieb and his colleagues (Gottlieb et al., 1977). They used a series of four-point rating scales, filled out by the clinician, to evaluate chronic pain patients across multiple dimensions. Ten of the scales measured functional improvement along both physical (mobility, walking distance), behavioral (medication reduction, pain behaviors), and cognitive dimensions (comprehension of pain-anxiety relationship). Vocational restoration was measured using a 7-point rating scale ranging from 1—"patient not yet able to consider vocational concepts due to physical disability and/or incapacitation by pain" to 7—"patient actually placed in gainful employment and sustained for a minimum 30-day period with evidence that pain is not limiting factor." Measurements were made at hospital admission and discharge. Similar clinician rating scales for chronic pain have been described by others (Sarno et al., 1973) and have long been used by rehabilitation specialists (Carey and Posavac, 1978).

Rybstein-Blinchik (1979) described a direct observation procedure designed to measure various pain behaviors. Each patient was greeted by a therapist. The pain behaviors occurring during the next 30 seconds are recorded. Behaviors observed include grimacing, touching the painful area, talking about pain, isolation, and guarded movement. For each 30-second observation period, a total frequency for each behavior is computed. Rybstein-Blinchik reports interrater reliability (percentage agreement) of 90 percent. The brevity of the observation period, coupled with the bias introduced when the therapist is present, reduces the validity of this technique. Although similar direct observation procedures have been described in the literature (Bourhis et al., 1978), rating scales are more frequently used.

Observation by family or peers.   Those who spend a great deal of time with the patient can function as observers. Fordyce (1976) has instructed the pain patient's spouse to record certain pain behaviors, such as verbal complaints of pain. Covert frequency counts are taken; the spouse is also asked to record the number of times they respond to the complaints. While this is an interesting technique that may foster behavior change, such observations have not been systematically applied.

Automatic recording devices.   Major difficulties are involved in having staff, therapists, or family members conduct direct observations. Observers are often biased and substantial time and effort is required. Several investigators have attempted to eliminate these problems by using automatic electromechanical recording devices. Cairns and coworkers (1976) described an ''uptime'' clock that is displayed over the patient's bed. This clock is activated by a microswitch placed under the mattress of the bed: when the patient is up, the clock counts the number of hours out of bed. The face of the clock also has descriptor labels such as poor, fair, and good, indicating criterion targets for particular patients. Saunders and coworkers (1978) used pedometers to record activity in patients hospitalized on a rehabilitation ward. The pedometers are about the size of a small matchbox, can be worn clipped to the belt, and can be calibrated and adjusted to foil cheating. Variations in physical activity were easily evident using this technique. One interesting finding of the pedometer study is that nurses' daily ratings of patient activity did not significantly correlate with the distances walked. Another device, the actometer, is worn like a wrist watch (McFarlain and Hersen, 1974; Bell, 1968; Bass and Schulman, 1967; Massey et al., 1971). As described in the literature, it appears to provide an accurate and highly reliable measure of physical activity. The pedometer, however, is widely available and is less expensive than the actometer. The pedometer and actometer have not been used with chronic low back pain patients, but electromechanical devices could provide better data than are currently available drom direct behavioral observation techniques, such as rating scales.

Comments.   While observation procedures are crucial to behavioral assessment, since the mid 1970s they have only begun to be used routinely in clinical settings with chronic pain patients. Self-observation techniques are most widely used (Fordyce, 1976). The reasons for this are several: First, self-observation is inexpensive. Second, it can be carried out across various treatment settings, thus facilitating assessment over long time periods. Third, self-observation can increase the patient's awareness of target behavior and promote the sense of self-control crucial to behavior change.

One of the most striking aspects of the application of self-observation is the number of behaviors that patients are asked to monitor at any given time. For example, a typical self-observation procedure might involve the patient monitoring "uptime" on an hourly basis, recording exercise frequency once or twice a day, and medication intake throughout the day. The frequency with which patients are asked to make observations as well as the range of behaviors to be observed is staggering. Fordyce (1976) has indicated that compliance with such extensive self-recording tasks can be increased if several practical details are considered, including providing the patient with a personal packet of material (including pens, data sheets, a notebook, etc.), public posting of data, and systemic reinforcement for data collection efforts. Nevertheless, in our experience the validity of data from such schemes is questionable. Even if the patient systematically records on an inpatient basis, the quality of data collected on an outpatient basis may be poor (Keefe, Kopel & Gordon, 1978). In addition, the pressure to provide ongoing data may result in falsification of data. We have received follow-up data sheets from patients that have obviously been filled in at one sitting and some in which the patients "forgot" the date. Whenever a self-observation strategy is used, questions as to the validity of the data gathered are present (Keefe et al., 1978). As the complexity of the patient's self-observation task is increased, the validity typically is decreased.

Direct and frequent behavioral observations have just begun to be used in the assessment of chronic pain patients. This is unfortunate since observable pain behaviors have long been the major target of intervention efforts. The practical difficulties inherent in this approach likely are responsible for this deficiency. Swanson and coworkers (1976) have shown that nurses can make periodic ratings of behavior on a practical basis. Simple time-sampling techniques can yield even better data. The available data have primarily been gathered through patient observations in ward environments. There are no data available on the behavior of patients in their naturalistic home environment, nor are there data available from behavioral observations taken in simulated natural environments in the laboratory. Such laboratory observations might provide important information as to how a patient interacts with a spouse, his or her doctors, etc. Direct behavioral observation has rarely been used in the assessment of chronic pain patients. Since this is one of the best assessment methods available, development of such direct measures is sorely needed.

Physiological Responses

The psychophysiological approach in behavioral assessment has generated a great deal of enthusiasm and interest; the search for a physiological measure of pain has interested researchers for years (Sternbach, 1978), however. Researchers have long thought that physiological measures might provide a more objective and reliable measure of pain than more subjective measures, such as pain intensity. Two major avenues of investigation have been vigorously pursued: autonomic responses and musculoskeletal responses (Sternbach, 1978).

Autonomic Responses

Researchers have examined the relationship between autonomic responses (such as skin resistance response, heart rate, and respiration), and pain. The results of such investigations have generally shown that changes in autonomic nervous system activity occur in patients (Sternbach, 1978). However, "at present there is no single accepted physiological indicator of pain which can be counted on to vary in an orderly way with the degree of pain" (Hilgard, 1969). Changes in autonomic nervous system activity appear to reflect global physiological arousal rather than precise changes in pain level. The fact that autonomic indices do not perfectly correlate with pain intensity does not render these physiological responses invalid as targets for behavioral intervention. Sympathetic nervous system hyperactivity is believed to be one of the major physiologic mechanisms of chronic pain (Bonica, 1977). Such hyperactivity can produce vasospasm and a resulting sequence of ischemia, cellular damage, and the liberation of neurotransmitter substances (e.g., norepinephrine) that lower the sensitivity of peripheral pain receptors. Although various pharmacologic (sedative-hypnotic and psychotropic medications) and behavioral treatment procedures (progressive relaxation and biofeedback training) attempt to reduce chronic autonomic arousal in chronic pain patients, systematic, repeatable measures of relevant physiological responses are lacking.

Musculoskeletal Responses

Skeletal muscular overactivity is an important factor in the onset and course of chronic pain. Muscular spasms in the lumbosacral region, gastrocnemius, and hamstrings are common complaints in chronic back pain patients. Electromyography (EMG) is widely believed to be a valid measure of muscular hyperactivity.

In their classic study, Holmes and Wolff (1952) examined EMG activity in 65 patients who complained of back pain. EMG activity was recorded from a wide range of muscle groups, including the trapezius, lumbosacral spinalis, etc. Observations of muscle activity were made during light exercise and during interviews focusing on emotionally upsetting topics. Holmes and Wolff found that back pain patients had a very high level of generalized overactivity. This pattern of skeletal muscle hyperactivity was evident under conditions of physical activity and emotional stress. They postulated that these patients tended to engage in guarding, in which they tense muscles as a protective reaction against possible pain. This guarding, as reflected in high levels of EMG activity, was thought to exacerbate pain. Some researchers go beyond this data to postulate the existence of a "pain-spasm-pain" cycle (Travell et al., 1942). This hypothesis forms the rationale for certain therapeutic approaches to chronic pain.

Studies by Basmajian and Wolf raise questions as to the meaning of EMG as a measure of spasm in pain patients. Basmajian (1978) reported that low-back region painful muscle spasms are accompanied by profound reductions in EMG activity measured in the lumbar paraspinals. An absence of EMG activity at rest in patients who show definite, palpable muscle spasms has also been found in similar studies with cerebral palsy patients (Holt, 1966) and fibrositis-syndrome patients (Kraft et al., 1968). Taken together, these findings question the validity of EMG activity as a measure of muscle tension, if the only measure taken is the amount of activity at rest. EMG measures are more valid spasm indicators if measures are taken during various dynamic activities. This approach has been used recently by Wolf. In a study by Wolf and coworkers (in press), normative EMG activity and mobility measurements were taken in 121 normals grouped by age and gender. Electromyographic activity was recorded bilaterally from the erector spinal muscles at the L 3-4, L 4-5 level. EMG activity was most prominent during dynamic activity involving trunk extension, and much less prominent during rest. In a second study (Jones and Wolf, in press), EMG activity from identical sites was recorded in a low back pain patient. Early in biofeedback treatment, EMG activity was high on both sides of the spine during dynamic activity. As treatment progressed, readings on one side of the spine were high whereas readings on the other side were low. At the end of treatment, EMG levels equalized, with a resultant decrease in pain. Subsequent unpublished research by Wolf indicates that chronic low back pain patients may either show hyper- or hypoactivity in the low back muscles. Teaching the patient to bring this activity into a more normal range seems to produce reliable pain reductions.

There are varied causes of chronic pain. Some are related to the initial etiology of the pain, and some are secondary to the original pain. However, in chronic pain patients with primary muscle involvement pain, evidence suggests that laboratory-induced psychological stress produces increased EMG levels in the affected area (Scott and Gregg, 1980). For example, Thomas and coworkers (1973) used a frustration-inducing task with patients who suffered from chronic myofascial pain dysfunction syndrome (a muscle-contraction headache of the lower face). Compared to controls, the pain patients had higher EMG levels during the psychologically stressful procedure. This finding supports the thesis that psychological stress can produce muscle hyperactivity and chronic pain.

Comments.   The literature on behavioral assessment of physiological responses in chronic pain patients is limited and inconclusive. Perhaps one reason is the uncertainty of a direct relationship between our present measures of physiological activity and pain etiology. Behavior therapists, however, view both chronic autonomic arousal and musculoskeletal overactivity as targets that deserve modification. Decreasing autonomic activity associated with anxiety may likely help chronic pain patients reduce intake of sedative-hypnotic agents and muscle relaxants. Changing patterns of muscle activity may assist patients in reducing pain by reducing avoidance posturing or gait abnormalities that in turn reduce a patient's functional ability in work or social activities. Lowering muscle activity may also reduce or eliminate pain. It appears, however, that physiological measurements are not likely to be valid unless multiple responses can be monitored during various activities.

DISCUSSION

Several conclusions can be based on this review. First, of the various self-report measures of pain used with chronic pain patients, the use of magnitude estimation or visual analogue scales for pain intensity ratings appears warranted. Second, although self-observation or rating scale techniques have commonly been used to assess overt behavior, more objective direct-observation methods should be used whenever feasible. Third, physiological response patterns in chronic pain patients are idiosyncratic, and the relevance of EMG or autonomic indices can best be determined on an individual basis. We recommend that behavioral clinicians working with pain patients employ a comprehensive assessment approach, including a minimum: (1) pain intensity ratings one or two times daily; (2) daily self-observation of a goal-related activity, e.g., miles walked or hours spent at work; and (3) periodic direct observation of "pain" behaviors.

Numerous clinical, methodological, and ethical issues beg consideration whenever behavioral assessment techniques are used with chronic pain patients.

Clinical Issues

As we have seen, behavioral assessment techniques attempt to measure responses in the subjective, behavioral, and physiological response systems. While such a comprehensive evaluation has many advantages, it occasionally leads to problems in the clinical management of patients. One obstacle is that some chronic pain patients view the only relevant target behavior as their subjective report of pain intensity. These patients may refuse to carry out self-observation tasks or actively participate in treatment. It is often difficult to identify such patients during a preliminary evaluation, because they present as willing to "do anything" to deal with their pain. Swanson et al. (1978), reported that providing patients with a 3-day trial in a behavioral pain management program can screen out such patients. Asking patients to routinely rate their pain can cause a second clinical problem. Attending to pain in a systematic way may increase the perceived severity of pain. The likelihood that keeping pain ratings will exacerbate pain is increased when patients are asked to make frequent ratings, for example, every hour on the hour. This problem can be overcome if one or two pain intensity ratings are taken at standard times each day. A third clinical problem can result from overzealous demands for behavioral data. Data collection demands can overwhelm the patient or staff, and thereby decrease motivation. Assessment can only be a reinforcing event for the patient if clinicians show restraint and rely on practical methods. A final and related point, assessment must be seen by both the patient and involved staff as an integral part of treatment. The importance of assessment techniques needs to be communicated to everyone who uses them. The purpose of data collection and its related goals, such as increasing ''uptime'' or decreasing medication intake, need to be made quite explicit.

Methodological Issues

There are inherent methodological problems in attempting assessment of behavior across three response systems (Cone, 1979). This is especially evident in research on the measurement of human pain. The ''wild and variable'' relationship between pain as a subjective experience and its physiological correlates is considered by some to be the central problem in pain research (Wall, 1978). Since 1930, investigators have tried in vain to discover a reliable and objective behavioral measures of clinical pain. Overt behaviors or physiological responses measured in the assessment of chronic low back pain patients cannot be equated with pain. These responses only reflect behavioral patterns exhibited by the particular patient studied, and should not be misconstrued as objective measures of pain. A behavioral measure of medication intake, therefore, is valid if it accurately measures how much medication is ingested, and not if it precisely correlates with pain intensity. The best clinical outcome clearly occurs when improvements occur in all three response systems. However, in the absence of such findings, improvements in overt behavioral function represent significant clinical improvement.

Chronic pain syndromes are extremely complex. The behavioral techniques used to assess these syndromes do not seem to acknowledge this inherent complexity. The methods in use basically consist of outcome measures. There is a clear need to develop alternative assessment methodologies. One approach is to examine a variety of target behaviors other than those commonly measured. Of potential importance is assessment of behavioral assets and deficits occurring in more natural settings. A second approach is to evaluate subgroups of chronic pain patients, perhaps along the lines suggested by MacNab (1977). For example, a comparison of behavioral patterns in patients suffering from discogenic vs spondylogenic chronic low back pain may prove interesting. A third approach would be to make a more idiographic analysis of each case. Determining important environmental antecedents and consequences on an individual basis may lead to more efficacious treatment. Finally, there is a need to integrate behavioral assessment with other approaches. An exciting example of this approach is recent work which has examined the significance of endogenous morphine-like substances in analgesic affects obtained through cognitive hypnotic manipulations (Goldstein and Hilgard, 1975).

Ethical Issues

There are several potential ethical problems involved in behavioral assessment of chronic low back pain. One problem is that focusing an attention away from the pain sensation to behavioral indices may mean that the patient ignores a pain signal that warns of additional tissue damage. Psychologists and other nonphysicians who may be involved in setting up behavioral assessment programs with chronic low back pain patients do not have the training, expertise, or medical competence to evaluate the gravity of a pain signal. An additional ethical concern can stem from patient expectations about a behavioral treatment program. Patients may expect to feel less pain at the end of a program but, in fact, may only learn to complain less or walk more. A final ethical concern is that the expense, time, and equipment needed to carry out behavioral treatment programs for chronic low back pain may not be justified. Ethical safeguards need to be built into every behavioral assessment and treatment for chronic pain. The ethical problems raised above can be overcome if two basic conditions are met: informed consent is obtained from the patient, and if every behavioral program for chronic pain is an interdisciplinary effort involving physicians in both assessment and treatment decisions.

REFERENCES

Aitken, A. T. The present status of intervertebrae disc surgery. *Michigan State Medical Society,* 1959, *58*, 1121–1127.

Azrin, N. H., Holz, W., & Goldiamond, I. Response bias in questionnaire reports. *Journal of Consulting Psychology,* 1961, *25*, 324–326.

Awad, E. A. Interstitial myofibrosis: Hypothesis of the mechanism. *Archives of Physical Medicine and Rehabilitation,* 1973, *54*, 449–453.

Basmajian, J. V. Muscle spasm in the lumbar region and the neck: Two double-blind controlled clinical and laboratory studies. *Archives of Physical Medicine and Rehabilitation,* 1978, *59*, 58–63.

Bass, H. N., & Schulman, J. L. Quantitative assessment of children's activity in and out of bed. *American Journal of Disabled Children,* 1967, *113*, 242–244.

Bell, R. Q. Adaptation of small wristwatches for measuring recording of activity in infants and children. *Journal of Experimental Child Psychology,* 1968, *6*, 302–305.

Blumetti, A. E. and Modesti, L. M. Psychological predictors of success or failure of surgical intervention for intractable back pain. In J. J. Bonica, & D. Albe-Fessard (Eds.), *Advances in pain research,* Vol. I. New York: Raven Press, 1976.

Bonica, J. J. (Ed.). *Advances in Neurology,* Vol. 4, International Symposium on Pain. New York: Raven Press, 1974.

Bonica, J. J. Neurophysiologic and pathologic aspects of acute and chronic pain. *Archives of Surgery,* 1977, *112*, 750–761.

Bond, M. R. *Pain: Its nature, analysis, and treatment.* New York: Churchill Livingstone, 1979.

Bourhis, A., Bourdouresque, W. P., Fondarai, J., Ponzio, J., & Spitalier, J. M. Pain infirmity and psychotropic drugs in oncology. *Pain*, 1978, *5*, 263–274.

Brena, S. F., & Unikel, I. F. Nerve blocks and contingency management in chronic pain states. In J. J. Bonica, & D. Albe-Fessard (Eds.), *Advances in pain research and therapy*, Vol. I. New York: Raven Press, 1976.

Caillet, R. *The low back pain syndrome*. Philadelphia: F. A. Davis, 1968.

Cairns, D., Thomas, L., Mooney, V., & Pace, J. B. A comprehensive treatment approach to chronic low back pain. *Pain*, 1976, *2*, 301–308.

Carey, R. G., & Posavac, E. J. Program evaluation of a physical medicine and rehabilitation unit: A new approach. *Archives of Physical Medicine and Rehabilitation*, 1978, *59*, 330–337.

Caslyn, D. A., Spengler, D. M., & Freeman, C. W. Application of the somatization factor of the MMPI-168 with low back pain patients. *Journal of Clinical Psychology*, 1977, *33*, 1017–1020.

Chaffin, D. B. Human strength capability and low back pain. *Journal of Occupational Medicine*, 1974, *16*, 248–251.

Cone, J. D. Confounded comparisons in triple response mode assessment research. *Behavioral Assessment*, 1979, *1*, 85–96.

Copp, L. A. The spectrum of suffering. *American Journal of Nursing*, 1974, *74*, 494–495.

Craig, C. Social modeling influence on pain. In R. A. Sternbach (Ed.), *The psychology of pain*. New York: Raven Press, 1978.

Crockett, D. J., Prkachin, K. M., & Craig, K. D. Factors of the language of pain in patients and volunteer groups. *Pain*, 1977, *4*, 175–182.

Crown, S., & Crisp, A. H. A short clinical diagnostic self-rating scale for psychoneurotic patients: The Middlesex Hospital questionnaire. *British Journal of Psychiatry*, 1966, *112*, 917–923.

Derogatis, L. R., Rickels, K., & Rock, A. The SCL-90 and the MMPI: A step in the validation of a new self-report scale. *British Journal of Psychiatry*, 1975, *128*, 280–289.

Elton, D., Burrows, G. D., & Stanley, G. V. Clinical measurement of pain. *Medical Journal of Australia*, 1979, *1*, 109–111.

Fernbac, J. C., Langer, F., & Gross, A. E. The significance of low back pain in older adults. *Canadian Medical Association Journal*, 1976, *115*, 898–900.

Finneson, B. *Low Back Pain*. Philadelphia: J. B. Lippincott Co., 1973.

Folkard, S., Glynn, C. F., & Lloyd, J. W. Diurnal variation and individual differences in the perception of intractable pain. *Journal of Psychosomatic Research*, 1976, *20*, 289–301.

Fordyce, W. E. *Behavioral methods for chronic pain and illness*. St. Louis, Missouri: C. V. Mosby, 1976.

Fordyce, W. E. Learning processes in pain. In R. A. Sternbach (Ed.), *The psychology of pain*. New York: Raven Press, 1978.

Fordyce, W. E., Fowler, R. S., Lehmann, J. R., DeLateur, B. J., Sand, P. L. & Trieschmann, R. B. Operant conditioning in the treatment of chronic pain. *Archives of Physical Medicine and Rehabilitation*, 1973, *54*, 399–408.

Freeman, C., Caslyn, D., & Louks, J. The use of the MMPI personality inventory with low back pain patients. *Journal of Clinical Psychology*, 1976, *32*, 294–298.

Gentry, W. D., Newman, M. C., Goldner, J. L., & vonBaeyer, C. Relation between graduated spinal block technique and MMPI for diagnosis and prognosis of chronic low back pain. *Spine*, 1977, *2*, 210–213.

Gentry, W. D., Shows, W. D., & Thomas, M. Chronic low back pain: A psychological profile. *Psychosomatics*, 1974, *15*, 174–177.

Goldstein, A., & Hilgard, E. R. Failure of opiate antagonist naloxone to modify hypnotic analgesia. *Proceedings of the National Academy of Sciences*, 1975, *72*, 2041–2043.

Gottlieb, H., Laban, C. S., Koller, R., Madorsky, A., Hackersmith, V., Kleeman, M., & Wagner, J. Comprehensive rehabilitation of patients having chronic low back pain. *Archives of Physical Medicine and Rehabilitation*, 1977, *58*, 101–108.

Gracely, R. H., McGrath, P., & Dubner, R. Ratio scales of sensory and affective verbal pain descriptors. *Pain*, 1978, *5*, 5–18.

Gracely, R. H., McGrath, P., & Dubner, R. Validity and sensitivity of ratio scales of sensory and affective verbal pain descriptors: Manipulation of affect by diazepam. *Pain*, 1978, *5*, 19–29.

Greenhoot, J. H., & Sternbach, R. A. Conjoint treatment of chronic pain. *Advances in Neurology*, 1974, *4*, 595–603.

Halpern, L. M. Analgesic drugs in the management of pain. *Archives of Surgery*, 1977, *112*, 861–869.

Hanvik, L. J. MMPI profiles in patients with low back pain. *Journal of Consulting Psychology*, 1951, *15*, 350–353.

Hendler, N., Derogatis, L., Avella, J., & Long, D. EMG biofeedback in patients with chronic pain. *Diseases of the Nervous System*, 1977, *38*, 505–509.

Hilgard, E. R. Pain as puzzle for psychology and physiology. *American Journal of Psychology*, 1969, *24*, 103–113.

Hilton, J. *On the influence of mechanical and physiologic rest in the treatment of accidents and surgical diseases, and the diagnostic value of pain*. London: Bell and Daldy, 1863.

Hirsch, C. Efficiency of surgery in low back disorders. *Journal of Bone and Joint Surgery*, 1965, *47A*, 991–998.

Holmes, T. H., & Wolff, H. G. Life situations, emotions and backache. *Psychosomatic Medicine*, 1952, *14*, 18–33.

Holt, K. S. Facts and fallacies about neuromuscular function in cerebral palsy as revealed by electromyography. *Developmental Medicine and Child Neurology*, 1966, *8*, 255–268.

Huskisson, E. C. Measurement of pain. *Lancet*, 1974, *2*, 1127–1131.

Ignelzi, R. J., Sternbach, R. A., & Timmermans, G. The pain ward follow-up analyses. *Pain*, 1977, *3*, 277–280.

International Association for the Study of Pain, Subcommittee on Taxonomy. The need of a taxonomy. *Pain*, 1979, *6*, 247–252.

Jones, A. L., & Wolf, S. L. Treating chronic low back pain: EMG biofeedback training during dynamic movement. *Physical Therapy*, in press.

Joyce, C. B., Zutshi, D. W., Hrubes, V., & Mason, R. M. Comparison of fixed interval and visual analog scales for rating chronic pain. *European Journal of Clinical Pharmacology*, 1975, *8*, 415–420.

Kanfer, F. H. Report on outcome measures in behavior therapy. In I. Waskow, & M. Parloff (Eds.), *Psychotherapy Change Measures*. DHEW Publication No. (ADM) 74–120, 1975.

Keefe, F. J. & Brown, C. J. Behavioral treatment of chronic pain syndromes. In P. Boudewyns & F. J. Keefe. *Behavioral medicine in general medical practice*. Menlo Park, CA: Addison-Wesley, 1982.

Keefe, F. J., Kopel, S., & Gordon, S. *A practical guide to behavioral assessment*. New York: Springer, 1978.

Keefe, F. J., Schapira, B., Brown, C., Williams, R. B., & Surwit, R. S. EMG-assisted relaxation training in the management of chronic low back pain. *American Journal of Clinical Biofeedback*, 1981, *4*, 93–103.

Keele, K. D. The painchart. *Lancet*, 1948, *2*, 6–8.

Kraft, G. H., Johnson, E. W., & LaBan, M. M. The fibrositis syndrome. *Archives of Physical Medicine and Rehabilitation*, 1968, *49*, 155–162.

Leavitt, F., Garron, D. C., D'Angelo, C. M., & McNeill, T. W. Low back pain in patients with and without demonstrable organic disease. *Pain*, 1979, *6*, 191–200.

Leavitt, F., Garron, D. C., Whisler, W. W., & Sheinkop, M. B. Affective and sensory dimensions of back pain. *Pain*, 1978, *4*, 273–281.

Leavitt, S., Johnston, R., & Beeper, R. The process of recovery: Patterns in industrial back injury. *Industrial Medicine*, 1972, *41*, 5–9.

Loeser, J. Low back pain. In J. J. Bonica (Ed.), *Pain*. New York: Raven Press, 1980.

Massey, P. S., Lieberman, A., & Batarseh, G. Measure of activity level in mentally retarded children and adolescents. *American Journal of Mental Deficiency*, 1971, *76*, 259–261.

MacNab, I. *Backache*. Baltimore, Maryland: Williams and Wilkins, Co., 1977.

McCreary, C., Turner, D., & Dawson, E. Differences between functional versus organic low back pain patients. *Pain*, 1977, *4*, 73–78.

McCreary, C., Turner, J., & Dawson, E. The MMPI as a predictor of response to conservative treatment for low back pain. *Journal of Clinical Psychology*, in press.

McFarlain, R. A., & Hersen, M. Continuous measurement of activity level in psychiatric patients. *Journal of Clinical Psychology*, 1974, *30*, 37–39.

McGill, C. M. Industrial back problems. *Journal of Occupational Medicine*, 1968, *10*, 174–177.

Melzack, R. The McGill Pain Questionnaire: Major properties and scoring methods. *Pain*, 1975, *1*, 277–299.

Melzack, R., & Wall, P. D. Pain mechanisms: A theory. *Science*, 1965, *150*, 971–979.

Merskey, H. The perception and measurement of pain. *Journal of Psychosomatic Research*, 1973, *17*, 251–256.

Mooney, V., Cairns, D., Robertson, J. A system for evaluating and treating chronic back disability. *Western Journal of Medicine*, 1976, *124*, 370–376.

Moore, P. A., Duncan, G. H., Scott, D. S., Gregg, J. M., & Ghia, J. N. The submaximal effort to tourniquet test: Its use in evaluatory experimental and chronic pain. *Pain*, 1979, *6*, 375–382.

Nelson, R., & Hayes, S. Some current dimensions of behavioral assessment. *Behavioral Assessment*, 1979, *1*, 1–16.

Newman, R. I., Seres, J. L., Yospe, L. P., & Garlington, B. Multidisciplinary treatment of chronic pain: Long-term follow-up of low back pain patients. *Pain*, 1978, *4*, 283–292.

Ohnhaus, E. E., & Adler, R. Methodological problems in the measurement of pain: A comparison between the verbal rating scale and the visual analogue scale. *Pain*, 1975, *1*, 379–384.

Pearce, J., & Moll, J. M. H. Conservative treatment and natural history of acute lumbar disc lesions. *Journal of Neurology, Neurosurgery and Psychiatry*, 1967, *30*, 13–17.

Peck, C., & Kraft, G. H. Electromyographic biofeedback for pain related to muscle tension. *Archives of Surgery*, 1977, *112*, 889–895.

Pheasant, H. C., Gilbert, D., Goldfarb, J., & Herron, L. The MMPI as a predictor of outcome in low back surgery. *Spine*, 1979, *4*, 78–84.

Ransford, A. O., Cairns, D., & Mooney, V. The pain drawing as an aid to the psychologic evaluation of patients with low back pain. *Spine*, 1976, *1*, 127–134.

Reading, A. E., & Newton, J. R. A card sort method of pain assessment. *Journal of Psychosomatic Research*, 1978, *22*, 503–512.

Rybstein-Blinchik, E. Effects of different cognitive strategies on the chronic pain experience. *Journal of Behavioral Medicine*, 1979, *2*, 93–102.

Sarno, J. E., Sarno, M. T., & Levita, E. The functional life scale. *Archives of Physical Medicine and Rehabilitation*, 1973, *54*, 214–220.

Saunders, K. J., Goldstein, M. K., & Stein, G. H. Automated measurement of patient activity on a hospital rehabilitation ward. *Archives of Physical Medicine and Rehabilitation*, 1978, *59*, 255–257.

Scott, D. S., & Gregg, H. M. Myofascial pain of the temporomandibular joint: A review of the behavioral-relaxation therapies. *Pain*, 1980, *9*, 231–241.

Seres, J. L., & Newman, R. I. Results of treatment of chronic low back pain at the Portland Pain Center. *Journal of Neurosurgery*, 1976, *45*, 132–36.

Smith, G. M., & Beecher, H. K. Experimental production of pain in man: Sensitivity of a new method to 600 mg of aspirin. *Clinical Pharmacology and Therapeutics*, 1969, *10*, 213–216.

Smith, G. M., Egbert, L. D., Markowitz, R. A., Mosteler, F., & Beecher, H. K. An experimental pain method sensitive to morphine in man: The submaximum effort tourniquet technique. *Journal of Pharmacology and Experimental Therapeutics*, 1966, *154*, 324–332.

Smith, G. M., Lowenstein, E., Hubbard, J. H., & Beecher, H. K. Experimental pain produced by the submaximum effort tourniquet technique: Further evidence of validity. *Journal of Pharmacology and Experimental Therapeutics*, 1968, *163*, 468–474.

Spangfort, E. V. The lumbar disc herniation. *Acta Orthopaedica Scandinavia*, 1972, Suppl. No. 142, *43*, 1–42.

Sternbach, R. A. *Pain patients: Traits and treatments*. New York: Academic Press, 1974.

Sternbach, R. A. Clinical aspects of pain. In R. A. Sternbach (Ed.), *The psychology of pain*. New York: Raven Press, 1978.

Sternbach, R. A., Deems, L. M., Timmermans, G., & Huey, L. Y. On the sensitivity of the tourniquet pain test. *Pain*, 1977, *3*, 105–110.

Sternbach, R. A., Murphy, R. W., Timmermans, G., Greenhoot, J. H., & Akeson, W. H. Measuring the severity of clinical pain. *Advances in Neurology*, 1974, *4*, 281–288.

Sternbach, R. A. Varieties of pain games. In J. J. Bonica (Ed.), *Advances in Neurology*, Vol. 4. New York: Raven Press, 1974.

Sternbach, R. A., & Timmermans, G. Personality changes associated with reduction of pain. *Pain*, 1975, *1*, 177–181.

Sternbach, R. A., Wolf, S. R., Murphy, R. W., & Akeson, W. H. Traits of pain patients: the low back 'loser.' *Psychosomatics*, 1973, *14*, 226–229.

Swanson, D. W., Maruta, T., & Swenson, W. M. Results of behavior modification in the treatment of chronic pain. *Psychosomatic Medicine*, 1979, *41*, 55–61.

Swanson, D. W., Swenson, M. W., Maruta, T., & McPhee, M. C. Program for managing chronic pain: I. Program description and characteristics of patients. *Mayo Clinic Proceedings*, 1976, *51*, 401–408.

Thomas, L. J., Tiber, N., & Schireson, S. The effects of anxiety and frustration on muscular tension related to temporomandibular joint syndrome. *Oral Surgery*, 1973, *36*, 763–768.

Timmermans, G., & Sternbach, R. A. Factors of human chronic pain: An analysis of personality and pain reaction variables. *Science*, 1974, *184*, 806–808.

Toomey, T. C., Ghia, J. N., Mao, W., & Gregg, J. M. Acupuncture and chronic pain mechanisms: The moderating effects of affect, personality and stress on response to treatment. *Pain*, 1977, *3*, 137–145.

Travell, J., Rinzler, S., & Herman, M. Pain and disability of the shoulder and arm. Treatment by intromuscular infiltration with procaine hydrochloride. *Journal of the American Medical Association*, 1943, *120*, 417–422.

Tsushima, W. T., & Towne, W. S. Clinical limitations of the low back scale. *Journal of Clinical Psychology*, 1979, *35*, 306–308.

Tursky, B. The development of a pain perception profile: A psychophysical approach. In M. Weisenberg, & B. Tursky (Eds.), *Pain: New perspectives in therapy and research*. New York: Plenum, 1976.

Wall, P. D. The gate control theory of pain mechanisms. *Brain*, 1978, *101*, 1–18.

Waring, E. M., Weisz, G. M., & Bailey, S. I. Predictive factors in the treatment of low back pain by surgical intervention. In J. J. Bonica, & D. Albe-Fessard (Eds.), *Advances in pain research and therapy*, Vol. 1. New York: Raven Press, 1976.

Wiltse, L. L., & Rocchio, P. D. Preoperative psychological tests as predictors of success of chemonucleolysis in the treatment of the low back syndrome. *Journal of Bone and Joint Surgery*, 1975, *57A*, 478–483.

Wolff, B. Behavioral measurement of human pain. In R. A. Sternbach (Ed.), *The psychology of pain*. New York: Raven Press, 1978.

Wolf, S. L., Basmajian, J. V., Russe, C. T. C., & Kutner, M. Normative data on low back mobility and activity levels: Implications for neuro-muscular reeducation. *American Journal of Physical Medicine*, 1979, *58*, 217–229.

Wolkind, S. N., & Forrest, A. J. Low back pain: a psychiatric investigation. *Postgraduate Medical Journal*, 1972, *48*, 76–79.

Woodforde, J. M., & Merskey, H. Some relationships between subjective measures of pain. *Journal of Psychosomatic Research*, 1972, *16*, 173–178.

Zborowshi, M. *People in pain*. San Francisco: Jossey-Bass, 1969.

Ziesat, H. A. Correlates of the tourniquet ischemia pain ratio. *Perceptual and Motor Skills*, 1978, *47*, 147–150.

Richard Lucas
Charles Brown

12

Assessment of Cancer Patients

Cancer poses difficult and complex problems for patients, their families, and professional staff involved in treatment. These problems, including those of the health care provider assessing the cancer patient, are perhaps more variable than those associated with any other illness. There are many forms of cancer, many types of treatment, and a variety of symptoms caused both by the disease and by treatment. The patient, the patient's family, and the professional staff often confront dramatic and unpredictable reverses. As a result, the professional staff must be flexible, ever-alert to change, and aware of the effects that cancer can have on the thoughts and behaviors of the patient, as well as all of those individuals personally and professionally involved in the cancer patient's treatment.

Cancer patient assessment can make great emotional demands upon the professional staff. The unpredictability and variability frequently associated with cancer can make it difficult to feel confidence in one's own efficacy. Both hopes and fears are confounded, and the staff person heavily invested in the patient may find him- or herself on an emotional roller coaster. Further, cancer elicits a variety of primitive fears; death, pain, bodily disfigurement, and loneliness are not invariably associated with cancer, but they do occur and are hard to dispassionately confront. There is a poignant mystique about cancer which is dually apparent, both in our culture's obsession with cancer and the euphemistic manner in which the disease is frequently discussed. It is the very fearfulness and threat of cancer that make it essential for staff members to understand patients and keep them from feeling abandoned. Professional staff can effectively and sensitively treat patients only when they carefully assess the patient's thoughts, feelings, behavior, and physical symptoms.

Principles of behavioral assessment are particularly useful in such careful assessment. The following guidelines, based on behavioral assessment principles can be helpful to keep in mind when working with cancer patients.

Assessment is comprehensive and specific.   Cancer patients often are reluctant to talk honestly about their symptoms: whether out of fear, shame, or a desire
not to burden others, patients may be unwilling to express their deepest concerns
and needs. The staff person can try, in an unobtrusive and non-directive manner,
to help patients explore and articulate their goals, desires, and unfinished business. These goals may include talking to an estranged family member, decreasing
pain, being able in some way to more effectively work or trying to feel less lonely.
Goals will vary from person to person, but many goals, if not all of them, can be
concretely expressed and in detail. Such specificity allows both the patient and
staff to set up intermediate goals, and also makes it easier for the patient and staff
to see if the goals are being achieved or at least approached over time. It is important for patients to explore existential issues, such as fear and loneliness. Such
responses are sometimes inadequately emphasized by behavioral psychologists.
To the degree possible, however, such discussion should lead to articulation of
specific goals associated with more global concerns and the description of behaviors that can lead to achieving those goals.

Assessment is ongoing.   Traditional approaches to psychological assessment
frequently involve a battery of psychodiagnostic tests given over a short time span.
Since personality is seen as enduring over time, frequent reassessment is deemphasized. In contrast, behavioral assessment is predicated on the belief that
behavioral patterns can be changed. Behavioral therapists continually monitor variations in behavior, thoughts, and symptoms that can change over time. Particularly
important with cancer patients is reassessment, with some constancy, their needs
and desires. These issues may change over time, or the patient may feel comfortable in discussing a problem that previously was either too difficult to discuss or
unrecognized and unarticulated. All too often, professionals will make inaccurate
inferences and implicit demands of patients, based on initial assessments that may
be outmoded or inaccurately drawn from inadequate data.

Psychopathology is deemphasized.   Behavioral assessment is concerned with
the uniqueness of the individual, and the particular kinds of thoughts, feelings,
and behavioral patterns that occur for that person in specific environments. Diagnostic categories can predispose professionals to overemphasize the patient's
weaknesses. Perhaps more important is the danger that only those patients showing severe psychopathological symptoms will be behaviorally assessed and treated. Patients who are not considered ''mentally ill'' may benefit from behavioral
assessment, perhaps more than the minority of severely disturbed patients.

The patient's coping skills are assessed.   By knowing how the cancer patient has effectively coped with past stress, especially stress related to illness, and
how the patient is successfully coping with current problems associated with cancer, professional staff can assist the patient in augmenting and extending these
skills. The professional's concern with, and focus on, skills can also keep assess-

ment from becoming a demeaning and alienating experience, in which the patient may feel the victim of inexorable forces. Behavioral assessment does involve confrontation with unpleasant realities; it also orients the patient to strengths which may have previously been ignored or deprecated.

The patient engages in self-monitoring.   Like many other seriously ill patients, cancer patients sometimes obsessively ruminate over their symptomatology and distressing situation. Behavioral assessment can transform this tendency rather than remove it altogether. The patient is an active, important participant in assessment and treatment. Active involvement tends to decrease feelings of passivity and helplessness. The patient learns, through careful observation, that even though the course of the disease and treatment are largely unpredictable, behaviors, thoughts, feelings, and symptoms can nonetheless be associated with particular antecedents. The patient also learns first-hand through self-assessment what methods alleviate specific problems personal to each patient.

The patient's environment is assessed.   It would be difficult to overemphasize the impact of the cancer patient's familial and treatment environment upon his or her well-being. Behavioral assessment involves observation of environmental events and behaviors by significant others that consistently lead to patient responses. Staff members who assess patients will become ombudsmen, representing the patient's needs to those who so critically affect that patient. By observing and influencing the patient's environment and family, the professional staff member may not only obtain better treatment for the patient but also can heighten the respect the patient has for the staff and strengthen the therapeutic relationship. The patient, however, will ideally learn how to modify the actions of family and medical staff, and not become overly dependent on staff members involved in assessment.

QUALITIES OF THE EFFECTIVE PROFESSIONAL

For professionals to be simply conversant in behavioral principles is obviously insufficient; the effective assessment of the cancer patient can only occur within the context of a relationship that is at once professional and personal. The cancer patient is likely to have ambivalent or negative attitudes towards both treatment and staff. Along with technological advances in the treatment of cancer, treatment has become, or at least can seem, more and more impersonalized. Like the cancer itself, the staff and the treatment can cause pain, circumscribe the patient's life, and leave the patient with feelings of impotence. The staff person may be perceived as invading the patient and callous in dealing with the patient. After all, the cancer patient rarely requests the services of the staff members making a behavioral assessment; the staff person in the course of assessment is likely to question behaviors and thoughts that may be considered painful or humiliating to discuss.

The staff person should appear to be caring and sensitive at the very least. Despite the constraints of time, institutional demands, and personal feelings of discomfort or helplessness, staff members should put the patient and his or her needs first. Throughout medical treatment, the patient may feel that he or she is being capriciously ordered about, rather than being served by, the medical system. Staff assessing the patient should strive to preserve the patient's integrity; the patient's need should be considered primary, and the patient should be respected as an autonomous person. The goals of behavioral treatment should be enhancing the ability of the patient to do what he or she desires, despite limitations caused by the disease, and maximizing the patient's physical and emotional comfort in the wake of the disease and the anticipated loss. Personal obligations, whether to the patient's family, the staff, or "science," should never interfere with the primary responsibility to the patient.

Over the course of several years work within a large medical system, the senior author (Richard Lucas) typically has introduced himself to cancer patients by making the following points:)1) he is a member of the patient's medical treatment team; (2) he has known and worked with seriously ill patients for many years; and (3) he hopes that the patient, if he or she wishes, may come to find use in seeing him as both a psychologist and a friend. In so doing, he hopes neither to undermine the medical staff nor his own credentials, but he also communicates that the patient's needs and desires will largely determine the direction of their interactions. The professional should suggest that it is the patient's decision to engage the professional if and when the patient so wishes. The professional must acknowledge personal experience and expertise in tandem with genuine concern and respect for the patient.

Warmth, genuineness, and accurate empathy are widely considered as important qualities for professionals engaging in therapeutic relationships, yet it is not uncommon for medical or psychotherapeutic professionals to be perceived as cold and self-important. The professional is all the more likely to distance him- or herself because of the nature of the problems that can accompany cancer, such as pain, disfigurement, and death. The professional, however, should endeavor to recognize and overcome personal fears and express honesty, expressiveness and caring.

A common protection against fears elicited by the situation of the cancer patient is to espouse particular scheme or concepts. Many professionals have treated Kubler-Ross's (1969) stages of dying, for example, as if they were etched in stone; other professionals will adhere with equal tenacity to psychodiagnostic classification or behavior principles. Yet others will see all cancer patients as undergoing experiences similar to their own or those personally close to them. Experience and knowledge are useful, but the professional should not use them to insulate him- or herself from the patient and acknowledging the patient's uniqueness.

Another problem faced by many professionals is how honest to be with patients. It used to be common neither to tell patients about the diagnosis of cancer, nor to fully inform them about their prognosis and the likely experiences of the near future. The pendulum has swung in the opposite direction; it has become popular to fully inform the patient, with the professional too-frequently being "brutally honest," or at least lacking in humane tact. Reluctance to be honest and overly explicit, grim prognostic communication share one element: they are both apt to indicate the professional's discomfort with the issues of death and pain, and that professional's inability to fully consider and appreciate the needs of the patient.

When assessing patients, professional staff cannot help but make implicit suggestions about the patient's life situation. They indirectly or directly will be asked by the patient about prognosis. There is no pat answer for how to respond. The patient, at such a critical time, typically is highly susceptible to suggestion. In fact, there is evidence that the expectations and beliefs of the patient not only influence the quality of life, but may prolong or shorten life (Stoll, 1980). Thus, when discussing cancer with a patient, it is best to point out how unpredictable the disease can be for each individual patient, and how it is very often true that patients do not experience many of the effects that they expected. If possible, give a personal example of someone who had a similar kind of cancer from which he or she either recovered or with which he or she did remarkably well. When the patient contemplates pain, nausea, or disfigurement, the professional can point out that such consequences often do not occur, and when they do occur, may not be severe. In short, the professional can be honest while offering realistic information tempered with hope. The professional should explore his or her personal fears, fantasies, and experience with cancer, and work to avoid insensitivity, defensiveness, or the notorious experience of "burn out."

Interactions with cancer patients can be both demanding and extraordinarily rewarding. Professionals should encourage evaluative feedback from colleagues, friends, patients, and families. Physicians owe it to our patients and to ourselves to be engaged in ongoing self-monitoring, in particular reflecting upon how we deal with our own mortality, our limitations, and the professional repercussions of such reflections. These issues can be discussed with colleagues or even pursued through psychotherapy. Books like *Personal Death Awareness* (Worden, 1976), can provide further insight. Also potentially useful are peer support groups, related workshops, and conferences on the issues of illness, loss, death, and grieving. It is inevitable that professionals sometimes feel as if they have personally and/or professionally failed when our patients worsen or die. Such irrational thoughts, however, can overwhelm and impede the professional's ability to effectively function, as individuals as well as professionals.

PROBLEMS FACED BY CANCER PATIENTS

Over the course of the illness, a number of maladaptive behaviors, painful emotions, and physical symptoms may appear. This is not to say that they *will* or *must* appear. It should again be emphasized that expected difficulties often do not appear or can appear and be relatively minor and manageable. Minor problems are exacerbated by patient fears, pessimistic communication, or suggestion from the staff. Still, because of the unexpected changes which so often occur with cancer patients, staff should remain aware of the possible occurrence or recurrence of such problems, which include the following:

Denial

One of the most widely reported behaviors of cancer patients is the unconscious suppression of unpleasant thoughts or strong emotions. Dansak and Cordes (1979) have clinically observed that patients rarely totally deny their cancer, but very often will consciously and voluntarily suppress aversive thoughts about the disease. Patients will sometimes talk and act as if they do not know that they have cancer. This suppression of thoughts about the disease may be a useful and, at times, necessary means of coping, giving the patient a sense of control in the face of what may understandably seem to be a terrifying reality (Abrams, 1971). Denial, however, becomes a serious problem when it leads to poor judgment in everyday living and non-compliance with the treatment regimen.

Even when patients are willing to talk about their diseases, they may deny or try to deny other emotion-laden issues. They may be particularly unwilling to talk about fears of isolation, and they may be unwilling to ask others for support and affection. Reluctance to address these issues can cause unhappiness and misunderstanding within the patient's family, and can impede the expression of affection which the patient and the family may both want and fear.

This is not to suggest that professional staff be confrontative or intrusive, forcing the patient to "open up." Denial can be useful. Even when it is not employed, when the patient wants to discuss painful subjects, doing so may be difficult for the patient. In many cases, emotional expressiveness and openness, especially about fears or anger, can be novel behaviors to the patient. Some researchers claim that those people who are psychologically predisposed to develop cancer are characterized by inexpressiveness and emotional suppression (Fox, 1976; Grossarth-Maticek, 1980a).

Staff can help the patient become more expressive, and can do so without being "brutally" honest. Direct confrontation will likely confirm the patient's belief that expressiveness is painful, and may increase the patient's reluctance to honestly communicate. Staff should instead attempt:

1. to develop a caring and understanding relationship with the patient which can make communication easier for both patient and staff.
2. to model expressive and open communication about feelings in a considerate way.
3. to gently reflect some of the feelings they believe the patient may be indirectly expressing.

4. to reinforce through words, gesture, and/or touch any appropriate ex-
    pressiveness manifested by the patient.
5. to openly state that there are things the patient may not be willing to
    immediately discuss and that the staff members recognize and respect
    this desire.
6. to seriously consider problems expressed by the patient and to teach
    problem-solving techniques.
7. to teach the patient, if he or she wishes, assertiveness and communica-
    tion skills.
8. to teach or direct other staff members and the patient's family to inter-
    act with the patient in a similar manner.

Inactivity

Both physical symptoms and a sense of hopelessness predispose many cancer patients to live much less actively than they did prior to their illness, but a
retreat into passivity or complete inactivity is rarely necessary. Patients should be
encouraged to sit up, to stay out of bed, to walk, or to do whatever physical tasks
their physical condition and good sense suggest that they can do. They should try
to do those things that have been fulfilling, pleasurable, and/or important in their
lives, or discover previously overlooked activities. These should be based on the
patient's desires rather than on the values of the staff or family. In assessing the
patient, it can be helpful to determine what the patient used to do on a typical day
prior to the illness, what he or she does now, and what the patient would like to be
doing. The staff can encourage the patient and reinforce (at least verbally) successive approximation of desired behaviors and activity levels. The patient may
be able to increase gradually such activities as walking, reading, cooking, gardening, or involvement in family outings. Increases in pleasurable activities have
led to mood changes among depressed patients (Lewinsohn and Graf, 1973). Cancer patients are frequently surprised and pleased over how active they can be with
staff support and reinforcement.

Anxiety

Cancer patients may complain of anxiety, reporting that they feel "jumpy"
or feel like they have "bad nerves." They may identify anxiety as a cause of headaches, dizziness, or insomnia. Further discussion usually reveals that anxiety is
not free-floating, but rather based on real and understandable fears of death, pain,
mutilation, or isolation. The treatment of anxiety begins with specifying the antecedent thoughts and experiences that led to increased feelings of nervousness.
Through open discussion of specific fears and reassurance from staff members
the patient can become desensitized to these fears, although they may not entirely
disappear. The use of relaxation and other cognitive coping techniques can also

reduce fear and manifestations of anxiety. Such techniques should not be applied until antecedents of increased anxiety have been explored and discussed; otherwise, the patient may communicate less honestly, and further suppress or deny fears without reducing anxiety.

Depression

Using a symptom checklist to compare ratings of cancer patients made by physicians and patients, Derogatis and coworkers (1976) found that the physicians were more likely to observe anxiety, and the cancer patients were more likely to see themselves as depressed. In a brief interaction with a cancer patient, the staff member frequently will notice the patient's anxiety, because the patient may want to communicate, directly or indirectly, his or her need for attention and help. In more extended contact, however, the staff member probably will be more aware of the patient's depression. Despair and grief over current or anticipated losses and a pervasive sense of helplessness can lead to depression. If the depression is severe or long-standing, psychotropic medications may be useful. The use of positive imagery and the reinforcement of gradual increases in patient activity also can lead to improvement.

Hostility

Hostility, like depression, is associated with feelings of helplessness and a lack of control. This sense of helplessness can elicit anger and frustration, rather than the fatalism that typically accompanies depression. The hostile patient may scapegoat staff and family, and may alienate others by incessant complaining. While this is unsettling to the staff, it should be noted that patients who express hostility and criticism may have a more favorable prognosis than patients who deny such feelings (Stavraky et al., 1968; Derogatis et al., 1979). Treatment should therefore aim not to suppress hostility, but rather to help the patient talk about the hostile feelings and communicate needs in a forthright, constructive manner. One way to help is to carefully and sympathetically listen to angry patients; staff and family frequently further alienate these patients by arguing with them, unwittingly encouraging the patient to become more angry and to even more emphatically complain. By listening and not explicitly or implicitly rejecting the patient, staff members foster a greater willingness on the part of the patient to more calmly communicate. Such communication should be noted and reinforced. Training in assertiveness, effective expressiveness, and self-management of anxiety and anger also assist the hostile patient in more effectively controlling the environment and in decreasing feelings of helplessness.

Psychotic Behaviors

Psychosis occurs infrequently among cancer patients. When it does occur, it involves delusions more often than hallucinations. The delusions are commonly paranoid in nature, with ideas of reference involving staff or family, who may be perceived as harmful to the patient. Such cognitive disturbances are often aggravated, if not caused by, medication, e.g., steroid-induced psychoses. Such cognitive disturbances can be reversed by changes in pharmacological treatment.

Manifest actions of depression as well as an organic brain syndrome can also be side effects of some cancer chemotherapy medications (Levine et al., 1978)). Whenever severe depression is noted, the patient's cognitive functioning might also be tested, since organicity is very commonly misdiagnosed as depression. As loss of functioning continues, the patient may manifest childish behaviors, e.g., crying, screaming, hiding under bedding, incontinence. Behavioral treatment may reduce the frequency and intensity of regressive behavior, even when the deterioration is organic. Periods when the patient does not show these behaviors should be noted and reinforced.

Pain

Among cancer patients, pain is rarely severe (McCorkle and Young, 1978) but frequently feared. Sometimes patients will focus on pain when they are really concerned about isolation and have no other way of indicating their need for contact. In other cases, cancer pain behavior may be reinforced by attention and medication. Discussion of issues associated with pain and the use of hypnotic and other imagery techniques may ameliorate pain. There is also some evidence that psychotropic medication may decrease pain (Bourhis et al., 1978).

Nausea

Nausea, vomiting, anorexia, and other gastrointestinal (GI) disorders often occur when patients undergo chemotherapy, and to a lesser extent, when patients undergo radiation therapy. By eating small amounts of foods which are both bland and enjoyable over time, the patient may reduce the incidence and severity of nausea and vomiting. Staff should discuss appropriate eating habits that also fit the patient's tastes. Pleasant imagery, relaxation, and other hypnotherapy techniques can reduce these GI problems. Ideally, such techniques should be taught before the patient has begun chemotherapy or radiation therapy. Redd (1980) has demonstrated the usefulness of extinction and differential reinforcement by staff members in ameliorating retching and coughing. Staff members consistently remained in the patient's room and chatted for about 10 minutes when the patient did not display the symptomatic behavior. When the patient displayed the undesirable behavior, staff members in the patient's room briefly performed the necessary tasks and left, minimally involving themselves in conversation. Retching (for one patient) and vomiting (for another patient) were dramatically reduced, and remained at a low rate of occurrence at 6-months follow up.

Insomnia

As a result of anxiety, depression, and/or physical symptoms, some patients may have difficulty sleeping. This may lead to a feeling of fatigue during the day, exacerbating psychological and physical symptoms. Sometimes patients get into the habit of sleeping during the day and staying up much of the night. By teaching patients relaxation techniques, noting and reinforcing nighttime sleep, and discouraging daytime sleep and napping, insomnia may be reduced.

Sexual Dysfunction

Patients often are concerned about an inability to sexually perform, or a loss of sexual attractiveness to their partner. In cases where there has previously been a satisfactory sexual relationship, it is often sufficient to assist couples and discuss these issues, since sexuality frequently is a subject that couples may complain about but avoid discussing. When the deterioration of the patient leads to sexual inability or extreme discomfort, spouses are often willing to have sexual contact without intercourse. Open discussion with staff members can help patients continue to express sexual feelings and realize a degree of sexual functioning satisfactory to patient and partner.

SPECIFIC INFORMATION TO ASSESS

It is not enough to simply assess the presence or absence of a particular problem. Assessment of the patient with regard to a problematic behavior, belief, emotion, or physical symptom should involve the following:

1. the antecedent thoughts, feelings, and experience which intensify the particular problems.
2. the nature and severity of the problems as differentially perceived by the patient, the staff, and the family.
3. a history-taking of when the problems first appeared.
4. the duration of the problems and their patterns of occurrence.
5. past medical and behavioral interventions attempted to resolve problems, and the degree of success realized.
6. coping responses used by the patient and the effects of these responses both for the patient and significant others.

INTERVIEWING THE PATIENT

The interview is a very flexible assessment technique that can be used in attempting to understand the patient's behavior and his or her experience of the problems discussed above. Equally important, the interview can help the patient see the staff member as caring. The relationship that develops over the course of several assessment interviews can be a source of hope and strength for the patient. This is most likely to happen when the staff member is willing to *stop, look, listen,* and *touch.*

Stop. The cancer patient may be understandably reluctant to complain of or report new problems. For an interview to be effective, the staff member ought to stop and talk to the patient for at least 10 minutes, preferably much longer. We have found that any shorter interview time tends to evoke stereotypical responses from the patient; he or she is "doing fine." In 10 or more minutes, through face to face contact or even in telephone conversations, the staff member gives the patient the time necessary to see that he or she is remembered and cared for. Accurate self-monitoring and participation in treatment activities is reinforced by this show of concern.

Look. The staff person should assess the patient's dress, posture, gestures, and the state of the patient's immediate surroundings. This non-verbal information can provide critical clues as to needs the patient may have that would otherwise go unnoticed or unreported by the patient. It is at least as important, however, for the staff members to make eye contact with the patient. The staff member who is tempted to look at an inpatient's chart ought to look, with some regularity, at the patient, conveying the idea that the patient is perceived as a person and not simply as a cluster of symptoms. With disfigured or emaciated patients, it may at times be difficult to make eye contact, but these patients may be precisely those most in need of caring and natural contact. Often the patient is seated or lying down when interviewed by the staff member. If no chair is available, the staff member crouches down beside the patient or, with permission, sits on the bed, so that the patient does not have to adopt an uncomfortable position or literally feel "beneath" the staff member. This simple, non-verbal action demonstrates courtesy and concern for the patient's comfort.

Listen. The staff member should actively listen to the patient, and to the extent possible give the patient full and undivided attention. For some staff, it may be easy to adhere to a rigidly structured set of questions, or to primarily focus on a specific problem for which the patient was referred. We find it most helpful to be flexible, and respond to patient-initiated content. This gives the interviewer a better idea about what is most important for the patient, and it also reflects his or her desire to listen and truly understand the patient. After establishing rapport, the questioning during an initial interview can begin by asking, "what is it like to be seriously ill?" or "tell me, in your own words, what's been happening?" As the relationship continues to develop over time, the staff person can continue to show a desire to share, to understand, and to learn, giving permission and encouraging the patient to be expressive. The staff person can also indicate that he or she does not have any preconceived notions; the patient is encouraged to discuss whatever he or she is moved to discuss. Silence may be the necessary order of the day.

The staff person should not, however, avoid asking specific questions. When the patient is self-monitoring, and when the staff and patient are working on a specific problem, it is important to ask, preferably early in the interview, for concrete data. For example, the staff members might ask about hours of sleep, communication with family, assertiveness with staff, degree of gastrointestinal comfort, hours spent out of bed, and similar questions aimed at obtaining data regarding targeted problems. The staff member, however, should continue the interview in such a way that the patient has the opportunity and is encouraged to bring up other issues.

Touch. Cancer patients sometimes feel like they are being considered as objects for study or, somehow, less than human; such feelings can lead to resistance, non-compliance, loneliness, and fears of abandonment. Touching is another way for staff members to humanize their relationship with the patient, and make it easier for the patient to honestly communicate. By touching the patient, the staff member can demonstrate that he or she cares enough to risk touching and being touched. To the degree the staff member and patient feel comfortable, they can shake hands, hold hands, or even embrace, on occasion. If a staff member is uncomfortable about physical contact, it may be helpful to first experiment with touching under the following circumstances: when first greeting the patient or leaving the patient; when the patient mentions a particular part of the body causing problems; or when making a point that can be punctuated or expressively underscored through a touch.

OTHER ASSESSMENT STRATEGIES

Although the interview has many advantages, it may not provide sufficient or reliable data by which to assess the needs of the patient or the efficacy of treatment. Other assessment strategies can supplement the interview, including questionnaires, self-monitoring, and observation in a naturalistic setting.

Questionnaires. The most widely used questionnaire with cancer patients is the MMPI. While useful for a clinical understanding of the patient, it does not easily lend itself to identification of specific problematic behaviors or symptoms, nor does it adequately assess treatment effects or changes over time. It is more helpful for understanding patients who are seriously emotionally disturbed, and less helpful for the less-disturbed patient with symptomatic and behavioral problems.

An instrument that has been widely used, but nonetheless shows promise, is the Symptom Checklist-90 (SCL-90) (Craig and Abeloff, 1974). This instrument is much easier to administer than the MMPI, having only 90 questions, and refers to problems over a short time span. It is appropriate for repeated use, and because of the time-limited nature of the questions, it is likely to be sensitive to changes over time, though this has not been tested with cancer patients. This checklist can easily be filled out by staff or family members to compare their impressions of the patient with the patient's own self-rating.

Self-monitoring. When specific problems are targeted, the patient can monitor his or her own behavior and symptomatology. Self-monitoring, though helpful, is often difficult for patients to perform. In many cases they do not have the motivation, desire, or self-confidence to fill out the lengthy forms; in many instances, the patient may not be literate. These problems usually can be overcome with questionnaires, since the more lengthy forms usually are completed only once. Self-monitoring requires daily observation. Thus, it is important for self-monitoring to be as simple as possible, and for staff to reinforce the self-observing patient, and frequently check in with him or her.

McCorkle and Young (1978) devised a symptom checklist for daily monitoring of symptoms. Unlike the SCL-90, it is specifically intended for cancer patients, is extremely brief, and is suitable for daily administration. The instrument consists of 10 cards dealing with problems frequently encountered by cancer patients: nausea, mood, appetite, insomnia, pain, mobility, fatigue, bowel pattern, concentration, and appearances. The cards give the patient a choice of numbers between 1 and 5 to measure the feelings of the patient. Thus, for mobility, "1" represents "able to do everything"; "5" represents "not able to get around." Daily or weekly ratings of some or all of these symptoms can provide useful information on changes regarding different problems, as well as changes in the main problems faced by the patient. This checklist has not, however, been extensively used, and it does not adequately represent different kinds of emotions which may trouble the patient.

Patients can also monitor desirable behaviors, such as time out of bed, assertive statements, or number of times during the day they use relaxation or anxiety-reduction techniques. Such information should ideally be written down by the patient, since written data provide the staff and the patient with documents to review and compare over time. If the patient is reluctant or unable to write down this information, staff members can obtain verbal data from patients during daily interviews and chart the data, or patients can record data via cassette.

Naturalistic observation.   Symptom checklists can be filled out by observers, but in many cases this requires inferences about the patient rather than direct observation of manifest behavior. Bourhis et al. (1978) devised a relatively simple method for daily assessment of the communication and activity level of the patient. Communication is rated by nursing staff on a five-point scale according to whether: (1) there is no complaint; (2) there is only complaint when questioned; (3) there is complaint once or twice a day to staff; (4) there is complaint three or four times a day; and (5) there is complaint five or more times a day. Unfortunately, this assessment of communication assumes degree of distress, which ideally should be low, and willingness to complain, which for cancer patients is often desirable. More useful is the activity level assessment, which is rated on a five-point scale according to whether: (1) the patient is able to leave the hospital and normally function; (2) the patient is able to leave the ward; (3) the patient is able to move about within the ward; (4) the patient is able to get out of bed to eat and go to the toilet; and (5) the patient is unable to get out of bed.

Redd (1980) describes another method for assessing symptomatology and bed behavior of cancer patients. In order to assess retching and coughing, tape recorders were hidden in patient rooms and were turned on every other hour for 60 minutes during day and evening shifts for 2 consecutive days. Controls were outside the patient rooms and the times during which the tape was recording was unknown to the patients. Occurrence or non-occurrence of the targeted behavior during 3-minute segments was noted. Assessment was conducted before, during, and after a therapeutic intervention. A second assessment technique involved having seven nurses enter the patient's room three times a day, only when the tape was off, and observing whether or not the behavior occurred. This gives an idea of the behavior as a response to involvement with staff, while the first technique measures the overall behavior level. These are obviously highly expensive techniques in terms of staff time and energy; however, less-frequent recording of behavior, as well as fewer occurrences of nurse-patient interaction, might provide useful data without overworking the staff.

The assessment strategies that are appropriate for cancer patients are quite variable. They should always be kept as simple as possible, and relevant to the needs of the patient. More important than particular assessment techniques are attending to specific data and sustaining a caring and constructive alliance between staff members and the patient.

ASSESSING THE FAMILY

Family responses to the cancer patient may range from denial to exaggerated identification with the patient. Families sometimes develop what Glaser and Strauss (1968) referred to as a "conspiracy of silence" or "mutual pretense." Although staff members may want to disrupt the family pattern of inexpressiveness, direct confrontation is no more advisable with the family than it is with the individual patient. Overidentification may lead to excessive emotionality on the part of family members, or even psychosomatic symptoms and the exacerbation of health problems. This may result in the patient feeling guilt or resentment. Staff members thus should be attuned to family problems, particularly to behaviors on the part of the family which lead to negative behavior, affect, and symptoms for the patient, and vice versa. Often it is necessary to follow the family over long periods of time and to attend to the quite different circumstances and difficulties which arise.

One couple, seen by the senior author, Richard Lucas, for over 4 years, illustrates the way one family reacts to cancer. A summary of the case is also intended to suggest the everchanging context of the cancer patient in which assessment and therapeutic intervention must be accomplished with flexibility, patience, and perseverance.

Mr. H. died at 55 years of age, after surviving Hodgkin's Disease, which had been suspected in 1960, 20 years earlier, when he discovered a pea-sized mass in the right side of his neck. By 1964, it had become the size of a quarter. Only when the node became grapefruit-sized, in 1971, did he seek medical diagnosis of the symptom. He complained of fevers, night sweats, and a 40-pound weight loss from his earlier weight of 280 pounds. Cervical and inguinal nodes were discovered. Following a year of chemotherapy and radiation therapy, there was, by 1973, no evidence of Hodgkin's Disease. In 1976, nodular sclerosing Hodgkin's Disease and left cervical adenopathy were diagnosed; Mr. H. appeared only partially responsive to irradiation efforts.

In January 1976, the patient initiated contact with Dr. Lucas, who was psychologist for the Hematology Clinic, which the patient now frequented once monthly. The patient spontaneously ventilated concerns about growing fears of loss of control relative to business and financial problems, marital tensions, and medical problems, and confided the sense that friends were "leaning away" from him.

Mr. H. was a self-made black businessman who had lived most of his life in the northern U.S.; in his forties, he moved south. Through the strength of his intellect and will, he had become a highly respected and successful general contractor, in spite of continuing racial tensions in the southern community in which he lived and worked. With their eight children grown, Mrs. H. worked full-time as a seamstress. Communication problems between them were aggravated by the Hodgkin's Disease. Mr. H. perceived himself as considerate in trying to be stoic and unexpressive about his medical problems; Mrs. H. tried to be even more nurturing to her husband as she became more apprehensive regarding his disease.

The psychologist made himself available to the patient during his outpatient visits to the Hematology Clinic. In February 1976, the patient and his wife became active in that clinic's patient/family group meetings. Since both spouses were articulate and attractive, imposing physical figures, they were perceived by other participants as strong leaders. Although encouraged by the psychologist to meet in marriage therapy, the wife initially preferred to ventilate in the groups. She complained of depression, increasing problems with obesity, alcohol abuse, and tension growing out of her fears that her husband would die. She insisted that she would rather die than face his death. In individual meetings with the psychologist, Mr. H. complained of depression and growing exasperation with both his cancer and his wife's response to it. As the patient's disease appeared to improve, the couple's complaints diminished by the end of 1976 and into 1977, and the wife began to lose weight through a weight reduction program.

In May 1978, Mr. H. presented with recurrence of Hodgkin's Disease, manifested by a cervical mass and right hip pain. In subsequent medical efforts the patient proved unresponsive to chemotherapy. With the recurrence of the disease and behavioral problems recurring, the couple began marriage therapy with the psychologist and a psychology intern. Both spouses now seemed tenaciously intent on accomplishing a more satisfactory marital relationship and more effectively coping with the disease. The MMPI suggested that both spouses were experiencing considerable anxiety, feeling different and apart from others, and moderately-to-severely depressed. When together, the husband tried to maintain a cool, intellectualized, articulate stance while critically soliloquizing about his wife and his medical care. Mrs. H. expressed resentment of her husband's criticisms and general feelings of inadequacy in interacting with him and attempting to do things for him at home. Each spouse was reinforced for behavioral changes each spontaneously began to make that were more agreeable to the other. For example, the husband would genuinely listen to his wife and speak for briefer periods of time, beginning to include positive statements about her. The wife began to ask less frequently how her husband was doing, and would also check her impulses to do things for him. The conjoint sessions were included as a part of their regular biweekly Hematology Clinic visits. By the end of 1978, the patient had lost 70 pounds and massive lymph node enlargement in the neck continued. As a person who had always taken fierce pride in his ability to achieve through effectively controlling himself and others, he now became more intent on struggling to control his disease. He was very disappointed that neither he nor the medical staff were able to control his cancer.

As the disease progressed through 1979, patient and wife reported fewer dissatisfactions with the marriage. The husband was more open to his wife's efforts to help him, and she was feeling more satisfied with herself. By late spring of 1979, she accepted the imminence of his death and felt strong enough to tolerate it. Marriage therapy was discontinued and the patient saw the psychologist for support in preparation for death and for pain control through hypnosis. By December 1979, Mr. H. weighted 170 pounds; over 100 pounds less than when he had considered himself healthy. He increasingly manifested severe necrosis below his right ear, his right facial area drooped badly and appeared contorted, his right ear remained clogged, considerable sputum aggravated a chronic cough and dysphagia, and subcutaneous tumors in the right axilla and hemithorax progressively pained him. A laparotomy with gastrojejunostomy and gastrostomy were done at the patient's request to prevent death from starvation due to gastric outlet obstructions. The primary fear of staff was that the patient would die of airway compression by tumor.

By January 1980, the patient acknowledged for the first time that he had lost his will to live. He said that he went to sleep each night praying that he would die and tried to will himself to do so. Both he and his wife were ready for his death and all of us who had known him for so many years wished it for him too. Four years to the day after he met the psychologist, Mr. H. said goodbye to him on his last Hematology Clinic visit and died the following afternoon of a suspected cerebral vascular accident (stroke) while napping in his bed with his wife attending him at home. Their marriage had survived more satisfactorily than before, with the patient relinquishing more control and the wife feeling more able to assume more control not only in the patient's care but in matters of business and financial management which had been exclusively his. Mrs. H. had made significant gains: her moods improved, her eating was better controlled with no alcohol consumption, she had greater relaxation with reduced blood pressure problems, and fewer apprehensions regarding death and dying. Mr. H. remained remarkable in his manifestation of his courage and continued ability to tolerate growing chronic pain, swallowing, eating, and breathing problems. His fears of a loss of control and being alienated from others continued to decline. While he was embarassed about his facial appearance, he made it clear that the attentions of his wife and medical staff were critical to him.

The patient had been assessed through the psychologist's ongoing dialogues with the patient and/or wife over the last 4 years of the patient's life. MMPIs were administered only once, in 1977 when the couple seemed most stressed and depressed. The results confirmed suspicions that their overt behaviors were deceptive, in that neither initially felt as elevated in moods nor as secure as they tried to appear to be to others. They had both survived and coped with probably two decades of a life-threatening cancer, with all of its disturbingly irregular developments that imposed everincreasing demands. These two people showed themselves to be more courageous and better able to cope as the disease worsened.

The approaches staff took in assisting the couple in the behavioral management of their predicament were flexible and varied from individual and conjoint contexts that included humanistic and behavioristic techniques for the management of such problems as depression, anger, anxiety, obesity, pain, and insomnia.

CONCLUSION

It is far from clear that cancer patients suffer unusual amounts of emotional disturbance (Plumb and Holland, 1977), and as we have noted, physical symptomatology, particularly pain, is less prevalent than commonly believed. Still, behavioral assessment can be useful in helping cancer patients improve the quality of their lives. Further, behavioral assessment and intervention are likely to decrease side effects of medical treatment, thereby increasing compliance with procedures that can extend life. Finally, tentative evidence supports the following.

1. The growth and remission of tumors are related to the patient's endocrinological system and immunological defenses, both of which are themselves influenced by the emotions and behavior of the patient (Stoll, 1980).
2. People with certain personality types appear to be predisposed to having cancer later in life (Grossarth-Maticek, 1980a; Fox, 1976; Dattore et al., 1980).
3. Cancer patients with these same predisposing characteristics appear to be likely not to survive as long as cancer patients with different characteristics (Achterberg et al., 1978; Derogatis et al., 1979; Stavraky et al., 1968; and Rogentine et al., 1979).
4. Cancer patients involved in supportive and behavioral therapy may live almost twice as long once diagnosed as having cancer as patients not involved in such therapy (Simonton et al., 1980; Grossarth-Maticek, 1980b).

Those patient characteristics associated with longer life include hopefulness and a sense of self-confidence; expressiveness of feelings, including negative feelings; the willingness and opportunity to be involved in meaningful activity; and the willingness and opportunity to be involved in fulfilling relationships with others. Behavioral interventions which improve the quality of the patient's life may also increase lifespan; such intervention may well be almost as important as medical treatment. Staff members and behavioral scientists who work with cancer patients should learn more about the kinds of behaviors which improve and possibly lengthen the patient's life, how to assess these behaviors, and how to intervene in order to encourage and reinforce these behaviors.

REFERENCES

Abrams, R. Denial and depression in the terminal patient. *Psychiatric Quarterly,* 1971, *45,* 394–404.

Achterberg, J., Matthews, S., & Simonton, O. C. Psychology of the exceptional cancer patient: A description of patients who outlive predicted life expectancies. *Psychotherapy: Therapy, Research, and Practice,* 1978, *14,* 24.

Bourhis, A., Boudsuresque, G., Pellet, W., Fondarai, J., Ponzio, J., & Spitalier, J. Pain infirmity and psychotropic drugs in oncology. *Pain,* 1978, *5,* 263–274.

Craig, R., & Abeloff, M. Psychiatric symptomatology among hospitalized cancer patients. *American Journal of Psychiatry,* 1974, *131,* 1323–1325.

Dansak, D., & Cordez, R. Cancer: Denial or suppression? *International Journal of Psychiatry in Medicine,* 1978-1979, *9,* 257–262.

Dattore, P., Shontz, F., & Coyne, L. Premorbid personality differentiation of cancer and noncancer groups: A test of the hypothesis of cancer proneness. *Journal of Clinical and Consulting Psychology,* 1980, *48,* 388–394.

Derogatis, L., Abeloff, M., & McBeth, C. Cancer patients and their physicians in the perception of psychological symptoms. *Psychosomatics,* 1976, *17,* 197–201.

Derogatis, L., Abeloff, M., & Melisaratos, N. Psychological coping mechanisms and survival time in metastatic breast cancer. *Journal of the American Medical Association,* 1979, *242,* 1504–1508.

Fox, B. H. The psychosocial epidemiology of cancer. In J. W. Cullen, B. H. Fox & R. N. Isom, (Eds.), *Cancer, the behavioral dimension.* New York: Raven Press, 1976.

Glaser, B., & Strauss, A. *Time for dying.* Chicago: Aldine, 1968.

Grossarth-Maticek, R. Psychosocial predictors of cancer: An overview. *Psychotherapy and Psychosomatics,* 1980a, *33,* 122–128.

Grossarth-Maticek, R. Social psychotherapy and course of the disease: First experiences with cancer patients. *Psychotherapy and Psychosomatics,* 1980b, *33,* 129–138.

Kubler-Ross, E. *On death and dying.* New York: MacMillan Publishing Company, Inc., 1969.

Levine, P., Silberfarb, P., & Lipowski, Z. J. Mental disorders in cancer patients: A study of 100 psychiatric referrals. *Cancer,* 1978, *42,* 1385–1391.

Lewinsohn, P., & Graf, M. Pleasant activities and depression. *Journal of Consulting and Clinical Psychology,* 1973, *41,* 261–268.

McCorkle, R., & Young, K. Development of a symptom distress scale. *Cancer Nursing,* 1978, *1,* 373–378.

Plumb, M., & Holland, J. Cooperative studies of psychological function in patients with advanced cancer. I: Self-reported depressive symptoms. *Psychosomatic Medicine,* 1977, *39,* 264–275.

Redd, W. Stimulus control and extinction of psychosomatic symptoms in cancer patients in protective custody. *Journal of Consulting and Clinical Psychology,* 1980, *48,* 448–455.

Rogentine, G. N., van Kammen, D., Fox, B., Decherty, J., Rosenblatt, J., Boyd, S., & Bunney, W. Psychological factors in the prognosis of malignant melanoma: A prospective study. *Psychosomatic Medicine,* 1979, *41,* 647–655.

Simonton, O. C., Matthews-Simonton, S., & Sparks, T. Psychological intervention in the treatment of cancer. *Psychosomatics,* 1980, *12,* 226–233.

Stanfiel, J., Tompkins, W., & Brown, H. A daily activities list and its relation to measures of adjustment and early environment. *Psychological Reports,* 1971, *28,* 691–699.

Stavraky, K. M., Buck, C. N., Lott, J. S., & Wanklin, J. M. Psychological factors in the outcome of human cancer. *Journal of Psychosomatic Research,* 1968, *12,* 251–259.

Stoll, B. *Mind and cancer prognosis.* New York: Wiley, 1979.

Worden, J. W. *Personal death awareness.* New Jersey: Prentice Hall, 1976.

PART VI

Assessment Strategies for
Sexual Disorders

Sandra R. Leiblum

13

Assessment of Sexual Dysfunction

Despite the ever-increasing media coverage given to all aspects of human sexuality, a surprising degree of reticence about discussing sexual matters persists in the ranks of physicians and mental health workers. Yet the incidence of sexual problems is quite high in the normal population. Masters and Johnson (1970) have estimated that 50 percent of the American population have sexual difficulties of one kind or another. Frank and coworkers (1978), in a survey of sexual adjustment in a group of self-defined "happily married" couples found considerable evidence of general sexual difficulties, as well as actual sexual dysfunction. More than 50 percent of the women reported difficulty reaching orgasm, while nearly that many indicated sexual arousal difficulties. While the men admitted to fewer sexual problems than the women, nearly 40 percent reported problems with ejaculation, and 10 percent complained of erectile difficulties. Other common sexual complaints included an inability to relax prior to intercourse, insufficient foreplay, and sexual disinterest.

Most research investigators agree with these estimates and the conclusions of surveys of sexual problems that sexual problems are quite common and, furthermore, that these problems can lead to unfavorable consequences.

CONSEQUENCES OF SEXUAL PROBLEMS

Among the unfortunate consequences of sexual problems are relationship conflicts. At times, unresolved sexual difficulties become the basis for separation and divorce. The incidence of extramarital affairs among couples with distressed relationships is high and usually exerts a disruptive impact on family life. Physical complaints are often associated with long-standing sexual problems. Complaints of headaches, fatigue, apathy, backache, and "genital" aches are not unusual along with the more obvious symptoms of depression, guilt, shame, and anxiety. In severe cases, these feelings so deleteriously affect self-esteem that they disturb occupational and interpersonal functioning. Finally, problems with infertility may be directly linked to sexual dysfunction. The woman with vaginismus (the reflexive contraction of the vaginal entrance when penetration is attempted) will clearly have a problem conceiving; the man with chronic erectile failure or ejaculatory inability will have little success with impregnation. Given, then, that the incidence of sexual problems is high and the consequences serious, how does one assess sexual functioning?

THE CLINICAL INTERVIEW

Considerable information about sexual attitudes, beliefs, and behaviors can be collected in a relatively brief time period by the skillful interviewer. Sexual inquiry requires a relaxed, comfortable, and sensitive attitude on the part of the interviewer. Burnap and Golden (1967) found that the incidence of sexual problems reported by patients was twice as high among those individuals who were questioned by physicians who were comfortable discussing sexual matters than among those physicians who were not. These authors concluded that ''there is little doubt that the variability in the reported incidence of sexual problems is related more to the physician than to his [or her] patients.''

Style is as important as content in taking a sexual history. The interviewer must first establish rapport with the client before delving into intimate material. Discussion of less personal matters should precede questions about sexual functioning. Beginning the interview with a review of the patient's medical or family history is a helpful ice-breaker. As the patient becomes more relaxed, the interviewer can introduce the arena of sexual functioning with a general statement which gives the patient permission and encouragement to discuss sexual material, e.g., ''Sexual health is as important as physical health. I will be asking you questions about your sexual life and then you will have the opportunity to raise any questions you may have.'' Any statement indicating the ubiquity of sexual concerns can prove reassuring to the patient who feels unique and stigmatized about having problems. Open-ended questions are preferable to yes-or-no questions in generating informative replies. ''Tell me about sexual relations with your wife,'' for instance, is a better question than ''is sex with your wife satisfactory?''

For most purposes, a brief sexual overview is generally sufficient. General content areas to be covered include:

Current sexual function and satisfaction.   Is the patient able to satisfactorily perform in current sexual relationships? Included here is the ability to obtain erection, control ejaculation, and achieve orgasm without pain or discomfort, as well as the ability to become sexually aroused or lubricated. Is the patient content with the current frequency and quality of sexual encounters?

Partner function and satisfaction. Is the patient able to stimulate and satisfy the partner, and vice versa? Does the patient experience sexual and social compatability with the partner?

Brief relationship/marital history. Duration, satisfaction, and major events in the relationship should be covered. Divorce, separation, pregnancies, etc., are all relevant.

Effects of contraception, pregnancy, illness, medication, and aging on sexual response. For example, has a recent hospitalization or trauma interfered with sexual interest or performance? Special attention should be paid to instances of venereal disease, rape, molestation, abortion, miscarriage, etc. The interviewer should employ special sensitivity when inquiring about the impact of such experiences.

Current sexual concerns and difficulties. The brief overview should conclude with an opportunity for the patient to raise questions about any aspect of sexuality, including anatomy, physiology, "normality" of certain sexual behaviors, etc. In the event that the brief overview suggests significant sexual difficulties, a more detailed evaluation may be undertaken along the following lines.

Detailed History

History of the presenting problem. This should include onset, duration, and severity; contributing factors and patient's explanation of problem; and previous attempts at overcoming problem and outcome.

Early sexual development. Examine parental, religious, and peer influences on sexual beliefs, attitudes, and behaviors. Pubertal milestones and subjective responses should be noted, including masturbation and menstruation, as well as adolescent social and sexual development, homosexual experiences, and dating behavior. Pre- and post-marital sexual history, including extra-marital relationships, should be included here.

Patient goals and expectations, with respect to the problem. How does the patient expect to deal with the difficulty? Does the patient expect it to resolve without treatment? Evaluate the patient's interest in and appropriateness for counseling, and consider referral options.

A patient's current level of sexual function and satisfaction should always be seen in the context of his or her overall physical and emotional level of health. Sexual problems can represent "the tip of the iceberg," and the physician's judgment in interpreting the significance of sexual symptoms is always important.

Interview Format

Respect for the client's privacy and comfort during the sexual interview is essential. Closed doors, a minimum of distractions (e.g., jingling telephones or other interruptions), and assurance about the confidentiality of the information gathered is important. It is generally good policy to first see a couple together, and then to separately interview each individual, in order to secure balanced views of both the integrity of the relationship and the individual. Often what emerges during conjoint interviews is very different from what is disclosed in individual sessions.

Case Study

Martha and Bob were initially seen together, at Bob's request. He indicated that he was dissatisfied and frustrated with Martha's aversive reaction to his sexual overtures. He felt repeatedly rebuffed by her and at a loss as to why she found sex so distasteful. Martha agreed with Bob's description of her behavior. She was deferential to Bob throughout the session and, in fact, vigorously defended her husband when the interviewer inquired about Bob's possible contribution to their current difficulties. However, an individual interview with Martha revealed that she felt that Bob belittled her, unfavorably compared her to other women, and disregarded her emotional and sexual needs. Martha's description of their sexual foreplay indicated that Bob provided little in the way of tenderness or sensuality, but rather moved rapidly to genital fondling and penetration with lengthy intromission, which was uncomfortable for her. When Bob was interviewed alone, he presented himself as an arrogant, perfectionistic, hard-driving individual who was quite unaware of Martha's feelings and complaints. He placed the entire responsibility for the unsatisfactory sexual relations on Martha's inadequacies as a woman and mate. This couple obviously needed to be seen both together and separately to obtain a full picture of their life together.

BEYOND THE INTERVIEW

Psychogenic versus Organic Factors in the Etiology of Sexual Problems

Sexual difficulties can be caused by both physical and psychogenic factors, but sexual dysfunction most commonly is psychogenic in origin. Yet many specific dysfunctions have physical concomitants or causes and, invariably, when physical factors are involved, psychogenic variables interact with them to complicate the clinical picture. Any assessment of sexual function must include a determination of the role organic and physical factors play in creating and maintaining difficulties so that appropriate treatment interventions can be implemented. At times, a complete workup by a physician is integral to the initial assessment.

In women, the overwhelming majority of sexual problems are psychogenic in origin (Kaplan, 1974). However, dyspareunia, or pain during intercourse, quite commonly is the result of physical factors. The woman reports pain upon penetration or with thrusting of the penis in the vagina. The pain may be located in the vagina or lower pelvic area. There is reported a high association, 30–40 percent, of physical disease and dyspareunia (Fordney, 1978). Chronic pelvic infection, endometriosis, advanced pelvic carcinoma, extensive prolapse, scars from episiotomies, acute vulvovaginitis, cystitis, and introital, vaginal, and cervical scarring may be the culprits (Fordney, 1978). Other physical causes include estrogen-deprivation common in post-menopausal women, spermicidal jellies or douches, allergic reactions to the rubber used in condoms, and certain drugs (e.g., sympathomimetic agents, amphetamines, and cocaine) (Fordney, 1978). The likelihood that physical factors are indeed responsible for the pain women report must be ruled out or, if present, treated before sex therapy is attempted. In psychogenic dyspareunia, the report of pain is more generalized than with physical dyspareunia, and difficult to locate and replicate during the gynecological exam. If organic factors are eliminated as causal agents, it is likely that the pain is psychogenic in origin; such factors as conflict with a partner, anxiety, fear, sexual disinterest, or intrapsychic conflict are implicated. In such cases, the clinician must undertake a detailed sexual history, since it is unlikely that there is a single specific precipitant, but rather multiple factors interacting to create and maintain the dyspareunia.

Vaginismus, the involuntary, spasmodic contraction of the vaginal outlet and abductor muscles when penetration is attempted, is not caused by physical malfunction, yet physical factors can be associated with the development of the problem. For instance, history taking sometimes reveals an early vaginal trauma involving painful gynecological surgery, an imperforated hymen that caused the woman considerable discomfort when vaginal penetration was first attempted, or a long history of vaginal infections or cysts. While such factors did not specifically cause the conditioned phobic reaction to penetration, vaginismus often occurs secondarily to such problems.

Sometimes anatomical difficulties, such as a particularly small vaginal introitus, can interact with psychological factors to create vaginismus.

Case Study

Susan had been married for 5 years, although she technically was a "virgin." Intercourse had never been successfully accomplished because of her phobic reaction to the thought of, or attempt at, vaginal penetration. Nevertheless, Susan loved her husband, reported a satisfactory marital relationship, and engaged in a wide variety of sexual activities other than intercourse. She was orgasmic both with manual and oral stimulation.

Assessment of her sexual history revealed that Susan had been repeatedly warned while growing up that intercourse "hurt." This was first suggested by her mother, and later reinforced by her older sisters. When, as an adolescent, she complained of menstrual discomfort, her mother retorted that childbirth was, by far, a more excruciating experience. When Susan went for a gynecological exam following an initial sexual therapy session, her gynecologist reported that Susan's vaginal outlet was exceptionally small, and even though Susan was relaxed during the examination, passage of two fingers into the vagina was impossible. Although psychotherapy was recommended, surgical enlargement of Susan's vaginal introitus proved helpful in facilitating therapeutic progress.

Other common female sexual dysfunctions are inhibited sexual desire, sexual aversion, general arousal difficulties, and orgasmic dysfunction. These are infrequently associated with physical factors (Masters & Johnson, 1970). Rather, significant etiological variables include intrapsychic or interpersonal conflict; ignorance; anxiety; guilt; fears of losing control, or receiving pleasure, or intimacy with another; as well as a host of specific psychosexual developmental experiences. Careful history-taking generally provides clues about the factors that may be instrumental in causing or maintaining the sexual problem, although one can never be certain about which variables were critical in creating the problem.

In men, a number of physical factors can cause the complaint of erectile failure. Although the incidence of actual anatomical defects in the reproductive or central nervous system is quite low (Masters & Johnson, 1970), functional impotence may be caused by nervous disorders, excessive use of alcohol or certain drugs, deficient hormonal functioning, circulatory problems, or the aging process per se. Physical examination for erectile dysfunction includes assessment of urological, neurological, endocrinological, and vascular functioning. Although most investigators tend to underemphasize the role of reduced or inadequate testosterone in causing erectile problems, a study by Spark and coworkers (1980) reported that in 105 patients with impotence, 37 patients had previously unsuspected disorders of the hypothalamic-pituitary-gonadal axis. Evaluation of the neuroendocrine/hormonal component of sexual functioning is seen to be important. Relevant assessment should include plasma testosterone levels (best taken on two separate occasions), estrogen and prolactin levels, estrogen–testosterone ratio, and the percentage of unbound testosterone. Evaluation of possible diabetes and thyroid malfunctioning may reveal the cause of the erectile dysfunction.

Generally, intelligent history-taking provides salient clues as to whether the erectile difficulty is psychogenic or organic in origin. For instance, inquiring about the presence of early morning erections or whether erections are obtained under *any* circumstances, such as during masturbation, erotic reading, or with some partners, is helpful. If erections occur in some contexts but not others, the likelihood is very great that the erectile failure is caused and maintained by psychogenic factors. However, sometimes interview material fails to adequately clarify the basis for the problem, since both physical and psychogenic factors seem equally implicated. In such cases, differential diagnosis via assessment of nocturnal penile tumescence is indicated.

NOCTURNAL PENILE TUMESCENCE ASSESSMENT

Nocturnal penile tumescence (NPT) assessment is based on the observation that adult males have regularly occurring episodes of erection during sleep, approximately every 90 to 100 minutes, which are closely associated with rapid-eye-movement (REM) sleep (Fisher et al., 1965; Karacan, 1969, 1978). These REM periods last from 20 to 40 minutes on average and are characterized by autonomic activation and dreaming. NPT is not necessarily related to sexual dreaming, although many men erroneously believe that their early morning erection is due to erotic dreams or bladder pressure.

In NPT assessment, the assumption is made that the man who complains of erectile failure but who has normal NPT for his age is suffering from psychogenic rather than organic impotence. On the other hand, if on several successive nights, a man displays reduced or absent NPT, the erectile failure is likely to be of organic origin.

NPT assessment is quite straightforward, although it must be done in specially equipped sleep laboratories or clinics. The individual initially undergoes an extensive clinical interview and then is invited to come to the sleep lab. At that time, electrodes are placed for electroencephalogram assessment of eye movement activity. Changes in penile circumference are monitored by means of two mercury-filled strain gauges that are positioned around the penis. Penile circumference changes are recorded throughout the night on the polygraph recorder, as are periods of REM sleep. If the man has difficulty sleeping and the sleep is disrupted or abnormally brief, the NPT data cannot be interpreted because of the possibility of false negatives and the test is repeated on a subsequent evening. Assessment of physical factors contributing to the sexual dysfunction must also include the possible etiological role of various medications. Drugs can interfere with the desire, arousal, and orgasmic phases of the sexual cycle. Assessment should include a complete inventory of all drugs, including alcohol, that the individual is taking.*

The other major male dysfunctions, i.e., aversion toward sex or inhibited sexual desire and early or retarded ejaculation, are less commonly associated with physical factors. In most cases, the sexual problem stems from conflicts regarding sexuality, developmental inhibitions, and/or unfortunate conditioning of maladaptive behavior (e.g., learning to ejaculate quickly by virtue of having one's early sexual experiences occur in environments where speed rather than pleasure was reinforcing). As in women, the major etiological agents in causing and maintaining these problems include fear, guilt, and anxiety.

RELATIONSHIPS: STRENGTHS AND WEAKNESSES

Couples who are having conflict in their relationship will often begin to experience sexual difficulties: loss of sexual interest, difficulty with arousal or erection, or problems achieving orgasm. Similarly, the presence of sexual problems often creates tensions in what may have been a viable and compatible relationship. Therefore, the couple's relationship should be assessed in terms of conflict and compatibility.

---

*A useful appendix that describes the effect of various drugs on sexual functioning may be found in *Disorders of sexual desire* (Kaplan, 1979). A more complete description of the effect of various medications on sexuality is in *Textbook of sexual medicine* (Kolodny, Masters, & Johnson, 1979).

Behavior During Interviews

The couples' behavior during the assessment interview is an important behavior sample. How close or far apart couples sit during the interview may provide clues as to the degree of warmth existing between them. The amount of touching the couple does when talking, the facial expressions or grimaces that are made during problem description, and the degree of attentiveness and respect paid to each other provide tentative indications about the state of the relationship.

For instance, if the husband softly groans and raises his eyes to the ceiling as his wife complains of his lack of personal hygiene, he is conveying both exasperation with the wife and disagreement and impatience with her complaints. When observing such body messages, the interviewer may comment on it: "I notice you groaned when your wife said that. I wonder what you're thinking?" Doing so permits further discussion of exactly what constitutes the conflict.

In addition to the couple's non-verbal behavior, certain important parameters of the relationship must be assessed in order to plan treatment interventions.

Communication.   Can this couple talk about conflictual as well as non-conflictual topics? Do they talk to each other in a way that conveys respect and empathy or do they display hostility and sarcasm? Do they hear each other out, or do they constantly interrupt each other? Do they spend sufficient time alone together, or are there constant distractions to any real sharing? Are they each satisfied with the quality of communication in their relationship?

Commitment.   Is this couple committed to remaining together, or are they seeking counseling as a last-ditch attempt to save a floundering relationship? Is one partner committed while the other is privately planning an exit from the relationship?

Conflict management.   What areas of conflict exist for the couple? How is conflict resolved? Does this couple repeat the same argument, or can they resolve problematic issues?

Relationship history.   What is the shared history of this couple? Have there been long periods of harmony and companionship, or has the relationship always been punctuated by conflict and stress? Has there been outside sexual involvement by either of the partners? If so, what were the consequences? Is it current?

The clinician must also assess such variables as the power conflicts, and the degrees of trust, dependency, and intimacy in the relationship. Assessment may suggest that individual or relationship counseling must precede or be concomitant with sex therapy.

Case Study

A young couple requested sex counseling because of the wife's complaint that she had lost all interest in sex. She explained that she had always enjoyed sex until the birth of her baby, who was now 10 months old. He had been born with a defective heart valve and required considerable medical and parental attention. He was irritable, slept poorly, and was a source of worry for both the parents. The wife described herself as an outgoing, sociable person who found herself angry at the strange new role she was living, that of a home-bound wife and mother. Her husband was supportive and loving toward her, and expressed much sympathy and understanding for her position. He was disappointed at her sexual rejection, since he found her appealing and desirable, yet he was willing to accommodate to her current needs. She viewed him as a "Casper Milktoast," and spoke disparagingly of him and of her feelings toward him. After three assessment sessions, it was apparent that the wife's loss of sexual interest had more to do with her current life situation and with unresolved issues in the couples' relationship than any intrinsic sexual conflict. She was angry and bitter about having a "defective" child, blamed her husband for the baby's heart ailment, and felt dissatisfied with the rewards of being a wife and mother. Relationship therapy seemed the best place to start with this couple.

COGNITIVE ASSESSMENT

Humans are thinking animals; cognitive beliefs, expectations, and mediational processes critically influence and guide our sexual behavior. Ellis (1962, 1975) has repeatedly emphasized the catastrophic consequences the self-injunctions "can, must, and should" have on sexual behavior. Masters and Johnson (1970) elaborated on the negative impact that performance demands place on sexual arousal. Sexual belief systems are idiosyncratic; each person's collection of facts and fictions about sex have a considerable impact on what that person is willing to "do" sexually, as well as on how one "does it," and the resulting satisfaction or dissatisfaction. The woman who believes that swallowing semen is perverse and physically harmful is likely to gag during fellatio, while her neighbor who believes that semen is loaded with protein and good for the complexion is likely to enthusiastically engage in oral sex.

Zilbergeld (1978) has highlighted several of the devastating sexual myths that many males endorse. These include the following injunctions:

1. Men should not have, or at least not express, certain feelings. (These feelings include feelings of vulnerability, fear, sadness, and tenderness.)
2. In sex, as elsewhere, it's performance that counts. (The insidious emphasis on goals rather than process.)
3. The man must assume charge of and orchestrate sex. (The sheer responsibility that this imposes on men can be disastrous.)
4. A man always wants, and is always ready to have, sex. (The ever-ready model of male sexuality that ignores male right to say "no," to feel sexual disinterest, or to be "just plain pooped.")

5. All physical contact must lead to sex. (The belief that sensuality is less important and less respectable than genital sex.)
6. Sex equals intercourse (The overly narrow view of what constitutes "real" sexuality.)
7. Sex requires an erection (This relates to myths 5 and 6.)

These male myths are mirrored by a whole collection of beliefs that affect female sexuality.

1. "Sexy" is how you look, not who you are or what you do.
2. A beautiful body is all it takes to feel sexually confident.
3. Being outspoken about one's sexual preferences is certain to threaten or "turn off" men.
4. Love is the only justification for engaging in sex.
5. It is up to the man to direct sexual interaction; it's better to be passive than active.
6. Only men masturbate.
7. Knowledge about sex destroys its mystery and spontaneity; good sex "just" happens.

And finally, a myth both genders believe: With love and good will, all sexual problems can be overcome.

Assessment of an individual's cognitive beliefs may be accomplished in many ways: through questionnaires, true–false "quizzes" about sex, even reactions to films and tapes. Simple interviewing though, usually reveals an individual's governing beliefs and expectations about sex.

Case Study

A 54-year-old divorced man consulted a sex therapist because of his recent inability to sustain an erection. Although he had been troubled by early ejaculation during the 25 years of his first marriage, he had never experienced erectile failure. This new symptom enormously distressed him. It was especially unnerving since he had recently met and fallen in love with a warm, sympathetic woman with whom he felt comfortable and whom he was thinking of marrying. During the evaluation interviews, several assumptions emerged which appeared to exert a damaging effect on his sexual functioning. He indicated that he was "already over the hill" in age, so what could you expect anyway? He believed that self-stimulation at any time was immature and prohibitive, even during those periods when he did not have access to a partner. Further, he felt that he should attempt intercourse every time his new girlfriend indicated "interest," since "she expected it."

Clarifying some of these erroneous beliefs did not eliminate this patient's erectile problem, but it did relieve some of his performance anxiety and permitted a more relaxed approach to sex.

SEXUAL SCRIPT ASSESSMENT

In assessing the sexual repertoire of a patient or couple, investigation of the specific sexual "script" adhered to is invaluable. The sexual script consists of covert cognitive plans that guide sexual action and serve as a standard of performance in sex, and the actual sexual behavior that occurs during a sexual encounter (Gagnon, 1973; Rosen et al., 1979). In script analysis, the interviewer identifies the *who, what, when, where,* and *why* of the patient's sexual encounters, permitting a better understanding of the patient's motivations for sex, the meanings attached to sex, and the behavioral sequences engaged in. Script assessment includes attention to several parameters.

1. Complexity—both the range and diversity of overt sexual behaviors that comprise the script, as well as the covert intentions, motivations, and cognitions of the participants.
2. Rigidity—the predictability or degree of routinization in the time, place, or actions of the participants. The script may be invariant in certain respects (e.g., the same partners are always involved), but relatively flexible with respect to the setting, sequence, or actions.
3. Conventionality—is the script conventional (that is, in conformity with general social values), or unconventional (includes activities society or the law finds unacceptable, e.g., sex with children)?
4. Competence or adequacy of the script—refers to the degree to which the script meets the sexual and emotional needs of the partners.

Script assessment may be accomplished either through the interview or questionnaire (Rosen et al., 1980). The patient is typically asked to describe the total sexual encounter, from initiation to termination, providing detailed and specific information on the who, what, where, when, and why of their sexual interaction. If the assessment involves a couple, each individual is asked to describe in writing two scripts, i.e., the typical sexual script, and their ideal sexual script, or what they would like to have occur during sex. The partners then compare scripts: Do they agree on what typically occurs? How close or discrepant are their ideal sexual scripts? Such material provides valuable information for understanding sexual dissatisfaction, as well as providing a jumping off place for script rewriting.

Case Study

A middle-aged couple entered sex therapy because of the wife's sexual disinterest. In the last 2 years, the frequency of sexual encounters had dropped from once or twice a week to less than once a month. Both husband and wife said they could become aroused and orgasmic without difficulty, but the wife said she just wasn't "in the mood" for sex. Script assessment provided valuable clues as to the cause of the difficulty. In describing their actual sexual encounter, the couple agreed that the husband initiated sex abou 90 percent of the time. He usually initiated sex in bed at about 11 PM. He would generally engage in some breast and genital caressing, and when his wife failed to rapidly respond with high levels of arousal, he tried to excite her through detailed description of his own sexual fantasies which involved having her dress up in sheer, sexy clothing, dance seductively with him, and then, have another woman join the two of them in their actual sexual contact. His fantasy included a close female friend or relative of his wife in sexual threesomes. His wife, hearing these fantasies, not only failed to become aroused, but became upset and angry with her husband. She responded either by passive submission to his sexual overtures in order to ''get it over with,'' or refused sex altogether. Her own ideal sexual script involved a congenial, shared time, after the children were asleep, with an opportunity to talk and touch in the living room before going to the bedroom. She preferred quiet lighting and soft music, with considerable sensual foreplay prior to intercourse. She disliked any talking during sex but was responsive to gentle body massage. Helping this couple negotiate a sexual script that was agreeable to both of them resulted in a return to their former frequency of sexual activity.

SPECIALIZED ASSESSMENT METHODS

Psychophysiological Assessment

Psychophysiological assessment, involving such physiological measures as heart rate, blood pressure, temperature, muscle tension, skin conductance, and penile or vaginal vasocongestion is useful in the determination of erotic preferences and sexual arousal. Using penile strain gauge assessment, heterosexuals have been discriminated from homosexuals (Bancroft, 1971; Steinman et al., 1979). Arousal to pedophiliac stimuli has been assessed (Freund, 1965; 1965; 1967), and differential arousal to various violent and non-violent sexual stimuli has been measured (Abel et al., 1977; Malamuth and Cheek, 1979). Psychophysiological assessment is particularly important when working with individuals who display sexually deviant behavior, since objective measures of sexual arousal are more valid than self-report, and arousal to deviant stimuli can have potentially serious legal and social consequences.

In men, penile tumescence is readily assessed via mercury-filled or mechanical strain gauges that stretch with tumescence. To assess arousal or erotic preferences, film or slide presentations depicting various erotic activities or stimuli may be shown, and the patient is asked to rate his subjective feelings of arousal to the material at the same time the objective recording of erection is taking place. The correlation between the subjective and objective measures of arousal may thus be determined; if discrepancy exists, useful information is obtained for both the therapist and patient.

There are several ways of assessing sexual arousal in women. Vaginal vasocongestion can be reliably measured with a vaginal photoplethysmograph, a tampon-like acrylic tube that uses a photocell and light source to measure blood volume and pressure pulse changes in the vagina (Sintchak and Geer, 1975). Another measure of female sexual arousal uses surface temperature changes as the indicator of genital vasocongestion, by attaching a thermistor to a minor labium with a small clip (Henson et al., 1977). While many investigators fail to find a correlation between objective and subjective estimates of arousal (Geer et al., 1974; Wilson and Lawson, 1976; Heiman, 1977; Wincze et al., 1977), Henson and Rubin (1978) reported vaginal blood volume to be significantly correlated with subjective arousal in five of six subjects in whom subjective arousal was continuously monitored by changing the position of a lever. Wincze and coworkers (1976) also found lower levels of vaginal blood volume and pressure pulse in women reporting sexual disinterest.

Ongoing assessment of arousal may be useful in research designs when trying to teach women to recognize their own sexual arousal, or if one wants before-and-after measures of the effectiveness of sex therapy. Certainly when working with sexual deviants, objective assessment of sexual arousal is critical. For example, in one case (Rosen and Kopel, 1977, 1978), a homosexual transvestite who had been arrested and convicted several times reported that he was quite free from deviant arousal and was discharged from treatment after several months of therapy. Several months later, he was arrested for another episode, with more serious consequences than his earlier convictions. Obviously, ongoing psychophysiological assessment might have averted this patient's early termination from treatment and, possibly, his next offense.

Questionnaires

One of the most popular means of assessment is through the administration of sexual and marital relationship self-report questionnaires (Keefe, Kopel & Gordon, 1978). A host of such questionnaires are in common use (cf. Keefe et al., 1978) and are helpful for the assessment of the repertoire and frequency of various sexual behaviors, marital satisfaction, conflict areas in relationships, etc. Among the more useful instruments are the Locke and Wallace Marital Adjustment Test (Locke and Wallace, 1959); the Sexual Arousability Inventory (Hoon et al., 1976); the Sexual Interaction Inventory (LoPiccolo and Steger, 1974); and the Derogatis Sexual Functioning Inventory (Derogatis, 1976). (For a complete listing of measures commonly used in sexual assessment, see the 1979 issue of the *Journal of Sex and Marital Therapy.*)

Such "paper and pencil" self-report questionnaires and inventories permit rapid, systematic retrieval of a wide array of assessment material that patients might not otherwise volunteer or interviewers might neglect to investigate. For example, the Sexual Intake Inventory used at the Rutgers Medical School Sexual Counseling Service (New Jersey) invites patients to provide information about significant sexual trauma, such as rape or molestation. Such information is quite obviously relevant, and yet patients often fail to offer such information without direct questioning.

Behavioral Recording

During assessment as well as during treatment, patients can be asked to record behaviors that are of focal interest. For example, an individual who complains of "constant" intrusive imagery involving deviant sexual acts may be asked to record the daily frequency of such distracting images. Additionally, he or she may be asked to provide an A-B-C analysis of the behavior, that is to record the *a*ntecedents of the *b*ehavior (the deviant fantasy), and *c*onsequences of thinking about such material. Patients can also be asked to record the frequency and intensity of various sexual urges or behaviors, deviant or non-deviant. Such assessment provides a valuable baseline for determining change over time.

Audio/Video Taping

An assessment technique that is becoming more popular involves the use of video- or audio tape recording. Videotape recording of initial interviews helps pinpoint specific individual and couple interactions that may be dysfunctional. Videotapes are especially relevant to the assesment of individuals requesting gender reassignment, since they provide valuable data on the ease, naturalness, and authenticity the patient displays with cross-gender motor, postural, and vocal behavior.

Audio tapes can be helpful in analyzing a couple's communication and conflict resolution skills. For instance, if a couple complains they can never agree on when or how often to have sex, the interviewer can ask them to discuss the issue at home while a tape recorder is playing. They are asked to bring the tape to the next session so that their particular negotiation problem can be identified.

STATE OF THE ART

Sex therapy as a specialized discipline has a brief history. It is only since the 1970s that short-term, directive approaches to sexual dysfunction have gained popularity and extensive professional attention. In short-term therapy, rapid but accurate assessment is critical, since the clinician does not have the luxury of time to permit the evaluation of the full clinical and medical picture, but rather must promptly integrate material from diverse sources and develop a viable treatment plan.

Despite the decade's tremendous strides, little is understood about the causal factors and antecedent events of sexual problems (Pervin and Leiblum, 1980). Many people with problematic sex histories have no sexual difficulties, while others with seemingly positive (i.e., nonproblematic) family and developmental backgrounds develop problems. It is often perplexing to discern which of many developmental events significantly contributed to the emergence of a problem. At times, no precipitant seems obvious. Consequently, assessment in sex therapy must rely less on accurately formulating the "right" explanation for the present problem and more on assessing the current conditions that maintain the difficulty. Whether a conflictual marriage caused the sexual problem, or the sexual problem caused the marital stress, is not at question. What is *now* important is the current degree of relationship distress, and how that may be maintaining the current dysfunction.

Furthermore, assessment in sex therapy must cover many areas of functioning and must include various assessment approaches. While the most popular and useful assessment technique remains the clinical interview, other sources of information are important. Medical evaluation, endocrinological assessment, NPT, psychophysiological assessment, "paper and pencil" questionnaires, and behavioral records all play a role in comprehensive assessment. Assessment for research purposes and for increasing knowledge is broader in focus than what one needs for planning treatment. Nevertheless, multidimensional assessment is always useful and usually justifies itself in the long run.

In cases involving sexual deviation, psychophysiological assessment during and following treatment is necessary. Where differential diagnosis for erectile dysfunction is an issue, nocturnal penile tumescence is indicated. Where couple communication is poor, audio and videotape recordings can add valuable data. Flexibility both in what is assessed and how assessment is accomplished marks the current approach to assessment in sex therapy.

While sex therapy was initially viewed as a panacea for a variety of chronic sexual problems, greater humility exists today. We know very little about the causes of sexual problems, about why one person develops a problem with premature ejaculation and another with erectile failure, why one woman is anorgasmic and another has arousal difficulties. Similarly, our assessment methods are in a state of flux. We recognize the importance of a broad-spectrum approach to assessment with utilization of various assessment methods and coverage of various areas of functioning. Nevertheless, we have a long way to go, both in determining how to integrate the material we collect so that a sensible treatment plan may be devised, and how to utilize assessment in an ongoing fashion, so that different approaches can be adopted when treatment runs into difficulty. Assessment in sex therapy never stops.

REFERENCES

Abel, G. G., Barlow, D. H., Blanchard, E., & Guild, D. The components of rapists' sexual arousal. *Archives of General Psychiatry*, 1977, *34*, 395–403.

Bancroft, J. The application of psychophysiological measures to the assessment-modification of sexual behavior. *Behaviour, Research and Therapy*, 1971, *8*, 119–130.

Burnap, D., & Golden, J. Sexual problems in medical practice. *Medical Education*, 1967, *42*, 673–680.

Derogatis, L. R. Psychological assessment of the sexual disabilities. In J. K. Meyer (Ed.), *The clinical management of sexual disorders*. Baltimore, Maryland: Williams & Wilkins Co., 1976.

Ellis, A. The rational-emotive approach to sex therapy. *Counseling Psychologist*, 1975, *5*, 14–21.

Ellis, A. *Reason and emotion in psychotherapy*. New York: Lyle Stuart, 1962.

Fisher, C., Gross, J., & Zuch, J. Cycle of penile erection with dreaming (REM) sleep. *Archives of General Psychiatry*, 1965, *12*, 27–45.

Fordney, D. S. Dyspareunia and vaginismus. *Clinical Obstetrics and Gynecology*, 1978, *21*, 205–221.

Frank, E., Anderson, C., & Rubinstein, D. Frequency of sexual dysfunction in "normal" couples. *New England Journal of Medicine*, 1978, *299*, 111–115.

Freund, K. Diagnosing heterosexual pedophilia by means of a test for sexual interest. *Behavior Research and Therapy*, 1965, *3*, 229–234.

Freund, K. Diagnosing homo- and heterosexuality and erotic age preferences by means of a psychophysiological test. *Behavior Research and Therapy*, 1967, *5*, 209–228.

Freund, K. A laboratory method for diagnosing predominance of homo- and hetero-erotic interests in the male. *Behavior Research and Therapy*, 1965, *1*, 85–93.

Gagnon, J. H. Scripts and the coordination of sexual conduct. In J. K. Cole & R. Dienstbier, *Nebraska Symposium of Motivation* Lincoln Nebraska: University of Nebraska Press, 1973.

Geer, J., Morokoff, P., & Greenwood, P. Sexual arousal in women: The development of a measurement device for vaginal blood volume. *Archives of Sexual Behavior*, 1974, *3*, 559–564.

Heiman, J. R. A psychophysiological exploration of sexual arousal patterns in females and males. *Psychophysiology*, 1977, *14*, 266–274.

Henson, D. E., & Rubin, H. B. A comparison of two objective measures of sexual arousal in women. *Behavior Research Therapy*, 1978, *16*, 143–151.

Henson, D. E., Rubin, H. B., Henson, C., & Williams, J. R. Temperature change of the labia minora as an objective measure of human female eroticism. *Journal of Behavior Therapy and Experimental Psychiatry*, 1977, *8*, 401–410.

Hoon, E. F., Hoon, P. W., & Wincze, J. The SAI: An inventory for the measurement of female sexual arousal. *Archives of Sexual Behavior*, 1976, *5*, 209–215.

Kaplan, H. *Disorders of sexual desire*. New York: Brunner/Mazel, 1979.

Karacan, I. Advances in the psychophysiological evaluation of male erectile impotence. In J. LoPiccolo, & L. Lopiccolo (Eds.), *Handbook of sex therapy*. New York: Plenum Press, 1978.

Karacan, I. A simple and inexpensive transducer for quantitative measurements of penile erection during sleep. *Behavior Research Methods and Instrumentation*, 1969, *1*, 251–252.

Kolodny, R., Masters, W., Johnson, V. *Textbook of sexual medicine*. Boston: Little, Brown & Co., 1979.

Locke, J. H., & Wallace, K. M. Short marital adjustment and prediction tests: Their reliability and validity. *Marriage and Family Living*, 1959, *21*, 251–255.

LoPiccolo, J., & Steger, J. C. The sexual interaction inventory: A new instrument for assessment of sexual dysfunction. *Archives of Sexual Behavior,* 1974, *3,* 585–595.

Malamuth, N. M., & Cheek, J. U. *Penile tumescence and perceptual response to rape as a function of victim's perceived reactions.* Paper presented at the Annual Meeting of the Canadian Psychological Association, Quebec City, 1979.

Masters, W. H., & Johnson, V. E. *Human sexual inadequacy.* Boston: Little, Brown & Co., 1970.

Pervin, L. A., & Leiblum, S. R. Conclusion: Overview of some critical issues in the evaluation and treatment of sexual dysfunctions. In S. R. Leiblum, & L. A. Pervin (Eds.), *Principles and practice of sex therapy.* New York: Guilford Press, 1980.

Rosen, R. C., & Kopel, S. A. Penile plethysmography and biofeedback in the treatment of a transvestite-exhibitionist. *Journal of Consulting and Clinical Psychology,* 1977, *45,* 900–916.

Rosen, R. C., & Kopel, S. A. Role of penile tumescence measurement in the behavioral treatment of sexual deviation: Issues of validity. *Journal of Consulting and Clinical Psychology,* 1978, *46,* 1519–1521.

Rosen, R. C., Leiblum, S. R., & Gagnon, J. H. *Sexual scripts: Assessment and modification in sex therapy.* Paper presented at the 4th Annual Meeting of the Society for Sex Therapy and Research, Philadelphia, 1979.

Rosen, R. C., Leiblum, S. R., & Weis, D. Sexual script questionnaire. Unpublished research instrument, 1980.

Sintchak, F., & Geer, J. A. A vaginal photoplethysmography system. *Psychophysiology,* 1975, *12,* 113–115.

Spark, R., White, R., & Connolly, P. Impotence is not always psychogenic: Newer insights into hypothalamic-pituitary-gonal dysfunction. *Journal of the American Medical Association,* 1980, *243,* 750–755.

Steinman, D. L., Sakheim, D. K., Wincze, J. P., & Barlow, D. H. *A psychophysiological investigation of sexual responding in heterosexual males and females and homosexual males.* Paper presented at the Annual Convention of the Association for the Advancement of Behavior Therapy, San Francisco, 1979.

Wilson, G. T., & Lawson, D. M. Effects of alcohol on sexual arousal in women. *Journal of Abnormal Psychology,* 1976, *85,* 489–497.

Wincze, V., Hoon, E., Hoon, P. A comparison of the physiological responsibility of normal and sexually dysfunctional women during exposure to erotic stimulus. *Journal of Psychosomatic Research,* 1976, *20,* 44–50.

Wincze, J. P., Hoon, P., Hoon, E. F. Sexual arousal in women: A comparison of cognitive and physiological responses by continuous measurement. *Archives of Sexual Behavior,* 1977, *6,* 121–133.

Zilbergeld, B. *Male sexuality.* New York: Bantam Books, 1978.

Elaine Crovitz

14

Assessment of Gender Dysphoria

Interest in transsexuals has burgeoned since Christine Jorgenson's conversion from male to female in the early 1950s and, more recently, since the conversion of Renée Richards. By contrast, the medical, scientific, and psychological literature on transsexualism is meager, as the "condition" named by Cauldwell in 1949 was rarely recognized as a distinguishable entity before Benjamin's paper in 1953 (Benjamin, 1953). Since that time, gender identity or gender dysphoria clinics and programs have been created at large university hospitals throughout the United States. (In addition, private clinics exist for transsexual diagnosis and treatment.) The incidence and prevalence of transsexualism are matters of guess-work, ranging from 1 person in 50,000, or 4,300 transsexuals in the United States, to 1 in 10,000 (Leff, 1977). The number of patients with this condition is small compared to those with other illnesses and abnormalities; attempts to define the term or condition have either led to clinical disagreement (Kubie and Mackie, 1966), or abandonment of the concept of transsexualism. An argument has been made that "transsexualism" be restricted as a diagnosis to those who have received sex reassignment surgery (Meyer, 1973), while others propose that "gender dysphoria syndrome" replace the classification of transsexualism (Fisk, 1973; Lothstein, 1977). Some clinicians believe that a population of "pure" transsexuals exists, for whom sex reassignment surgery is indicated (Benjamin, 1966; Stoller, 1968; 1970–1971; Person and Ovesey, 1974a,b). Other clinicians (Lothstein, 1977) find that patients requesting sex-conversion surgery constitute a diverse group of individuals, suffering from a broad range of gender identity disorders. The common plea of such patients is that they have the attitudes, thoughts, and feelings of one sex, while they possess the body of the other. According to Meyer (1973; 1974), patients desiring sex reassignment surgery reflect the following charac-

Acknowledgment is due Dr. John Rhoads of Duke University, Department of Psychiatry, for design of a standardized interview for evaluation of patients with gender dysphoria.

teristics: (1) an inability to function in the anatomically congruent sex role, (2) a belief that improvement will occur with role reversal, and (3) homoerotic interest and heterosexual inhibition.

The diagnosis of transsexualism or gender dysphoria syndrome is a phenomenon of the past thirty years. In making such a diagnosis the practitioner is faced with conceptual difficulties arising from diverse theoretical positions regarding the etiology and disturbance of gender identity. Are individuals requesting sex-conversion surgery transsexuals, transvestites, or homosexuals? Are they deluded, and suffering from a monosymptomatic psychotic state? Is the problem of gender dysphoria mental or genital? Is its etiology psychic or somatic? Clinicians disagree about why some adults are convinced that the gender-identity success of the fetuses they once were was a mistake, and thus there is no concensus on how to help patients with gender dysphoria. Treatments range across psychotherapy, behavior therapy, sex-conversion surgery, to no treatment at all. However, suicide and self-mutilation are real risks to frustrated and despairing patients, and gender dysphoria can make a shambles of family life. It is not known how many untreated, perhaps undiagnosed gender-dysphoric individuals have taken their own lives, nor how many have performed self-mutilation. Suicidal attempts and self-mutilation of genitalia have been reported by clinicians; the reports often are the basis for referral to gender identity clinics or to psychiatrists, psychologists, and social workers.

FACTORS THAT DETERMINE GENDER IDENTITY

Four factors have been identified as affecting the development of gender identity: *genetics, hormone levels, genital anatomy,* and *socialization.* Normally, each of these factors is sequentially expressed: i.e., genetics determines hormone levels, hormone levels determine genital anatomy, and genital anatomy determines sexual identity. Sexual identity, based on the anatomy of the external genitalia, is established at birth and is the criterion by which society denotes an individual to be male or female.

Once sexual identity is extablished, parents and others shape the child's behavior through a variety of casual and unplanned learnings toward behaviors considered appropriate for the specific sex. Expectations for sex roles begin immediately at birth. In an ingenious experiment, Rubin and coworkers (1974), demonstrated that sex-typing and sex-role socialization have already begun by birth. Thirty pairs of primiparous parents, 15 with sons and 15 with daughters, were interviewed within the first 24 hours post-partum. Although male and female infants did not significantly differ in birth length, weight, or Apgar scores,* daughters were significantly more likely than sons to be described as little, beautiful,

---

*Apgar score is a numerical expression of the condition of a newborn infant 60 seconds after birth. It is the sum of points acquired on assessment of the heart rate, respiratory effort, muscle tone, reflex irritability, and color.

cute, pretty, and as resembling their mothers. Fathers made more extreme and stereotyped rating judgments of their newborns than did mothers. These attitudes set the stage for differential treatment of boys and girls. Parental treatment of children based upon the child's gender is known as *sex of rearing*.

Sex of rearing usually influences the inner image the child develops of itself as male or female. This inner image, or *gender identity*, seems to be formed during the first 18 to 36 months of life. Gender identity, an individual's sense of maleness or femaleness, is thus a fundamental psychological phenomenon. As gender identity is established, the child enacts a sexual role. Recent evidence suggests that sex-role learning is accomplished through powerful and deep-seated pressures which force conformity: Males are expected to exhibit, and are taught, instrumental, aggressive, work, and task-oriented behaviors based on the ability to compete, and to be strong, dominant and independent. Females are expected to perform, and to learn, nurturant, supportive, and care-taking functions. The sexual role is the part one plays in society as a male or female, and is usually in accord with gender identity. Thus, *sexual identity* is the gender that society imposes on a person, while *gender identity* is the gender a person accepts as his or her own. While sex and gender seem to be synonymous, the two realms are not inevitably bound together in a one-to-one relationship. Each may go its independent way: a male transsexual, for example, may act the role of a man while feeling like a woman. Biological sex does not completely determine gender identity; gender identity can be viewed as a system that may emerge out of assigned sex and sex-role learning. Gender identity usually relates to biologic sex and sex-role definitions, but depends upon neither. Gender identity and sex-role performance have unique individual properties, and reflect the malleability of human behavior.

A genetic male with male sex hormones may be born with the external genital anatomy of a female, be sexually identified as female, and raised to be a woman. Such a woman may not understand why she cannot conceive unless she goes to a fertility clinic, where she might learn that she is genetically and hormonally a male, with internal male organs. Conversely, a genetic male with male sex hormones, internal male organs, and the external genital anatomy of a male may be raised as a male, but become convinced of belonging to the female sex and experience a torment in inhabitating "the wrong body."

Boys born without penises do not doubt they are males if their parents also believe this without question; similarly, girls who are genetically, anatomically, and physiologically normal except for being born without a vagina do not have gender-identity disturbances if parental attitudes are certain with regard to the femaleness (Stoller, 1972). Expression of XY genetic sex may be interrupted after birth by surgical removal of the testes and penis (e.g., where the penis is accidentally destroyed during circumcision or where the penis is considered too small to grow and function as a phallus). With the construction of a functional vagina in infancy, the children are raised as females, treated at puberty with female sex hormones, and often marry, report orgasm, and adopt children (Money and Erhardt, 1972).

Disorders in normal development of genetic XX females can arise from the presence of inappropriate androgen levels in utero. Excess adrenal androgens will make external genitalia ambiguous or masculinized. This disorder, *congenital adrenal hyperplasia,* is treated with cortisone and corrective surgery. Many patients have been sexually identified and reared as females and develop female gender identities. There are genetic XX females, with female sex hormones, internal female organs, and external female genitalia, who are reared as females but develop a sincere belief that they are a member of the opposite sex. Female transsexuals, just as male transsexuals, seek hormonal and surgical sex reassignment.

Males seeking sex reassignment outnumber females by almost six to one, although figures range from eight-to-one to three-to-one (Ihlenfeld). The fact that fewer females make requests for sex transformation surgery has been variously interpreted: The development of maleness has been viewed, from a biological point of view, as a complex process, a continuing struggle against a basic trend toward femaleness. Thus biological anomalies along the route to maleness may be greater. Another suggested reason for the lower frequency of female transsexuals may be that females can take on part of the opposite sex's societal role with greater ease and with less social disruption than can the male transsexual (Rubin et al., 1974). "Tomboyishness" in women is more easily accepted by society than "sissy" behavior in men. Yet another hypothesis is that information regarding operative procedures on female transsexuals rarely appears in the literature; indeed, such operative procedures are not easily accomplished and are fraught with hazards (Hopes, 1969). Phalloplasty, the corrective surgery that female-to-male transsexuals seek, is far from perfected. In every attempt, surgeons must compromise between fashioning a pseudopenis long enough to look adequate and short enough to permit urinary voiding standing up; sensation and erectility generally elude surgical skills. An artificial vagina can become part of a patient's body image, but a neopenis typically remains an alien appendage, nonnormal in appearance and nonfunctional.

TRANSVESTITES, HOMOSEXUALS, AND TRANSSEXUALS

Transvestites, effeminate homosexuals and "queens," and male transsexuals may share a common overt behavior, e.g., putting on women's clothes, or a common fantasy, e.g., conscious or unconscious desires for homosexual relations. While differences in gender identity have been identified, they are by no means agreed upon by clinicians. Since effeminate homosexuals have strong identifications with certain aspects of femininity, many professionals regard tranvestism and transsexualism as variants of homosexuality. Transvestism is fetishistic, intermittent cross-dressing as a female by a biologically normal male who does not usually question that he is a male—that is, the possessor of a penis. Transvestites usually stress that they prefer sexual relations with women and are not effeminate when not dressed as a woman. Some transvestites are gratified by intermittently dressing and passing as a woman, while other transvestites consider themselves to be males who get sexually excited by women's garments. Transvestism as seen in males is practically unknown in females. Many effeminate homosexuals (queens) question whether they are transsexual or homosexuals: at times they question whether they possess the feelings, attitudes, desires, interests, and traits of females and have a simultaneous preference for same-sex individuals as sexual partners. Usually, effeminate homosexuals accept the fact that they possess a penis. The male transsexual typically seeks sex-change surgery so as to physically alter his body to correspond to an unalterable state of mind, consciously and unconsciously feeling certain of belonging to the opposite, female, sex.

It is around the differences in gender identity, manifested by the overwhelming desire to transform the external genitalia, that the differentiations between transvestism, effeminate homosexuality, and transsexualism can be made. Usually, the male transsexual is disgusted and deeply distressed by possessing a penis, and horrified by erections. Another feature differentiating among these conditions is sexual object choice. The transvestite prides himself on his heterosexuality, the effeminate homosexual who has homosexual relations recognizes them as homosexual, whereas male transsexuals say their sexual experiences with same-sex are *not* homosexual, since they occur between a male and female trapped in a male body (or vice versa, for female transsexuals). Male transsexuals often report daily fantasies of having become a normal woman who is married to a normal man and usually resent and object to the label homosexual. Many male transsexuals not only fantasize about having a body that appears completely female, but wish to have internal organs changed in order to have functioning ovaries and uterus, and ultimately, to bear a child. Similarly, female transsexuals imagine themselves able to become normal men, to marry normal women, and to acquire not only a penis but the capacity to impregnate. Female transsexuals are digusted by their breasts and genitalia and are made miserable by menstruation. Removal of offending organs of transsexuals causes no regret in statements made in the assessment procedure.

The differences among individuals suffering from gender identity dysphoria are easier to outline on paper than to assess in a clinical situation. Transvestites, ashamed of their compulsive cross-dressing behavior, often believe that they can assuage guilt and shame by being diagnosed as "transsexual," and they present themselves to professionals with statements which suggest gender-identity crises. Effeminate homosexuals often appear in clinics, hospitals, and professional offices with grave confusion over gender identity and sex-role performance; they often believe they would be more acceptable in society as transsexuals, but tend to worry over sexual rejection by males if they become females.

ETIOLOGY OF GENDER DYSPHORIA

Several schools of thought exist in the etiology of gender dysphoria. They range from purely psychosocial to the extreme of purely biological, and reflect most often hunches as to the source(s) of explanation rather than empirically verified data which can explain the broad range of gender problems. Erhardt maintains that psychosocial factors, mainly sex at rearing, are the primary determinants of gender identity and gender dysphoria (Money and Erhardt, 1972). Her coworker, John Money, has altered a purely psychosocial view to one in which "it takes a specifically programmed protoplasm subjected to a special life circumstances to produce a transsexual" (Leff, 1977). Thus, any espousal of either nature or nurture as the cause of transsexualism is seen by Money as a futile dichotomy. Stoller (1968a) offers a psychoanalytic interpretation, seeing the dissonance of anatomic sex and psychosocial gender as caused by a disturbance in the mother–child bond early in life. The explanation portrays a depressed mother who binds her son too closely to her in a symbiotic relationship. This relationship evolves in the absence of an effective father figure. A similar psychoanalytical explanation suggests an early childhood defect in separation and individuation from the mother.

Another school, emphasizing biological contributions proposed by Imperato and coworkers (1979), believes that gender identity is largely a function of hormone levels. In the Dominican Republic, endocrinologists have identified "guevedoces," literally, penis-at-twelve youngsters, suffering from male pseudohermaphroditism. The children failed to form a hormone in utero, DHT, from testosterone as normally occurs in males, so that the external genitalia fail to be fully masculinized. They are born with a clitoris-like phallus with no urethral opening, a labial-like bifid scrotum, a urogenital sinus with blind vaginal pouch, and bilateral inguinal or labial testes. At about 12 years of age, these children experience the normal burst of testosterone secretion—the enlarged clitoris grows to a small penis, the testes descend, muscle mass increases markedly, and the voice deepens. Some of these "men" have erections and sexual intercourse. Despite their upbringing as "girls," researchers indicate that they have unequivocally male psychosocial orientation and gender identity as adults, suggesting that testosterone secreted at puberty alters not only anatomy and physiology but gender identity as well. Money and Erhardt (1972) believe that these children with ambiguous genital anatomy had ambiguous gender identification as well. Indeed, their name, "guevedoces," suggests that these children were expected to undergo this change by family and others in their society. This bizarre genetic defect with its drastic deficiency of an enzyme that converts testosterone to DHT has led some who believe the fundamental cause of gender problems to be biological to believe that the fruitful approach to understanding gender identity and dysphoria lies in hormonal studies. No one has yet identified biological abnormalities such as endocrine or central nervous system mechanisms which might influence cross-gender identity, with the exception of Imperato et al. (1979), whose work has been met with criticism. There is no acceptable evidence of any genetic, constitutional, or biochemical abnormality amongst those individuals who label themselves as transsexual. On the other hand, there is no agreement upon psychosocial factors or mechanisms which lead to transsexualism. Disturbed mother–child relationships (as symbiotic ties or replacement of a husband with a son in maternal affections), and family dynamics (as unconscious exchange of a daughter for a defective son, to be reared as a "father's son") in infancy are postulated as causes based upon reconstruction in adulthood of early experiences of patients (Stoller, 1968). Whatever the cause or causes, the phenomenon of gender dysphoria exists, and troubled individuals seek genital reversal.

ASSESSMENT STRATEGIES

The ability to evaluate which patients, by virtue of their gender identification, previous life experience, physical appearance, and psychological status can be expected to make a satisfactory postoperative adjustment rather than experience postoperative disappointment, depression, and continued inability to assimilate into society remains a considerable challenge. The strategy in assessment involves evaluating the patient's reality-testing abilities, the motivation for sex reassignment, the extent to which the individual can demonstrate the capacity to "pass" in society and to support himself or herself in the desired sexual role, and the degree to which life expectations after reassignment appear realistic. To what extent the individual is emotionally stable outside the area of gender identity must be considered, as well as the choice of treatment, e.g., psychological, behavioral, or surgical therapy.

The current availability of gonadal hormones and refinement of surgical techniques have made it partly possible to realize the fantasies and aspirations of individuals with gender dysphoria, and have brought about an increased demand for sex reassignment. Perplexing questions beyond mere strategies for assessment and diagnosis exist, such as the patient's right to self-determination and the peculiarity that the diagnosis and treatment of transsexualism is often seen by patients as being determined by themselves, not by the professionals they are consulting. Assessment is carried out in a clinical situation where many patients are determined to have professionals affirm their self-diagnosis of transsexualism, and patients may become irritated or provoked by the necessity for a concurring opinion by staff in their attempts to gain sex reassignment.

The extent to which the individual can demonstrate his or her capacity to "pass" in society in the desired sex role can be assessed by *observation of appearance*. To this end in the initial interview, general appearance, gait and gestures, hair, make-up (for male transsexuals), clothing, and speech are noted. Some individuals, as a result of past experience in assuming the desired sex role or a striking physical resemblance to the opposite sex, are easily accepted by others in the coveted sex role. However, other individuals appear so similar to the stereotype of the gender they wish to escape that attempts, even with hormonal treatment and surgery, will not suffice to aid them in being accepted in the desired sex role in society.

An indepth clinical interview is used to obtain a comprehensive picture of the patient's personality. The examiner is particularly interested in obtaining information on the psychosexual development of the patient, early experiences and his or her reaction to them, the structure of the patient's family, and the patient's feelings toward key family members. Further knowledge is sought of emotional difficulties experienced, and their precipitating circumstances; the patient's objectives, goals, and ideals; defensive maneuvers the patient prefers; and sexual attitudes, thoughts, conflicts, and experiences. Biographical information can initiate the interview; age of patient, birthplace, residences while growing up, religion, parental education, occupations, health, personalities, and relationships to the patient are important, as well as the ages, religion, and attitude(s) toward life of the parents. The relationship between the parents can be explored, as well as the issue of whether the patient was a wanted child and, if so, which sex was desired and by whom. The composition of the family of origin can be explored, including siblings and their relationship to the patient. A vocational history, military history, criminal history and drug-abuse history will provide information about the patient's stability (or lack of it), social adaptiveness or social deficiency, and degree of behavioral control.

A developmental history, including sleeping arrangements or habits, play habits, education, religion, and personal philosophy should be obtained. Of interest are preferences for playing with males or females, as well as preferred friends and games. Religious training and ethics, especially regarding surgery and sex-reassignment, should be obtained. A sexual history is extremely relevant in the assessment of gender dysphoria. Questions should address the following: early sexual knowledge, prepubertal activity, parental attitudes toward sex, sex education, puberty (when did it occur; what was the reaction to this event), masturbation and accompanying fantasies, dating patterns (if any), first sexual experience, and subsequent sexual experiences. Sexual experiences are to be dealt with in detail; types of sexual activity and emotions accompanying sexual experiences are discussed. Sexual preference is noted (preferred sex of partner), and past or present marriage(s). Cross-dressing experience should be elicited, including the first time, how it was accomplished, and present cross-dressing patterns.

The body image of the patient is significant in the assessment of transsexuals; many patients report that *self-image,* rather than libido, is the key motivation for seeking sex reassignment. Many transsexuals do not display strong sex drives but report strong motivation to possess a body which is integrated with their mental picture of themselves. Comcepts of breasts, genitals, hips, face, hair, and voice are critical body parts to those suffering from gender dysphoria. Pre- and expected postoperative thoughts and fantasies regarding body image should be explored, as well as general expectations from surgery. What does the patient envision surgery will accomplish, with respect to self-feelings and satisfaction, interpersonal relationships, vocational and social success? Another important consideration with regard to attitudes toward alteration of sex is parental attitudes, family views, and the existence of social support (either individual or group). Any dreams or daydreams which are repetitive or significant to the patient shed additional light upon internal motivations.

For clinical purposes, flexibility is one of the strengths of the interview method of assessment. The skillful practitioner can adapt a standardized interview to the variations found in patients with gender dysphoria. But for many patients who diagnose themselves as transsexuals and who view psychological assessment as a barrier to be overcome in seeking surgical sex change, the interview has important weaknesses. Individuals may either consciously or unconsciously withhold and distort significant personal information. To obtain the valid picture of relevant aspects of personality needed to diagnose gender dysphoria, objective psychological tests and projective techniques are used.

One objective test of personality, the Minnesota Multiphasic Personality Inventory (MMPI), serves the purpose of evaluating mental dysfunction by reflecting the type of psychiatric disorder present and the severity of the problem. A critical question to be answered early in the assessment of gender dysphoria is the presence or absence of psychosis, either in the form of a thought disorder or a serious affective disturbance which can produce delusions. Impaired reality-testing capacities and psychiatric disability unrelated to gender dysphoria problems can be screened with the utilization of the MMPI. If the MMPI and/or interview findings hint at personality disorganization of severe proportions behind a "good front," the Rorschach, a projective technique, can be used to assess major qualitative disturbances of thinking. Once assured that the request for sex reassignment does not reflect general disordered thinking or psychotic self-punitive delusional processes, extensive use of projective techniques are introduced to evaluate inner dynamics, i.e., motivations, conflicts, emotional balance, and relative degree of maturity in personality development. (Body image, relatively unfettered by verbal control, is tested by use of figure drawing techniques.) The patient's fantasies, past, present, and future, with regard to him- or herself and interpersonal relationships, are assessed in a sentence completion test and a fantasy stimulating test.

The Sacks Sentence Completion Test contains 60 incompleted sentences which the patient must complete. When an individual is put under pressure to respond with the first idea that occurs, he or she usually offers significant, uncensored material. When faced with the problem of completing or structuring an ambiguous situation, an individual's responses are considered to be more indicative of that individual's reactions and sentiments. Sentence completion test data content are categorized as follows:

1. Attitude toward mother
2. Attitude toward father
3. Attitude toward family unit
4. Attitude toward women
5. Attitude toward men
6. Attitude toward heterosexual relationships
7. Attitude toward friends and acquaintances
8. Attitude toward authority

9. Fears
10. Guilt feelings
11. Attitude toward own abilities
12. Attitude toward past
13. Attitude toward future

The Inquiry Test, a fantasy-stimulating test suggested by Dr. Paul A. Walker and extensively used with gender-dysphoric individuals solicits responses to a variety of unusual and dramatic conditions. Induced fantasy is highly suggestive of crucial motivations, goals, aspirations, conflicts, and other aspects of personality that may be difficult to discern in other overt behavior. Because many people seem to intuitively recognize that fantasy life is highly revealing, they are often hesitant to volunteer the content of dreams or daydreams. Induced fantasy can provide an illumination of wishes that the individual perceives as forbidden by others, forbidden by his or her own psychology or requiring expenditures of energy or skills that the individual believes he or she does not possess. Similarly, induced fantasy suggests inner ideas of how needs may be met, satisfied, or how the tension associated with needs may be reduced. The relationship between fantasy and reality, from bizarre to near-real, is significant in the assessment of gender dysphoria patients, as some may imagine that sex change will magically produce instant happiness and success, in contradistinction to interview verbalizations which are more constrained with regard to expectations.

Responses to the Figure Drawing Test can serve as a projection of the body image, crucial to the complaints of people with gender dysphoria. Individuals are asked to draw a person. If the first picture drawn is male, the individual is asked to draw a female, and vice-versa (i.e., if a female is drawn first, a male figure is requested). Additional figure drawings which may be solicited are: (1) ''draw yourself and a friend,'' (2) ''draw yourself and your family,'' (3) ''draw your ideal self,'' and (4) ''draw your ideal social self.'' The drawings are analyzed with regard to figure sequence (i.e., male or female drawn first); precision of form, and body parts omitted, distorted, or exaggerated. A comparison of figures is made, which reveals aspects of psychosexual attitudes. Does the gender-dysphoric patient first draw disputed gender or wished-for sex? Are the drawings reflective of verbalized lack of integrity of body and mind? Who is the friend drawn, and what is the nature of the relationship between the friend and the patient? Similarly, how does the patient ''fit in'' with the family drawn? Are the drawings projections of self-concept or of idealized self-concept? The patient's drawings and responses to questions about them constitute a method of discovering body-image concepts and feelings less defensive and more purposeful than the patient's comments about body-image when he or she is attempting to impress the evaluator with the necessity for sex-change surgery.

While observation, interview, use of objective psychological tests, and projective techniques make up the assessment strategy for gender dysphoria patients and represent varying modes of obtaining information, each method, in varying degrees, is subject to interevaluator differences. The clinical judgment of the evaluator plays a considerable role in interpreting the results of this variety of assessment techniques.

To enhance the effectiveness of assessment of gender dysphoria patients whose diagnosis is incompletely accepted and whose problems lie in the subjective realm of personal dissatisfaction, it is advisable that several practitioners evaluate the individual who is being assessed. In the setting in which the author has seen gender dysphoria patients, interviews have been performed by a surgeon, a psychiatrist, and a psychologist. Gender identity and sex-role preference are psychological phenomena best illuminated by a variety of assessment methods, including depth interview, observation, psychological testing, and the collection of fantasy data. Independent evaluations of these elusive phenomena performed by different practitioners lessens the possibility of error or bias by utilizing practitioners of different sexes and varying principlines. Clinical experience has shown that gender dysphoria patients present different aspects of themselves to practitioners of different disciplines as well as to sexually different evaluators. The effect of the evaluator's gender on gender-dysphoric patients has not been reported in the literature, but Masters and Johnson (1970) indicate that in the diagnosis and treatment of sexual dysfunction it is imperative to have male-female representation on a diagnostic-therapeutic basis. Furthermore, the psychological literature (Easly, 1978; Kimble, 1945) indicates that the gender of the evaluator affects projective test responses and undoubtedly influences interview communications. Careful review of independent interview findings, in conjunction with psychological test results, considered in the light of the conditions under which the patient asked to be evaluated, offers a comprehensive evaluation in terms of the various possibilities and contingencies under which the diagnosis and treatment of gender dysphoria are likely to be valid.

In summary, the various assessment strategies (observation, interview, obtaining of biographical information, and use of both objective and projective tests) have as their goals the identification of degrees of mental and emotional stability, the fluidity or rigidity of gender identification, the motivations for sex reassignment, and the capacity for adaptation.

Long-term studies using objective criteria for outcome of sex reassignment surgery and a control group are almost non-existent. The sole approximation to such a study used measures of a patient's ability to form relationships and succeed at work, with no difference being found in long-term progress between 15 transsexuals who had received surgery and 35 who had not (Meyer and Reter, 1979). Both groups registered the same small improvement in social adjustment. The lack of random assignment of patients to the non-treatment group (composed of people who had before them the 2 years of cross-dressing stipulated as a condition of surgery) is a flaw which makes the conclusions less than authoritative. Follow-up reports of patients after sex-change surgery, without control group data, indicate little improvement in both social situations or mental health, and small positive changes in relationships and work status. Unpublished reports suggest deterioration of mental health and social adjustment. Currently there are no adequate control studies that adjudicate between the views that sex-reassignment surgery confers no advantages to patients and that there are a group of people for whom such surgery is the only option.

CASE STUDIES

The following two case studies are samples of gender dysphoric patients who have been evaluated by the means (observation, biographical information, objective psychological tests, projective psychological tests) previously described.

Case 1. A 40-year-old patient was referred for psychological evaluation with the complaint that he be helped to ''. . . live as a female, as I asked to be 20 years ago.'' The patient, a victim of adrenal-genital syndrome, was born with ambiguous genitalia, and the parents were advised by physicians to give the child a female name, and to rear the baby as a female. The patient was raised as a ''girl'' until 5½ years of age, at which time another physician recommended that ''clothes and hair'' and expectations be changed to male. At age 11, the patient was given reconstructive genital surgery, which ''failed,'' and between ages 11 and 13 a bilateral salpingo-oophrectomy and a total abdominal hysterectomy were performed in an attempt to aid in the ''masculinization'' of the patient. The patient was told he had had an appendectomy, and did not learn until age 21 that he had had surgery to remove internal female organs.

The patient's mother indicated that the patient was not told of the reason for his change in sex at 5½, but ''the doctor'' suggested this change; she ''didn't understand the reason either.'' At the same time, the family moved, so there was no apparent influence from neighborhood children, and there were few children in the new neighborhood. The patient's father was an alcoholic, abusive person, and the mother had to work to support the family. After unsuccessful penis-reconstructive genital surgery at 11, the patient ran away from his father's home to stay with his mother (the parents were separated); after surgery at 13, the patient was expelled from the eighth grade for drawing pictures of naked women. The patient ''tried'' to live and work as a male, but complained that others did not respond to him as if he were male. At 17, he moved in with an older homosexual for ''financial reasons,'' stating that he did not like the homosexual relationship. At age 21, while being evaluated for a 4-F draft classification, a physician told him that womb and ovaries had been removed; since then the patient has had problems with drinking, depression, poor work performance, and has had three psychiatric hospital admissions. Five years ago he met his present roommate, and is involved in occasional sex (once a month) acting as the ''passive female partner.'' He and his roommate plan on being married after sex conversion surgery returns the patient to his female identity.

At age 19 the patient was evaluated at an out-patient psychiatric clinic for a depressive condition. At this time a battery of psychological tests was administered to the patient, including the following: Wechsler-Bellevue Intelligence Scale; Minnesota Multiphasic Inventory; Interpersonal Check List; Rorschach; Thematic Apperception Test; Michigan Sentence Completion Test; and Draw-a-Person Test. Reports from this evaluation, found in hospital files, revealed a passive, feminine life orientation. The patient was described as identifying with women in both fantasy and drawing, and as revealing the attitude that life as a woman would be happy and self-respecting. He was said to find the assertive male role as extremely confusing, difficult to fulfill, and distasteful. Test responses reflected a hope for the future which lay in "becoming a female completely."

From age 19 to age 40 the patient sought, intermittently and fruitlessly, medical help which would reconvert him nonambivalently to his former, female gender identity. At 40, he was consumed by the notion that he must resolve this gender dysphoria in order to derive some satisfaction from the years which remain in his life; his fortieth birthday had reminded him of life's limits. To this end, he sought help at a medical center which recently had begun to perform sex reassignment surgery. The patient was once more seen in a psychological evaluation; tests similar to those performed 20 years before were administered. Again, both objective and projective techniques revealed a gender identity as female. Well-developed fantasies and ideation of himself as a woman are most clearly reflected on the figure drawing test. When asked to draw a person, he drew a woman; when asked to draw an ideal self, he drew a female who appears pregnant; when asked to draw an ideal social self, he drew a glamorous woman bedecked in a gown (see Fig. 14-1). Throughout projective testing, he reflected a concern about being accepted as a female by others, although he seemed to experience little subjective distress regarding his female gender identity. Since being accepted for what he is (namely, "female") has been a continual problem for the patient, his projected fears appear to be bound in reality. Personality, at ag 40, was appraised, again, as essentially passive and dependent. At ages 19 and 40, Rorschach percepts were well-formed, displayed domestic interests, and involved such elaborations as clothing or personal decoration. Rorschach percepts were congruent with reported interests of cleaning house, washing, sewing, listening to the radio and stereo music, and interest in fashion.

Despite documented exposure to high androgen levels in utero, at birth, and prepuberty, the patient retained a female gender identity and a preference for female sex role in accordance with sex assignment at birth and sex-rearing as a female until 5½ years of age. The 20-year mission of the patient to reemerge as a "complete female" had involved numerous consultations with physicians and social agencies, repeated psychiatric hospitalizations, and a plethora of defeats, yet the patient still insisted upon a female gender identity. Sex reassignment surgery was recommended after a period of hormonal treatment, supportive psychotherapy, and living in the female sex-role.

Case 2. The patient was a 27-year-old male referred for psychological evaluation because of gender dysphoria. The patient was tastefully dressed in feminine garb: dress; hose; high heels; make-up (not excessive); shoulder-length, brownish-red hair (natural color); long fingernails; with a somewhat deep voice and a slightly prominent Adam's apple. Being on the thin side, the patient was a bit angular, although the skin appeared to have more subcutaneous fat than the average male of thin habitus. Gait and gestures observed were feminine and not caricatured. The patient sought sex conversion surgery, reporting maintenance for 6 months on Prolactin®, with small breast development. The patient had been on Premarin® for 14 months, summing to a total of 20 months of hormonal treatment. With Premarin®, there was more breast development, minimal voice change, some increase

a.   b.   c.

Fig. 14-1.   Patient's response to the instructions: (a) "draw a person"; (b) "draw your ideal self"; and (c) "draw your ideal social self."

in hips and thighs, and softening of skin and body contours. The hair on the patient's head was fuller (there had been some previous thinning of hair, in a male pattern). Sex drive was almost totally lost with hormonal treatment.

The patient was the second of five children and was teaching at a university. His father was in his early fifties, a retired and land-based Navy pilot. His longest absence from family was a 6-week period during the early 1950s. His mother was also in her fifties, now a housewife; she had been a hairdresser during the patient's childhood, returning to work 6 weeks after each child was born. The oldest brother, 18 months the patient's senior, was a married chemical engineer. The patient was followed by another brother, 14 months younger, who was the director of a hospital, and married. Yet another brother was 18, a recent high school graduate, and very sports-minded and interested in girls. The youngest child, a girl 17, was a cheerleader and dated frequently.

The patient was a wanted child, with a normal, healthy childhood. Throughout childhood, the two brothers closest in age to the patient would "gang up" on him. The mother reports the patient was quieter and more creative than the two brothers. The patient played, but not with the brothers. His mother enjoyed household tasks, such as painting and gardening, and the patient delighted in helping her with these activities, and did not seem as interested in father's interests. The patient reports that his childhood was "not happy;" his father was described as a "hard, insensitive, rigid Roman Catholic and authoritarian. I was always in opposition to him. He was always trying to force me into things I wasn't interested in. He made me go into Little League baseball, but I made a point of joining the worst team in the league. Mother let me out of it, and I got into pottery and crafts. I was always pressured to eat more so I would grow more. It makes me upset to think of it." The patient reports that his relationship with his mother was much better; his mother was "more sensitive and more responsive . . . and more concerned about what would make me happy than about what I should develop into. She was less of a religious fanatic. She did have a lot of thyroid trouble, cried a lot, and was upset with father, who had a short temper." The patient believes the eldest brother was "Father's child," while the patient was "Mother's child," and that the "eldest brother and I were in pressure positions, but the younger three were not."

The first awareness of wanting to be a girl was in the first grade; "the nuns would punish boys by making them wear a dress. I was always well-behaved and never punished, but can recall being jealous of the boys being punished." The patient avoided boys' games and tried to be friendly with the girls. Puberty occurred at age 14, with unhappiness over the growth of body hair and embarrassment of genitalia, especially erections. Sex dreams in early adolescence involved dreams of being a female. Sexual aspects of dreams were usually vague, and did not involve intercourse. One dream involved the patient as a little girl in a fluffy dress with no underwear, which revealed male sex organs. Cross-dressing began at age 11, when the patient would insert objects into his shirt to simulate breasts; later, he would wear his mother's clothes when she was out of the home. Later, when he was working, the patient bought dresses. At age 17, the patient was arrested for wearing women's clothes.

The first sexual experience occurred at age 19 with a prostitute. The patient reported trouble in becoming aroused, finally imagining he was a woman. The patient was uncertain as to whether or not he ejaculated. At 20, the patient began a sexual relationship of a month's duration with a female: "I enjoyed companionship, enjoyed snuggling and hugging . . . sex was as before, a little more fulfilling, except that I still had to imagine myself as a female in order to get an erection and perform." The first homosexual experience also occurred at 20, when the man performed fellatio on the patient: "I was excited by his caresses, but not by fellatio." The patient married at age twenty. The following year the wife became pregnant, and an abortion was performed. By the fourth year of marriage, the patient was openly cross-dressing and, after a separation of 6 months, was divorced.

The patient reports sexual interest in men, and not in women. Depression over the "double life" led to crying spells, loneliness, withdrawal, suicidal thoughts and self-pity. Suicide was attempted, but the patient stopped short at the last minute. The decision to seek sex change brought an apparent end to his depressive affect. The patient says, "I could live without sex with men. I have no interest in women. I know that I am feminine and female. I don't use the word 'woman,' because a woman is capable of childbirth and I never will be. If I continue as a male, the tensions are too great; I would think of suicide again. My goal is to be feminine with the elimination of 'that thing,' that growth."

Psychological tests performed revealed no signs of major psychiatric disturbance, such as a psychotic affective condition or a thought disorder. On the contrary, the patient possessed ample ego strength, including the abilities to reflect, plan, organize, be resilient, self-appreciative, and to effectively defend against anxiety. The patient is likely to be seen as natural, buoyant, and free in social relations, confident in taking on tasks, and effective in a variety of activities. Freedom of expression leads to initiative in social relations and to persuasive and verbally facile bahaviors. Projective techniques revealed guilt feelings with respect to parental unhappiness about sex transformation, and realistic fears of not being accepted as a female by colleagues. The patient preferred to be female, fantasizing the possibility of marriage to a man with whom life and love could be shared. The patient portrayed ''herself'' in the future as an elegant, professional woman. The patient took responsibility for what befalls ''her'' in life, and was, to a large extent, self-directed. Body-image, seen in figure drawing tests, is unclear, with the patient defining femininity by externals. The patient was expected to show a preoccupation with make-up and clothing and ways of affirming femininity (see Fig. 14-2). Sex reassignment was recommended after an 18-month period of living in the female sex-role, continuing hormonal treatment, and gaining every chance to learn firsthand about living in the coveted sex-role. If the patient response is favorable, in terms of social and occupational adjustment and feelings of satisfaction, then surgery may be considered.

SUMMARY

Since 1965 when the Johns Hopkins Medical School began surgical sex changes in the United States, clinicians have been faced with the demands of patients, more aware than ever before of the possibility of surgical transmogrification, for this surgery. Some 40 American medical centers either perform sex reassignment surgery or provide preoperative evaluations. The surgerical technique is relatively new and *irreversible*. Caution is needed in diagnosing a transsexual, as well as the knowledge that there is disagreement about such a diagnosis. While the belief exists that transsexualism is a single diagnostic category for which surgery is applicable, there is also the belief that psychotherapeutic and behavioral treatments can rehabilitate transsexuals. Others take the position that while surgery may be an appropriate treatment for some gender-dysphoric individuals, the problem is in identifying who they are within a larger population complaining of gender dysphoria. Permitting the troubled individual to make his or her own di-

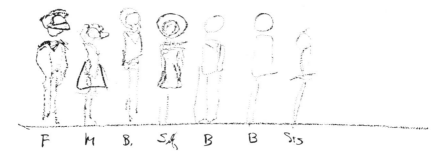

Fig. 14-2. Patient's response to the instruction, ''draw yourself and your family.''

agnosis and prescribe treatment is simplistic and can lead to tragic events. The assessment strategy advocated as the most reasonable approach is one which investigates the individual's mental and emotional stability, the fears, conflicts, or unconscious desires which may be producing the belief that the body needs to be changed, the fluidity or rigidity of gender identity, and the capacity for adaptation. The current state of the art in evaluating gender dysphoria requires a broad-based, multifaceted approach to understanding the thinking, feeling, motivations, and personality functioning of individuals who believe that they have the wrong sexual anatomy.

REFERENCES

Benjamin, H. The transsexual phenomenon. New York: Julian Press, 1966.

Benjamin, H. Transvestism and transsexualism. *International Journal of Sexology,* 1953, *7,* 12–14.

Easly, A. H. Sex differences in influenceability. *Psychological Bulletin,* 1978, *85,* 86–118.

Fisk, N. Gender dysphoria syndrome. In D. R. Laub, & P. Gandy, (Eds.), *Proceedings of the Second Interdisciplinary Symposium on Gender Dysphoria Syndrome.* Palo Alto, California: Stanford University Medical Center, 1973.

Hoopes, J. E. Operative treatment of the female transsexual. In R. Green and J. Money (Eds.), *Transsexualism and sex reassignment.*

Ihlenfeld, C. L., When a woman becomes a man. *Sexology,* June 1972.

Imperato-McGinley, J., Peterson, R. E., Goutier T., et al. Androgens and the evolution of male gender identity among male pseudohermaphrodites with 5a-reductase deficiency. *New England Journal of Medicine,* 1979, *300,* 1233–1237.

Kimbler, G. A. Social influence on Rorschach records. *Journal of Abnormal Social Psychology,* 1945, *40,* 89–93.

Kubie, L. S., & Mackie, J. B. Critical issues raised by operations for gender transmutation. *Journal Nervous and Mental Disorders,* 1966, *147,* 431–443.

Leff, D. N. Genes, gender, and genital reversal. *Medical World News,* 1977, 45–58.

Lothstein, L. M. Psychotherapy with patients with gender dysphoria syndromes. *Bulletin of the Menninger Clinic,* 1977, *41,* 563–582.

Masters, W., & Johnson, V. *Human sexual inadequacy.* Boston: Little, Brown & Co., 1970.

Meyer, J. K. Clinical variants among applicants for sex reassignment. *Archives of Sexual Behavior,* 1974, *3,* 527–558.

Meyer, J. K., & Reter, D. J. Sex reassignment. *Archives of General Psychiatry,* 1979, *36,* 1010–1015.

Meyer, J. K. Some thoughts on nosology and motivation among "transsexuals," in D. R. Laub, & P. Gandy (Eds.), *Proceedings of the Second Interdisciplinary Symposium on Gender Dysphoria Syndrome.* Palo Alto, California: Stanford University Medical Center, 1973.

Money, J., & Erhardt, A. *Man and woman: Boy and girl.* Baltimore, Maryland: Johns Hopkins Press, 1972.

Person, E., & Ovesey, L. The transsexual syndrome in males: I. Primary transsexualism. *American Journal of Psychotherapy,* 1974a, *28,* 4–20.

Person, E., Ovesey, L. The transsexual syndrome in males: II. Secondary transsexualism. *American Journal of Psychotherapy,* 1974b, *28,* 174–193.

Rubin, J., Provenzano, F. J., & Luria, Z. The eye of the beholder: Parents' views on sex of newborns. *American Journal of Orthopsychiatry,* 1974, *44,* 512–519.

Stoller, R. J. The "bedrock" of masculinity and femininity: Bisexuality. *Archives of General Psychiatry,* 1972, *26,* 207–212.

Stoller, R. J. Male childhood transsexualism. *Journal of the American Academy of Childhood Psychiatry,* 1968a, *7*(2), 192–209.

Stoller, R. J. Psychotherapy of extremely feminine boys. *International Journal of Psychiatry,* 1970–1971, *9,* 278–282.

Stoller, R. J. *Sex and gender.* New York: Science House, 1968.

PART VII

Assessment Strategies for Disorders of Special Populations

Robert J. Thompson, Jr.

15

Assessment of Developmental Disabilities

In order to consider assessment strategies for developmental disabilities it is first necessary to gain an appreciation of what constitutes a developmental disability. The term *developmental disabilities* does not refer to a specific disorder or any one dimension of dysfunction. Rather, it encompasses disorders of a number of systems, some of which are entities in themselves, such as epilepsy or mental retardation.

First, the continuing evolution of the concept of developmental disabilities will be considered. Next, a schema useful for assessment and for integrating information will be presented. Then there will be a consideration of the interdisciplinary team process as the necessary and essential assessment procedure used with developmental disabilities. Finally, future directions will be discussed.

DEVELOPMENTAL DISABILITIES—AN EVOLVING CONCEPT

The starting point for the evolution of the concept of developmental disabilities can reasonably be considered to be the appointment of the President's Panel on Mental Retardation by John F. Kennedy on October 16, 1961 (Thompson and O'Quinn, 1979). The panel consisted of 28 outstanding physicians, lawyers, psychologists, social scientists, and educators. Their mandate was to prepare a national plan to combat mental retardation.

A year later, the panel reported what was then known about the etiology of mental retardation, as well as views then current regarding services and training. Mental retardation was presented as a major national health, social, and economic problem. The proposed program of action was based on the panel's conclusion that mental retardation is a complex phenomenon stemming from multiple causes, many of which are known and can either be prevented or treated. In the majority of cases, however, a specific cause can not be identified (Hormuth, 1963). The panel did point out the heavy correlation between the incidents of mental retardation, particularly in its mildest manifestations, and the adverse social, economic, and cultural status of groups of our population.

Central to the panel's recommendations are several concepts and findings. First, prevention and the need for sustained and mutual stimulation of mother and child were dually emphasized. The panel concluded that mentally retarded infants can be cared for at home, provided mothers are given skilled advice and encouragement. There was a strong conviction that the mentally retarded person should be served with as little dislocation from the normal environment and as consistent with the special character of his or her needs, and that these needs be met as close to home as possible, and in such a way as to maintain relationships with family and peers. Second, the panel endorsed what is perhaps its most critical finding and concept in developing services for the mentally retarded, that is, the concept of *continuum of care*. This concept stressed "the selection, blending, and use in proper sequence and relationship, of medical, educational, and social services required by a retarded person to minimize disability at every point in his life span." Third, because effective care is a continuum, the panel asserted that the problems of the mentally retarded cannot be the sole domain or responsibility of any one discipline or agency. Because of the focus on a continuum of care and on interdisciplinary and multiagency approaches, a premium was placed on careful planning and coordination of diagnostic and therapeutic services.

The panel's report on mental retardation was used by President Kennedy to promote legislation to combat mental retardation and mental illness. The major piece of legislation to be enacted was Public Law 88-164, entitled the Mental Retardation Facilities and Community Mental Health Centers Construction Act of 1963. This bill launched the first major federal program for construction of facilities for the mentally retarded and mentally ill, and launched major federal programs in the area of mental retardation.

The legislative process of continuing the 1963 legislation and broadening the scope of its coverage provided the catalyst for the evolution of the concept of handicapping developmental disabilities (Thompson and O'Quinn, 1979). Professionals and associations testified regarding this legislation, and several key points were made. First, many common needs of individuals were classified under different diagnostic labels. Second, many of the retarded also suffer other handicaps. Third, individuals with multiple handicaps required attention to all their physical and mental problems. Fourth, many people whose diagnostic label was different than "mental retardation" had needs and required services closely related to those of the mentally retarded. The proposed legislation incorporated these points and was considered an ecumenical bill, which brought under one umbrella disabled persons with common needs but different diagnostic labels.

The legislative result was Public Law 91-517, entitled the Developmental

Disabilities Service and Facilities Construction Amendments of 1970. It was in this law that we first see a definition for developmental disabilities:

> Disabilities attributable to mental retardation, cerebral palsy, epilepsy, or another neurological condition or an individual found by the Secretary of (Health, Education, and Welfare) to be closely related to mental retardation or to require treatment similar to that required for a mentally retarded individual, which disability originates before such individual attains age 18, which has continued or can be expected to continue indefinitely, and constitutes a substantial handicap in the individual.

During subsequent Congressional hearings, it was recommended that the definition be expanded to include autism and specific learning disabilities. The definition was broadened to include autism, but not all specific learning disabilities. Furthermore, because considerable disagreement arose regarding the definition, a task force was assembled in 1976–1977 to consider the matter (Thompson and O'Quinn, 1979).

The task force clarified that the term developmental disabilities was not a catch-all for an arbitrary collection of existing labels or conditions: ''Rather, the 'developmental disabled' are a group of people experiencing a chronic disability which substantially limits their functioning in a variety of broad areas of major life activity central to independent living'' (Thompson and O'Quinn, 1979). The majority of the task force advocated the following functional definition that cut across specific categories or conditions. A developmental disability is a severe, chronic disability of a person that

1. is attributable to a mental or physical impairment or constellation of mental or physical impairments.
2. is manifested before age 22.
3. is likely to continue indefinitely.
4. results in substantial functional limitations in three or more of the following areas of major life activities: self care, receptive and expressive language, learning, mobility, self direction, capacity for independent living, or economic self sufficiency.
5. reflects the need for a combination and sequence of special, interdisciplinary, or generic care, treatment, or other services which are either of lifelong or extended duration or individually planned and coordinated.

The major changes over the existing definition involved the replacement of specific references to categories of disabling conditions, such as mental retardation and epilepsy, with an emphasis on substantial functional limitations attributable to mental and/or physical impairments. This definition became part of the Public Law 95-602, entitled Rehabilitation, Comprehensive Services, and Developmental Disabilities Amendment of 1978.

A SCHEMA FOR ASSESSMENT AND
INTEGRATION OF INFORMATION

The broad, continually evolving definition of developmental disabilities arising out of the legislative process provides only a general outline that must be fleshed out to be clinically useful. What has been needed is a conceptual schema that would reflect the multiple interactions of many factors that can affect the individual at various periods of development, and that can have functional manifestations in various systems. The developmental disabilities cube, depicted in Figure 15-1, presents such an integrating schema. One axis represents etiological factors, broadly considered as genetic or environmental. The second axis represents time, with the prenatal, perinatal, and postnatal developmental periods depicted. The third axis represents the interdependent systems of human functioning, such as the cognitive, language, and neuromotor systems. The consequences of an etiological factor depends upon many things, including the factor type and the developmental period in which it occurs. An etiological factor, such as an inborn error of metab-

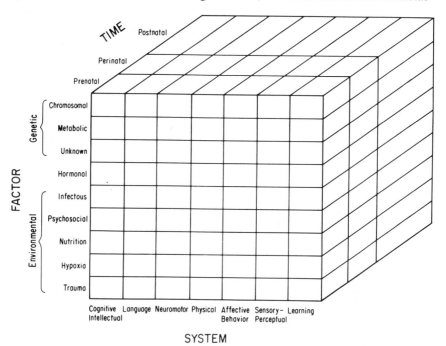

Fig. 15-1. Developmental Disabilities Cube, depicting the interaction of etiologic factors occurring during a time period of development resulting in manifestations in various systems. (From Thompson, R. J., Jr., and O'Quinn, A. N. Developmental disabilities: Etiologies, manifestations, diagnoses and treatment. New York: Oxford University Press, 1979, p. 17. Reproduced with permission.)

olism, may be operative during one developmental period but the consequences may not manifest until a later period. The consequences, or manifestations, associated with an etiologic factor may affect only one system, such as language, or a number of dimensions, such as cognitive, neuromotor, and affective functions. We thus see that the various etiological factors act singly or together during one or more developmental periods, resulting in manifestations in one or more dimensions of functioning.

It is also necessary to differentiate between developmental delay and developmental disorder. Whenever a child is not demonstrating an aspect of functioning when the majority of children of similar age are demonstrating it, that child may be exhibiting either a developmental delay or a developmental disorder. The differentiation depends upon the intactness of the system in question. If the system is appropriately functioning, the discrepancy between performance and expectancy may reflect a delay in development rate. If the system is not appropriately functioning, a developmental disorder may be present. For example, a child may be demonstrating a developmental delay if he or she is not talking by 24 months of age. Later, if it persists, it may be determined that the language problem is not a delay but an aphasic disorder. Any disorder that persists throughout a person's life and substantially hampers functioning or adjustment is a developmental disability.

The functional emphasis reflected both in the current definition of developmental disabilities and in the developmental disabilities cube schema is not meant to obscure the conceptual and clinical utility of subgroup categories, such as epilepsy and mental subnormality. While it has been useful and necessary to recognize that handicapped individuals share common needs, this does not mean that differential diagnosis is no longer needed or that, as some have advocated, mental retardation is synonymous with learning disability. In fact, one of the main reasons for assessment with the developmentally disabled is not to apply a diagnostic label but to appreciate possible, etiologic factors, delineate involved systems, and differentiate between *delay and disorder.* Such an assessment process often leads to a recognition that the individual's difficulties cluster into a recognizable subgroup, such as epilepsy or cerebral palsy, and this can lead to specificity of intervention and remediation.

THE INTERDISCIPLINARY TEAM PROCESS

Great advances in biomedical and behavioral sciences as well as in patient care have been accomplished through the intensity of focus afforded by specialization. However, there has been little emphasis on integrating specialized findings into holistic formulations of the patient. Team approaches—first, multidisciplinary and then, interdisciplinary—evolved as practitioners recognized the need for both gathering and integrating specialized information and findings (Thompson and O'Quinn,

1979). As noted above, early in the evolution of developmental disabilities it was recognized that providing a continuum of care required diverse knowledge and skills that no single practitioner could possess. The comprehensiveness and integration deemed necessary for competent care necessitated an interdisciplinary approach. It can be said that the interdisciplinary team process is the method of assessment with the developmentally disabled.

At this point, it is necessary to differentiate the interdisciplinary approach from other team approaches, primarily the multidisciplinary approach (Thompson and O'Quinn, 1979). Interdisciplinary is a fashionable term, and is sometimes indiscriminately used to refer to any situation in which individuals representing two or more disciplines associate. However, in terms of health care teams, *interdisciplinary* and *multidisciplinary* denote distinct group processes.

If the person responsible for a patient, typically a physician, feels the need for input, either in terms of assessment or treatment, a team composed of specialists from medical and nonmedical disciplines may be assembled. Input requested by the physician is relayed to him or her and may be used in the diagnosis, recommendation, and treatment plan as the physician thinks best. This is a multidisciplinary team process. The ultimate responsibility rests with the team captain, usually a physician, for ascertaining what information or assessments are needed to arrive at a diagnosis and treatment plan, e.g., what is required outside his or her area of expertise, and who can provide it. The team may have a more or less permanent composition, but the relationship of team members is primarily consultative, with respect to their area of expertise, to the captain.

In an interdisciplinary approach, case managership exclusively rests neither with one person nor with one discipline. Instead, responsibility varies as a function of the nature of the patients' needs and the skills of the team members. For example, a physical therapist might be the most appropriate case manager for a child with cerebral palsy, while a neurologist or psychologist might be most appropriate for a child with a seizure disorder and behavior problems. "In contrast to the multidisciplinary approach, one person does not decide what disciplinary input is needed in a particular case. It is the responsibility of each disciplinary representative on the team to determine what their role in each case needs to be" (Thompson and O'Quinn, 1979). Likewise, integrating the assessment findings and data into diagnosis, formulation, and treatment plan is not the responsibility of one individual, but of the entire team. This group process is collaborative rather than consultative, with the team having ultimate responsibility and each individual being responsible to the team for representing an area of expertise.

Team composition is important in achieving adequate comprehensiveness. The Developmental Disabilities Cube, presented in Figure 15-1, is useful in depicting the dimensions of functioning knowledge that need to be represented on the interdisciplinary team. Despite a blurring of traditional disciplinary boundaries with respect to roles and skills, most interdisciplinary teams are composed of representatives of medicine, psychology, communication disorders, occupational therapy, speech pathology, special education, physical therapy, social work, nursing, and nutrition (Palmer and Thompson, 1976; Thompson et al., 1976).

Initiating a Data Base

The process of bringing the expertise of the interdisciplinary team to bear in assessment, planning, and treatment in a particular case has been greatly facilitated by the advent of the problem-oriented approach to patient management and clinical record-keeping (Hurst, 1971). Any complaints the patient has, or any functional deficits that require management or diagnostic work-up, are considered problems. A problem list is generated for each patient and becomes part of the clinical record. It serves as a summary index of the patient's status, and is supplemented or changed as new problems emerge or as existing ones resolve. A data base is compiled for each patient that includes all relevant history, review of systems, lab, and other disciplinary findings. The data base is typically initiated through an interview conducted with the child's parents. A standard format is utilized which requires the interviewer to gather information about the child's past and current functioning in various areas. The standard interview format used at the Duke Developmental Evaluation Center is depicted in Table 15-1. The objective is for the interviewer, who can be any team member, to collect sufficient information to enable a determination of specific problems.

Enhancing the Data Base

The data base needs to be sufficient to arrive at a treatment plan for each problem. If it is insufficient, it frequently can be enhanced through an assessment procedure conducted by one or more team members. The existing data base might already contain a detailed history and a physical exam. The psychologist may decide to increase the data base by doing an intellectual and personality assessment. The special educator may decide that the data base needs to be augmented by specific achievement measures in reading and math, and by observation of the child's behavior in the classroom. Thus, specific disciplinary evaluations are conducted; these include assessment of specific dimensions of functioning, such as receptive language, intellectual, or neuromotor functions, as well as behavior demonstrated under specified situations. That is, each team member utilizes assessment procedures commensurate with their training and specific to the problem being evaluated, and writes a report of their findings, which then becomes part of the data base.

Disciplinary Perspectives on Assessment

Although the interdisciplinary team process itself is the method of assessment for developmental disorders, it is necessary to consider assessment from the component disciplinary perspectives. (At this point one can appreciate the magnitude of the task of considering the assessment strategies and methods used by

Table 15-1.

Interdisciplinary Case History Interview Outline

I. Birth History
  A. *Pregnancy:* length, condition of mother, unusual factors
  B. *Birth conditions:* mature or premature, duration of labor, weight, unusual circumstances
  C. *Conditions following birth*
II. Physical and Developmental Data
  A. *Health history:* accidents, high fevers, other illnesses
  B. *Present health:* habits of eating and sleeping, energy and activity level, medications
  C. *Developmental history:* held head up, crawled, sat alone, walked, babbled, first words, (2-word) sentences, language difficulties.
III. Speech and Language
  Parents' description of child's speech and language skills at the present time with regard to:
  A. *Sound production:* How easy is it to understand the child?
  B. *Sentence construction:*
    1. Sentence length
    2. Words in proper order
  C. *Grammar:*
    1. Usage of pronouns
    2. Usage of plurals
    3. Usage of verb tenses
  D. *Voice quality:*
    1. Nasality
    2. Hoarseness
    3. Breathiness
  E. *Rate and rhythm*
    1. Speaks too fast
    2. Speaks too slow
    3. "Stuttering" behavior
  F. *Language comprehension:* Does the child understand what is said to him or her?
    1. Does he or she follow instructions, with or without gestures?
    2. Can he or she answer questions appropriately?
    3. Does he or she relate verbally what has happened?
  G. Are the parents concerned about the child's speech and language skills?
  H. Are the child's speech and language skills as good as those of other children the same age?
  I. What languages are spoken at home?
IV. Motor Skills
  A. Clumsiness, awkwardness, lack of coordination and balance
  B. Ability to plan and execute skilled gross motor acts (ride a tricycle, put on clothing, etc.)
  C. Abnormal types of movements, abnormal muscle tone, or orthopedic problems

       D.   Eye–hand coordination for fine motor tasks (using a pencil, cutting with scissors, putting toys together, etc.)

V.   Nutrition

       A.   Does the child have any unusual food habits? (e.g., pica, eating snacks only, eating no vegetables, etc.)

       B.   Does the child have any difficulty in sucking, swallowing, chewing, or frequent drooling?

       C.   Does the child frequently suffer from any of the following conditions: diarrhea, vomiting, constipation, colds, or fevers?

       D.   Is the child excessively over- or underweight, or very pale?

       E.   Does the child have rough, dry, or puffy skin?

VI.   Social and Personal Factors

       A.   Friends

       B.   Sibling relationships

       C.   Hobbies, interests, recreational activities (toy and play activities)

       D.   Home and parent attitudes

       E.   Acceptance of responsibilities

       F.   Attitude toward learning problems

       G.   Self-care activities (degree of independence in dressing, feeding, toileting, etc.)

VII.   Educational Factors

       A.   *Preschool education:* nursery school, kindergarten

       B.   *School experience:* skipped or repeated grades, moving, change of teachers

           1.   Teacher's report

           2.   Child's attitude toward school

       C.   Special help, if any, previously received

VIII.   Personality Characteristics, especially regarding:

       A.   Anxieties

       B.   Fears

       C.   Dependence

       D.   Mood swings

       E.   Aggression tantrums

       F.   Reliability

       G.   Enuresis

IX.   Impressions

X.   Recommendations

From Thompson, J. R., Jr., and O'Quinn, A. N. Developmental disabilities: Etiologies, manifestations, diagnoses and treatment. New York: Oxford University Press, 1979, pp. 270–271. (Reprinted with permission.)

disciplines in relation to a number of dimensions of functioning.) Several key points will be made; the interested reader is directed to a more extensive presentation (Johnston and Magrab, 1976). All the basic methods of assessment, i.e., interview, observation, and testing (Keefe et al., 1978), are utilized in varying degrees by each individual discipline. Not only do disciplines vary in their reliance upon one or more assessment methods, but there is tremendous individual variability among professionals within disciplines. With these cautions about the ability to make generalized statements clearly in mind, some broad statement about roles, goals, and methods can be ventured, discipline by discipline.

Medicine. The primary representatives of the medical discipline on the interdisciplinary team are pediatricians and neurologists. Their goals are diagnostic and functional assessment of the child, and their methods generally are interview (history) and observation (clinical exam). The purpose of the physical exam "is to see how the various organ systems of the body are structured and functioning, as well as to determine whether there are clues to the underlying nature of any neurodevelopmental problems (Johnston, 1976). Neurodevelopmental assessment seeks "to determine the level and degree of refinement of function acquired by the nervous system as it progresses toward maturation" (Johnston, 1976). In addition to the delineation of strengths and weaknesses in dimensions of functioning, medical assessment strives for a statement of etiology. While from some assessment perspectives, knowledge of etiology is thought to be of little utility, this is untrue from a medical perspective. There are two main reasons: First, as previously mentioned, the nature of developmental manifestations are influenced by the type of etiological factor and the time period in which it is operative. Second, specification of a diagnosis affords access to the accumulated knowledge about a given syndrome or disorder, which enables an understanding of prognosis and could facilitate treatment. In conjunction with the clinical exam, a host of tests can be employed as needed. Among others there include electroencephalogram (EEG), computerized axial tomographic (CAT) scan, and karyotyping, to discover chromosomal abnormalities.

Physical therapy. Assessment of development in posture and locomotion is the focus of the physical therapist. This is primarily accomplished in the neurodevelopmental examination, with particular emphasis on the presence and maturity of primitive and automatic reflexes (Harryman, 1976). Determinations are made of muscle tone and strength as well as coordination and the presence, range, quality, and effectiveness of active movement. Any limitations in passive range of movement are also noted.

Occupational therapy. The occupational therapist typically focuses on assessment of fine-motor, sensorimotor, personal-social, and perceptual motor skills (Gorga, 1976). Methods include neurodevelopmental examinations, informal tests, and formal tests such as the Southern California Sensory Integrative Test battery (Ayers, 1972) which are standarized visual-motor, kinesthetic, tactile, and motor coordination tasks.

Nutrition. Nutritionists have an integral role on the interdisciplinary team. In assessing clinical status, one or more of the following methods is used: dietary assessment, feeding assessment, anthropometric measures, biochemical or laboratory tests, and clinical assessment of physical signs (Ekvall, 1978). The most widely used method of dietary assessment is to obtain a 1-, 3-, or 7-day record of food intake, which is then analyzed by the nutritionist in terms of recommended dietary allowance (RDA) of major food groups, calories, protein, etc. Feeding problems, such as refusals or inabilities to eat certain foods, lend themselves to applied behavior analysis as a method of feeding assessment (Thompson and Palmer, 1974; Palmer et al., 1975). Anthropometric measures include height, weight, head circumference, skinfold, and bone or skeletal age. Biochemical or laboratory tests can detect marginal nutritional deficiencies but interpretation is often difficult. The clinical exam focuses on physical signs of malnutrition.

Social work.   The primary method of assessment utilized by the social worker is the interview. The focus is typically on gathering an extensive psychosocial family history, and specific assessment of the functioning of each parent and of the marriage and family systems.

Psychology.   The psychologist typically focuses on cognitive-affective-behavioral-and-learning dimensions of functioning, and utilizes interview, observations, and testing. Testing is both objective and projective and involves informal procedures, such as play evaluation, as well as standardized and norm-referenced procedures. Various behavior checklist or rating scales are utilized for assessment of broad- and/or narrow-band behaviors. For example, studies at the Duke Developmental Evaluation Center using the Missouri Children's Behavior Checklist (Thompson et al., 1979) have demonstrated: homogeneity of parents' behavior ratings of children from two different developmental disabilities clinics; differences in ratings of children referred to a developmental disabilities clinic, a child psychiatry clinic, and non-referred controls; and differences in behavior ratings among developmentally disabled children on the basis of presenting problems (Thompson et al., 1979; Curry and Thompson, 1979).

Communication disorders.   Communication encompasses language, speech, and hearing. The speech pathologist uses observation and testing in assessing the speech and language dimensions of functioning. Standardized articulation, expressive, and receptive language tests have been developed. In addition, language samples are frequently elicited and subjected to either formal or informal analysis. The audiologist assesses hearing in terms of sensitivity, discrimination, and integration (Smith, 1976), and the results are reflected via audiogram. In addition to the standard technique of having the individual respond to sounds presented through earphones, special techniques, such as operant audiometry and impediance audiometry, have been developed (Smith, 1976).

Special education.   The focus of educational assessment is typically upon specific skills, such as reading, as well as upon achievement and readiness levels.

Both standardized and informal procedures are used. Some standardized tests are norm-based; others are criterion based.

Formulation and Recommendation

After the initial patient data base has been developed, specific problems listed, and all corresponding efforts to increase the data base through specific disciplinary evaluations have been completed, a complete course of action needs to be planned for each problem, and all the findings need to be integrated into a holistic picture. At this point, the team reconvenes and the data base, in terms of history, problems, and findings is discussed. It is the team's responsibility to arrive at a formulation. This is a dynamic statement about the current functioning of the patient, strengths as well as weaknesses, that specifies the relevant contexts, the probable etiology, and implications for habilitation and rehabilitation efforts. If possible, a diagnosis is made. Subsequently, members of the team meet with the family to discuss findings and recommendations.

FUTURE DIRECTIONS

The interdisciplinary team as the method for the provision of a continuum of assessment, planning, and intervention services is well-established. It is also expensive, and needs to be efficiently utilized. This efficiency comes about by triaging patients, so that those with complicated problems have priority over those with simple and straightforward problems in access to this type of service. Efficiency also comes about by appropriately utilizing the interdisciplinary team. Not all team members feel compelled to perform disciplinary evaluations with each patient; input can be achieved by observing and/or commenting on the evaluations of other team members. The problem-oriented approach has facilitated efficient utilization by focusing attention on the questions that need answers rather than automatically having each and every patient evaluated by each and every discipline. In the future, we are likely to see one procedure utilized by representatives from two or more separate disciplines, rather than the current process of each disciplinary representative adding his or her procedure to those employed by others. This utilization of a common procedure may first be accomplished by collaboration between special educators and speech pathologists as they focus upon learning problems that may be language-based.

The effectiveness of interdisciplinary team assessment depends upon the skills and procedures of each individual team member. Advancement in assessment strategies and methods will thus require increased sophistication in the assessment methodology associated with some disciplines, particularly in terms of norms and standardization of procedures. Informal procedures are fine for hypothesis generation, but lack replicability and a framework for interpretation based on known response distributions and patterns as a function of age. For example, in our center, an effort is currently underway to derive a standard procedure for testing and scoring minor neurological signs for which norms will subsequently be developed. In addition, criteria-referenced, in addition to norm-referenced, procedures will need to be developed for the proper assessment of some dimensions of functioning, especially skill-acquisition dimensions, such as learning problems. The strength of the interdisciplinary process lies in its heterogeneity of perspectives, but these must rest on valid and reliable assessment strategies and methods. In turn, these assessment strategies and methods must be based upon good clinical judgment, so that essential questions can be formulated, and the meaningfulness of results appreciated.

REFERENCES

Ayers, A. J. *Southern California sensory integrative tests*. Los Angeles: Western Psychological Services, 1972.

Curry, F. J., & Thompson, R. J., Jr. The utility of behavior checklist ratings in differentiating developmentally disabled from psychiatrically referred children. *Journal of Pediatric Psychology*, 1979, *4*, 345–352.

Ekvall, S. Assessment of nutritional status. In S. Palmer, & S. Ekvall (Eds.), *Pediatric nutrition in developmental disorders*. Springfield, Illinois: Charles C. Thomas, 1978.

Gorga, D. I. Occupational therapy. In R. B. Johnston, & P. R. Magrab (Eds.): *Developmental disorders: Assessment, treatment, and education*. Baltimore, Maryland: University Park Press, 1976.

Harryman, S. E. Physical Therapy. In R. B. Johnston, & P. R. Magrab (Eds.), *Developmental disorders: Assessment, treatment, education*. Baltimore, Maryland: University Park Press, 1976.

Hormuth, R. P. A proposed program to combat mental retardation. *Children*, 1963, *10*, 29–31.

Hurst, J. W. How to implement the Weed system. *Archives of Internal Medicine*, 1971, *128*, 456–462.

Johnston, R. B. Medicine. In R. B. Johnston, & P. R. Magrab (Eds.), *Developmental disorders: Assessment, treatment, education*. Baltimore, Maryland, University Park Press, 1976.

Johnston, R. B., & Magrab, P. R. (Eds.). *Developmental disorders: Assessment, treatment, education*. Baltimore, Maryland: University Park Press, 1976.

Keefe, F. J., Kopel, S. A., & Gordon, S. B. *A practical guide to behavioral assessment*. New York: Springer, 1978.

Palmer, S., & Thompson, R. J., Jr. Nutrition: An integral component of the interdisciplinary health care team. *Journal of the American Diatetic Association*, 1976, *69*, 138–142.

Palmer, S., Thompson, R. J., Jr., & Linscheid, T. R. Applied behavior analysis for childhood feeding problems. *Developmental Medicine and Child Neurology*, 1975, *17*, 333–339.

Smith, K. E. Audiology. In R. B. Johnston, & P. R. Magrab (Eds.), *Developmental disorders: Assessment, treatment, education*. Baltimore, Maryland: University Park Press, 1976.

Thompson, R. J., Jr., Curry, J. F., & Yancy, S. W. The utility of parents' behavior checklist ratings with developmental disabled children. *Journal of Pediatric Psychology,* 1979, *4,* 19–27.

Thompson, R. J., Jr., Garret, D. J., Striffler, N., Rutins, I. A., Palmer, S., & Held, D. A model interdisciplinary diagnostic and treatment nursery. *Child Psychiatry and Human Development,* 1976, *6,* 224–232.

Thompson, R. J., Jr., & O'Quinn, A. N. *Developmental disabilities: Etiologies, manifestations, diagnoses and treatment.* New York: Oxford University Press, 1979.

Thompson, R. J., Jr., & Palmer, S. Treatment of feeding problems—a behavioral approach. *Journal of Nutrition Education,* 1974, *6,* 63–66.

Alan D. Sirota

16

Assessment of Asthma

Asthma has long been of interest to behavioral scientists. Asthma was historically considered to be a disease of psychogenic etiology and as such, was an obvious target for psychological investigation. While asthma is now understood to be a physiologically based illness, the interest of psychological investigators has remained strong. Through the influence of the recent growth of interest in behavioral approaches to medical problems, research has shifted from trying to discover unique elements in the personality or family dynamics of asthmatics to developing strategies for treating asthmatics. Behavioral medicine interventions have been developed for influencing psychological variables that precipitate, exacerbate, and/or maintain asthmatic episodes. While emphasis was initially placed on the value of behavioral interventions, such as relaxation and biofeedback for ameliorating pulmonary status per se, that emphasis has shifted to focus on affecting asthma-related behaviors and emotional concomitants, such as anxiety (Creer, 1979). Detailed behavioral analyses lead to the understanding of the behaviors and cognitions of the patient that precede, accompany, and follow an asthmatic episode.

The early growth of behavioral medicine interest in asthma yielded some positive results, but numerous problems remain unsolved. Many pertain to the ways in which we evaluate the disorder and our impact on it, i.e., assessment strategies. Asthma, as an intermittent disorder, presents unique assessment-strategy challenges for the scientist and practitioner. Issues are as basic as the need for adequate diagnosis, and measurement of the disease and its severity. The purpose of the present chapter is to examine these and other assessment problems, to indicate how investigators have attempted to address them, and to suggest needs for future research. Intervention strategies, as they highlight assessment issues, will also be discussed. Before dealing in detail with the problems of particular concern to behavioral medicine, the nature of asthma and historical perspectives on the role of psychological variables will be briefly considered.

ASTHMA: SYMPTOMS AND ETIOLOGY

Bronchial asthma can be conceptualized as an organically based disease process which is probably genetically linked. Distressing symptoms of dyspnea arise from acute, recurrent, chronic or protracted hyperactivity of the respiratory apparatus. They can be induced by infectious, allergic, or emotional triggers. In some instances, the three triggers may be operative singly or in combination, whereas in others, the trigger may be obscure (Kapotes, 1977). To the patient, asthma means labored breathing accompanied by wheezing and a sense of chest constriction, as well as coughing, gasping, and apprehension. To the physician, asthma refers to reversible obstruction of the large and/or small airways caused by smooth muscle constriction, mucosal edema, and the retention of secretions with resultant symptoms and signs of respiratory insufficiency (Mathison, 1976). *Extrinsic, or allergic, asthma* usually affects children and young adults and refers to attacks in reaction to specific allergens such as pollens, dander, or dust. *Intrinsic asthma* exists when the trigger cannot be specified. *Idiopathic asthma* is so labelled when infection is involved, usually found in persons over 35. *Mixed asthma* refers to a combination of extrinsic and intrinsic asthma (Creer, 1979).

Until the allergic phenomena in asthma were discovered, asthma was considered primarily a nervous disease and was referred to in medical texts as "asthma nervosa." As early as the fourth century, Hippocrates pointed out the relationship between asthma and emotions and advised that an asthmatic must "guard against his own anger" (Chong, 1977). While asthma is now regarded as a medical disorder involving biological vulnerability with a probable genetic component (Knapp et al., 1976), the symptoms of the disorder usually are multiply triggered. In an individual case, asthma precipitated by a physically defined stimulus almost invariably coexists with asthma precipitated by psychological stimuli. Thus a high score on biological characteristics does not rule out the importance of emotional stimuli, and vice versa (Purcell and Weiss, 1970). The principal psychological stimuli implicated in asthmatic episodes are affective states, associated with major endocrine and autonomic nervous system alteration, and certain respiratory behavior, such as crying and hyperventilation. The role of emotions will be considered in more detail later.

Asthma is a widespread illness. It is the most common chronic disease of childhood. One quarter of school absenteeism and of the restricted activity of schoolage children can be attributed to asthma (American Lung Association, 1979). It is found in approximately 1 percent of the population and results in 2- to 3 thousand yearly deaths.

As an intermittent disorder with marked variability in the intensity and duration of symptoms, asthma presents many assessment challenges for the clinician-investigator. Perhaps the most crucial primary issue in the assessment and treatment of asthmatic patients is the importance of an accurate diagnosis, unfortunately overlooked by many investigators. If appropriate diagnostic tests had been administered in many of the studies reported in the literature, a diagnosis of asthma would not be confirmed in a high percentage of subjects. In order to confirm a diagnosis of asthma, techniques such as challenging the patient with a number of stimuli like foods, exercise, allergens, aspirin, etc., a radioallergosorbent test to establish the presence of specific IgE antibodies (circulating in the blood), or a methacholine challenge may be employed. Accurate diagnosis is essential to provide validity for whatever dependent variables are used in assessing treatment effects (Creer, 1979). Further classification of the disease as extrinsic or intrinsic, seasonal or perennial, acute-intermittent or chronic, may also be helpful in treatment planning (Richerson, 1974).

EMOTIONAL FACTORS AND ASTHMA

The importance of psychological factors in asthma has been recognized since antiquity. Years of research, however, have yielded "no convincing evidence that the biological pathology which results in the hypersensitive airway characteristic of asthma can in any way result from psychological influences" (Alexander, 1977). That is, emotional factors per se are not involved in the etiology of the disease. On the other hand, psychological disturbance may be one result of some patients' constant struggle with a chronic illness. The confusion regarding the role of emotions in asthma has been in distinguishing cause from effect. A patient's response to his or her symptoms may be mistakenly interpreted as the cause of those symptoms. The two are not always easy to separate; asthmatic symptoms may lead to acting-out behavior, such as refusal to take medications, which might in turn lead to an increase in symptoms (Purcell and Weiss, 1970). An asthmatic attack, irrespective of the initial trigger, can be aggravated and prolonged by emotional responding. Intense emotions may precipitate an asthmatic episode, and may therefore be primary antecedents in an attack, an invariable secondary reaction to an attack, or both (Kapotes, 1977). The importance of the behaviors involved in emotional responses are undeniable. What the person actually does when "emotional" may be functionally related to an attack. While asthma may be mechanically induced as a function of certain behaviors, more typically, emotional behaviors act upon the respiratory system (similar to the effects of exercise). This illustrates that the behavioral components of emotional-responding trigger asthma, either through mechanical means (e.g., stimulation of the vagus nerve), or through exercise (Creer, 1979). The failure to recognize the importance of the behavioral components of emotional responding (in contrast to the emotion per se) may reflect inadequate assessment and observation. For example, the observation that anger may precipitate an asthmatic episode has led to unproductive exploration of the psychodynamic significance of anger as a causal factor in asthma. What has been ignored is the screaming, storming about, crying, and muscle tensing behaviors that often accompany anger and in fact, may be the actual triggers of the attack (Purcell and Weiss, 1970).

Anxiety is particularly associated with asthmatic episodes. Anxiety reactions are frequently interwoven into all aspects of the disease, whether they occur antecedent to, concurrent with, or as a consequence of asthma attacks (Creer, 1979).

Of all the bodily symptoms that can affect a patient, dyspnea is one of the most fearful. Many patients respond to their difficulty in breathing with panic and feel that they may be dying as they gasp for air. This pattern of arousal with cognitive, motor, and physiological components of anxiety may exacerbate the dyspnea, creating a vicious and escalating cycle of symptoms. The assessment and treatment of anxiety related to asthma has been a major focus of clinical investigation and will be considered in this chapter.

Several investigations attempted to directly relate emotional arousal to decreased pulmonary functioning in asthmatics. In one study (Miklich et al., 1974), portable radio transmitters monitored naturally occurring emotions in 18 asthmatics. Periodic assessments of peak expiratory flow rate (PEFR) were made while the subjects were monitored. In six instances, negative correlations were found between emotional arousal and subsequent peak flow. Knapp and Mathe (1971), used a mental arithmetic task with imposed time constraints, continuous criticism, and surgical and autopsy films to produce emotional arousal, which led to decreases in asthmatics pulmonary functioning. More recently, Tal and Miklich (1976) demonstrated that vividly remembered incidents of anger and fear decreased pulmonary performance in 60 asthmatic children. Decreases following anger and fear correlated with increases due to relaxation. The amount of change in each condition correlated with history of emotionally precipitated asthma. These studies suggest that it is arousal, and not psychopathology, which may trigger an attack. In summary, although emotions have not been found useful in understanding the etiology of asthma, assessing them with particular attention to their behavioral components is important in understanding the onset and maintenance of, as well as the reaction to, an asthmatic attack.

PERSONALITY FACTORS IN ASTHMA

In addition to the attempt to causally relate emotions to asthma, another traditional approach has been the search for the "asthmatic personality." Numerous studies purport to show that asthmatics have particular personality traits that differentiate them from others and presumably are related to the etiology of their illness (Chong, 1977). However, as stated by Purcell and Weiss, a careful examination of the literature does not suggest that any specific personality constellation, nuclear conflict, or form of interpersonal relationship is uniformly and etiologically associated with asthma. Behavioral maladjustment which is present for the asthmatic and his or her family may instead be related to the existence of chronic illness.

Some researchers have strongly argued for the concept of distinct subgroups of asthmatic patients, and stressed the importance of categorizing patients away from the total population as crucial both to research and before forming treatment strategies. Numerous schemes have been developed, including how patients score on an asthma symptom checklist, developed by Kinsman and colleagues (Kinsman et al., 1973). This then relates to other data, such as scoring pattern on the MMPI, pulmonary function data, and patient requests for medication. One way of classifying asthmatic children into subgroups is based on how they respond to a structured interview designed to elicit the precipitants of their attack. One group of investigators (Purcell et al., 1969) dichotomized the children they studied into those who listed emotional precipitants and those who did not. They predicted that the former group would respond to separation from their parents differently than those in the later group; the hypothesis was confirmed. This division of patients based on behavioral data may have implications for other types of interventions. The data bearing on the utility of dividing patients into subgroups, however, are equivocal. Many researchers have argued, based on their investigations, that this practice is neither warranted nor of value; they assert that distinct subgroups do not exist. Creer and coworkers (1976) argued rather convincingly that the behaviors to be altered through intervention can be targeted only through behavioral analysis and not through a preconceived classification scheme.

BEHAVIORAL TREATMENT OF ASTHMA

Nearly every psychological or behavioral intervention strategy has been applied to asthma, including psychoanalysis, group therapy, hypnosis, environmental manipulations, family therapy, play therapy, and behaviorally oriented techniques (such as relaxation, systematic desensitization, biofeedback, and assertiveness training).

Three types of behavioral intervention may be considered, although these distinctions rarely are clear-cut: those that alter the abnormal pulmonary function per se, those that alter maladaptive emotional concomitants (e.g., panic), and those that alter asthma-related behaviors and family patterns (Alexander, 1977).

Widely employed strategies in behavioral approaches to asthma are relaxation training or biofeedback-assisted relaxation, to lessen anxiety or reduce sensitivity to stimuli that appear to elicit asthmatic responding. Systematic desensitization may be employed for the latter, with hierarchies focusing on events in the asthmatic attack itself (e.g., fighting for breath), stimuli which evoke attacks (e.g., a very hot day in a stuffy room), or stressful events of an idiosyncratic nature (e.g., interpersonal difficulties) (Knapp and Wells, 1978).

Numerous studies investigate the effects of relaxation training and report improvements in pulmonary functioning and/or positive changes in such target behaviors as number of attacks, medication use, and hospital visits; the actual clinical significance of the pulmonary changes produced has been questionable.

In their investigation of 14 severely asthmatic children, Alexander and colleagues (1979) found that relaxation training did not lead to clinically meaningful improvements in lung function. While the value of relaxation for ameliorating pulmonary function may be doubtful, its value as an adjunct technique in asthma treatment is not. This may be particularly true for less-severe asthmatics. It should also be emphasized that the therapeutic efficacy of relaxation seems to be increased through long-term, intensive practice of abbreviated exercises which the patient gradually incorporates into daily life situations. The distinction has been made that the maladaptive anxiety responses to asthma are altered by relaxation techniques and not by lung function itself. Although this distinction is important, both anxiety and asthmatic symptoms can be quite interwoven during an attack, with increases in one producing increases in the other, in an escalating fashion. Therefore, reducing anxiety at the onset of an attack may abort this escalation, and perhaps prevent further airway obstruction.

Relaxation exercises have been used for target behaviors other than pulmonary functioning. Medication abuse is often encountered in asthmatics. Overuse of inhalers, for example, can be serious. The proper use of an inhaler is occasional, for acute exacerbations when quick relief is needed. A frequency of inhaler use much greater than four to six times daily should be discouraged (Richerson, 1974). However, some patients abuse these medications and take them at the slightest discomfort. Excessive misuse has been linked to increased mortality among asthmatic patients (Creer, 1979). Psychological dependence on the nebulizer can also be a problem, with the patient's awareness that the nebulizer is not at hand precipitating a panic reaction and asthmatic attack.

Sirota and Mahoney (1974) report a case study in which frequency of nebulizer use was the major dependent measure. A 41-year-old woman with severe asthmatic difficulties was given brief training in muscular relaxation as a means of avoiding and reducing bronchospasm. A portable timer was used to cue naturalistic self-monitoring of muscle tension and self-relaxation. In addition, the timer was used to help the patient postpone the use of her nebulizer and substitute relaxation. Medication was used only if it was still needed after 3 or 4 minutes of relaxation practice. Patient records of medication frequency indicated a dramatic decrease in number of asthmatic attacks and medication use, and excellent maintenance at 6-month follow-up. While relaxation has many applications in asthma, additional work is required to answer questions concerning its mechanism and the therapeutic rationales for its use.

ASSESSMENT OF BEHAVIORAL FACTORS IN ASTHMA

We will now take a more detailed look at the assessment methods in behavioral medicine approaches to asthma. Various techniques have been employed to evaluate behavioral factors. The assessment of sequences of behavior displayed during asthmatic attacks is of primary importance.

Assessment of Behavioral Sequences

In developing measures of behavior during an asthmatic attack, sequences of behavior must be carefully examined. Assessment efforts focus on identifying the antecedents and consequences of attacks that may serve to control them, as well as behaviors exhibited during the actual asthmatic episode.

Antecedents of Asthmatic Episodes

In assessing the behavior of the asthmatic patient, the essential first step is to obtain a detailed history. Historical data verbalized by the patient is the most important diagnostic tool to isolate the precipitants of the asthmatic process. As in medical history taking in general, the interviewer should begin in an open-ended manner, asking the patient to list those things he or she has noticed may precipitate an attack, as well as the time interval between the noted event and the attack. An additional list of typical precipitants may then be presented (e.g., overexertion, weather, excitement, worry, upset, anger, sadness, laughing, crying, hard breathing, coughing, foods, colds, dust, etc.). The patient may be asked to rank the precipitants in order of importance separately, once for frequency and again, for severity. Asking the patient for an illustration allows the interviewer to make a distinction between the patient's perception of what actually occurs and what others have told the patient (Purcell and Weiss, 1970). The asthmatic's usual methods of intervening in an attack and their effectiveness should be explored (e.g., distracting one's attention, relaxing, etc.)

The conditions antecedent to an attack must be carefully assessed. While various investigators have devised questionnaires to explore asthmatic precipitants, no one instrument is universally used for this purpose. (One excellent format for interviewing is described by Creer (1979), from which most of the following suggestions are taken.)

General antecedents that may occur considerably before an actual attack should be investigated. These include such things as the patient's compliance with medical advice, e.g., adhering to medication instructions and attempting to avoid known precipitants, such as cigarette smoke. Careful exploration of more immediate antecedent conditions should then be undertaken, examining such things as if the patient or family member can predict an attack, if the patient's behavior changes just prior to an attack, and what events or stimuli seem to relate to the onset of symptoms. Among the cues sometimes listed by patients or their families as signifying the beginning of an attack are: behavior changes (becoming moody, quiet, or aggressive); facial changes (red face, flaring of nostrils, sweating); breathing changes (shallow breathing, voice changes); verbal reports (feeling tired or clammy); or physical changes (changes in posture, scratching throat or nose). Peak flow changes may also be used as cues. One might initiate treatment when values are at 50 percent of predicted performance.

In assessing asthma and asthma-related behavior, antecedent conditions of three types need to be considered: those which have occurred for prolonged periods before the disease is diagnosed (e.g., smoking), those that occur after the onset of the disease and affect the overall health of the patient (e.g., misuse of medication), and those that occur just prior to an asthmatic attack (e.g., exercise). Some illustrations follow.

Smoking is an exceedingly difficult behavior to eliminate (Pomerleau and Pomerleau, 1977). While smoking is contraindicated for asthmatics in general, it is a particular problem for young patients, both because it can precipitate an attack and because smokers require approximately double the dosage levels of theophylline as nonsmokers. Medication abuse is an example of the second category of antecedent conditions. It may result in harmful side effects (as in the overuse of nebulizers), lead to habituation to the medicine, or present problems in contraindicated use of drug combinations (Creer, 1979). Medication abuse may result from the patient's ignorance of available alternative actions that alleviate an attack, such as drinking fluids, engaging in relaxation exercises, or from the patient's desire to avoid what he or she expects will be a more serious attack. Psychological attachment to the nebulizer itself may also account for the problem. Appropriate behavioral analyses, including patient self-monitoring, must be done to determine what maintains the pattern of medication abuse so that effective interventions can be devised. So, for example, if phobic anxiety about a possible attack has produced overuse of medications, systematic desensitization might be the treatment of choice. Underuse of medication or lack of compliance is also a serious problem.

Compliance is affected by a number of factors, including the nature of the regimen given to the patient. For example, when marked changes in normal routine are called for, compliance is decreased. Taste, cost, schedule, side effects, beliefs that the patient holds about the illness and treatment, and certain features of the patient–physician interactions are other factors affecting compliance (Matthews and Hingson, 1977). Interventions can be offered for each problem area revealed by assessment: for example, education about the disease, its management and the role of specific medication. The reinforcement of appropriate beliefs and the alteration of erroneous theories about asthma by medical personnel, modeling, social pressure, and support are other ways to foster compliance. At the National Asthma Center, there is a multifaceted program for increased compliance (Creer, 1979). Patients are taught to assume responsibility for their own medication. Self-monitoring and self-control strategies are emphasized and are assessed by behavioral records and theophylline levels.

When assessing the patient's ability to trace events that result in an asthmatic attack, the investigator can evaluate the patient's awareness of physiological, behavioral, or cognitive cues signalling an impending attack. Knowning these cues might allow for early interventions, such as relaxation or environmental manipulation, and eliminate the need for further treatment, such as medication. However, many patients do not recognize the early signs of an asthmatic episode and therefore cannot initiate proper treatment while symptoms are relatively mild (Taplin and Creer, 1978). Rubinfeld and Pain (1976) have shown that 15 percent of patients do not even sense the presence of severe airway obstruction. How quickly a patient recognizes the onset of asthmatic attacks can have important implications for management. Symptom discrimination is important, as attacks can rapidly intensify, and because of the usual lack of correlation between verbal report of asthma and objective measures (Creer, 1979). Patients, particularly children, may exaggerate their degree of distress to avoid something unpleasant or minimize their symptoms to avoid missing out on a pleasant activity. Because early symptom detection is so important, studies have been conducted which have attempted to increase this ability in patients. Renne and coworkers (1976) taught asthmatic children to monitor their symptoms in order to discriminate small changes in their respiration. Peak expiratory flow rate was used to measure pulmonary function.

The children not only learned to self-monitor and to seek assistance at earlier points in the course of asthmatic episodes but also maintained this behavior beyond the duration of the training program (Renne et al., 1976). Rubinfeld and Pain (1977) also taught patients to become more sensitive monitors of their pulmonary functioning, after challenging them with methacholine. Taplin and Creer (1978) attempted to use PEFR data to increase the predictability of asthmatic episodes. They reported that typical correlations between a child's rating of asthma severity and peak expiratory flow rate is only $-.25$ to $-.70$. One reason offered by these investigators why even severe pulmonary dysfunction may go unrecognized is that some asthma patients may adapt to their symptoms by markedly reducing their activity level, thereby making symptom discrimination difficult.

Consequences of Asthmatic Episodes

In addition to the primary focus on events that occur prior to and during an asthmatic attack, assessment must also be concerned with the behavioral consequences of asthma. A person afflicted with asthma may experience consequences associated with the disease, its treatment, and the response of others. Research thus far has not devoted as much systematic attention to the assessment and treatment of these consequences as to antecedent factors (Creer, 1979).

An examination of the behavioral consequences of asthma addresses a wide variety of issues. The disease may become the center of the patient's life, severely restricting normal daily functioning (Creer, 1979). Children are particularly prone to developing behavioral deficits and excesses related to their asthmatic condition: frustration due to activity restriction and a perceived sense of being different from others is not uncommon. Anxiety reactions, as previously discussed, are prevalent. These may not be confined to the patient but also displayed by family members and persons in the community, such as teachers or coworkers. Aggressiveness, denial, malingering, and excess body preoccupation are other possible consequences. An asthmatic youngster may become overly concerned with the weight gain associated with the side effects of corticosteroids, leading to yet another behavioral consequence, reduced compliance with medication. The potential embarassment of taking medication at school or work may also result in a compliance problem.

Asthma may lead to withdrawal and isolation by the patient, or isolation may be imposed by family, peers, or school personnel (Creer, 1979). Feelings of worthlessness and depression may result. Social isolation in turn may lead to deficits in social skills and lack of assertiveness, creating further isolation and depression, describing a vicious circle. A detailed history must assess these potential problems.

The patients' responses to the physiological effects of asthma and the medications used to treat it, such as delayed growth and sexual development, are important to assess. It is necessary to help and support asthmatic children to function at levels commensurate with their physical capacity, neither restricting them from acitivities of which they are capable nor forcing them to participate at a level beyond their abilities. Overprotectiveness of family and teachers can be as likely a consequence as pushing the youngster, based on denial of the illness. Careful assessment of the patient and the expectations and demands of others on the patient can identify the problems which exist.

The responses of family members are crucial to assess. Do parents, for example, respond in a manner that facilitates efficient management of attacks, or is there panic and confusion? Anxiety responses of family members can be severe complicating factors in the treatment of the asthmatic patient. Other maladaptive responses may present targets for intervention, such as rejection, hostility, overindulgence, reinforcement of socially inappropriate behavior, etc. (Creer, 1979). Parent's failure to reward the asthmatic child for socially appropriate behavior, such as joining in normal social activities, is an all too frequent problem. Education of family members and family therapy aimed at shaping more appropriate behavior may be necessary. Responses of the greater community merit assessment when feasible. Attempts to ostracize the asthmatic and exclude him or her from school activities is common.

The behavioral consequences described above are not always present in every asthmatic. In addition, for any individual with asthma, a consequence may be absent at the time of initial history taking but appear at a later time. Since asthma affects so many youngsters, new problems may be expected to arise with growth and development, as new situations in life are encountered. Periodic reassessment is therefore extremely important. Depending on the findings of detailed assessment, appropriate treatment programs can be implemented. Social skills and assertiveness training, exercise and weight control programs, relaxation techniques, education, and supportive counseling, etc., may all be indicated during the management of asthma.

Measurement of Target Behaviors

When detailed history-taking reveals problem areas, more intensive assessment may have to be undertaken. Behaviors that reliably precipitate an attack or help to exacerbate or maintain attacks, or are a maladaptive response to the attack, may be suitable targets for intervention. Detailed behavioral analysis is then required for each such problem. Whenever feasible, the clinician should obtain supporting information from someone other than the patient in order to corroborate a particular pattern of behavior. Direct observation, whenever possible, is a valuable assessment tool. Self-monitoring by the patient may be helpful in providing baseline information. Other objective indices of asthma related behaviors, to be described later, should be employed where appropriate.

While the importance of a detailed history has been stressed in discovering asthma precipitants, it should be noted that verbal reports of patients are generally less valuable in judging the efficacy of a therapeutic procedure. For example, Chai and colleagues (1968) examined five types of measurements: (1) verbal reports of asthmatic children and their parents; (2) clinical examination; (3) physiological measurements; (4) medication requirements; and (5) activity restriction. The methods were intercorrelated, resulting in the finding that verbal reports are the weakest in providing an accurate index of the asthmatic state. Neither parents nor children's self-reports accurately reflect clinical findings or degree of airway obstruction.

After selecting target behaviors, the clinical investigator must choose the dependent measures he or she will employ to assess the impact of his interventions. Two sets of dependent measures have been widely used: (1) physiological measures of respiratory functioning, and (2) asthma-related behaviors.

Physiological measures of respiratory functioning. Physiological indices of respiratory functioning have been used as dependent measures in behavioral intervention strategy studies with asthmatics. Some measures are obtainable by means of simple pulmonary tests which can be performed in the patient's home and lend themselves particularly well to psychological investigation; others require the sophistication of a computer, a laboratory, and trained technicians.

The spirometer, the most fundamental piece of equipment for the evaluation of pulmonary physiology, assesses several measures. Forced vital capacity (FVC) is the maximal amount of air that can be expelled following a maximal inspiration. Forced expiratory volume in 1 second (FEV_1) refers to the amount of air expelled in the first second after the start of expiration; FEV_1 reflects what is happening in a patient's large airways. Maximum midexpiratory flow rate (MMEF) is the average rate of airflow during the middle half of the forced expiration, and reflects both large- and small-airway capacity. Spirometric measures can be speedily and readily obtained in any doctor's office, and represent the most useful test of pulmonary function. They are, however, subject to limitations. Because the intensity of response is being measured, the measures obtained are dependent to some degree on patient motivation. MMEF is less effort-dependent than FEV_1.

The peak flow meter, a relatively simple instrument consisting of a mouthpiece attached to a meter, measures peak expiratory flow rate (PEFR), which is the rate of air outflow at the peak of the expiration curve. Obtaining this measure has its advantages, since the apparatus is simple, inexpensive, and portable. It has for these reasons been the most frequently reported dependent measure in behavioral studies (Kotses et al., 1978). However, the use of this measure as the sole index of respiratory functioning is open to much criticism. Extensive cooperation is required of the patient (Knapp and Wells, 1978), and excessive exertion on repeated trials may actually lead to pulmonary distress. The value is also highly effort-dependent, relatively insensitive to small-airway obstruction (Jones, 1976), and is related to some aspects of body size (Kotses et al., 1978). The maximum level obtained may interact with the flow rate immediately preceding it, such that lower initial flows are associated with higher maximum flow rates. Thus, PEFR values may be spuriously high for asthmatics who frequently produce low initial flow rates as a result of airway obstruction (Bouhuys, 1974). Despite these criticisms, the measure has been shown to correlate well with FEV_1 (Creer, 1979).

An alternative measure of pulmonary functioning is total respiratory resistance (TRR), by the forced oscillation technique (Dubois et al., 1956; Levenson, 1974). This measure is not effort-dependent, does not require maximum exertion, and requires only minimal patient cooperation (Knapp and Wells, 1978). The patient, wearing a nose clip, breathes through a mouthpiece on a tube in which air is pulsating. Vachon and Rich (1976) reported high correlations between this measure and whole-body plethysmography. TRR has served as the dependent measure in two studies of biofeedback and asthma (Vachon and Rich, 1976; Feldman, 1976). This measure, which is sensitive to small changes in airway constriction and relaxation, does not require the tightly confining environment of a body plethysmograph which may produce anxiety in some patients (Strupp et al., 1974).

Despite the limitations of using a peak flow meter or spirometer, the measures provided by these instruments are adequate for most purposes. While more sophisticated tests of pulmonary functioning might be desirable, they are not always available to the behavioral scientist.

Asthma-related behaviors.   Measuring the amount of medication used is a frequently employed outcome measure. Since the actual drugs, as well as their frequency and amounts, can be quantified, these measures would appear to represent a particularly good objective measure of the efficacy of behavioral intervention. A number of difficulties are involved with using medications as a dependent measure. Medication use may, in fact, be a highly deceptive measure. "Medication scores not only result in questionable outcome data but the agents interact and interfere with the other dependent measures of a study" (Creer, 1979). Rather than being a valid dependent measure, they may be an uncontrolled independent variable. Consider the issue of non-compliance. A study by Eney and Goldstein (1976) demonstrated that only 11 percent of a sample of asthmatic children achieved therapeutic theophylline levels. A researcher cannot assume that a prescribed medication is being taken as directed. The schedule by which medications are taken is another consideration. If drugs are taken regularly, resulting in a stable baseline of use, any change in this baseline could represent the effects of intervention. If, on the other hand, the medication is taken only when needed, it is impossible to obtain a stable baseline and therefore, medication use represents an uncontrolled variable. Another problem is the use of corticosteroids. Their powerful effects may mask more subtle changes produced by other measures, such as pulmonary physiology, by techniques such as relaxation. Creer (1979) suggests two possible solutions to these difficulties: (1) looking for immediate pre- and post-differences in pulmonary functioning produced by relaxation, and (2) selecting patients for behavioral studies who do not suffer severe enough asthma to be using steroids for long periods of time, constituting the substantial majority of asthmatics.

Medication use should always be recorded in an asthma study, but whether it can serve as a useful dependent measure depends on the establishment of a stable baseline. An indirect measure of medication use was recently employed by Sirota and Vachon (1977). They were specifically interested in reducing the frequency of nebulizer use by asthmatic patients through the gradual substitution of relaxation techniques. The reduction of preventricular contractions (PVCs) evidenced in the electrocardiogram record of one patient corroborated the self-report of reduced use of adrenergic medication. Rate of PVCs may serve not only as an index of medication use, but as a target behavior for patients so affected.

Another measure used to assess changes in asthmatic functioning is the frequency and duration of hospital admissions. While this relatively easy-to-obtain measure can be an indication of the severity of the disease and may permit an analysis of the pattern of attacks, it too has inherent disadvantages (Creer, 1979). These variables are subject to influence by factors unrelated to disease severity, as it has been demonstrated that reducing reinforcements in the hospital setting can lead to reductions in the frequency and duration of hospitalizations (Creer, 1979). Parental panic, rather than asthmatic severity, might be the underlying reason for increased hospitalization.

Activity restriction can be an important measure, as the number of days missed from work or school usually can be objectively verified. Absenteeism may reflect school adjustment problems or job dissatisfaction more than severity of illness. Individual differences also may result in persons with equally severe symptoms either severely restricting their activity or persisting in following their usual daily routine (Creer, 1979).

The correct use of inhalation therapy equipment was the target behavior in an innovative study (Renne and Creer, 1976). Through shaping and reinforcement, asthmatic children learned to appropriately use the equipment, resulting in the need for less medication.

In addition to assessing the observable behavioral events that precede, precipitate or follow an asthmatic episode, one must assess the cognitive activity that occurs prior to and during an attack. "Thinking about my asthma" is a not uncommon report made by patients when asked about the things that seem to cause or aggravate the symptoms. Patients who are thinking about their asthma, (e.g., because they are worried that they may get an attack, detect the onset of respiratory distress, or they see another individual having an attack) may begin to develop symptoms or worsen an ongoing attack. "Getting my mind off it" is a commonly reported technique for subjective relief (Weiss et al., 1976).

Some patients develop bronchial narrowing or asthma as a reaction to their own thoughts. What likely occurs is that patients become hypersensitive to slight changes in pulmonary functioning and become anxious in anticipation of having an attack. This anxiety mediated by such thoughts as, "Oh no, I'm going to have a bad attack," further reduces pulmonary functioning, creating a rapidly escalating vicious circle. In the initial phases of assessment, not all patients may report that their own thoughts relate to an asthmatic episode, but later self-monitoring of thoughts often makes the patient aware of this relationship. When assessment reveals a cognitive trigger or intensifier of asthmatic episodes, appropriate intervention may begin to assist the patient in controlling symptom-exacerbating cognitions and substituting more calming and self-controlling thoughts (Sirota and Vachon, 1977).

Other targets for assessment are the patient's overall psychosocial assets—e.g., a vital interest in life; adequate financial resources and housing; social support; being loved; feeling esteemed; being part of a mutual "defense system" which one can utilize in time of need; ability to cope with environmental changes; flexibility; freedom from oversensitivity; congeniability; reliability; good judgment; ability to handle responsibility; etc. (Dudley et al., 1980). De Araujo and colleagues (1973) reported that those asthma patients with the greatest psychosocial assets require the least medication and more readily adapt to emotionally-triggered physiological changes in ventilation and/or CO_2 level than patients with fewer psychosocial assets. Those with many assets seemed more aware of the effect of emotions on symptom development, and were thus able to exercise greater control over their symptoms. While the therapist may not be able to offer interventions for all deficient areas, knowledge of these assets may help in individualizing treatment and predicting which patients will most benefit. The lack of objective measures of these global factors is a problem; they lack the behavioral precision of other target behaviors. But rather than ignore them completely, investigators should try to use them when possible.

The more objective the outcome measures, the more reliable measurement will be. Thus such measures as duration of bedtime coughing and number of attacks, while less precise than measures of pulmonary functioning, are nevertheless more reliable than clinical ratings of improvement or self-evaluative mood questionnaires. Of critical importance is that multiple-dependent measures be utilized whenever possible. While measurement of asthma-related behaviors may not be especially valuable in determining the immediate outcome of behavioral interventions, they may be useful in evaluating both long-term follow-up and asthmatic response in the natural environment (Knapp and Wells, 1978).

CRITICAL ISSUES IN BEHAVIORAL ASSESSMENT OF ASTHMATICS

Numerous critical issues exist in the behavioral assessment of asthmatics. Most relate to the nature of the disorder, with its inherent difficulties of accurate diagnosis and measurement. Many characteristics of asthma and asthma-related behaviors and their treatment result in unique assessment problems. Since the condition is chronic and long-term, repeated assessment over extended periods is necessary. The degree of severity of the disease, as well as the presence or absence of various asthma-related behaviors, may fluctuate with the growth and development of the patient. Since asthmatics constitute a markedly heterogeneous population, differing in such factors as severity of disease, medication use, precipitants of attacks, etc., selection criteria of subjects for group studies are crucial.

The aperiodic and unstable nature of asthmatic symptoms means that careful evaluation is required to obtain reasonably accurate assessments of frequency and severity. Objective measures are extremely important. Studies that lack them are problematic, because of the repeated gross discrepancies between subjective and objective measures, with the former typically overestimating the effectiveness of treatment (Purcell and Weiss, 1970). So, for example, patients whose flow rates remain unchanged after treatment may report feeling better, experiencing a decrease in frequency and/or severity of attacks, and increasing activity, etc. In such cases, these subjective estimates might reflect a withdrawal or redirection of attention, which gives rise to faulty reporting. Alternatively, while pulmonary function between attacks may remain unchanged, the range of triggering agents may be narrower due to treatment. Clinical improvement and subjective reports may in fact highly correlate while physiological functioning remains unimproved. McFadden and coworkers (1973) found that 22 patients recovering from acute asthmatic episodes became symptom-free, although airway conductance remained less than 50 percent of predicted normal values.

Asthma is aperiodic; it is thus difficult to assess events that occur on such an intermittent schedule. Further complicating the picture are behaviors accompanying the attacks that may not consistently occur during all attacks. A target behavior may thus be observed only once in several weeks, creating an assessment problem of great proportions. Two specific pitfalls which may occur in asthma related behaviors are "sampling jackpot," wherein a target behavior never occurs again after baseline data are gathered, and "fade-away baseline," in which the baseline level gradually decreases during observation suggesting that the behavior in question might already have been decreasing when the patient was referred for treatment (Creer, 1979). The spontaneous remission of symptoms is a fact of life in working with asthmatics; it can frequently complicate the findings of studies, making it difficult to attribute changes to the effects of intervention.

A major assessment issue throughout behavioral medicine concerns the generalization and maintenance of therapeutic effects (Russo et al., 1980). This is a particularly important issue for asthma. So, for example, it is crucial that relaxation skills initially acquired in the clinic be employed in diverse natural settings if they are to be of benefit. All too frequently, investigators are content to limit their efforts at furthering generalization and maintenance to instructing their patients to continue to practice their new skills. Long-term follow-ups, booster sessions, and attempts to include family and community members in reinforcing adaptive behaviors are all too rare. The problem of adequate assessment of generalization of initial treatment effects is far from solution. Studies that have measured pulmonary functioning at various times throughout the day outside of the training environment are necessary (Scherr & Crawford, 1978). Few such studies have been done and considerable further effort is required.

Throughout this chapter, reference has been made both to asthma itself and asthma-related behavior, e.g., the variety of antecedents, concurrent conditions, and consequences related to asthma. While it is important to consider the distinction in conceptualizing investigations, in terms of actual clinical consideration, it is often blurred. So, for example, behavioral interventions for asthma (such as relaxation) probably work in part by breaking the anxiety-dyspnea-decreased pulmonary function vicious circle. It is a difficult and perhaps somewhat academic question as to whether asthma or asthma-related behavior is actually being affected. The main concern is that the patient's ability to function in the environment has been in some way improved. Or, as Purcell and Weiss (1970) have so aptly stated, ". . . when asthma has resulted in severe anxiety and social maladjustment, there is little reason to limit the assessment of therapeutic effectiveness to demonstrably improved physiologic function. If good results are even purely subjective but have important behavioral ramifications, the application of psychological techniques will be warranted." This highlights the importance of assessing clinical as well as statistical improvements. It might in some ways be easier to focus assessment efforts on small changes in pulmonary function, but everyday functioning should be the crucial assessment issue.

The mechanisms by which behavioral approaches work need considerable further examination. How, for example, relaxation exercises produce beneficial results for asthmatics is not well understood. The degree of direct impact on pulmonary function of long-term practice in mild asthmatics is not a settled issue. While it is reasonable to speculate that reductions in anxiety, mediated by reduced autonomic activity, are responsible for the benefits, other mediators, such as the patient's perception of increased self-control over symptomatology, need to be explored.

SUMMARY

Although progress has been made in the behavioral assessment and treatment of asthma and asthma-related behavior, a great deal of work remains to be accomplished. Much of the published work in the field suffers from the assessment deficiencies discussed in this chapter, despite the fact that many of the problems noted were outlined before 1970 (Purcell and Weiss, 1970). The use of multiple-dependent measures in all clinical studies is essential. Standardized diagnostic work-ups and detailed asthma histories are essential as well, if researchers are to be able to select patients who may benefit from behavioral intervention. The understanding and eventual alteration of antecedents, concurrent conditions, and consequences of asthmatic respondings depends on finely-tuned and detailed behavioral analyses, which must begin with such diagnostic procedures and history-taking.

Direct observations, data collection by significant others, and patient self-monitoring of behaviors, cognitions, and physiological state should be utilized when possible. Pulmonary function measures taken at frequent intervals are indispensable to assessment and treatment. Indices in addition to effort-dependent ones should be employed when feasible. The commendable use of portable measuring devices in the natural environment is a trend which hopefully will continue. While this begins to address the need for maintenance and generalization of treatment effects, much remains undone in meeting this challenge. Therapists should program generalization strategies into their treatment packages and assess their effectiveness, rather than simply "hoping" that effects will generalize on their own. Increasing the predictability of attacks so that self-regulatory techniques may be used for early intervention is an important direction for future research.

The evaluation and treatment of behavioral problems related to asthma must be accomplished from a broad clinical base. Single-treatment approaches, such as biofeedback alone or psychotherapy alone, are destined for failure. In this regard, assessment of the role of family members (and, when feasible others in the community), should always be undertaken. Involvement of family members in helping to carry out treatment strategies is often essential.

An important area for further investigation is the identification of patients for whom behavioral intervention is most appropriate. It might be, for example, that the lungs of some asthmatics are particularly sensitive to psychological influence (Alexander, 1977). Better understanding of, and methods for, distinguishing these individuals could yield greater benefits. This important area, the identification of suitable patients, is in its infancy.

One final point deserves mention. This chapter has outlined many criticisms of the assessment strategies currently in use for asthma. The need for behavioral medicine to be characterized by high scientific standards of objective, thorough assessment and intervention makes these criticisms warranted. However, despite the limitations and problems noted, the need for increasing sophistication and refinement of our techniques, we should not lose sight of the real contributions already made to asthma evaluation and treatment. As an example, self-regulatory relaxation strategies have been shown to be of considerable value. Unfortunately, the use of such procedures seems to be primarily limited to teaching and research centers. In addition to devoting our efforts to further refining and extending our assessment and treatment tools, we should also be concerned with communicating these established techniques to general clinical medical practice.

REFERENCES

Alexander, A. B. Behavioral methods in the clinical management of asthma. In W. D. Gentry, R. B. Williams (Eds.), *Behavioral approaches to medical practice*. Cambridge, Massachusetts: Ballinger, 1977.

Alexander, A. B., Cropp, G. J. A., & Chai, H. Effects of relaxation training on pulmonary mechanics in children with asthma. *Journal of Applied Behavior Analysis*, 1979, *12*, 27–35.

American Lung Association. *Asthma: Facts about your lungs—patient education materi-al*. American Lung Association, 1979.

Bouhuys, A. *Breathing: Physiology, environment, and lung disease*. New York: Grune and Stratton, 1974.

Chai, H., Purcell, K., Brady, K., Falliers, C. J. Therapeutic and investigational evaluation of asthmatic children. *Journal of Allergy*, 1968, *41*, 23–26.

Chong, T. M. The management of bronchial asthma. *Journal of Asthma research*, 1977, *14*, 73–89.

Creer, T. L. *Asthma therapy: A behavioral health care system for respiratory disorders*. New York: Springer, 1979.

Creer, T. L., Renne, C. M., Christian, W. D. Behavioral contributions to rehabilitation and childhood asthma. *Rehabilitation Literature*, 1976, *37*, 226–232.

De Araujo, G., Dudley, D. L., Holmes, T. H. Life change, coping ability and chronic intrinsic asthma. *Journal of Psychosomatic Research*, 1973, *17*, 359–363.

Dubois, A. B., Brody, A. W., Lewis, D. H., Burgess, B. F. Oscillation mechanics of lungs and chest in man. *Journal of Applied Physiology*, 1956, *8*, 587–592.

Dudley, D. L., Glaser, E. M., Jorgenson, B. N., & Logan, D. L. Psychosocial concomitants to rehabilitation in chronic obstructive pulmonary disease: I. Psychosocial and psy-chological considerations. *Chest*, 1980, *77*, 413–420.

Eney, R. D., & Goldstein, E. O. Compliance of chronic asthmatics with oral administra-tion of theophylline as measured by serum and salivary levels. *Pediatrics*, 1976, *57*, 513–517.

Feldman, G. M. The effect of biofeedback training on respiratory resistance of asthmatic children. *Psychosomatic Medicine*, 1976, *38*, 27–34.

Jones, R. S. Asthma in children. Acton, Massachusetts: Publishing Sciences Groups, 1976.

Kapotes, C. Emotional factors in chronic asthma. *Journal of Asthma Research*, 1977, *15*, 5–14.

Kinsman, R. A., Laparello, T., O'Bannon, K. O., & Spector, S. Multidimensional anal-ysis of the subjective symptomology of asthma. *Psychosomatic Medicine*, 1973, *35*, 250–267.

Knapp, P. H., Mathe, A. A., Vachon, L. Psychosomatic aspects of bronchial asthma. In E. B. Weiss, M. S. Segal (Eds.), *Bronchial asthma: Mechanisms and therapeutics*. Boston: Little Brown & Co., 1976.

Knapp, T. J., & Wells, L. A. Behavior therapy for asthma: A review. *Behavior Research and Therapy*, 1978, *16*, 103–115.

Kotses, H., Glaus, K. D., Bricel, S. K., Edwards, J. E., & Crawford, P. L. Operant mus-cular relaxation and peak expiratory flow rate in asthmatic children. *Journal of Psy-chosomatic Research*, 1978, *22*, 17–23.

Levenson, R. W. Automated system for direct measurement and feedback of total respira-tory resistance by the forced oscillation technique. *Psychophysiology*, 1974, *11*, 86–90.

Mathé, A. A., & Knapp, P. H. Emotional and adrenal reactions to stress in bronchial asthma. *Psychosomatic Medicine*, 1971, *33*, 323–340.

Matthews, D., Hingson, R. Improving patient compliance: A guide for physicians. *Medi-cal Clinics of North America*, 1977, *61*, 879–889.

Mathison, D. A. In H. F. Conn (Ed.), *Current therapy*. Philadelphia: W. B. Saunders, 1976.

McFadden, E. R., Jr., Kiser, R., & DeGroot, W. J. Acute bronchial asthma: Relations between clinical and physiologic manifestations. *New England Journal of Medicine,* 1973, *28,* 221–225.

Miklich, D. R., Chai, H., Purcell, K., & Brady, K. Naturalistic observation of emotions preceding low pulmonary flow rates. *Journal of Allergy and Clinical Immunology,* 1974, *53,* 102–106.

Pomerleau, O. F., & Pomerleau, C. S. *Break the smoking habit: A behavioral program for giving up cigarettes.* Champaign, Illinois: Research Press, 1977.

Purcell, K., Brady, K., Chai, H., Muser, J., Molk, L., Gordon, N., & Means, J. The effect on asthmatic children of experimental separation from the family. *Psychosomatic Medicine,* 1969, *31,* 144–164.

Purcell, K., Weiss, J. H. Asthma. In C. C. Costello (Ed.), *Symptoms of psychopathology.* New York: Wiley & Sons, 1970.

Renne, C. M., & Creer, T. L. The effects of training on the use of inhalation therapy equipment by children with asthma. *Journal of Applied Behavioral Analysis,* 1976, *9,* 1–11.

Renne, C. M., Nau, E., Dietiker, K. E., & Lyon, R. Latency in seeking asthma treatment as a function of achieving successively higher flow rate criteria. Paper presented at Tenth Annual Convention of The Association for the Advancement of Behavior Therapy, New York, 1976.

Richerson, H. B. Symptomatic treatment of adults with bronchial asthma. *Medical Clinics of North America,* 1974, *58,* 135–145.

Rubinfeld, A. R., & Pain, M. C. F. Bronchial provocation in the study of sensations associated with disordered breathing. *Clinical Science and Molecular Medicine,* 1977, *52,* 423–428.

Rubinfeld, A. R., & Pain, M. C. F. Perception of asthma. *Lancet,* 1976, 7965(1), 882–884.

Russo, D. C., Bird, B. L., Masek, B. J. Assessment issues in behavioral medicine. *Behavioral Assessment,* 1980, *2,* 1–18.

Scherr, M. S., & Crawford, P. L. Three-year evaluation of biofeedback techniques in treatment of children with chronic asthma in a summer camp environment. *Annals of Allergy,* 1978, *41,* 283–292.

Sirota, A. D., & Mahoney, M. J. Relaxing on cue: The self-regulation of asthma. *Journal of Behavior Therapy and Experimental Psychiatry,* 1974, *5,* 65–66.

Sirota, A. D., & Vachon, L. Unpublished case studies conducted through the Lung Clinic of Boston City Hospital, Boston, 1977.

Strupp, H. H., Levenson, R. W., Manuck, S. B., Shell, J. D., Heinrichsen, J. J., & Boyd, S. Effects of suggestion on total respiratory resistance in mild asthmatics. *Journal of Psychosomatic Research,* 1974, *18,* 337–346.

Tal, A., & Miklich, D. R. Emotionally induced decreases in pulmonary flow rates in asthmatic children. *Psychosomatic Medicine,* 1976, *38,* 190–200.

Taplin, P. S., & Creer, T. L. A procedure for using peak expiratory flow data to increase the predictability of asthma episodes. *The Journal of Asthma Research,* 1978, *16,* 15–19.

Vachon, L., & Rich, E. S. Visceral learning in asthma. *Psychosomatic Medicine,* 1976, *38,* 122–130.

Weiss, J. H., Lyness, J., Leizer, R. J. Induced respiratory changes in asthmatic children. *Journal of Psychosomatic Research,* 1976, *20,* 115–123.

Eric M. Ward

17

Assessment of Self-injurious Behaviors

Self-injurious behaviors, such as eye-gouging, head-banging, and lip-biting, while easy to observe, are difficult to assess and treat. Some aspects of the assessment of self-injury are rather straightforward: identification and description of the more dramatic and obvious forms of self-injury can be relatively simple. Other aspects of the analysis are much more complex. For example, self-injurious behaviors initially appearing because of central nervous system dysfunction may eventually come under the control of environmental factors; these environmental factors may become so potent as to mask the contribution of organic factors. An issue that complicates both assessment and treatment concerns the fact that individuals from several disciplines may be involved with self-injurious patients, each approaching the problem from a different perspective. Criminology, psychiatry, psychology, suicidology, emergency medicine, psychoanalysis, dermatology, and plastic surgery are just a few of the specialties involved. A final complicating factor is that misplaced staff and parental attention to the obvious and confusing behaviors displayed by self-injurious patients may serve to maintain the problem.

The purpose of this chapter is to review the approach that behavioral medicine specialists have taken to assessing the self-injurious patient. The chapter begins with a brief description of the scope of the problem in order to provide guidelines to the practicing clinician in identifying high-risk individuals. Commonly used behavioral assessment methods are then described and evaluative comments on these methods are provided. Finally, important future directions for clinical practice and research are outlined.

SCOPE OF THE PROBLEM

It is a common fallacy that self-injury is limited to mentally retarded, autistic, or psychotic individuals. While one study of a population of institutionalized mentally retarded individuals showed a prevalence of 10 percent (Schroeder et al., 1978), healthy, normally intelligent individuals ranging in age from infancy to late adulthood have been observed to injure themselves. Self-injury may be quite common in infancy with an 11–18 percent incidence among infants 9 to 18 months of age (Shintoub and Soulairac, 1961). Self-injury in this group is normally limited to relatively benign head-banging on the floor or crib, which normally resolves over time and without acute or chronic sequelae. In one study of 100,000 persons, an overall prevalence rate of 1,400 cases of broadly defined self-injury was found (Whitehead and Ferrence, 1973). Percentages are highest for mentally retarded, autistic, and otherwise neurologically impaired or emotionally disturbed patients. For example, 5 percent of individuals screened at a neuropsychiatric clinic were found to be self-injurious (Frankel & Simmons, 1976), and a 4–6 percent prevalence was found in one study of institutionalized mentally retarded patients (Bachman, 1972).

PROBLEM DEFINITION

It may be best to begin a discussion of description and classification of self-injurious behaviors with a word about terminology. Terms such as "auto-aggression," which reflects a psychodynamic, self-directed aggression-interpretation of the behavior, are being gradually replaced by more behaviorally specific and neutral terms. Tate and Baroff (1966) used "self-injury" as a more specific term free of presumed explanatory meaning related to the patient's suspected motives.

Two broad classes of self-injurious behavior have been described by Ross and McKay (1980). *Direct forms* are those in which bodily damage occurs as an immediate and clear consequence of self-injury. The self-hitting of retarded individuals or the arm-cutting or self-burning of delinquent youths are common examples. *Indirect self-injury* occurs when the physically damaging consequences of self-injury are more delayed and equivocal. Refusing or interfering with medical treatments or the even more delayed consequences of various substance abuses are examples.

Problems secondary to self-injury may develop, and the nature and extent of physical trauma due to self-injury may need to be assessed. Head-banging of sufficient frequency and intensity may produce concussion, hematomas or tissue loss. As the condition becomes chronic, sutures may reopen and wounds may become infected. Retinas have been detached (Russo et al., 1979), and in at least one case (Williams, 1981) so-called "punch drunk syndrome" has developed. Known as traumatic encephalopathy of boxers (Johnson, 1969), symptoms of mental deterioration, marked dysarthria, parkinsonian-like features of the hands, and ataxia of gait are seen in adults who engage in activities resulting in multiple cerebral injuries. When restraints are prescribed, chafing and bruising may develop; muscle atrophy can occur over longer periods of time.

In addition to physical problems which may develop secondarily to self-injury, behavioral deficits need consideration. Individuals in physical restraints have obvious limitations on their ability to perform self-help and other adaptive behaviors. Both restraint and self-injury may render some patients less responsive to teaching and, therefore, at risk for developing many functional limitations as highly frequent self-injury comes to interfere with, or replace, adaptive behaviors.

ETIOLOGY

Genetic and sensory defects, infectious agents, and other organic conditions are associated with self-injury. Diagnosis is complicated if symptoms caused by organic factors come under the control of social and environmental influence. On the other hand, some self-injury may be both initiated and maintained by environmental factors.

Organic Causes of Self-injury

Most children with *Lesch-Nyhan syndrome* repeatedly bite themselves (Hoefnagel, 1965; Lesch and Nyhan, 1964). Lips, tongue, fingers, shoulders, and arms are common sites of injury. Found only in males, the x-linked genetic disorder is marked by enzyme deficiencies which produce hyperuricemia. It has been thought that high uric acid levels in saliva might, in some way, mediate the characteristic biting. However, symptomatic treatment of high uric acid levels with allopurinol (Marks et al., 1968) and L-5-hydroxytryptophan (L-5-HTP) has not proved reliably beneficial in controlling self-biting. Research continues in this area (Frith, 1976).

Diagnosis of the syndrome can often be clinically made. These children appear normal at birth, though all develop hypotonia by 1 year of age (Gilroy and Meyer, 1975). Psychomotor retardation is usually noted by that age as well. Extrapyramidal movements are manifested by 2 years of age, though these movements eventually are masked by progressive generalized spasticity. Characteristic self-biting appears to begin with the eruption of teeth. This is the prominent clinical feature, but all Lesch-Nyhan patients do not show self-biting; others show more conventional forms of self-injury, such as head-banging. While Menkes (1980) suggests that the retardation is never severe and that at least some individuals with the disorder have normal intelligence, others cite severe retardation as a common feature (Gilroy and Meyer, 1975). Confirmation is best obtained from a urinalysis; uric acid content is usually elevated to 10 mg./100 ml. (Menkes, 1980). Diagnosis through prenatal enzymatic analysis is also possible (Milunsky, 1973).

Children with *Cornelia de Lange syndrome* are also at increased risk for self-injury (Bryson et al., 1971). Patients can be distinguished by small hands, face, nose and stature; long eyelashes; low-set thumbs; hirsutism; thin lips; and mental and growth retardation. The etiology of the disorder is unknown, although a chromosomal abnormality is suspected. A higher-than-average proportion of these children were found to injure themselves in studies of institutionalized retarded children (Bryson et al., 1971). While picking of the eyelids and lip-biting are commonly reported, other forms of self-injurious behavior, such as face hitting, are also seen.

Behavior therapy techniques that involve manipulation of environmental factors (e.g., operant conditioning) have been successful in modifying self-injury in patients with both Lesch-Nyhan syndrome (Anderson and Herrmann, 1975; Duker, 1975) and Cornelia de Lange syndrome (Shear et al., 1971). Russo and colleagues (1979) point out that the utility of behavioral techniques with these disorders does not necessarily indicate that self-injury is caused by environmental factors. Thus, assessment of patients who are at risk for self-injury because of organic conditions, such as Lesch-Nyhan or Cornelia de Lange, should not end with a medical diagnosis of their syndrome. Possible social determinants of self-injury should routinely be assessed, using the methods described below.

Children with otitis media may also be at increased risk. In one sample, 6 of 15 young children who banged their head were found to have a history of this painful middle-ear infection (de Lissovoy, 1963). Since a large number of developmentally normal young children have otitis—one review indicated that one-third of a prospectively studied group of 2,565 children had experienced three or more episodes of otitis media (Howie, 1980)—it cannot be said that such children are at high prospective risk for self-injury. When dealing with patients who already exhibit self-injury (particularly head-banging), however, it is wise to check for otitis media.

Patients with autism, brain damage, dysautonomia, and childhood schizophrenia have also been identified as at risk for self-injury (Russo et al., 1979). The hypothesis of a direct organic link between these conditions and self-injury is less tenable. The incidence of self-injury is much lower in these conditions than in cases of Lesch-Nyhan syndrome.

Self-injury among these lower-incidence at-risk groups may be due to a number of factors. Self-injury may be mediated by deficient language and behavioral repertoires. Self-injury is more prevalent among schizophrenic children who are language deficient (Shodell and Reiter, 1968), and among children with more severe mental retardation (Baumeister and Forehand, 1973). Second, self-injury is thought by Frankel and Simmons (1976) and others to develop among low-functioning, language-deficient children as a coercive means of modifying adult attention. Third, children from intellectually and emotionally impaired subgroups may be at greater risk for self-injury because some display abnormal reactions to pain. One study of institutionalized schizophrenic children suggested that a majority did not respond normally to pain stimuli (Goldfarb, 1958). Clinical observation confirms that many children who self-injure do not display concommitant indications of pain. Russo et al. (1979), however, note that an abnormal pain reaction may be the result, rather than the cause, of self-injurious behavior, since pain is known to be influenced by social factors and modified by learning (Fordyce, 1976). Attempts to screen self-injurious patients for abnormal pain reactions are not likely to be fruitful, since most self-injury patients are language deficient and pain is a subjective experience.

Referral to a pediatric neurologist for diagnosis of at-risk organic conditions may be the best starting point for an evaluation when there is suspicion that organic conditions exist. The use of psychometric instruments to assess intellectual deficits is an obvious aid in screening for conditions associated with mental retardation.

Efforts to screen for organic bases of self-injury may yield diagnostic information but do not always yield definitive treatment recommendations. With each of the organic conditions described above, a thorough behavior analysis of social learning influences on self-injury is needed before behavioral treatment begins. It is to that analysis that we now turn our attention.

A number of behavioral and environmental factors can influence self-injurious behavior. These include: (1) social factors, (2) physical environment factors, (3) the developmental of behavioral chains, and (4) physiological arousal.

Social Factors which Control Self-injury

Numerous studies indicate that once begun, self-injury can be maintained as a learned response by its effects on those who interact with the patient. No studies reviewed, however, provide proof that the initial presentation of self-injury in humans was due to learning. Animal studies have shown that rhesus monkeys can be taught through operant reinforcement methods to first touch their heads with a paw, then to gradually increase the intensity of head-touching until only severe head-hitting produces reinforcers. Verbal expressions of sympathy or instructions to stop hitting by the experimenter initially given with food rewards were eventually sufficient to maintain self-injury without food.

In one study by Levison (1970), it was noticed that a food-deprived monkey accidently bumped his head as he was learning to move from one cage to another for food rewards. Subsequently, the animal began to "superstitiously" bang his head during training sessions. Months later, when the same animal was inadvertently fed last instead of first among other monkeys, head-banging appeared in the home cage. A reversal to the old schedule and reinitiation of the new feeding schedule eliminated then reinstated head-banging, respectively. Thus, self-injury might first be learned "accidently" if rewards are inadvertently given contingent on a randomly occurring self-injurious event.

In humans, there at least exists a possibility that normally occurring mild forms of self-injury might, through misplaced parental attention, come under social control. Frankel and Simmons (1976) suggest that self-injurious behavior can function to *produce* adult attention which is sufficiently positive to override the pain of the injury, or *remove* adult attention in the form of demands on the child which are more aversive than self-injury. In the latter case, the parent presumably drops their demands if the child self-injures. The development of self-injury through parental attention may be gradual over time, as adults inadvertently require increasingly intense varieties of self-injury before ceasing demands or attending to the child (Ferster, 1961). If developmentally appropriate forms of self-injury could accidently come under social control, it is at least logical that self-injury with an organic etiology could come under partial or full environmental control.

While these paradigms of learned self-injury are speculative when applied to the acquisition of symptoms, they appear to be valid in describing the maintenance of self-injury. Several studies of schizophrenic and mentally retarded children and adults (Corte et al., 1971; Lovaas et al., 1965) indicate that the temporary removal of adult attention produces reliable increases in self-injury. Well-intentioned efforts to stop self-injury by comforting (Lovaas et al., 1965), distracting (Lovaas and Simmons, 1969), verbally persuading the child, or other forms of positive reinforcement have been shown to actually worsen self-injury. The contention that self-injury may function to terminate adult attention in the form of demands which are aversive to the child is also well-documented (Carr et al., 1976; Solnick et al., 1977). If the child's self-injury causes adults to modify or drop their demands, the child learns to avoid future demands by self-injuring. Such self-injury is said to be negatively reinforced by a reduction of aversive adult demands. In fact, such children do decrease the rate of self-injury when adult demands are reduced. The decrease is unfortunately short-lived, as the next legitimate demand the parent makes is more likely to cause additional self-injury, perhaps at a more intense level. The ways in which the positive and negative reinforcement paradigms operate to increase the direct forms of self-injury displayed by the intellectually impaired are often obvious. The mode of action in more subtle and indirect forms of self-injury is often less clear. As an example, careful observation of the self-carving of delinquent young women by Ross and McKay (1979) revealed that social isolation and confinement following self-injury, designed to limit adult and peer attention, actually caused the behavior to increase. It was subsequently concluded that the attention of peers rather than adults served as effective reinforcers for these adolescents. Peer attention was reliably given if self-carving caused adults sufficient consternation. When adults subsequently showed less concern for self-injury and the adolescents' peers were given responsibility to control self-injury, the behaviors dramatically decreased.

Hair-pulling may be reinforced if the positive aspects of the attention received are sufficient to overcome the nagging that may accompany this attention (Keefe and Ward, 1981). As another example, patients may refuse to comply with medical treatments, which, if successful, would lead to the patients' return to stressful school or work environments. Thus, while other factors may maintain these more subtle forms of self-injury, the efforts of both positive and negative reinforcement can be operative (Ross and McKay, 1979).

Physical Environment Factors

Recent evidence indicates that the environmental factors that control self-injury are not always social. The self-stimulation hypothesis for the generation of self-injury, reviewed by Russo and co-workers (1979), suggests that self-injury may function to provide sensory feedback to stimulus-deprived individuals. Patients in unstimulating institutional environments display higher rates of a variety of stereotyped behaviors, including self-injury (Berkson and Mason, 1964; Davenport and Berkson, 1963). In those studies, enriched play environments were found to reduce stereotypic and self-injurious behavior: toys and furnishings helped control self-injury.

The use of mechanical restraints as a health maintenance measure to prevent self-hitting has produced iatrogenic effects, in that some patients actually increase their rate of hitting over baseline levels when restraints are withdrawn (Favell et al., 1978). For such individuals, restraints may function as a positive reinforcer. One case involved a 30-year-old, instituionalized, retarded woman, who attempted to restrain herself in her clothing by placing her hands through openings in wooden furniture, or by holding her arms behind her back when unrestrained. When firm elbow splints, mechanically preventing movement of her arms and thus self-injury, were first applied and later withdrawn, self-injury increased dramatically; the patient made repeated attempts to reapply the elbow splints herself. Only through a gradual reduction in the size and strength of the splints over many months was the patient's self-injury controlled without the aid of restraints. Studies have shown that brief periods of restraint can be used to increase such patient's performance on arbitrarily selected fine motor tasks. This suggests that restraints may function as positive reinforcement for not only the motor tasks, but self-injury as well (Favell et al., 1981).

Self-injury as Part of a Behavioral Chain

Self-injury may be maintained by environmental consequences, which operate on a chain of behaviors that includes self-injury. A child's non-compliance, for example, may escalate to whining and complaining, tantrums, aggression, and finally, self-injury. One study of a child who was both non-compliant and self-injurious indicated that a teaching strategy designed to improve the child's ability to follow instructions decreased both non-compliance and self-injury (Russo et al., 1981). Azrin and Nunn (1977) identified a large number of behaviors that may be part of a behavioral chain that culminates in nail-biting and hair-pulling. Virtually any face-touching behavior, such as rubbing the chin, touching the lips with a finger, straightening or raising eyeglasses, rubbing of the eyes, stroking a mustache or beard, or pushing stray strands of hair back in place, can play a generative role. Behaviors that reliably precede self-injury are often important in the maintenance of self-injurious symptoms.

Self-injury Mediated by Psychophysiological Responses

Psychophysiological responses have been neglected in the etiology of self-injury. There is at least face validity to the notion that self-injuring patients are more likely to display their symptoms during high arousal states. Romanczyk (1981; Romanczyk and Goren, 1975) has hypothesized that self-injury itself produces high physiological arousal, which in turn may cause further self-injury. In a complex but instructive analysis, Romanczyk and Goren (1975) suggest that patients whose self-injury developed as a means of avoiding external aversive events may also attempt to avoid aversive internal high arousal. Such patients may uncontrollably follow the high physiological arousal produced by an initial self-injurious response with a second self-injury, in a futile attempt to avoid unpleasant internal arousal. This self-defeating pattern could thus continue, accounting for the characteristic ''bursts'' of self-injury seen in many such patients. Treatments in which such arousal is kept low by judicious use of restraint have been proposed but not yet tested. Initial experimental attempts to measure skin conductance from a restrained limb while another limb is free to self-injure may solve the problem of movement artifacts in the assessment of arousal (Romanczyk, 1981).

BEHAVIORAL ASSESSMENT OF SELF-INJURY

There are five basic steps in a comprehensive assessment of self-injury, including: (1) the identification of the target behavior and its specification in measurable terms; (2) baseline measurement of the target behavior(s); (3) a functional analysis of the symptoms and the selection of an appropriate treatment strategy; (4) repeated measurement over time; and (5) assessment of maintenance and generalization of treatment gains.

Identification of the Target Behavior

Individuals who self-injure normally are referred by concerned parents, teachers, treatment workers, or primary care physicians. Since these patients may have various medical, psychological and educational needs, they daily interact with a large number of persons. The patterns of social interaction may vary considerably, as some care-givers attempt to ignore the behavior, others nag or punish it, while still others are quite solicitous. Each care-giver may have his or her own description of the presenting symptoms. It may be necessary to convene a meeting of relevant care-givers and others who interact with the patient to gather information on the patient's problem. For example, with a schoolage child, teachers, therapists, the school nurse, the child's parents, and even the school bus driver may be given the opportunity to describe self-injury, its rate in their presence, and their reaction to it. A pattern of discussion often emerges, in which rates appear to vary as a function of certain settings, activities, or types of social interaction. Characteristics of the response itself may accordingly vary. For example, a mentally retarded child may rock back and forth and only occasionally slap his face in one classroom where the behavior is being ignored, but he may engage in highly frequent face slapping with occasional bursts of head-banging in a second class, where his teacher makes more demands, or attempts to restrain the child's self-injury. On the basis of such descriptions, commonalities emerge: the clinician can begin to pinpoint relevant characteristics of the patient's self-injury. Such descriptions help the clinician to determine whether the particular behavior is self-injurious because it occurs with high frequency (e.g., rapid face-slapping), high intensity (e.g., self-cutting), or prolonged duration (e.g., finger-sucking). Care-givers may include in their description other problem behaviors which are not strictly self-injurious under a general category of "disruptiveness." For example, a retarded child might intersperse hits to the face with fist-pounding on her desk, hitting others, or screaming. These behaviors may, in fact, be in a reliable chain. Intervention on any one may thus decrease self-injury.

Individuals whose self-injury is on a continuum with benign, self-stimulatory behavior pose a particular challenge to defining self-injury in measurable terms. An autistic child's rapid stroking of her face with a finger may quickly change to eye-poking and face-slapping, and as rapidly return to self-stimulation. If changes in topography are too rapid, separate measurement of the two self-injuring behaviors may be impossible. A definition in which any hand-to-face contact is considered self-injury, while not wholly valid, will yield more reliable measurement. In the next step, the clinician performs a preliminary observation of the patient. Such observation will help confirm or resolve differences in staff and/or parent reports regarding topography, frequency, and intensity of the response. The clinician may be additionally able to eliminate irrelevant aspects of the behavior as it was first defined. Finally, other behaviors which can be targeted for modification can be identified. It is important that behaviors which covary with self-injury are identified in cases where low frequency but severely health-threatening self-injury cannot be readily observed. For example, a hospitalized child who on rare occasions removes an intravenous line may be found to be noncompliant with a variety of self-care routines and instructions by care-givers. These less-serious problem behaviors may be functionally related to self-injury and therefore are critically important targets for intervention.

Appropriate behaviors which covary with self-injury can likewise be assessed. If behaviors such as toy play, success in school, positive interactions with parents, or, for more intellectually impaired individuals, simply folding the hands, are reliably associated with the absence of self-injury, programs designed to increase these behaviors may be indicated. Participation by the client or the care-givers in the identification of alternative appropriate behavior may help them to focus more on behavioral strengths, and not simply on deficits and problems. In addition, specification of alternative appropriate behaviors may be required as part of a written treatment protocol to control self-injury in state-operated facilities (May et al., 1975).

A final step in defining self-injury is to have those who will be involved in the patient's treatment employ the agreed-on definitions. Two observers may be asked to simultaneously record the patient's behavior so that definition differences can be made explicit, thereby enhancing reliability. Changes in the definition may have to be made following a trial run. For instance, only face slaps which are audible may be included in the definition if less-intense varieties cannot be distinguished from self-stimulatory behavior. Before proceeding with the assessment, it may be wise to assess the subjective emotional reaction of the individual care-givers to the patient's self-injury. Some may be quite overwhelmed by the problem; others may believe that their current method of management is the only helpful one. These individuals may require special reassurance before they are able to participate in a consistent alternative program to control self-injury. Care-givers often need assurances from involved medical personnel before they are willing to participate in further assessment.

Measurement of the Target Behavior

Treatment of self-injury can often not be delayed to allow for adequate baseline observations. However, even a minimum of repeated measurements of the behavior prior to treatment provides critically important information on whether treatments are sufficiently effective to warrant their continuation. This is particularly true when assessments during treatment reveal only gradual changes and the patient's care-givers become demoralized. The extraordinarily high rates of certain self-injurious responses and the low frequencies of others present special assessment problems. In a well-known example, an 8-year-old's head-hitting with his fist occurred some 10,000 times during 15 hours in which the behavior was ignored (Lovaas and Simmons, 1969). Rates of face-hittings of over 80/minute have been observed (Carr et al., 1976). Mechanical counters and stop watches have been used by trained observers to reliably record rates that high, although alternatives to frequency recording have been used, either when well-trained observers are unavailable or when behaviors occur too rapidly to reliably measure.

In many instances, the simple occurrence of the behavior during a standard number of consecutive timed intervals can be recorded and expressed numerically as the *percent occurrence*. An example is found in a study by Ball and coworkers (1980): A young, mentally retarded child's finger-sucking was associated with chronic salivary dermatitis. The authors chose to record the occurrence of finger-sucking during any part of each consecutive 10-second interval of a standard re-cording session. This was done since finger-sucking varied from short, relatively discrete intervals to longer, continuous intervals. Thus, whether finger-sucking was observed as several discrete behaviors or a single continuous response within an interval, its occurrence was recorded.

Direct measurement of the duration of relatively continuous self-injurious responses may also provide an accurate measure. A 3-year-old's trichotillomania (Massong et al., 1980) was assessed by the child's mother who used a stop watch to record the duration of her daughter's hands touching her hair.

Once an appropriate dimension of behavior has been selected, the timing and number of daily observation sessions must be agreed upon. For low-rate but quite noticeable varieties of self-injury, day-long recording of each episode may be possible, even without continuous monitoring. If a child's self-induction of seizures is always preceded by highly visible hand-waving to strobe sunlight or by loud hyperventilation, each episode could simply be entered into a daily log. With highly frequent self-injurious behavior, as few as three, daily, 10-minute samples may be sufficient to adequately reflect response patterns and rate changes as a result of treatment. Behavior which occurs in relatively infrequent "bursts" may be most efficiently measured by sampling the occurrence of behavior during ex-tended intervals.

While the number and length of recording sessions is important, their place and timing may be most critical. Based on the care-giver reports and the clini-cian's initial observations, separate measurements may be taken in two or more settings which are thought to differentially control the occurrence of self-injury. When environmental antecedents and consequences are highly potent in control-ling self-injury, dramatic differences in rates of behavior may be observed when assessments are conducted in different settings. Carr and McDowell (1980) sam-pled a normally intelligent 10-year-old's self-scratching during play with peers, while talking with his parents, and while watching television each evening after dinner. A clear pattern of differential responding emerged after a few observation sessions. Scratching virtually never occurred while the child played with peers. Scratching was of moderate intensity while talking to his parents, and occurred more than once/minute during television-watching.

Table 17-1 lists the recording dimension, the daily recording interval, the settings in which measurements were conducted, alternative behaviors monitored, and the identity of the observers in several studies in which a variety of self-injurious behaviors were assessed and treated. Most measured self-injury and al-ternative behavior in more than one setting or during more than one activity.

While measurements prior to treatment normally are repeated at regular in-tervals, when self-injury represents a significant health risk to the patient, repeated measurement may be limited by demands that the treatment begin before further injury occurs. The patient may at this point be in restraint. If even a 2–3 minute

Table 17-1
Selected Measurement Strategies in the Assessment of Self-injury

Study	Population and Problem	Recording Dimension	Daily Recording Interval	Setting(s)	Alternative Behaviors Monitored	Observer
Jones, Simons, & Frankel, 1974	Mentally retarded child's self-biting and self-jabbing	Frequency	One 30-minute session	1. Isolation room 2. Day room	1. Self-feeding 2. School & recreational activities	Therapist, ward staff
Bucher, Reykdal, & Albin, 1976	Mentally retarded children's pica of dangerous objects	Frequency	Four 15-minute sessions	1. Ward: therapist present/absent 2. Bedroom: therapist present/absent	None	Therapist
Lovaas & Simmons, 1969	Mentally retarded children's fist-to-head hitting and head-to-object hitting	Frequency	1. One 90-minute session 2. Three 5–10 minute sessions	1. Bedroom 2. Ward room with nurse 3. Ward room alone 4. Walking in hall with therapist	1. Whining 2. Withdrawal from adults	Therapist
Linscheid & Cunningham, 1977	9-month-old child's rumination and emesis	occurrence/10-sec intervals	Three post-meal hours	1. Hospital room/ observer present 2. Hospital room/ observer absent	Body weight	1. Therapist 2. Mother

Balaschak, & Mostofsky, 1980	Normally intelligent child's nocturnal head banging	Frequency & duration of "bursts"	All night	1. Home 2. Summer camp 3. Dayroom 4. Simulated apartment	None	1. Mother 2. Child 3. Camp roommates
Massong, Edwards, Silton, & Hailey, 1980	3-year-old's trichotillomania	Duration	Ten 5-minute observations	Home	Appropriate play	Mother
Ball, Campbell & Barkemeyer, 1980	Mentally retarded child's finger sucking with salivary dermititis	1. Occurrence during 10-sec partial interval 2. Frequency during partial interval	1. Two 20-minute sessions 2. Four 10-minute	1. Dormitory/alone 2. Group room	Arms at sides	Not specified
Carr, & McDowell, 1980	Normally intelligent 10-year-old's self-scratching following contact dermititis	1. Frequency of 2-sec intervals of scratching 2. Number of body sores	Three 10–45 minute sessions	With/without parent attention: 1. Play with friends 2. Watching television 3. Talking with parents	1. Body sores 2. Parental attention to scratching	Mother

sample of highly frequent self-injury can be safely allowed, it may offer some basis on which to evaluate the importance of what may be small but consistent changes during the early stages of treatment.

A final consideration, the selection of an appropriate measurement strategy, should reflect the resources and skills of the observers who will conduct the measurements. Assessment methods should be as simple and as practical as possible. Overly complex behavioral definitions and extended observation periods are likely to be disregarded, particularly by parents and care-givers who are already stressed by the patient's self-injury. Initial definitions are likely to be crude (Bijou et al., 1969), and the settings selected may have little apparent effect on rates of behavior. In the course of using a measurement system, more relevant aspects of the behavior may emerge, necessitating modifications in definition and measurement methods.

Assessments are often carried out by those who spend the most time with the patient. Parents and teachers are often selected as observers. Self-reporting is sometimes employed with capable patients. Self-monitoring alone may, for milder forms of self-injury, be sufficient to control the behavior. Children and adults who have relevant skills can be taught to record the occurrence of their self-injury on a wrist counter or on an index card.

Observation of self-injury in naturally occurring settings and its direct measurement by the several methods discussed above are fundamental to the many treatment breadkthroughs that have been witnessed in this area since 1960. The gradual rate changes which many behavioral treatment programs have produced might never have been noticed if clinicians had not had a thorough, long-term commitment to reliable repeated measurement. Anecdotal reports of improvement, which once dominated the field, are particularly susceptible to bias when behavior is variable. Given its normally overt nature, variability in rate, and susceptibility to environmental control, self-injury is, among the behavioral-medicine treatment areas, one of the most relevant to a rigorous applied behavior analysis.

Functional Analysis

Often a consistent pattern emerges from measurement of self-injurious behavior in various settings. Perhaps, a child's hair-pulling may occur at high rates in the home shortly before school; after-school and evening observations show low rates. Such habitual consistency helps direct the clinician to treatment strategies. The appearance of response rates which reliably vary with different activities or settings does not by itself suggest a *differential* treatment. Knowing that a child self-injures more at school than at home is important information but does not necessarily indicate how the school environment produces higher rates of self-injury. The clinician must complete a functional analysis in which several hypotheses are carefully considered as to how situational and/or organic factors relate to the observed rates of behavior.

As discussed, self-injury often has a learned component. A variety of effective treatment approaches have been devised, each based on modifying particular types of learning that may be responsible for observed patterns of self-injury. Among the most important hypotheses about the function of self-injury are those regarding motivational control. Carr (1977) describes a protocol to sequentially consider not only organic causes of self-injury but several motivation sources as well. Devised for work with children, the protocol, shown in Table 17-2, may

Table 17-2

A Screening Sequence to Determine the Motivation of
Self-injurious Behavior

Step 1

Screen for genetic abnormalities (e.g., Lesch-Nyhan
   and de Lange syndromes), particularly if lip,
   finger, or tongue biting is present.
Screen for nongenetic abnormalities (e.g., otitis
   media), particularly if head banging is present.
If screening is positive, motivation may be organic.
If Step 1 is negative, proceed to Step 2.

Step 2

Does self-injurious behavior increase under one or
   more of the following circumstances:
   (a) When the behavior is attended to?
   (b) When reinforcers are withdrawn for behaviors
      other than self-injurious behavior?
   (c) When the child is in the company of adults
      (rather than alone)?
If yes, motivation may be positive reinforcement.
Does self-injurious behavior occur primarily when
   demands or other aversive stimuli are presented?
If yes, motivation may be negative reinforcement.
If Step 2 is negative, proceed to Step 3.

Step 3

Does self-injurious behavior occur primarily when
   there are no activities available and/or the environment is barren?
If yes, motivation may be self-stimulation.

(From Carr, E. G. The motivation of self-injurious behavior: A review of some hypothesis. *Psychological Bulletin*, 1977, *84*, 800–816. Reprinted with the permission of the American Psychological Association, Inc., © 1977.)

have some applicability to adults as well. Step 1 in Carr's protocol involves screening for organic causes, such as Lesch-Nyhan and Cornelia de Lange syndromes, and otitis media. If this screening is negative, or if positive social factors also seem present, the clinician proceeds to step 2. Several questions to determine if the patient self-injures to attract social attention, win back previously withdrawn attention, or other reinforcers are asked. If rates (or percent occurrence) of self-injury increases when the behavior is attended to, when attention is withdrawn, and when the child is in the general company of adults, the motivation to respond is likely to be based on positive reinforcement. If, on the other hand, the behavior increases when demands are made, self-injury may function to avoid demands or other unpleasant events.

The sources of positive and negative reinforcement may be obscure. A retarded child who self-injures to avoid a teacher's demands to participate in school activities may, after repeated successful experiences in eliminating demands, begin to self-injure whenever that teacher enters the classroom. The behavior may mistakenly appear to be attention-getting when in fact its function is the avoidance of an anticipated command. If the teacher is told to ignore self-injury, which is the recommended treatment when the behavior is attention-getting, the response is likely to be strengthened, since it again functions to avoid an anticipated demand.

Clinicians may have to observe the patient in various settings, evaluate information provided by care-givers, and, if possible, self-reported by the patient, to determine if reinforcing events are presented or aversive events are removed following self-injury. Initial observations or staff reports might, for example, suggest a retarded adult's eye-pressing increases when demands are made at his sheltered workshop. Comparisons of frequencies collected during both supervised work and a more relaxed lunch break on each of several days might reveal the occurrence of expected differences.

Step 3 in Carr's assessment protocol aims at determining if an individual's self-injury relates to an unstimulating environment. Individuals residing in institutional settings have been found to self-injure less in more stimulating surroundings. This etiology is unlikely among home-bound patients.

An example of how the screening sequence can be used is nicely provided in a study cited earlier by Carr and McDowell (1980). A 10-year-old child's self-scratching did, in fact, have a clear organic etiology, beginning during an episode of poison oak contact dermatitis. The dermatitis cleared following standard medical treatment, but scratching continued and varied in each of several settings. Data was simultaneously collected on the rate of parental social attention in which the child was told to stop scratching or was physically restrained from scratching. The data indicated that social attention was more frequent in settings where self-scratching was high. To provide a more definitive answer as to how parental attention may have controlled self-injury, a single additional measurement session was scheduled. During that three-phase, 65-minute session, parents were first instructed to completely ignore scratching ("extinction"), then to attend to it as before by telling the child to stop, then to return to the extinction procedure. Data on the frequency of both parental attention and self-scratching showed a close correlation. Since parental attention was found to exert so complete a control of the symptoms, other sources of motivation or organic factors, such as irritation from previous scratching, could be viewed as contributing little to the maintenance of the child's symptoms.

Whether one adheres to a formal protocol such as Carr's or not, careful consideration of a variety of hypotheses regarding the etiology and maintenance of self-injury is the essence of a functional analysis. When the functional analysis is thorough, the clinician is likely to clearly identify organic factors, if any, and the particular types of learning which maintain the patient's self-injury. Only then can individualized treatments be appropriately matched to a particular patient.

Matching Treatment

Once the behavior has been specified and measured, and functional analysis has revealed probable causes, the task of selecting the appropriate treatment strategy begins. Based on the functional analysis, a number of potentially effective treatments can often be selected. For both child-implemented or mediator-assisted treatments, the simplest, least disruptive treatment which is still potentially effective is obviously the treatment of choice. Consideration of the most effective and efficient treatment must be balanced by careful review of the resources and skills of the patient and/or the care-givers in using the methods prescribed. Treatment of children or adults with limited language ability, mental retardation, or a history of poor compliance, will certainly require one of several mediators who are able and willing to consistently insure that decided-upon changes in environmental consequences are implemented, and that the effects of a behavior-change program are measured.

While it is not the purpose of this review to detail the range of possible treatments (Russo et al., 1979), brief descriptions and special assessment considerations of each follow. Two broad classes of treatment techniques have been described (Keefe and Ward, 1980). Those which promote new relationships between overt behavior and environmental events (largely independent of consideration of the individual's internal cognitions and physiological responses) fall under the general heading of *contingency management procedures*. Those which promote new relationships between internal behavior and its determinants fall under the heading of *self-control procedures*. In contingency management programs, there is an attempt to modify the relationship between an overt self-destructive behavior, such as face-hitting, eye-poking, skin-biting, or head-banging, and its consequences. Treatments which change the contingencies between self-destructive behaviors and their environmental consequences include "extinction" and "time-out" procedures, in which specific or all normally occurring consequences, respectively, are interrupted or withheld following self-injury. Adult attention or other events (food, toys, etc.) noted during assessment and functional analysis to be probable conse- quences are consistently programmed not to occur (Bucher and Lovaas, 1968; Jones et al., 1974). While effectiveness has been documented (Russo et al., 1979) the use of both procedures may be contraindicated. The temporary increase in in- tensity and frequency of self-injury that may initially occur, and the long number of treatment sessions often required for gradual reduction, may result in a significant health risk to the patient. If an adult intervenes during the initial acceleration of self-injury, the problem can become even worse, as the child may learn that higher frequencies and intensity of self-injury are required to win back adult attention. Ongoing assessment of the child's physical condition and simultaneous assessment of the care-giver's use of attention may be critically important.

Alternative behaviors that can compete with self-injury are sometimes estab- lished by making adult attention and other potential reinforcers contingent on them. As examples, a severely retarded child who slaps his face may be reinforced with food and praise to keep his hands at his sides or to play with toys; or, a normally intelligent adolescent who carves his flesh when he is depressed might agree, in a contract with his therapist, to engage in a variety of social activities which might combat depression and thus self-injury. It is important in such cases to take objec- tive, repeated measurements of these alternative behaviors, as well as self-injury. Differential reinforcement procedures may only partially suppress self-injury and often must be used in combination with other techniques to produce significant change.

Aversive consequences, such as a loud "no," noxious-tasting substances, the noxious odor of ammonia capsules, and peripheral electric shock programmed to follow each occurrence of self-injury, have been effective (Russo et al., 1979). Contingent shock procedures have been credited with a number of rapid and dra- matically successful outcomes (Bucher and Lovaas, 1968; Corte et al., 1971; Lovaas and Simmons, 1969; Romanczyk and Goren, 1975), but reductions are highly situation-specific to the treatment setting. In addition, work by Romanczyk and Goren (1975) suggests that electric shock may not be effective in suppressing "bursts" of extremely frequent self-injury. The electric shosks may actually in- crease rates. These authors advocate first the prevention of high rates of respond- ing by the use of restraint and then discrete-trial punishment of episodes of self-injury, which are allowed to occur. Romanczyk (1981) has hypothesized that increased arousal produced by high rates of self-injury may render patients unre- sponsive to shock, which itself increases arousal.

Legal, ethical, and professional competency concerns have placed constraints on the widespread use of aversive procedures. Published guidelines (May et al., 1975; Thomas, 1979) are available; these aid the practioner in making ethical, legal, and clinical treatment decisions. When strictly followed, the therapist must complete assessments not only of the failure of more benign techniques, includ- ing the effectiveness of programs to promote alternative adaptive behavior, but the competencies of each clinician who administers the program (May et al., 1975; Stolz, 1977; Thomas, 1979).

Overcorrection techniques (Foxx and Azrin, 1973; Epstein et al., 1974) involve components of all of the above methods. The procedure requires that the patient repeatedly practice exaggerated or overly correct alternatives to self-injury after each episode. It is thought that the positive practice of such movements (i.e., holding the arms to the sides or behind the back) functions as a "time-out" from other reinforcers, and as aversive stimulation while competing responses are being established. Studies suggest that overcorrection has been effective (Foxx and Azrin, 1973). However, there is some evidence that attempts to use the technique with highly resistive or assaultive patients has led untrained therapists to modify the technique, resulting in injury to patients and staff (Duda, 1976). Ongoing assessment of not only procedural consistency but the physical status of patients and staff is advised.

Mechanical restraints have traditionally been used as a health maintenance measure. As mentioned, the treatment itself may have harmful effects. Bruising and chafing may result and careful use of padding and regular monitoring may be required (Ball et al., 1980; Rogers, 1981). The application and removal of restraints are not necessarily neutral stimulus events which simply prevent the occurrence of self-injury. The timing and duration of the use of restraint may profoundly affect the continued maintenance of symptoms. Favell and coworkers (1978) have shown that for certain individuals who appear to be highly dependent on restraints, brief periods in restraint were an effective reinforcer for progressively longer periods without self-injury when the patient was unrestrained. There is anecdotal evidence that patients released from restraint may become more agitated than during periods before restraints were prescribed. While theory and research is limited in this area, clinicians may wish to carefully evaluate the effectiveness of alternative procedures before restraints are used.

The decision to consider use of self-control procedures in the treatment of self-injury has numerous assessment implications for the clinician. Since self-control methods place primary responsibility for behavior change on the patient, they are not appropriate for individuals with limited intellectual and motivational skills. Self-control techniques help patients learn to identify the relationship between their behavior and certain environmental antecedents that elicit the behavior. Once patients learn to identify a response pattern, they are instructed in some technique which allows them to break the almost automatic pattern of self-injury that follows the eliciting antecedent.

The treatment of less-injurious, but painful and cosmetically damaging behaviors, such as hair- and eyelash-pulling, biting the fingernails, or picking at the skin has been aided by a combination of self-control strategies. Azrin and Nunn (1977) have described a comprehensive self-control package for dealing with many self-injurious behaviors, called Habit Reversal Training. It involves several steps. In the first step, "Awareness Training," patients are taught to identify and closely monitor the occurrence of symptoms and behaviors which precede or follow self-injury. For example, a patient with trichotillomania may practice with a mirror to closely observe the topography of the hair pulling. Hair pulling may begin with hand-tensing, followed by face-touching and hair-stroking of a particular area of the scalp. Occasionally, awareness training and self-recording of each episode is sufficient to modify the behavior. A folded index card can be used to record the frequency of the behavior. More often, additional procedures are required. The patients are taught to recognize situations in which responses are likely to occur, and then taught behaviors incompatible with their symptom, such as folding their hands or grasping a chair. These competing responses reduce ongoing self-injury or interrupt the chain of behaviors leading to self-injury. Patients are also taught how to reward themselves and enlist the support of others for their improvement. Relaxation training also may be included in the treatment package. For example, a patient who engages in severe self-scratching of his arm might be taught not only general relaxation strategies but to specifically relax muscles near the affected areas of the arm and in the hands as well.

While some patients may profit from simply reading a popularized description of the program (Azrin and Nunn, 1977) and require virtually no therapist contact, others require repeated contact.

Repeated Measurements

The introduction of treatment following careful measurement and functional behavior analysis probably represents the first attempt to assess the consistent use of a single intervention in the patient's treatment history. Prior to this, no doubt various procedures were inconsistently applied over brief periods of time. Repeated measurement of a single, consistently applied approach to treatment over a longer period of time, while critically important, faces certain impediments. First, care-givers and other professionals who view the symptoms with alarm may not be oriented to accept the gradual decrease in frequency and severity that often occurs. Having adopted a "prevention-at-all-costs" attitude, they may need careful reorientation, stressing the fact that if self-injury is learned it may be unlearned in a more gradual fashion. Care-givers should be prepared for the possibility that as behavior decreases, it may remain variable, reaching baseline levels on certain days.

If extinction or time-out programs are used to control self-injury, self-injury is likely to initially increase. Care-givers need to be aware of this likelihood and contingency plans to address more intense forms of self-injury which may temporarily develop have to be outlined in advance.

Careful daily measurement, represented graphically, which shows even slight trends toward expected changes from baseline levels may be critically important in motivating care-givers and the patients themselves to continue use of agreed-on procedure.

Simple single-case experimental designs (Herson and Barlow, 1976) can be effective in verifying that observed changes are in fact due to treatment interventions. The importance of this point is well-illustrated in a case in which functional analysis of a severely retarded, obese woman's severe self-injury suggested that medical interventions were sufficiently reinforcing to the patient to maintain her symptoms. Large wounds on her cheeks and on the top of her head, when reopened by self-injury, led this woman to be taken from her understaffed ward to a medical treatment room where her requests for food were granted while her wounds were restitched. Treatments in which all medical intervention was conducted on her ward with minimal social attention and the patient was given favored low-calorie foods and praise for keeping her hands at her sides were dramatically effective. Free of restraints, the patient was transferred to a ward for more independent clients and remained free of self-injury for several months. The patient's successful treatment was explained to medical and other staff in the new setting and a treatment protocol was circulated. When a single episode of self-injury occurred and the patient was taken to the medical treatment room, medical staff on call who had not read the protocol granted the patient's request for food over the objections of ward staff. A rapid increase in self-injury followed, but control was regained in a matter of weeks. This naturally occurring reversal of contingencies was helpful in pointing out to all staff the importance of consistently adhering to the standard protocol.

An A–B design in which repeated measurements during a baseline (A) phase are compared with measurements during treatment (B) under identical conditions can convincingly demonstrate that changes occurred simultaneously with the onset of treatment. It cannot, however, be used to rule out the possibility that extraneous events coincident with the onset of treatment were responsible or contributed to the changes. To deliberately withdraw an effective treatment and then reinstate it as part of an A-B-A-B or withdrawal design is ethically inappropriate in the treatment of self-injury.

The multiple baseline design which measures the effects of sequentially applied treatments is not only an ethically appropriate alternative to a withdrawal design but often fits nicely with practical treatment goals. For instance, a child who both slaps his face and bangs his head may be best treated by using an overcorrection procedure which is initially used only for head-banging. Continued baseline measurement of face-slapping while head-banging is successfully treated might well reveal little or no change. If subsequent treatment of face-slapping with overcorrection also produces a decrease, the change would not appear to be due to extraneous events, since their effects are unlikely to be staggered with each onset of treatment.

Since treatment of self-injury is often highly situation-specific, a multiple baseline design in which the same behavior is treated in first one, then another setting is another useful alternative to a withdrawal strategy.

Documentation that treatments do not change the rate of self-injury from baseline levels is, of course, a possible outcome of the assessments. This information may aid the clinician in the revision of the original functional analysis of the problem and in devising an alternative treatment. While there are no strict criteria for terminating an unsuccessful treatment, this clinician has had experience in which small but reliable data trends did not become apparent until a procedure was consistently applied over 2 weeks or more. As self-injury improves, frequencies may precipitiously drop, then show a more gradual decline to zero rates. For example, a child's face-slapping may decline by as much as 90 percent during the first few days in treatment, but zero rates may not be reached for several weeks. To accentuate differences during the final stages of treatment, data may be better graphed on semi-logarithmic paper such as the Standard Behavior Chart (Pennypacker et al., 1972; White and Haring, 1976), which magnifies differences in rate closer to zero. Time sampling methods may have to be modified during the latter stages of treatment as well. Where brief 10-minute samples were sufficient to assess changes when behavior occurred hundreds of times daily, longer samples (i.e., an hour or more, or even day-long recordings of each episode) may be required to monitor change when rates are low.

As mentioned, the topography and intensity of the behavior is likely to change as well. This may necessitate a change in definition and retraining of observers to reestablish reliable recording.

Assessment of Maintenance and Generalization of Treatment Gains

Planning for the maintenance of change over time and generalization of improvements to new settings is an important final step. Numerous strategies are employed to directly promote carryover of gains. The structured and intensive procedures often required to produce change during initial stages of treatment when self-injury is severe can be carefully faded to approximate conditions available in more naturalistic settings. For instance, powerful but inconvenient rewards for alternatives to self-injury, such as candy given numerous times each hour, can be gradually replaced with more naturally occurring rewards, such as praise and access to toys. Rewards can be less-frequently available and less predictably awarded over time. Where treatments were initially conducted by the therapist alone, the use of peers, siblings, parents, or the patients themselves can enhance carry-over to new settings. Since the patient, free of restraint and less disfigured, can now more actively participate in a variety of new settings, these "mediators" can aid the therapist in applying the treatment regimen in novel situations. Simple assessments repeated at longer intervals can thus be conducted by care-givers in one or more such settings. For example, a child who formerly banged his head may, for the first time, be left in the company of grandparents, attend a less restrictive school environment, and accompany his parents on shopping trips. Simple records could be mailed to the therapist or discussed by telephone.

Generalization of gains to new *behaviors* also occurs. Increases in toy play, social responsiveness to adults and peers, and various other appropriate behaviors have been noted as side effects of successful treatment of self-injury (Bucher and Lovaas, 1968; Epstein et al., 1974; Tate and Baroff, 1966). While it is difficult to preselect which appropriate behaviors are likely to improve, once noted, follow-up assessments of behaviors that can compete with self-injury can provide useful information to the therapist.

The therapist may wish to terminate follow-up by insuring that all parties are given written protocols describing simple assessment and treatment methods to use if and when self-injury reoccurs.

SUMMARY

The questionnaires, checklists, hard- and soft-ware physiological recording devices, and widely adopted behavioral observation systems which characterize assessment in some areas of behavioral medicine are unavailable for the evaluation of self-injurious behavior. An individualized analysis in which each patient is essentially treated as a single-case experiment has long been a hallmark of behavioral assessment for this population. The normally high rate and clearly discrete motor responses of the self-injury patient are well-matched with the direct observational recording methods of applied behavior analysis (Baer et al., 1968). Some of the earliest and most convincing examples of the behavioral approach involved assessment and treatment of self-injury (Ferster, 1961; Lovaas et al., 1965). Observational measurement systems have become more reliable (Herson and Barlow, 1976), and our expanded knowledge of possible sources of motivation for self-injury has led to assessment in a wider number of settings and activities.

However, standardized measurement systems for a wide variety of patients have not developed. There are a number of reasons why this may be so: First, self-injury is a rare disorder. It is an important problem because of the severity and chronicity of the symptoms, the costs of health maintenance measures, the shock and demoralization of care-givers, and the ethical implications of leaving a patient in restraint when treatments are unsuccessful. Second, self-injury involves symptoms varying in topography and frequency; a single clinician is unlikely to encounter the same problem more than a few times. Third, a large number of behavioral and environmental factors have been implicated in the etiology and maintenance of self-injury. An attempt to list, in a standard assessment device, the bewildering array of social and non-social stimuli which could come to control self-injury would indeed be a formidable task. It is doubtful that standardized assessment devices would aid the clinician in measuring these diverse behaviors or in selecting from an array of specific causal or maintaining factors. Thus, it seems likely that evaluation of self-injury patients will remain an individualized process.

In evaluating the adequacy of the assessment methods themselves, it may be well to reiterate Ross and McKay's (1980) concern regarding the need for better classification of symptoms. Classifying symptoms on the basis of outcome rather than intent is helpful in conceptualizing the problem. Direct forms of self-injury in which there is nothing that appears inherently reinforcing about the response can be contrasted with the addictive properties of various forms of substance abuse (Miller, 1980; Nathan, 1980).

New theory and treatment breakthroughs will likely come from careful investigations of physiological responses that accompany self-injury. Problems with movement artifact in electrophysiological recording from a patient who is rapidly self-injuring present a significant challenge to reliable measurement. Measurement of physiological responses from a restrained limb while another limb is free to self-injure, and measurement of changes in arousal which precede self-injury (Romanczyk, 1981), may partially circumvent problems with movement artifact. There are important reasons why physiological variables need to be considered. There can be little doubt that intense forms of self-injury, application of restraint, release from restraint, and punishment techniques (e.g., electric shock), produce significant changes in a patient's arousal. How these changes relate to overt self-injury or to a patient's responsiveness to a given treatment deserves careful study (Romanczyk, 1981).

While standardized assessment methods may not be viable, standardization of the process by which clinicians sequentially consider organic, environmental, and behavioral factors in the etiology and maintenance of self-injury is helpful. The sequential screening protocol of Carr (1977) is a first step in this direction, and is important in drawing the attention of behaviorally oriented clinicians to organic factors which may have been neglected. It also highlights the importance of the "negative reinforcement hypothesis," in which self-injury is thought to function to terminate aversive events, such as adult demands. The protocol needs to be expanded to include several other considerations, including the maintaining effects of physical restraint; the role of awareness with particular regard to milder forms of self-injury; relationships to precursive or covarying behavior; the contribution of verbal responses; and, perhaps, the role of physiological arousal that is secondary to self-injury or the treatments prescribed. For example, Favell and colleagues (1981), have developed a five-item rating scale based on earlier observations by Frieden (1977), which should aid practitioners in identifying restrained patients who appear to enjoy restraint.

In sum, self-injurious behavior presents a paradox for behavioral assessment. The behavior is usually quite overt and easy to measure. The development of these apparently simple patterns of behavior may, however, be related to complex organic and environmental factors. Advances in behavioral assessment will undoubtedly further our understanding of these factors, and thus our ability to treat this serious and disturbing disorder.

REFERENCES

Anderson, L. T., & Herrmann, L. Lesch-Nyhan disease: A specific learning disability. Paper presented at the meeting of the Association of Advancement of Behavior Therapy, San Francisco, 1975.

Azrin, N. H., & Nunn, G. R. *Habit control in a day.* New York: Pocket Books, 1977.

Bachman, J. A. Self-injurious behavior: A behavioral analysis. *Journal of Abnormal Psychology,* 1972, *80*, 211–224.

Baer, D. M., Wolf, M. M., & Risley, T. R. Some current dimensions of applied behavior analysis. *Journal of Applied Behavior Analysis,* 1968, *1*, 91–97.

Ball, T. S., Campbell, R., & Barkemeyer, R. Air splints applied to control self-injurious finger sucking in profoundly retarded individuals. *Journal of Behavior Therapy and Experimental Psychiatry,* 1980, *11*, 267–272.

Berkson, G., & Mason, W. A. Stereotyped movements of mental defectives: IV. The effects of toys and the character of the acts. *American Journal of Mental Deficiency,* 1964, *68*, 511–524.

Baumeister, A. M., & Forehand, R. Stereotyped acts. In N. R. Ellis (Ed.), *International review of research in mental retardation* (Vol. 6). New York: Academic Press, 1973.

Bijou, S. W., Peterson, R. F., Harris, F. R., Allen, K. E., & Johnson, M. S. Methodology for experimental studies of young children in natural settings. *Psychological Record,* 1969, *19*, 177–210.

Bryson, V., Sakati, N., Nyhan, W. L., & Fish, C. H. Self-mutilative behavior in the Cornelia de Lange Syndrome. *American Journal of Mental Deficiency,* 1971, *76*, 319–324.

Bucher, B., & Lovaas, O. I. Use of aversive stimulation in behavior modification. In M. Jones (Ed.), *Miami Symposium on the Prediction of Behavior, 1967: Aversive Stimulation.* Coral Gables, Florida: University of Miami Press, 1968.

Carr, E. G. The motivation of self-injurious behavior: A review of some hypotheses. *Psychological Bulletin,* 1977, *84*, 800–816.

Carr, E. G., Newsom, C. D., & Binkoff, J. A. Stimulus control of self-destructive behavior in a psychotic child. *Journal of Abnormal Child Psychology,* 1976, *4*, 139–153.

Carr, E. G., & McDowell, J. J. Social control of self-injurious behavior of organic etiology. *Behavior Therapy,* 1980, *11*, 402–409.

Corte, H. E., Wolf, M. M., & Locke, B. J. A comparison of procedures for eliminating self-injurious behavior of retarded adolescents. *Journal of Applied Behavior Analysis,* 1971, *4*, 201–213.

Davenport, R. K., & Berkson, G. Stereotyped movements of mental defectives: II. Effects of novel objects. *American Journal of Mental Deficiency,* 1963, *7*, 879–882.

de Lissovoy, V. Head banging in early childhood: A suggested cause. *Journal of Genetic Psychology,* 1963, *102*, 109–114.

Duda, T. Personal communication and enclosure: Grievances #76-114 through 76-119; in the matter of arbitration between the State of Illinois, Department of Mental Health and Developmental Disabilities, and the American Federation of State, County and Municipal Employees, 1976.

Duker, P. Behavioral control of self-biting in a Lesch-Nyhan patient. *Journal of Mental Deficiency,* 1975, *19*, 11–19.

Epstein, L. H., Doke, L. A., Sajwaj, T. E., Sorrell, A., & Rimmer, B. Generality and side effects of overcorrection. *Journal of Applied Behavioral Analysis*, 1974, *4*, 201–213.

Favell, J. E., McGimsey, J. F., & Jones, M. L. The use of physical restraint in the treatment of self-injury and as positive reinforcement. *Journal of Applied Behavior Analysis*, 1978, *11*, 226–241.

Favell, J. E., McGimsey, J. F., Jones, M. L., & Cannon, P. R. Physical restraint as positive reinforcement. *American Journal of Mental Deficiency*, 1981, *85*, 425–432.

Ferster, C. B. Positive reinforcement and behavioral deficits of autistic children. *Child Development*, 1961, *32*, 437–456.

Fordyce, W. E. *Behavioral methods for chronic pain and illness*. St. Louis, Missouri: V. C. Mosby Co., 1976.

Foxx, R. M., & Azrin, N. H. The elimination of autistic self-stimulatory behavior by overcorrection. *Journal of Applied Behavior Analysis*, 1973, *6*, 1–14.

Frankel, F., & Simmons, J. Q. Self-injurious behavior in schizophrenic and retarded children. *American Journal of Mental Deficiency*, 1976, *80*, 512–522.

Frieden, B. Clinical issues on the physical restraint experience with self-injurious children. *Research and the Retarded*, 1977, *4*, 1–6.

Frith, C. D. Double blind clinical trial of 5-hydroxytryptophan in a case of Lesch-Nyhan Syndrome. *Journal of Neurology, Neurosurgery and Psychiatry*, 1976, *39*, 656–659.

Gilroy, J., & Meyer, J. S. *Medical neurology*, New York: MacMillan, 1975.

Goldfarb, W. Pain reactions in a group of institutionalized schizophrenic children. *American Journal of Orthopsychiatry*, 1958, *28*, 777–785.

Herson, M., & Barlow, D. *Single-case experimental designs*. New York: Pergamon Press, 1976.

Hoefnagel, D. The syndrome of athetoid cerebral palsy, mental deficiency, self-mutilation, and hyperuricemia. *Journal of Mental Deficiency Research*, 1965, *9*, 69–74.

Howie, V. M. Developmental sequelae of chronic otitis media: A review. *Developmental and Behavioral Pediatrics*, 1980, *1*, 34–38.

Johnson, J. Organic psychosyndromes due to boxing. *British Journal of Psychiatry*, 1969, *115*, 45–53.

Jones, F. H., Simmons, J. Q., & Frankel, F. An extinction procedure for eliminating self-destructive behavior in a 9-year-old autistic girl. *Journal of Autism and Childhood Schizophrenia*, 1974, *4*, 241–250.

Keefe, F. J., & Ward, E. M. Behavioral approaches to the management of self-destructive children. In I. R. Stuart, & C. E. Wells (Eds.), *Self-destructive behavior in children and adolescents*. New York: Van Nostrand Reinhold, 1981.

Lesch, M., & Nyhan, W. L. A familial disorder of uric acid metabolism and central nervous system function. *American Journal of Medicine*, 1964, *36*, 561–570.

Levison, C. The development of head banging in a young rhesus monkey, *American Journal of Mental Deficiency*, 1970, *75*, 323–328.

Lovaas, O. I., Freitag, G., Gold, V. J., & Kassorla, I. C. Experimental studies in childhood schizophrenia. I: Analysis of self-destructive behavior. *Journal of Experimental Child Psychology*, 1965, *2*, 67–84.

Lovaas, O. I. & Simmons, J. Q. Manipulation of self-destruction in three retarded children. *Journal of Applied Behavior Analysis*, 1969, *2*, 143–157.

Marks, J. F., Baum, J., Keele, D. K., Kay, J. L., & MacFarlen, A. Lesch-Nyhan Syndrome treated from the early neonatal period. *Pediatrics*, 1968, *42*, 357–359.

Massong, S. R., Edwards, R. P., Sitton, L. R., & Hailey, B. J. A case of trichotillomania in a three-year-old treated by response prevention. *Journal of Behavior Therapy and Experimental Psychiatry*, 1980, *11*, 223–226.

May, J. G., Risley, T. R., Twardosz, S., Friedman, P., Bijou, S. W., & Wexler, D. Guidelines for the use of behavioral procedures in state programs for retarded persons. *Mental Retardation Research*, 1975, *1*, 12–26.

Menkes, J. H. *Textbook of child neurology* (Ed. 2). Philadelphia: Lea & Feibiger, 1980.

Miller, P. M. Theoretical and practical issues in substance abuse assessment and treatment. In W. R. Miller (Ed.), *The addictive behaviors*. New York: Pergamon Press, 1980.

Milunsky, A. *The prenatal diagnosis of heridatary disorders*. Springfield, Illinois: Charles C. Thomas, 1973.

Nathan, P. Etiology and process in the addictive behaviors. In W. R. Miller (Ed.), *The addictive behaviors*. New York: Pergamon Press, 1980.

Pennypacker, H. S., Koenig, C. H., & Lindsley, O. R. *Handbook of the standard behavior chart*. Kansas City, Kansas: Precision Media, 1972.

Rogers, J. Tissue tolerance guidelines. 1974 Annual Reports of Progress Rehabilitation Engineering Center at Rancho Los Amigos Hospital, University of Southern California, Downey, California, 1973–1974.

Romanczyk, R. Self-injurious behavior: The development of an appropriate conceptual framework. Paper presented at the Gatlinburg Conferences on Research in Mental Retardation and Developmental Disabilities, Gatlinburg, Tennessee, 1981.

Romanczyk, R. G., & Goren, E. R. Severe self-injurious behavior: The problem of clinical control. *Journal of Consulting and Clinical Psychology*, 1975, *43*, 730–739.

Ross, R. R., & McKay, H. B. *Self-mutilation*. Toronto: D. C. Health and Co., 1980.

Russo, D. C., Carr, E. G., & Lovaas, O. I. Self-injury in pediatric populations. In J. Ferguson, & C. B. Taylor (Eds.), *Advances in Behavioral Medicine*. Holliswood, New York: Spectrum Publications, 1979.

Russo, D. C., Cataldo, M. F., & Cushing, P. J. Compliance training and behavioral covariation in the treatment of multiple behavior problem. *Journal of Applied Behavior Analysis*, 1981, *14*, 209–222.

Schroeder, S. R., Schroeder, C. S., Smith, B., & Dalldorf, J. Prevalence of self-injurious behaviors in a large state facility for the retarded: A three year follow-up study. *Journal of Autism and Developmental Disorders*, 1978, *8*, 261–269.

Shear, C. S., Nyhan, W. L., Kirman, B. H., & Stern, J. Self-mutilative behavior as a feature of the de Lange Syndrome. *Journal of Pediatrics*, 1971, *78*, 506–509.

Shintoub, S. A., & Soulairac, A. L'enfant automutilateur. *Psychiatrie de l'Enfant*, 1961, *3*, 111–145.

Shodell, M. C., & Reiter, H. H. Self-mutilative behavior in verbal and nonverbal schizophrenic children. *Archives of General Psychiatry*, 1968, *19*, 453–455.

Solnick, J. V., Rincover, A., & Peterson, C. R. Some determinants of the reinforcing and punishing effects of timeout. *Journal of Applied Behavior Analysis*, 1977, *10*, 415–424.

Stolz, S. Why no guidelines for behavior modification. *Journal of Applied Behavior Analysis*, 1977, *10*, 541–547.

Tate, B. G., & Baroff, G. S. Aversive control of self-injurious behavior in a psychotic boy. *Behavior Research and Therapy,* 1966, *4,* 281–287.

Thomas, D. R. Certification of behavior analysts in Minnesota. *Behavior Analyst,* 1979, *2,* 1–3.

White, O. R., & Haring, N. G. *Exceptional teaching* (Ed. 2). Columbus, Ohio: Charles E. Merrill Publishing Co., 1976.

Whitehead, P., & Ferrence, R. Measuring the incidence of self-injury: Some methodological and design considerations. *American Journal of Orthopsychiatry,* 1973, *43,* 142–148.

Williams, R. Personal communication, 1981.

Steve Herman
Denise Barnes

18

Behavioral Assessment in Geriatrics

At present, the elderly (defined as those individuals age 65 and older) comprise about 11 percent of the United States citizenry, and represent the fastest-growing segment of the population. In comparison, at the turn of the century only 4 percent of the population was 65 or over. This shift in the population's age profile, occasioned by increasing life expectancy and declining birth rates, has gained increasing recognition by social forecasters in both government and the private sector. Among those most concerned about this development are health care professionals, who have long been aware of the prominent position of the elderly as consumers of health care services.

For its part, psychology has come relatively late to a recognition of its present and future role as a provider of services to the elderly (Gatz et al., 1980). Professional training in psychology traditionally paid little attention to the mental health needs of the elderly, and few graduates were prepared for, or inclined to, work with this population. This is paralleled by a persistent underusage of mental health services (other than institutionalization) by the elderly, despite ample evidence attesting to the continuing and/or increasing need for such services in the later years of life (Kramer et al., 1973). This mutual avoidance by mental health professionals and the elderly has been attributed to various factors, including "ageism" (or negative attitudes towards aging) on the part of professionals; the stigma attached to mental health services by the elderly; financial and logistical limitations; and so on. These factors notwithstanding, numerous legislative and executive actions (summarized comprehensively by Gatz et al., 1980), have set the stage for an increasingly effective future provision of mental health services to the elderly. At present, however, conditions largely reflect the past, and relatively few elderly persons seek help for problems that they define as emotional or psychological in nature (Kulka and Tamir, 1978).

Realistically speaking, the mental health professional who adheres to a traditional position with respect to the elderly, expecting the patient to appear in the consulting room with a suitable neurotic complaint, is in for a long wait. The clinician experienced in working with the elderly knows that a more active, "outreaching" approach is often needed in identifying and assessing emotional and behavioral problems in this age group. The mental health specialist must take the "shop" to where the "action" is: to the medical clinics, the rest homes and nursing facilities, the senior centers, the congregate housing units. The clinician needs to closely coordinate his or her efforts with other health care providers and social agencies that deal with the elderly. Finally, the clinician needs to adapt both the scope and the methodology of the assessment scheme to conform with the special needs and challenges presented by the older patient.

This chapter will focus on that adaptation, and is intended to be a guide for clinicians interested in readying themselves for work with the elderly. A rationale will be presented for pursuing behavioral assessment within a multidimensional framework, and a number of general issues affecting geropsychological assessment will be discussed. The remainder of the chapter will be devoted to a selective survey of available assessment instruments and strategies relating to the dimensions of mental health, physical health, social needs and resources, and activities of daily living.

THE DESIRABILITY OF MULTIDIMENSIONAL ASSESSMENT

Any discussion of assessment must deal with one central question: *assessment of what?* When the object is the older patient, and the agent is the mental health practitioner, this question permits of a variety of answers (reviewed by Schaie and Schaie, 1979). The realities of aging and its associated stresses dictate a necessity for a broadly-based assessment framework that can encompass the older person's functioning in various, key life areas. Some of these areas, such as cognitive functioning and affective status, are familiar and traditional domains to the mental health practitioner. Others, such as social resources, patterns of health-care utilization, and ability to carry out necessary activities of daily living, may be unfamiliar. The *multidimensional assessment model* that emerges from this conception should not be confused with a *multidisciplinary approach,* in which specific assessment areas are delegated to appropriate specialists. Rather, the multidimensional model emphasizes concurrent assessment of a variety of life areas by a single clinician, with an eye toward identifying interconnecting impairment patterns which become most visible when the "total picture" is held in focus.

The rationale for this model is its consistency with the pattern of multiple impairments especially prevalent among the elderly. In an extensive survey of health and functional status among community-residing elderly in Durham, North

Carolina, about 1,000 subjects were interviewed and rated on five dimensions of well-being: (1) physical health, (2) mental health, (3) social resources, (4) economic resources, and (5) activities of daily living (Blazer, 1978). Impairment ratings correlated quite highly among most of these areas, with intercorrelations between physical health, mental health, and activities of daily living ranging from .55 to .72. These findings, verified by clinical observations of Older American Resources and Services (OARS) clinic patients, indicate that older patients who are impaired in one area are at high risk for impairment in another area. Commonly encountered examples of multiple impairments are the demented older person who is socially isolated and increasingly unable to carry out necessary activities of daily living; or the disabled, chronically ill elder who develops depressive symptoms and socially withdraws. Under such circumstances an assessment strategy that focuses too highly on specific symptom areas will likely overlook issues critical to the older patient's general well-being.

The multidimensional assessment approach has been the basis for the development of two instruments for geriatric assessment: the OARS Multidimensional Functional Assessment Questionnaire (MFAQ), and the Comprehensive Assessment and Referral Evaluation (CARE) (Gurland et al., 1977). The MFAQ was developed as a survey instrument and involves a structured interview with forced-choice responses. This yields ratings of physical health, mental health, social resources, economic resources, and activities of daily living. The validity and reliability of the MFAQ have been documented, and it has been extensively employed in both research and applied settings. The MFAQ is most appropriate when applied as an initial screening or survey instrument, providing an overall profile of relative impairment in critical life areas. It is no accident that these areas essentially coincide with the later sections of this chapter, and subsections of the MFAQ will be described at appropriate points.

The CARE battery is also a structured interview of demonstrated reliability, which, like the MFAQ, can be used as a geriatric screening instrument. In addition, however, the CARE format includes provision for optional follow-up questioning to elaborate identified problem areas and identify factors relevant to the etiology and disruptiveness of the problem. This represents a significant advantage over the more structured MFAQ in clinical settings, as it adds a dimension of sensitivity to individually-significant problem areas, an aspect of value both in initial and follow-up assessments.

The clinician seeking guidelines to multidimensional assessment of the elderly would be well advised to review the MFAQ and CARE protocols, for they represent an accumulation of the most important elements to assess in a geriatric setting, alongside the usual medical evaluations. Both approaches have been of value in sensitizing young clinicians to special needs and concerns of the elderly, which otherwise may have eluded their consideration.

Within the general multidimensional framework outlined above, there is ample room for more specialized assessment procedures where indicated. Before reviewing these, however, let us consider some general problems one often faces in the evaluation of the geriatric patient.

SPECIAL PROBLEMS IN ASSESSING THE ELDERLY PATIENT

Strictly speaking, there are no assessment problems in behavioral geriatrics which are not encountered in assessment of younger groups. Age alone does not create unique problems in the assessment situation. There are, however, certain functional difficulties that tend to be more prevalent in impaired, elderly persons and which require modification of assessment strategy and technique. In addition, there are special problems in the use of standard assessment instruments with this group.

Confusion and disorientation of varying degrees are often present in elderly patients referred for mental health services; such persons typically take longer to adjust to new situations and to respond to new demands placed on them. In working with confused patients, it is essential to allow time to establish rapport and to orient the patient to the task at hand before proceeding further. Initial observation of the patient's response capability can inform the clinician of the appropriate level on which to begin the assessment. It is important to avoid introducing excessive demands at the outset, as they might confuse and disturb the patient. Patience, repetition, and reinforcement are important interviewer attributes in such situations.

A second set of problems involves the securing of adequate cooperation and motivation, and several factors may play a part. Many older patients do not understand or perceive the value of psychological assessment and may feel that it is of little relevance to their lives and their problems. Geriatric researchers have pointed out that the elderly have a lower tolerance for ambiguity and shorter attention span (Salzman and Shader, 1975), and that face validity is an important factor in maintaining appropriate task involvement (Gurland et al., 1977). Probably more important, however, are the negative connotations of mental health assessment for the elderly—connotations that may generate much resistance and non-cooperation in the clinical situation. Elderly persons tend to perceive inquiry into their mental health status as implying that they are thought of as "crazy" or incompetent. For the elderly, especially, this may be a highly threatening prospect, for any of the following reasons: First, they grew up in an era which had little or none of our present positive resources for mental health care, and in which the popular notions of psychiatry involved the spectre of permanent institutionalization; there is a definite stigma attached to mental health in the minds of many elderly persons. Second, older persons with chronic physical illnesses may perceive psychological assessment as signaling a minimization of their physical symptoms by the physician; this could be perceived as a threat to the continuity of needed medical care. Finally, the prevailing view of mental disorder in old age is that it presages inevitable, terminal deterioration and loss of personal and environmental control. Older persons with such associations are understandably adverse to projecting themselves into the ''mental disorder'' status.

It is not uncommon, then, that such anxieties cause older persons to retreat from involvement in psychological assessment. Resistance may be overt, as when a patient refuses to cooperate, or it may involve more subtle avoidance maneuvers designed to deny or suppress pathological symptomatology. The clinician needs to be aware of such anxieties when they appear to be present, and must take appropriate steps to dispel the tension. The patient can usually be reassured by explaining that the assessment is a routine part of the evaluation, and designed to help his or her doctors know the patient as ''a whole person.'' In other cases, the issues may better be confronted by open discussion of feelings about psychologic evaluation. If the patient is reluctant to share personal feelings, the interviewer can reflect on how ''many people'' feel under similar circumstances.

Another common set of problems presented by elderly patients involves physical limitations. Visual and auditory deficits of varying degrees are quite frequent in normal older persons (Fozard et al., 1977; Corso, 1977), and have been shown to have a significant detrimental effect on cognitive test performance (Granick et al., 1976). Recognized visual deficits may be compensated for by using large-print formats for written material or alternate, verbal forms of test administration. A partially deaf patient can better be communicated with by adopting a slow, clearly enunciated speech delivery with lips plainly visible, and with ample redundancy. Merely speaking louder does not help. Interference from extraneous stimuli is especially disruptive to elderly persons (Rabbitt, 1965); a quiet environment is conducive to optimum performance.

The impaired elderly patient is also easily subject to fatigue, which in turn affects cognitive, perceptual, and motor functioning (Furry and Baltes, 1973). Although fatigability varies with several factors, including general physical health and degree of cognitive deterioration, it is often the case that fatigue will diminish performance after a relatively brief period; it may thus be necessary to spread the assessment over several short sessions. Medications can influence energy level and speed of cognitive processes as well, and should be taken into account when analyzing performance.

Finally, the biological components of anxiety and depression often have a considerable effect on level of functioning in the elderly patient (Eisdorfer et al., 1970; Miller, 1979). Such affective conditions are common among the impaired elderly and special care must be taken to assess their contribution to observed performance deficits. This can often be accomplished by repeated testing, permitting fluctuations in affective status to be compared with changes in level of functioning.

In addition to the cognitive, emotional, and physical limitations so far described, there also are significant limitations in the test instruments available for use with the elderly. The most obvious of these is the relative lack of appropriate norms for older people. Most psychological tests have been standardized on younger groups, and aged norms, when available, typically are based on much smaller sample sizes. Moreover, as Gurland (1980) points out, norms for the elderly may need to be frequently updated, as successive cohorts of elderly are performing increasingly well on tests, probably as a result of better health and education (Schaie and Gribbin, 1975). Test norms, therefore, may generally be less reliable for older groups.

Another psychometric issue is that of construct validity: is a given test or scale measuring the same data in an older person as it does in a young person? For example, depression scales, such as the Zung Self-Rating Depression Scale (Zung, 1965), typically include items relating to somatic symptoms and complaints, which tend to be present in older persons independent of depressive symptomatology. This has led some researchers to warn against relying on the Zung scale as a measure of depression in the very old (Gallagher et al., 1978). This problem underscores the need for development and validation of assessment instruments designed with specific reference to geriatric symptomatology.

These limitations notwithstanding, an increasing body of clinical and research evidence is available to guide the selection, application, and interpretation of assessment instruments for use with the elderly. A review of this evidence underlies the topical survey of assessment strategies presented below.

COGNITIVE ASSESSMENT

Brief Screening Instruments

In various clinical geriatric settings there is an urgent need to conduct quick screenings of patients for gross evidence of cognitive impairments. This screening may be used to identify patients requiring more extensive neuropsychological evaluation. It may also be useful in alerting primary clinicians to cognitive limitations impacting on a patient's reliability as an informant, his or her ability to understand and comply with treatment instructions and to function independently, and other issues critical to case management.

A number of brief screening instruments of this type have been reported in the literature, many of which are variants of the Mental Status Questionnaire (MSQ) (Kahn et al., 1960), a 10-item scale tapping orientation and memory functions. The MSQ, along with six analog scales developed for special purposes, is comprehensively reviewed with respect to item content, reliability, and validity by Gurland (1980). These screening devices have been proven consistently effective in detecting the presence and degree of organic impairment in elderly subjects. One particularly systematic study (Haglund and Schuckit, 1976) subjected several screening instruments to a regression analysis, and found that one measure, the Short Portable Mental Status Questionnaire (SPMSQ) (Pfeiffer, 1975) accounted for almost all of the variance. The SPMSQ is reproduced in Figure 18-1 as it

```
[ASK QUESTIONS 1-10 AND RECORD ALL ANSWERS.  (ASK QUESTION 4a.
ONLY IF SUBJECT HAS NO TELEPHONE.)  CHECK CORRECT (+) OR
INCORRECT (-) FOR EACH AND RECORD TOTAL NUMBER OF ERRORS BASED
ON TEN QUESTIONS.]
```

+	-	
		1. What is the date today? _____
		Month Day Year
		2. What day of the week is it? _____
		3. What is the name of this place? _____
		4. What is your telephone number? _____
		a. [ASK ONLY IF SUBJECT DOES NOT HAVE A PHONE.] What is your street address?
		5. How old are you? _____
		6. When were you born? _____
		Month Day Year
		7. Who is the president of the U.S. now? _____
		8. Who was the president just before him? _____
		9. What was your mother's maiden name? _____
		10. Subtract 3 from 20 and keep subtracting 3 from each new number you get, all the way down.

[CORRECT ANSWER IS: 17, 14, 11, 8, 5, 2.]

_____ Total number of errors.

RATINGS:

0-2 errors - Intact intellectual functioning.

3-4 errors - Mild intellectual impairment.

5-7 errors - Moderate intellectual impairment.

8 + errors - Severe intellectual impairment.

Note: The above ratings are for persons with 9-12 years
    of education. For persons with less education, one more
    error is allowed for each category. For persons with
    more education, one less error is allowed.

Fig. 18-1. The Short, Portable Mental Status Questionnaire (SPMSQ). Reprinted with permission from *Multidimensional functional assessment: The OARS methodology* (Ed. 2.). Durham, North Carolina: Center for the Study of Aging and Human Development, Duke University Press, 1978.

appears in the OARS MFAQ, together with Pfeiffer's impairment rating scale and correction factor for educational level (Pfeiffer, 1975).

The advantages of the SPMSQ are its speed and ease in administration and scoring, and its proven reliability and discriminative validity (Pfeiffer, 1978). There is a danger of false-negatives, however, when the test is used with mildly to moderately impaired persons of superior intelligence and education. Where this is suspected, a low SPMSQ score should be interpreted with caution.

A different sort of screening test with demonstrated usefulness is the Face-Hand Test (FHT) (Fink et al., 1952). This procedure, which involves repeated trials of simultaneously touching the patient on the cheek and contralateral hand (see Fig. 18-2), is highly discriminative between functionally- and organically-impaired patients. The latter frequently detect only one of the two stimuli, or displace a stimulus to a different location (usually hand to face). Such responses are extremely rare both in normals or the functionally impaired. Irving and colleagues (1970) found that the FHT correctly identified 92 percent of the functionally impaired and 76 percent of organically impaired elderly patients. Its culture-free, relatively language-independent format enhances its clinical usefulness in a range of situations where performance on a measure such as the SPMSQ would be suspect. For instance, Fink and colleagues (1952) report that by 10 trials, 87 percent of brain-damaged patients, compared with only 3 percent of schizophrenics, continued to make errors.

A final cognitive screening instrument which bears special mention is the Mini-Mental State (MMS) (Folstein et al., 1975). The MMS is comprised of 11 items that cover a wider range of intellectual functions than the SPMSQ and similar instruments. The items assess orientation, verbal learning, attention and calculation (serial 7s), verbal recall, language functioning, and visual-motor integration (design copying). The MMS may be the screening instrument of choice where identification of focal neuropsychological signs is of particular importance, for it includes items sensitive to lateralized brain functions.

Other cognitive screening instruments successfully used with older patients include Libow's FROMAJE Test (1981), and Plutchik's GIES scale (1971).

Intelligence Testing

The Wechsler Adult Intelligence Scale (WAIS) (Wechsler, 1955) has been extensively used as a measure of intelligence with geriatric populations. Norms for persons over 65 were developed by Doppelt and Wallace (1955), and are included in the WAIS test manual. Subsequent experience has shown, however, that these norms do not generalize to most elderly populations. Price and colleagues (1980) point out that seven of eight studies subsequent to the initial standardization study have found that elderly persons achieve significantly lower scaled scores on performance than on verbal subtests. It appears clear that an adjustment in the aged WAIS norms is necessary; until this is accomplished on a large scale, it is best to

---

FACE-HAND TEST: ADMINISTRATION

The patient is seated facing the examiner, eyes
closed, with hands resting palm down on the knees.
The examiner touches the patient lightly on the cheek
and back of the hand simultaneously, asking him/her to
indicate what was felt.   Ten trials are given in the
following sequence;

      1. Left cheek/ Right hand
      2. Left hand/ Right cheek
      3. Left cheek/ Left hand
      4. Right cheek/ Right hand

      5. Left cheek/ Right cheek
      6. Left hand/ Right hand

      7-10. (Repeat #1-4)

The main types of error which occur are **extinction**,
where only one stimulus is reported; and **displacement**,
where two stimuli are reported but one or both are incorrectly located.   A patient is scored POSITIVE on the test
if he/she consistently fails to identify the correct stimuli over trials #1-4 and #7-10.   A patient is scored
NEGATIVE if trials #7-10 are negotiated correctly, regardless of possible errors on trials #1-4.   Trials #5-6 are
to orient the patient to the occurance of double stimulation, and are not counted.   Repetition of the test with
eyes open will usually replicate the original performance.

Fig. 18-2.   Procedures for administering the Face-hand test.

use the subtest profiles reported by various researchers (Birren et al., 1963;
Eisdorfer and Cohen, 1961; Overall and Gorham, 1972) as a basis for judging the
normalcy of WAIS profiles for the aged in a clinical setting. In selecting an appropriate reference group, care should be taken to achieve the best match with
regard to age, educational level, socioeconomic status, cultural background, and
general health. The Duke OARS Clinic, for instance, might do well to rely on

normative data from the Duke longitudinal studies (Eisdorfer and Cohen, 1961), gathered from local community residents.

One common question underlying the assessment of intellectual functioning in the older patient is the determination of the presence, degree, and rate of cognitive decline. The ideal way to assess this process is to compare equivalent performance measures taken prior to and during the illness. Unfortunately, this is rarely possible, as premorbid test data are not often available. Instead, an estimate of premorbid intellectual level must usually suffice. Among the estimation methods suggested are Vocabulary score (Yates, 1956); reading ability (Nelson and O'Connell, 1978); "deterioration index" derived from WAIS subtest scores (Wechsler, 1958); and estimation based on prior educational or occupational levels. These alternatives are reviewed by Gurland (1980), who points out serious limitations in each. In the absence of any generally applicable formula, the assessment of intellectual decline remains a matter of clinical judgment based on whatever data are available in a particular case. Relevant historical information includes educational and occupational accomplishments, interests and hobbies, and reading habits. Valuable evidence occasionally emerges when the patient is asked how he or she was as a student, or how easy it was to learn new things as a youngster. Test data is often helpful to the extent that certain WAIS subtests tend to hold up better than others in the presence of brain dysfunction (Overall and Gorham, 1972). For the most part, however, estimation of premorbid level of functioning is a matter of clinical judgment that requires creative investigation.

The WAIS is a long test, and requires special training to administer and score. In many clinical situations there is a need for a quick, global estimate of current level of intellectual functioning. The test of this sort which has been most thoroughly evaluated with elderly patients is the Quick Test (QT) (Ammons and Ammons, 1962). The QT is a picture vocabulary test requiring only a non-verbal response. A correction factor for ages 45–75 + is contained in the test manual. Levine (1971) found very high correlations between the QT and the WAIS in a small sample of normal elderly subjects, while Gendreau and colleagues (1973) provided additional narrative data for very old institutionalized patients. The QT is brief, easy to administer and score, and usable with hearing-impaired patients and those patients with very brief attention spans.

Memory Assessment

The importance of memory assessment in the geriatric setting cannot be overemphasized, as memory impairment is probably the single most common symptom among the cognitively-impaired elderly. The DSM-III *(Diagnostic and Statistical Manual of Mental Disorders, third edition)* lists memory impairment as a criterial symptom of both delirium and dementia, and it is typically one of the earliest indicators of the progressive intellectual decline one sees in Alzheimer's type senile dementia. At the same time, however, laboratory studies with normal adults have demonstrated a significant age decrement in certain memory functions beyond the fifth decade (Craik, 1977; Botwinick & Storandt, 1974). Other data suggest a positive correlation between self-reported memory problems and depressive affect (Kahn et al., 1975). In older adults, the relationship between memory complaints and actual memory impairment is complex, and the assessment task is to determine the presence and degree of memory impairment, and to differentiate decline indicative of organic pathology from that attributable to normal age changes and/or depression or other psychopathology.

An excellent and comprehensive review of the current memory assessment literature is provided by Erickson and Scott (1977), and the reader seeking extended discussion of theoretical issues and empirical findings would do well to begin there. The present treatment takes a pragmatic approach focusing on memory assessment procedures applicable to general clinical settings.

For the clinician seeking a quick measure of memory functioning, we recommend the "Set Test" procedure (Isaacs and Akhtar, 1972). This procedure involves asking the patient to name as many items within a given category as possible. Isaacs used four categories: colors, animals, fruits, and towns or cities, and counted up to 10 responses for each, yielding a maximum score of 40. If the patient gives up, or repeats a previous item, the count is stopped at that point. We have found that almost all subjects will cooperate with this procedure if it is introduced as a test of memory and if the interviewer is patient and supportive. For special purposes, alternative categories can be added to test the limits. For example, a retired mechanic might be asked to name as many tools as he can, or a gardener to name flowers. Failure on these tailor-made categories indicates severe impairment of free recall, while success suggests the continuing retention of overlearned material and permits completion of the task on a positive note.

Isaacs reported set test results from 64 community-residing men and women aged 65 and over. His overall mean score of 31.3 contained an age difference of five points between the 65–74 and 75 + age groups, which indicates that clinical norms will have to be age-corrected. If we apply the customary criterion that a "normal score" on this measure should fall within one standard deviation of the mean, the normal range of Set Test performance would be as follows:

Age Group	Normal Range (Max = 40)
65–74	27–40
75 +	20–37

Preliminary data from 32 outpatients seen at the OARS Geriatric Evaluation and Treatment Clinic yielded a prorated mean score of 25.2 out of 40.0. When patients were grouped as to organic versus functional diagnosis, the organic group (n = 21) had a mean score of 20.8; the mean score for the functional group (n = 11) was 34.0. These early findings support the potential usefulness of the Set Test as a memory screening device.

The Wechsler Memory Scale (WMS) (Wechsler, 1945) is a familiar, widely used battery comprised of seven subtests: personal and current information; orientation; mental control; logical memory; memory span; visual reproduction; and associate learning. Initially the test was standardized for 25–50-year-olds, and it was not until the mid-1960s that empirically derived norms for older persons appeared (Hulicka, 1966; Klonoff and Kennedy, 1965; Meer and Baker, 1965). Criticism of the WMS, as reviewed by Erickson and Scott (1977) is widespread, and has focused on the scale's erroneous conception of memory as unitary (as represented by the concept of a ''memory quotient''), and its tendency to measure learning rather than memory per se. The consensus appears to be that in its original form the WMS is less than desirable as a memory assessment tool.

More recently, however, Russell (1975) has produced a modified WMS that answers some of the criticisms of the original scales. The revised form utilizes only the logical memory (paragraph recall) and visual reproduction (copying designs from memory) components of the WMS, and includes repetition of the two subtests—without re-presentation of stimuli—after a 30-minute delay. The comparison of delayed and immediate recall yields a retrieval score, which theoretically represents a measure of memory relatively independent of learning factors. The Russell revision of the WMS includes three separate scores for both the semantic and visual test modalities: immediate recall; delayed recall; and percent retention. Raw scores are converted to ratings on a 6-point impairment scale (Russell, 1975), ranging from outstanding (0) to severely impaired (5). Logue and Wyrick (1979) have published a validation of the Russell revision of the WMS in a comparison of normal and demented elderly patients. A significant difference was found between these groups on all six memory scores, thus providing norms which can be used as an initial guide for identifying memory impairment associated with dementia.

Another memory test battery, the Guild Memory Test (Gilbert et al., 1968; Gilbert and Levee, 1971), has been extensively standardized with older age groups, and has also been corrected for verbal intelligence level. The Guild Test, which includes subtests similar to the WMS, has not yet been published, and is thus of limited availability.

Digit-span tests have long been used as a measure of immediate recall, or, perhaps more correctly, as reflecting attention or concentration. It has been found, however, that digit span does not decline much with age, and does not differentiate well between normal and impaired older subjects (Inglis, 1958). Crook and coworkers (1980) introduced a variant of the digit span test that requires the subject to dial, from memory, visually-presented 10-digit numbers on a standard telephone. The number is presented in a 3-3-4 grouping typical of long-distance telephone numbers. This procedure emphasizes the performance deficit of memory-impaired elderly persons, and its incorporation as part of a clinical memory assessment battery is recommended.

Finally, it should be noted that a number of memory assessment items are included in the cognitive screening instruments reviewed earlier. These items tend to tap orientation and long-term recall. The following questions, and others may be useful as a brief initial screening for memory impairment: How old are you? When were you born? What was your mother's maiden name? Who is the President now? What did you have for breakfast? What day of the week is it?

Given the prevalence of memory complaints among the elderly, and the wealth of experimental data available concerning normal age changes in memory, there is likely to be much interest generated in this area in the future. Erickson and coworkers (1980) have generated a set of recommendations intended to guide the development of more clinically useful memory tests in coming years.

Neuropsychological Evaluation

The primary goal of neuropsychological assessment is to differentiate between normal and impaired brain function. With the elderly patient, this becomes a very tricky business, as impairment of certain brain functions appears to be a common occurrence in normal aging. The fact that most neuropsychological tests have been standardized on young and middle-aged adults has led to an unfortunate situation where a large proportion of the elderly would be identified as brain-impaired by prevailing norms (Price et al., 1980; Reed and Reitan, 1963; Davies, 1968; Cauthen, 1978). Neuropsychological assessment of older persons must be able to differentiate between the impairment patterns typical of normal aging and those indicative of brain pathology.

One successful attempt to differentiate the effects of age from those of chronic brain syndrome is reported by Overall and Gorham (1972), who found through multiple discriminant analysis that the two groups show differential patterns of impairment on WAIS similarities, vocabulary, and object assembly subtests, on the one hand, and comprehension, arithmetic and picture completion subtests on the other. The three former measures were much more affected by organic brain disease than by age. Another report (Goldstein and Shelly, 1975), suggests that age and diffuse brain damage exert similar effects on motor abilities but dissimilar effects on language functions, non-verbal memory, and psychomotor problem-solving.

No comprehensive norms for the elderly have been forthcoming for either of the two most widely used neuropsychological test batteries, the Halstead-Reitan and the Luria. Until such necessary work is done, clinicians are advised to interpret test results of elderly patients with caution. Logue (1981) is conducting neuropsychological evaluations of patients with Alzheimer's dementia using a modified Halstead-Reitan Battery. The publication of these results will hopefully provide a reference point for comparison with the performance of older persons with suspected brain impairment.

PERSONALITY AND PSYCHOPATHOLOGY

Self-rating and Questionnaire Measures

Assessment instruments employing self-ratings or self-descriptive responses have found wide application in psychological test batteries, due at least in part to their ease in administration and efficient use of staff time. At the same time, however, self-report measures entail numerous potential problems that can limit their usefulness with older populations: they may be long and tiring; complicated and confusing; lacking in face validity; and easily distorted by denial. In addition, norms for the elderly and verification of reliability and validity may be inadequately documented. Plutchik (1979) discusses these limitations at length, and presents useful guidelines to follow in evaluating and selecting scales for use with the elderly. We will provide an overview of three general categories of self-report instruments: (1) multidimensional inventories; (2) measures of specific affect or symptom categories; and (3) brief screening devices for preliminary assessment of psychopathology.

Multidimensional Inventories

The Minnesota Multiphasic Personality Inventory (MMPI) (Hathaway and McKinley, 1943) is the multidimensional instrument most frequently used with elderly patients, and it is the one for which the most extensive descriptive data are available.

Figure 18-3 shows composite profiles (with demarcation of the ± 2 S.D. "normal range") for a massive sample of 13,748 medical outpatients aged 60 and over who were treated at the Mayo Clinic (Swenson et al., 1973). These data, and reviews of other studies (Bernal et al., 1977; Lawton et al., 1980), indicate that normal elderly patients tend to score appreciably higher on the neurotic triad (hypochondriasis, depression, and hysteria), and lower on the psychotic triad (paranoia, psychaesthenia, and schizophrenia) and acting-out scales (psychopathic deviate, and mania). It is recommended that clinicians interpreting elderly MMPI profiles keep the age-appropriate norms in mind. Evidence regarding reliability and validity is scanty, but generally supportive of the MMPI's usefulness as a diagnostic aid with the elderly (Lawton et al., 1980).

The 556-item MMPI, in either its booklet or questionnaire form, presents a long and potentially confusing task for the impaired older person; patients of limited intelligence or education, or with visual deficits, may be particularly unable to respond appropriately. Some clinicians have recommended using the card-sorting version of the MMPI, which is simpler for the patient to handle, but the card-sorting test is tedious and more time-consuming to score. Another approach is the use of shortened forms of the MMPI, such as the 71-item "Mini-Mult" (Kincannon, 1968). These short forms can be orally administered or given in written form. Again, there has been little psychometric analysis of MMPI short forms with the elderly, although a report by Fillenbaum and Pfeiffer (1967) raises questions concerning the reliability and validity of the Mini-Mult for use with elderly subjects. Readers are encouraged to refer to this publication before interpreting elderly Mini-Mult profiles.

The Maudsley Personality Inventory (MPI) (Eysenck, 1959), a 48-item questionnaire yielding scores on extraversion and neuroticism, has, in Great Britain, been widely used with the elderly. Norms for various clinical groups and normal elderly are provided by Bolton and Savage (1971). Clinically, the MPI may be useful primarily as a general measure of neuroticism. The availability of a short form (Eysenck, 1970) and a simplified-language version (Eysenck, 1969) extend its applicability to a wider range of impaired elderly patients.

Another clinically useful inventory, the Hopkins Symptom Checklist (HSCL), is available in several versions (Derogatis et al., 1974), and has been factor-analyzed, yielding five distinct factors: somatization; anxiety; depression; interpersonal sensitivity; and obsessive-compulsive traits. Although further work is needed to confirm the factor-structure of the HSCL with elderly patients, the symptom-checklist approach has received strong endorsement as a valuable measure of response to treatment in the elderly (Gatz, 1978).

Special Purpose Instruments

In clinical geriatrics, the evaluation and differential diagnosis of depression is a common and particularly complex problem. (For an excellent overview, see Salzman and Shader (1979).) From an assessment standpoint, a critical issue concerns possible differences between elderly and non-elderly depressed patients, and the discrimination of depressive symptoms from complaints attributable to increasing age and ill health (e.g., somatic problems, fatigability, etc.) (Raskin, 1979). The most familiar self-rating depression scales—the Zung Self-Rating Depression Scale (SDS) (Zung, 1965), the Beck Depression Inventory (BDI) (Beck et al., 1961), and the MMPI Depression Scale (Hathaway and McKinley, 1943)—were developed and standardized on younger patients, and yield differing norms and factor structures when applied to the elderly (Zung, 1967; Zemore and Eames, 1979; Harmatz and Shader, 1975). There is specific evidence that items relating to somatic symptomatology may be less discriminating of depression in elderly patients, who tend to score higher than younger patients on all current self-rating depression inventories. A review of depression scales suitable for use with elderly patients is provided by Salzman and coauthors (1972).

As a clinical syndrome, anxiety has also been found to manifest variously in a geriatric population. Verwoerdt (1981) provides a valuable schema for understanding and classifying anxiety reactions in the elderly. No measures have been devised especially for assessing anxiety in the elderly, although three self-report anxiety measures have been successfully administered to elderly subject groups

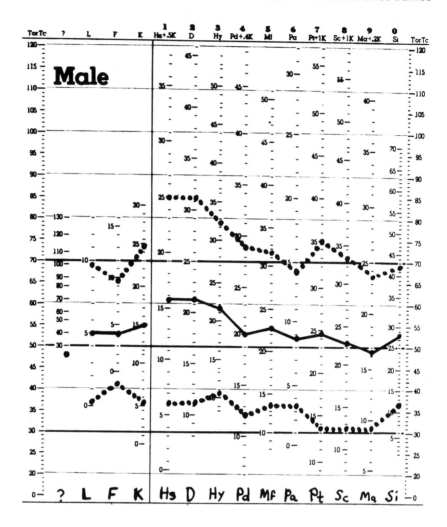

in research settings—the Taylor Manifest Anxiety Scale (1955), the Zung Self-Rating Anxiety Scale (1971), and the tension factor of the Profile of Mood States Scale (1979). In contrast to depression scale norms, there is a general tendency for elderly subjects to score *lower* than younger subjects on self-rating anxiety scales (Salzman and Shader, 1979).

Hypochondriasis, frequently encountered in geriatric settings, is often difficult to differentiate, given the frequency of multiple chronic disorders in this population. Busse and Pfeiffer (1977) provide a useful guide to assessment and treatment of the hypochondriacal older patient, while Brink et al. (1979) describe the development of a six-item self-report scale for detecting hypochondriacal tendencies in an institutionalized geriatric setting.

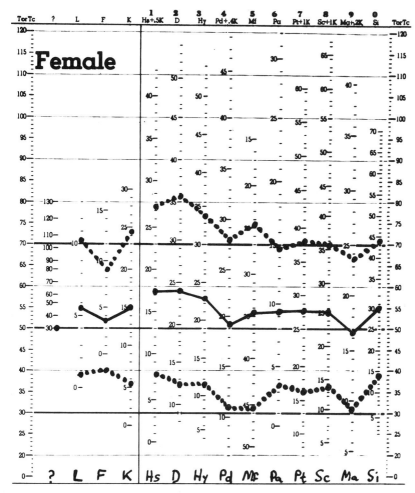

Fig. 18-3. Composite MMPI profiles of male (n = 7048) and female (n = 6700) medical outpatients age 60 and over. Dotted lines represent ±2 S.D. Adapted from: Swensen, W.M., Pearson, J.S., & Osborne, D., *An MMPI sourcebook*. Minneapolis, Minnesota: University of Minnesota Press, 1973.

Brief Screening Instruments

Several brief self-rating scales have been developed for the purpose of detecting the presence of psychiatric impairment in the elderly. Savage and Britton (1967) and Pfeiffer (1979) independently developed scales employing 15 MMPI items. Of the two scales, the Pfeiffer scale, identified as the Short Psychiatric Evaluation Schedule (SPES), has received wider use in the United States and has been incorporated into the OARS Multidimensional Functional Assessment Protocol (1978). The SPES is reproduced in Figure 18-4, with Pfeiffer's rating scale.

Please answer the following questions "Yes" or "No" as they apply to you now. There are no right or wrong answers, only what best applies to you. Occasionally a question may not seem to apply to you, but please answer either "Yes" or "No", whichever is more nearly correct for you.

[CIRCLE "YES" OR "NO" FOR EACH.]

(1) Do you wake up fresh and rested most mornings?...............yes NO

(2) Is your daily life full of things that keep you
     interested?...yes NO

(3) Have you, at times, very much wanted to leave home?..........YES no

(4) Does it seem that no one understands you?....................YES no

(5) Have you had periods of days, weeks, or months when you
     couldn't take care of things because you couldn't "get
     going"?...YES no

(6) Is your sleep fitful and disturbed?..........................YES no

(7) Are you happy most of the time?..............................yes NO

(8) Are you being plotted against?...............................YES no

(9) Do you certainly feel useless at times?......................YES no

(10) During the past few years, have you been well most of
     the time?...yes NO

(11) Do you feel weak all over much of the time?..................YES no

(12) Are you troubled by headaches?...............................YES no

(13) Have you had difficulty in keeping your balance in
     walking?..YES no

(14) Are you troubled by your heart pounding and by a
     shortness of breath?..YES no

(15) Even when you are with people, do you feel lonely much
     of the time?..YES no

                    Sum of Responses in Capital letters _____

RATINGS:

0-3 items - Absence of significant psychopathology.

4-5 items - Borderline.

6+ items - Definite psychopathology.

10+ items - Extensive psychopathology.

Fig. 18-4. The Short Psychiatric Evaluation Schedule (SPES). Reprinted with permission from *Multidimensional Functional Assessment: The OARS Methodology* (Ed. 2.). Durham, North Carolina: Center for the Study of Aging and Human Development, Duke University Press, 1978.

490

Our own experience with the SPES has found it generally consistent with clinical assessment of psychiatric impairment, although it may not detect the disturbed elderly patient who is denying impairment and defensively responding. The addition of a subset of items designed to identify defensiveness, as in the L or K scales of the MMPI, would enhance the discriminative power of the SPES.

PROJECTIVE MEASURES

Some of the greatest drawbacks to self-report measures of personality and psychopathology are the defensive patients or the patients who clearly attempt to put forward an overly-positive self-image. Projective measures are often helpful under such conditions, as they tend to resist conscious bias and assess deeper levels of personality structure. Unfortunately, however, the literature is relatively sparse that reports the projective test performance of elderly persons, especially with respect to clinical issues.

Lawton and colleagues (1980) reviewed numerous studies employing the Rorschach test, and found some consensus that elderly persons showed fewer responses, higher W percent, higher F percent, few M and C responses, and more rejections. They point out, however, that these so-called "age changes" in Rorschach responses tend to correlate with cognitive deficits and are not present in certain healthy community samples (Eisdorfer, 1963). Validity studies of the Rorschachs of elderly populations have been limited to correlations with cognitive measures, and do not provide any guide to their use in assessing psychodynamic processes. A similar problem compromises the usefulness of the House-Tree-Person Test as a projective measure of geriatric personality (Wolk, 1972); sensory and motor limitations tend to overshadow the more subtle contributions of cognitive and personality factors.

The Thematic Apperception Test (TAT) (Murray, 1938) has probably been the most frequently used projective technique in gerontological research (Chown, 1968), and several TAT analogs have been developed especially for use with the elderly. The first of these was the Gerontological Apperception Test (GAT) (Wolk and Wolk, 1971). The GAT consists of 14 pictures depicting older people in situations "frequently encountered by the elderly," thought likely to maximize identification and evoke personally meaningful themata. The most prevalent GAT stimulus theme involves generational relations, with others depicting loneliness; loss of youth, sexuality, and intimacy; and physical dependency. The GAT has been criticized with respect to both form and content by Starr and colleagues (1979), who found it overly depressive in tone, limited in the range of depicted situations, and stereotyped in its view of aging. They also pointed out that many stimuli are too structured, and leave insufficient ambiguity to nurture the projection of personal feelings.

A second TAT analog is the Senior Apperception Test (SAT), developed by Bellak and Bellak (1973). This version consists of 16 pencil drawings whose themes partially overlap, but also expand upon, those of the GAT. Some of the same criticisms leveled at the GAT apply as well to the SAT, but its biggest drawback may be the technically poor quality of the drawings, which presents perceptual problems for persons with visual deficits.

A third test has been published, the Projective Assessment of Aging Method (PAAM) (Starr et al., 1979); it is, in all respects, superior to the two others. It consists of 28 stimulus cards (14 standard and 14 alternates) which cover a wide range of situations relevant to the aging experience. The pictures are clearly and tastefully drawn, and carefully engineered to provide an optimum balance of ambiguity and structure. Three of the most useful cards are provided in virtually identical male and female versions, differing only in the gender of the main figure. As a stimulus set for the projective assessment of elderly patients, the PAAM clearly represents the state of the art.

The question remains, however, as to the clinical usefulness of these specialized projective measures. The test manuals contain examples of stories and interpretations, and present suggestions for clinical applications, but there is little provided or available in the way of standard scoring procedures, norms, or evidence of construct validity. (See Kahana (1978), for a detailed review of these and other projective measures used with the elderly.) Nevertheless, these authors agree with Gallagher and colleagues (1980) that projective techniques are worthy of inclusion in any comprehensive assessment procedure undertaken with the elderly. TAT-analog procedures offer an intimate view of the older person's perceptions and feelings about the world around him or her, and may also provide an index of functions such as judgment, reality testing, affective status, and response to unstructured situations.

OBSERVER RATING SCALES

Rating scales designed for standardized description or evaluation of behavior and symptomatology can be of frequent, great use in clinical geriatric settings. One reason for this is that older patients, and especially those with cognitive impairments, tend to under-report symptomatology or problem behaviors that are readily apparent to family members, professionals, and staff (Reifler et al., 1981). In addition, decisions regarding diagnosis, prognosis, and required level of care heavily depend on behavioral observations and the subsequent generalizations. Thus it is not surprising to note that the rating scale has been the predominant format among specially-designed geriatric assessment instruments.

The most widely used geriatric rating scales assess multiple dimensions of psychopathology and functional impairment; we will focus on these. More specialized scales for rating symptom categories such as depression (Zung, 1972; Hamilton, 1967), and anxiety (Zung, 1971) have also been used with the elderly, and are reviewed by Kochansky (1979).

One group of rating scales are those designed for use by nurses, psychiatric aides, or other institutional personnel. These scales presume no specialized psychiatric training on the part of the observer. Of these scales, extensively reviewed by Smith (1979) and by Salzman and coworkers (1972), two stand out in terms of comprehensiveness and demonstrated reliability and validity: the Geriatric Rating Scale (GRS) (Plutchik et al., 1970), and the Physical and Mental Impairment-of-Function Evaluation (PAMIE) (Gunel et al., 1972).

The GRS is a 31-item scale primarily dealing with social functioning, self-care capability, and the presence of disruptive behaviors. Each item is rated on a three-point scale, indicating degree of impairment; the ratings are then summed to yield an overall impairment score. In addition, three factors have been isolated—withdrawal/apathy, antisocial disruptive behavior, and deficits in activities of daily living—which may be scored separately to derive corresponding indices of impairment (Smith et al., 1977). The GRS is brief, easy to rate, and of high face validity to staff, insofar as it taps dimensions of practical importance in day-to-day patient management.

The PAMIE is a somewhat longer inventory developed for use with institutionalized geriatric patients and designed to assess disabilities in the physical, psychological, and social realms. The PAMIE is composed of 77 items rated *yes* or *no*, and yields scores on the following empirically-generated factors: self-care/dependent; belligerent/irritable; mentally disorganized/confused; anxious/depressed; bedfast/moribund; behaviorally deteriorated; paranoid/suspicious; sensorimotor impaired; withdrawn/apathetic; and ambulatory. The PAMIE is by far the most comprehensive rating scale available for use by ward personnel, and is particularly well suited for indicating the level of care required by institutionalized patients (Smith, 1979).

A second group of geriatric rating scales are multidimensional instruments incorporated within a structured psychiatric interview framework. This type of scale usually emphasizes the differentiation of psychopathological symptomatology, and assumes specialized training on the part of the interviewer. Three such instruments have received wide use with elderly patients: the Geriatric Mental Status interview (GMS) (Gurland et al., 1976); the Brief Psychiatric Rating Scale (BPRS) (Overall and Gorham, 1962); and the Sandoz Clinical Assessment-Geriatric Scale (SCAG) (Shader et al., 1974).

The GMS is a structured interview that consists of about 100 core questions and about the same number of additional questions which are added as needed for elaboration of identified problem areas. The interview includes a mixture of objective, subjective, and performance items, and takes about an hour to administer. Based on the patient's answers and observed behavior, the interviewer then assigns ratings to almost 500 scale items, which have been factored out to 21 factors encompassing a wide range of clinical psychiatric syndromes. The GMS is a vigorously designed instrument intended to standardize differential diagnosis of geriatric psychopathology; its primary application is in clinical research studies.

The BPRS, though designed for use with a general inpatient psychiatric population, has been successfully used with geriatric patients in a number of drug studies (Kochansky, 1979). This brief instrument is comprised of 16 "symptom constructs" to be rated on a seven-point scale of severity, on the basis of a structured psychiatric interview. Ratings are then totalled to yield a single impairment score. The BPRS may be of use as a measure of the extent and severity of psychopathology in psychiatrically impaired elderly patients.

The newest of these instruments, the SCAG, was especially designed for differentiating between early dementia and depression in the elderly. Like the BPRS, it involves interview-based ratings of discrete symptom areas (in this case, 18 areas, plus a global assessment), using a seven-point scale of severity. The SCAG variables appear well-suited to geriatric symptomatology, and include the following: mood depression; confusion; mental alertness; motivation initiative; irritability; hostility; bothersome; indifference to surroundings; unsociability; uncooperativeness; emotional lability; fatigue; self-care; appetite; dizziness; anxiety; impairment of recent memory; disorientation; and overall impression of patient. The SCAG was developed under the auspices of Sandoz Pharmaceuticals, who employed it widely in tests of the effectiveness of Hydergine® in the treatment of dementia (Hughes et al., 1976). No published studies document the validity, reliability, or factor structure of the SCAG.

ASSESSMENT OF SOCIAL NEEDS AND RESOURCES

Assessment of the older person's social needs and resources encompasses two related areas; the instrumental and the emotional. *Instrumental needs* refer to those activities of daily life which an older person is unable to carry out without some degree of assistance from another individual. Instrumental needs vary considerably among older persons, and tend to closely correlate with both mental and physical health status. The persons and/or agencies available to meet an individual's instrumental present and future social needs may be regarded as that person's *instrumental social resources*. In assessing such resources, the key questions include: *who* is available to do *what*, and for *how long* (or *how often)?*

Emotional social needs refer to the older person's desire for interpersonal contact, companionship, and intimacy, as an end in itself. Old age is often considered to be a time of relative social isolation and withdrawl. In many instances, it is, but there is also a great range of variation in the older person's desire for social contact and in the availability of same. An assessment of social functioning from this perspective would focus on the adequacy of current social relationships in terms of the person's (1) desired level and extent of social involvement, and (2) actual and potential relationships with significant others.

One difficulty in assessing these two general areas of social functioning in the elderly is that to date, no instrument has been developed that takes a comprehensive view of social functioning unique to this age group. The absence of such an instrument may be due, in part, to ambiguities in the definition of adequate social functioning for the elderly in this society. Other age groups have particular goal-directed roles that are clearly defined and broadly encouraged, but these may not be generalizable to the older population. A prime example concerns the position that activity holds in determining social strengths: In the young, social activity and social adjustment tend to be viewed as one and the same. All too often, enthusiastic health-care providers overwhelm older persons with programs to increase social activity. Little or no consideration is given to the possibility that an apparently isolated individual may actually enjoy solitude and resent uninvited manipulation of lifestyle. Conversely, an active individual consumed in community activities who appears not to need any intervention may nevertheless experience acute loneliness brought on by loss of family members or close friends. A comparison of recent studies on the effect of activity on general well-being of the elderly yields conflicting reports (Cutler, 1973; Bull and Aucoin, 1975; Graney, 1975).

Given this variability, a good starting point in assessing social adjustment is taking a detailed social history to place the individual's current situation within the context of past social relationships and preferences. A clear picture should be gained of the closeness of family ties, the extent and depth of friendships, and involvement over the years in religious and community activities. Such data will often reveal the intensity of affiliative needs, and may also illustrate how the person responded in the past when help was needed.

In assessing current social needs and resources one attempts to establish: (1) the extent and quality of current social involvements; (2) the person's satisfaction with current social involvements; and (3) the availability of supportive help, should it be needed. These issues are focused on in the social resources section of the OARS MFAQ (1978), which includes questions such as the following: How many times did you talk with someone on the telephone in the past week? How many people do you know well enough to visit in their homes? Is there someone you can trust and confide in? Do you feel lonely quite often, sometimes, or almost never? Is there someone who would take care of you as long as needed, or only for a short time?. In addition, a similar, though briefer, set of questions is asked of an informant, as data obtained from impaired older persons can be times unreliable and may require verification. Data obtained from patient and informant are then used as a basis for rating social resources on a six-point scale reflecting adequacy of social relationships and availability of supportive help, if needed. This scale provides a good overall indication of social supports and is a helpful supplement to the detailed social and family history obtained through interviews.

Other scales have been developed which are especially appropriate for social assessment in specific situations. The Sheltered Care Environment Scale (SCES) (Moos and Lemke, 1979) assesses resident and staff perceptions of the social milieu. The scale can be used to determine three different perceptions: (1) how staff and residents feel things really are, (2) how they would like things to be, and (3) what the future holds for all. The SCES assesses relationships, personal growth, system maintenance, and change. Response analysis can yield a better understanding of what an elder views as "necessary ingredients" for a satisfying social environment, offering clues for modification of staff behavior.

Other scales measure the deinstitutionalized elder's social functioning upon return to the community setting. The Social Adjustment Inventory (Berger et al., 1964) is a follow-up instrument which assesses the effect of treatment on the elder's community adjustment. This questionnaire yields four scores: (1) family/social adjustment, (2) social productivity, (3) self-maintenance, and (4) antisocial behavior. It does not inquire into the elder's personal satisfaction, but relies on members of the elder's social group for insights into his or her behavior, as it relates to adjustment in the community. The Katz Adjustment Scale (KAS) (Katz and Lyerly, 1963) is a widely employed measure of treatment outcome similar to the social adjustment inventory. The scale is of demonstrated validity and reliability (Katz and Lyerly, 1963), and distinguishes levels of social behavior and performance by age, marital status, gender, and social class. The authors view adjustment from personal as well as social reference points, and accordingly include sections to be completed by the patient and an informant. The KAS is a lengthy scale, and tends to heavily focus on maladaptive behaviors.

The Social Dysfunction Rating Scale (SDRS) (Linn et al., 1969) involves a half-hour semistructured interview that stresses the patient's personal satisfaction with, rather than mere amount of, activity. Adjustment is self-defined through a determination of significant roles, goals, and the degree to which a person has been able to adapt to achieve these. This instrument is sensitive to change and involves factor scores of: apathetic/detachment; dissatisfaction; hostility; health/finance concern; and manipulation/dependency.

Isolation and withdrawal stereotypically but erroneously characterize the social environment of the elderly. This misconception is perpetuated among health-care providers who rarely look past the boundaries of their institutions to the majority of healthy, active elderly. Although the elderly are particularly vulnerable to isolation, it remains the exception rather than the rule. Palmore reported that 80 percent of the elderly in the United States live with someone, 75 percent say they are not often alone, and 76 percent had contact with relatives during the week previous to inquiry (1980). In the event that the health-care provider suspects alienation, the Anomie Scale (Strole, 1956) is a useful tool to assess this aspect of social functioning, aiding the health-care provider in determining whether or not to intervene.

Another set of measures often utilized in assessing social adjustment are the life satisfaction or morale measures (reviewed by George and Bearon, 1980). The most familiar of these are the Life Satisfaction Index (LSI) (Neugarten et al., 1961) and the Philadelphia Geriatric Center Morale Scale (PGC) (Lawton, 1975). Both scales were specifically developed for use with the elderly, and both may be used to derive either multidimensional or global ratings of life satisfaction. The factors comprising the LSI are: zest vs apathy; resolution and fortitude; congruence between desired and achieved goals; positive self-concept; and mood tone. The PGC factors are: surgency; attitude toward aging; acceptance of status quo; agitation; easygoing optimism; and lonely dissatisfaction.

The issues addressed in conducting a social assessment are often of critical importance in evaluating an older person's total situation. A frequent key question concerns future living arrangements: a complete view of social resources is a necessity. In other cases, social assessment uncovers factors contributing to mental or physical disorders, and points out obvious remedial opportunities. The evaluation of social factors should occupy a central and permanent place in the overall geriatric assessment strategy.

ACTIVITIES OF DAILY LIVING

In the previous section, the concept of instrumental needs was introduced with reference to the elderly person's available social resources. Instrumental needs refer to the degree and type of help required in negotiating life's daily demands. The greater the need for help, the greater the strain placed on available social resources. The importance of assessing degree of social dependence from this perspective should be obvious, for the adequacy of social resources to meet present and future needs is a key factor in assessing optimal level of care required by impaired elderly persons, both in the community and in institutional settings.

The behaviors focused on in assessment of activities of daily living include basic physical functions, such as eating; dressing and undressing; grooming; walking; getting in and out of bed; bathing; and toileting. Another set of necessary functions require a certain degree of cognitive intactness, and include using the telephone; shopping; traveling to places out of walking distance; cooking meals; doing housework; taking appropriate medicine; and handling financial matters. These lists are taken from the OARS MFAQ (1978) activities of daily living section, where each item is rated on a three-point scale indicating complete, partial, or no dependency. Individual ratings are then combined to yield an overall index of functional capacity to perform necessary activities of daily living (ADL) rated on a six-point scale, ranging from "excellent ADL capacity: Can perform all of the activities of daily living without assistance and with ease," to "completely impaired ADL capacity: Needs help throughout the day and/or night to carry out the activities of daily living."

Several other scales for ADL assessment are available, which are quite similar to the MFAQ ADL scale; they can be used interchangeably. Most notable are Katz' Index of Independence in Activities of Daily Living (Katz et al., 1963), and the Instrumental Activities of Daily Living Scale (Lawton and Brody, 1969).

One problem with ADL rating scales is their tendency to heavily depend on the patient's self-report, which is often found to be at odds with reality. When this occurs, it most often reflects an older patient's defensive attempt to deny dependency. The frequent discrepancy between objective and subjective evidence of functional impairment was demonstrated in a study by Kuriansky and colleagues (1976). They employed a performance test of activities of daily living, in which elderly patients were observed as they attempted various simple tasks. Their actual performance measure was then compared with the patient's self-rating of capacity for home self-care. The degree of agreement between these measures was found to be zero, thus underscoring the potential dangers of taking patients' self-ratings at face value.

Given the advantages of behavioral observation over self-report, it is best to assess ADL capacity in person. When community-residing elderly are involved, the most desirable setting for ADL assessment is in the home. Home visits, a common feature of geriatric evaluation as practiced in Great Britain (Currie, 1980), provides an opportunity to gather visible evidence of both how the patient has been managing at home, and how the environment is likely to affect future health problems. A preliminary version of a home assessment protocol is employed at the OARS Clinic and will be publicly available.

PHYSICAL HEALTH

It has been said that if growing old is not a disease, it may just as well be. National Institute of Health statistics indicate that about 86 percent of persons 65 years of age and over have one or more chronic illnesses, with many experiencing associated limitations in their activities. Not only is chronic illness in the elderly associated with increased mortality and functional impairment, but it is also known to contribute to social isolation and mental disorders, most notably, reactive depression. The assessment of health status of the elderly patient should be a primary concern not only for the physician or geriatrician but for the mental-health practitioner as well. Medical examinations asimed at diagnosis and treatment of physical disorders are an essential component of comprehensive geriatric evaluation, but there is also a broad range of assessment issues which could be gathered under the heading of ''health-related behavior.'' These will be surveyed, with recommendations for appropriate assessment strategies.

Self-perceived Health Status

The older person's perception of his or her own physical well-being is of importance in two respects: First, because of its known correlation with general morale or life-satisfaction. Secondly, because it reveals information predictive of an older person's likelihood to seek medical care. A number of studies (Friedsam and Martin, 1963; Heyman and Jeffers, 1963; Suchman et al., 1958; Maddox and Douglass, 1973) have demonstrated the general agreement between physician ratings and patient self-ratings of overall physical health. This degree of concordance tends to support the validity of several health indices, such as the Index of

Illness and Disability (Rosencranz and Pihlblad, 1970), and the Scale of Physical Capacity (Rosow and Breslan, 1966), which generate assessments of physical health based only on interview data. Such indices can be useful where detailed medical examinations are not possible.

Assessment of self-perceived health may involve no more than asking for a general rating on a continuum of health and illness. When this direct approach is taken, it is often helpful to ask the patient how their current health compares with 5 years ago; this will often uncover concerns about declining health. More specific information may be obtained by reading out a list of common chronic illnesses and asking the patient to identify any which affect him or her, together with an estimate of the degree to which the illness interferes in daily life activities. An example of such an approach can be found in the OARS MFAQ (1978). Perceived health status should be contrasted with physician ratings, as large discrepancies might help identify persons manifesting somatic overconcern (hypochondriasis) or underconcern (denial).

Patterns of Health-Care Usage

The somatically over- and underconcerned older patients typically represent two extremes in their patterns of health-care use. The hypochondriac often ''doctor shops,'' and may be under the concurrent care of multiple physicians, who may or may not know of other physician involvement. Other somatically overconcerned patients abuse emergency room services, and, with time, run the risk of Aesop's *Boy Who Cried Wolf*. The denier, on the other hand, may avoid contact with medical personnel, placing himself or herself at risk of suffering from undetected and untreated conditions.

Assessment of health-care use should focus on the following questions: What has been the patient's recent (i.e., the last 6 months) extent of contact with various medical care providers? Is there a primary physician the patient identifies as his or her doctor, and is this physician aware of other specialists the patient has been consulting? Is there provision for regular check-ups, or is help sought only as needed? Is the patient adequately financially covered to meet medical emergencies? Is the patient aware of alternative community-based sources of medical care?

Medication Use

Many older persons, but particularly the somatically overconcerned and those with multiple chronic illnesses, have accumulated an extensive array of prescription and non-prescription medications which they often consume in unfortunate combinations: a condition referred to as ''polypharmacy.'' To assess this dangerous practice, the older patient should be requested to bring all medications on hand (prescription and non-prescription; current and otherwise) with them for examination. This often yields surprising results; one OARS client appeared with two shopping bags stuffed with the remains of over 200 prescriptions accumulated over a 30-year period!

Another problem which frequently occurs with cognitively-impaired elderly patients is non-compliance with recommended medication dosages. This can be assessed in part by asking the patient to demonstrate which medicines are taken, in what amounts, and when. The patient's account can then be compared with prescribed instructions. If the patient lives with others, it is worth inquiring as to whether the patient ever "borrows" medications from others; this is not an uncommon practice.

Exercise, Nutrition, and Alcohol Use

The role played by exercise and diet in restoring and maintaining health has garnered increasing attention from health-care professionals, and routine inquiry in these areas makes particular sense in geriatric assessment. Older persons with physical infirmities are often at risk of developing muscular and systemic weakness secondary to poor nutrition and inactivity. While relevant information can often be obtained by interview, a home visit (with a quick glance in the refrigerator and pantry) is often more revealing.

While it is true that many alcoholics never reach old age, alcohol does constitute a health problem for many older persons. Alcohol abuse is particularly evident in the geriatric population of psychiatric hospitals (Gaitz and Baer, 1971). Its prevalence in the community-based population is also significant (Calahan, 1970; Calahan et al., 1969). Most of the geriatric abusers are maintaining a chronic condition established in their younger years, although late onset of alcoholism may occur in response to age-related stresses (Drollar, 1964; Rosen and Glatt, 1971). In such cases, alcohol abuse may cease with relief of stress (Zinberg, 1974). Since alcoholism plays a significant role in arrests of older persons (Epstein et al., 1970) and mortality (Metropolitan Life, 1977), its detection is crucial. Inquiry concerning alcohol abuse can be introduced through questions such as: Has your doctor ever advised you to cut down on your drinking for health reasons? and How often do you drink alcoholic beverages? Since alcoholics often deny or minimize their drinking problem, additional data from informants should be sought in questionable cases.

Sensory Impairments

Sensory impairments, especially involving hearing and sight, are quite common among the elderly (Fozard et al., 1977; Corso, 1977), and may have a significant impact on both physical and mental functioning (Granick et al., 1976). The interviewer should be alert to behavioral signs of sensory impairment, and a routine question or two concerning how well the person is able to hear and see is worth including. When feasible, brief sensory screening tests are advisable.

The five issues reviewed above constitute a domain of concern for all health-care providers, medical and non-medical alike, working in the geriatric community. Those readers wishing an introduction to the strictly medical aspects of geriatrics are referred to a text by Libow and Sherman (1981).

REFERENCES

Ammons, R. B., & Ammons, C. H. The quick test: Provisional manual. *Psychological Reports*, 1962, *11*, 111–161.

Beck, A. T., Ward, C. H., Mendelson, M., Mock, S. E., & Erbaugh, J. An inventory for measuring depression. *Archives of General Psychiatry*, 1961, *4*, 561–571.

Bellak, L., & Bellak, S. S. *Senior apperception test*. New York: C.P.S., Inc., 1973.

Berger, D. G., Rice, C. E., Sewall, L. G., & Lemkau, P. N. The posthospital evaluation of psychiatric patients: The social adjustment inventory method. *Psychiatric Studies and Projects*, 1964, *2*, 1–30.

Bernal, G. A. A., Brannon, L. J., Belar, C., Lavigne, J., & Cameron, R. Psychodiagnostics of the elderly. In W. D. Gentry (Ed.), *Geropsychology: A model of training and clinical service*. Cambridge, Massachusetts: Ballinger, 1977.

Birren, J. E., Butler, R. N., Greenhouse, S. W., Sokoloff, L., & Yarrow, M. R. *Human aging: A biological and behavioral study (DHEW Pub No. 986)*. Washington, D.C.: US DHEW, 1963.

Blazer, D. The OARS Durham surveys: Description and application. In *Multidimensional functional assessment: The OARS methodology. A manual* (Ed. 2). Durham, North Carolina: Center for the Study of Aging and Human Development, 1978.

Bolton, N., & Savage, R. D., Neuroticism and extraversion in elderly normal subjects. *British Journal of Psychiatry*, 1971, *118*, 473–474.

Brink, T. L., Belanger, J., Bryant, J. et al. Hypochondriasis in an institutional geriatric population: Construction of a scale (HSIG). *Journal of the American Geriatrics Society*, 1979, *26*, 557–559.

Bull, C. N., & Aucoin, J. B. Voluntary association, participation and life satisfaction: A replication note. *Journal of Gerontology*, 1975, *30*, 73–76.

Busse, E. W., & Pfeiffer, E. Functional psychiatric disorders in old age. In E. W. Busse, & E. Pfeiffer (Eds.), *Behavior and adaptation in late life* (Ed. 2). Boston: Little, Brown and Co., 1977.

Cahalan, D. *Problem drinkers*. San Francisco: Jossey-Bass, 1970.

Cahalan, D., Cisin, I. H., & Crossley, H. M. *American drinking practices*. New Brunswick, New Jersey: Rutgers University Press, 1969.

Cauthen, N. Normative data for the tactual performance test. *J Clinical Psychology*, 1978, *34*, 456–460.

Chown, S. M. Personality and aging. In K. W. Schaie (Ed.), *Theory and methods of research on aging*. Morgantown, West Virginia: University Press, 1968.

Corso, J. F. Auditory perception and communication. In J. E. Birren & K. W. Schaie (Eds.), *Handbook of the psychology of aging*. New York: Van Nostrand Reinhold, 1977.

Craik, F. I. M. Age differences in human memory. In J. E. Birren & K. W. Schaie (Eds.), *Handbook of the psychology of aging*. New York: Van Nostrand Reinhold, 1977.

Crook, T., Ferris, S., McCarthy, M., & Rae, D. Utility of digit recall tasks for assessing memory in the aged. *Journal of Consulting and Clinical Psychology*, 1980, *48*, 228–233.

Currie C., Personal communication, 1980.

Cutler, S. J. Voluntary association, participation, and life satisfaction. *Journal of Gerontology*, 1973, *28*, 96–100.

Davies, H. D. M. The influence of age on trail-making test performance. *Journal of Clinical Psychology*, 1968, *24*, 96–98.

Derogatis, L. R., Lipman, R. S., Rickels, K., Uhleuhuth, F. H., & Cori, L. The Hopkins symptom checklist (HSCL): A measure of primary symptom dimensions. In P. Pichot (Ed.), *Psychological measurements in psychopharmacology: Modern problems in pharmacopsychiatry, Vol. 7*. Basel, Switzerland: S. Kanger, 1974.

Doppelt, J. E., & Wallace, W. L. Standardization of the Wechsler adult intelligence scale for older persons. *Journal of Abnormal and Social Psychology*, 1955, *51*, 312–330.

Drollar, H. Some aspects of alcoholism in the elderly. *Lancet*, 1964, *18*, 137–139.

Eisdorfer, C. Rorschach performance and intellectual functioning in the aged. *Journal of Gerontology*, 1963, *18*, 358–363.

Eisdorfer, C., & Cohen, L. D. The generality of the WAIS standardization for the aged: A regional comparison. *Journal of Abnormal and Social Psychology*, 1961, *64*, 520–527.

Eisdorfer, C., Nowlin, J., & Wilkie, F. Improvement of learning in the aged by modification of autonomic nervous system activity. *Science*, 1970, *170*, 1327–1329.

Botwinick, J., & Storandt, M. *Memory, related functions, and age*. Springfield, Illinois: Charles C. Thomas, 1974.

Epstein, L. J., Mills, C., & Simm, A. Antisocial behavior of the elderly. *Compr Psychiatry*, 1970, *11*, 36–42.

Erickson, R. C., Poon, L. W., & Walsh-Sweeney, L. Clinical memory testing of the elderly. In L. W. Poon, J. Fozard, L. Cermak, L. Arenberg, & L. W. Thompson (Eds.), *New directions in memory and aging: Proceedings of the George A. Talland Memorial Conference*. Hillsdale, New Jersey: Lawrence Erlbaum, 1980.

Erickson, R. C., & Scott, M. L. Clinical memory testing: A review. *Psychological Review*, 1977, *84*, 1130–1149.

Eysenck, H. J. *Manual of the Maudsley personality inventory*. London: University of London Press, 1959.

Eysenck, H. J. A short questionnaire for the measurement of two dimensions of personality. *Journal of Applied Psychology*, 1958, *42*, 1–10.

Eysenck, S. B. *Manual of the Eysenck-Withers personality inventory for subnormal subjects*. London: University of London Press, 1969.

Fillenbaum, G. G., & Pfeiffer, E. The mini-mult: A cautionary note. *Journal of Consulting and Clinical Psychology*, 1976, *44*, 698–703.

Fink, M., Green, T., & Benda, M. The face-hand test as a diagnostic sign of organic mental syndrome. *Neurology*, 1952, *2*, 46–58.

Folstein, M. F., Folstein, S. E., & McHugh, P. R. "Mini-mental state": A practical method for grading the cognitive state of patients for the clinician. *Journal of Psychiatric Research*, 1975, *12*, 189–198.

Fozard, J. L., Wolf, E., Bell, B., McFarland, R. A., & Podolsky, S. Visual perception and communication. In J. E. Birren & K. W. Schaie (Eds.), *Handbook of the psychology of aging*. New York: Van Nostrand Reinhold, 1977.

Friedsam, H., & Martin, H. A comparison of self and physician's health ratings in an older population. *Journal of Health and Human Behavior*, 1963, *4*, 179–183.

Furry, C. A., & Baltes, P. B. The effect of age differences in ability-extraneous performance variables on the assessment of children, adults, and the elderly. *Journal of Gerontology*, 1973, *28*, 73–80.

Gaitz, C. M., & Baer, P. E. Characteristics of elderly patients with alcoholism. *Arch Gen Psychiat*, 1971, *24*, 372–378.

Gallagher, D., McGarvey, W., Zelinski, E., & Thompson, L. Age and factor structure of the Zung depression scale. Paper presented at the 31st Annual Meeting of the Gerontological Society, Dallas, Texas, November 1978.

Gallagher, D., Thompson, L. W., & Levy, S. M. Clinical psychological assessment of older adults. In L. W. Poon (Ed.), *Aging in the 1980's: Psychological issues*. Washington, D. C.: American Psychological Association, 1980.

Gatz, M. Measures of change in the assessment of psychotherapy with older adults. Paper presented at the 31st Annual Meeting of the Gerontological Society, Dallas, Texas, November 1978.

Gatz, M., Smyer, M. A., & Lawton, M. P. The mental health system and the older adult. In L. W. Poon (Ed.), *Aging in the 1980's: Psychological issues*. Washington, D. C.: American Psychological Association, 1980.

Gendreau, L., Roach, T., & Gendreau, P. Assessing the intelligence of aged persons: Report on the quick test. *Psychological Reports*, 1973, *32*, 475–480.

George, L. K., & Bearon, L. B. *Quality of life in older persons: Meaning and measurement*. New York: Human Sciences Press, 1980.

Gilbert, J. G., & Levee, R. F. Patterns of declining memory. *Journal of Gerontology*, 1971, *26*, 70–75.

Gilbert, J. G., Levee, R. F., Catalano, F. L. A preliminary report on a new memory scale. *Perceptual and Motor Skills*, 1968, *27*, 277–278.

Goldstein, G., & Shelly, C. H. Similarities and differences between psychological deficit in aging and brain damage. *J of Gerontology*, 1975, *30*, 448–455.

Granick, S., Kleban, M. H., & Weiss, A. D. Relationships between hearing loss and cognition in normally hearing aged persons. *Journal of Gerontology*, 1976, *31*, 434–440.

Graney, J. J. Happiness and social participation. *Journal of Gerontology*, 1975, *30*, 701–706.

Gunel, L., Linn, M. W., & Linn, B. S. Physical and mental impairment-of-function evaluation in the aged: The PAMIE scale. *Journal of Gerontology*, 1972, *27*, 83–90.

Gurland, B. J. The assessment of the mental health status of older adults. In J. E. Birren & R. B. Sloane (Eds.), *Handbook of mental health and aging*. Englewood Cliffs, New Jersey: Prentice-Hall, 1980.

Gurland, B. J., Copeland, J. R. M., Sharpe, L., & Kelleher, M. The geriatric mental status interview (GMS). *International Journal of Aging and Human Development*, 1976, *7*, 303–311.

Gurland, G., Kuriansky, J., Sharpe, L., Simon, R., Stiller, P., & Birkett, P. The comprehensive assessment and referral evaluation (CARE)—Rationale, development, and reliability. *International Journal of Aging and Human Development*, 1977, *8*, 9–42.

Haglund, R., & Schuckit, M. A. A clinical comparison of tests of organicity in elderly patients. *Journal of Gerontology*, 1976, *31*, 654–659.

Hamilton, M. Development of a rating scale for primary depressive illness. *British Journal of Social and Clinical Psychology*, 1967, *6*, 278–296.

Harmatz, J., & Shader, R. Psychopharmacologic investigations in healthy elderly volunteers: MMPI depression scale. *Journal of the American Geriatrics Society*, 1975, *23*, 350–354.

Hathaway, S. R., & McKinley, J. C. *The Minnesota multiphasic personality inventory manual*. Minneapolis: University of Minnesota Press, 1943.

Heyman, D., & Jeffers, F. Effects of time lapse on consistency of self-health and medical evaluations of elderly persons. *Journal of Gerontology*, 1963, *18*, 160–164.

Hughes, J. R., Williams, J. G., & Currier, R. D. An ergot alkaloid preparation (Hydergine) in the treatment of dementia: Critical review of the literature. *Journal of the American Geriatrics Society*, 1976, *24*, 490–497.

Hulicka, I. M. Age differences in retention as a function of interference. *Journal of Gerontology*, 1967, *22*, 180–184.

Hulicka, I. M. Age differences in Wechsler memory scale scores. *Journal of Genetic Psychology*, 1966, *109*, 135–145.

Inglis, J. Psychological investigations of cognitive deficit in elderly psychiatric patients. *Psychological Bulletin*, 1958, *55*, 197–214.

Irving, G., Robinson, R. A., & McAdam, W. The validity of some cognitive tests in the diagnosis of dementia. *British Journal of Psychiatry*, 1970, *117*, 149–156.

Isaacs, B., & Akhtar, A. J. The set test: A rapid test of mental functioning in old people. *Age and Ageing*, 1972, *1*:222–226.

Kahana, B. The use of projective techniques in personality assessment of the aged. In M. Storardt, I. C. Siegler, M. F. Elias (Eds.), *The clinical psychology of aging*. New York: Plenum Press, 1978.

Kahn, R. L., Goldfarb, A. I., Pollack, M., & Peck, A. A brief objective measure for the determination of mental status of the aged. *Am J of Psychiatry*, 1960, *117*, 326–328.

Kahn, R. L., Zarit, S. H., Hilbert, N. M., & Niederehe, G. M. Memory complaint and impairment in the aged. *Archives of General Psychiatry*, 1975, *32*, 1569–1573.

Katz, S., Ford, A. B., Moskowitz, R. W., Jackson, B. A., & Jaffe, M. W. Studies of illness in the aged: The index of ADL, a standardized measure of biological and psychosocial function. *Journal of American Medical Association*, 1963, *185*, 914–919.

Katz, M. M., & Lyerly, S. B. Methods of measuring adjustment and social behavior in the community. *Psychological Reports*, 1963, *13*, 503–535.

Kincannon, J. C. Prediction of the standard MMPI scale scores from 71 items: The minimult. *Journal of Consulting and Clinical Psychology*, 1968, *32*, 319–325.

Klonoff, H., & Kennedy, M. Memory and perceptual functioning in octogenerians and nonagenarians in the community. *Journal of Gerontology*, 1965, *20*, 328–333.

Kochansky, G. F. Psychiatric rating scales for assessing psychopathology in the elderly: A critical review. In A. Raskin, & L. F. Jarvik (Eds.), *Psychiatric symptoms and cognitive loss in the elderly: Evaluation and assessment techniques*. Washington, D. C.: Hemisphere, 1979.

Kramer, M., Taube, C. A., & Redick, R. W. Patterns of use of psychiatric facilities by the aged: Past, present, and future. In C. Eisdorfer, M. P. Lawton (Eds.), *The psychology of adult development and aging*. Washington, D. C.: American Psychological Association, 1973.

Kulka, R. A., & Tamir, L. Patterns of help-seeking and formal support. Paper presented at the meeting of the Gerontological Society, Dallas, Texas, 1978.

Kuriansky, J., Gurland, B. J. & Fleiss, J. L. The performance test of activities of daily living. *International Journal of Aging and Human Development*, 1976, *7*, 343–352.

Lawton, P. The Philadelphia geriatric center morale scale: A revision. *J of Gerontology*, 1975, *30*, 85–89.

Lawton, M. P., & Brody, E. Assessment of older people: Self-maintaining and instrumental activities of daily living. *Gerontologist*, 1969, *9*, 179–186.

Lawton, M. P., Whelihan, W. M., & Belsky, J. K. Personality tests and their uses with older adults. In J. E. Birren, & R. B. Sloane (Eds.), *Handbook of mental health and aging*. Englewood Cliffs, New Jersey: Prentice-Hall, 1980.

Libow, L. S. A rapidly administered, easily remembered mental status evaluation: FROMAJE. In L. S. Libow, & F. T. Sherman (Eds.), *The core of geriatric medicine: A guide for students and practitioners*. St. Louis: C. V. Mosby, 1981.

Libow, L. S., & Sherman F. T. (Eds.). *The core of geriatric medicine: A guide for students and practitioners*. St. Louis: C. V. Mosby, 1981.

Linn, M. W., Sculthorpe, W. B., Evje, M., & Slater, P. H. A social dysfunction rating scale. *Journal of Psychiatric Research*, 1969, *6*, 299–316.

Logue, P. Personal communication, 1981.

Logue, P., & Wyrick, L. Initial validation of Russell's revised Wechsler memory scale: A comparison of normal aging versus dementia. *Journal of Consulting and Clinical Psychology*, 1979, *47*, 176–178.

Maddox, G. L., & Douglass, E. B. Self-assessment of health: A longitudinal study of elderly subjects. *Journal of Health and Social Behaviors*, 1973, *14*, 87–93.

McNair, D. M., Low, M., & Droppleman, L. F. *Profile of mood states: Manual*. San Diego, California: Educational and Industrial Testing Service, 1971.

Meer, B., & Baker, J. A. Reliability of measurements of intellectual functioning of geriatric patients. *Journal of Gerontology*, 1965, *20*, 110–114.

Miller, W. Psychological deficit in depression. *Psychological Bulletin*, 1979, *82*, 238–260.

Moos, R., & Lemke, S. *Multiphasic environmental assessment procedure—preliminary manual*. Palo Alto, California: Social Ecology Laboratory, Veterans Administration Medical Center and Stanford University School of Medicine, 1979.

———. *Multidimensional functional assessment: The OARS methodology. A manual* (Ed. 2). Durham, North Carolina: Center for the Study of Aging and Human Development, 1978.

Murray, H. *Explorations in personality*. New York: Oxford University Press, 1938.

Neugarten, B. L., Havighurst, R. J., & Tobin, S. S. The measurement of life satisfaction. *J of Gerontology*, 1961, *16*, 134–143.

Metropolitan Life Insurance Company. Mortality from alcoholism. Statistical bulletin 58:3–7, 1977.

Overall, J. E., & Gorham, D. R. The brief psychiatric rating scale. *Psychological Reports*, 1962, *10*, 799–812.

Nelson, H. E., & O'Connell, A. Dementia: The estimation of premorbid intelligence levels using the new adult reading test. *Cortex*, 1978, *14*, 234–244.

Overall, J. F., & Gorham, D. R. Organicity versus old age in objective and projective test performance. *Journal of Consulting and Clinical Psychology*, 1972, *45*, 412–416.

Palmore, E. The social factors in aging. In E. W. Busse & D. Blazer (Eds.), *Handbook of geriatric psychiatry*. New York: Van Nostrand Reinhold Co., 1980.

Pfeiffer, E. A short portable mental status questionnaire for the assessment of organic brain deficit in elderly patients. *Journal of the American Society*, 1975, *23*, 433–441.

Pfeiffer, E. A short psychiatric evaluation schedule: A new 15-item monotonic scale indicative of functional psychiatric disorder. In F. Hoffmeister, & C. Muller (Eds.), *Brain function in old age*. Berlin: Springer-Verlag, 1979.

Plutchik, R. Conceptual and practical issues in the assessment of the elderly. In A. Raskin & L. F. Jarvik (Eds.), *Psychiatric symptoms and cognitive loss in the elderly*. New York: John Wiley & Sons, 1979.

Plutchik, R., Conte, H., & Lieberman, M. Development of a scale (GIES) for assessment of cognitive and perceptual functioning in geriatric patients. *Journal of the American Geriatric Society*, 1971, *19*, 4, 614–623.

Plutchik, R., Conte, H., Lieberman, M., Bakur, M., Grossman, J., & Lehrman, N. Reliability and validity of a scale for assessing the functioning of geriatric patients. *Journal of the American Geriatrics Society*, 1970, *18*, 491–500.

Price, L. F., Fein, G. & Feinberg, I. Neuropsychological assessment of cognitive function in the elderly. In L. W. Poon (Eds.), *Aging in the 1980's: Psychological issues*. Washington, D. C.: American Psychological Association, 1980.

Rabbitt, P. An age decrement in the ability to ignore irrelevant information. *Journal of Gerontology*, 1965, *20*, 233–238.

Raskin, A. Signs and symptoms of psychopathology in the elderly. In A. Raskin & L. F. Jarvik (Eds.), *Psychiatric symptoms and cognitive loss in the elderly: Evaluation and assessment techniques*. Washington, D. C.: Hemisphere Publishing Co., 1979.

Reed, H. B. C., & Reitan, R. M. Comparison of the effects of the normal aging process with the effects of organic brain damage in adaptive abilities. *Journal of Gerontology*, 1963, *18*, 177–179.

Reifler, B. V., Cox, G. B., & Hanley, R. J. Problems of mentally ill elderly as perceived by patients, families and clinicians. *Gerontologist*, 1981, *21;* 165–170.

Rosin, A. J., & Glatt, M. M. Alcohol excess in the elderly. *Quarterly Journal of Studies on Alcohol*, 1971, *32*, 53–59.

Rosencranz, H. A., & Pihlblad, C. T. Measuring the health of the elderly. *Journal of Gerontology*, 1970, *25*, 129–133.

Rosow, I. & Breslau, N. A Guttman health scale for the aged. *Journal of Gerontology*, 1966, *21*, 556–559.

Russell, E. W. A multiple scoring method for the assessment of complex memory functions. *Journal of Consulting and Clinical Psychology*, 1975, *43*, 800–809.

Salzman, C., Kochansky, G., Shader, R., & Cronin, D. Rating scales for psychotropic drug research with geriatric patients: II. Mood ratings. *Journal of the American Geriatrics Society*, 1972, *20*, 215–221.

Salzman, C., & Shader, R. I. Methodology for the evaluation of psychotropic agents in geriatric patients. In F. G. McMahon (Ed.), *Principles and techniques of human research and therapeutics (Vol VIII): Psychopharmacological agents*. Mt. Kisco, New York: Futura, 1975.

Salzman, C., & Shader, R. I. Clinical evaluation of depression in the elderly. In A. Raskin & L. F. Jarvik (Eds.), *Psychiatric symptoms and cognitive loss in the elderly: Evaluation and assessment techniques*. Washington, D. C.: Hemisphere Publishing Co., 1979.

Salzman, C., Shader, R. I., Kochansky, G. E., & Cronin, D. M. Rating scales for psychotropic drug research with geriatric patients. I. Behavior ratings. *Journal of the American Geriatrics Society*, 1972, *20*, 209–214.

Savage, R. D., & Britton, P. G. A short scale for the assessment of mental health in the community aged. *British Journal of Psychiatry*, 1967, *113*, 512–523.

Shader, R. I., Harnatz, J. S., & Salzman, C. A new scale for clinical assessment in geriatric populations: Sandoz clinical assessment-geriatric (SCAG). *Journal of the American Geriatrics Society*, 1974, *22*, 107–113.

Schaie, K. W., & Gribbin, K. Adult development and aging. *Annual Review of Psychology*, 1975, *26*, 65–96.

Schaie, K. W., & Schaie, J. P. Clinical assessment and aging. In J. E. Birren & K. W. Schaie (Eds.), *Handbook of the psychology of aging*. New York: Van Nostrand Reinhold, 1979.

Smith, J. M. Nurse and psychiatric aide rating scales for assessing psychopathology in the elderly: A critical review. In A. Raskin, & I. F. Jarvik (Eds.), *Psychiatric symptoms and cognitive loss in the elderly: Evaluation and assessment techniques*. Washington, D. C.: Hemisphere, 1979.

Smith, J. M., Bright, B., & McCloskey, J. Factor analytic composition of the geriatric rating scale (GRS). *Journal of Gerontology*, 1977, *32*, 58–62.

Starr, B. D., Werner, M. B., & Rabetz, M. *The projective assessment of aging method (PAAM)*. New York: Springer-Verlag, 1979.

Srole, L. Anomie. *American Sociological Review*, 1956, *21*, 709–716.

Suchman, E., Streib, G., & Phillips, B. An analysis of the validity of health questionnaires. *Social Forces*, 1958, *36*, 223–232.

Swenson, W. M., Pearson, J. S., & Osborne, D. *An MMPI source book: Basic item, scale, and pattern data on 50,000 medical patients*. Minneapolis: University of Minnesota Press, 1973.

Taylor, J. A. A personality scale of manifest anxiety. *Journal of Abnormal and Social Psychology*, 1955, *48*, 285–290.

Verwoerdt, A. *Geropsychiatry* (Ed. 2). Baltimore, Maryland: Williams & Wilkins Co., 1981.

Wechsler, D. *Manual for the Wechsler adult intelligence scale*. New York: Psychological Corporation, 1955.

Wechsler, D. *The measurement and appraisal of adult intelligence*. Baltimore, Maryland: Williams & Wilkins, 1958.

Wechsler, D. A standardized memory scale for clinical use. *Journal of Psychology*, 1945, *19*, 87–95.

Wolk, R. L. Refined projective techniques with the aged. In D. P. Kent, R. Kastenbaum, & S. Sherwood (Eds.), *Research planning and action for the elderly: The power and potential of social science*. New York: Behavioral Publications, 1972.

Wolk, R. L., & Wolk, R. B. *The gerontological apperception test*. New York: Behavioral Publications, 1971.

Yates, A. J. The use of vocabulary in the measurement of intellectual deterioration—A review. *Journal of Mental Science*, 1956, *102*, 409–440.

Zemore, R., & Eames, N. Psychic and somatic symptoms of depression among young adults, institutionalized aged and non-institutionalized aged. *J of Gerontology*, 1979, *34*, 716–722.

Zimberg, S. The elderly alcoholic. *The Gerontologist*, 1974, *14*, 221–224.

Zung, W. W. K. Depression in the normal aged. *Psychosomatics*, 1967, *8*, 287–291.

Zung, W. W. K. The depression status inventory: An adjunct to the self-rating depression scale. *Journal of Clinical Psychology*, 1972, *28*, 539–543.

Zung, W. W. K. A self-rating depression scale. *Archives of General Psychiatry*, 1965, *12*, 63–70.

Zung, W. W. K. A rating instrument for anxiety disorders. *Psychosomatics*, 1971, *12*, 371–379.

Index